PARKER SCHOOL OF
FOREIGN AND COMPARATIVE LAW
COLUMBIA UNIVERSITY

LAW AND LEGAL SYSTEM OF THE RUSSIAN FEDERATION

by

GENNADY M. DANILENKO
Professor of Law
Wayne State University Law School and
Senior Research Fellow
at the Institute of State and Law,
Russian Academy of Sciences

and

WILLIAM BURNHAM
Professor of Law
Wayne State University Law School
Research Associate
Center for Russian and East European Studies
University of Michigan

Juris Publishing

Library of Congress Cataloging-in-Publication Data

Danilenko, G. M. (Gennadiĭ Mikhaĭlovich)
Law and legal system of the Russian Federation / by Gennady M. Danilenko and William Burnham.
p. cm.
Includes bibliographical references and index.
ISBN 1-57823-053-5
1. Law—Russia (Federation) 2. Justice, Administration of—Russia (Federation) 3. Courts—Russia (Federation) I. Burnham, William, 1947- . II. Title.
KLB68.D36 1998
349.47–dc21 98-18219
CIP

Manufactured in the United States of America.

PARKER SCHOOL OF
FOREIGN AND COMPARATIVE LAW
COLUMBIA UNIVERSITY

LAW AND LEGAL SYSTEM OF THE RUSSIAN FEDERATION

by

GENNADY M. DANILENKO
Professor of Law
Wayne State University Law School and
Senior Research Fellow
at the Institute of State and Law,
Russian Academy of Sciences

and

WILLIAM BURNHAM
Professor of Law
Wayne State University Law School
Research Associate
Center for Russian and East European Studies
University of Michigan

Juris Publishing

Library of Congress Cataloging-in-Publication Data

Danilenko, G. M. (Gennadiĭ Mikhaĭlovich)
Law and legal system of the Russian Federation / by Gennady M. Danilenko and William Burnham.
p. cm.
Includes bibliographical references and index.
ISBN 1-57823-053-5
1. Law—Russia (Federation) 2. Justice, Administration of—Russia (Federation) 3. Courts—Russia (Federation) I. Burnham, William, 1947- . II. Title.
KLB68.D36 1998
349.47–dc21 98-18219
CIP

Manufactured in the United States of America.

* * * *

This book is dedicated to our families,
Olga Danilenko, Helen Danilenko and Marcia Major,
for tolerating weekends
and other times when our minds and bodies were elsewhere.

* * * *

ACKNOWLEDGMENTS

This book could not have been completed without the assistance and support of many people. We would especially like to thank Elizabeth Condon, Maria Rodriguez, Marian Dent, Paul McFarling, Vladimir Zaistev, Oleg Zaistev, Irina Reshetnikova and especially Olga Danilenko. Of particular help on the chapters on criminal law and procedure were Stephen Thaman, Todd Fogelsong, Peter Solomon, Jane Picker, Peter Henning and Edward Wise. Expressions of thanks are also due to students in Russian Law classes at the law schools of the University of San Diego and Wayne State University.

TABLE OF CONTENTS

PREFACE

The purpose of this book is to introduce the law student, practicing lawyer or academic lawyer to the principal features of the law and legal institutions of present-day Russia. It is likely to be of special interest to three types of readers within these broad groupings.

First, knowledge of the Russian legal system is essential for lawyers with business clients entering or already involved in the Russian market. Such knowledge is necessary not only for any direct use it might have, but also to understand the legal culture from which Russian co-counsel come from. Of particular interest to these readers will be the chapters that deal with aspects of Russian and international law as they relate to business transactions with Russian companies.

Second, lawyers working with the government and non-governmental agencies dealing with Russia must have at least a basic grasp of its law. The development of the rule of law over the last seven years means among other things that, unlike the past, actions of the Russian government will increasingly be governed by law. These and other readers with a public law or comparative law bent will find much of interest in the chapters on the institutions of the legal order, constitutional law, protection of human rights and criminal procedure. And, both for this group and business lawyers, knowledge of both public and private Russian law is directly transferable to the study of other members of the Commonwealth of Independent States and the former "socialist block" countries in Eastern and Central Europe. Many of them face the same problems as Russia in their transition from a command economy and society to a market economy and a democratic law-based society.

A third use of this book is not restricted to such a specific focus on Russia or even Eastern Europe. Russia's legal system follows the civil law tradition as do the great democracies of continental Western Europe. Given that the civil law tradition is the oldest, most widely distributed and most influential legal tradition in the world, American lawyers ignore it at their peril in the modern world of growing globalization of the legal order and of law practice. Lawyers who study comparative legal institutions are not only better equipped to deal with their foreign counterparts from different legal cultures; they gain a deeper knowledge of and appreciation for their own legal system and its place in the world.

The approach we have adopted in this book should ease the law-trained American reader's entry into the Russian legal world. We have adopted the familiar "casebook" approach—appellate decisions followed by notes and questions designed to stimulate thought and class discussion. Although we have provided narrative explanatory text as well, the focus of the book is primarily on decisions of the Russian Constitutional Court, Supreme Court and Supreme Arbitration Court. Aside from providing a familiar format, court decisions provide the opportunity to view real-life examples of the factual contexts in which legal disputes arise and illustrate the mode and style of legal analysis. Moreover, the study of judicial decisions has some direct applicability because of the increasingly important role that judicial precedent plays in the Russian legal system.

This book covers most of the important areas of Russian law. However, it is not intended to be comprehensive. In addition, the presentation of the material in the book is analytical and systematic rather than historical. Although some historical overview is provided in connection with specific problems, the focus of the book is on contemporary Russian law.

Our general approach is also more descriptive and comparative than evaluative. Our hope is that our account is a balanced one that is neither apologist nor hypercritical—poles toward which some writing on Russian and Soviet law has tended to gravitate. Our intent is to provide a sufficiently detailed picture of the principal institutions and workings of the present Russian legal system that readers can form their own opinions of that system. Where opinions have been voiced on particular controversial issues, we try to address both sides of the question.

It must be admitted that for the Russia of today, the rule of law remains more a challenge for the future rather than a present-day reality. And in thinking about that challenge and how it can become a reality, we must remember the limits of laws and legal systems, the subjects of our study here. In Russia, no less than any other country, it is not through tinkering with these things that the rule of law will ultimately emerge. To paraphrase Learned Hand, "a society so riven that the spirit of moderation is gone," no legal system can save, while "a society where that spirit flourishes," no legal system *need* save.[1] Beyond the issue of specific legal reforms described in this book, one can only hope that Russia will avoid the extremism, polarization and strife that has brought so much suffering to its people in this century. If it does, then

[1] Learned Hand, The Contributions of an Independent Judiciary to Civilization, The Supreme Court of Massachusetts 1692-1942, Massachusetts Bar Association, reprinted in Ruggiero J. Aldisert, The Judicial Process: Text, Materials and Cases 147 (2d ed.1996).

perhaps it will emerge in the twenty-first century—not simply with just laws and a fair legal system in place—but with an entire legal culture that enjoys the confidence of its people and the respect of the international legal community.

Gennady Danilenko
William Burnham

Detroit, Michigan
March 1998

CHAPTER I

RUSSIAN LAW IN A COMPARATIVE PERSPECTIVE

Before we start a detailed discussion of the modern Russian legal system, it may be useful to discuss where it stands in the existing systematic classifications of legal systems on a global scale. Locating it "on the legal map" in this way will assist us because it will tell us where the Russian system stands in relationship to the US and other common law systems. We will also be able to locate the Russian legal system within a group or family of legal systems which operate according to the same basic principles. It is essential for us to determine which doctrines, procedures or techniques exist in all legal systems belonging to the same family and which ones are uniquely Russian.

A. Methods of Classification

Comparative lawyers have spent much time and energy in trying to arrive at a systematic classification of legal systems of the world. Although there is much disagreement as to the criteria to be used, all the existing legal systems have traditionally been classified into groups or families. Until recent revolutionary changes in Russia and Eastern Europe, there were three major groups or families: civil law, common law and socialist law.

In classifying legal systems as a whole, some commentators rely on formal criteria, such as sources of law. Principal distinctions based on sources have concentrated on whether judicial decisions are a source of law in a particular system. Others use extra-legal criteria, such as the type of civilization or political ideology. Some writers use a combination of several criteria. For example, an influential book on comparative law[1] suggests that two independent criteria must be used: (1) legal method and (2) the philosophical, political and economic foundations of the legal system. Another approach relies on the "style" of legal systems.[2] According to the proponents of this approach, the elements determining the style of a legal system are (1) historical origin; (2) method of legal reasoning; (3) particularly characteristic legal

[1] See R.David, J.E.C. Brierly, Major Legal Systems in the World Today 20 (1985).

[2] See K.Zweigert, H.Koetz, An Introduction to Comparative Law 63-75 (2nd ed. 1992).

institutions; (4) nature and treatment of sources of law; and (5) ideological factors.

B. Why "Socialist" Law?

The contrast between civil law and common law draws primarily on formal criteria, such as sources of law, organization of the law and ways of handling legal materials. However, the socialist legal system was singled out by using extra-judicial factors, namely ideology and political structure.

Prior to "socialist" revolutions, countries of the socialist legal family belonged to the civil law world and, from a purely technical perspective, the socialist legal system was not much different from the civil law family. Indeed, during its Soviet period Russian law preserved many characteristics of civil or Romano-Germanic law. These characteristics encompassed basic concepts of law, civil law institutions, methodology and general organization. The same was true of the "socialist" countries of Eastern Europe. It is therefore understandable that any attempt to distinguish the socialist family from the rest of the civil law world had to rely on ideological criteria. Although such an approach is vulnerable to the criticism of inconsistency in applying different set of criteria for the same classification, it had its merits. Indeed, while the law of the imperial Russia belonged to the civil law world, far-reaching changes in the Soviet period made it quite different from the traditional civil law systems. The Soviet legal system operated in a state that had socialized all means of production, established an all-embracing state control over all aspects of social life, was dominated by a "vanguard communist party" and proclaimed Marxism as official state ideology. This was bound to affect the legal system.

Marxists always regarded law and state as elements of the society's "superstructure" or an ideological expression of economic relations at a particular point in time. Law was also considered a product of the political process. In fact, it was regarded as both policy and politics. According to Marxist theory, law is an instrument of economic and social policy. Communists regard law as a means of social engineering aimed at creation of a communist society.

Following the October Revolution of 1917, the communists declared all Russian imperial law to be no longer in force. According to Marx, the abolition of private ownership of the instruments and means of production was an absolute prerequisite for a just society. Guided by this theory, the Soviet communists nationalized all means of production and almost all private property. The only exception was the inconsequential "personal" property of citizens necessary for their own use or consumption.

On the economic plane, the first priority of the new ruling elite was to turn an economically backward country into an industrialized state. Large-scale and rapid industrialization required tight state control and planned concentration and allocation of available resources. The Soviet state assumed full control over the industry and agricultural production. As a command economy replaced private industry and commerce, the Russian imperial civil law, which used to govern commerce in the Russian empire, practically disappeared.[3] The field of operation of traditional civil law remained restricted to private law relationships between citizens (such as marriage, inheritance, and ownership of private residences). The centralized command economy did not require traditional civil law contracts. As a result, freedom of contract in relations between state-owned enterprises was abolished. Contractual relations between these entities were governed by a new set of rules that emphasized the role of the state plan. Private law was largely absorbed by public law.

On the political plane, the Marxist doctrine required the establishment of a new type of state - the dictatorship of the proletariat. The dictatorship of the proletariat was not bound by any formal rules of law as it pursued its principal domestic goals and accelerated economic development. The concept of dictatorship of the proletariat resulted in the establishment of a totalitarian state which controlled all aspects of social life and engaged in gross and massive violations of human rights to accomplish its goals. The state itself was dominated by a single political party - the Communist Party of the USSR. Although in the early 1960s the concept of the dictatorship of the proletariat was officially replaced with that of "a state of the whole people" or "an all-people's state," the repressive nature of the regime did not change.

Marxists also believed that law would die out under communism. Soviet theorists maintained that at the highest level of socialist development the state would rely less on coercion and more on persuasion. Under communism the state would divest its functions to non-state bodies, such as social organizations. Law would be replaced by other means of social control. Although these theories were of a rather abstract character, they made their impact on the official and popular attitudes concerning the nature and significance of law. From a practical perspective, the theory meant that law was not to be taken seriously during the transition to communism. Legal

---

[3] The term "civil law" is used here not as a reference to the entire legal system, but as a reference to a separate branch of Russian law which dealt with the law of persons, property, contracts, torts, inheritance and similar civil law subjects. On the differences in the usage of the term "civil law," see J.H. Merryman, The Civil Law Tradition 6-7 (1985).

nihilism prevailed in state administration and in the mass consciousness.[4] Legal studies were neglected and the number of lawyers was very small.

To a large extent, these concepts and practices of the Russian communists reflected the traditional Russian attitudes towards the law and the state. The Russian imperial state had always been authoritarian and arbitrary. The Russian Emperor agreed to emancipate the serfs only in 1861. The first parliamentary institution - the State Duma - was created only after the 1905 revolution. Although the State Duma had the power to legislate, the Tsar was able to adopt laws when the State Duma was not in session. The professional judiciary was established in 1775 under Catherine the Great who established courts staffed by judges, rather than by administrative officials. But the court reform of 1775 envisioned different courts for different social classes. Furthermore, the courts did not have the power to limit the executive branch of government. Life tenure for judges and jury trial for serious criminal offences were instituted only by the 1864 court reform. The Russian state had always had difficulties in instilling respect for the rule of law. The lack of legal rights, particularly of the serfs and working people, led to an anti-legalistic frame of mind. As Alexander Herzen, the Russian writer and philosopher of the 1840s wrote, "The Russian, whatever his social status, subverts or violates the law wherever he can do so without being punished, and the government acts precisely the same way."[5]

We might agree that a family of law or a legal tradition is not a set of technical rules of law about property, contracts or juridical persons, but a set of deeply rooted attitudes about the nature of law, about the role of law in the society and the polity, about the proper organization and operation of a legal system, and about the way law is or should be made, applied, perfected and taught.[6] If so, the remaining technical similarities between the Soviet legal system and the legal systems of countries belonging to the civil law family become unimportant. It is clear that there were several important political and ideological features that distinguished Soviet law from the civil law tradition. Hence, the theory that socialist law had become a new and separate legal family alongside the common law and civil law. By imposing the principles of Marxist ideology on pre-existing civil law structures and on the civil law tradition, the communists created a new legal tradition of an essentially hybrid nature.[7]

---

[4] See V.A. Tumanov, *O pravovom nigilizme* (On the Legal Nihilism), 10 *Soventskoe gosudarstvo I pravo* 21 (1989).

[5] A.I.Herzen, 7 *Sobranie sochinenii* (Collected Works) 251 (1956).

[6] See Merryman, *supra,* note 3, at 2.

[7] Id., at 4.

C. Continuation of the Civil Law Tradition

The nature of the Soviet Russian hybrid legal system meant that it retained many features of a typical civil law system. The major factor, of course, was the imperial civil law legacy. The law of imperial Russia was connected to the system of European civil law, although the civil law tradition in Russia did not have the same historical roots as in other European countries.

This is not the place to discuss the historical origin of the Russian imperial civil law. However, it should be kept in mind that Roman law was not received directly. At a time when Western Europe was experiencing the revival of Roman law and some Western European countries (e.g. Germany) had formally received Roman civil law as binding law, Russia adhered to its local laws and customs. The Russian legal system came under the influence of Roman law through the reception of Byzantine and German texts. Christianity brought an additional imported body of canon law. However, during the Mongol subjugation (1240-1480) Russia remained largely isolated from the rest of Europe. It did not participate in the European Renaissance. Some reception of Western European law occurred during the reign of Tsar Aleksei Mikhailovich and the "westernization" of Russian society under Peter the Great. More systematic reception of Roman and civil law became possible through the study of western legal texts during the 18th , 19th and early 20th century. The 1845 Criminal Code drew on Western European codes. Russian civil legislation, in particular the 1913 Draft Civil Code, was drafted on the model of the civil codes of Western Europe. Although it came late and by an indirect route, the civil law tradition in Russia was well established by the time of the Revolution of 1917.

Russian communists managed to repeal all imperial law, but they were not able to abolish the civil law tradition as such. The legal rule was still conceived in the form of a general rule of conduct. The rules of the Soviet legal system were highly codified. While written codes remained the predominant source of law, the judiciary did not participate in law-making: the concept of *stare decisis* was never recognized. Judges and attorneys based their decisions and arguments on rules contained in the codes. They also relied on commentaries of the codes prepared by scholars. Civil procedure continued to be based on the inquisitorial system of the civil law countries. Criminal procedure emphasized the preliminary investigation which was supposed to prepare a detailed written dossier for the court, like in other civil law countries.

A particularly interesting aspect of the continued reliance on the civil law tradition was the technique of codification. While common law countries also feel need for statutes, in the civil law countries comprehensive codes are the predominant source of law. In Soviet Russia, the rejection of the imperial order was accompanied by the enactment of new civil and criminal codes. When these new codes were prepared in the early 1920s, the drafters drew on the imperial codes. As in other civil law countries, the new codes were treated as comprehensive, that is as integrated systems containing rules applicable to all situations. Soviet courts were not supposed to fall back on imperial law nor were judicial decisions considered a source of law. Imperial law did not recognize precedent and Russian judges never used the case-law method.

Soviet legal scholarship was also extremely positivistic. The accepted theory of sources of law recognized only statutes and regulations. Custom was considered reactionary and did not play any significant role in the operation of the Soviet legal system. Judges always tried to decide cases on the basis of written codes or regulations. They avoided references to prior judicial decisions, legal doctrine or natural law.

This dogmatic concept of the law may appear strange to a common lawyer who is brought up on the case-law method. At the same time, it is quite familiar to a civil law lawyer who likes a clear, systematic and hierarchical theory of sources of law. As a result of these similarities, lawyers trained in Russia in the Soviet period had no difficulties understanding, for example, the legal concepts, organization, techniques and procedural institutions of such traditional civil law countries as France or Germany.

It should be noted, however, that Soviet law did not adopt some of the features of the Western European civil law that developed in the 20th century. In Western civil law countries, written constitutions became the superior sources of law and those countries introduced systems of judicial review of the constitutionality of legislative action. Judges were given the power to declare that a statute in conflict with the constitution is void. By contrast, in the Soviet Union written constitutions were regarded as instruments of ideology. Although they were proclaimed to be the supreme law of the land, they were never considered to be self-executing. Russia embraced the idea of constitutionalism only after the collapse of the communist regime in 1991.

While the majority of comparatists divided the world's legal systems into three major groups (civil law, common law, and socialist law) and agreed that the Russian Soviet law should be classified as belonging to a socialist legal tradition, some commentators claimed that, notwithstanding all the changes introduced by the communists, the Soviet law remained within the civil law family. The proponents of this theory believed that civil law rules, methods, institutions and procedures that were retained by the Soviet legal system were far more important than the broad political-legal features distinguishing it from other civil law systems. They argued that despite the many innovative features of the Soviet legal system, it remained within the Romanist, or civil law, tradition.[8]

D. The Contemporary Russian Legal System: The Civil Law Tradition with Some Special Russian Characteristics

Recent developments in Russia have made the controversy over the proper classification of Russian law largely moot. The "Second Russian Revolution" of the early 1990s resulted in fundamental changes in the country's legal system. These changes began with the elimination of the constitutional basis for the communist party's monopoly on state power, the disintegration of the USSR and the introduction of a massive program of privatization. The movement from a planned to a free market economy required the abandonment of central planning and massive transfer of state enterprises to private ownership.[9] It also required the creation of a whole set of new institutions and laws needed for the operation of a modern market economy.

Another major development was the institutionalization of democracy and constitutional government. The 1993 Constitution proclaimed the goal of establishing a state based on the rule of law. The Constitution provided strong guarantees for individual rights based on internationally recognized human rights standards. Judicial reform resulted in the establishment of an independent and active Constitutional Court, as well as two other courts - the Supreme Court and the Supreme Arbitration Court. Private property was guaranteed by the Constitution and protected by the reinvigorated judiciary. A new Civil Code, drafted on the model of the modern civil codes of Western Europe, restored the fundamental importance of civil and commercial law for the emerging free market economy.

Comprehensive political and legal reforms have largely reunited the Russian legal system with the civil law family. The following chapters will demonstrate how the on-going legal reforms concern not only substantive law, but also legal structures, sources of law, legal actors and legal procedures.

At the same time, the remaining relics of the socialist past make Russia different from other members of the modern civil law family. These

---

[8] See, in particular, J. Quigley, Socialist Law and the Civil Law Tradition, 37 *American Journal of Comparative Law* 781 (1989).

[9] On Russian economic reforms, see A. Aslund, How Russia Became a Market Economy (1995).

relics affect not only the content of legal institutions and rules, but also underlying attitudes about the nature and significance of law and the way it should be reformed and enforced. For example, there is still resistance to the notion of private ownership of land. Popular resistance to recent attempts aimed at dismantling the socialist welfare state became one of the major problems for the reformers. Despite massive privatization, the government's role in the economy is much more visible than in other civil law countries.

The traditional authoritarian style continues to pose a serious threat to the emerging democratic government. While the 1993 Constitution established a democratic form of government, it represents a continuation of the imperial and Soviet pattern of a strong executive. The juridical nihilism in the mass consciousness, described by Herzen in the 19th century,[10] continues to undermine efforts to install legality as a principle on which both society and the state should be based. The elimination of these and other residual elements of both imperial and socialist past will remain a predominant challenge for Russia in the years ahead.

An important factor in Russia's efforts to join the modern family of civil law countries will be European integration. The implementation of the rule of law principle in Russia became the subject of much debate in the Council of Europe, which Russia joined in 1996. Member states of the Council of Europe were impressed by Russia's progress in adopting new legislation. However, it is well known that the enactment of new laws is not enough. The ability of the government to implement the laws is the crucial element.[11] And most important, as the Council of Europe emphasized, one of Russia's major tasks is to develop a "legal culture" or "a broad awareness of, and respect for, the rule of law in all its aspects: political, legal and administrative - and at all levels: national, regional and local."[12] While recognizing the dynamics and direction of many positive legal and political developments across the Russian Federation, the Council of Europe noted that Russia's progress in this field will "take many years."[13]

---

[10] See *supra* note 5 and accompanying text.

[11] As Montesquieu wrote, "*Quand je vais dans un pays, je n'examine pas s'il y a des bonnes lois, mais si on execute celles qui y sont, car il y a des bonnes lois partout,*" Montesquieu, *Notes sur l'Angleterre*, in *Oeuvres Completes* 331-332 (1964). (Translation: "When I come to a country, I am not interested in whether there are good laws; I am interested in whether they are enforced, because good laws are available everywhere").

[12] Resolution No. 1065 "On Procedure for an Opinion on Russia's Request for Membership of the Council of Europe" (Adopted by the Parliamentary Assembly of the Council of Europe on September 26, 1995, Doc. H/INF (96) 1, at 103).

[13] Id.

E. Alternative Approaches to the Categorization of Legal Systems: Where Does Russia Fit?

Many comparativists reject the common law-civil law dichotomy as too simplistic and try to develop groupings on a variety of criteria other than the opposition between common and civil law. Some comparativists have traditionally treated the "Western legal tradition" as a single entity. For our purposes, it is interesting to look at alternative criteria that define Russia as falling outside the same group as other European civil law countries.

One contemporary alternative approach emphasizes the importance of law in the functioning of human societies. It is based on the idea that law plays a vital role in the actual life of individuals and groups only in "Western law" countries. In "non-Western" systems the law plays a much more limited role in ordering social and political life. Some comparativists suggest that all contemporary legal systems can be divided into three groups: (1) Western systems (both common and civil law); (2) the legal systems of developing and post-socialist countries and (3) legal systems dominated by non-Western traditions or ideology. The first group (the "Western legal tradition") is characterized by the predominance of the idea of law. The law is distinct from both politics and religious or philosophical traditions. In the second group (the "law of development and transition") these ideas have not taken root. As a result, the political process and the legal process cannot be separated. In these countries, the legal process is often determined by political relationships and policy considerations tend to prevail over the requirements of law. The third group (the "Eastern legal tradition") includes countries (such as Japan, China, Iran and India) where Confucianism or Islam play a major role.[14] Under this approach, the second group encompasses developing countries and the majority of post-socialist states, including Russia.[15]

Some Russian scholars also reject the idea that Russia is simply returning to the civil law family. They emphasize the profound cultural and religious differences between the Western European countries and Slavic nations. As a result, they have proposed a new classification which distinguishes Russia from other civil law countries. The proponents of this view argue that there is a separate "Slavic legal family" which has its own cultural, religious and moral values.[16] Important characteristics of the proposed new

---

[14] See U. Mattei, Three Patterns of Law: Taxonomy and Change in the World's Legal Systems, 45 *American Journal of Comparative Law* 5 (1997).

[15] Id., at 29, 30.

[16] See, V.N. Sinukov, *Pravovye sistemy I pravovye sem'i* (Legal Systems and Legal Families), in N.I. Matuzova, A.V. Mal'ko, *Teoriya gosudazstva I prava* (Theory of State and Law) 168, 175 (1997).

family include "elements of collective consciousness" and traditions of the Russian Orthodox Church.[17]

However, from a broad theoretical perspective, both these new global legal maps exaggerate the extent to which cultural differences affect the operation of legal systems. In practical terms it appears impossible to measure with any degree of certainty the extent of cultural differences between, for example, Southern and Northern Europe, on the one hand, and Western and Eastern Europe, on the other. As a result, it appears that the proposed new classifications are determined not by legal criteria, but largely by contemporary and traditional political theories (such as the "coming clash of civilizations" or Slavophilism).

The first of the above classifications is particularly problematic because it lumps together in the so-called "law of development and transition" such diverse countries as the less developed countries of Africa and Latin America, Eastern European countries and Cuba. Although transitional economies of Eastern Europe have encountered many problems, they are quite different from those of the developing world in terms of their responsiveness to "politics" or "policy" rather than law. And the nature of the political processes in these states must count for something. The fact that Cuba, a socialist totalitarian country, is included in the same group with post-Soviet era Eastern European countries should raise some serious doubts as to how useful this categorization is.

We believe that Russian law is gradually returning to the civil law family from which it came. However, it does not mean that there are no transitional problems that distinguish Russia from other civil law countries. From a micro-comparative perspective, Russia may fall into the category of transitional civil law systems that are primarily influenced by either Germanic or French civil law. As we will see later, different branches of Russian law may borrow from different models. For example, with respect to the organization of the executive branch of government, Russia has largely borrowed from the French model. In contrast, the ongoing codification of civil law has been influenced by the Germanic civil codes.

Be that as it may, the readers are advised to make their own judgment as to the precise categorization of Russian law after they have read the following chapters of this book.

---

[17] Id., at 180.

CHAPTER II

SOURCES AND HIERARCHY OF LAWS

A. Introduction

In all civil law systems there is a concept that is thought essential to the study of law. It is the theory or doctrine of "sources of law." While common law lawyers may attach less significance to formalistic theories about sources of law, lawyers from civil law countries have always emphasized the importance of a neat delineation of different sources of law and their interrelationship. This "grammar of law" is the first legal topic taught to Russian law students, usually in a course called "Theory of State and Law."

The Russian doctrine of sources has been developed under the influence of several general concepts. State positivism, as expressed in the concept of the sovereignty of the state, led to the recognition of an absolute state monopoly on law-making. As a result, "sources of law" are only those rules or norms that have been created or sanctioned by the Russian state. Separation of powers demands that only specially designated state organs are entitled to make law. As a general principle, all law-making power is lodged in the Russian parliament. Russian courts are empowered only to apply and to interpret the law in deciding cases, and hence they can not make law. Court judgments in individual cases, at whatever level of the judicial hierarchy rendered, are normally not considered as precedent for future cases. Consequently, as a general principle court decisions are not regarded as sources of law.

It is important to note that in Russia "sources of law" are only those legal acts that prescribe *general rules of conduct*. These acts are called "normative acts" since they establish norms of behavior for people. (In contrast, non- normative acts concern individual situations or specific matters and rely on the already established legal norms.)[1] Russian lawyers usually distinguish between two categories of "normative acts" - statutes or laws (*zakon*) and legislation *(zakonodatel'stvo)*. The term "statute" (*zakon*) refers to a form of law which has been promulgated by a parliamentary process.[2] In

---

[1] The distinction between normative and non-normative acts is discussed *infra* p. 17-22.

[2] The term "statute" (*zakon*) has been defined by the Constitutional Court as "an act of the highest legal force emanating from the highest organ of state power." See *Case Concerning the Decree of the RSFSR Supreme Soviet On the Interpretation of Art. 183 of the Constitution, VKS*, 1993, No. 2/3, p. 4.

contrast, the broader term "legislation" *(zakonodatel'stvo)* usually means any form of normative act which has been enacted by a state organ competent to promulgate or enact general rules of conduct. It may include statutes as well as various forms of secondary legislation of general application.

Recent revolutionary changes in the Russian legal system have resulted in several important innovations in the traditional doctrine of sources. The most important innovation has been the movement toward constitutionalism. While the Russian parliament remains the principal source of enacted rules, its legislative power is limited by the Constitution. The 1993 Constitution is considered not as a mere political guideline but as directly applicable fundamental and supreme law. An entirely new element and level of law in the system of sources has been introduced by judicial review of constitutionality of legislation. The Constitutional Court has been granted the power to annul unconstitutional legislation. At least in the civil law mind, this power undermines the traditional doctrine of sharp separation of legislative and judicial power.

Another major change in sources of law concerns the distribution of government power effected by the 1993 Constitution. It provides for a decentralization of government powers among the Russian Federation and its constituent units thus resulting in a more complex system of sources that includes not only federal, but also local legislation.

B. Domestic Sources of Law

The principal domestic sources of Russian law in order of their hierarchy are as follows: the Constitution, constitutional laws, statutes and sub-laws. Each of these sources will be discussed below.

1. The Constitution

The 1993 Russian Constitution was adopted by a popular referendum and is now considered to be the supreme law of the land. According to Art. 15 of the Constitution, "the Constitution of the Russian Federation shall have supreme legal force and direct effect, and shall be applicable throughout the entire territory of the Russian Federation."

Adopting the Constitution by referendum, in itself, was a major innovation because it involved the transfer of law-making power from the legislature to the people. As a result, the law-making power of the legislature as the sole source of law has been weakened. The power of legislation has been further weakened by the constitutional amendment procedure, that, among other things, provides that fundamental constitutional provisions cannot be revised by the Federal Assembly.[3]

In contrast to all Soviet constitutions, which were largely considered as instruments of ideology (and which, as a result, were not applied by courts), the new Constitution has direct legal effect. Although the 1993 Constitution includes some aspirational clauses, the majority of its provisions are self-executing and therefore may be applied both by the Constitutional Court and by courts of general jurisdiction.

The Supreme Court emphasized the significance of direct application of the Constitution by courts of general jurisdiction in its Ruling ("Explanation")[4] *"On Some Questions Concerning the Application of the Constitution of the Russian Federation by Courts."*[5] The Supreme Court ruled, among other things, that "the supreme legal force and direct effect of the Constitution means that all constitutional norms have priority over laws and subordinate legislation." The Supreme Court instructed the lower courts that "when hearing individual cases the courts must be guided by the Constitution of the Russian Federation." The lower courts were also instructed to evaluate the contents of applicable laws or other normative acts for their conformity to the Constitution and "to apply the Constitution of the Russian Federation as an act of direct effect in all necessary cases."[6] Judicial practice indicates that challenges to federal and local laws based on the 1993 Constitution before the Constitutional Court and ordinary courts have been increasingly successful.

2. Constitutional Laws

Constitutional laws are enacted in the most important areas of constitutional law as determined by the Constitution.[7] Adoption of these laws requires special majorities in both chambers of the Federal Assembly[8].

It is important to emphasize that constitutional laws do not become a part of the Constitution. In its ruling concerning interpretation of Art. 136 of the Constitution,[9] the Constitutional Court pointed out that constitutional laws cannot change the provisions of the Constitution and "cannot become its

---

[3]Constitution, Art. 135.

[4]The significance of the "explanations" of the Supreme Court will be explained *infra* p. 25-27.

[5]*BVS*, 1996, No. 1, p. 3.

[6]Id.

[7]See, e. g., Constitution, Arts. 56, 114, 118.

[8]Constitution, Art. 108.

[9]*Case Concerning Interpretation of Art. 136 of the Constitution, VKS*, 1995, No. 6, p. 10.

constituent part." The Constitutional Court also ruled that constitutional laws cannot be regarded as an appropriate vehicle for adopting constitutional amendments "because federal constitutional laws are supposed to be adopted only to govern issues specifically determined by the Constitution of the Russian Federation." According to the Court, amendments to the Constitution could be made only by promulgation of "a special legal act on constitutional amendment; this act differs from both federal laws and federal constitutional laws." At the same time, constitutional laws enjoy a higher hierarchical status with respect to ordinary laws. According to the Constitution, "federal laws may not contravene federal constitutional laws."[10]

3. Statutes

Statutes are the predominant source of law in Russia. Statutes are the unquestionable basis of all legal discourse. As in other civil law countries, there is a general tendency to believe that statutory language is supposed to provide answers in most cases. Again, as in other civil law countries, the Russian legislator is striving for comprehensive statutory rules. This tendency is particularly evident in the enactment of major codes.

The Russian codes are supposed to be a complete statement of the entire law in a particular area. New codes always replace the entire body of the preexisting law on a given matter. Although basic codes are usually supplemented by large bodies of special legislation, which develop provisions of the codes, codes retain their preeminence as major sources of law in a given area.

Since codes are supposed to be comprehensive - to contain all the rules applicable to all cases in the given area of law, the function of a judge is limited to selecting the code provision that applies to the dispute at hand. Nonetheless, gaps exist even in the most detailed of codes. But even in situations where a particular dispute is not directly governed by a specific code provision, judges should always find a basis for deciding a given case within the code. As a result, judges tend to resort to a rather flexible interpretation of the codes; they may also base their decisions on "general principles" of the applicable code (such "general principles" are usually contained in the first chapters of each code).[11] In addition, the Russian legal system (like other civil law systems) allows reasoning by analogy from statutory rules.[12]

Because all preexisting Soviet codes are outdated, the Russian

---

[10] Constitution, Art. 76.

[11] The "general principles" of the 1994 Civil Code will be discussed in Chapter VI.

[12] See *infra* p. 28-29.

parliament - the Federal Assembly - has the enormous task of reforming the existing legal system to meet the needs of the new society and the new government. Several new codes, including the Land Code, the Civil Procedure Code and the Criminal Procedure Code are still under debate. Some codes, including the Criminal Code and the Family Code have already been adopted. The most important Russian code adopted in recent years is the 1994 Civil Code.[13] The Civil Code is considered to be the "constitution" of the market economy and is designed to repeal all prior civil law and establish an entirely new system of market-oriented rules. The Civil Code enjoys a special hierarchical status among other codes and laws. It provides that "rules of civil law laid down by other laws shall be consistent with the present Code."[14] This means that while the Civil Code is not a "federal constitutional law," it has to be regarded as "the first among equals."[15]

The enactment of numerous new codes and statutes raises an important question about the legal status of pre-existing laws. The problem is of great practical significance because the Russian parliament sometimes fails to abolish old rules when enacting new ones. If there is a conflict between statutory rules on the same level, the later statute regulating the same subject matter supersede earlier ones. However, there may be exceptions to this general rule, for example, in cases where the older statute is expressly preserved.

4. Sub-Laws: Presidential Decrees and Agency Rules

The President may issue decrees and different federal agencies may adopt regulations that play a very important role as sources of Russian law. The power to enact the relevant subordinate acts (*podzakonye akty*) may be based on a general delegation when enacting the pertinent acts as part of the agency's competency, or it may be based on an ad hoc delegation.

The 1993 Constitution grants the President the power to issue both "normative" and "non-normative" decrees.[16] While Art. 90 of the Constitution does not restrict the President's power to issue normative decrees on certain topics, it states that they "may not contravene the Constitution of the

---

[13] The first part of the Civil Code was enacted in 1994 (*Sobranie*, No. 32, item 3301 (1994)). The second part - in 1995 (*Sobranie*, No. 5, item 410 (1996)). The third and final part of the new Civil Code is still under discussion.

[14] Civil Code, Art. 3.

[15] Courts have already started to emphasize the priority of the 1994 Civil Code over conflicting legislation. See, e.g., *Trukhina v. UPP VOS* (*BVS*, 1995, No. 9, p. 3) (1992 legislation concerning compensation for harm could not apply because it contravened Art. 208 of the new Civil Code).

[16] See Constitution, Arts. 90, 125 (2 (a)).

Russian Federation and federal laws." The President's power to issue "normative" decrees and regulations containing general rules of conduct became the subject of the most heated debate throughout the drafting process of the new Civil Code. Although the 1994 Civil Code confirmed the President's power to promulgate decrees that would govern "civil legal relations," the Code placed clear restrictions on that power. Art. 3 of the Code states that "The [civil law] relations defined in Art. 2 para. 1 and 2 of the present Code shall also be regulated by the decrees of the President of the Russian Federation, which shall not contradict the present Code and other laws." Art. 3 further states that if a decree of the President "contravenes the present Code or any other law, the present Code or the relevant law shall apply."

After the 1993 Constitution was adopted, the Federal Assembly was divided and managed to pass only a few laws that touched on economic reform. The sluggishness of Parliament's legislative work opened the doors for the President to fill the normative vacuum and, in particular, to regulate economic issues. Consequently, the President issued numerous "normative decrees" to fill gaps in the existing legislation. For a certain period of time the President became the principal legislator on economic matters, including privatization. Because of the gaps in the law, the President was able to legislate by decree in several areas without worrying about whether his acts would conflict with federal laws. Although the President's eagerness to legislate by decree became quite controversial, there was a general agreement that the decrees would remain in effect only until the adoption of relevant laws by the Federal Assembly.[17]

The Government of the Russian Federation is also granted the power to issue directives that may have a "normative" character.[18] According to Art. 3 of the Civil Code, "on the basis of and in execution of the present Code and other laws, and of the decrees of the President of the Russian Federation, the Government of the Russian Federation shall have the right to enact directives (*postanovleniya*) containing rules of civil law." Again, Art. 3 of the Civil Code provides that if "a directive of the Government of the Russian Federation contravenes the present Code or any other law, the present Code or the relevant law shall apply."

The power of different federal agencies to issue "normative" regulations in their areas of activity is generally recognized. Art. 3 of the Civil Code

---

[17] See *Case Concerning the Decree of the President "On Measures to Strengthen the Unified System of Executive Power in the Russian Federation," VKS*, 1996, No. 3, p. 15 (We will discuss this case in Chapter IV).

[18] Constitution, Art. 115.

provides that "in cases envisioned by the present Code, by other laws and other legal acts and within limits established by these legislative enactments, the ministries and other federal organs of federal executive power may issue acts containing rules of civil law." An example of the general delegation based on the Civil Code are delegations to transportation ministries and agencies, which may promulgate regulations concerning the carriage of goods and passengers[19] and to the Russian Central Bank, which may issue normative acts (instructions) governing money transfers by commercial banks.[20]

Sub-statutory regulations raise important questions about the limits of executive power. If the power of administrative agencies to enact subordinate legislation is not strictly defined, the delegation of law-making authority may be misused. New policies aimed at restricting excesses and misuses of administrative power resulted in attempts to limit the ability of executive organs to enact generally binding secondary legislation. One way to establish limits on agency rule-making is to permit enactment of the relevant rules solely by statute. The new Civil Code may serve as an illustration of this technique. As all other Russian codes, the Civil Code requires the promulgation of supplementary legislation. The form of such legislation is determined by the Code itself which may refer either to "statutes" or "legislation." Although the Civil Code still includes many references to "legislation" (that is, references to both statutes and various forms of secondary legislation), the number of clauses requiring promulgation of the supplementary rules by statute has increased. This means that the supplementary rules may be enacted only by the Russian parliament. For example, Art. 49 of the 1994 Civil Code, which deals with legal capacity of juridical persons, provides that juridical persons may engage in certain commercial activities only if they obtain a special authorization or licence. According to Art. 49, the list of such activities may be determined only by "a statute" (*zakon*). This means that in this area administrative agencies can no longer impose any restrictions on the activities of domestic or foreign juridical persons.

5. Sources of Russian Law in Judicial Practice: *Nuclear Fuel Cases*

At this stage it may be useful to turn to cases which illustrate some practical applications of concepts of the hierarchy and sources of law. One of the most challenging problems for the common law lawyers is the distinction between "normative" and "non-normative" acts. As noted earlier, normative acts are statutes and other acts of legislation that contain general rules of conduct. Non-normative acts deal with specific situations and specific actors.

[19] Civil Code, Art. 784.
[20] Civil Code, Art. 862.

While in some cases it is difficult to draw a clear line between these two types of acts, the distinction is extremely important for the operation of the Russian legal system. One area is the power of state bodies to enact normative acts containing rules of general application. Another area concerns the power of the courts to review the constitutionality of normative or non-normative acts, as will be discussed in Chapter III. Russia has a complicated court structure which includes the Constitutional Court, the Supreme Court and the Supreme Arbitration Court. These courts have different powers with respect to judicial review of normative or non-normative acts. Here we will consider two cases which illustrate the importance of the distinction under discussion for the jurisdiction of different courts.

The Constitutional Court: *Case Concerning the Decree of the President of the Russian Federation "On the State Support of the Structural Reconstruction and Conversion of Nuclear Industry in the City of Zheleznogorsk" (Konstitutsionnyi Sud Rossiiskoi Federatsii. Postanovlenia, opredelenia* 1992-1996, at 160 (1997))

[In 1995 the Russian President issued a Decree "On the State Support of the Structural Reconstruction and Conversion of Nuclear Industry in the City of Zheleznogorsk." The Decree envisioned, among other things, the continuation of the construction of a Plant PT-2 which was designed to regenerate used nuclear fuel. It also allowed the Krasnoyarsk mining-chemical enterprise to receive used nuclear fuel from foreign nuclear plants. The Decree became extremely controversial. Environmental activists claimed that it violated Art. 42 of the Constitution which provides that "everyone shall have the right to a favorable environment." Furthermore, the Decree violated several provisions of the 1991 Law "On the Protection of the Natural Environment,"[21] in particular Art. 50 of this Law, which prohibits any import "for purposes of storage or burial [of] radioactive wastes and materials from other countries."

The State Duma (the lower chamber of the Federal Assembly - the parliament of the Russian Federation) challenged the constitutionality of the Decree before the Constitutional Court.]

The challenged provisions constitute only a part of the Decree of the President of the Russian Federation on the main directions for the reconstruction and conversion of the military production of a mining-chemical enterprise located in the city of Zheleznogorsk of the Krasnoyarsk region. These provisions envision, among other thing, the continuation of the construction of Plant PT-2 designed to regenerate used nuclear fuel from certain types of

---

[21] *Vedomosty RF*, No. 10, item 457 (1992).

nuclear plants. . . The same mining-chemical enterprise had been given the right to receive used nuclear fuel from foreign nuclear plants which were built by using Russian designs, as well as from other plants. . .

The provisions of the Decree under discussion are of an operative and directive character; they contain specific instructions directed to specific subjects and are valid for only a limited period of time. They concern the development and operation of only one specific industrial plant, namely the Krasnoyarsk mining-chemical enterprise. Therefore, they do not have a normative character.

Under Art. 125(2)(a) of the Constitution of the Russian Federation and Art. 3(1)(a) of the Federal Constitutional Law "On the Constitutional Court of the Russian Federation," the Constitutional Court resolves cases concerning the compliance with the Constitution of only normative acts of the President. . . Therefore, the resolution of the question raised by the application of the State Duma. . . does not fall within the jurisdiction of the Constitutional Court. . .

The Supreme Court: *I.P. Blokov, A.V. Kisilev, O.N. Kuznetsov v. The President of the Russian Federation* (*Sudebnayia praktika po grazhdanskim delam* 1993-1996, at 69 (1997))

[Because the Constitutional Court dismissed the case, several environmental activists challenged the controversial Decree before the Supreme Court.]

The petitioners believe that the [challenged] Decree allows environmentally dangerous activities which violate the rights of citizens of the Russian Federation, including the rights of the petitioners to a favorable environment guaranteed by Art. 42 of the Constitution of the Russian Federation and Art. 11 of the Law "On the Protection of the Natural Environment.". . . [They] ask the Supreme Court to annul the part of the Decree which allows the mining-chemical enterprise to receive used nuclear fuel from foreign nuclear plants which were built using foreign designs. . .

The petitioners base their argument on the fact that under the Decree the reprocessing of the used nuclear fuel imported from other countries must be carried out at Plant PT-2 of the mining-chemical enterprise, which is still under construction. Because at this stage the enterprise lacks any facilities for reprocessing, the petitioners believe that permission to import nuclear fuel from foreign nuclear stations for reprocessing amounts to permission to import radioactive material for storage, which is prohibited by the law [Art. 50 of the Law "On the Protection of the Natural Environment"]. . .

The representative of the President rejected the claim by stating that the importation of used nuclear fuel from foreign stations for the purposes of subsequent reprocessing is not prohibited by the Law; therefore, the Decree of the President does not violate the Law "On the Protection of the Natural Environment." The technological process of regeneration always contemplates preliminary maintenance of the nuclear fuel in special containers. The above enterprise does have the necessary containers. . .

The Judicial Collegium for Civil Cases of the Supreme Court of the Russian Federation grants the petition in part for the following reasons:

Under Art. 50(3) of the RSFSR Law "On the Protection of the Natural Environment," any importation of radioactive wastes and materials for purposes of storage or burial is prohibited. The Court finds that the challenged Decree of the President of the Russian Federation does not have a normative character; as a result, the petition challenging the Decree must be considered, in accordance with Art. 116 of the Civil Procedure Code, by the Supreme Court of the Russian Federation.

The materials of the dossier indicate that the mining-chemical enterprise does not have any facilities for reprocessing the nuclear fuel. The Plant PT-2, which is still under construction. . ., has a storehouse for only short-term storage of nuclear fuel in the amount of 6000 tons. . . In view of this, the Judicial Collegium for Civil Cases of the Supreme Court finds that the provisions of the Decree allowing the mining-chemical enterprise to receive used nuclear fuel from foreign nuclear plants for the purpose of subsequent reprocessing violate Art. 50(3) of the RSFSR Law "On the Protection of the Natural Environment"; this part of the Decree is declared invalid. . . In the absence of the reprocessing plant, the permission given by the Decree to the mining-chemical plant to receive used nuclear fuel from foreign stations, even if this permission was given exclusively for the purposes of short-term maintenance and subsequent reprocessing, must be considered by the Court as a permission to receive such fuel for storage, which violates the requirements of the above Law and Art. 90 of the Constitution of the Russian Federation, according to which the decrees and orders of the President of the Russian Federation may not contravene the Constitution of the Russian Federation and federal laws.

At the same time, the Judicial Collegium finds that under the existing legislation of the Russian Federation the mining-chemical enterprise has the right to receive used nuclear fuel from foreign nuclear stations for the purposes of reprocessing from those countries, which conclude, within the framework of the established procedure, international treaties on the subject with the Russian Federation. This is because, in accordance with Art. 15(4) of the

Constitution of the Russian Federation the generally recognized principles and norms of international law and the international treaties of the Russian Federation shall constitute an integral part of its legal system, and if an international treaty of the Russian Federation establishes rules other than those stipulated by the law, the rules of the international treaty shall apply. . .

QUESTIONS AND COMMENTS

1. What is the significance of the difference between normative and non-normative act for the subject-matter jurisdiction of the Constitutional Court and the Supreme Court?

2. What is the essence of the definition of a non-normative act formulated by the Constitutional Court? Do you agree that a Decree authorizing importation of nuclear fuel from foreign nuclear plants to a Russian plant is a non-normative legal act? Why did the Constitutional Court put forward a rather narrow definition of a non-normative act in this case?

Note that in other cases the Constitutional Court appears to have used a broader definition. In the *Tatarstan Case* (*VKS,* 1993, No. 1, p. 43) the Court found that a resolution of the Tatarstan's legislature on the date and proposed questions for the local referendum on independence from Russia was of a normative character. The Court argued that the resolution under discussion "serves as a means to establish major legal consequences. . . Hence, the aforementioned resolution is not only a law-applying act but also an act of normative significance which presages the direction and meaning of the law-making process. The normative character of this resolution is also determined by the consequences of its implementation - the direct influence of the results of the referendum on the future constitutional process in the Republic and Russia as a whole." Is it possible to use this same argument in the *Nuclear Fuel Cases?*

In its Ruling "*On Some Issues Arising During the Judicial Consideration of Cases Upon Procurators' Applications Concerning the Recognition of Legal Acts as Contrary to the Law*" (*BVS*, 1993, No.7, p. 8), the Supreme Court formulated the following definition of "normative acts": "Such acts may be of a normative nature, i.e. setting forth legal rules (rules of conduct) binding on an indefinite number of people, intended for repeated application and remaining in force irrespective of whether particular legal relations envisioned by the act have begun or ceased to exist, and may also be of an individual nature, i.e. establishing, changing or revoking the rights and duties of particular persons." The Supreme Court also defined the non-normative act as an act which is "addressed to specific persons or a group of persons" (See *Rossi v. Deputy Head of Orenburg Regional Administration* (*BVS*, 1995, No. 12, p. 2)). How does the nuclear fuel decree fare under these two definitions?

3. Note that although the Supreme Court relied on some constitutional provisions, it ignored the arguments of the petitioners based on Art. 42 of the Constitution. Why did it do that? Some commentators believe that broad constitutional clauses guaranteeing the right to a favorable environment are non-justiciable. Do you agree?

4. What is the Supreme Court's view on the hierarchical significance of presidential decrees? How would you characterize the technique of interpretation used by the Supreme Court when it addressed the challenged presidential Decree and the Law "On the Protection of the Natural Environment?"

5. Note the importance of international treaties in the legal system of the Russian Federation. How did international treaties change the assessment of the legality of the challenged Decree?

We will discuss the importance of treaties and other international instruments for the Russian domestic order matter in some detail *infra* section C.

6. Judicial Decisions, Judicial Practice and "Explanations" of Supreme Courts

(a) The Traditional Understanding of Judge-Made Law

As noted earlier, under the traditional civil law approach only a democratically elected legislature is supposed to make law. The judicial function is restricted to applying the law. Law can not be made, either directly or indirectly, by judges.

The traditional attitude of most Russian lawyers is that judges are supposed to use only written law contained in codes, statutes or regulations in deciding a case. Although attorneys may use prior judicial decisions in their arguments, judges never refer to prior cases in their decisions. Court judgments in individual cases, even if rendered by the Supreme Court, are not precedents for future decisions.

(b) Some Inroads into the Tradition

Despite the fact that Russia follows the traditional civil law approach, certain contemporary changes in the responsibilities of the courts tend to undermine the traditional theory of sources. The most important innovation has been the movement toward judicial review.

(1) Judicial Review for Constitutionality

Decisions of the Constitutional Court in individual cases are now regarded as sources of law. The Constitutional Court of the Russian Federation has been granted the power to review the constitutionality of laws and other normative acts.[22] In reviewing challenged statutes and other normative acts, the Court is empowered to declare an unconstitutional act void.[23] Decisions of the Constitutional Court are binding on the entire territory of the Russian Federation and upon all representative, executive and judicial organs.[24] Because any declaration concerning unconstitutionality of normative acts would inevitably have an *erga omnes* (generalized) effect, it is generally recognized that the power to hold statutes and other normative acts invalid is a form of judicial law-making. It has been long accepted that judicial annulment of a statute enacted by the parliament has the same general character as its adoption, "but with a negative sign."[25] In other words, when the Constitutional Court annuls a statute enacted by the Russian parliament it functions as a "negative" legislator.

The law-making role of the Constitutional Court is recognized by leading Russian lawyers. The former Chairman of the Constitutional Court, V.A. Tumanov, notes in this connection that although as a formal matter the Constitutional Court is not a law-making body, its decisions change the law. They must be regarded as having "the character of a precedent that has a prescriptive rule or directive, which in the future must be followed by the law-making or other organs."[26] However, beyond the "negative" legislative

---

[22] Constitution, Art. 125.

[23] According to Art. 79 of the Federal Constitutional Law on the Constitutional Court of the Russian Federation (*Sobranie*, No. 13, item 1447 (1994)), "acts or their individual provisions judged unconstitutional shall become null and void."

[24] Id., Arts. 6 and 79. Note also that the Constitutional Court's interpretation of the Constitution is binding on all state bodies. Under Art. 106 of the Constitutional Law on the Constitutional Court, "the interpretation of the Constitution of the Russian Federation given by the Constitutional Court of the Russian Federation shall be official and binding upon all representative, executive and judicial agencies of state power, local self-government, enterprises, institutions, organizations, officials and citizens and their associations."

[25] The "negative" legislative function of constitutional courts was first emphasized by the father of the Austrian Constitutional Court, Hans Kelsen. See H. Kelsen, *La garantie jurisdictionelle de la constitution (la justice constitutionelle), Revue du droit public et de la science politique en France et à l'etranger*, at 206, 224, 226 (1928).

[26] V.A. Tumanov, *Predislovie* (Preface), *in Konstitutsionnyi sud Rossiiskoi Federatsii. Postanovleniya, Opredeleniya* 1992-1996 (The Constitutional Court of the Russian Federation. Decisions and Opinions 1992-1996) 5 (1997). Some judges of the

function, the precise bounds of the legal effect of a Constitutional Court decision in analogous cases is as yet unclear. There is evidence of the Court citing prior decisions for their analogical effect. At the same time, other evidence suggests that the Court may ignore what it has done in prior cases.[27]

(2) Judicial Invalidation of Normative Regulations Inconsistent with Statutes

Another instance of "negative" legislation is the power of the courts to decline to apply normative regulations, in particular subordinate regulations, that contravene statutes. The 1993 Constitution proclaims that courts of law shall "obey only the Constitution of the Russian Federation and federal law."[28] As a result, courts are instructed to apply only "the law" (and, of course, "legislation" enacted in accordance with it). Under Article 120(2) of the Constitution, "a court of law, having established during the consideration of a case that any act of a governmental or other organ does not correspond to the law, shall render a ruling in accordance with the law."[29]

The 1995 Arbitration Procedure Code[30] became the first procedural code to confirm this new court power. According to this Code, if an arbitration court finds that an act relied upon by a party in a given case does not correspond to "the law," the court must set aside the regulation in question and apply "the law." Although as a formal matter the ordinary or arbitration courts do not have the power to annul regulations contravening laws with an *erga omnes* effect, they do have the power to change, at least for the case at hand, the sub-laws or legislation in force. Judicial determinations that a particular regulation contravenes the law may gradually affect the operation of the whole legal system, if it is applied in other cases. The extent to which this

---

Constitutional Court believe that it is inappropriate to speak about the opinions of the Constitutional Court as precedents, because they are binding on all persons in all cases involving the relevant norm. By contrast, precedents control only cases that involve similar facts. See the statement of the Deputy Chairman of the Constitutional Court T.G. Morshchakova, in 5 *Gosudarstvo I pravo* 8 (1997). Cf. B.S. Ebzeev, *Konstitutsiya, pravovoe gosudarstvo, Konstitutsionnyi sud* (Constitution, Law-Based State, Constitutional Court) 163 (1997).

[27] Cf., for example, the various definitions of a normative act put forward by the Constitutional Court in different cases discussed *supra*.

[28] Constitution, Art. 120 (1).

[29] It is interesting to note that the entire system of judicial review in the United States is based on exactly this concept of constitutional review. See *Marbury v. Madison*, 5 U.S. 137, 178 (1803) ("[Since] the constitution is superior to any ordinary act of the legislature; the constitution, and not such ordinary act, must govern the case to which both apply.")

[30] See *Sobranie*, No. 19, item 1709 (1995).

will happen is, as yet, unclear. However, it is natural that courts will wish to assure that their decisions are consistent with one another.

Russia has also enacted a new law allowing judicial review of acts of organs or officials that contravene the law and violate the rights and freedoms of citizens.[31] Under the 1993 Law on Appeals citizens may challenge not only administrative action, but also normative acts issued by different state organs. Judicial practice indicates that, in controversies involving different types of normative acts issued by governmental agencies and local authorities, court judgements are playing a creative and important role in the development of the law.

(c) Settled Judicial Practice

Although these innovations have undoubtedly increased the law-making or law-changing power of the courts in certain situations, the majority of Russian lawyers would still argue that decisions of ordinary or arbitration courts in individual cases are not sources of law. At the same time many commentators would agree that *the established judicial practice* is becoming one of the important sources of Russian law.

Just as Western European civil lawyers discovered long ago,[32] many Russian lawyers realize that even if the legislature tries to enact absolutely complete, coherent and clear codes, written law still needs to be interpreted by judges in specific cases and that each interpretation adds some new meaning to the law. The judicial interpretation of codes inevitably results in the codes being adapted to changing conditions or applied to problems that the legislature did not envision. The role of the courts in shaping the law has become particularly evident at the present time, when the Russian legislation is in considerable flux and is full of contradictions.

(d) Judicial "Explanations" of the Law

The issue of judicial law-making is particularly interesting because, in Russia, the plenary session of the Supreme Court and the plenary session of the Supreme Arbitration Court have the power to provide so-called "explanations on issues pertaining to judicial practice."[33] The explanations' purpose is to

---

[31] See "Law on Appeals to Court Against the Actions and Acts Violating the Rights and Freedoms of Citizens," *Vedomosty RF*, No. 19, item 685 (1993) (as amended in 1995, see *Sobranie*, No. 51, item 4970 (1995)).

[32] Cf. M. Cappelletti, The Judicial Process in Comparative Perspective 3-8, 53-56 (1989).

[33] The term "Explanations" was introduced by Art. 126 of the 1993 Constitution. Prior to the adoption of the 1993 Constitution the "Explanations" of the Supreme Court were called "Guiding Explanations," which emphasized their binding character for lower courts. In the former Soviet Union, the "Guiding Explanations" were also issued by the plenary sessions of the USSR Supreme Court. Note that, in its

authoritatively interpret the law in controversial or unclear areas and instruct the entire court system on matters concerning the current application of the law. Often these explanations simply codify formally what is the already established "judicial practice," while others address relatively new issues. "Explanations" are addressed directly to the lower courts and often instruct them to interpret and to apply specific rules of law in a specific manner. By this method, the highest courts maintain uniformity in the approach of lower courts applying laws.

It is not clear to what extent "explanations" are formally binding on lower courts. On the one hand, Arts. 126 and 127 of the Constitution recognizes that part of the Supreme Courts and the Supreme Arbitration Court's powers involve issuing such "explanations on issues pertaining to judicial practice." On the other hand, Art. 120 of the Constitution provides that judges "shall obey only the Constitution of the Russian Federation and federal law." However, even if as a formal matter "explanations" are not binding on the courts, in reality they may be considered as a source of Russian law. The texts of all the "explanations" are published in the official bulletins of the Supreme Court and of the Supreme Arbitration Court, and are also published cumulatively in book form. (In contrast, only selected individual case opinions of the Supreme Court and of the Supreme Arbitration Court are published). "Explanations" are frequently cited by the courts, together with legislation, when deciding cases. All this is support for the proposition that the "explanations" constitute an important source of law.

The Deputy Chairman of the Supreme Court, V.M. Zhuykov, argues that the judicial practice consolidated in the "explanations" is a recognized source of law, because "explanations" are often cited by judges and may serve as an independent basis for a court's decision.[34] In his authoritative book Zhuykov cites many examples in which "Explanations" have created new rules of law. Furthermore, he also describes several interesting cases in which individual decisions of the Supreme Court created new rules of law. One such case is *Hublein, Inc. v. The Appellate Chamber of the Committee of the Russian*

1992 Ruling "*On the Application of the Guiding Explanations of the Plenary Sessions of the Supreme Court of the USSR,*" the Supreme Court of the Russian Federation stated that "pending the adoption of the relevant legislative acts of the Russian Federation, the norms of the former USSR and explanations concerning their application embodied in the guiding explanations of the plenary sessions of the Supreme Court of the USSR may be applied by courts in so far as they do not contradict the Constitution of the Russian Federation, legislation of the Russian Federation and the Agreement on the Creation of the Commonwealth of the Independent States" (*BVS*, 1992, No. 7, p. 11). Arbitration courts follow the same rule.

[34] See V.M. Zhuykov, *Sudebnaya zashchita prav grazhdan I juridicheskikh lits* (Judicial Defense of the Rights of Citizens and Juridical Persons) 145 (1997).

Federation on Patents and Trademarks.[35] This case established that Art. 46 of the Constitution, which guarantees the right of everyone to judicial enforcement of his or her rights, applies not only to citizens, but also to organizations, including foreign organizations.[36]

Zhuykov also points out that published decisions of the Supreme Court in individual cases are often taken into account by judges when resolving cases before them and, as a result, often serve as a de facto source of law. He believes that it is necessary to officially recognize that the decisions of the Supreme Court in individual cases are precedents and that courts have the right to cite them in their judgments.[37]

Other prominent jurists are more cautious. An example of such an attitude are the views of the Chairman of the Supreme Arbitration Court, V.F. Yakovlev. In discussing the role of the judgments of the Supreme Arbitration Court, Yakovlev points out that they are not binding for lower arbitration courts that consider similar cases.[38] At the same time he acknowledges that these judgments "play an important role in ensuring the consistency of practice of Russia's arbitration courts." He adds that "the opinions of the Presidium [of the Supreme Arbitration Court] in individual cases formulate the practice of interpretation and application of legal norms, which indeed becomes a general practice of all arbitration courts of Russia."[39]

7. Other Sources of Law

(a) USSR Legislation

It is clear that reform of the Russian legal system will take many years. It is also clear that a total rejection of Soviet laws would have created serious gaps in legal regulation. As a result, all newly independent states, including Russia, have had to rely on the legislation of the former Soviet Union. Soviet laws and regulations are applicable only insofar as Russian domestic law presently lacks such laws and the Soviet law does not conflict with any existing Russian law. In general, former Soviet law should be considered purely

---

[35] See *VKS*, 1995, No. 1, p. 11 (We will study this case in Chapter IV).

[36] Zhuykov, *supra* note 26, at 168-169.

[37] Id., at 189.

[38] V.F. Yakovlev, *Vstupitel'naya stat'ia* (Introduction), in 1 *Sbornik postanovlenii Prezidiuma Vysshego Arbitrazhnogo Suda* (Compilation of Opinions of the Presidium of the Supreme Arbitration Court) 1 (1996).

[39] Id. For a comparison of how Western European civil law countries deal with judicial decisions as precedent, see M. Shapiro, Courts: A Comparative and Political Analysis 143-150 (1981).

transitional - existing only until the Russian Parliament has enacted Russian laws in those areas.

The application of Soviet Union legislation on Russian territory is governed by the 1990 Law "On the Application of Acts of Organs of the USSR on the Territory of the RSFSR"[40] and the Supreme Soviet's decree ratifying the Agreement on the Creation of the Commonwealth of Independent States.[41] According to these enactments, Soviet laws apply only if they do not contradict the legislative acts of the Russian Federation adopted after June 12, 1990 (i.e. after the Russian Federation's proclamation of sovereignty). The 1993 Constitution adopted the same approach.[42]

An illustration of Soviet legislation's continued importance is the 1991 Fundamentals of Civil Legislation of the USSR and Union Republics of May 31, 1991.[43] Until legislative work on the third part of the new Civil Code is completed, almost all fundamental questions of private international law will continue to be governed by the 1991 Fundamentals.

(b) Analogy

In contrast to American judges who dislike reasoning by analogy from statutory provisions,[44] Russian judges feel much more comfortable with analogy. Although codes are supposed to be comprehensive statements of the entire law on the subject at hand, the written law cannot cover all possible situations that arise. The first instinct of a civil law judge would be to try to base the decision on the general principles included in the code or to interpret a specific statutory provisions in a broad manner. If flexible interpretation is not possible, the judge reasons by analogy. Although analogy is excluded in certain areas of law (such as criminal law), some codes expressly provide that judges may apply the code's rules by analogy to situations not covered by the specific content of the rule. The use of analogy is expressly allowed by the Civil Code. Art. 6 of the Civil Code provides:

---

[40] See *Vedomosty RF*, No. 21, item 237 (1990). At the time this law was enacted, "RSFSR" stood for the "Russian Soviet Federated Socialist Republic." After the dissolution of the Soviet Union, Russia became the "Russian Federation."

[41] See *Vedomosty RF*, No. 51, item 1798 (1991); See also the Decree of the Supreme Soviet of July 14, 1992 "On the Regulation of Civil Legal Relations During the Implementation of the Economic Reform," *Vedomosty RF*, No. 30, item 1800 (1992).

[42] See Constitution, Part II, Art. 2.

[43] *Vedomosty SSSR*, No. 26, item 733 (1991).

[44] See W. Burnham, Introduction to the Law and Legal System of the United States 62-64 (1995).

1. In cases where [civil law] relations defined in Art. 2 para. 1 and 2 of the present Code are not directly regulated by the legislation or by a contract between the parties and where an applicable commercial custom does not exist, the civil legislation governing similar relations shall apply, in so far as such an application will not contravene the nature of the relevant relation (analogy of statutes).

2. If it is not possible to resort to analogy of statutes, the rights and duties of the parties shall be determined on the basis of general principles and meaning of civil legislation (analogy of law) and the requirements of good faith, reasonableness and justice.

An analysis of Art. 6 indicates that there are two types of analogy available to a Russian judge: analogy of statutes and analogy of law. While Russian courts are not entirely reluctant to reason analogically from statutes, there are only a few examples of reasoning from the "meaning of civil legislation" (analogy of law).

A well-known example of the application of procedural rules by analogy is the *Communist Party Case* decided by the Constitutional Court. [45] The Court had to determine whether the Communist Party of the USSR was constitutional. However, the Constitutional Court rules governing the procedures to be followed by the Court did not contain any specific provisions on the matter. As a result, the Court held that "the procedure for the constitutional review of the constitutionality of political parties or any other public association may be established in accordance with the basic rules of procedure of the Constitutional Court, and, if necessary, on the basis of analogy of procedural law. . ."[46] In another case, in which the Court declared a clause of the Criminal Procedure Code unconstitutional, the Court added that the resulting gap "may be filled in by the judicial organs on the basis of procedural analogy."[47]

(c) Legal Consciousness, Natural Law, Good Faith and General Principles of Law and Justice

The prevailing doctrine of legislative positivism in principle precludes any reliance on natural law or similar broad concepts. According to Art. 120 of

---

[45] See *VKS*, 1993, No. 4/5, p. 37. We will discuss this fascinating case in Chapter IV.

[46] Id.

[47] *Case Concerning Art. 418 of the Criminal Procedure Code, VKS*, 1996, No. 5, p. 15, 20.

the Constitution, judges obey only Constitution and federal "law." It should be noted that the term "law" in this context means not written and unwritten law, but only statutes. The Russian version of Art. 120 of the Constitution uses the term *"zakon."* It does not use the broader term *"pravo."* Although both terms can be translated as "law," "*zakon*" is a narrower and more technical term. Usually it is used in connection with statutes. "*Pravo,*" on the other hand, encompasses both written and unwritten law. In a less positivist sense it may mean "justice."

A Russian judge would try to find broad principles of legislation not outside written law but within it. This task is facilitated by the standard structure of the codes which always contain introductory parts proclaiming certain general principles. However, from time to time even a Russian judge has to rely on certain broad notions of unwritten law. The analogy-of-law provisions of the Civil Code quoted above explicitly refer to reliance on "the requirements of good faith, reasonableness and justice." In times of change in a legal system these notions can become particularly important.

An interesting example on a recent non-positivistic attitude was the 1991 "Law on the Constitutional Court of the RSFSR."[48] It stated that the Constitutional Court "shall settle disputes and issue advisory opinions on the basis of the Constitution of the RSFSR and *legal consciousness*"[49] (emphasis added - eds.). Note, however, that the 1991 Law ceased to operate after the adoption of the 1993 Constitution. The 1994 Constitutional Law on the Constitutional Court[50] instructs the Court to apply the Russian Constitution only.[51]

Nevertheless, a careful analysis of the practice of the Constitutional Court indicates, that it does rely on certain general principles of law or logical propositions. Although sometimes these principles can be traced to practice or existing pieces of legislation, in some cases they are abstractions no longer directly connected with practice. For example, in the *Case Concerning Compensation in Cases of Unlawful Dismissal*[52] the Court held that the prevailing practice to pay compensation for only a limited period of time contradicts "the general legal principles of fairness and equality before the law." In the *Communist Party Case*[53] the Court stated that "in accordance with the general principles of law, any legal act of a general nature affecting the

[48] *Vedomosty RF*, No. 19, item 621 (1991).
[49] Law on the Constitutional Court of the RSFSR, Art. 1.
[50] *Sobranie*, No. 13, item 1447 (1994).
[51] 1994 Constitutional Law on the Constitutional Court, Art. 3.
[52] *VKS*, 1993, No. 2/3, p. 56, 60.
[53] *VKS*, 1993, No. 4/5, p. 37, 49.

rights, freedoms and duties of the human being, enters into force only after its publication or dissemination for public knowledge by other means." In the *Case Concerning Some Normative Acts of the City of Moscow,*[54] the Court referred to "the principles of equality and fairness" in connection with the establishment of local taxes. In the *Case Concerning Art. 97(5) of the Criminal Procedure Code*[55] the Court relied on the "principle of proportionality" which means that the government can enact "only such limits [on rights and freedoms] as are sufficient to vindicate the state's legitimate goals." Finally, in the *Case Concerning the Law On Excise Duties,*[56] the Court mentioned a "principle" according to which any law that negatively affects the rights of citizens or associations could not have retroactive effect.

(d) Custom

Because of the predominance of legislation, the role of custom in Russian law has been insignificant. Until recently, custom was applied only when the law expressly called for its application. While the existing statutory provisions contain certain direct references to custom,[57] it was generally assumed that custom had largely lost its role as a separate source of law.

While this traditional attitude is strong, the 1994 Civil Code sought to change the situation by expressly recognizing custom as a separate source of law. Under Art. 5 of the Civil Code, custom may apply in many situations not governed by legislation. Yet, even this recognition expressly excludes applying custom that contradicts written law. Art. 5 of the Civil Code provides:

1. An established and widely applicable rule of conduct in a particular area of entrepreneurial activity, not codified by the legislation and irrespective of whether or not it is laid down in a particular document, shall be recognized as commercial custom.

2. Commercial customs contravening the imperative provisions of legislation or of a contract binding upon the parties shall not apply.[58]

---

[54] *VKS,* 1996, No. 2, p. 42.

[55] *VKS,* 1996, No. 4, p. 2.

[56] *VKS,* 1996, No. 5, p. 2.

[57] As a rule, direct references relate to international customary rules. Thus, the 1991 Fundamentals of Civil Legislation provide that foreign law may be applied "on the basis of an international custom." (Art. 156). Cf. also the reference to "customs of international merchant shipping" in the 1968 USSR Merchant Shipping Code (Art. 15) (*Vedomosty SSSR,* No. 39, item 351 (1968)) (this Code is still in effect).

[58] Compare the above provisions on custom with Art. 9 of the United Nations Convention on Contracts for the International Sale of Goods (UN Doc. a/CONF.97/18 (1980)):

1. The parties are bound by any usage to which they have agreed and by any practices which they have established between themselves.

An analysis of custom's role must also take into account that lawyers may need to appeal to custom to clarify the ideas of the legislature. In other words, custom may play a certain role in interpreting or applying enacted law. Furthermore, customary practice may be taken into account in contract interpretation.[59]

An interesting new development is the reference to constitutional usages or traditions in the practice of the Constitutional Court. In a recent case, the Constitutional Court relied on constitutional "usage," which, according to the Court, established "a rule" that legislative organs of the constituent units of the Russian Federation could be elected for any period of time but not longer than for five years.[60]

(e) Academic Commentary

Individual scholars may have a formative influence on the content of the law when they prepare draft legislation or participate in public debates concerning legislative changes. However, academic commentary (often called "doctrine" in civil law countries) is not regarded as a source of law in Russia. Civil law scholars always played a prominent role in explaining the codes. The opinions of commentators of the major codes are widely used by attorneys and judges, but courts never cite such commentaries when issuing a decision.

C. International Law in the Russian Domestic Legal System

Compared to the United States, where international law plays a relatively minor role in the domestic legal system, international law is an important source of Russian law. According to Art. 15 (4) of the 1993 Constitution "the generally recognized principles and norms of international law and the international treaties of the Russian Federation shall constitute an integral part of its legal system." Art. 15(4) also states that "if an international treaty of the Russian Federation establishes rules other than those stipulated by the law, the rules of the international treaty shall apply."

---

2. The parties are considered, unless otherwise agreed, to have impliedly made applicable to their contract or its formation a usage of which the parties knew or ought to have known and which in international trade is widely known to, and regularly observed by, parties to contracts of the type involved in the particular trade concerned.

[59] See 1994 Civil Code, Art. 431 (which provides that contracts may be interpreted in the light of "commercial customs").

[60] See *Case Concerning the Postponement of Elections of the Legislative Organs of Certain Subjects of the Federation, Sobranie*, No. 20, item 2383 (1997).

Two principal features of Art. 15 must be pointed out. First, Art. 15 states that *all* international law is part of the Russian domestic legal system. In contrast to many contemporary constitutions, which usually refer to either treaties or to custom, Art. 15 incorporates both treaty law and "the generally recognized principles and norms of international law." This formulation includes sources of general international law, in particular general customary law. Second, Art. 15 establishes a higher normative status for treaty rules than for contrary domestic laws. Consequently, laws in force within Russia do not apply if their application is incompatible with treaty provisions. Domestic courts must give precedence to treaty norms over domestic law, be it antecedent or later-enacted, or federal or republic-level/provincial law. Art. 15, while it incorporates them, does not confer such superior status on "the generally recognized principles and norms of international law." It may be assumed that the main reason for this is the fact that customary law often lacks a sufficient degree of specificity. Another consideration may be the lack of parliamentary participation in customary law-making.[61]

Art. 15 of the 1993 Constitution is an important step toward wider application of international law in Russia. Russia embraced the idea of direct incorporation of international law as part of a general policy aimed at advancing the rule of law at the international and domestic level. The 1993 Constitution represents a bold political commitment to the international community and its fundamental values expressed in principles and norms of international law. From the domestic law perspective, international law, especially the international law of human rights, reinforces the legitimacy of the constitutional and other legal norms adopted in recent years. In cases where Russian constitutional or statutory laws fall below international standards, international law may become an important direct source of law for the protection of human rights and fundamental freedoms. International standards may be used as a highly legitimate and readily available legal instrument for abolishing outdated statutory norms. This function of international law is particularly important when one considers that the comprehen-

---

[61] While these two considerations may have affected Art. 15, "the generally recognized principles and norms of international law" of human rights may enjoy a higher status than contrary domestic legislation. The human rights section of the new Constitution includes Art. 17, which provides that human rights in Russia are recognized and ensured "according to the generally recognized principles and norms of international law." At first glance this reference to international law appears to be mere statement of policy. Yet it is still possible to interpret it as envisioning a higher hierarchical status for "the generally recognized principles and norms of international law" concerning human rights than for other "generally recognized principles and norms" mentioned in Art. 15. Recent court decisions appear to support the view that in the human rights area "the generally recognized principles and norms of international law" enjoy a higher status than contrary domestic law.

sive reform of Russian laws to eliminate inconsistencies with international norms is likely to take many years.[62]

It is well known that the actual status of international law in various domestic legal orders is determined not only be constitutional clauses but also by the willingness of courts to rely on that body of law. Judicial practice indicates that international law can be invoked before Russian domestic courts. Ordinary courts, which have little experience in applying international law, are still cautious about resorting to it, but the Constitutional Court has relied on international law in many cases.

The first case in which the Constitutional Court relied on international law is the *Labor Code Case*. This case concerned the controversial practice, sanctioned by a provision of the Labor Code, of using a simplified procedure to annul labor contracts with persons who had reached pension age - effectively a mandatory retirement law. Consider the relevant paragraphs of the Court's opinion:

The Constitutional Court: *The Labor Code Case* (*VKS*, 1993, No. 1, p. 29)[63]

[62]The significance of constitutional provisions concerning the relationship between international and Russian domestic law can be fully appreciated only against the background of the previous experience of the former Soviet Union. See G.M. Danilenko, The New Russian Constitution and International Law, 88 *American Journal of International Law* 451, 458 (1994) (The former Soviet Union never considered international law as something that might be invoked before, and enforced by, its domestic courts. The 1977 Constitution did not allow the direct operation of international law in the domestic setting. Although the Constitution proclaimed that the relations of the USSR with other states should be based on the principle of "fulfillment in good faith of obligations arising from the generally recognized principles and rules of international law, and from international treaties signed by the USSR," this broad clause was never interpreted as a general incorporation of international norms into Soviet domestic law. The application of international norms was envisaged in some exceptional cases of statutory references to international treaty law, but as a general constitutional principle the Soviet legal order remained closed to international legal norms. The Soviet legal system was protected from any direct penetration of international law by its conception of international law and municipal law as two completely separate legal systems. As a result of this dualist approach, the international obligations of the Soviet state would be applicable internally only if they were transformed by the legislature into a separate statute or administrative regulation. By relying on the doctrine of transformation, the Soviet Union was able to sign numerous international treaties, including treaties on human rights, and still avoid implementing some or all of their provisions into its domestic legal order.) (Citations omitted).

[63]Note that this ruling was rendered on the basis of the 1978 Constitution.

The complainants, B. A. Altgovzen and M. F. Stadnikova, appeal in the Constitutional Court the decision to terminate their labor contracts adopted in accordance with Art. 33(1.1) of the Labor Code, and all the court decisions related to their case, on the grounds that their constitutional right to employment was violated and that it was not protected by the court in accordance with the existing legal procedures. The labor contracts were terminated because the plaintiffs had reached pensionable age and were eligible for a full old-age pension.

B.A. Altgovzen, a foreman of the Orgstroi Production Association, Leningrad, was dismissed by his employer on February 1, 1990. Altgovzen filed a lawsuit in the Smolninsky district court requesting reinstatement in his job. On March 20, 1991, the court rejected his claim. On April 25, 1991, the Collegium for Civil Cases of the Leningrad City Court reviewed and affirmed the decision of the district court. The appeals of this decision in accordance with the supervisory procedures were rejected by both the Leningrad City Court and the Supreme Court of the Russian Federation.

Similar court decisions were rendered in the case of M. F. Stadnikova, a barge-skipper who was dismissed by the management of the Astrakhan port on March 29, 1991. The decision of the Kirovsky district court, which rejected Stadnikova's request for the recovery of her job, was affirmed by the Collegium for Civil Cases of the Astrakhan City Court on January 2, 1992. The appeal to the Supreme Court of the Russian Federation in accordance with supervisory procedures was also rejected.

All the decisions in these cases stated that the dismissals were made strictly in accordance with Art. 33(1.1) of the Labor Code of the Russian Federation. . . However, in accordance with the meaning of the Constitution of the RSFSR this norm should not have been applied.

According to Art. 32 of the Constitution, "all citizens of the Russian Federation are equal before the law regardless of origin, social and property status, race, nationality, gender, education, language, religion, type and nature of occupation, place of residence and other circumstances. The equality of Russian Federation citizens shall be ensured in all spheres of economic, political, social and cultural life."

Art. 38 of the Constitution, which proclaims the right to work, guarantees "the right to choose a profession, type of occupation and job in accordance with one's calling, capabilities, professional training and education, and taking into account social needs." In accordance with Art. 14 of the Constitution, the law ensures that all people engaged in production enjoy fair conditions of employment, dismissal, remuneration for work and safety in the workplace.

It follows from these constitutional provisions that, first, any discrimination of citizens is inadmissible, not only on the grounds stated in Art. 32, but also on other grounds. Second, the law ensures the equality of citizens in the exercise of their right to work. Third, pensionable age may not constitute an obstacle to the exercise of this right (indeed, the Constitution specifies other criteria that should be considered when concluding and canceling labor agreements, namely: one's calling, capabilities, professional fitness and education, as well as social needs).

Far from restricting the list of reasons for which a person may not be subject to discrimination, the Constitution suggests that it should be further specified by follow-up legislation and rules of law. Like the Constitution, the Declaration of the Rights and Freedoms of the Individual and Citizen, adopted by the Supreme Soviet on November 22, 1991, which also proclaims the principle of the equality of people before the law, does not provide an exhaustive list of grounds of discrimination; it only introduces some grounds, such as one's convictions, affiliation with any public association and job status. It should also be noted that the Law of the Russian Federation "On Employment," adopted on April 19, 1991, provides such a guarantee for the right to work as equal employment opportunities without regard to age (Art. 5).

Given that the Constitution and the follow-up laws that clarify it contain an open list of discriminating grounds, age may not be regarded as a reason for discrimination in the exercise of the right to work. . .

It follows from Art. 28 of the Constitution that Russia ensures good faith fulfillment of obligations arising from the generally recognized principles and norms of international law and from international treaties and agreements signed by Russia. The latter's supremacy over Russian laws is confirmed by the Declaration of the Rights and Freedoms of the Individual and Citizen. The rule codified in Art. 33(1.1) of the Labor Code, whereby a labor contract may be canceled on the initiative of the employer when a person reaches pensionable age, contradicts several international acts concerning human rights.

This rule contravenes Art. 7 of the 1948 Universal Declaration of Human Rights which proclaims that all are equal before the law and are entitled to equal protection against any discrimination. It also contradicts Art. 2 of the 1966 International Covenant on Economic, Social and Cultural Rights, concerning the duty of the state to guarantee the exercise of the relevant rights without discrimination of any kind.

Art. 33(1.1) of the Labor Code is incompatible with the obligations assumed by the states that signed and ratified the International Labor Organization's Convention No. 111 (adopted in 1958) concerning discrimination in the field of employment. In accordance with Art. 2 of the Convention, states are obliged to pursue national policies to encourage equal opportunity for employment in order to eradicate any discrimination in this field. Under Art. 1(2) of the same Convention, only distinctions, exclusions and preferences based on specific requirements (qualifications) of concrete jobs are not regarded as discrimination. Dismissal on the ground that a person has reached pensionable age is not connected to such requirements and therefore may be classified, in accordance with international legal standards, as impermissible discrimination in the field of employment, which, according to Art. 1(1 "a" and "b") of Convention No. 111, is defined as any distinction, exclusion or preference resulting either in the elimination or violation of equal opportunities in the field of employment.

Prevention of discrimination on the grounds of age is also the aim of several recommendations adopted by the International Labor Organization. Thus, ILO Recommendation 162 "On Elderly Workers" (adopted in 1980) proceeds from the inadmissibility of any discrimination against senior citizens in the field of employment (Paragraph 3) and the need to guarantee them equal opportunities in the field of employment and access to work in accordance with their choice (Paragraph 5). It qualifies rules of law allowing termination of labor contracts on the grounds of age, if it is not connected to the character of work in question, as discrimination in the field of employment (Paragraph 22). In accordance with Paragraph 5 of the ILO's Recommendation No. 166 "On the Termination of Labor Contracts On the Initiative of the Employer" (adopted in 1982) the age of a worker may not serve as grounds for canceling his labor contract.

Therefore, international legal documents classify the termination of labor contracts on grounds of age as impermissible discrimination, if the termination is not required by the type and specifics of the relevant work.

The social-legal consequences of the cancellation of the labor contract of a worker who has reached pensionable age and is entitled to a full old-age pension and the usage of law-applying practice based on Art. 33(1.1) of the Labor Code confirm the discriminatory nature of this rule. Because of the low pensionable age established in the Russian Federation, the application of Art. 33(1.1) of the Labor Code results in the violation of the right of a very large social group to equal opportunities in the field of employment and protection against unemployment. It also restricts their opportunities to earn a living and maintain decent living standards, especially in a situation when old-age pensions are rather low. At the same time, in accordance with international legal documents and related domestic legislation, pensioners are referred to as a category of people who need social protection and additional employment guarantees (Art. 13 of the Law "On Employment"). The absence of such guarantees leads to real discrimination against pensioners in the field of employment. . .

Furthermore, when dismissed on the grounds of pensionable age the worker is deprived not only of many guarantees and compensation benefits, but also of the right to court review of the circumstances of the dismissal. When considering a labor dispute over the termination of a labor contract on the grounds that the worker has reached pensionable age and is entitled to a full old-age pension, the courts tend to qualify such dismissals as lawful, because such a ground is expressly mentioned by Art. 33(1.1) of the Labor Code. . . The courts that considered Altgovzen's and Stadnikova's requests to be reinstated also restricted themselves to verifying the fact that the plaintiffs had reached pensionable age and were entitled to a full old-age pension. After verifying these facts the courts ruled that there were sufficient grounds for confirming the legitimacy of the plaintiffs' dismissals in accordance with Art. 33(1.1) of the Labor Code. . . In the case of Altgovzen and Stadnikova, as well as in other cases concerning Art. 33 of the Labor Code, the courts did not evaluate whether this rule was compatible with the Constitution of the Russian Federation.

Such an application of the law contradicts the obligation of state bodies and officials to observe the Constitution, laid down in Art. 4 of the Constitution. It follows from this constitutional provision that the Constitution must be directly applied by the courts should they discover contradictions between constitutional norms and other laws. The courts should also assess the applicable law from the point of view of its conformity with the principles and rules of international law, because the Constitution requires good faith observance of obligations arising from them. In addition, in accordance with the 1991 Declaration of the Rights and Freedoms of the Individual and Citizen, which develops these constitutional provisions, the generally recognized international human rights norms directly create rights and obligations for the citizens of Russia. . .

QUESTIONS AND COMMENTS

1. It is important to keep in mind that the present opinion was based on the 1978 Constitution which, like the 1977 Constitution of the USSR, did not contain any clause declaring international law to be part of the law of the land. It included only Art. 28 according to which, as the Court noted, "Russia ensures good faith fulfillment of obligations arising from the generally recognized principles and norms of international law and from international

treaties and agreements signed by Russia." As noted earlier, this broad clause was never interpreted as a general incorporation of international law into the Soviet or Soviet Russian law. Yet even in this situation the Court based its decision not only on the Constitution, but also on a variety of international instruments, in finding that the simplified procedure envisioned by the Labor Code violated the principle of nondiscrimination. Furthermore, the Court held that in the Russian domestic context Art. 28 required the courts to "assess the applicable law from the point of view of its conformity with the principles and rules of international law." What might explain the Court's novel approach?

2. Art. 28 of the 1978 Constitution did not establish any supremacy of "the generally recognized principles and norms of international law" over the Russian domestic law. At that time, such supremacy was proclaimed only by the 1991 Declaration of the Rights and Freedoms of Person and Citizen adopted by the then existing legislature - the Congress of People's Deputies(See *Vedomosty RF*, No. 52, item 1865 (1991)). Art. 1 of the Declaration proclaimed that "the generally recognized international norms concerning human rights have priority over laws of the Russian Federation and directly create rights and obligations for the citizens of the Russian Federation." However, the Declaration was not adopted as a legally binding instrument. How would you explain the holding of the Court that "the generally recognized principles and norms of international law" override contrary Russian domestic law? Which norms, if any, may have such higher hierarchical status?

3. The practice of international courts and tribunals indicates that "the generally recognized principles and norms of international law" include general customary principles and rules. For example, the International Court of Justice held that the generally recognized principles of international law proclaimed in the United Nations Declaration on Principles of International Law (U.N. General Assembly Resolution 2626 (1970)), are "the general rules of international customary law" (*Nicaragua Case*, I.C.J. Reports, 1986, pp. 92-98). (Art. 38 of the Statute of I.C.J. defines international customary law "as evidence of a general practice accepted as law"). How would you interpret the phrase "the generally recognized principles and norms of international law" as used in the present opinion of the Constitutional Court and in the 1993 Constitution?

4. What evidence of the "the general principles and rules of international law" prohibiting discrimination on the ground of age was cited by the Court? Is this evidence persuasive or sufficient?

5. Note the extensive reliance by the Court on non-binding international instruments - the Universal Declaration of Human Rights, ILO recommendation No. 162 and the ILO recommendation No. 166. Why did the

Court cite these legally non-binding instruments? Can an ILO *recommendation* prevail over contrary provisions of Russian domestic law?

6. The Court also relied on international treaties - the International Covenant on Economic, Social and Cultural Rights and the International Labor Organization Convention No. 111. However, both treaties are essentially aspirational. Furthermore, they require the adoption of domestic legislative measures to be effective in any given country.

Consider Art. 2 of the Covenant: "Each state party to the present Covenant undertakes to take steps, individually and through international assistance and co-operation, especially economic and technical, to the maximum of its available resources, with a view to achieving progressively the full realization of the rights recognized in the present Covenant by all appropriate means, including particularly the adoption of legislative measures."

Further, Art. 2 of the ILO Convention No. 111 provides that each member state undertakes to pursue a national policy designed to promote elimination of any discrimination in employment "by methods appropriate to national conditions and practice." Under Art. 3 of the Convention, state parties assume an obligation to enact "legislation" to secure the acceptance and observance of the policy and "to repeal any statutory provisions" which are inconsistent with the policy.

In view of this, can these treaties or their provisions be considered to be self-executing? If these kinds of treaty provisions have direct effect, what other kinds of treaties might apply?

7. Under the first Law on the Constitutional Court (see *Vedomosty RF,* No. 19, item 621 (1991), no longer in force), decisions of the Court on individual complaints only affected the parties involved. If the constitutional Court declared a practice based on the application of a law unconstitutional, it was not authorized to annul the law. The Court usually required the organ that issued the law to repeal it. In this case, the Court asked the then-existing parliament - the Supreme Soviet - to abolish Art. 33(1.1) of the Labor Code. Art. 33(1.1) was abolished by the Supreme Soviet on March 12, 1992 (see *Vedomosty RF,* No. 14, item 712 (1992)).

8. The concept of self-executing treaties was first elaborated in 1952 by the California Supreme Court in the case of *Sei Fujii v. State* (38 Cal.2d 718, 242 P2d 617 (1952)). The California Supreme Court held that the human rights provisions of the U.N. Charter were non-self-executing because they were merely aspirational and lacked "the mandatory quality and definiteness which would indicate an intent to create justiciable rights in private persons immediately upon ratification." Since then the concept of self-executing

treaties crossed the Atlantic and became common legal doctrine in Europe. The following article will, among other things, discuss the emerging Russian concept of self-executing or directly applicable treaties.

***

G.M. Danilenko, International Law in the Russian Legal System (*Proceedings of the 91st Annual Meeting of the American Society of International Law* 295 (1997))[64]

Lawyers in the fields of international and comparative law who follow developments in Eastern Europe know that this region has become the world's most exciting laboratory of constitutional reform. From the international perspective, the most interesting aspect of Eastern European developments is the gradual "opening" of the domestic legal systems of countries in this region to international law.

In many respects, Russia is an illustration of the Eastern European trend. Russia is particularly interesting for at least two reasons. First, the "opening" to international law represents a radical departure from Russia's traditional isolationism. Second, the "opening" began several years ago. As a result, one can see how the techniques of direct incorporation have been tested and implemented in practice.

When Russia engaged in constitution drafting, most participants in the debate agreed that the country needed to abandon its traditional dualistic approach. In 1992, for the first time in its history, Russia adopted a constitutional principle incorporating "the generally recognized international norms concerning human rights" into its domestic law.[65] By introducing the concept of direct relevance of international law to the internal legal process, the country took a giant step away from its previous isolationist stand. It should be noted that the 1992 constitutional amendment focused on international human rights law. This is quite understandable in view of the massive violations of human rights that took place in the Soviet Union. By incorporating the whole body of international human rights law into the Russian domestic law, the drafters of the 1992 amendment hoped to effect rapid changes in the legal environment.

The 1993 Constitution confirmed the trend of giving a prominent

---

[64] Copyright by the American Society of International Law. Reproduced with permission.

[65] For details, see G.M. Danilenko, The New Russian Constitution and International Law, 88 *American Journal of International Law* 451, 461 (1994).

place to international legal standards in the domestic legal setting. . . I will now turn to recent Russian court decisions dealing with incorporation of international law into the Russian domestic legal system. From a broad political-legal perspective, an examination of judicial practice may indicate whether Art. 15 has any practical effect on the operation of the Russian domestic legal system. While the 1993 Constitution represents an important step toward wider application of international law in Russia, it cannot in itself be considered a guarantee that international law will enjoy the status envisioned for it by its framers. The actual status of international law in the Russian domestic legal system is and will continue to be determined not only by the constitutional clauses, but also by the willingness of courts to rely on that body of law.

In many countries constitutional rules remain a dead letter. There are many instances of domestic courts simply ignoring broad constitutional clauses referring to international law. It is not surprising that with respect to Russia, which lacks any experience in the direct implementation of constitutional norms, there is much skepticism as to the possible practical effect of Art. 15. An example of such skepticism is the report of the group of eminent experts of the Council of Europe who stated in 1994 that with respect to the implementation of international human rights in Russia Art. 15 seems "to be more theory than practice."[66] I will try to show that this pessimistic assessment of the situation was incorrect in 1994 and remains incorrect today.

An examination of judicial practice is also interesting from a technical perspective. It is always interesting to investigate how the courts ascertain applicable international law (and whether there is any executive's intervention in the process) or whether the courts develop any judicial doctrines aimed at avoiding direct application of international norms. I will focus on only one problem - the emerging Russian doctrine of directly applicable or self-executing treaties.

Judicial practice indicates that Russian courts do rely on international law. The Constitutional Court invokes international law in almost all of its decisions concerning human rights. In fact, the Court started to rely on international law even before the enactment of the constitutional provision declaring international law part of the Russian domestic law. For example, the *Labor Code Case*[67] was decided by the Constitutional Court before the adoption of the 1992 constitutional amendment. Yet even in that situation the

---

[66] Report on the Conformity of the Legal Order of the Russian Federation with the Council of Europe Standards, Doc. AS/Bur/Russia (1994), reprinted in 15 *Human Rights Law Journal* 249, 250 (1994).

[67] See *VKS*, 1993, No. 1, p. 29.

Court based its decision on a variety of international instruments. In searching for a constitutional basis for the direct application of international norms, the Court innovated by broadly interpreting a very general reference to international law in the Soviet-era Constitution. This example indicates that, in a favorable political environment open to international standards, even vague references to international law may be interpreted by courts as requiring direct application of that body of law.

The Constitutional Court often relies not only on treaties, but on "the generally recognized principles and norms of international law." In so doing, the Court appears to regard "the generally recognized principles and norms" concerning human rights as having a higher hierarchical status than contrary domestic law. For example, in the *Moscow Residence Permits Case*[68] the Court declared the local regulations requiring residence permits unconstitutional by referring not only to human rights treaties, but to the "generally recognized principle and norms of international law."

Ordinary Russian courts have much less experience in applying international law. However, even here there is progress. In 1995, the Russian Supreme Court issued a ruling on the matter in the form of an "Explanation."[69] "Explanations" are abstract opinions that are binding on all lower courts. The 1995 ruling instructed all lower courts to apply international law directly.

The developments described above indicate that Art. 15 of the new Russian Constitution is not a dead letter. International law can be invoked before the Russian domestic courts.

I now turn to the emerging Russian concept of directly applicable or self-executing treaties. The issue may become crucial for the entire regime of incorporation in Russia because an extensive use of the doctrine could effectively "close" the domestic legal order and, in extreme situations, turn a monistic state into a dualistic one.

An analysis of decisions of the Constitutional Court indicates that it makes no distinction between self-executing and non-self executing treaties. The *Labor Code Case* is probably the best illustration of this trend. In declaring age discrimination in labor relations unconstitutional, the Court relied, among other things, on the International Covenant on Economic, Social and Cultural Rights (ICESCR) and the International Labor Organization (ILO) Convention No. 111. I doubt that the courts of the majority of monistic

---

[68] See *VKS*, 1996, No. 2 p. 42.
[69] See *BVS*, 1996, No. 1, at 3.

countries would consider these treaties to be self-executing, because they are essentially programmatic. Both Art. 2 of the ICESCR and Art. 2 of ILO Convention No. 111 provide for progressive realization of these treaties. It appears that state parties to these treaties intended merely to assume a commitment to work towards the achievement of certain policy objectives. Such programmatic commitments, by their very nature, cannot be self-executing. Therefore they are incapable of overriding conflicting domestic legislation. However, one could argue that only the realization of the substantive rights guaranteed by the ICESCR was intended to be progressive. By contrast, the obligation of non-discrimination provided for in Art. 2(2) of the Covenant must be realized immediately. Even if we would agree that the essentially programmatic nature of obligations under the Covenant does not necessarily mean that the prohibition against discrimination cannot have direct effect, it is much more difficult to advance this type of argument with respect to ILO Convention No. 111.

Other evidence of the non-self-executing nature of these treaties is the requirement that state parties adopt domestic "legislative measures." The argument based on the obligation to adopt domestic legislative measures seems particularly strong with respect to the ILO Convention No. 111. Under Art. 2 of the ILO Convention, each member state undertakes to pursue a national policy designed to promote elimination of any discrimination in employment "by methods appropriate to national conditions and practice." Under Art. 3 of the Convention, state parties assume an obligation to enact "legislation" to secure the acceptance and observance of the policy and "to repel any statutory provisions" which are inconsistent with the policy. Express provisions of this kind seem to undermine any claim that the relevant international standard is self-executing.

The Constitutional Court used a slightly different approach in the *Collective Labor Disputes Case.*[70] The Court did recognize that under the ICESCR the regulation of the right to strike must be effected by domestic legislation. Indeed, under Art. 8 of the Covenant, state parties undertake to ensure "the right to strike, provided that it is exercised in conformity with the laws of the particular country." However, the Court still held that the limits of permissible restrictions established by the Covenant are directly applicable or self-executing.

While in the cases described above the Constitutional Court refused to draw any distinction between self-executing and non-self-executing treaties, the Russian legislature took the initiative. The 1995 Law on International

[70]See *VKS*, 1995, No. 2/3, p. 45.

Treaties[71] includes a clause which states that "the provisions of officially published international treaties of the Russian Federation, which do not require the promulgation of domestic acts for application, shall operate in the Russian Federation directly. In order to effectuate other provisions of international treaties of the Russian Federation, the relevant legal acts shall be adopted." This clause is based on the idea that as a matter of principle there are two categories of treaties and that certain treaties must be transformed into the domestic legal system in order to be effective. At the same time, the clause does not reveal much about the characteristics that make a treaty non-self-executing. One thing is clear, however: Any treaty provision that expressly requires states to adopt legislative measures cannot be considered directly applicable or self-executing.

It appears that the Constitutional Court is also moving toward recognition of the distinction between different categories of treaties and of the importance of this distinction for their effective domestic implementation. In the *Chechnya Case*[72] the Court noted that the absence of the relevant domestic regulations that would have transformed the provisions of the Additional Protocol II to the Geneva Conventions into domestic law "became one of the reasons for non-compliance with [its] rules."

It will be interesting to see whether the Russian courts apply the doctrine of self-executing treaties broadly or restrictively. Different political-legal considerations will influence further developments in this area. Russia embraced the idea of direct incorporation of international law primarily because it wanted to improve the domestic human rights situation. This consideration will continue to favor direct application of international norms. At the same time, there are political-legal considerations which may push Russia in the opposite direction. While at this stage we cannot exclude the possibility of isolationism and nationalism, Russia may encounter difficulties with domestic implementation of certain norms of international law in any political environment. For example, Russia is trying to enter international markets and join international regulatory regimes that govern international trade. It may soon discover that some of the rules and practices established by trading nations could create serious problems for its economy. It may then try to restrict the direct applicability of the relevant trade rules in its domestic legal order by relying on a broad version of the doctrine of non-self-executing treaties.

An important factor favoring direct application of treaties will be Russia's participation in international institutions. Indeed, I think that

[71] See *Sobranie*, No. 29, item 2757 (1995), Art. 5.
[72] See *VKS*, 1995, No. 5, p. 3.

Russia's integration into the existing global and regional organizations will be a decisive factor. Experience indicates that, if a country joins international institutions to which aggrieved individuals may appeal against breaches of treaty obligations on the domestic level, national authorities tend to take treaty obligations seriously. We know, for example, that the jurisprudence of the European Court of Human Rights exerts a strong influence on the attitude of domestic courts of the members of the Council of Europe. As soon as the domestic authorities, including judges, realize that the European Court is emerging as a kind of Pan-European Constitutional Court, they start to pay much closer attention to the European Convention on Human Rights and to the case-law of the European Court of Human Rights. As a result, there is much more willingness than before to apply the European Convention directly.

Russia is bound by the Optional Protocol to the International Covenant on Civil and Political Rights and recently joined the Council of Europe. I believe that the interaction between Russian domestic courts and the European Court of Human Rights will have a particularly significant impact on the direct domestic application of human rights treaties.

It is appropriate to mention here that under Art. 15 of the Russian Constitution it is possible not only to invoke rules of treaties before domestic courts but to rely on the interpretation of such treaties by international organs. As a result, once Russia ratifies the European Convention on Human Rights,[72a] there will be no bar to the domestic use of the interpretation of the Convention advanced by the European Court of Human Rights. The case-law of the European Court may thus be gradually transformed into Russian domestic jurisprudence.

In this connection, I would like to draw your attention to Art. 46 of the Russian Constitution. Art. 46 reinforces the direct applicability of international human rights standards by providing that all persons enjoy a constitutionally protected right to submit petitions to "inter-state organs concerned with the protection of human rights and freedoms" after exhausting domestic remedies. In a recent case concerning the Criminal Procedure Code, the Constitutional Court held that decisions of these organs may lead to domestic reexamination of previously decided cases.[73] Because Art. 46 does not expressly refer to international courts, it appears that a request for the re-opening of the case could be successful even on the basis of "the views" adopted by the Human Rights Committee under the Optional Protocol. Although the legislature has yet to adopt new procedural codes that would add a new ground for re-opening

---

[72a] Russia ratified the European Convention on Human Rights in early 1998, see *Sobranie*, No. 14, item 1514 (1998).

[73] See *Sobranie*, No. 7, item 701 (1996).

proceedings with express reference to findings of international organs,[74] the innovative interpretation of Art. 46 advanced by the Constitutional Court established an obligation to give direct domestic effect to decisions of international human rights bodies. This provides additional guarantees of Russia's compliance with international obligations. In practice only a small percentage of cases could be referred to the Human Rights Committee or to the European Court of Human Rights. However, Russian judges are beginning to realize that there are international institutions which can verify their interpretation of international human rights principles and norms. Thanks to the recent holding of the Constitutional Court, Russian judges will also know that decisions of these international organs may lead to domestic reexamination of previously decided cases. . .

***

As indicated earlier, the Supreme Court of the Russian Federation has instructed all lower courts to apply international law directly. Consider the following paragraphs from the "explanation" issued by the Plenary Session of the Supreme Court:

The Supreme Court: *Ruling of the Plenary Session of the Supreme Court of the Russian Federation "On Some Questions Concerning the Application of the Constitution of the Russian Federation by Courts"* (*BVS*, 1996, No. 1, p. 3).

When administering justice, courts shall take into account that the generally recognized principles and norms of international law, laid down in international covenants, conventions and other documents (particularly in the Universal Declaration of Human Rights, the International Covenant on Civil and Political Rights, and the International Covenant on Economic, Social and Cultural Rights) and the international treaties of the Russian Federation are, under Art. 15 para. 4 of the Constitution of the Russian Federation, a part of Russia's legal system. The same constitutional norm stipulates that if an international treaty of the Russian Federation establishes rules other than those established by the law, the rules of the international treaty shall apply.

In view of this, when hearing a case, a court cannot apply rules of law governing the relevant relationship if an international treaty that came into force and became binding on the Russian Federation through enactment of a

---

[74] Under the existing Criminal Procedure Code, it is possible to request the review of a conviction following a finding by international organs by referring to a "new circumstance" or a breach of "the law," a formula which may include violations of international law. Similar considerations may be invoked in civil cases.

federal law lays down other rules than those stipulated by the law. In those cases the rules of the international treaty of the Russian Federation shall apply.

In these situations the courts shall bear in mind that, according to Art. 5 para. 3 of the Federal Law on International Treaties of the Russian Federation, the provisions of officially published international treaties of the Russian Federation that do not require the promulgation of domestic acts for application, shall operate in the Russian Federation directly. In other cases it is necessary to apply, along with the international treaty of the Russian Federation, the relevant domestic legal act that was enacted for effectuating the provisions of the said international treaty.

QUESTIONS AND COMMENTS

1. What is the Supreme Court's definition or concept of "the generally recognized principles and norms of international law?"

2. The Court stated that "when hearing a case, a court cannot apply rules of law governing the relevant relationship if *an international treaty, that came into force and became binding on the Russian Federation through enactment of a federal law*, lays down rules other than those stipulated by the law" (Emphasis added - eds.). How does this statement correspond to Art. 15(4) of the Constitution? According to this Ruling, can a Russian court apply an international treaty that was not ratified by the Russian Federation?

3. Note that the 1995 Law "On International Treaties of the Russian Federation" (See *Sobranie* No. 29, item 2757 (1995)) requires ratification of a wide category of treaties. Art. 15 of the 1995 Law provides that the Federal Assembly must ratify the following categories of treaties:

a) the implementation of which requires modification of the existing federal laws or the adoption of new ones, as well as those treaties which set forth rules different from rules provided by a law;

b) the subject of which is the fundamental rights and freedoms of the person and the citizen;

c) concerning the territorial delimitation of the Russian Federation with other states, including treaties on the precise demarcation of the state boundary of the Russian Federation, as well as treaties on the delimitation of the exclusive economic zone and the continental shelf of the Russian Federation;

d) on the basic principles of inter-state relations, regarding questions affecting the defense capability of the Russian Federation, regarding questions of disarmament or international control over armaments, regarding questions of ensuring international peace and security, as well as peace treaties and treaties on collective security;

e) on the participation of the Russian Federation in inter-state unions, international organizations and other inter-state associations, if such treaties provide for the transfer to them of the effectuation of part of the powers of the Russian Federation or establish the legal mandatory force of decisions of their organs for the Russian Federation.

4. Note that the Ruling of the Court, by referring to the 1995 Law "On International Treaties of the Russian Federation," draws a distinction between self-executing or directly applicable and non-self-executing treaties. The distinction between these two categories of treaties had also been made by the 1994 Civil Code. Art. 7 of the Civil Code provides that "international treaties of the Russian Federation shall directly apply to [civil] relations defined in Art. 2 para. 1 and 2 of the present Code with the exception of those cases where it follows from the international treaty that its application requires the enactment of a domestic act." At the same time, Art. 5 of the 1995 Law on International Treaties stipulates that "the provisions of officially published international treaties of the Russian Federation, which do not require the promulgation of domestic acts for application, shall operate in the Russian Federation directly. In order to effectuate other provisions of international treaties of the Russian Federation, the relevant legal acts shall be adopted." Is there any difference between these two clauses? Which factors should be taken into account when we try to determine the self-executing or non-self-executing character of a treaty?

5. The Court stated that in cases of non-self-executing treaties "it is necessary to apply, *along with the international treaty of the Russian Federation,* the relevant domestic legal act that was enacted for effectuating the provisions of the said international treaty" (Emphasis added - eds). Does the Court require *simultaneous* application of domestic laws and underlying non-self-executing treaties? If there is a conflict between the two, what rule should apply?

6. In 1995 the Supreme Court adopted an "explanation" instructing the courts to apply Art. 9 of the International Covenant on Civil and Political Rights directly. The Ruling of the Plenary Session of the Supreme Court of the Russian Federation "*On the Judicial Practice Concerning Verification of the Legality and Justification of Arrests or the Extension of Periods of Detention*" (*BVS*, 1995, No. 1, p. 3) stated:

> 2. The courts must take into account that, in accordance with Art. 9 of the International Covenant on Civil and Political Rights, which entered into force on May 23, 1976, and the rules of which, under Art. 15 para. 4 of the Constitution of the Russian Federation, are a part of the legal system of the Russian Federation and have priority over its domestic legislation, everyone who is deprived of his liberty by arrest or detention has the right to institute proceedings before a court in order that the court may decide, without delay, the lawfulness of his detention and order his release if the detention is unlawful.
>
> In view of this, the complaint of anyone detained on the suspicion of committing a crime, or the complaint of her or his lawyer or legal representative, concerning the lawfulness and well-foundedness of the detention must be considered and resolved by the court in the manner established by the criminal procedure legislation.[75]

7. The Supreme Court also relies on international treaties in individual cases. In *Re Komarov* (*BVS*, 1997, No. 2, p. 1) involving a dispute about an *in camera* hearing of a criminal case the Supreme Court relied on Art. 14 of the Covenant on Civil and Political Rights according to which the public may be excluded from all or a part of a trial "when the interest of the private lives of the parties so requires."

D. The Effects of Federalism

Because Russia is a federal state, its legal system has a complex character. Under the 1993 Constitution,[76] the Russian Federation retains expansive legislative powers. For example, the Federation retains exclusive jurisdiction over criminal, criminal-procedural, civil, civil-procedural and arbitration-procedural legislation. As a result, much of the Russian law is federal law. All the major codes, such as the Civil Code, the Civil Procedural Code, the Criminal Code, and the Criminal Procedure Code, are federal law. Almost all commercial law is federal law. The formation, structure and activities of joint stock companies and other business entities are also governed by federal law.

---

[75] Note that under the Russian Criminal Procedure Code (Arts. 220(1) and 220(2) (*Vedomosty RF*, No. 40, item 592 (1960) (as amended)) only persons *arrested* (not simply detained) on a criminal charge have the right to bring proceedings before a court].

[76] Constitution, Art. 71.

1. Law-Making Power of the "Subjects" of the Russian Federation

At the same time, the "subjects"[77] of the Russian Federation "enjoy full state power" in all areas that have not been expressly delegated to the Federation or defined as spheres of joint competence.[78] In areas of their exclusive jurisdiction as well as in matters of concurrent jurisdiction, the constituent republics and other "subjects" of the Federation may enact their own laws and other normative acts. This may result in a mix of federal laws and laws of the "subjects" on matters on concurrent jurisdiction. However, laws and other normative legal acts of the "subjects" in areas falling within joint jurisdiction may not contravene federal laws. In case of a conflict, federal law would prevail both in areas of exclusive federal jurisdiction and joint jurisdiction. In areas within the exclusive jurisdiction of "subjects," their own regulation should prevail.

From a technical perspective, nothing prevents the "subjects" of the Federation from adopting their own laws even in areas of exclusive federal jurisdiction if the local laws would have exactly the same wording as federal laws. However, the Constitutional Court stated in the *Case Concerning the Law of the Kabardin-Balkar Republic On the Status of Judges*[79] that the constituent republics should not reproduce, in their own laws, the provisions of federal laws on matters of exclusive federal jurisdiction because the latter had direct effect on the entire territory of the country. The Court added that "the confirmation of the validity of federal laws with respect to the territory of republics by special legislative acts of the republics contravenes the nature of the exclusive federal competence; furthermore, it is redundant from the point of view of the economy of legislative efforts and legislative technique."

Republics within the Russian Federation also enact their own constitutions. These are considered to be fundamental laws for the respective republics. Other "subjects" of the Russian Federation enact "charters" or "fundamental laws." The constitutions or fundamental laws enjoy status superior to other local laws. Constitutional courts of the republics are usually given the power to review the constitutionality of all normative acts of the relevant republic.

---

[77] The 1993 Constitution uses the phrase "subjects of the Russian Federation" to describe the component units (republics, regions, territories etc.) of the Federation. All the "subjects" of the Federation are listed in Art. 65 of the Constitution.

[78] Constitution, Art. 73.

[79] See *VKS*, 1994, No. 6, p. 29, 31-32.

2. The Court System and "Subjects" of the Russian Federation

Although the Russian version of federalism diffuses some law-making power, judicial power is largely unified. Under the 1996 Federal Constitutional Law on the Judicial System of the Russian Federation[80] almost all courts in Russia are federal courts. Republics and other "subjects" may establish only "justices of the peace" and their own constitutional courts. This means that federal courts must apply not only federal law but also the laws enacted by the "subjects."

At the time of the adoption of the 1993 Constitution the future of the court system in Russia was unclear. As a result, Art. 120 of the Constitution provides that judges obey "only the Constitution of the Russian Federation and *federal law*." In contrast, the 1996 Law on the Judicial System states that judges obey "only the Constitution of the Russian Federation and *the law*"[81] (Emphasis added - eds.). Art. 3 of the 1996 Law expressly instructs all judges to apply not only federal laws but also "constitutions (charters) and other laws of the subjects of the Russian Federation." It appears that, within the federal court system, higher courts would always have the power to reverse judgments of lower courts based on local constitutions and laws.

We will discuss issues concerning the law-making power of the Federation and its "subjects" in more detail in Chapter IV.

E. The Hierarchy of Sources of Law

Taking into account all sources of law discussed, the hierarchical relationships between various sources are governed by the following principles:

- federal law of all kinds prevails over laws of the constituent "subjects" of the Russian Federation in areas of joint and exclusively federal jurisdiction;

- the federal Constitution prevails over federal constitutional laws and ordinary statutes;

- federal constitutional laws take priority over ordinary statutes;

- international treaties and "in some cases the generally recognized principles and norms of international law" prevail over ordinary statutes;

---

[80] See *Sobranie*, No. 1, item 1 (1997).
[81] 1996 Law on the Judicial System, Art. 5.

- federal statutes prevail over presidential decrees and regulations promulgated by administrative agencies.

In addition, rulings of the Constitutional Court can invalidate any unconstitutional statute. "Explanations" issued by the Supreme Court and by the Supreme Arbitration Court are not supposed to change statutes; but they would probably occupy a higher place than administrative regulations. Custom is always at the bottom of the hierarchy of sources. The Constitution leaves all law-making power in the "subjects" in areas not falling within the exclusive federal and concurrent jurisdiction. In those areas local laws would prevail.[82]

F. Legal Research of Russian Law

1. Russian-Language Sources: Publication of Legislation and of Court Judgments

Official publication of laws and regulations is an indispensable prerequisite for the smooth operation of legal rules in any society governed by the rule of law. In Russia, publication is governed by the 1993 Constitution and the 1994 Federal Law "On the Procedure for the Publication and Entry Into Force of Federal Constitutional Laws, Federal Laws and Acts of the Chambers of the Federal Assembly."[83]

According to Art. 15(3) of the 1993 Constitution, "the laws shall be officially published. Unpublished laws shall not be applicable." Furthermore, Art. 15(3) of the Constitution provides that "no normative legal act affecting the rights, freedoms or duties of the human being and citizen shall be effective if they have not been published officially for general knowledge." The new constitutional requirement that any enactment affecting the rights, liberties or duties of the human being and citizen must be brought to the information of the general public created serious problems for some administrative agencies. Many regulations of federal agencies and local authorities did not appear in any official publication. This practice of "secret" or "semi-secret" legislation has come to an end. Failure to publish a legal act for general knowledge makes the relevant regulation inapplicable. There are several cases in which the courts refused to apply regulations that were not published.[84]

---

[82] For details, see Chapter IV.

[83] See *Sobranie*, No. 8, item 801 (1994).

[84] See, e.g., *O.V. Prokhodtsev v. The Ministry of Defense* (*Sudebnaya praktika po grazhdanskim delam* 1993-1996, at 61-63 (1997)) (The Supreme Court refused to apply several unpublished regulations of the Ministry of Defense); *Victims of Chernobyl Accident v. The Ministry of Finance and the Ministry of Labor* (Id., at 89-93) (The Supreme Court refused to apply unpublished regulations which established restrictive rules concerning monetary compensation to the victims of Chernobyl nuclear disaster). See also *Case Concerning the Law "On Excise Duties," VKS,* 1996, No. 5, p. 2, 5-7 .

The 1994 Publication Law provides that federal constitutional laws, federal laws and other enactments of the Federal Assembly are to be published in the official government newspaper *Rossiiskaya Gazeta* and in the official federal compilation of legislation called "*Sobranie zakonodatel'stva RF*."[85] Presidential decrees and Government regulations also appear in *Sobranie*.[86] The 1994 Law further provides that Constitutional Court decisions "concerning the interpretation of the Constitution and the compatibility with the Constitution of laws, normative acts issued by the President, the Federation Council, the State Duma and the Government" must also be published in *Sobranie*.[87]

International treaties ratified by the Federal Assembly are published simultaneously with the relevant ratification laws in *Sobranie*. They are also published in the Bulletin of International Treaties (*Biulleten' mezhdunarodnykh dogovorov*).

Normative acts issued by ministries and other governmental agencies appear in the Bulletin of Normative Acts of Ministries and Agencies of the RF (*Biulleten' normativnykh aktov ministerstv I vedomstv RF*) published by the Ministry of Justice. Some ministries and agencies also issue their own official gazettes. Legislative acts of the constituent republics and other subjects of the federation are published in the official gazettes of the respective "subjects."

Publication of laws usually provides a precise point of reference in time from which the relevant laws take effect. Under the 1994 Publication Law, a law normally enters into effect ten days after its publication either in *Sobranie* or *Rossiiskaya Gazeta*. However, the Constitutional Court held the

---

[85] Cited in these materials as *Sobranie*. Before the adoption of the 1993 Constitution, the parliamentary official gazette was the Official Gazette of the Congress of People's Deputies and Supreme Soviet of the Russian Federation (*Vedomosty Siezda Narodnykh Deputatov Rossiiskoi Federatsii I Verkhovnogo Soveta Rossiiskoi Federatsii*). Before February 6, 1992 it was published as the Official Gazette of the Congress of People's Deputies and Supreme Soviet of the RSFSR (*Vedomosty Siezda Narodnykh Deputatov RSFSR I Verkhovnogo Soveta RSFSR*). These publications, as well as the official gazette of the pre-reform Supreme Soviet of the RSFSR are cited in these materials as *Vedomosty RF*; the official gazette of the legislative agencies of the former Soviet Union is referred to as *Vedomosty SSSR*.

[86] Until 1993 Presidential decrees were published in Vedomosty RF. The Government published its enactments in Sobranie postanovlenii pravitel'stva RF (RSFSR). In 1993-1994 the official gazette of the President and of the Government was Sobranie aktov Presidenta I pravitel'stva RF (cited in these materials as *Sobranie aktov*).

[87] Before 1994 all decisions of the Constitutional Court were published in *Vedomosty RF*.

Case Concerning the Law "On Excise Duties,"[88] that there is a difference between a publication in *Sobranie* and a publication in *Rossiiskaya Gazeta.* While *Rossiiskaya Gazeta* is a daily newspaper, *Sobranie* is published weekly. The Court noted that a law published in *Sobranie* cannot be deemed to be in effect as of the date of sending *Sobranie* to the printers: "At this stage there is no guarantee that the addressee of the law would in effect receive information about the content of the law."[89] The best point of reference with regard to the actual date of the entry of legislation into force is therefore the date of publication of the relevant law in *Rossiiskaya Gazeta.*[90]

The official gazette of the Constitutional Court is the Herald of the Constitutional Court of the Russian Federation (*Vestnik Konstitutsionnogo Suda RF*).[91] The Supreme Court publishes the Bulletin of the Supreme Court of the Russian Federation (*Biulleten' Verkhovnogo Suda RF*).[92] The Supreme Arbitration Court has the Herald of the Supreme Arbitration Court of the Russian Federation (*Vestnik Vysshego Arbitrazhnogo Suda RF*).[93] While all decisions of the Constitutional Court are published in full (including dissenting opinions), only selected judgments of ordinary and arbitration courts are published; and even then only excerpts of them are generally published.

2. English-Language Sources

Translation of Russian laws and regulations may be obtained from a variety of sources. Some Russian periodicals publish English translation of major laws, especially those affecting foreign relations or foreign trade. These include *The Moscow Journal of International Law* and *Journal of International Private Law*. In the US, translations of Russian laws are published, among other things, in *International Legal Materials* and in *Statutes and Decisions: The Laws of the USSR and Its Successor States.*[94] Translations of major codes, such as the Civil Law Code,[95] are often published as separate books.

---

[88] See VKS, 1996, No. 5, p. 2 .

[89] Id., at 7.

[90] There is now a move to create a separate *Parlamentskaya Gazeta*, a parliamentary newspaper. Under the proposed amendments to the 1994 Publication Law the right to publish laws will be transferred from the official government newspaper *Rossiiskaya Gazeta* to *Parlamentskaya Gazeta.*

[91] Cited in this book as *VKS.*

[92] Cited in this book as *BVS.*

[93] Cited in this book as *VVAS.*

[94] For further useful information, see Th.H. Reynolds, Some Recent English Language Sources for Current Russian Legislation, 22 International Journal of Legal Information 80 (1994).

[95] See The Civil Code of the Russian Federation (English translation by P.B. Maggs) (1997); Civil Code of the Russian Federation (English translation by W.E. Butler) (1997).

Many US law journals publish academic commentary on Russian legal developments. There are several scholarly English-language journals devoted to legal developments in Eastern Europe (*Review of Central and Eastern European Law, East European Constitutional Review, The Parker School Journal of East European Law, Journal of Constitutional Law in Eastern and Central Europe* and *Sudebnik).* These specialized journals may be a very useful source of information on current legal developments in Russia.

LEXIS and WESTLAW contain a wide variety of materials on Russian law. Both LEXIS and WESTLAW give access to English-language translations of Russian legislation and administrative regulations. Some Russian legal resources may also be obtained on the Internet.[96]

[96] For information concerning Russian Laws on Internet, see 3 The Parker School Journal of East European Law 247 (1996).

CHAPTER III

COURTS AND OTHER INSTITUTIONS IN THE LEGAL ORDER

A. Structure and Jurisdiction of the Courts

1. Introduction

Judicial reform is an indispensable element of Russia's efforts to become a democratic state based on the rule of law. The basic principles and purposes of comprehensive judicial reform were articulated in the 1991 Concept of Judicial Reform in the Russian Federation.[1] Although the 1991 Concept of Judicial Reform was not intended to be a legally binding document, it was officially approved by the then existing parliament.[2]

The 1991 Concept of Judicial Reform, which derives inspiration not only from foreign legal systems but also from pre-revolutionary Russian tradition, provides a blueprint for a new judicial system. It enumerates several important principles as constituting the foundations of reform. These principles, among other things, include: creation of a federal court system in Russia; recognition of the right to a jury trial,[3] reaffirmation of the principles of independence of the courts and the subordination of judges only to the law. The principal goal of reform is the creation of an independent judiciary which will enjoy the trust of the people and enforce the rule of law. This is a difficult task for Russia whose imperial and Soviet era cultural legacies include, as one commentator put it, "a cynical and condescending attitude toward law on the part not only of the public but also of officials."[4]

According to the Concept of Judicial Reform, judicial reform was supposed to be given top priority in the legislative activities of the Russian parliament. The Russian parliament has already enacted several fundamental

[1] *Kontseptsiya sudebnoi reformy v Rossiiskoi Federatsii* (The Concept of Judicial Reform in the Russian Federation) (1992).

[2] See *Vedomosty RF*, No. 44, item 1435 (1991).

[3] The proponents of the judicial reform believe that the twelve-person jury trial system which was introduced in the imperial Russia in 1864 is the best model to follow. Jury trials will be discussed in Chapter X.

[4] P.H. Solomon, Courts and Their Reform in Russia History, in P.H. Solomon ed., Reforming Justice in Russia, 1864-1996 3, 18 (1997).

laws on judicial reform. They include the Constitutional Law on the Constitutional Court,[5] the Constitutional Law on the Arbitration Courts,[6] and the Constitutional Law on the Judicial System of the Russian Federation.[7]

However, reform is still far from being completed. In order to comply with the 1991 Concept, Russia will have to adopt several new laws. For example, under the 1993 Constitution, the Russian parliament must enact new laws on the Supreme Court and the Supreme Arbitration Court.[8] Furthermore, Russia needs new codes of civil and criminal procedure. More importantly, Russian reformers need to overcome social legacies of the past, in particular, popular attitudes toward law and legal institutions shaped by the Soviet experience, that continue to remain critical impediments to the development of a rule-of-law state in Russia.

2. An Independent and Impartial Judiciary

One of the fundamental elements of the 1991 Concept of Judicial Reform is the recognition of the independent role of the courts as a separate branch of government. Art. 10 of the 1993 Constitution states the doctrine of separation of powers as follows: "State power in the Russian Federation shall be exercised on the basis of separation of the legislative, executive and judiciary branches."

In contrast to the Soviet concept under which courts were treated as hierarchically inferior to parliament and to the executive, the 1993 Constitution recognizes that the courts are an independent branch of government that is equal to the legislative and executive branches. According to Art. 10 of the Constitution, "the organs of legislative, executive and judiciary power shall be independent." Art. 120 of the Constitution confirms the independent status of the judiciary by stating that "judges shall be independent and shall obey only the Constitution of the Russian Federation and federal law."

The 1996 Constitutional Law on the Judicial System provides additional guarantees of judicial independence. The traditional Soviet system contained many organizational and procedural features which undermined the independence of courts. One of these features was the traditional "oversight" over courts of general jurisdiction by the Ministry of Justice. The Ministry of Justice used to "provide for" and "oversee" the "ordinary" courts. The courts, especially the lower "ordinary" courts, depended on the Ministry of Justice

---

[5] *Sobranie*, No. 13, item 1447 (1994).
[6] *Sobranie*, No. 19, item 1709 (1995).
[7] *Sobranie*, No. 1, item 1 (1997).
[8] See Constitution, Art. 128 (3).

and its local offices for court space and other needs. Experience shows that the support of the courts of general jurisdiction was dependent on the discretion of the organs of the Ministry of Justice. As a result, the courts were subject to pressure.[9]

The 1996 Constitutional Law on the Judicial System eliminated the previous system of oversight by the Ministry of Justice. The 1996 Law envisions the creation of a Judicial Department Within the Supreme Court.[10] The structure and functions of the Judicial Department are specified by the 1998 Law On the Judicial Department Within the Supreme Court.[11] The Judicial Department is to be responsible for personnel, organizational and resource support of all "ordinary" courts. In addition, it will provide for the logistical needs of "the organs of the judicial community."[12] This new approach means that the organizational, personnel and material support for the activities of "ordinary" courts will finally be fully independent from the discretion of the executive branch.

Another serious problem is financial guarantees of judicial independence. Although the 1993 Constitution established strong legal guarantees for the independence of the judiciary, it failed to provide any financial guarantees. The economic crisis of the 1990s resulted in a serious underfinancing of Russian courts, especially courts of general jurisdiction, by the Russian government. The problem of insufficient financing became one of the major obstacles in the implementation of the judicial reform. Because the federal budget failed to provide adequate funding for the maintenance of existing court facilities, the condition of many court buildings deteriorated dramatically.[13] By the middle of 1990s, the judicial system was in a state of serious

[9] While prior to the 1996 Constitutional Law on the Judicial System the Ministry of Justice obviously played an important role in providing logistical support to the courts, it would be absolutely wrong to believe, as some commentators did, that the Ministry of Justice was "at the pinnacle of the judicial system in Russia." See G.B. Smith, Reforming the Russian Legal System 130 (1996) ("At the pinnacle of the judicial system in Russia is the Ministry of Justice").

[10] See Law on the Judicial System, Art. 31. Art. 38 of the 1996 Law provides, that "the staff of subdivisions of the Ministry of Justice of the Russian Federation in proportion to that part of their work which is connected with the financing and maintenance of the work of the courts, with the exception of the military courts, shall be transferred to the Judicial Department."

[11] *Sobranie,* No. 2, item 223 (1998).

[12] These organs will be discussed *infra* p. 112.

[13] The Concept of Judicial Reform (*Kontseptsiya sudebnoi reformy v Rossiiskoi Federatsii, supra* note 1, at 7) described the working conditions of the justice system as "deplorable." A recent article chronicles similar conditions as of 1997 based on interviews with judges. *See* W. Patrick Murphy, The Russian Courts of General Jurisdiction: In Crisis, Undergoing Reform, or Both?, 4 Parker Sch. J.E. Eur. L. 207 (1998). Cf. also E. Huskey, Russian Judicial Reform After Communism, in Reforming

financial crisis. Some courts of general jurisdiction were not able to function because of the lack of funds.[14]

The drafters of the 1996 Constitutional Law on the Judicial System decided to deal with the problem by changing the principles underlying the formation of the judicial system budget. The major change is the participation of the judiciary in the budget process. Art. 33 of the 1996 Law provides that the financing of the Constitutional Court, the courts of general jurisdiction, the arbitration courts and of justices of the peace is to be done on the basis of standards established by federal law and according to separate line items in the federal budget. This means that the relevant budget items providing money for the judiciary will be mandatory: payments will be made even if the government revenues fall short of expectations. Art. 33 also provides that the Government will draw up a draft federal budget for financing the courts in concert with the chairmen of the Constitutional Court, the Supreme Court and the Supreme Arbitration Court. The chairman of these courts will have the right to participate in the discussion of the federal budget in the Federal Assembly. All these new provisions provide some ground for hope that the efforts to obtain adequate funding for the judiciary will be more successful in the future.

Finally, judicial independence has to be ensured by the procedural legislation. An important impediment to full independence of courts is the traditional prosecutorial bias of the courts. The current Criminal Procedure Code contains numerous clauses which run counter to the very notion of judicial independence and impartiality. In criminal cases, courts often have to assume prosecutorial functions.

The Concept of Judicial Reform envisions a radical reform of criminal procedure. It includes the strengthening of the independence of the judiciary, the introduction of adversary procedure in criminal cases and the right to trial by jury. The major task in this area is the elimination of the traditional prosecutorial bias of the courts. The reintroduction of trial by jury in nine

---

Justice in Russia, 1864-1996 325, 332 (1997) ("The condition of court buildings has been a perennial source of embarrassment for the judiciary. Unlike executive and legislative accommodations, court facilities have none the dignity or gra ndeur of buildings of state").

[14]The Collegium for Criminal Cases of the Supreme Court stated in its recent review of the problem that "many courts have no money for postal expenses, business trips, payments to people's assessors, attorneys, experts, witnesses and victims. As a result, they stop their work, sometimes for long periods of time, and seek donations. They use not only acceptable but also unacceptable means to achieve this goal. . . Court chairmen often seek donations from the heads of local administrations. As a rule, these requests are granted. . ., but there is danger that courts will become dependent on local authorities." *BVS*, 1998, No. 2, p. 22-23.

"subjects" of the Russian Federation[15] has resulted in a new adversarial procedure in criminal cases.[16]

3. Structure of the Judicial System

The Russian court structure is complex. The Russian courts have been set up to deal with specialized subjects. As a result, there are three separate court systems: the Constitutional Court, the courts of general jurisdiction (including military courts) and arbitration (or commercial) courts. The 1991 Concept of Judicial Reform also envisions the creation of a separate system of administrative courts (at present, administrative disputes are dealt with by "ordinary" courts and arbitration courts). The 1996 Law on the Judicial System endorses this idea by contemplating the creation of specialized federal courts that would resolve civil and administrative cases.[17]

Although the presence of several court systems may be confusing for a common law lawyer, it is useful to keep in mind that Russian judicial reform is fully consistent with the practice of other European civil law countries, in particular France and Germany. These countries have also established several sets of courts, each with its own jurisdiction, its own hierarchy of tribunals and its own procedure. According to this model, a case falling within one jurisdiction would not be considered in the other.

The most important of these jurisdictions in Russia is the system of so-called "ordinary" courts (or courts of general jurisdiction). Such courts hear and decide the great range of civil and criminal litigation, and, as a result, affect most frequently the life of the ordinary Russian citizen. In civil matters the "ordinary" courts apply the law found in the Civil Code and in the legislation that supplements it. Their procedure in such cases is governed by the Civil Procedure Code. In criminal cases these courts apply the law found in the Criminal Code; their procedure in such cases is governed by the Criminal Procedure Code.

The creation of a separate system of arbitration (commercial) courts became an important innovation in the Russian judicial system. The Russian name for these courts - *arbitrazhnye sudy*- is translated in this book as "arbitration courts." This translation may be slightly misleading in that arbitration courts is not a system of arbitration with the parties consenting to have their claims heard by an arbitrator. It is a system of *special state courts*

---

[15] As of 1993 in Ivanovo, Moscow, Riazan and Saratov Regions and Stavropol Territory and as of 1994 in Rostov-on-Don and Ul'ianovsk Regions and Altai and Krasnodar Territories.

[16] For details, see Chapter X.

[17] 1996 Law on the Judicial System, Art. 26.

with compulsory jurisdiction over commercial and some administrative disputes. From this perspective, they may be called commercial courts. While these courts, like "ordinary" courts, apply the Civil Code and legislation supplementary to it, their procedure is governed by the new 1995 Arbitration Procedure Code. A number of complicated issues arise in this connection, such as the exact delineation of the jurisdictional boundary between "ordinary" courts and arbitration courts.

The adoption of the idea of constitutional review as a constituent element of democracy based on the rule of law has resulted in the creation of a separate court to review the constitutionality of legislation. Following the lead of a number of other civil law countries, Russia created a Constitutional Court. Under the 1993 Constitution and the 1994 Constitutional Law on the Constitutional Court, the Court not only has the power to review the constitutionality of laws and other normative acts, but also may settle other constitutional disputes. However, "ordinary" courts also have the power to review the constitutionality of legislation. The exact line between the jurisdiction of "ordinary" courts and the Constitutional Court in this area is another matter that raises many controversies.

4. One Judicial System or Three?

Although according to Art. 3 of the 1996 Law on the Judicial System the judicial system of Russia is supposed to be "unified," in reality there is no "unified" system in the common law sense of the word. A judicial system that has several sets of independent courts has no "supreme" court that would be able to resolve a dispute for all the courts of the country. Such a system has its drawbacks, primarily because of the danger of conflicting interpretations of the existing codes.[18]

Another problem is the inevitable competition between different systems for a more prominent position within the judicial community. For example, many judges of the Constitutional Court believe that the Court is the

---

[18]The Supreme Court and the Supreme Arbitration Court try to avoid the danger of conflicting interpretations of basic codes or laws by adopting "Joint Explanations." See, for example, the Joint Ruling of the Plenary Session of the Supreme Court and the Plenary Session of the Supreme Arbitration Court "*On Certain Aspects of the Jurisdiction of Courts and Arbitration Courts*," *VVAS*, 1992, No. 1, p. 84; The Joint Ruling of the Plenary Session of the Supreme Court and the Plenary Session of the Supreme Arbitration Court "*On Some Questions Concerning the Application of the First Part of the Civil Code of the Russian Federation*," *BVS*, 1996, No. 9, p.1 (1996); The Joint Ruling of the Plenary Session of the Supreme Court and the Plenary Session of the Supreme Arbitration Court "*On Some Questions Concerning the Application of the Law On Joint-Stock Companies*," *BVS*, 1997, No. 6, p. 1.

highest court of the country. There are basically two arguments in favor of this position. The first argument relates to the legal force of the Constitutional Court's opinions. According to Arts. 6 and 79 of the Law on the Constitutional Court, decisions of the Constitutional Court are binding on the entire territory of the Russian Federation upon all "representative, executive and judicial organs."[19] The reference to "judicial organs" obviously includes other courts. The second argument is based on Chapter 7 of the Constitution. Although the Supreme Court and the Supreme Arbitration Court are described as the "highest judicial organs" in their respective court systems, this does not mean that they are the highest courts of the country. Some commentators argue that an important piece of evidence that the highest court is the Constitutional Court is the fact that it is listed first in Chapter 7 of the Constitution ("Judicial Power").[20]

As one might expect, judges of the Supreme Court - the highest court in the system of "ordinary" courts - disagree. They argue that the enumeration of different courts in Chapter 7 of the Constitution has no legal significance. More importantly, they point out that both the Constitutional Court and the arbitration courts are *specialized* courts with limited jurisdiction. In contrast, the "ordinary" courts have general jurisdiction over all disputes with the exception of those that are specifically routed to specialized courts.[21] Furthermore, the Constitutional Court does not have exclusive competence to review the constitutionality of legal acts. All courts have the duty to apply the Constitution in all cases properly within their jurisdiction. Finally, the Constitutional Court has no power to review the judgments of other courts.[22] We will return to the ongoing controversy over the power of different courts shortly.

---

[19] The Constitutional Court's interpretation of the Constitution is also binding on all state bodies. Under Art. 106 of the Constitutional Law on the Constitutional Court, "the interpretation of the Constitution of the Russian Federation given by the Constitutional Court of the Russian Federation shall be official and binding upon all representative, executive and judicial agencies of state power, local self-government, enterprises, institutions, organizations, officials and citizens and their associations."

[20] Cf.. B.S. Ebzeev, *Konstitutsiya, pravovoe gosudrstvo, Konstitutsionnyi sud* (Constitution, Law-Based State, Constitutional Court) 120 (1997). See also N.B.Vitruk, L.V. Lazarev, B.S. Ebzeev eds., *Federal'nyi konstitutsionnyi zakon o Konstitsionnom sude Rossiiskoi Federatsii. Kommentarii* (Federal Constitutional law on the Constitutional Court of the Russian Federation. Commentary) 22 (1996).

[21] See V.M. Zhuykov, *Sudebnaya zashchita prav grazhdan I juridicheskikh lits* (Judicial Defense of the Rights of Citizens and Juridical Persons) 191-192 , 210-211(1997).

[22] Id., at 211.

5. What Courts are "Federal" Courts

For a certain period of time, another controversial area was the structure of the court system in a federal state. The Concept of Judicial Reform was based on the assumption that federalism would result in a major modification of the existing court structure. Traditionally all courts in Russia were federal. There were no judicial systems of the constituent units of the Federation. In the early 1990s it was assumed that the reform of Russia's federal structure implied that all "subjects" of the Federation would create their own courts. However, the rearrangement of preexisting federal structures which culminated in the adoption of the 1993 Constitution did not result in any major shift in the structure of the courts.

The framers of the 1993 Constitution envisioned the creation of several federal courts. Art. 128 (1) mentions the most important among these: the Constitutional Court, the Supreme Court and the Supreme Arbitration Court. Although Art. 128(2) mentions "other federal courts," they were never defined in the Constitution. The Constitution did not mention any courts of the constituent "subjects" of the Federation. Given this ambiguity, some of the "subjects" made attempts to establish their own court systems . This was motivated in large part by the desire to have more control over the selection of the personnel for the judiciary. The following excerpt from the *Case Concerning the Charter - Fundamental Law of Chitinskaya Region* illustrates the controversy over this fundamental issue.

The Constitutional Court: *Case Concerning the Charter - Fundamental Law of Chitinskaya Region* (*VKS,* 1996, No. 1, p. 34)

The petition [filed by the administration of Chitinskaya Region] challenges the constitutionality of Art. 74(1) of the Charter [of the Region] which provides that the court system of the Region is part of the court system of the Russian Federation. The petitioner has doubts about the notion "the court system of the Region" and about the right of the regional legislative organ to define the court system.

According to Art. 71 of the Constitution of the Russian Federation, the establishment of the system of federal organs of judicial power (para. d) and the organization of the courts (para. n) fall within the jurisdiction of the Russian Federation (and not of its subjects). Art. 118(3) of the Constitution of the Russian Federation provides that the judicial system of the Russian Federation shall be established by the Constitution of the Russian Federation and by federal constitutional law. Pending the enactment of such a law, the existing judicial system is also governed by the law of the Russian Federation; according to this law, it is a unified judicial system because it does not contemplate independent judicial systems of the subjects of the Russian Federation.

However, the challenged provision has to be considered in the context of all provisions of Art. 74 of the Charter - it enumerates only those courts of the Region that are envisioned by federal legislation; it must also be considered in conjunction with Art. 73(1) which provides that the administration of justice in the Region is conducted by the courts which are established and operate in accordance with the Constitution of the Russian Federation and federal laws. In view of this, the notion of a "court system of the Region" does not signify the establishment of a special regional court system alongside the unified court system of the Russian Federation, which is established and operates in accordance with the relevant provisions of the Constitution and legislation of the Russian Federation. . .

For these reasons. . . the Constitutional Court of the Russian Federation finds:

(1) The following provisions of the Charter - Fundamental Law of Chitinskaya Region conform to the Constitution of the Russian Federation: . . . 74(1). . .

Dissenting Opinion of Judge N.B. Vitruk

According to Art. 71 (para. d) of the Constitution of the Russian Federation, the establishment of the system of federal organs of judicial power, procedure for the organization and activities thereof, as well as the organization of the courts (para. n) fall within the jurisdiction of the Russian Federation; under Art. 72 (para. k), questions concerning personnel of the judiciary fall within the joint jurisdiction of the Russian Federation and the subjects of the Russian Federation.

It does not follow from these constitutional provisions that the judicial system of the Russian Federation is only a federal one (judicial organs of the subjects of the Russian Federation may be established alongside the federal organs of judicial power; the possibility of the creation of judicial organs by the subjects of the Russian Federation is envisioned by the officially approved Concept of Judicial Reform) or that the subjects of the Federation cannot promulgate legal norms that would specify the provisions of federal laws, for example, on the procedure of the formation of federal organs of judicial power.

Given the absence of federal laws that would have fully governed the system and the procedure for the organization and activities (administration of justice) of the federal organs of judicial power, it is very difficult to determine, with any degree of certainty, the constitutionality of the provisions of the Charter concerning the judicial system and personnel of the judiciary. . .

QUESTIONS

1. The principal question in this case was whether Chitinskaya Region's Charter established "a special regional court system alongside the unified court system of the Russian Federation." Why did the Court come to the conclusion that this was not the case?

2. Do you agree with Judge Vitruk's dissent that Arts. 71(a, n) and 72(k) of the Constitution do not mean that "the judicial system of the Russian Federation is only a federal one" or that "judicial organs of the subjects of the Russian Federation may be established alongside the federal organs of judicial power?"

6. Courts of the "Subjects" of the Russian Federation

Under the 1996 Law on the Judicial System the "subjects" of the Federation may establish only two kinds of courts of the "subject": constitutional courts and justices of the peace.[23]

Several republics within the Russian Federation have already established their own constitutional courts. These courts have jurisdiction over controversies involving constitutions of the relevant republics. While jurisdiction over constitutional questions may thus be divided in accordance with the federal structure of Russia, there is no formal hierarchical relationship between the federal Constitutional Court and the constitutional courts of the republics.[24] This remains an interesting question in light of the *Chitinskaya Region Case*. The Constitutional Court of the Russian Federation interpreted "the court system of the Region" to refer to the normal Russian Federation courts and as not establishing regional court system. If the Constitutional Court (or the Charter Court) of the Chitinskaya Region decided that its Charter or Fundamental Law meant the opposite, it is not clear whether this finding could be appealed in the Russian Federation Constitutional Court.

[23] 1996 Law on the Judicial System, Art. 4.

[24] In is interesting to note that despite the uncertainty of the hierarchical relationships, the Herald of the Constitutional Court of the Russian Federation (*VKS*) publishes some of the decisions of the constitutional courts of the subjects of the Federation. See, e.g., *VKS*, 1995, No. 5, p. 46 (Ruling of the Constitutional Court of the Republic of Buryatia); Id., p. 49 (Ruling of the Constitutional Court of the Kabardin-Balkar Republic); Id., p. 53 (Ruling of the Constitutional Court of the Republic of Karelia).

Justices of the peace existed in the pre-revolutionary Russia. The 1996 Constitutional Law on the Judicial System reintroduced them. Art. 28 of the Law provides that the authority and activities of the justices of the peace "shall be established by federal law and by law of the subject of the Russian Federation." Under Art. 28, justices of the peace will hear civil, administrative and criminal cases as a court of first instance. Justices of the peace will hear misdemeanor cases and certain categories of civil cases, for example, property settlements and divorces. Under Art. 13 of the 1996 Law on the Judicial System justices of the peace may be appointed or elected to their positions.

All other courts of the Russian Federation are *federal* courts. Only constitutional courts of the "subjects" of the Federation are really independent. Although justices of the peace are considered to be judges of the constituent units of the Federation, their judgments are reviewed by the lowest courts in the *federal* system of "ordinary" courts. The essentially unitary nature of judicial proceedings in all Russian courts is further emphasized by the fact that all courts apply the same federal procedural law - the Civil Procedure Code and the Criminal Procedure Code.

Practice indicates that the only constitutional provision that gave certain power to the constituent units over courts of the Federation is Art. 72 (k) of the Constitution, according to which questions concerning personnel of the judiciary fall within the joint jurisdiction of the Russian Federation and the "subjects" of the Russian Federation. Under the 1996 Law on the Judicial System, the appointment of judges of all "ordinary" and arbitration courts located in the "subjects" of the Federation requires the assent (*po soglasovaniu*) of "the legislative (representative) organs of state power of the respective subject of the Russian Federation."[25] During the debates on the 1996 Law some "subjects" of the Federation promoted the idea that judges holding court on their territories must be appointed by the legislatures of the "subjects." These far-reaching proposals met with strong opposition of those who believed that judges needed to be protected from the influence of local authorities. The 1996 Law preserved the unified judicial power throughout Russia. At the same time, the final version of the Law is a compromise between the proponents of a strong and unified federal judicial system and the supporters of greater local control of courts.

B. The Three Principal Court Systems

1. The Constitutional Court

(a) Reasons for a Constitutional Court

The creation of the Constitutional Court - the first court in Russian

---

[25] 1996 Law on the Judicial System, Art. 13.

history to be given the competence to decide constitutional issues - became one of the most important developments of Russian legal reform. For many observers the creation of the Constitutional Court became the first credible evidence that Russia was poised to become a genuine law-based state. Indeed, the adoption of the concept of constitutional review implies that governmental power is limited by constitutional norms. The Constitutional Court is designed to guarantee the supremacy of the Constitution and ensure institutional protection of democracy and fundamental human rights.

Orthodox communist constitutionalism rejected the concept of constitutional or judicial review of legislation. All Soviet constitutions were viewed as symbolic acts reflecting communist ideology. Courts were not permitted to review statutes because this would have rendered the judiciary superior to parliament. While the official position was that the legislature was the supreme expression of the will of the people, in reality the rejection of judicial review preserved the domination of the Communist Party which exercised total control over the state machinery.

Like other European countries emerging from oppressive or totalitarian regimes, Russia entrusted the enforcement of the Constitution to a new judicial body. Constitutional review exercised by the Constitutional Court has become an important mechanism which guarantees direct effect of the Constitution and imposes checks on the legislative and executive branches of the government.[26]

From a comparative perspective, the creation of the Constitutional Court means that Russia moved toward the "centralized" system of judicial review of legislation. The "centralized" system of judicial review based on a Constitutional Court confines the power to determine the constitutionality of legislation to a single judicial organ. In contrast, the "decentralized" (or American) system gives this power to all "ordinary" courts.[27]

Russia favored the adoption of the "centralized" system of judicial review for the same reasons as other European countries.[28] The first reason is the traditional conception of the separation of legislative and judicial powers. Under this conception, judges must accept and apply the law as enacted by the all-powerful legislature. As mere interpreters of the law judges were never

[26] Cf. M. Cappelletti, The Judicial Process in Comparative Perspective 187 (1989) ("Indeed, it seems as though no country in Europe, emerging from some form of undemocratic regime or serious domestic strife, could find a better answer to the exigency of reacting against, and possibly preventing the return of, past evils, than to introduce constitutional justice into its new system of government.")

[27] Id., at 132-133.

[28] Id., at 137-146.

supposed to challenge the validity of legislative enactments. However, by adopting the ideas of constitutionalism and inalienable human rights Russia admitted that even popularly elected parliaments can pose a serious threat to these values. As a result, Russia started to look for a means of guaranteeing both government's and parliament's obedience to the Constitution.

While the framers of the Russian Constitution admitted the need for some sort of judicial control of legislation, they were reluctant to give this power to the "ordinary" judges. The professional training of these judges became the second major reason for adopting the "centralized" system. Russian "ordinary" judges have always been trained to interpret and apply written codes. As a result, they tend to avoid policy-oriented decision-making. Because constitutional adjudication is value-laden and largely political, the creation of a single Constitutional Court staffed by specially selected judges became the only viable option.

Still another important reasons for Russia's choice is the absence of any well-established *stare decisis* principle. In the "decentralized" (American) system, the principle of *stare decisis* ensures that the determination of the constitutionality of statutes by different judges would be more or less consistent because courts are bound to follow their own prior decisions and the decisions of higher courts in the same jurisdiction. As Mauro Cappelletti noted, in the United States "the existence of a single supreme court, combined with the lower courts' duty to follow superior precedents, insures the uniformity of constitutional adjudication."[29] In the absence of a developed system of *stare decisis,* determinations of constitutionality or non-constitutionality by some Russian judges would not bind other judges. In fact, the same court might adopt conflicting decisions on matters of constitutionality in different cases. The problem of inconsistency becomes even more serious in view of the fact that Russia has two entirely independent court systems - the system of "ordinary" courts and the system arbitration (commercial) courts. In such a situation, the establishment of a workable system of judicial review required the creation of a special court whose decisions would have an *erga omnes* (generalized) effect.

(b) Some Lessons From the Recent History of the Constitutional Court

While the idea of constitutional review won quick approval, its implementation in Russia met with serious difficulties. The first Constitutional Court was established in 1991. It was granted wide powers to review the constitutionality of legislation. Because the Court had to review the relevant

---

[29] Id., at 139.

legislation under the old Soviet 1978 Constitution, its activities became quite controversial and politicized. The 1991 Law on the Constitutional Court[30] did not limit the political activities of the Court. Indeed, it encouraged them by allowing the Court to issue advisory opinions on its own initiative outside the context of an actual case or controversy. As a result, the first Constitutional Court became an active participant in the country's political process.[31] On many issues the Court took sides with the conservative Congress of People's Deputies which resisted President Yeltsin's attempts to adopt an entirely new Constitution by referendum. When President Yeltsin issued a Decree announcing a new plan for constitutional reform and dissolving the Congress in September 1993,[32] the Court pronounced the Decree unconstitutional.[33] During the "Second October Revolution" of 1993 President Yeltsin issued another Decree which stripped the old Court of its key powers. The Decree ordered the Court "not to convene its sessions until the adoption of the new Constitution of the Russian Federation."[34] The controversial Decree asserted that the Court "had played a negative role, actually that of an accomplice, in the tragic developments of October 3 and 4, 1993, in Moscow" and that the Court "had transformed itself into an instrument of political struggle, posing extreme danger to the state."[35]

The new Russian Constitution, adopted by a popular referendum in December 1993, redefined the powers of the Constitutional Court. The 1993 Constitution and the 1994 Constitutional Law on the Constitutional Court[36] made an attempt to block the politicization of the new Court. Art. 3 of the 1994 Law on the Constitutional Court expressly states that the Court "shall rule exclusively on questions of law." Although constitutional courts cannot avoid policy considerations because constitutional adjudication is always value-laden, procedural rules may prevent unnecessary politization of constitutional adjudication. An example of this approach in Russia is the abolition of

---

[30] *Vedomosty RF*, No. 19, item 621 (1991).

[31] As Judge N.V. Vutruk put it, the Court "had gradually transformed itself from an organ of justice into an organ of politics." N.V. Vitruk, *Vstupitel'naya stat'ia* (Introduction), in Vitruk, Lazarev, Ebzeev, *supra* note 20, at 10.

[32] Decree "On the Progressive Constitutional Reform in the Russian Federation," *Sobranie aktov*, No. 39, item 3597 (1993).

[33] See *VKS*, 1994, No. 6, p. 40.

[34] Some judges of the Constitutional Court do not think that Yeltsin's Degree did really order the Court not to convene its sessions again. In their view, Yeltsin's Decree simply described the existing situation, because after Yeltsin's Decree announcing a new plan for constitutional reform several judges of the Courts refused to participate in the activities of the Court pending the adoption of a new constitution. See Vitruk, *supra* note 31, at 11.

[35] *Sobranie*, No. 41, item 3921 (1993).

[36] *Sobranie*, No. 13, item 1447 (1994).

the right of the new Constitutional Court to examine cases on its own initiative.

(c) Structure

The Constitutional Court consists of 19 judges appointed by the Federation Council upon nomination by the President. The judges of the Constitutional Court are quite different from "ordinary" judges. Many constitutional judges come not from the ranks of the professional judiciary but from the law faculties of Russian universities. As a result, constitutional judges tend to produce (in contrast to the generally terse judgments of "ordinary" courts) more elaborate and reasoned opinions.

The Court considers and resolves cases in its plenary session or in sessions of its two chambers composed of ten and nine judges. Certain matters may be resolved only in the plenary session of the Court. According to Art. 21 of the Law on the Constitutional Court, the Court resolves some issues, such as "cases concerning the constitutionality of the constitutions of the republics and charters of the subjects of the Russian Federation" or "interpretation of the Constitution," exclusively in its plenary session.

(d) Jurisdiction

The jurisdiction of the Court is defined by Art. 125 of the Constitution and the 1994 Constitutional Law on the Constitutional Court. The Constitutional Court has jurisdiction over four major categories of cases.

The first category of cases involves abstract review of the constitutionality of federal laws, normative acts of the President, constitutions, laws and other "normative acts" of the republics and of other "subjects" of the Federation and international treaties that are not yet in force.

Constitutional review of these different normative acts may be initiated by the President, the Federation Council, the State Duma, one-fifth of the members of the Federation Council or deputies of the State Duma, the Government, the Supreme Court, the Supreme Arbitration Court and organs of legislative and executive power of the "subjects" of the Russian Federation.[37]

The second category of cases involves incidental or concrete constitutional revue of statutes. The Constitutional Court has the power to review the constitutionality of "laws" in response to complaints filed by individuals and juridical persons alleging violations of constitutional rights and freedoms. This

---

[37] Constitution, Art. 125 (2).

important procedure, based on the model of the German Federal Constitutional Court, means that individuals and juridical persons have direct access to constitutional review. In view of the expansive list of human rights protected by the Constitution,[38] the Court may consider a variety of topics ranging from property rights of individuals and juridical persons (such as partnerships and companies) to the right of everyone to "a favorable environment."

In contrast to the German model, where an individual must exhaust all other remedies in the "ordinary" court system before she or he can bring a case before the Constitutional Court, Russian law does not impose this requirement. An aggrieved individual dissatisfied with the judgment of the lowest "ordinary" court has the right to file a constitutional complaint directly with the Constitutional Court. And it may be that no other court has been previously involved, so long as some government organ has acted pursuant to an allegedly unconstitutional law. Practice indicates that Russians take advantage of the right of an individual to file a constitutional complaint in increasing numbers. In fact, as a consequence of these extremely permissive "standing" rules, the Constitutional Court has been flooded with complaints.

The Constitutional Court has also been granted the power to rule on constitutional issues arising in specific court cases at the request of "ordinary" or arbitration (commercial) courts.

The third category of cases involves disputes over competence between different organs of the Russian Federation and the "subjects" of the Federation. The Constitutional Court is empowered to determine controversies between various organs of government with respect to their rights and powers. The Court may resolve competence disputes between: (1) "the federal organs of state power" (such as the President and the Federal Assembly); (2) "the organs of state power of the Russian Federation and organs of state power of the subjects of the Russian Federation" and (3) "the highest organs of state power of the subjects of the Russian Federation."

The fourth category of cases involves requests of the President, the Federation Council, the State Duma, the Government or the organs of legislative power of the "subjects" of the Russian Federation that the Court give an authoritative interpretation of the Constitution.

In addition, the Constitutional Court plays an important role in the impeachment of the President. At the request of the Federation Council, the Constitutional Court renders opinions concerning the observance of the

[38] See Constitution, Arts. 17-64.

established procedure for bringing charges against the President of the Russian Federation for high treason or other serious crime.

(e) Applicable Law

In rendering its rulings, the Constitutional Court applies the Constitution. However, the Court also decides questions of conflicts between federal laws and substatutory normative acts or laws of the "subjects" of the Federation.

This might not be considered by some to be a "constitutional" question. However, ordinary laws often implement applicable constitutional principles. Furthermore, the Constitution provides that all normative acts must conform to the Constitution and federal laws. Thus, a substatutory normative act that violates the requirements of a federal statute also violates the Constitution. This type of review of constitutionality have been described as "indirect."[39] Similar considerations explain the Court's frequent references to the generally recognized principles and norms of international law and international treaties of the Russian Federation. Although the Court has no express power to review laws and other normative acts for conformity with international treaties, it often applies international law directly because the Constitution requires that those laws comply with international rules.

(f) Process

The proceedings before the Constitutional Court have all the characteristics of a trial. Hearings are open to the public and are adversarial in nature. Because judges of the Constitutional Court have the power to declare void a wide variety of laws and other "normative acts," their work enjoys more publicity than the activities of any bench within the system of "ordinary" courts. Decisions of the Court attract attention of the public and the media and often become the subject of public debate.

All rulings of the Constitutional Court (again, in contrast to judgments of even the highest "ordinary" court) are published. Individual and dissenting opinions of constitutional judges are published as well.

(g) Caseload and Impact

During its first years of operation, the Court issued many rulings

---

[39] The term "indirect" constitutional review in cases when the Constitutional Court relies on federal statutes has been used by Judge N.V. Vitruk in his dissenting opinion in the *Case Concerning Arts. 74 and 90 of the Constitution of the Republic of Khakasiya*. See *Sobranie*, No. 26, item 3145 (1997).

resolving questions of great political importance. Most of the Court's political jurisprudence resulted from abstract review proceedings initiated by different organs designated by Art. 125(2) of the Constitution and from conflicts between the Federation and its "subjects." The Constitutional Court also resolved numerous cases initiated by individuals and juridical persons alleging violations of constitutional rights and freedoms.

There is no doubt that the Court has made a notable contribution to the development of constitutional doctrine and Russian law.[40] Although the Court has had two phases in its development, it has striven to develop a coherent body of jurisprudence. Strictly speaking , the Court does not recognize the doctrine of precedent. However, it does try to maintain judicial consistency and in its opinions it frequently refers to earlier decisions. The concern over judicial consistency undoubtedly underlies Art. 73 of the Law on the Constitutional Court, which deals with the transfer of cases from the chambers of the court to the plenary session. Art. 73 states that "if the majority of judges participating in the session of a chamber favor the adoption of a decision inconsistent with the legal position expressed in prior decisions of the Constitutional Court of the Russian Federation, the case shall be transferred to the plenary session."

The substance of the Constitutional Court's work and the effects of its decisions make it the most influential court in Russia. However, as noted earlier, the Constitutional Court is not considered to be a superior instance to other Russian courts.

(h) The Effect of Constitutional Court Decisions

Decisions of the Constitutional Court are binding on the entire territory of the Russian Federation upon "all representative, executive and judicial organs of state power, local self-government, enterprises, institutions, organizations, officials, citizens and their associations."[41] According to Art. 79 of the same Law, decisions of the Court are final. More importantly, "the legal force of a ruling rendered by the Constitutional Court of the Russian

[40] Note, however, that the quality of the Court's opinions has varied considerably. Some discretion is needed in handling old opinions because they were rendered on the basis of the 1978 Constitution.

[41] See 1994 Constitutional Law on the Constitutional Court, Art. 6. As noted earlier, the Constitutional Court's interpretation of the Constitution is also binding on all state bodies. Under Art. 106 of the Law on the Constitutional Court, "the interpretation of the Constitution of the Russian Federation given by the Constitutional Court of the Russian Federation shall be official and binding upon all representative, executive and judicial agencies of state power, local self-government, enterprises, ins titutions, organizations, officials and citizens and their associations."

Federation, declaring an act unconstitutional, may not be overruled by the readoption of the same act."[42] Acts or their individual provisions judged unconstitutional become null and void. Art. 79 also states that "the decisions of the courts or other bodies, based on the enactments pronounced unconstitutional, shall not be executed and shall be reconsidered in cases established by the federal law."

Although the Constitutional Court is not designated as the highest judicial organ of the country, its activities inevitably affect the operation of other courts, including the Supreme Court and the Supreme Arbitration Court. A Constitutional Court's decision on the unconstitutionality of a statute may affect any prior judicial decisions made on the basis of the invalidated law. Under Art. 100 of the 1994 Constitutional Law on the Constitutional Court, a specific case based on an invalidated law must be "reconsidered by the competent organ according to the established procedure." Thus, civil and arbitration proceedings in such a case may be reopened and criminal cases may be annulled.

However, the situation is not as simple as it might appear at first sight. First, it is important to keep in mind that the Constitutional Court has no power to review the judgments of other courts. As the Constitutional Court noted in the *Case Concerning Arts. 180, 181, 187(1) and 192 of the Arbitration Procedure Code*,[43] it does not review "the legality of judicial acts." Second, it must be noted that, according to Art. 3 of the 1994 Constitutional Law on the Constitutional Court, "the Constitutional Court of the Russian Federation shall rule *exclusively on questions of law*" (Emphasis added - eds.). Art. 3 also states that "in administering constitutional justice, the Constitutional Court of the Russian Federation shall refrain from establishing and investigating *factual circumstances* in any case when this falls within the competence of other courts or other organs." (Emphasis added - eds.) This means that rulings of the Constitutional Court are binding on ordinary courts only with respect of the constitutionality or unconstitutionality of the challenged law. If a particular law is declared unconstitutional, an ordinary court cannot apply it to the case at hand. All other pertinent issues of the case, including the question as to whether the decision of the Constitutional Court has any significance for the case, are decided by the "ordinary" courts.[44]

Another problem is retroactivity. If the parties in a case decided by the Supreme Court challenge the constitutionality of the law applied in the case before the Constitutional Court, and the Constitutional Court declares the law

---

[42] 1994 Constitutional Law on the Constitutional Court, Art. 79.
[43] *Sobranie,* No. 6, item 782 (1998).
[44] Cf. Zhuykov, *supra* note 21, at 224.

unconstitutional, it may be argued that the declaration of unconstitutionality may apply only to cases arising in the future. Because the declaration of unconstitutionality may only have prospective effect to new cases, the courts of general jurisdiction have no obligation to reopen old cases. However, it may also be argued that the unconstitutional provision may be deemed unconstitutional from the moment the new Constitution was adopted, that is, from December 25, 1993. As a result, a new rule may apply not only to all cases arising in the future, but also to the parties in the case decided by the Supreme Court or by the Supreme Arbitration Court if the case arose after December 25, 1993. This line of argument becomes particularly persuasive if a rule declared unconstitutional concerns a procedural obstacle that the parties to the case tried to overcome. Although the new rule would apply retroactively to the parties in that very case, the changes do not concern substantive standards of conduct. They affect only the procedure to deal with the case.

A case still pending may clarify some aspects of retroactivity and the Constitutional Court's powers. In 1996 the Constitutional Court declared Arts. 371, 347 and 384 of the Criminal Procedure Code unconstitutional because they contained a limited list of grounds for review or reopening of criminal cases by the Supreme Court.[45] The Constitutional Court ruled that criminal cases of the several petitioners in that case convicted by "ordinary" courts "must be reconsidered."[46] It may well be argued that there is no problem of retroactive application of that ruling to the parties in the relevant criminal cases decided by "ordinary" courts. However, the Supreme Court refused to reconsider these cases. As a result, in June of 1997 the Constitutional Court issued an opinion in which it renewed its demand to reopen the cases.[47] While at this stage the result of the on-going controversy between the two courts is unknown, it is clear that it will define the exact effect of the rulings of the Constitutional Court on previously decided cases in the system of "ordinary" courts.

2. Courts of General Jurisdiction

The traditional system of the "ordinary" courts or courts of general jurisdiction is governed by the 1996 Constitutional Law on the Judicial System of the Russian Federation[48] and to some extent by the old 1981 Law on the

---

[45] See *Case Concerning Arts. 371, 374 and 384 of the Criminal Procedure Code*, *VKS*, 1996, No. 2, p.2.

[46] Id.

[47] See *Sobranie*, No. 25, item 2950 (1997).

[48] *Sobranie*, No. 1, item 1 (1997).

Judicial System of the RSFSR.[49] The 1981 Law is applicable only insofar as it does not conflict with the 1996 Law.

Under the 1996 Law, the system of ordinary courts is composed of the courts of the "subjects" of the Russian Federation and district courts. At the apex of the system of general jurisdiction courts is the Supreme Court of the Russian Federation. Military tribunals, which hear cases concerning all crimes committed by servicemen, by officers as well as certain crimes designated by criminal procedure legislation (e.g., espionage) operate separately at first instance, at cassational (second) and supervisory (third) instance. However, military tribunals merge with the system of "ordinary" courts at the Supreme Court level. The activities of the military tribunals are supervised by the Military Collegium of the Supreme Court.

(a) District Courts

District courts are established in each rural or urban district. They function as courts of first instance and courts for de novo appeals from decisions of justices of the peace. District courts usually have several professional judges and a number of lay (people's) assessors for each judge. Although in theory lay assessors participate in the proceedings and take part in the making of rulings on an equal footing with the professional judge,[50] in practice professional judges always dominate the proceedings and decision-making. Judges may specialize in a particular area of law, the main divisions being civil and criminal cases. Civil and criminal cases may be heard by individual professional judges or by a judge and two lay assessors. Although superior courts may hear certain civil and criminal cases at first instance, the overwhelming majority of all cases are decided initially by the district courts.

(b) Second-Level Courts

The second-level courts have various names depending on the territory on which they are located. Some "subjects" of the Russian Federation have the status of "republics" or states and the second-level courts in those instances are called the "Supreme Courts" of those republics. The territorial jurisdiction of other second-level courts may extend to other "subjects" of the Russian Federation - "provinces," "regions" or federal cities (Moscow and St. Petersburg). In that case, the second-level courts are referred to as "provincial courts," "regional courts" or "city courts." Other second-level courts cover

---

[49] *Vedomosty RF*, 1981, No. 28, item 976 (1981) (as amended in 1992 and 1993).

[50] According to Art. 11 of the 1981 Law on the Judicial System of the RSFSR, "in administering justice people's assessors shall enjoy all the rights of a judge."

autonomous republics or territories and their name will reflect the name of the relevant constituent entity as well. Whatever their name, the second-level courts have these functions.

First, they serve as trial courts in civil and criminal cases designated by the Civil Procedure Code and the Criminal Procedure Code. These cases are generally more serious crimes and civil matters other than those assigned to district courts. Civil and criminal cases may be heard by a judge and two lay assessors or by three professional judges. As noted earlier, in several regions of the country judges may conduct criminal trials with a jury. Although Art. 47 of the 1993 Constitution proclaims the general right to a court hearing "with the participation of jurors," at this stage jury trials are available only in those areas of the country where the system has been implemented. Further expansion of jury trials in serious criminal cases is expected in the near future.

Second, these second-level courts act as appellate courts reviewing district court judgments (second or cassational instance). In this case, second-level courts review judgments of district courts which have not entered into legal force on cassational appeals of interested parties or protests of procurators. Appeals are heard by three professional judges.

In contrast to many other European civil law countries, where "courts of cassation" usually decide only questions of law and operate by remand to the lower courts, Russian "ordinary courts of cassation" may review both questions of law and fact. The "court of cassation" always receives a file of the case which contains all documents and written record. It then reviews all the factual evidence contained in the file. In addition, the court may receive new evidence on the factual issues in the case if the interested party proves that it was not able to present it to the court of first instance. The powers of the cassational instance are broad and include the right to send the case for new consideration by the district court, the right to vacate the judgment of the lower court and the right to render a new judgment. Because in Russia cassational appeal may lead to a trial de novo, Russian "courts of cassation" have far more supervisory powers than their Western European counterparts and American appellate courts.

The third function of second-level courts is to act as courts of supervisory review (third instance). Review by way of supervision is a special procedure which allows additional reexamination of judgments which have already entered into legal force and may have already been decided on cassational appeal. As a formal matter, supervisory review can not be initiated by the interested parties. Cases are reexamined only upon protests of chairmen of the courts of the "subjects" of the Federation and the procurators. The powers of the court of supervisory instance are the same as the powers of the court of cassational instance.

The second-level courts are divided into the judicial collegiums for civil cases and judicial collegiums for criminal cases. Each court has a chairman and a court presidium which is composed of the court chairman, deputy chairmen and several members of the court. While the judicial collegiums hear cases as courts of first instance and on cassation, the court presidiums exercise primarily supervisory functions by considering protests against judgments that have already entered into force. They may also consider cases which have been reopened because of newly discovered facts.

(c) The Supreme Court of the Russian Federation

The Supreme Court, described by Art. 126 of the Constitution as "the highest judicial organ on civil, criminal, administrative and other cases falling within the jurisdiction of courts of general jurisdiction," is divided into three collegiums - the Judicial Collegium for Civil Cases, the Judicial Collegium for Criminal Cases and the Military Collegium. The Supreme Court has a Chairman and a Presidium which is composed of the court chairman, deputy chairmen and several members of the court. In addition to the Presidium it also has a Plenum. The Plenum consists of the court chairman, deputy chairmen and all members of the court.

Although the Supreme Court may hear certain very important or complex civil and criminal cases as a trial court (first instance), its main task is the supervision of the activities of all lower courts. It may review all judgments of lower courts by way of cassational appeal (second instance) or supervision (third instance). Supervisory review in the Supreme Court may be initiated by protests of the Chairman and Deputy Chairmen of the Supreme Court or protest of the Procurator General and his deputies. Because in both cassation and supervisory instances the Supreme Court in principle may hear the whole case de novo, it enjoys very broad supervisory powers over all lower courts scattered across the vast territory of the country.

The Supreme Court also has the broader task of overseeing the development of judicial practice and of the law in general. The plenary session of the Supreme Court has two unique powers:

(1) it may issue "explanations" on questions pertaining to judicial practice, and

(2) it may exercise the Court's "right of legislative initiative" by formulating the relevant "legislative proposals" for their subsequent submission to the parliament.

These powers raise interesting questions about sources of Russian law and the limits of judicial power.

3. The Arbitration (Commercial) Courts

Arbitration courts are separate state commercial courts designed to resolve economic and certain administrative disputes. These courts were established on the basis of the former *State Arbitrazh*, a system of quasi-judicial bodies that settled economic disputes between state enterprises in accordance with simplified rules of procedure. The traditional role of state arbitrators in a planned economy combined the functions of judge, mediator and state economic administrator. The introduction of a free market economy required the establishment of true commercial courts. The former quasi-judicial organ (that was subordinate to the Council of Ministers) was transformed into a new system of independent courts by the 1991 the Law "On the Arbitration Court."[51] The new courts were granted jurisdiction over commercial disputes and disputes between commercial enterprises and governmental agencies.

The first Arbitration Procedure Code was enacted in 1992.[52] The 1992 Code retained many simplified rules of procedure of the former *State Arbitrazh*. After a period of initial experimentation, the present structure and jurisdiction of arbitration courts were established by the 1995 Federal Constitutional Law on the Arbitration Courts[53] and the 1995 Arbitration Procedure Code.[54] These new laws expanded the jurisdiction of arbitration courts and introduced more elaborate rules of procedure. As a result, the new system of arbitration courts was turned into a system of true commercial courts capable of resolving different types of economic disputes in the emerging market economy. Former state arbitrators became independent judges, and the new courts became a part of the Russian judicial system.

The system of arbitration courts is comprised of the Supreme Arbitration Court, ten federal arbitration courts of the circuits (circuits unite several "subjects" of the Federation) and arbitration courts for the constituent republics and other "subjects" of the Federation.

(a) Trial Arbitration Courts

The first level of arbitration courts may be established in each "subject" of the Russian Federation with jurisdiction coextensive with the

[51] *Vedomosty RF*, No. 30, item 1013 (1991).
[52] See *Vedomosty RF*, No. 16, item 836 (1992).
[53] *Sobranie*, No. 18, item 1589 (1995).
[54] *Sobranie*, No. 19, item 1709 (1995).

territory of that subject. These arbitration courts are called arbitration courts of the "subjects" of the Russian Federation. However, the 1995 Constitutional Law on the Arbitration Courts also allows the establishment of several courts in each republic, or the establishment of one court for several republics. Arbitration courts of the first level are courts of original jurisdiction.

Each arbitration court of the first level is made up of a presidium and two collegiums: the collegium for the examination of disputes arising from civil and other legal relations and the collegium for the examination of disputes arising from administrative legal relations. While the presidium exercises only administrative functions, the judicial collegiums examine in the first and the appellate (second) instances economic disputes falling within the jurisdiction of arbitration courts. Arbitration courts of the first level have been granted original jurisdiction over almost all cases falling within the jurisdiction of these courts. In contrast to the "ordinary" court system, where different types of cases may be considered at first instance by different levels of the court hierarchy, the Supreme Arbitration Court has been given the power to consider at first instance only a very limited category of cases.

Cases in the first instance are usually examined by a sole professional judge. However, complicated cases may also be considered by three professional judges. Bankruptcy cases are always tried by a panel of three judges. The 1995 arbitration reform envisions the gradual introduction of lay arbitration assessors. The 1996 Law on the Judicial System legitimized arbitration assessors by including them in the list of other lay people who participate in the administration of justice (These are jurors, people's assessors and arbitration assessors). The Supreme Arbitration Court adopted special regulations governing the participation of arbitration assessors in arbitration proceedings.[55] Under these Regulations cases may be tried at first instance by panels composed of one professional judge and two arbitration assessors. In contrast to lay assessors in "ordinary" courts arbitration assessors are required to possess specialized knowledge and experience in the sphere of business and commerce.

Arbitration courts have a very interesting system of appeals which may be described as a limited version of the trial de novo. Parties have the right to submit appeals of decisions which have not entered into legal force. However, the "appeal" is heard by the same court that considered the case at first instance. All cases at the appellate level are reviewed by a new panel of three or more professional judges (if there are more than three judges, the number must always be uneven). Because appellate review means reconsideration of the case as a whole (with respect to both questions of law and fact), the

[55] See *VVAS*, 1997, No. 6, p. 23.

new panel may receive new evidence on the factual issues in the case. Certain restrictions have been imposed, however. An appellate court may receive new evidence only if the interested party proves that it was not able to present it to the court of first instance. At the same time, the appellate court cannot consider those legal claims or demands which have not been submitted to the arbitration court of first instance. Because the appellate court is supposed to decide the whole case all over again, it has no power to remand the case for reconsideration. The new panel of appellate judges always renders a new final ruling binding on the parties.

(b) Federal Arbitration Courts of the Circuits

Federal arbitration courts of the circuits function as intermediate appellate arbitration courts. They are structured similarly to the first tier of courts. These are courts of cassational (third) instance. A panel of three or more professional judges reviews decisions of lower courts which have entered into legal force. At this stage, there is no appeal by trial de novo. In principle, cassational review, which may be initiated by the parties, concerns only questions of law. As noted earlier, "courts of cassation" in other civil law countries, which decide only questions of law, usually operate by remand to the lower courts. Russian circuit arbitration courts function in a different way. Although these "courts of cassation" are supposed to decide only special questions of law, they often reexamine the whole written record of the file. The circuit court may always refuse to accept lower courts findings of fact and substitute their own fact-finding under the guise of law finding.[56] Circuit courts may not only send the case back to the lower court if the ruling is "unfounded," but also issue a new judgment. This means that they enjoy extremely broad supervisory powers.

(c) The Supreme Arbitration Court

The Supreme Arbitration Court, which is described by Art. 127 of the Constitution as "the highest judicial organ resolving economic and other disputes within the jurisdiction of the arbitration courts," is structured similarly to the lower courts, but with the addition of a Plenum.

The Supreme Arbitration Court considers cases by way of supervision (fourth instance). In the arbitration court system, review by way of supervision is considered to be exceptional. The right to lodge protests against decisions of lower courts has been granted only to the Chairman of the Supreme Arbitration Court, the Procurator General and their deputies. Cases are reviewed by the Presidium of the Supreme Arbitration Court. As the court of

[56] For details, see Chapter VII.

supervisory instance, the Supreme Arbitration Court has the right to review the case as a whole, i.e. to reconsider not only legal but also factual issues. The Presidium of the Supreme Court has both the power to vacate the judgment and send the case for new consideration and the power to vacate the judgment and render a new judgment.

In addition, the Supreme Arbitration Court has original jurisdiction with respect to two types of cases:

1) cases concerning invalidation of those non-normative acts of the President, the Federation Council, the State Duma and the Government which "contravene the law and violate the rights and lawful interests of organizations and citizens;"

2) economic disputes between the Federation and its "subjects" and those between the "subjects."

Decisions of the Supreme Arbitration Court rendered at first instance are final and not subject to either appellate or cassational review (however, review by way of supervision is possible).

The plenary session of the Supreme Arbitration Court has the same powers as the Plenary session of the Supreme Court. It may issue "explanations on questions pertaining to judicial practice" and initiate legislation.

4. Summary: Diagram of the Russian Court System(s)

The above presentation indicates several important differences in the structure and operation of ordinary and arbitration courts. Differences between civil and arbitration procedure will be discussed in Chapter VII. The following is a diagram summarizing the court system just described.

DIAGRAM OF THE RUSSIAN COURT SYSTEM(S)

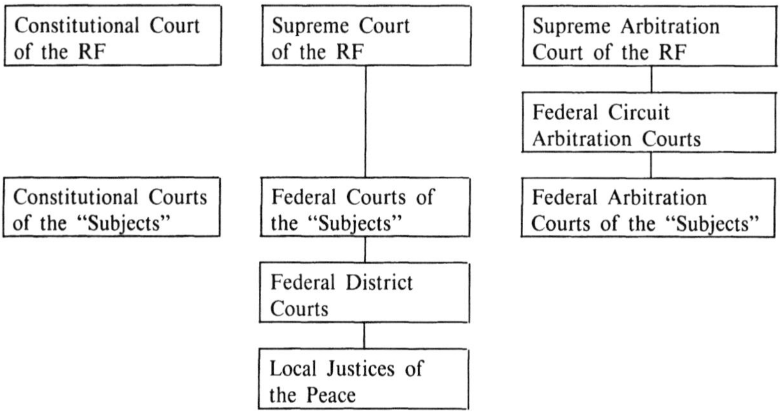

C. Jurisdictional Divisions Between Court Systems

The existing court system presents a lawyer with three different courts of law from which to choose. Any decision of where to file a suit or complaint must take into account the established division of jurisdiction between the Constitutional Court, "ordinary" courts and arbitration courts. While in the US complexities arise from the concurrent overlapping competence of state and federal courts, in Russia they result from the overlapping competencies of the Constitutional Court, "ordinary" and arbitration courts.

1. The Subject-Matter Jurisdictional Division Between the Constitutional Court and the Courts of General Jurisdiction

(a) Individual Complaints to the Constitutional Court

The exact delineation of the competence of the Constitutional Court and "ordinary" courts in the review of the constitutionality of normative acts is fairly complicated. A careful analysis of Art. 125 of the Constitution indicates that citizens can directly initiate only review of "a law that has been applied or is due to be applied in a specific case." There are many examples of this kind of action before the Constitutional Court. Consider the pertinent extracts from the following cases:

The Constitutional Court: ***Case Concerning Art. 54 of the Housing Code*** (*VKS*, 1995, No. 2/3, p. 32)

1) For five years L.N. Sitalova cohabited with V.N. Kaderkin and lived in his apartment; at the same time she remained registered at another place of residence with her daughter and her son-in-law. After the death of

Kaderkin's parents, she raised the question of obtaining a permit to reside in his apartment, but failed to obtain his consent.

The petitioner brought suit with the Narimanov people's court of the Astrakhan region which granted her claim. The Judicial Collegium for Civil Cases of the Astrakhan Regional Court vacated the decision of the people's court and denied the claim stating that she moved into the apartment in violation of registration rules envisioned by Art. 54 of the Housing Code of the RSFSR and that the petitioner was not a member of the tenant's family.

Believing that these actions violated her constitutional right to a home, L.N. Sitalova filed a complaint with the Constitutional Court of the Russian Federation to review the constitutionality of paras. 1 and 2 of Art. 54 of the Housing Code of the RSFSR.

2) According to Art. 97 of the Federal Constitutional Law on the Constitutional Court of the Russian Federation, a complaint about a law's violation of constitutional rights and freedoms is admissible, if the challenged law, first, affects the constitutional rights and freedoms of citizens, and, second, has been applied or may be applied in a concrete case, whose consideration has been completed or begun in a court.

The above Constitutional Law implies that the decision concerning the admissibility of the petition does not depend on the substance of decisions rendered by courts of general jurisdiction in the given case; it is also of no significance whether the case has been considered by all judicial instances. The Constitutional Court of the Russian Federation does not review decisions of the courts. A citizen has the right to petition the Constitutional Court of the Russian Federation only in cases if he or she believes that there is uncertainty as to whether the law affecting his or her interests is in conformity with the Constitution.

The petitioner believes that the Judicial Collegium for Civil Cases of the Astrakhan Regional Court, when applying paras. 1 and 2 of Art. 54 of the Housing Code in her case, "assumed that moving in accordance with the established procedure means moving into a dwelling premises with the observance of the residence permit (*propiska*) regulations." The petition states that this law is incompatible with the Constitution of the Russian Federation and that its application affects the constitutional rights of L.N. Sitalova. Therefore, her complaint is admissible and the resolution of the issue raised in the complaint falls within the jurisdiction of the Constitutional Court of the Russian Federation. When considering the case, the Constitutional Court of the Russian Federation, in accordance with paras. 2 and 3 of Art. 3 and para. 3 Art. 74 of the Federal Constitutional Law on the Constitutional Court of the

Russian Federation, shall not be bound by the arguments advanced in the petition and shall rule exclusively on questions of law, refraining from establishing and investigating factual circumstances, including those which confirm the violation of a citizen's rights in the specific case, in all cases when this falls within the jurisdiction of other courts. . .[57]

The Constitutional Court: *Case Concerning Arts. 220(1) and 220(2) of the Criminal Procedure Code* (*VKS*, 1995, No.2/3, p. 39)

1) Criminal prosecutions for violations of Art. 122 (intentional non-payment of support) and Art. 130 (criminal libel) of the Criminal Code of RSFSR were brought against citizen V.A. Avetian and an order for pretrial detention was issued to be executed on him, but it was not executed. This order, dated August 16, 1990, remained unchanged right up to the time that the criminal case was dismissed on April 16, 1994. Thus, the order for Avetian's arrest and detention was in effect for the period of four years; in connection with that order, he was listed as wanted by the police and this was reported in the local newspaper.

Citizen V.A. Avetian filed a complaint to the local court of general jurisdiction challenging the legality of the order and seeking its reversal. However, the complaint was dismissed two times on the ground that under Arts. 220(1) and 220(2) of the Criminal Procedure Code of RSFSR such complaints may be brought only by persons who are actually in custody and that those complaints are heard by a court of the place where the person is detained.

2) In his complaint to the Constitutional Court of the Russian Federation, the petitioner asserts that Arts. 220(1) and 220(2) of the Criminal Procedure Code of RSFSR applied in his case limit his right to freedom and personal inviolability and his right to judicial protection, violate equality of everyone before the law and courts, guaranteed by the Constitution of the Russian Federation and therefore contravene Arts. 19, 22, 45, 46 and 47 of the Constitution of the Russian Federation.

The Constitutional Court of the Russian Federation granted the petition, because, pursuant to Art. 97 of the Federal Constitutional Law on the Constitutional Court of the Russian Federation, the challenged provisions of the law were applied in his case and affect his constitutional rights. . .

Courts of general jurisdiction recognized the limitation of the right to appeal to court introduced by the Criminal Procedure Code of the RSFSR and

[57] We will return to the merits of this case in Chapter V.

yet did not make use of their right to request the Constitutional Court of the Russian Federation to review the constitutionality of the above clauses of the Criminal Procedure Code of RSFSR envisioned by Art. 125(4) of the Constitution of the Russian Federation as well as by Arts. 3(1), 101 and 103 of the Federal Constitutional Law on the Constitutional Court of the Russian Federation. At the same time, a court of general jurisdiction has no right to declare unconstitutional a law that is supposed to be applied in a specific case considered by it. This falls within the exclusive jurisdiction of the Constitutional Court of the Russian Federation which, in its turn, does not verify the legality and justification of the decisions of courts of general jurisdiction; it rules exclusively on questions of law. . .[58]

QUESTIONS AND COMMENTS

1. What are the jurisdictional prerequisites for an individual complaint filed with the Constitutional Court?

2. In its ruling in the *Case Concerning Art. 54 of the Housing Code,* the Court stated that "according to Art. 97 of the Federal Constitutional Law on the Constitutional Court of the Russian Federation, a complaint about a law's violation of constitutional rights and freedoms may be brought, if the challenged law, first, affects the constitutional rights and freedoms of citizens, and, second, has been applied or may be applied in *a concrete case, whose consideration has been completed or begun in a court"* (Emphasis added - eds.). Does this mean that the relevant law has to be applied only by *a court*? Compare this statement with Art. 125(4) of the Constitution. Can we find any clarification of this issue in the ruling of the Court in the *Case Concerning Arts. 220(1) and 220(2) of the Criminal Procedure Code?*

3. Note that in the *Case Concerning Arts. 220(1) and 220(2) of the Criminal Procedure Code* the order for pretrial detention was repealed and the criminal case dismissed prior to the petition to the Constitutional Court. Why did the Court consider the complaint?

4. Does a person have to exhaust all the remedies within the system of "ordinary" courts before filing a constitutional complaint?

5. What is the nature of the relationship between the Constitutional Court and "ordinary" courts according to these cases? Why are "ordinary" courts supposed to turn to the Constitutional Court if there is any doubt about the constitutionality of a law? Why can't they declare the law unconstitutional themselves? (Note that under Art. 120 of the Constitution "judges shall be

[58] We will return to the merits of this case in Chapter V and Chapter X.

independent and shall obey only the Constitution of the Russian Federation and federal law." Art. 120 also states that "a court of law, having established during the consideration of a case that any act of a governmental or other organ does not correspond to the law, shall render a ruling in accordance with the law").

6. In its ruling in the *Case Concerning Art. 54 of the Housing Code*, the Courts stated that "the Constitutional Court of the Russian Federation does not review decisions of the courts." It also noted that it "shall rule exclusively on questions of law, refraining from establishing and investigating factual circumstances, including those which confirm the violation of a citizen's rights in the specific case, in all cases when this falls within the jurisdiction of other courts." How does the ruling of the Constitutional Court on the unconstitutionality of a law applied in a specific case affect the judgments of "ordinary" courts based in this law?

7. Note that under of Art. 125(4) of the Constitution citizens cannot challenge presidential decrees. They can only initiate judicial review of the constitutionality of "laws." Nor can they challenge the constitutionality of sub-laws or other normative acts of the "subjects" of the Federation. In the *Case of Mrs. Grishchenko*, the petitioner wanted to challenge in the Constitutional Court regulations of the Council of Ministers of the former USSR concerning foreign travel. However, she was not able to do so because the Constitutional Law on the Constitutional Court, which is based on Art. 125 of the Constitution, does not give the citizens the right to challenge sub-laws. The petitioner then asked the Court to verify the constitutionality of the restrictive Law on the Constitutional Court because in violates Art. 46 of the Constitution. The Court refused to consider the petition because the normative acts in question could be challenged in "ordinary" courts. The Court also added, that the Court may not review provisions of the Constitution (i.e. Arts. 46 and 125) for mutual conformity (see *Sobranie*, No. 24, item 2803 (1997)).

(b) Judicial Review for Constitutionality by "Ordinary" Courts

(1) Individual Complaints

We have established that citizens may initiate judicial review of the constitutionality of "a law that has been applied or is due to be applied in a specific case." We also have established that citizens cannot initiate review of normative acts of the President or normative acts of the "subjects" of the Federation mentioned in Art. 125(2) (a and b) of the Constitution. Nor can they initiate review of all kinds of normative regulations issued by the governmental agencies. This is a very serious restriction because these regulations may affect interests of millions of people.

As the Constitutional Court noted in *Mrs. Grishchenko's* case, however, the ordinary courts are available to aggrieved citizens in these situations. Thus, the limitations of Art. 125 of the Constitution open the door for a more active role of "ordinary" courts in constitutional litigation. The normative basis for court action is Art. 46 of the Constitution which proclaims that "everyone shall be guaranteed protection of his or her rights and freedoms in a court of law." Although the Constitutional Court has exclusive power to declare statutes unconstitutional, "ordinary" courts also have the power to review the constitutionality of laws or other normative acts that litigants seek to apply. Such review takes place principally in two situations.

First, because the Constitutional Court cannot verify the constitutionality of regulations issued by governmental agencies, citizens must turn to "ordinary" courts. The matter is now governed by Art. 116 of the Civil Procedure Code. According to Art. 116, complaints about the normative acts of the federal ministries and agencies affecting the rights and freedoms of citizens must be filed with the Supreme Court. The Supreme Court hears these case as a court of first instance.

The second situation is which "ordinary" courts assess the constitutionality of statutes and other normative acts is when those laws are sought to be applied in the case at hand. Courts are not supposed to apply a statute or other normative act if it contradicts the Constitution.[59] As a result, "ordinary" courts asserted the power to review the conformity of legislation with the Constitution and to disregard, in the concrete case, any normative act held unconstitutional. The Supreme Court, in its Ruling "*On Some Questions Concerning the Application of the Constitution of the Russian Federation by Courts*,"[60] has emphasized that the Constitution has supreme legal force and direct effect. Consequently, "when hearing individual cases the courts must be guided by the Constitution of the Russian Federation. "The Supreme Court instructed all lower courts to evaluate the contents of applicable laws or other normative acts for their conformity to the Constitution and" to apply the Constitution of the Russian Federation as an act of direct effect in all necessary cases. Thus, "normative decrees" of the President should be applied by courts only if they do not contravene the Constitution and federal laws.

The Supreme Court ruled that the courts must apply the Constitution in all cases, and, in particular:

---

[59]This argument also applies to arbitration courts which, according to Art. 120 of the Constitution, may also refuse to apply unlawful or unconstitutional acts in specific case at hand.

[60]*BVS*, 1996, No. 1, p. 3.

> when a court reaches the conclusion that a federal law in effect on the territory of the Russian Federation prior to the effective date of the Constitution of the Russian Federation contravenes the Constitution;
>
> when a court reaches the conclusion that a federal law enacted after the effective date of the Constitution of the Russian Federation is in conflict with the relevant provisions of the Constitution;
>
> when a law or any other normative legal act promulgated by a subject of the Russian Federation on matters of joint jurisdiction of the Russian Federation and subjects of the Russian Federation contravenes the Constitution. . .[61]

These trends indicate that the emerging system of constitutional review does not exclude constitutional review by "ordinary" courts. From a comparative standpoint, the Russian judicial review system in "ordinary" courts may be described as "decentralized." As noted earlier, the decentralized (or American) system gives all "ordinary" courts the power to determine the constitutionality of legislation.[62] In contrast, the centralized system based on a Constitutional Court confines this power to a single judicial organ. Because in Russia both the Constitutional Court and the "ordinary" courts have the power to review the constitutionality of different normative regulations it appears that in reality the emerging Russian model of judicial review is mixed.[63] While citizens may file complaints about the constitutionality of statute-level laws with the Russian Constitutional Court under Art. 125(4) of the Constitution, there exists a general right of review of all normative acts violating human rights and freedoms in "ordinary" courts under Art. 46 of the Constitution. Clearly, there is the potential for overlap in these cases, since laws that are unconstitutional could also affect human rights and freedoms.

The delineation of the jurisdiction of the Constitutional Court and "ordinary" courts with respect to non-normative (as well as normative) acts of the President is illustrated by the *Nuclear Fuel Cases* discussed in Chapter II, section B(5). Please read and analyze these cases again.

As noted earlier, another area where the citizens must turn to "ordinary" courts is the review of the constitutionality of regulations issued by the "subjects" of the Russian Federation. The following cases deal with

---

[61] Id.

[62] See Cappelletti, *supra* note 26, at 132-133.

[63] For a comparative analysis of other mixed systems of judicial review, see A.R. Brewer-Carias, Judicial Review in Comparative Law 263-326 (1989).

constitutional complaints initiated by citizens against various normative acts promulgated by the "subjects" of the Russian Federation:

The Supreme Court: *Potapov v. The Legislative Assembly of the Altai Region* (*Sudebnaya praktika po grazhdanskim delam* 1993-1996, at 113-115 (1997))

By a decision of May 26, 1995, the Legislative Assembly of the Altai Region enacted a Charter (Fundamental Law) of the Altai Region. According to Art. 83(2) of the Charter, the Head of the Administration of the Region is elected by the Legislative Assembly of the Region. . .

Mr. Potapov brought suit in court to declare the above-mentioned clause of the Charter unlawful, because, in his opinion, it contradicts the Constitution and violates his constitutional right to directly elect the head of the executive branch of the Region.

A ruling issued by the judge of the Altai regional court dismissed the suit because the court held that the dispute did not fall within the jurisdiction of the courts of general jurisdiction; the court noted that cases concerning compliance with the Constitution of the Russian Federation of charters of the subjects of the Russian Federation are resolved by the Constitutional Court of the Russian Federation.

Having considered the case upon the appeal of Mr. Potapov, the Judicial Collegium for Civil Cases of the Supreme Court of the RF, vacated the ruling for the following reasons:

In terminating the proceedings, the court held that the case did not fall within the jurisdiction of the court because, as the court stated, the petitioner challenged the compatibility of Art. 83(2) of the Charter of the Region with the Constitution of the Russian Federation; according to Art. 125 of the Constitution of the Russian Federation, resolution of this issue falls within the jurisdiction of the Constitutional Court of the Russian Federation.

This argument cannot be accepted.

Indeed, the petitioner based its request to annul the challenged Art. 83(2) of the Charter of the Region on the fact that it contravened the Constitution of the Russian Federation and legislation of the Russian Federation. However, he also claimed that Art. 83(2) of the Charter violated his electoral rights, in particular the right to elect and be elected; in this connection, he believed that the Charter infringed upon his subjective rights and liberties in violation of Art. 55 of the Constitution of the Russian Federation. In this case, proceeding from the guarantee of court protection of rights and freedoms for everyone, established by Art. 46 of the Constitution of the Russian Federation, he had the right to appeal in court the decision of the Legislative Assembly of the Altai Region, which, in his opinion, resulted in the promulgation of an unlawful act. . .

The Supreme Court: *Citizens of Uglitch v. Vice-Governor and Governor of the Yaroslavl Region* (*BVS*, 1995, No. 9, p. 1).

On February 25, 1995 the Vice-Governor of the Yaroslavl Region issued a ruling by which he dismissed C. as the head of administration of the town of Uglitch and appointed S. as a new head. . .

The petitioners - citizens of Uglitch - filed a complaint with the court stating that in accordance with the Constitution of the Russian Federation, the 1991 "Law on the Local Self-Government in the Russian Federation" and the 1991 "Law on the Election of the Heads of Administrations," the organs of local self-government and their heads are directly formed by the people of the region where such organs are established; at the same time, the organs of state power of the Russian Federation have no right to interfere with municipal affairs, in particular, to appoint the head of the local administration. . .

The Collegium for Civil Cases of the Yaroslavl Regional Court granted the claim with respect to the recognition as void of all acts challenged by the petitioners; it also ordered the Governor of Yaroslavl Region to organize elections of the head of the administration of the town of Uglitch. . .

The Collegium for Civil Cases of the Supreme Court of the RF, which considered the case by way of cassation, confirmed on March 1, 1995 that the lower court was right when it declared illegal the ruling of the Vice-Governor of the Yaroslavl Region concerning the appointment of S. as the head of the administration of the town of Uglitch, because this position is supposed to be filled on the basis of the results of elections.

According to Art. 12 of the Constitution of the Russian Federation, local self-government operates independently within the limits of its authority. The bodies of local self-government are not part of the system of the organs of state power. The appointment of the head of local administration by the head of the administration of the subject of the Russian Federation violates the self-governance of the territory and is an attempt to establish a local organ of state power; this violates Art. 130 (1) of the Constitution of the Russian Federation which ensures that people will independently resolve questions of local importance. . .

The Deputy Procurator General of the RF filed a protest in this case and asked to vacate the relevant court decisions and terminate the proceedings because the Yaroslavl Regional Court, in considering the case, acted beyond the limits of its jurisdiction.

The Presidium of the Supreme Court of the RF rejected the protest on July 5, 1995 and stated the following:

The protest's argument about the lack of jurisdiction of the court refers to the fact that the complaint of the petitioners amounted to a demand to verify the constitutionality of the rulings, issued by the Vice-Governor and the Governor of the Yaroslavl Region, on the establishment of general principles of local self-government on the territory of a subject of the Russian Federation; according to Art. 125 of the Constitution of the Russian Federation, such a verification falls within the exclusive jurisdiction of the Constitutional Court of the Russian Federation.

These arguments of the protest cannot be accepted.

The complaint of the petitioners - citizens of the town of Uglitch - "did not amount" to a demand to review the constitutionality of the rulings issued by the Governor of Yaroslavl Region.

Indeed, the petitioners demanded that challenged rulings be voided for their inconsistency with the Constitution and legislation of the Russian Federation. However, they argued that the above rulings violated their constitutional rights, in particular the right to elect and be elected to organs of self-government and independently solve all questions of local importance . . . (Arts. 130, 131 and 132 of the Constitution of the Russian Federation).

It is thus clear that the petitioners believed that their subjective rights and freedoms had been violated. In that case, pursuant to Art. 46 of the Constitution of the Russian Federation which guarantees protection of everyone's rights and freedoms in a court, they had the right to appeal in court actions of the Governor of Yaroslavl Region which, in their opinion, resulted in the issuance of illegal acts (Art. 46(2) of the Constitution of the Russian Federation). . .

This petition of citizens cannot be classified as a petition falling within the exclusive jurisdiction of the Constitutional Court of the Russian Federation. In accordance with Art. 125(2) of the Constitution of the Russian Federation, the Constitutional Court of the Russian Federation, in response to applications of a limited number of subjects (citizens are not included in this group), resolves cases about compliance with the Constitution of the Russian Federation of normative acts of the subjects of the Russian Federation, issued on questions within the joint jurisdiction of the organs of state power of the

Russian Federation and the organs of state power of the subjects of the Russian Federation (the protest correctly notes that the establishment of general principles for the organization of local self-government falls, under Art. 72 of the Constitution of the Russian Federation, within the joint jurisdiction of the Russian Federation and its subjects).

In that case the court did not resolve issues concerning compliance of normative acts with the Constitution of the Russian Federation. The petitioners did not raise before the court the question concerning review of the constitutionality of the ruling issued by the Governor of the Region; they appealed actions of the official which resulted in the issuance of, in their view, illegal acts violating the rights and freedoms of citizens. Whether or not these rights had indeed been violated, was the question for the court to determine during the consideration of the case; that was exactly what the court did.

In that formulation, the complaint of the petitioners falls within the jurisdiction of courts of general jurisdiction; so the Yaroslavl Regional Court had the right to consider the complaint and correctly stated that there was no reason to classify the above complaint as a complaint falling within the exclusive jurisdiction of the Constitutional Court of the Russian Federation. . .

QUESTIONS AND COMMENTS

1. What were the major arguments in favor of asserting jurisdiction of "ordinary" courts in both cases?

2. Why did the Supreme Court place such an emphasis on the alleged violation of *the subjective rights and freedoms* of citizens by *actions* of officials or *decisions* of local bodies which resulted in the issuance of illegal *acts*? Consider Art. 46 and Art. 120 of the Constitution. Do they establish the right of every citizen to challenge unlawful acts of any governmental official or local authorities? Can this right be restricted by jurisdictional and procedural rules, for example by Art. 125 of the Constitution?

3. In *Citizens of Uglitch v. Vice-Governor and Governor of the Yaroslavl Region,* the Deputy Procurator General believed that the Rulings of the Vice-Governor and the Governor of the Yaroslavl region concerned the establishment of general principles of local self-government on the territory of a "subject" of the Russian Federation. In other words, he thought that the regulations were of a normative character. Do you agree? What did the Court say in this connection?

(2) Procurator Protests of Unconstitutionality of Local Laws

Another way that the "ordinary" courts get involved in constitutional matters is when the case arises from the institution of Procurator's protest.[64] Art. 125 of the Constitution contains a fairly restricted list of official or organs which may lodge constitutional complaints with the Constitutional Court. This list does not include Procurators. While the Procurator General had been granted the power to challenge the constitutionality of laws before the Constitutional Court under the revised version of the law "On the Procuracy of the Russian Federation,"[65] lower-ranking procurators can only turn to "ordinary" courts. Local procurators started to lodge protests against unconstitutional charters, laws and other normative acts of the republics and other "subjects" of the Federation with "ordinary" courts. While some lower courts held that these matters belong to the exclusive jurisdiction of the Constitutional Court, the Supreme Court issued several opinions which asserted the jurisdiction of ordinary courts over these constitutional disputes. The Supreme Court emphasized the importance of the Procuracy's activities in this area and stated, among other things, that procurators may demand that the courts review the constitutionality and legality of "legal" or "normative" acts issued by ministries and other government departments and regional legislative organs.[66] Examples of Procuracy activism - challenging the constitutionality of various normative acts, especially acts promulgated by the subjects of the Russian Federation, abound.[67]

(3) Different Effects of Constitutional Adjudication by the Constitutional Court and "Ordinary" Courts

Although "ordinary" courts have no power to declare a controversial law unconstitutional (and, therefore, officially void), they have the power to assess the constitutionality of the relevant law, or any other normative act, and independently decide (either negatively or positively) on its constitutionality

[64] We will discuss the Procuracy and functions of Procurators *infra* p. 117-123.

[65] See *Sobranie*, No. 47, item 4472 (1995).

[66] Ruling of the Plenary Session of the Supreme Court of the Russian Federation " *On Some Issues Arising During the Judicial Consideration of Cases Upon Procurators' Applications Concerning the Recognition of Legal Acts as Contrary to the Law*" (*BVS*, 1993, No. 7, p. 8).

[67] See *Procurator v. the Administration of the Vologda Region* (*BVS*, 1995, No. 5, p. 6); *Procurator v. the Belgorod Regional Duma* (*BVS*, 1996, No. 5, p. 1) (In both cases, the challenged regional acts were invalidated by the Supreme Court because they contradicted Art. 76 of the Constitution). The latest compilation of decisions of the Supreme Court includes three additional cases on constitutional disputes initiated by the Procurators. See *Sudebnaya praktika po grazhdanskim delam* 1993-1996 (Judicial Practice in Civil Cases 1992- 1996), at 26, 119, 123 (1997).

(and, therefore, apply or not apply it in the case at hand). In addition, "ordinary" courts often must make the initial judgment as to whether a constitutional issue ought to be referred to the Constitutional Court.[68]

As a result, the Constitutional Court and the Supreme Court may hand down rulings on substantially the same constitutional questions. This is illustrated by two recent decisions of these courts dealing with regional regulations that imposed extremely heavy taxes for residence registration. Both the Constitutional Court[69] and the Supreme Court[70] held that the restrictive regulations promulgated by the City of Moscow contravene the constitutional right to choose a place of residence, guaranteed by Art. 27 of the 1993 Constitution.

At the same time, the effects of constitutional adjudication in the Constitutional Court and in "ordinary" courts are different. While the Constitutional Court is capable of giving rulings of general binding effect, the impact of "ordinary" courts' determinations of unconstitutionality is limited because their decisions in individual cases are not precedents. "Ordinary" court's determination of unconstitutionality is binding only for the parties in the case. The effect may become much stronger if the Supreme Court issues "explanations" on constitutional issues. However, as a formal matter even "explanations" cannot repeal the law. As the Constitutional Court observed in its Ruling in the *Case Concerning Arts 220(1) and 220(2) of the Criminal Procedure Code,*[71] "a court of general jurisdiction has no right to declare unconstitutional a law that is supposed to be applied in a specific case considered by it. This falls within the exclusive jurisdiction of the Constitutional Court of the Russian Federation. . ."

(4) The Duty of "Ordinary" Courts to Refer Constitutional Issues to the Constitutional Court

Because both the Constitutional Court and the Supreme Court have become active in matters of constitutional control, the relations between them is not without a certain amount of friction. Indeed, some aspects of the relationship are quite controversial.

One of the most controversial areas is the power of ordinary courts to assess the constitutionality of laws. The question is whether they can render

---

[68] See *infra* p. 96-98.

[69] See *Case Concerning Some Normative Acts of the City of Moscow, VKS*, 1996, No. 2, p. 42 (We will study this case in Chapter V).

[70] *Onischenko vs. Directorate of Internal Affairs of Moscow, BVS*, 1996, No. 3, p. 4.

[71] *VKS*, 1995, No.2/3, p. 39.

decisions on constitutionality of laws independently or whether they must always turn to the Constitutional Court. Art. 101 of the Constitutional Law on the Constitutional Court provides:

> Should a court, in considering a case in any instance, come to the conclusion that a law that has been applied or should be applied in that case violates the Constitution of the Russian Federation, it shall request the Constitutional Court of the Russian Federation to review the constitutionality of the law.

Three points must be emphasized in connection with Art. 101. First, it obviously recognizes the power of "ordinary" (as well as arbitration) courts to decide that the relevant law is constitutional and therefore applicable to the case at hand (positive determination). Second, it also recognizes the power of "ordinary" (as well as arbitration) courts to make an independent initial determination that there are doubts about the constitutionality of the law (negative determination). Third, in cases of doubt Art. 101 makes the appeal to the Constitutional Court mandatory. The authoritative "Commentary" to the Federal Constitutional Law on the Constitutional Court of the Russian Federation emphasizes that in cases of doubt courts must submit the question to the Constitutional Court.[72]

The above proposition has been met with serious objections from the Supreme Court, which wants to retain the power of "ordinary" courts to independently make both positive and negative determinations of constitutionality. In its Ruling "*On Some Questions Concerning the Application of the Constitution of the Russian Federation by Courts,*"[73] the Supreme Court noted that according to Art. 125(4) of the Constitution, courts should request the Constitutional Court to review the constitutionality of "a law that has been applied or is due to be applied in a specific case" only in cases of "uncertainty" regarding its constitutionality. It follows that in all other cases courts are supposed to make their independent evaluation of the situation and apply the Constitution directly.

Judges of the Supreme Court argue that under the Constitution the courts have only *the right and not an obligation* to submit requests to the Constitutional Court.[74] Indeed, Art. 125 (4) of the Constitution does not provide for any obligation on the part of the courts to submit requests to the Constitutional Court to verify the constitutionality of the law that has been applied or due to be applied in a specific case. In his book "Judicial Defense of

---

[72] Vitruk, Lazarev, Ebzeev, *supra* note 20, at 314; Cf. Ebzeev, *supra* note 20, at 56.

[73] See *supra* note 60.

[74] See Zhuykov, *supra*, note 21, at 219-223 (1997).

the Rights of Citizens and Juridical Persons," the Deputy Chairman of the Supreme Court, V.M. Zhuykov, argues that Art. 101 of the Law on the Constitutional Court contravenes the Constitution.[75]

2. The Subject-Matter Jurisdictional Division Between the Constitutional Court and Arbitration Courts

The division of jurisdiction between the Constitutional Court and arbitration courts is very clear. Because under the 1995 Arbitration Procedure Code arbitration courts do not have any power to review the constitutionality of "normative acts," there is no conflict of jurisdiction between the Constitutional Court and arbitration courts.

3. The Subject-Matter Jurisdiction of "Ordinary" and Arbitration Courts

The subject-matter jurisdiction of "ordinary" courts and arbitration courts in civil law matters raises several controversial issues. Despite the efforts of the drafters of the 1995 Arbitration Procedure Code to clarify the applicable tests, some of the tests are not easy to apply. Regrettably, there is no single or ultimate authority on conflicts of jurisdiction between ordinary and arbitration courts. The court in which the action is brought is supposed to decide whether it has jurisdiction. Although its ruling can be appealed within the relevant system of courts, there is no impartial authority to settle the matter.

However, it is important to keep in mind that under Art. 5 of the 1995 Constitutional Law on Arbitration Courts, one of the main tasks of arbitration courts is the protection of the rights and interests of "enterprises, institutions, organizations and citizens in the sphere of entrepreneurial and other economic activity." The Supreme Arbitration Court stressed in one of its rulings that arbitration courts are *specialized courts* designed to resolve economic disputes arising out of entrepreneurial activity.[76] (Emphasis added - eds.)

(a) The Statutory Provisions

It is well established that while "ordinary" courts are supposed to have general jurisdiction in civil, family, labor and administrative legal relations if one party to the dispute is a citizen, arbitration courts have the power to handle economic disputes among enterprises or people engaged in business.

[75] Id., at 221.
[76] See *VVAS*, 1995, No. 2, p. 43.

The subject-matter jurisdiction of arbitration courts is defined by Art. 22 of the 1995 Arbitration Procedure Code as follows:

1. Arbitration courts shall have jurisdiction over cases concerning economic disputes arising from civil, administrative and other legal relations:

   1) between judicial persons (hereinafter referred to as organizations), citizens engaged in entrepreneurial activity without the formation of a judicial person and having the status of an individual entrepreneur, obtained in the procedure established by the law (hereinafter referred to as citizens);

   2) between the Russian Federation and the subjects of the Russian Federation and between the subjects of the Russian Federation.

2. Economic disputes subject to the jurisdiction of arbitration courts shall, in particular, include disputes over:

   - conflicts of opinion about the formation of a contract, the conclusion of which is required by the law or where the parties to the contract have agreed to refer to arbitration courts any dispute arising in connection with the contract;

   - the amendment of the terms or termination of contracts;

   - the failure to perform or improper performance of obligations;

   - the recognition of rights of ownership;

   - the demands by an owner or other lawful possessor to recover property from the unlawful possession of another;

   - the violation of the rights of an owner or other lawful possessor not connected with deprivation of possession;

   - compensation of losses;

   - the recognition as void (in full or in part) of non-normative acts of state organs, organs of local self-government and other organs that are inconsistent with the laws and other normative legal acts and that violate the legally protected rights and interests of organizations and citizens;

   - the protection of honor, dignity and business reputation;

- the recognition of writs of execution or other documents which allow the transfer of monetary resources in an uncontested procedure;

- the appeal of a refusal of state registration or avoidance of state registration within the established period of time of an organization or citizen, as well as in other cases when such registration is envisioned by the law;

- the imposition of fines on organizations and citizens by state organs, organs of local self-government and other control organs, if the federal law does not provide for the transfer of monetary resources in an uncontested procedure;

- refund from the budget of monetary resources imposed as sanctions by control organs in an uncontested procedure in violation of the requirements of the law or other normative legal act.

3. The arbitration courts shall also consider other cases, including:

   - the establishment of facts having legal significance for the creation, alteration and termination of the rights of organizations and citizens in the sphere of entrepreneurial or other economic activity;

   - the insolvency (bankruptcy) of organizations and citizens. . .

6. Cases subject to the jurisdiction of the arbitration court shall concern organizations and citizens of the Russian Federation, as well as foreign organizations, organizations with foreign investment, international organizations, foreign citizens, stateless persons engaged in entrepreneurial activity, unless otherwise stipulated by an international treaty of the Russian Federation.

(1) The Requirement of an "Economic Dispute"

The provisions of Art. 22 are complicated and require some clarification. Note that under Art. 22 arbitration courts have jurisdiction over cases concerning "*economic disputes* arising from civil, administrative and other legal relations." This means that arbitration courts, just as "ordinary" courts, may resolve civil and administrative disputes (but not criminal cases). The main criteria defining disputes falling within the jurisdiction of arbitration courts are (1) the notion of an *economic dispute* and (2) parties who may participate in the arbitration proceedings. Both criteria must be satisfied.

The notion of "economic disputes" is not defined by the Code. Only examples are given. A careful analysis indicates that economic disputes may arise from entrepreneurial activities. They also concerns property rights and interests.

(2) The Presence of Parties "Engaged in Entrepreneurial Activity"

Parties who participate in proceedings before arbitration courts are usually persons engaged in entrepreneurial activity. Art. 22 indicates that arbitration courts resolve economic disputes between juridical persons, primarily commercial entities.[77] As a general rule, citizens may become parties to the arbitration proceedings only if they are engaged in entrepreneurial activity and have the status of an individual entrepreneur. There are, however, some exceptions. For example, citizens who wish to become individual entrepreneurs may appeal refusals of state registration. Citizens may also become plaintiffs in suits concerning the insolvency (bankruptcy) of commercial entities.

In the majority of cases the determination of the personal status of the participant of the relevant relationship presents no problems. However some situations may be less clear. Consider the following case:

The Supreme Arbitration Court: *Joint Stock Company "M-GRATA" v. Joint Stock Company "NB-Trust"* (1 *Sbornik postanovlenii Prezidiuma Vysshego Arbitrazhnogo Suda 30* (1996)).

The joint sock company "M-GRATA" brought suit in Moscow City Arbitration Court against the joint stock company "NB-Trust" to declare an insurance contract void. . .

By a decision of 26.01.96, the Court upheld the claim. The case was not considered at either appellate or cassational instance. A protest was brought against the decisions to vacate the judgment and reject the suit. The Presidium [of the Supreme Arbitration Court] finds that the protest must be sustained for the following reasons:

The file of the case indicates that on 03.06.94 the plaintiff and the defendant signed an insurance contract; under Art. 1.1 of the contract, the plaintiff provided insurance to cover the liability of "NB-Trust" in cases of non-performance of obligations in connection with the accumulation of monetary resources. The insurance proceeds were supposed to be paid directly to the clients of "NB-Trust."

---

[77] See *infra*, p. 292-303.

In view of the fact that the above contract contained provisions in favor of third parties, who had transferred their monetary resources to the defendant, the present case may be resolved only if these third parties participate in the proceedings, because they are to receive benefits under the contract. The file of the case contains documents which indicate that depositors in the "NB-Trust" were citizens.

Under Art. 1(1) of the Arbitration Procedure Code of the Russian Federation, arbitration courts have jurisdiction over cases concerning economic disputes among judicial persons, citizens engaged in entrepreneurial activity without the formation of a judicial person and having the status of an individual entrepreneur. Disputes involving citizens who are not entrepreneurs do not fall within the jurisdiction of arbitration courts. Consequently, this case cannot be considered by the arbitration court. . .

QUESTIONS AND COMMENTS

1. Although the case involved a contractual dispute between two juridical persons, the Supreme Arbitration Court terminated the proceeding because of lack of jurisdiction. The major factor was the fact that third parties under the contact were citizens. Which court would have jurisdiction if the third parties were private companies? Which court would have jurisdiction if the third parties were both citizens and private companies?

2. Another important consideration in all jurisdictional disputes is the nature of the relations between the parties. For example, in a 1996 case the Supreme Arbitration Court affirmed all decisions of lower courts which refused to hear a case in which the Bank for Foreign Trade of the Russian Federation sued the Investigation Department of the Ministry of Internal Affairs. An investigator in a criminal case issued a ruling that lifted a ban on operations with certain securities, and the Bank wanted to retain the ban. The Supreme Arbitration Court noted that this dispute cannot be considered by arbitration courts because the legal relations between the parties are governed by the rules of the criminal procedural legislation (See 1 *Sbornik postanovlenii Prezidiuma Vysshego Arbitrazhnogo Suda 20-21*(1996)). Would the arbitration court have jurisdiction if a tax police investigator imposed a fine on the Bank for Foreign Trade? What court would have jurisdiction if it was alleged that the investigator's lifting of the ban was an unconstitutional *action*? If the *law* that empowered the investigator to decide whether to lift a ban was unconstitutional?

(3) Disputes Involving Foreign Businesses

Of particular interest is Art. 22(6) of the 1995 Arbitration Procedure

Code. It provides that disputes involving "foreign organizations, organizations with foreign investment, international organizations, foreign citizens, stateless persons engaged in entrepreneurial activity" are to be considered in arbitration courts. Traditionally these disputes were resolved by "ordinary" courts in accordance with Art. 25 of the 1964 Civil Procedure Code. Some commentators believe that Art. 22 of the Arbitration Procedure Code did not supplant Art. 25 of the 1964 Civil Procedure Code, because the Arbitration Procedure Code contains no provisions regarding repeal of Art. 25. Under this approach, disputes involving foreign entities may be heard by both "ordinary" and arbitration courts. Any foreign plaintiff would have a choice between two jurisdictions. However, this line of argument may be unsatisfactory because traditionally the later law on the same subject supplants earlier law even if the later law contains no explicit provisions to that effect. An argument could be made that the 1995 Arbitration Procedure Code supplanted provisions of the old 1964 Civil Procedure Code on the matter.[78] It could therefore be asserted that after 1995 disputes involving "foreign organizations, organizations with foreign investment, international organizations, foreign citizens, stateless persons engaged in entrepreneurial activity" must be considered by arbitration courts.

The situation may be clarified when the new Civil Procedure Code is enacted. It may allow "ordinary" courts to assert jurisdiction over disputes involving foreign business entities. Art. 22 of the 1997 Draft of the new Civil Procedure Code[79] provides that "courts shall resolve disputes involving foreign citizens, stateless persons, foreign juridical persons and other organizations." If Art. 22 of the 1997 Draft Civil Procedure Code is adopted by the Russian parliament, an argument could be made that the Civil Procedure Code provides an alternative forum for resolving disputes involving foreign business entities. A foreign party could probably challenge the assertion by an arbitration court of exclusive jurisdiction over foreign business entities.

(4) Pre-Contractual Disputes

Pre-contractual disputes are a category of disputes unknown to American law. Pre-contractual disputes arise in cases when the parties are obliged to conclude a contract but cannot agree on its specific terms. These disputes fall under the jurisdiction of arbitration courts only if the conclusion

---

[78] Cf. V.M. Sherstuk, *Novye polozheniya Arbitrazhnogo protsessual'nogo kodeksa Rossiiskoi Federatsii* (New Provisions of the Arbitration Procedure Code of the Russian Federation) 31-32 (1996); K.I. Komissarov, Y.K. Osipov, *Grazhdanskii protsess* (Civil Procedure) 474 (1996).

[79] *Grazhdanskii protsessual'nyi kodeks Rossiiskoi Federatsii (Proekt)* (Draft Civil Procedure Code of the Russian Federation) (1997).

of the relevant contract is "required by the law." At this stage, mandatory conclusion of contracts is an exception to the principle of freedom of contract proclaimed by the 1994 Civil Code.[80] Mandatory conclusion of contracts is required in very few situations. Examples are public contracts[81] and contracts for delivery of goods for certain areas of Northern territories and for state needs. Private parties may also be under an obligation to conclude a final contract if they have signed a "preliminary agreement" envisioned by Art. 429 of the 1994 Civil Code.[82] Finally, parties may agree to refer pre-contractual disputes to arbitration courts.

The following case provides an illustration of pre-contractual disputes:

The Supreme Arbitration Court: *Municipal Enterprise v. Joint Stock Company "Kurovskii Tekstil"* (1 *Sbornik postanovlenii Prezidiuma Vysshego Arbitrazhnogo Suda 33-34* (1996)).

The municipal enterprise "Production-Technical Union of the City Industry No. 2 of the Orekhovo-Zuev Region" brought suit in Moscow Regional Arbitration Court against the joint stock company "Kurovskii Tekstil" because the parties failed to agree on the terms of a contact concerning water supplies and sewage disposal for the year of 1995.

By a ruling of 11.04.95, the court refused to accept the statement of claim and cited Art. 85(1) of the Arbitration Procedure Code (the dispute is not subject to resolution in an arbitration court) because of the lack of either an agreement between the parties to transfer a pre-contractual dispute for resolution by an arbitration court or any legislative act providing for such a transfer. . .

A protest was filed to vacate the ruling of the Moscow Regional Arbitration Court and to send the case for new consideration on the merits.

The Presidium [of the Supreme Arbitration Court] finds that the protest must be granted for the following reasons:

Under Art. 22 of the Arbitration Procedure Code of the Russian Federation arbitration courts have jurisdiction over disputes concerning

[80] Civil Code, Art. 1.

[81] Public contracts are contracts concluded by commercial organizations serving the general public (retail trade, public transportation, communications etc.) and individuals. Under Art. 426 of the 1994 Civil Code, commercial organizations serving the general public cannot avoid (without valid reasons) the formation of a public contract with persons who turn to them. For details, see Chapter VI.

[82] The concept of "preliminary agreement" will be discussed in Chapter VI.

conflicts of opinion about the formation of a contract, the conclusion of which is required by the law or where the parties to the contract have agreed to refer to arbitration courts any dispute arising in connection with the contract. The materials of the file of the case indicate that the parties had reached an agreement to transfer disputes that arise during the formation of the contract for resolution by an arbitration court. This fact is confirmed by a contract signed by the parties together with a statement of differences of opinion. Art. 10.2 of the contact, which is not challenged by either of the parties, provides that all disputes that arise between the parties during the formation and implementation of the contract shall be resolved by arbitration courts of the Russian Federation. Another proof of the agreement is a letter sent by AOOT "Kurovskii Tekstil" on 08.02.95 No. 1717-1.

According to Art. 446 of the Civil Code, if the conflict of opinion about the formation of a contract is referred by the agreement of the parties for resolution by an arbitration court, the terms of the contract not agreed upon by the parties are determined by the decision of the court.

In view of this, the Moscow Regional Arbitration Court's conclusion that there was no jurisdiction is unfounded. . .

COMMENT

The agreement of the parties envisioned by Art. 22(2) means an agreement in writing. In contrast to international commercial arbitration,[83] where in certain situations an arbitration agreement may be reached by an exchange of the claim and response to the claim, state arbitration courts do not recognize the principle of *forum prerogatum* (a principle which confers jurisdiction by the tacit consent of the parties, deduced from their conduct in pleading to the merits of a claim without raising the question of jurisdiction).[84]

(b) A Clarifying "Joint Explanation" from the Supreme Court and the Supreme Arbitration Court

Some controversial jurisdictional issues were clarified by the Joint Ruling "*On Certain Aspects of the Jurisdiction of Courts and Arbitration Courts*" issued by the Plenary Session of the Supreme Court and the Plenary Session of the Supreme Arbitration Court.[85] The following sections of the "Joint Explanations" are particularly instructive:

[83] Cf. See *infra*, p. 423-432.
[84] Cf. *VVAS*, 1993, No. 1, p. 114.
[85] *VVAS*, 1992, No. 1, p. 84.

1. It is necessary to take into consideration that by entrepreneurial activity shall be recognized the independent activity initiated by citizens and their associations aimed at obtaining profits or other income and implemented at their own risk and under their own property liability. A citizen shall acquire the status of an entrepreneur by means of state registration in accordance with the Law "On the Registration Fee Levied on Physical Persons Engaged in Entrepreneurial Activity". The document confirming such a status shall be the certificate of state registration. . .

3. Civil cases . . . shall be subject to consideration in an [ordinary] court if at least one of the parties is a citizen who does not have the status of an entrepreneur, or if the citizen has such a status but the case arose not in connection with his or her entrepreneurial activities. . .

   [Ordinary] courts shall have jurisdiction over disputes arising from contracts for the transportation of freight via direct international railroad and air freight conveyance between enterprises, institutions, organizations, on the one hand, and railway and air transport authorities, on the other, that derive from corresponding international treaties (Article 25 of the Civil Procedure Code). . .

4. A citizen shall have the right to appeal in court any acts of state and other organs, as well as the actions of officials that infringe upon his or her rights.

   Disputes concerning the recognition as invalid of acts of state and other organs that do not conform to legislation and that violate the rights and legally protected interests of organizations and citizen-entrepreneurs shall be subject to resolution in an arbitration court. . .

   Disputes concerning the compensation of losses caused by acts of state and other organs and by the actions of officials that do not conform to legislation shall be settled in [ordinary] courts if the claims have been presented by a citizen, or in arbitration courts if the claims have been presented by an organization or a citizen-entrepreneur.

5. If several claims related to one another, one of which falls within the jurisdiction of an [ordinary] court and the others within the jurisdiction of an arbitration court, are combined, all of the claims

shall be subject to consideration in an [ordinary] court (Article 28 of the Civil Procedure Code). . .

QUESTIONS

1. Which provisions of the "Joint Explanation" reflect the understanding that arbitration courts are *specialized courts*, while "ordinary" courts have a general jurisdictional reach?

2. Which provision indicates that in some cases "ordinary" courts have priority jurisdiction?

(c) Disputes Involving "Normative" Acts

It is important to keep in mind that only non-normative acts can be challenged in arbitration courts. Challenges to normative acts fall under the jurisdiction of "ordinary" courts. Consider the following cases:

The Supreme Arbitration Court: *Trial v. Biisk City Soviet* (*Zakon*, 1994, No. 7, p. 82)

The enterprise "Trial" brought to the Altai regional arbitration court a suit against Biisk city Soviet concerning invalidation of paragraphs 1 and 3 of the city Soviet's resolution No. 172 of January 21, 1993, which established that enterprises, institutions and organizations should pay monthly taxes for city needs and contributions to the city fund of social support for the citizens. The Altai arbitration court upheld the claim in part and invalidated paragraph 3 of the resolution of the Biisk city Soviet.

The Deputy Chairman of the Supreme Arbitration Court lodged a protest against the said ruling . . . arguing that arbitration courts have no jurisdiction over the matter raised by the plaintiff's suit. . .The Supreme Arbitration Court reviewed the legality and justification of the judgment and quashed it for violations of procedural law. . .

The resolution of the Biisk City Soviet No. 172 laid down rules of conduct that address an unlimited number of persons and that are supposed to be applied many times; in other words, the resolution is of a normative character. According to Article 22 of the Arbitration Procedural Code of the Russian Federation, arbitration courts have jurisdiction over disputes concerning invalidation of acts issued by government or other agencies (addressed to particular persons or groups of persons), which are inconsistent with the law and violate legally protected rights and interests of organizations. . . In view of this, the arbitration court had no jurisdiction over the plaintiff's demand to invalidate the resolution of the Biisk city Soviet No. 172, which was of a normative character. . .

The Supreme Court: ***Rossi v. Deputy Head of Orenburg Regional Administration*** (*BVS*, 1995, No. 12, p. 2).

An individual private enterprise "Rossi" filed a complaint with the court against the ruling of the First Deputy Head of the Administration of the Orenburg Region "On Taxes" which, in its opinion, infringes upon the rights of the private enterprise.

By its ruling the Court of the Orenburg Region terminated the proceedings because of lack of jurisdiction. The Deputy Chairman of the Supreme Court of the RF filed a protest and asked to vacate the ruling as incorrect. The Collegium for Civil Cases of the Supreme Court of the RF sustained the protest on October 6, 1995 and stated the following:

The regional court terminated proceedings because it found that the complaint of the private enterprise was supposed to be considered by the arbitration court. The court based its conclusion on paragraph 4 of the Joint Ruling of the Plenary Session of the Supreme Court of the RF and the Plenary Session of the Supreme Arbitration Court of the RF "On Certain Aspects of the Jurisdiction of Courts and Arbitration Courts," which provides that complaints of organizations and citizens-entrepreneurs seeking invalidation of actions of officials that violate their rights and legally protected interests are not to be considered in [ordinary] courts, if the challenged actions have been formalized in executive or other documents.

Indeed, these disputes were supposed to be considered in arbitration court, but only if the relevant acts were addressed to specific persons or a group of persons and violated the legally protected rights and interests of organizations and citizens-entrepreneurs (Art. 22 of the 1992 Arbitration Procedure Code which was in force until July 1, 1995). According to the Arbitration Procedure Code which has been in force since July 1, 1995, arbitration courts have jurisdiction over disputes concerning the recognition as void (in full or in part) of non-normative acts of state organs, organs of local self-government and other organs that are inconsistent with laws and other normative legal acts and that violate the legally protected rights and interests of organizations and citizens engaged in entrepreneurial activity without the formation of a judicial person and having the status of an individual entrepreneur, obtained in the procedure established by the law (Art. 22).

An analysis of the text of the ruling of the First Deputy Head of the Administration of the Orenburg Region indicates that it has a normative character and does not belong to the category of acts mentioned in Art. 22 of the preexisting or Art. 22 of the existing Arbitration Procedure Code of the RF. Demands of a citizen, an organization or a citizen-entrepreneur seeking the recognition of an act of a normative character as unlawful are to be considered by courts of general jurisdiction because they do not fall within the jurisdiction of arbitration courts. . .

QUESTIONS AND COMMENTS

1. What were the major considerations which determined the subject-matter jurisdiction of "ordinary" and arbitration courts in these cases?

2. What is the essence of the definition of a normative act formulated by the Supreme Arbitration Court and the Supreme Court? Do you agree that a local regulation establishing the duty of enterprises, institutions and organizations is of a normative character?

3. The facts of *Rossi* indicate that the ruling of the First Deputy Head of the Administration of the Orenburg Region "On Taxes" infringed upon the rights of the private enterprise "Rossi."

Suppose that there is an actual controversy between "Rossi" and the local administration involving application of the challenged ruling. Could a lawyer contemplating an action bring a suit in the Orenburg Region Arbitration Court? When considering this question, read Art. 120(2) of the Constitution. Also note that under Art. 11 of the 1995 Arbitration Procedure Code "the arbitration court, having established during the consideration of a case that an act of a state organ, an organ of local self-government or any other organ does not correspond to the law, including situations when the relevant act was issued in violation of the organ's competence, shall render a decision in accordance with the law." Can you think of any advantage of going to arbitration courts instead of ordinary courts?

D. Judges, Organs of Judicial Community, and Methods of Judicial Selection

1. Applicable Law

The legal status of all Russian judges is established by the 1993 Constitution and the 1992 Law "On the Status of Judges."[86] Laws governing different court structures may contain additional normative prescriptions

[86] *Vedomosty RF*, No. 30, item 1792 (1992) (as amended in 1995, see *Sobranie*, No. 26, item 2399 (1995)).

concerning the status of judges. For example, the 1994 Federal Constitutional Law on the Constitutional Court determines the legal status and the process of appointment of judges of the Constitutional Court.

It is important to note that although, under Art. 72 of the 1993 Constitution, questions concerning "personnel of judiciary" fall within the joint jurisdiction of the Russian Federation and its "subjects," the legal status of judges of all federal courts and their selection is governed by federal laws. Federal law governs the status and selection of all judges of the Constitutional Court, courts of general jurisdiction and arbitration courts. Attempts of some republics within the Russian Federation to establish their own regulations concerning the status of judges of these courts have been rejected by the Constitutional Court. The Constitutional Court invalidated the law of the Kabardin-Balkar Republic concerning the status of judges because it violated provisions of the Constitution and the 1992 Law on the Status of Judges.[87] Under the 1992 Law on the Status of Judges, "subjects" of the Federation may enact laws affecting the status of certain categories of judges only in cases envisioned by federal laws.[88] The "subjects" of the Federation may adopt laws on the status and activities of the judges of their constitutional courts. The 1996 Law on the Judicial System also provides that the authority and activities of justices of the peace will be established not only by federal law, but also "by law of the subject of the Russian Federation."[89]

2. Methods of Judicial Selection

The Communist regime rejected as fundamentally flawed the notion of an independent and politically neutral judiciary. All Soviet judges received ideological indoctrination during their legal training. The process of judicial appointment and dismissals was designed to assure political reliability of judges. Although in theory all the judges were directly elected by the voters of their judicial districts or by the local legislatures, in practice they were carefully selected by the Communist Party. In accordance with the communist concept of "the unity of state power," all judges were part of the state's coercive apparatus, and the judicial branch, like other organs of state power, existed primarily to promote the political interests of the Communist Party.

In view of this heritage, the creation of legal and institutional guarantees for judicial independence became one of the main tasks of judicial reform.

[87] *Case Concerning the Law of the Kabardin-Balkar Republic On the Status of Judges*, *VKS*, 1994, No. 6, p. 29-39.

[88] 1992 Law on the Status of Judges, Art. 2.

[89] 1996 Law on the Judicial System, Art. 28.

The major steps in this direction were the adoption of the concept of the separation of powers and the establishment of strong constitutional guarantees for judicial independence. New procedures of appointment and the lifetime tenure of judges are designed to assure immunity from pressure from other branches of government and from political parties.

The Concept of Judicial Reform rejected the electoral system because it did not assure judicial independence. The electoral system in the form of a vote of the upper chamber of the parliament is preserved only for the selection of judges of the Constitutional Court, the Supreme Court and the Supreme Arbitration Court. In addition, justices of the peace may be elected by the voters of their judicial districts.

(a) Supreme Courts and Constitutional Court

According to the 1993 Constitution and the 1992 Law on the Status of Judges, judges of the Constitutional Court, of the Supreme Court and of the Supreme Arbitration Court are appointed by the Federation Council upon nomination by the President. The 1992 Law provides that the President's nomination of judges of the Supreme Court and of the Supreme Arbitration Court must take into account the opinions of the Chairman of the relevant court.[90]

(b) Other Federal Judges

The 1992 Law on the Status of Judges provides that judges of all other federal courts are appointed by the President following the recommendation of the chairmen of the Supreme Court and of the Supreme Arbitration Court. With the exception of federal arbitration courts of the circuits, all nominations were supposed "to take into account the opinions of the legislative (representative) organ of the relevant subject of the Federation."[91] In a 1996 case, the Constitutional Court emphasized that "taking into account the opinions of the legislative organs" of the respective subject of the Federation did not mean that the appointment of judges required their "assent."[92] However, the situation has changed with the enactment of the 1996 Law on the Judicial System. As noted earlier, under the 1996 Law, the appointment of judges of all "ordinary" and arbitration courts located in the "subjects" of the Federation

---

[90] 1992 Law on the Status of Judges, Art. 6.

[91] Id.

[92] *Case Concerning the Charter - Fundamental Law of Chitinskaya Region, VKS,* 1996, No. 1, p. 34.

requires "the assent" (*po soglasovaniu*) of "the legislative (representative) organs of state power of the respective subject of the Russian Federation."[93]

3. Additional Measures to Assure Quality Candidates

(a) Approval by Judicial Collegia

The current system of the selection of judges envisions certain additional measures to assure non-partisan selection of candidates based on merits. Under this system, judicial candidates are first screened by the qualification collegia composed of judges of the respective court system.[94] The President can appoint a judge only if there is approval by the respective "qualification collegium" of judges (Art. 13 of the 1996 Law on the Judicial System). The same procedure is contemplated by Art. 6 of the 1992 Law on the Status of Judges.

The qualification collegia of judges are formed by the so-called "organs of the judicial community." These organs were mentioned for the first time in the 1992 Law on the Status of Judges.[95] The 1996 Law on the Judicial System clarified the legal status of these organs. They include the Congress of Judges of the Russian Federation and an executive organ of the Congress - the Council of Judges.[96] The Congress represents the judicial community of all Russian judges, including judges of the Constitutional Court, "ordinary" courts, arbitration courts and military courts. Organizational and other support for the organs of the judicial community is provided by the newly established Judicial Department within the Supreme Court.[97] The powers and functions of the Congress and of the Council of Judges will be specified by a proposed new law "On the Organs of the Judicial Community."

The Supreme Qualification Collegium is elected by the Congress of Judges. Other qualification collegia are formed within each respective court system. The qualification collegia play an important role not only in the judicial selection, but also in the disciplining of judges. Under the concept of judicial independence adopted in Russia, any disciplining or removal of judges must be an exclusively internal judicial function administered by the qualification collegia. The oversight by the Ministry of Justice in this area has been

---

[93] 1996 Law on the Judicial System, Art. 13.

[94] The composition and activities of the qualification collegia of judges are governed by the Regulation on the Qualification Collegia of Judges. See *Vedomosty RF*, No. 24, item 856 (1993).

[95] 1992 Law on the Status of Judges, Art. 17.

[96] 1996 Law on the Judicial System, Art. 29.

[97] 1996 Law on the Judicial System, Art. 31.

eliminated. This means, that in these matters the executive has no control over the judiciary.

(b) Minimum Requirements to be Considered

Candidates for judicial appointment are required to have a law degree and law practice experience of at least 5 years (supreme court nominees must have at least 10 years of law practice experience). While the minimum age for judges of lower courts is 25 years, judges of the supreme courts must be older than 35 years. Under the 1994 Law on the Constitutional Court, candidates for the Constitutional Court must be persons "having recognized high qualifications in the field of law." In addition, they must have at least 15 years of law practice experience and be older than 40 years.[98]

4. Degree of Politization of Judicial Selection

Because judges of the Constitutional Court have the power to hold statutes unconstitutional, the process of their selection is highly politicized. The 1994 Law on the Constitutional Court recognizes the political nature of the process by stating that suggestions on nominees may be submitted to the President by deputies of the Federal Assembly, legislative organs of the subjects of the Federation, supreme judicial organs, federal legal agencies and law associations.[99] The list of nominees prepared by the President usually contains names of prominent lawyers who may not be members of the ordinary judiciary. Many of the current Constitutional Court judges came to the Court after a long law-teaching career.

By contrast, the appointment of "ordinary" and arbitration judges attracts little attention of the general public: these judges are not public figures. As a rule, the candidates for judges of higher courts are selected from the ranks of the professional judiciary. After several years of law practice, judges usually start their judicial careers at the bottom of the judicial system and move to higher courts after several years of court experience.

In general, judges are appointed for life. However, there are several exceptions. First, the judges of the Constitutional Court have a tenure of 12 years.[100] Judges of lower courts are appointed for 3 years for the first time;

[98] 1994 Law on the Constitutional Court, Art. 8.

[99] Id, Art. 9.

[100] Constitutional Law on the Constitutional Court, Art. 12. Art. 12 also provides that "a judge of the Constitutional Court may not be appointed for a second term." The single term limit is supposed to enhance judicial independence because judges would not be motivated to indulge political forces which may be responsible for their re-election. However, it may be argued that the ban on a second appointment does not guarantee absolute judicial independence: decisions may be influenced by the desire to obtain alternative employment at the end of the 12-year term.

after that they are re-appointed for life. Finally, justices of the peace are elected or appointed for five years.

5. Removal From Office

An important guarantee of judicial independence is the irremovability from office. Under the 1992 Law on the Status of Judges, a judge may be removed only in a very limited number of situations, which include health reasons, immoral behavior, activities inconsistent with judicial functions and conviction of a crime.

In contrast to federal judges in the United States who can be removed under extraordinary but unreviewable circumstances by impeachment in the House of Representatives and conviction in the Senate, Russian judges can be removed or suspended during their term of office only pursuant to the decision of other judges. The 1992 Law provides that in all these cases the power of the judge may be terminated only by the decision of the relevant qualification collegium of judges. Decisions of the collegium may be appealed in the Supreme Qualification Collegium. The decision of the Supreme Qualification Collegium may be appealed in the Supreme Court.[101]

6. Judicial Immunity

Under the 1993 Constitution and the 1992 Law, all judges enjoy broad immunity, including immunity from criminal proceedings. Criminal proceedings against a judge may be initiated only by the Procurator General of the Russian Federation with the consent of the relevant qualification collegium of judges.[102] The Constitutional Court has emphasized the importance of judicial immunity in a case in which several victims of a crime allegedly committed by a judge challenged the constitutionality of Art. 16 of the 1992 Law. The Court, in upholding judicial immunity, stated: "The constitutional provision on the immunity of judges, which establishes one of the essential elements of the status of a judge and an important guarantee of his or her professional activity, is aimed at ensuring the viability of the fundamentals of the constitutional system concerning the separation of powers as well as the autonomy and independence of judicial power (Arts. 10 and 120 of the Constitution of the Russian Federation)."[103]

---

[101] 1992 Law on the Status of Judges, Art. 14.

[102] 1992 Law on the Status of Judges, Art. 16.

[103] *Case Concerning Art. 16(3) of the Law on the Status of Judges*, *VKS*, 1996, No. 2, p. 21.

7. Political Activities of Judges

In order to prevent political interference and conflicts of interests, the 1992 Law imposes on judges several requirements concerning their extra-judicial activities. An important element is the prohibition on political activity. Judges cannot join "political parties or movements" or combine their position on the bench with a seat in the legislative organs.[104] In addition, judges are not supposed to engage in entrepreneurial activity or in most other remunerative activities except academic, educational, literary or other creative activities. Violations of these requirements may be qualified as "activities inconsistent with judicial functions" under Art. 14 of the 1992 Law.

8. Salaries

The judge's salary must be adequate to assure an appropriate standard of living: it is well known that judicial independence can be threatened by insufficient judicial salaries. Because of the problem of court financing, discussed above, the salaries of Russian judges are rather modest. Although judicial salaries were raised several times,[105] they certainly cannot be compared with the amounts of money that many private lawyers make. As a result, many judges leave the bench for private practice. Because of low salaries both "ordinary" and arbitration courts experience serious difficulties in attracting qualified professionals.[106] Those judges who remain tend to be attracted not by salaries, but by the power and prestige of the position of the judge. Some young judges remain on the bench because of housing benefits: under the existing housing law judges are provided with the subsidized municipal housing.

9. Judicial Independence

Because tenure and promotion of Russian judges are determined by a system of examinations and evaluations controlled by the judges themselves, the Russian judiciary is an almost completely self-contained and self-controlled service. At the same time, experience indicates that no judicial system can be absolutely immune from outside influence. Thus, in all countries

---

[104] 1992 Law on the Status of Judges, Art. 3.

[105] See, for example, the 1997 presidential Decree which increased judicial salaries by 65 percent, *Sobranie*, No. 4, item 526 (1997).

[106] In 1997 judicial vacancies in the arbitration court system reached 38 percent. See *Programma povysheniya effektivnosti deyatel'nosti arbitrazhnykh sudov v Rossiiskoi Federatsii v 1997-2000 godakh* (A Program to Increase the Effectiveness of the Activities of the Arbitration Courts in the Russian Federation For the Years 1997-2000), *VVAS*, 1997, No. 11, at 24.

politics may undermine judicial independence in different indirect and subtle ways.

The actual independence of Russian judges presents special problems because Russian judges are career civil servants who often perceive themselves to be government officials. This means that it may be overly optimistic to expect all Russian judges to act as independent watchdogs of government administration. Furthermore, as career civil servants Russian judges usually seek promotion from lower courts to higher judgeships. As a result, they may be subjected to influence of their superiors who often control their promotion in rank. It is also useful to keep in mind that there is always the potential for outside direct or indirect influence by federal and local politicians, in particular legislators, powerful economic organizations, mass media and even organized crime groups.

10. Competence of Judges

Russian judiciary has lost many experienced judges who left the bench for private practice. The competence of judges to implement new laws is also affected by the fact that the values of many Russian judges were formed during the Soviet era. While both "ordinary" and arbitration judges receive some training in the legal principles of a market-oriented system, experience indicates that this training is far from adequate. Lack of expertise in sophisticated commercial matters is particularly damaging to the prestige of arbitration (commercial) courts.

It appears that the Supreme Arbitration Court realized the magnitude of the problem. In 1997 the Chairman of the Supreme Court approved a special Program to Increase the Effectiveness of the Activities of the Arbitration Courts in the Russian Federation For the Years 1997-2000.[107] One of the major goals of the Program is the expansion of the existing judicial training workshops for arbitration court judges.[108]

The Program also emphasizes the need to improve the quality of opinions issued by arbitration court judges.[109] The quality of arbitration court decisions has raised serious concerns among litigants and commentators. Many arbitration judges have enormous work loads because of judicial vacancies. As a result, they fail to devote sufficient attention to the thorough preparation and drafting of opinions.[110] Although judges in all civil law

[107] Id.

[108] Id., at 24.

[109] Id., at 14-15.

[110] For details, see N. Materov, *O kul'ture sudebnogo resheniya* (On Professional Standards for Judicial Decisions), *VVAS*, 1995, No. 1, at 134.

countries tend to avoid detailed legal analysis and write short decisions, some arbitration court judges in Russia even fail to identify the legal basis for their opinions.[111] One can only hope that the Program adopted by the Supreme Arbitration Court will allow arbitration judges gain greater expertise in commercial matters and improve the quality of arbitration court decisions.

E. The Procuracy

1. The Procuracy in History

The Procuracy is one of the few organs of the state that modern Russia inherited from its imperial past. This uniquely Russian institution has a long history. Peter the Great created the Procuracy in 1722 and gave it the power to supervise the conformity to imperial laws of all governmental agencies and departments, officials and courts.[112] The Procuracy was supposed to act as the "Eye of the Tsar" and be independent of any local influence. Although Peter the Great may have studied German, French and Swedish organs similar in nature, he created a unique institution which is quite different from other bodies with analogous functions in other countries. The original Petrine model has been modified many times during the last centuries, but the Procuracy has always been an important instrument of the country's legal order.

2. The Need for Reform

The Procuracy model that Russia inherited from its Soviet past did not fit into the new design of the state based on the idea of separation of powers. During the Soviet period, the Procuracy was granted extremely broad powers which even included supervision over the execution of laws by courts. The procurator was both a participant in the court proceedings and a supervisor of the court's activities. For example, the procurator was given the power to file suits in court in civil matters. At the same time, during the court proceedings the procurator was supposed to give official opinions regarding the substance of the civil case as a whole. Furthermore, the procurator had a broader task to ensure that all judgements, sentences, rulings and orders rendered in the case were lawful and well-founded. In a way, the procurator, who participated in the hearing of cases at all stages, from the court of first instance to all cassational and supervisory instances, was placed above courts.

Economic reform highlighted another controversial area of the

---

[111] Id.

[112] For details, see N.B. Murav'ev, 1 *Prokurorskii nadzor v ego ustroistve I deyatel'nosti* (Procuracy Supervision in its Structure and Operation) 1889; V.I. Baskov, *Prokurorskii nadzor* (Procuracy Supervision) 12-19 (1996).

Procuracy's activities - the so-called "general supervision" over the execution of laws by ministries, organizations, enterprises, their officials and citizens. Critics of the Procuracy pointed out that in exercising "general supervision" the Procuracy often misused its powers by interfering with operational and economic activities. Critics of "general supervision" argued that it was unnecessary in a democratic society with a functioning market economy. In view of these and other considerations, the reformers pressed for a more precise definition of the Procuracy's powers. The Concept of Judicial Reform proposed to restrict the Procuracy's function to that of the state prosecutor in courts.[113] Many commentators also believed that the only task of the Procuracy should be investigation of crimes and criminal prosecution in courts.[114] Not all of these proposals have been accepted. The Procuracy, which, as some critics claim, "turned out to be the most conservative state institution of the Soviet period,"[115] managed to retain the powers of "general supervision." However, the scope of the former "general supervision" has been restricted (the term itself is no longer used by the new Law on the Procuracy).[116]

Another controversial area is the precise definition of the political-legal status of the Procuracy in the new system of state organs. Under the traditional model, the Procuracy is not considered to be a component part of any branch of government (some commentators claim that it is a fourth branch of government).[117] It is supposed to perform its functions independently of other federal organs, organs of the "subjects" of the Federation or organs of local self-government. Yet, Art. 129 of the Constitution, dealing with the Procuracy, is included in Chapter 7 of the Constitution which is entitled "Judicial Power." This is misleading because the Procuracy is not a judicial

---

[113] See *Kontseptsiya sudebnoi reformy v Rossiiskoi Federatsii* , *supra* note 1, at 47-52.

[114] See, e.g., V.M. Savitskii, *Organizatsiya sudebnoi vlasti v Rossiiskoi Federatsii* (Organization of Judicial Power in the Russian Federation) 54-70 (1996).

[115] Id., at 54.

[116] It is interesting to note that the current debate about the scope of the "general supervision" is nothing new. The issue had been raised in the second half of the 19th century. The traditional Petrine model of procurator was changed by the 1864 judicial reform. Supervisory functions over state administration were removed and the Procuracy was required to confine its activities to criminal prosecution. Many prominent lawyers raised objections to the reform. For example, the famous Russian lawyer A.F. Koni wrote that the elimination of "general supervision" was "a big mistake." See A.F. Koni, *Za poslednie gody* (During the Last Years) 69 (1889).

[117] See, e.g., V.I. Shvetsov ed., *Sudoustroistvo I pravookhranitel'nye organy v Rossiiskoi Federatsii* (The Court System and Law-Enforcing Agencies in the Russian Federation) 205 (1996).

body. It is a system of organs which perform supervisory functions over the execution of laws in the country.[118]

3. The Present-Day Procuracy

The powers and organization of the Procuracy are defined by the 1995 Law "On the Procuracy of the Russian Federation."[119] According to the 1995 Law, the Procuracy is a unified and centralized system of federal organs charged with supervision over the observance of laws on the entire territory of the country.

(a) Organization of the Office

The system of organs of the Procuracy consists of the Procurator General's office, the procurator's offices of the "subjects" of the Federation and the procurator's offices of towns and districts. The Procurator General of the Russian Federation is the head of the Procuracy. Local procurators are directly responsible to the superior procurators and to the Procurator General. The Procuracy system also includes the so-called "specialized" procuracies, such as the Military Procuracy, the Transport Procuracy or the Environmental Procuracy.

In many cases the legal powers of the procurators are carried out by their first deputies and deputies. A Procurators's office of a district usually consists of the procurator, first deputy procurator, several deputies, senior and junior assistants, senior and junior investigators. The structure of superior level of the Procuracy becomes much more complicated, and the relevant office would usually be divided into several departments according to the main "branches" of the Procuracy supervision. The Procurator's General office also forms a Collegium which consists of the Procurator General, his deputies and other executive personnel. The Collegium considers the basic state and orientation of Procuracy work, reports of various departments, drafts of major instructions and orders, as well as personnel appointments.

(b) Selection, Dismissal and Term of Office of Procurators

The Procurator General is appointed to office for a term of 5 years (and is removed from the post) by the Federation Council on nomination by

---

[118] Some commentators believe that the inclusion of Art. 129 in Chapter 7 of the Constitution is not only misleading but also dangerous. They contend that this dilutes the very notion of "judicial power." See, e.g., B.N. Topornin at al. eds., *Konstitutsiya Rossiiskoi Federatsii. Kommentarii* (Constitution of the Russian Federation. A Commentary) 499 (1994).

[119] *Sobranie*, No. 47, item 4472 (1995).

the President. Because the Procurator General has broad powers, the appointment procedure is highly politicized. The Procurator General is accountable to both the President and the Federal Assembly. All lower procurators are appointed by the Procurator General for a term of 5 years. According to Art. 129 of the Constitution, procurators of the "subjects" of the Russian Federation are appointed by the Procurator General with the consent (*po soglasovaniu)* of the relevant "subject" (the "subjects" themselves determine the organ which participates in the appointment process).[120] At the same time, the Procurator General may dismiss the procurators of the "subjects" without any consultations with the "subjects." All other inferior procurators down to the level of districts are also appointed and dismissed by the Procurator General independently of any local influence. District procurators are required to have a law degree, be older than 25 years and have a record of Procuracy service of at least 3 years. Procurators of the "subjects" of the Federation must also have a law degree, be older than 30 years and have a record of Procuracy service of at least 5 years.[121]

(c) Scope of Power of the Procuracy: Statutory Provisions

Art. 1 of the 1995 Law defines the tasks of the Procuracy in the following way:

> 2. In order to ensure the supremacy of the law, unity and effectiveness of legality, protection of the rights and freedoms of the individual and the citizen, as well as the legally protected interests of society and the state, the Procuracy shall exercise:
>
> - supervision over the execution of laws by federal ministries and agencies, representative (legislative) and executive organs of the subjects of the Russian Federation, organs of local self-government, organs of military administration, control organs, their officials, as well as over the consistency of legal acts issued by them with the law;
>
> - supervision over the implementation of the rights and freedoms of the individual and the citizen by federal ministries and agencies, representative (legislative) and executive organs of the subjects of the Russian Federation, organs of local self-

[120] Some commentators consider this new procedure of appointment of local procurators as a violation of the traditional principle that procurators must be independent of any local influence. See, e.g., Baskov, *supra* note 112, at 41. Others approve the new arrangement because it takes into account the fact that "modern Russia is a federal state." Savitskii, *supra* note 114, at 63

[121] 1995 Law on the Procuracy of the Russian Federation, Art.40.

government, organs of military administration, control organs, their officials, as well as the executive organs and the heads of commercial and non-commercial organizations;

- supervision over the execution of laws by organs which conduct intelligence-operational searches as well as by organs of enquiry and preliminary investigation;

- supervision over the execution of laws by the administration of organs and institutions charged with the execution of penalties and other measures of a coercive nature imposed by the courts, the administration of places where detainees are held in custody and of places of preliminary detention;

- criminal prosecution in accordance with the powers defined by the criminal procedure legislation of the Russian Federation;

- coordination of the activities of the law-enforcement agencies fighting crime.

3. In accordance with the procedural legislation of the Russian Federation, procurators shall participate in the consideration of cases in courts, file protests against those judgements, sentences, rulings and orders of courts which do not conform to the law.

(d) Major Activities of the Procuracy

An analysis of Art. 1 indicates, that there are three major areas of Procuracy activities. The first is the "general supervision" over the execution of laws by different state bodies, organizations and organs of local-self-government. The second deals with criminal investigation and criminal prosecution. The third is procurator's participation in civil proceedings.

To fulfill these broad tasks, procurators have been granted wide powers. The procurators use their powers in the area of "general supervision" by arranging "verifications and reviews" of the activities of the relevant organs and organizations. They have the right to require from the heads of the relevant organs and organizations and from other officials the presentation of all necessary documents, materials and information. In addition, they may summon officials and citizens and require explanations from them regarding violations of the law. Although the Procuracy is a powerful organization with thousands of employees, it is, of course, not able to supervise the execution of laws by all bodies mentioned in Art. 1. As a result, its "general supervision" tends to be selective.

The results of "verifications" often lead to formal protests or representations to the relevant organs. A procurator may file a protest against a legal act as contrary to the law with the issuing organ or official. The organ or official receiving the protest must consider it within ten days and notify the procurator of the results. A procurator may also send a representation regarding a violation of law to an organ or an official and demand elimination of the violation. The necessary measures must be taken within one month and the procurator informed of the results in writing.[122]

The procurators may also use the information obtained during "verifications" to initiate criminal proceedings. Procurators may file criminal charges for violations of criminal law. While preliminary investigation in criminal cases may be conducted not only by the Procuracy itself, but also by other agencies (for example, by agencies of internal affairs or by the Federal Security Service), the Procuracy supervises the investigation. Formal indictments are issued by the Procuracy which then refers the case to the appropriate court. The procurators also act as state prosecutors in courts.[123]

(e) The Role of the Procuracy in Civil Proceedings

Of particular interest is the participation of procurators in civil proceedings. Civil and constitutional review actions are possible in several situations:

1) The procurator may challenge the legality of different kinds of legal acts or action of different organs, organizations and officials mentioned in Art. 1 of the 1995 Law. This may be done two ways. First, procurators may initiate civil actions for judicial review of actions of both federal administrative agencies and local state organs or organs of self-government. Second, procurators may challenge the constitutionality of statutes or regulations of these organs. As noted earlier, procurators are particularly active in challenging the constitutionality of various normative acts, especially acts promulgated by the "subjects" of the Russian Federation.

2) The procurator may file suits in both "ordinary" and arbitration courts if it is necessary to protect state and public interests. In these suits, the procurators may represent the state as a whole, state organizations or enterprises. The procurator may also assume the role of a public plaintiff representing the aggrieved party if there are violations of the rights and freedoms of a large number of citizens (for example, in environmental cases).

---

[122] 1995 Law on the Procuracy of the Russian Federation, Arts. 23, 24.
[123] For details, see Chapter X.

3) The procurator may file suits in "ordinary" courts in the interests of individual aggrieved parties if for some reason (such as poor health or old age) they cannot prosecute their own claims. Plaintiffs often turn to the Procuracy to initiate an action in civil disputes because a procurator's involvement in a suit allows the plaintiff to participate in an action without paying court costs.

In addition, procurators have the right to participate in cases initiated by the parties to ensure that the interests of some of them or public interests are protected. In some civil cases, procurators are required by law to make an appearance in court (for example, in cases to terminate parental rights[124]).

4) The procurator has the right to lodge protests against judgments, sentences, rulings and orders of courts. This right may be exercised even with respect to cases where the procurators have not participated in the court proceedings. Furthermore, the right to lodge protests may be exercised even if decisions or judgments have already entered into force. The procurator may demand any case from a court and lodge a protest by way of supervision.

5) The Procurator General has the right to challenge in the Constitutional Court the constitutionality of a law that violates the constitutional rights and freedoms of citizens and that has been applied or due to be applied in a specific case.

(f) The Role of the Procuracy in Criminal Proceedings

The role of the Procuracy in criminal proceedings will be discussed in Chapter X.

F. The Advokatura

1. Colleges of Advocates

The Russian Advokatura, or "Bar," has changed in the last few years and is suffering a serious crisis. Traditionally lawyers who practiced law were organized in the "colleges of advocates." Under the 1980 Statute on the RSFSR Advokatura,[125] which still governs the matter, the "colleges of advocates are voluntary associations of persons who are engaged in advocacy activity," that is, in the representation of clients in civil or criminal cases. Each territorial subdivision in Russia used to have a single "college" to which all practicing advocates were required to belong.

---

[124] See Art. 70 of the Family Code, *Sobranie*, No. 1, item 16 (1996).
[125] *Vedomosty RF*, No. 48, item 1596 (1980).

Market reforms resulted in a enormous increase in the demand for legal advice. As a result, the number of lawyers has increased dramatically. Some of them organized law firms, others started to establish the so-called "parallel" "colleges of advocates." The 1980 Statute on Advokatura did not provide any barriers to the multiplication of new "colleges." Under Art. 3 of the 1980 Statute, colleges may be formed upon the application of a group of persons who have a higher legal education or upon the initiative of local administration. Art. 3 also provides that the Ministry of Justice may allow the formation of "interregional and other colleges of advocates." There were also economic reasons for this trend. Because "colleges of advocates" are defined as "associations of *persons,*" that is, not as corporate bodies, the new "colleges" were able to avoid the tax liabilities of enterprises or corporations.[126]

Another way to start a legal practice without joining the traditional "colleges" is the licencing procedure administered by the Ministry of Justice.[127] There is no monopoly on the practice of law by the members of the "colleges." Any person with a Russian higher legal education may obtain a licence to practice law and start his or her own practice. This may be a solo practice, a small law firm or a large law firm.

As a result of these trends and tendencies the legal profession in Russia is largely unorganized. Traditional "colleges" lost their former de facto monopoly as associations of advocates who provide legal representation in civil and criminal cases. New "parallel" colleges have emerged in many regions of the country. At the same time, there is a large number of solo practitioners and independent law firms.

2. Structure and Organization of Colleges of Advocates

Although the traditional "colleges" included only a part of the legal profession, they represented an organized structure that was able to maintain professional discipline and ethics. The traditional "colleges of advocates" are self-administering associations. Legal service is provided in subdivisions of the "college" called "legal consultation offices." With the substantial increases in demand and new opportunities for legal cervices, the "traditional" colleges also started to establish semi-independent legal firms or bureaus.[128] Legal

---

[126] For details, See M.Y. Barshchevskii, *Organizatsiya I deyatel'nost' advokatury v Rossii* (Organization and Activities of Advokatura in Russia) 198- 221 (1997).

[127] See Regulations on the Licencing Procedure Concerning Paid Legal Services on the Territory of the Russian Federation, *Sobranie*, No. 17, item 1550 (1995).

[128] For details, see M.Y. Barshchevskii, *Advokat. Advokatskaya firma. Advokatura* (Advocate. Advocate Firm. Advokatura) (1995). See also Barshchevskii, *supra* note 126, at 227-260.

firms or bureaus usually specialize in providing legal service in a particular area of law.

The internal affairs of each "college" are managed by a general meeting of the college. The general meeting elects the executive organ of the "college" - the presidium - and an audit commission. The membership of each "college" is controlled by the members themselves. Certain admission standards have always been maintained. All applicants to the "college" are required to have a law degree. They are usually admitted to the "college" after an exam administered by the presidium. Some "colleges" have also required a period of official apprenticeship before the new members of the "college" would be permitted to practice.[129]

In contrast to this traditional practice, the new "parallel" "colleges" do not maintain any strict standards of admission. Nor do they adhere to the traditional canons of professional ethics. As a result, there are calls for a stricter regulation of the conduct of advocates.

Greater competition for clients has resulted in serious friction between lawyers representing different types of organizations. A particularly serious source of friction is poor defendants in criminal cases. In the absence of any well-organized system of "public defenders," legal services for the poor in criminal cases are provided by members of the traditional "colleges" appointed by the court. Although the state compensates advocates for the work performed, the state fees are extremely low if compared to what the same layer could make with a client who is able to afford a lawyer. The substantial amount of this kind of semi pro-bono-work performed by advocates of the traditional "colleges" has a depressing effect on their income. At the same time, advocates of the new "parallel" "colleges" often manage to escape court appointments in criminal cases.

3. The Need for Reform

These and other problems require attention of the legal profession. However, efforts to establish a unified professional association that would be able to administer the affairs of the profession as a whole and enforce legal ethics have so far failed.

Major reforms are expected to be introduced by a new law on Advokatura. However, a draft of the new law has been deadlocked in the parliament for many years. The major reason for the delay is the conflict

[129] In the Moscow City "college of advocates" the period of apprenticeship is nine months. See Barshchevskii, *supra* note 126, at 65.

between the proponents of an "integrated" system of "colleges," which would be based on the traditional "colleges of advocates," and those who believe that Russia does not need any "integrated" system of bar associations.

The Draft Federal Law on Advokatura in the Russian Federation, submitted to the State Duma by the President in 1995 and approved by the Duma "in the first reading" in 1996,[130] envisions the creation of integrated bar systems in all the "subjects" of the Russian Federation. Art. 19 of the Draft Law states that "only one college of advocates exists on the territory of the subject of the Russian Federation." Under the Draft Law all existing "colleges" must be integrated within three years. In the meantime, they are supposed to agree upon a fair allocation of pro bono work. The Draft Law also contemplates the creation of a national organization - the Federal Union of Advocates of the Russian Federation to promote professional rights and formulate rules of professional ethics.[131]

4. Who is an "Advocate"?

It must be emphasized that even if Russia adopts an "integrated" system of "colleges," they will never resemble the organization of the bar in the United States. In the United States the overwhelming majority of law school graduates gain admission to the bar. This includes all practicing lawyers - solo practitioners, members of large corporate law firms, government lawyers, in-house counsel for corporations and even judges. The Russian "colleges of advocates" have always been associations of only one kind of practitioner - those who wish to practice law in association with others. Another major difference lies in the fact that members of the "colleges of advocates" do not enjoy any monopoly on the practice of law. Membership in the "colleges" is not mandatory. Many lawyers practice law without joining "colleges." For example, there is no requirement that government lawyers or in-house counsel for state or private corporations join the Russian "Bar." In fact, there is no prohibition on non-lawyers practicing law. Under the existing Civil Procedure Code and Arbitration Procedure Code every adult citizen who is entitled to vote has the right to represent another citizen or company in civil or arbitration proceedings. The Criminal Procedure Code is somewhat more restrictive in this respect. Lawyers may provide legal advice or draft documents in criminal matters without being members of the "Bar" and, with permission of the court, anyone - even a non-lawyer - may represent a criminal defendant in court. However, only members of the "colleges" have the right to represent clients in criminal cases before the organs of preliminary investigation.

---

[130]The Draft Law is reprinted in Savitskii, *supra* note 114, at 298.

[131]The Draft Federal Law on Advokatura in the Russian Federation, Art. 28.

The monopoly on representation in criminal proceedings was one of the major issues in the *Case Concerning Art. 47 of the Criminal Procedure Code.*[132] Art. 47 of the Criminal Procedure Code provides that only "advocates," or members of "colleges of advocates," are allowed to represent clients in criminal proceedings. The petitioners, who wanted to engage independent private attorneys who had licences to practice law, asked the Constitutional Court to declare the restriction unconstitutional. They relied on Art. 48(2) of the Constitution which provides that "every arrestee or detainee and the accused in a criminal case shall have the right to use the assistance of an advocate (defender) from the moment of arrest, detention or indictment, whichever comes first." The petitioners argued that the use of two words - "advocate" and "defender" - indicates that everyone may freely choose between engaging an "advocate" or engaging any other defense attorney. The Court, by a narrow majority, ruled that the restriction of Art. 47 of the Procedural Code does not violate the Constitution. In the view of the majority of five judges the state has the right to establish certain professional or qualification requirements for attorneys providing legal assistance in criminal cases. The Court focused on the interpretation of Art. 48(1) of the Constitution, according to which "everyone shall be guaranteed the right to qualified legal assistance." In the view of the majority the right of the state to impose certain qualification requirements, such as membership in a "college of advocates," follows from the words "qualified legal assistance."

The four dissenting judges advanced three major arguments against this interpretation of Art. 48 of the Constitution. First, they pointed out that the words "advocate" and "defender" are not synonymous. Therefore, everyone must have the right to choose the best attorney, even if this attorney is not a member of a "college." Second, private attorneys may practice law only if they obtain a licence from the Ministry of Justice. The licencing procedure satisfies Art. 48's concern with the "qualified legal assistance." Third, as judge E.M. Ametistov argued in his separate opinion, Art. 48 of the Constitution must be interpreted in the light of preparatory materials. He pointed out that the Constitutional Meeting rejected several proposals that were aimed at allowing only members of the "colleges" to represent clients in criminal cases. The drafters of the Constitution did not want to create "closed shops" for advocates who then would have a monopoly on the practice of law. They wanted to give the citizens the right to choose between different types of practicing lawyers.[133] Judge N.T. Vedernikov added that any monopoly on the practice of law would violate Art. 8 of the Constitution which guarantees support for competition and freedom of economic activity.[134]

[132] *VKS*, 1997, No. 1, p. 25
[133] Id., at 32.
[134] Id., at 37.

If the view of the dissenting judges had prevailed, even if an "integrated" bar system were established in Russia, lawyers practicing criminal law could not be required to join the official bar associations of the relevant "subjects" of the Federation.

5. Ethical Rules of Conduct of Advocates

In Russia, the conduct of advocates is subject to regulation by legislation and by standards of ethics established by "colleges." The 1980 Statute on Advokatura contains several important prescriptions governing the conduct of advocates. Under Art. 16, an advocate has a duty to provide competent representation. The advocate has the duty to "use all methods and means provided for by law to defend the rights and lawful interests of citizens and organizations who have applied to him for legal assistance."

An advocate also owes the client a duty of loyalty. An advocate may not accept a commission to give legal assistance in a case where she or he is giving or has given assistance to persons whose interests are contrary to the person seeking assistance. Nor may an advocate render assistance if he or she has participated in the case as a judge, procurator, investigator, expert, translator or witness or if a relative of the advocate took part in the investigation or consideration of the case.

Under the 1980 Statute, an advocate owes a client the important duty of confidentiality. An advocate may not disclose information communicated to him or her by the client in connection with the legal service. The existing legislation also provides that an advocate may not be questioned as a witness concerning facts which became known to her or him in connection with the performance of her or his duties.

Self-regulation by the "colleges" may take different forms. While formal regulations on professional ethics are rare, all "colleges" have their own disciplinary proceedings for misconduct which are based on certain unwritten standards of good behavior. In 1971, the Moscow Research Institute for Judicial Defense and Education of Advocates published a compilation of decisions of the Presidiums of the Moscow City "college of advocates" and the Moscow Regional "college of advocates."[135] The compilation contains many interesting decisions which illustrate the traditional canons of professional ethics.

The Draft Law on Advokatura continues the tradition of legislative

---

[135]See I.I. Skliarskii ed., *Distsiplinarnaya praktika Moscovskoi gorodskoi I oblastnoi kollegii advokatov* (Disciplinary Practice of the Moscow City and Regional Colleges of Advocates) (1971).

regulation of professional ethics. It incorporates practically all rules contained in the 1980 Statute and adds some new rules aimed at establishing tighter standards of professional behavior. However, the formulation of detailed standards of professional conduct for all advocates still remains an important challenge for the Russian "colleges of advocates."

6. Attorney's Fees

Lawyers are free to negotiate their fees with the client. Fees vary depending on the qualifications, work-load, and, of course, the financial status of the client. Contingent fee arrangements are practically non-existent. Certain categories of legal advice must be rendered free of charge (for example, in labor disputes cases). As noted earlier, there is also a substantial amount of court appointment work in criminal cases for members of the traditional "colleges" when the accused person is unable to afford a lawyer.

G. The Notariat

In all civil law countries notaries represent a separate branch of the legal profession. While in the US a notary usually has limited powers, such as administration of oaths to persons who sign sworn documents or verification of signatures on such documents, Russian and other civil law notaries perform many functions which in the US would be done by lawyers.

The structure and activities of the Russian Notariat are governed by the 1993 Fundamental Principles of Legislation on the Notariat.[136] Under the 1993 Principles, there are state notaries, who are civil servants, and private notaries. While state notarial offices are accountable to the Ministry of Justice, all private notaries are required to join the Notarial Chamber. Notarial Chambers are self-governing bodies which enforce rules of professional conduct and discipline notaries for misconduct. The national organization for all private notaries is the Federal Notarial Chamber.

State notaries are appointed by the Ministry of Justice. Private notaries are also appointed by the Ministry of Justice but on nomination of the Notarial Chamber. The candidates must have a higher legal education - the same level of education which advocates, procurators and judges have. They are also required to undergo an apprenticeship for at least one year. Furthermore they must pass a qualification exam and obtain a licence to practice as a notary. Licences are issued by the Ministry of Justice.

Functions of both state and private notaries are practically identical.

[136] See *Vedomosty RF*, No. 10, item 357 (1993).

Arts. 35 and 36 of the 1993 Principles contain a long list of different types of notarial activities. Notaries perform numerous functions. One of the most important functions is certification of legal transactions, such as powers of attorney and contracts. Public policy requirements of certainty have provided stricter formal requirements with respect to certain transactions. Some legal transactions must be certified by a notary before they become valid. For example, the 1994 Civil Code requires a notary certification of powers of attorney[137] and mortgage contracts.[138] In practice, however, many parties seek notarial certification even in cases not required by the law. The reason is simple: a certified contract constitutes irrefutable evidence that the contract has been formed. Furthermore, it may help to counter possible claims of one of the parties concerning incapacity, fraud or duress.

Notaries also certify wills and often perform important functions during the succession. For example, they issue certificates concerning the right to an inheritance and may take measures to protect inherited property. In addition, they may certify the accuracy of copies of documents and the accuracy of translations, issue certificates concerning the right of ownership in regard to a share in the common property of spouses, impose prohibitions against alienation of property, endorse documents of execution, certify nonpayment of checks, protest promissory notes and perform maritime protests.

While performing these and other functions, notaries often provide legal advice and assistance. Indeed, under the 1993 Principles, notaries are obliged to render to citizens and organizations assistance in exercising their rights and defending their legal interests. Notaries must explain to citizens and organizations "their rights and duties and inform them about the consequences of notarial activities performed so that lack of legal information can not be used to their detriment."[139] For example, the notary who certifies a contract must "explain to the parties the meaning and consequences of the draft contact submitted by the parties."[140] Quite often notaries draft the contract themselves. The notary must also ensure the legality of transactions. A notary must refuse certification if "a transaction contravenes the requirements of the law."[141] In view of this, Russian commentators note that notaries perform quasi-judicial functions and provide valuable "anticipatory control" over the legality of many transactions.[142]

---

[137] Civil Code, Art. 185.

[138] Civil Code, Art. 339.

[139] 1993 Fundamental Principals of Legislation on the Notariat, Art. 16.

[140] Id., Art. 54.

[141] Id., Art.48.

[142] Cf. M.K. Treushnikov ed., *Uchebnik grazhdanskogo protsessa* (Manual of Civil Procedure) 432-433 (1996).

It should be noted, however, that this valuable "anticipatory control" may be quite expensive. Because notaries enjoy monopoly on notarization, their fees are very high, especially in cases where notarization is required by the law. For example, Art. 339 of the Civil Code requires a notary certification of mortgage contracts. Notarization fees charged in connection with the pledging of assets represent 1.5 percent of the value of asset pledged.

CHAPTER IV

CONSTITUTIONAL LAW

A. Introduction

1. The Emergence of Independent Russia

Since the collapse of the Soviet Union in 1991, Russia has been undergoing a profound transformation in its political, economic and constitutional spheres. Until the autumn of 1993, the "supreme law of the land" in Russia was the 1978 Constitution of the Russian Soviet Federative Socialist Republic (RSFSR). The 1978 Constitution replicated the 1977 USSR Constitution and was designed for a constituent republic of a totalitarian country governed by the Communist Party. The emergence of a new, independent Russia was symbolized by three fundamental constitutional developments. First, on June 12, 1990, the First Congress of People's Deputies of Russia adopted a Declaration on the State Sovereignty of Russia,[1] which proclaimed Russia's sovereign and independent status. Second, the Congress of People's Deputies eliminated the Communist Party's legal monopoly on state power by modifying the relevant clauses of the 1978 Constitution. Third, following the August 1991 coup d'Etat, the Soviet Union gradually disintegrated and ceased to exist.[2]

2. The Adoption of a New Constitution

While the collapse of the Soviet Union made it clear that, as an independent country, Russia needed a new constitution, the then-existing legislature and the President were at odds over the best way to achieve this goal. The conservatives were entrenched in the former Congress of People's Deputies, which, under the old Constitution, had exclusive jurisdiction over constitutional changes. They favored the gradual reform of the existing constitution and were reluctant to adopt an entirely new text. Although the Congress decided to draft a new constitution and appointed a special Constitutional Commission to prepare the text, in fact it intended a step-by-

[1] *Vedomosty RF,* No. 2, item 22 (1990).

[2] As a formal matter, the USSR was dissolved when the Treaty of the Union concluded on 30 December 1922 was denounced by its initial participants on December 12, 1991. See Decree of the Supreme Soviet of the RSFSR on the Denunciation of the Treaty on the Formation of the USSR, *Rossiiskaya Gazeta,* December 17, 1991, at 1.

step reform of the 1978 Constitution. Revisions of the old text were hurriedly made and were largely perceived as instruments in the on-going political struggle with the President. While the President favored radical economic and legal reforms, the communist-dominated Congress of People's Deputies tried to preserve the Soviet economic and political system. Modifications of the 1978 Constitution were easy to make because the amendment procedure required only the assent of the Congress. In a short time, the Congress managed to rewrite almost 75 percent of the text. Yet, although the revisions concerned important sections dealing with human rights, federal structure and the judicial system, they did not radically reform the Soviet form of government.

In the meantime, the draft of an entirely new constitution, prepared by the Constitutional Commission of the Congress, remained in limbo, notwithstanding the fact that in 1992 the Congress approved its "basic provisions"[3] and even endorsed a proposal to submit them to a referendum scheduled for April of 1993.[4] The proposed referendum never took place, largely because enactment of the new constitution would have meant the demolition of the Soviet system of government and of the Congress of People's Deputies itself.

By 1993, the country had reached an impasse. The congressional leadership refused to carry out its earlier decision to adopt an entirely new constitution. The President pressed for the adoption of a new text that would have established a real separation of powers, replaced the unworkable Congress with a normal parliament and expanded the powers of the executive, in particular with respect to economic reform. As the tension mounted, President Yeltsin decided to deal with the situation in his own resolute way. On September 21, 1993, he issued Decree No. 1400 "On Progressive Constitutional Reform in the Russian Federation"[5] which suspended the operation of a number of provisions of the 1978 Constitution. In particular, it suspended the Constitution's provisions concerning the powers of the Congress of People's Deputies. Yeltsin also issued a decree that envisioned a national referendum on a new constitution.[6] The Congress refused to dissolve itself and the constitutional crisis resulted in armed clashes in downtown Moscow and subsequent arrest of the leaders of "the parliamentary coup."

The President's dissolution of the Congress and other actions leading to the adoption of the 1993 Constitution clearly violated the 1978 Fundamen-

---

[3] See *O proekte Konstitutsii Rossiiskoi Federatsii* (On the Draft Constitution of the Russian Federation), *Vedomosty RF*, No. 18, item 979 (1992).

[4] See *Vedomosty RF*, No. 51, item 3016 (1992).

[5] *Sobranie aktov*, No. 39, item 3597 (1993).

[6] *Sobranie aktov*, No. 42, item 3995 (1993).

tal Law.[7] These actions were labeled as dictatorial and unconstitutional by Yeltsin's political opponents, or as revolutionary and extra-constitutional by the reformers.[8] Be that as it may, the ultimate result of the 1993 constitutional crisis was the destruction of the system of Soviet power throughout the country and the adoption of an entirely new Constitution.

The text of the proposed new Constitution was prepared by a Constitutional Meeting[9] that based its work on a draft submitted by the President. The final draft of the new constitution incorporated some of the earlier patchwork revisions and many provisions of the Constitutional Commission's official draft, which had been approved by the Congress.

The new Russian Constitution was approved by a popular referendum on December 12, 1993.[10] It went into effect on December 25, 1993. Notwithstanding certain misgivings about the legitimacy of the process leading to the adoption of the 1993 Constitution, the majority of commentators agree that the reliance on the constitution-making power of the people secured the most complete democratic legitimation of the new Constitution.

---

[7] The Constitutional Court held that the Decree of the President No. 1400 violated ten articles of the 1978 Constitution. See *Case Concerning the Decree on the Progressive Constitutional Reform in the Russian Federation, VKS*, 1994, No. 6, p. 40.

[8] The Ministry of Justice of the Russian Federation issued a special statement justifying the President's action. The statement emphasizes that although the President "acted beyond the formal legal framework, he acted in accordance with the constitutional principles of government by the people, insurance of the country's security and protection of the rights and lawful interests of citizens. . . Although, as a formal matter, he exceeded his powers, he used this violation, not to usurp power (the elections of the President are scheduled for July 12, 1994) but to protect the will of the people." Statement of the Ministry of Justice at the Constitutional Meeting. See *Informatsionnyi bulleten'* (Information Bulletin), 1993, No. 2, p. 26.

[9] The composition and functions of the Constitutional Meeting were defined by President Yeltsin's decrees *O merakh po zavershenіu podgotovki novoi Konstitutsii Rossiiskoi Federatsii* (On Measures to Complete the Preparation of the New Constitution of the Russian Federation), *Sobranie aktov*, No. 20, item 1757 (1993) and *O sozyve Konstitutsionnogo soveshchaniya I zavershenii podgotovki proekta Konstitutsii Rossiiskoi Federatsii* (On the Convocation of the Constitutional Meeting and Completion of the Preparation of the Draft Constitution of the Russian Federation), *Sobranie aktov*, No. 21, item 1903 (1993). The Constitutional Meeting consisted of representatives of the federal administration, the subjects of the Russian Federation, the local councils, the political parties, the trade unions, the associations of businessmen, the groups of deputies of the former Congress of People's Deputies, the Russian Academy of Sciences, the Constitutional Court, the Supreme Court, the Supreme Arbitration Court and the Procuracy.

[10] Of the participants in the referendum, 58.4 percent voted in favor of the new Constitution, *Rossiiskaya Gazeta*, December 25, 1993, at 1.

3. The Concept of the Rule-of-Law State

From a broad political perspective, the 1993 Constitution signifies a complete departure from the communist dictatorship and a passage to democratic government. As a new basic law for a "democratic federal rule-of-law state",[11] the Constitution became an important step toward establishing the rule-of-law state in Russia.

The Constitution does not define the concept of "rule-of-law" state. However, the essential elements of such a state may be found in Chapter 1 of the Constitution which deals with "Fundamentals of the Constitutional System." These elements include provisions of Arts. 2, 3, 10 and 15 of the Constitution. They indicate that the Russian "rule-of-law" state is intended to be a state in which governmental action is not arbitrary but based on constitutional principles and legal rules enacted by the people who have certain inalienable rights and freedoms and who are the sole source of power in the state.

Under Art. 2 of the Constitution, the new Russia is directed to adhere to the fundamental principle that "human beings and their rights and freedoms shall be of supreme value." The state assumed an obligation to recognize, respect and protect the rights and freedoms of the human being and citizen. Art. 3 of the Constitution proclaims that "the multinational people of the Russian Federation shall be the bearer of its sovereignty and the sole source of power in the Russian Federation."

Art. 10 of the Constitution introduces the concept of separation of powers and affirms the independence of different branches of government. Of particular importance are the constitutional guarantees of the independence of the judiciary. The independent judiciary has to ensure submission of the state to the law. The constitutionality of the legal and actual behavior of the state and its organs is ensured by the power of constitutional and judicial review granted to the Constitutional Court and "ordinary" courts.

Art. 15(1) establishes the principle of constitutionalism by providing that "the Constitution of the Russian Federation shall have supreme legal force and direct effect." Art. 15(1) ensures that, first, the Constitution is a supreme and fundamental law of Russia binding upon even the legislature and, second, that it is a directly applicable and effective fundamental law. It follows that ordinary legislation becomes null and void if it contravenes the Constitution. Finally, Art. 15(4) provides that the generally recognized principles and norms of international law and the international treaties of the Russian Federation

---

[11] Constitution, Art. 1.

are an integral part of its legal system and therefore are binding on all governmental agencies.[12]

It should be emphasized that Art. 1 of the 1993 Constitution, which proclaims Russia as a "democratic federal rule-of-law state," must currently be viewed as a goal rather than a description of the actual state of affairs. Although Russia has embarked upon the road toward democracy and it is clearly making progress toward becoming a state based on the rule of law, its totalitarian past and the absence of a tradition of respect for the rule of law make achieving this goal difficult. The 1993 Constitution indicates that Russia managed to establish normative and institutional foundations for the "rule-of-law state." However, changes in social attitudes towards law and legal institutions, in particular the lack of "legal conscienceness" of the population as a whole, as well as of the political and intellectual elites, cannot be achieved by even most far-reaching constitutional or legislative reforms. It is well known that as a component of any legal system the social attitudes towards law and institutions change the most slowly.

4. The Concept of the Social State

Russia is also proclaimed to be "a *social* state, the policies of which shall aim at creating conditions ensuring dignified life and free development of every individual."[13] (Emphasis added - eds.). Again, Art. 7(1) must be viewed as a goal rather than a description of the actual state of affairs.

Art. 7(1) is an indication that a "welfare" state or a state which takes into account the requirements of social justice, is an ideal goal for Russia. During the Constitutional Meeting some participants objected to the notion of "a social state," because it reflected the traditional socialist ideology.[14] Others claimed that the notion had nothing to do with any form of ideology. It means that the state has a responsibility to promote economic, social and cultural rights of individuals.[15] Chapter 2 of the Constitution dealing with "Rights and Freedoms of the Human Being and Citizen" contains an extensive catalogue of economic, social and cultural rights based on the International Covenant on

---

[12] The Constitutional Court noted in the *Chechnya Case* (*VKS*, 1995, No. 5, p. 3) that "in accordance with the principles of a law-governed state laid down by the Constitution of the Russian Federation, the organs of power are bound in their activities both by internal and international law."

[13] Constitution, Art. 7 (1).

[14] See the statement of S.S.Alexeev at the Constitutional Meeting, *Informatsionnyi bulleten'* (Information Bulletin), 1993, No. 3, p. 7.

[15] See 18 *Konstitutsionnoe soveshchanie. Materialy. Dokumenty* (Constitutional Meeting. Materials. Documents) 83, 486 (1996).

Economic, Social and Cultural Rights.[16] These rights are far from being precise. This means that Russia has considerable latitude in implementing the required "social" programs in a way that is compatible with the actual state of its economy. At the same time it is clear that as a "social" state Russia has assumed an obligation to enact welfare-oriented legislation and to establish the necessary institutions to deal with many difficult post-communism socio-economic issues. The concept of the social state may also become a serious barrier to the dismantling of social programs already in force.

Under Art. 7(2) of the Constitution the state must "protect the work and health of its people, establish a guaranteed minimum wage, provide state support for the family, motherhood, fatherhood and childhood, and also for the disabled and elderly citizens, develop a system of social services and establish government pensions, benefits and other social security guarantees." These provisions are nothing but a very general directive to the legislature. The legislature is directed to enact legislation transforming the principle of social justice into specific and judicially enforceable rules. It is also the responsibility of the legislative branch to establish the procedures by which welfare-oriented legislation and economic and social rights are to be fulfilled. It is not entirely clear whether individuals could base their claims to welfare assistance directly on the broad policy goals proclaimed in Art. 7 of the Constitution.

As yet no law has been declared unconstitutional as a result of the application of Art. 7 of the Constitution. However, in the *Case Concerning Art. 28(1) of the Law on Employment of Peoples of the Russian Federation*[17] the Constitutional Court appears to have recognized that application of broad principles of social justice may invalidate laws. Art. 28(1) of the challenged Law on Employment provided that in the event of sickness unemployed people were entitled to social security compensations for only 30 days during the 12 months of unemployment. The Constitutional Court declared this restrictive provision unconstitutional by reference to Art. 39(1) of the Constitution which states that "everyone shall be guaranteed social security in old age, in the event of sickness, disability or loss of a breadwinner, for the raising of children and in other cases specified by law." Although the operative part of the ruling in this case did not refer to Art. 7 of the Constitution, the concept of social state played an important role in the reasoning. The Court emphasized that as a social state the Russian Federation "is obliged to take care of well-being of its citizens and their social security." If a person cannot work for reasons of age or health and therefore does not have any income, she or he "has the right to expect to receive appropriate help and material support from the state and the society." The Court also declared that "the establishment of the system of

---

[16] 993 UNTS 3.

[17] *Sobranie*, No. 51, item 5878 (1997).

social security as an integral part of social protection of the population constitutes an essential element in the fulfillment of the goals of the social state."

Be that as it may, even if the principle of social state is not self-executing, it may always influence interpretation and application of specific laws. In the *Case Concerning Art. 1(3) of the Law on the Social Security of Citizens - Victims of the Nuclear Accident of 1957*[18] the Constitutional Court held that the right to a "favorable environment"[19] imposed on the state an obligation to "take adequate measures to protect the environment and the people from nuclear accidents and catastrophes." The Court also noted that Art. 42 of the Constitution, taken in conjunction with Art. 7 of the Constitution, mandates the state to establish a "system of benefits and compensations" that would go beyond the limits of ordinary compensation of harm caused by environmental law violations.

5. The Concept of Democratic State: The Communist Party Case and Restrictions on Radical Political Parties

Art. 1 of the 1993 Constitution requires Russia to be a democratic state. The Constitution does not define the term "democracy." However, it establishes certain principles that are normally associated with the presence of democracy. Art. 3 of the Constitution states that people are "the sole source of power in the Russian Federation." It also provides that the people may exercise their power directly and through representative government. Under Art. 3, "referenda and free elections shall be the supreme direct manifestation of the power of the people." In addition to these basic principles, the Constitution guarantees other characteristics of democracy, such as majority rule, free opinion and speech, freedom of assembly, freedom of association and political plurality.

The Constitution also recognizes that a functioning democracy requires the creation of a multi-party political system and equality of chances for all political parties. In view of this, Art. 13 of the 1993 Constitution expressly states that "political diversity and a multi-party system shall be recognized in the Russian Federation." Furthermore, it proclaims that public associations, including political parties, are equal before the law.

At the same time, Art. 13(5) of the 1993 Constitution provides that "the establishment and the activities of public associations, whose aims or actions are directed at forcible alteration of the fundamentals of the constitu-

[18] *VKS*, 1996, No. 2, p. 26.
[19] Constitution, Art. 42.

tional system and disruption of the integrity of the Russian Federation, undermining of the security of the state, the forming of armed units, the incitement of social, racial, national or religious strife shall be prohibited." The major purpose of this far-reaching restriction is to prohibit political parties which may destroy democracy by misusing the existing political freedoms and democratic procedures.

The questions of whether the state has the right to prohibit anti-democratic public associations is important for all countries emerging from totalitarian rule. Experience indicates that totalitarian parties destroy democratic orders and freedoms of others by invoking their freedom to operate.

The Communist Party of the USSR always rejected political pluralism and popular democracy. The 1977 USSR Constitution expressly placed the Communist Party above the law. Art. 6 of the 1977 Constitution described the Communist Party as "the leading and guiding force of Soviet society and the nucleus of its political system." In practice, the Communist Party exercised total control over the state machinery, including the legislature, executive and judiciary. In view of this, the elimination of the legal monopoly on state power enjoyed by the USSR Communist Party became an indispensable element of democratic reform in Russia.

The Communist Party's role in the emerging Russian democracy became a particularly hotly debated issue after the failed 1991 coup d'Etat staged by a group of conservatives who wanted to turn back democratic reforms in the Soviet Union. Many reformers believed that the establishment of a democratic form of government in Russia was impossible without the total destruction of the Communist Party. The association of the Communist Party with the anti-democratic coup was cited by President Yeltsin as one of the major reasons for his decision to suspend and then ban the activities of the USSR Communist Party in the Russian Federation.

President Yeltsin's decrees outlawing the Communist Party in Russia became a highly contested legal issue. A group of Communist Party deputies filed a petition in the newly established Constitutional Court arguing that the Decrees were beyond President's constitutional authority. In response, a group of Yeltsin's supporters petitioned the Court to review the legality of the Communist Party. The *Communist Party Case*, reproduced below, deals with many political and legal issues concerning the legal status of the Communist Party, its distinctive characteristics as a totalitarian organization and the constitutionality of President Yeltsin's decrees.

The Constitutional Court: *The Communist Party Case* (*VKS*, 1993, No. 4/5, p. 37)[20]

1. The Decree of the President of the Russian Federation of August 23, 1991 suspended the activities of the Communist Party of the RSFSR, while the Decree of November 6, 1991 terminated the activities of the CPSU [Communist Party of the Soviet Union] and of the Communist Party of the RSFSR on the territory of the Russian Federation; and the Decree of August 23, 1991 instructed the Ministry of the Interior of the RSFSR to ensure the inviolability of the property of the Communist Party of the RSFSR, the Central Bank of the RSFSR to suspend transactions on the accounts of the bodies and organizations of the Communist Party of the RSFSR; the Decrees of August 25 and November 6, 1991 provided for a set of protective measures in respect to the property of the CPSU and the Communist Party of the RSFSR on the territory of the Russian Federation, which had been declared state property; in this connection, the state authorities were granted the right to utilize this property. . .

2. While the Constitutional Court was preparing the consideration of the petition [of a group of People's Deputies challenging the constitutionality of these decrees], another group of People's Deputies of the Russian Federation filed petitions on May 12 and May 25, 1992 with the Constitutional Court to test the constitutionality of the CPSU and the Communist Party of the RSFSR. The applications are based on Art. 165.1 of the Constitution of the Russian Federation in the edition of April 21, 1992; they argue that the CPSU and the Communist Party of the RSFSR must be recognized as unconstitutional organizations. . .

Art. 165.1, which was included in the Constitution of the Russian Federation on April 21, 1992 and entered into force on May 16, 1992, gives the Constitutional Court the power to consider cases concerning the constitutionality of political parties and other public associations. The Constitutional Court finds that sanctions concerning the unconstitutional practice of political parties were established on June 16, 1990 by a new version of Art. 7 of the Constitution of the Russian Federation, which prohibits and therefore restricts the unconstitutional activities of parties and other public associations.

The principle prohibiting retroactive effect of laws does not affect the change in jurisdiction, which is determined in accordance with the law in force at the time of the consideration of the case. . .

The procedure for the constitutional review of the constitutionality of

[20] Note that this ruling was rendered on the basis of the 1978 Constitution.

political parties or any other public association may be established in accordance with the basic rules of procedure of the Constitutional Court, and, if necessary, on the basis of analogy from procedural law. . .

The issue of the constitutionality of the CPSU and the Communist Party of the RSFSR is closely connected with the issue of their legal nature, which constitutes a starting point for evaluating the constitutionality of measures taken against them according to the decrees under review. Consequently, there is clear evidence of the common character of the subject matter of the applications filed with the Constitutional Court by various groups of People's Deputies of the Russian Federation. For these reasons. . . the Constitutional Court has consolidated the application concerning the verification of the constitutionality of the above decrees . . . and the applications concerning the verification of the constitutionality of the CPSU and the Communist Party of the RSFSR. . .

(I) The application of the first group of People's Deputies of the Russian Federation asserts that the Decree by the President, of August 23, 1991, "On the Suspension of Activities of the Communist Party of the RSFSR" is unconstitutional because the activities of a public association may be suspended only in an emergency, and since there was no emergency at the moment the Decree was signed, the President exceeded his authority.

The representatives of the President asserted that the Presidential decision to suspend the activities of the Communist Party of the RSFSR in the Russian Federation corresponded to his constitutional authority, the separation of powers established in the Russian Federation and the limitations on jurisdiction of the highest state organs of the Russian Federation established by the Constitution.

An analysis of the August 23, 1991 Decree indicates that the President assumed. . . that the Communist Party of the RSFSR enjoyed the status of a public organization. The Decree emphasized, in particular, that the Communist Party of the RSFSR had not been registered according to the established procedure, that organs of the Communist Party supported the State Committee for the State of Emergency and were directly involved in the establishment of emergency committees in a number of regions, thereby flagrantly violating the Constitution and laws of the Russian Federation. . .

The Declaration of State Sovereignty of the Russian Federation adopted on June 12, 1990 by the first Congress of People's Deputies of the Russian Federation provides that the Russian Federation guarantees all citizens, political parties and other public associations acting within the framework of the Constitution equal opportunities for the participation in the management of state and public affairs. . . The Communist Party of the RSFSR was established in 1990. . . All documents of the Communist Party of the RSFSR indicate that it considered itself a structural unit of the CPSU. The Communist Party of the RSFSR could, according to the CPSU rules, draft its own programs and regulations on the basis of the fundamental program and rules of the CPSU. . . Consequently, there were no plans to register the Communist Party of the RSFSR. It follows that the Communist Party of the RSFSR did not enjoy the rights of a legal entity. . . As an integral part of the CPSU, the Communist Party of the RSFSR could not become an independent property owner in disregard of the CPSU. . .

On August 19, 1991, Soviet leaders imposed a state of emergency in certain regions of the USSR. . . and formed a State Committee for the State of Emergency in the USSR (SCSE), i.e. an unconstitutional state organ, to manage the country and administer the state of emergency. The leaders of the CPSU and of the Communist Party of the RSFSR, and many party committees at the regional and provincial level directly or indirectly supported the activities of the unconstitutional SCSE. . .

The President of the Russian Federation issued several decrees aimed at protecting the Constitution, law and order which ensured state and public security. . . The President of the Republic [the Russian Federation] did not impose a state of emergency in the Russian Federation; and no such state was in effect as of the publication of the Decree "On the Suspension of the Activities of the Communist Party of the RSFSR." In view of this, the application of the group of People's Deputies of the Russian Federation asserts that the activities of the Communist Party of the RSFSR were suspended unlawfully because the activities of political parties could only be suspended in a state of emergency.

The legislation in effect at that time, and in effect now, does not contain general provisions specifying the grounds and procedure for suspending the activities of political parties. . . At the same time, the possibility of such a suspension was envisioned in Article 23 of the RF Law "On a State of Emergency" and in a similar USSR law relating to the imposition of a state of emergency. . .

A comparison of the said acts with Article 7(2) of the Constitution of the Russian Federation, and also with Articles 3 and 22 of the USSR Law "On Public Associations" gives one grounds for concluding that both Russian and Union legislation proceeded from the principle according to which the activities of political parties and other public associations, apart from cases of a state of emergency, may be suspended by the competent organs of state power on the same grounds that are contemplated by the law for preventing their activities. According to Art. 7(2) of the Constitution, the activities of political parties and other public associations may be banned in order to curtail the unlawful activities described in this provision.

Consequently, the suspension of the activities of public associations must be effectuated in the interests of ensuring the security of the people, state and public security and normal functioning of institutions of state power. In all these cases, the activity of public associations could be suspended pending a court decision. The suspension of the activities of a public association, if there are grounds to believe it is involved in unconstitutional actions, which must be subject to investigation, serves exactly these purposes. While there is no detailed regulation for such a procedure, the normative acts providing for the suspension of the activities of public associations vest such powers with the highest official of the state, the President.

The activities of the Communist Party of the RSFSR were suspended by Presidential Decree for the aforementioned purposes in the situation which emerged as a result of the coup d'Etat of August 19, 1991. The suspension complied with the provisions of Article 4 of the Constitution (in the May 24, 1991 edition) which provided that state organs must ensure law and order, the interests of society, rights and freedoms of citizens. . . It was also correlated with the constitutional status of the President, in particular his authority to take measures to ensure state and public security of the Russian Federation and, on its behalf, to participate in the maintenance of state and public security of the USSR. . . The law does not relate the implementation of such measures to the imposition of a state of emergency. . . The said authority implies the right of the President to acknowledge the existence of a threat to the state and public security of the country and, depending on the extent of the threat, to make decisions in accordance with his competency. . .

The August 23, 1991 Decree. . . directly applied Article 7(2) of the Constitution. . . which prohibits the activities of parties, organizations and movements whose aims or actions are directed, in particular, at forcible alteration of the constitutional system and undermining of the security of the state. At the same time, the Constitution does not provide for a court procedure for imposing limitations on the right of association. Yet, the Decree contemplated that, after the relevant investigation had been completed the judicial branch would render decisions on the constitutionality or unconstitutionality of the activities of the Communist Party. . . The Constitutional Court also notes that the Resolution of the Supreme Soviet of the USSR of August 29, 1991 "On the Situation in the Country In Connection With the Coup d'Etat" suspended the activities of the CPSU on the entire territory of the USSR. The Resolution provides that the relevant decision concerning the CPSU will depend on the results of the Procuracy investigation concerning the involvement of the leading bodies of the CPSU in actions aimed at forcible alteration of the constitutional system. Under this Resolution, if the facts of involvement of the leading bodies of the CPSU in actions aimed at forcible alteration of the constitutional system is confirmed, they will be examined by the supreme judicial organ.

Suspending the activities of the Communist Party of the RSFSR required the implementation of measures to protect its property. The relevant measures, specified in paragraphs 3 and 4 of the Presidential Decree of August 23, 1991, were indeed taken in order to prevent unlawful use of party property and assets. . . In particular, the Ministry of the Interior of the RSFSR was instructed to ensure the preservation of the property and monetary resources of organs and organizations of the Communist Party of the RSFSR pending final judgement of the judicial organs; the Central Bank of the RSFSR was instructed to block the accounts of organs and organizations of the Communist Party of the RSFSR until further notice. . .

(II) The application of the People's Deputies. . . asserts that the President's decision to declare the property of the CPSU and the Communist Party of the RSFSR to be state property amounts to "nationalization." It also asserts that the President's expropriation of the property contravened the Constitution (Arts. 10 and 49) and the existing laws, in particular, the Law "On Property in the RSFSR" (Arts. 1,2,17,30,31 and 32) and the Law "On Public Associations" (Arts. 18 and 22) which lays down guarantees of the right of ownership of public associations. . .

The Constitutional Court finds that the property possessed by the CPSU and the Communist Party of the RSFSR included objects which might belong to various owners, including the state. . . Precisely determining the holder of the right of ownership to various assets managed by the CPSU organs is difficult because of the general "etatisation" of most of the nation's wealth.

The 1977 Constitution of the USSR (Art.10) provided that the property of trade unions and other public organizations (as well as state (public), collective farm and cooperative property) was socialist property. . . The systematic interpretation of the provisions of the Constitution of the USSR and the Constitution of the Russian Federation, as well as the Fundamentals of Civil Legislation of the USSR and Union Republics, and the Civil Code of the Russian Federation leads the Constitutional Court to conclude that the notion "public organizations" in this context did not include the CPSU. . . The legislation at that time did not include the CPSU in the notion "other public organizations" because it would have contradicted the actual position of the CPSU as the "guiding and directing force of Soviet society." Art. 6 of the USSR Constitution defined the CPSU as the "nucleus of the political system [of Soviet society] and state and public organizations," whereas Art. 7 of the Constitution of the USSR did not mention the CPSU among public organizations. The CPSU's reluctance to be identified as a public organization is thus confirmed by the Constitution of the USSR.

The CPSU was not within the scope of civil regulation of relations in respect to its property. This thesis is confirmed by the materials of the case: it has been established that the state did not exercise financial control over CPSU property. The Procurator's Office's general supervision also did not cover activities of the CPSU. . . The CPSU organs or officials would issue binding instructions to other property owners concerning the disposal of property without its inclusion onto the records of property in the party's possession. Furthermore, there were cases of unjustified enrichment of the CPSU at the expense of the state and in violation of Art. 133 of the Fundamentals of Civil Legislation of the USSR and Union Republics.

The uncertainty regarding persons enjoying the right of ownership with respect to property managed by the CPSU and the Communist Party of the RSFSR does not allow one to recognize them unequivocally as owners of that property. The property was easily transformed from one form of socialist ownership to another at the will of those CPSU organs who managed the property, and not at the will of the formal owners. The civil law regulations had not evolved into specific property relations, and at the same time the CPSU organs acted consistently with a literal interpretation of Art. 6 of the Constitution of the USSR. . .

The Constitutional Court finds that it is impossible to establish, in the framework of these court proceedings, the actual will of the owner during the transfer of property from the state to the CPSU, and considers that the property at the CPSU's disposal was managed without any proper legal basis. This statement does not rule out the possibility that some of the property managed by the CPSU legally belonged to it on the basis of the right of ownership.

Consequently, in its assessment of the constitutionality of the Presidential Decree of August 25, 1991 "On the Property of the CPSU and the Communist Party of the RSFSR" the Constitutional Court proceeds from the fact that the property managed by the CPSU and the Communist Party of the RSFSR correspondingly belonged to three types of owners: a) the state; b) the CPSU; and c) other owners. However, there is a legal uncertainty in respect to where the ownership of one person ends and the ownership of another starts, and in some cases who the real owner is; these issues could be clarified only by a court or by an arbitration court. . .

The President's decision to declare as state property the part of property managed by the CPSU with respect to which it had the right of ownership (membership dues, income from publishing activities) and the part of property the owner of which was unknown cannot be recognized as lawful. Under the existing law, such property cannot be converted into state property by an act of the executive branch. . . The declaration of state ownership over the property that has never been state property cannot fall within the competency of the executive branch unless the executive is authorized to so declare it by a special act of the legislature. No authorizing act had been passed in the given case.

(III) A regime of unlimited power of a narrow group of communist functionaries, united in the Politburo of the Central Committee of the CPSU and headed by the General Secretary of the Central Committee of the CPSU, governed the country for a long time.

The documents in the case provide evidence that in the overwhelming majority of cases the leading organs and top functionaries of the CPSU acted secretly from the rank-and-file members of the CPSU. . . At different management levels the real power belonged to the first secretaries of the relevant party committees. It was only at the lower level organizations that the CPSU had the characteristics of a public association. . . The materials in the case and witness testimony reveal that the leading structures of the CPSU initiated (and local structures often carried out) a policy of repressions towards millions of Soviet people, including deported peoples. It continued in such a way for decades.

After the amendment of Art. 6 of the Constitution of the USSR.[21] the organizational structures of the CPSU continued, as in previous years, to make decisions on many issues which fell within the jurisdiction of the relevant state agencies. For example, . . . in 1990 the Central Committee of the CPSU discussed the transformation of USSR diplomatic missions, . . production of fire fighting equipment, activities of the military-industrial complex and the Ministry of Foreign Economic Relations, . . . bugging of office phone conversations, withdrawal of Soviet troops from Hungary, and maintenance of Soviet troops in Germany. . . Top officials were still appointed and the rank of General conferred only with the approval of the Central Committee of the CPSU . . .

---

[21] [As noted earlier, Art. 6 of the 1977 Constitution described the Communist Party as "the leading and guiding force of Soviet society and the nucleus of its political system." This amendment eliminated the legal basis for the Communist Party's monopoly on state power].

The Regulations on the Committee on State Security and its Local Agencies, of January 9, 1959 approved by the CPSU Central Committee Presidium were still in force. . . The Regulations emphasized that the KGB organs were political organs called upon to implement measures approved by the CPSU Central Committee and working under its direct guidance; KGB top officials were part of the party *nomenklatura* [party-nominated state officials]; the orders of the KGB chairman were issued upon the approval of the Central Committee of the CPSU. . .

The CPSU continued to keep the mass media under its control. In 1990 the party leadership instructed Gosteleradio of the USSR to create a regular television program devoted to the CPSU's problems, its role and place in modern society; in the same year, the ideological department criticized Goskino for a film featuring documentary shoots of the Nuremberg trial. In 1991 the CPSU Central Committee instructed the Foreign Ministry of the USSR to bring the attention of the Western powers to the inadmissible activities of the Voice of America, BBC and Svoboda radio stations. . .

All these activities were carried out by the leading structures of the CPSU and the Communist Party of the RSFSR, in particular their central and local committees as well as staff members of these committees. The mass of rank-and-file members, including the leaders of primary party organizations, were unable to engage in state affairs. . .

The leading bodies of the CPSU and of the Communist Party of the RSFSR misappropriated state powers and used them to hinder the normal functioning of constitutional organs of power. This provided the legal basis for the liquidation of the said bodies by the Decree of the highest official of the Russian Federation. The President's actions were motivated by an objective need to prevent a return to the situation of the past, to destroy an organization whose day-to-day practice was based on the CPSU's position in the state mechanism, which contravened the fundamentals of the constitutional system.

The legal basis for the termination of the activities of the CPSU and the CP RSFSR and the dissolution of their organizational structures is provided by Art. 4(1) of the Constitution of the Russian Federation (in the November 1, 1991 edition) which makes the state and its agencies responsible for the protection of law and order, of the interests of society and of rights and freedoms of citizens. . .

The unconstitutionality of the activities of the leading structures of the CPSU and the Communist Party of the RSFSR . . . prevents their restoration in the preexisting form. Members of the Communist Party of the Russian Federation may only set up new structures in full compliance with the provisions of the existing Constitution and laws of the Russian Federation and on equal conditions with other parties. . .

(IV) The Communist Party of the RSFSR, as mentioned earlier, had been an integral part of the CPSU and had not evolved into an independent political party when the President's decrees under consideration were published. . .

Because it is established that neither the CPSU nor the Communist Party of the RSFSR has existed for twelve months, it must be acknowledged that there is no grounds for considering the application of the second group of the People's Deputies of the Russian Federation who seek to recognize the CPSU as unconstitutional. . .

For these reasons . . . the Constitutional Court of the Russian Federation:

(I) On the issue of the constitutionality of the Decree of the President of the Russian Federation of August 23, 1991 No. 79 "On the Suspension of the Activities of the Communist Party of the RSFSR"

[The Court found that, with respect to all major issues discussed in the extract, the Decree was constitutional]

(II) On the issue of the constitutionality of the Decree of the President of the Russian Federation of August 25, 1991 No. 90 "On the Property of the CPSU and the Communist Party of the RSFSR"

Holds that paragraph 1 of the Decree conforms to the Constitution . . . as applied to the share of property owned by the state but actually possessed, used and disposed of by organs and organizations of the CPSU and the Communist Party of the RSFSR as of the time of publication of the Decree.

Holds that paragraph 1 of the Decree contravenes the Constitution. . . as applied to the share of property owned by the CPSU and also the share of property actually possessed, used and disposed of by organs and organizations of the CPSU and the Communist Party of the RSFSR as of the publication of the Decree but whose owner was not determined. . .

(III) On the issue of the constitutionality of the Decree of the President of the Russian Federation of November 6, 1991 No. 169 "On the Activities of the CPSU and the Communist Party of the RSFSR"

Holds that paragraph 1 of the Decree conforms to the Constitution. . . as it relates to the dissolution of the leading organizational structures of the CPSU and also of the Communist Party of the RSFSR to the extent that it was an integral part of the CPSU.

Holds that the provisions of paragraph 1 of the Decree on dissolution of organizational structures of the CPSU and the Communist Party of the RSFSR contravene the Constitution of the Russian Federation. . . insofar as they concern the lower level organizations of the Communist Party of the RSFSR formed on territorial principles, as the said organizations retained their public character and were not replacing the structures of state power. . .

(IV) On the accompanying issue of the constitutionality of the CPSU and the Communist Party of the RSFSR

Dismisses the case concerning verification of the constitutionality of the CPSU and the Communist Party of the RSFSR because the CPSU disbanded and lost its status as a public organization in August-September 1991, since the constitutionality of the dissolution of the leading organizational structures of the CPSU and the Communist Party of the RSFSR as an integral part thereof is confirmed by this Ruling, and the Communist Party of the RSFSR has not been organizationally established as an independent political party. . .

QUESTIONS AND COMMENTS

1. The *Communist Party Case* is the most important case heard by the first Constitutional Court. One of the controversial issues in this case were the powers of the Constitutional Court under the 1991 Law on the Constitutional Court. According to Art. 1(3) of the 1991 Law on the Constitutional Court, political questions did not fall within its jurisdiction. However, in a case like the *Communist Party Case* the judges had to enter into the political domain.

Another problem was the absence of any procedural rules governing the proceedings concerning the constitutionality of political parties. As a result, the Court had to resort to an analogy from procedural legislation ("The procedure for the constitutional review of the constitutionality of political parties or any other public association may be established in accordance with the basic rules of procedure of the Constitutional Court, and, if necessary, on the basis of analogy from procedural law. . .").

Finally, the Court had extremely limited powers to investigate and determine the necessary factual issues prior to formulating a decision.

2. What were the principal issues before the Court? What were the arguments of the Communist petitioners challenging the constitutionality of

President Yeltsin's Decrees? What was the Court's holding with respect to the presidential Decree banning the activities of the Communist Party?

3. Was the CPSU a "public organization" or "public association" under the Soviet law? Why was this question so important for the outcome of the case? How did the legal status of the Communist party affect the procedure for the termination of its activities? Why was it possible to expropriate part of its property by an act of the executive branch?

4. The Constitutional Court noted that "the materials in the case and witness testimony reveal that the leading structures of the CPSU initiated (and local structures often carried out) a policy of repressions towards millions of Soviet people, including deported peoples. It continued in such a way for decades." This means that it is difficult to draw a distinction between "the leading organs and top functionaries of the CPSU" and "the lower level organizations." Yet, the Court drew a distinction between top functionaries and the lower level organizations. It hold that the lower level organizations of the CPSU had the characteristics of a legitimate "public association." Is there any persuasive justification for the Court's view of the CPSU?

5. Note that under the USSR Law "On Public Associations" (which was in force at the time of the hearing) the activities of public associations could be terminated only by a court order. This means that the executive branch had no power to prohibit even public associations fighting against the constitutional system or violating criminal law. The Constitutional Court emphasized this fundamental principle in the 1992 *Case Concerning the Decree of the President On Measures to Protect the Constitutional Order of the Russian Federation* (see *VKS*, 1994, No. 1, p. 14). In this case a group of deputies challenged the presidential Decree which banned the "unconstitutional activities" of the National Salvation Front (a hard-line anti-reform party). The Court found that the National Salvation Front was a "public association." In view of this, it declared the Decree of the President unconstitutional because the activities of public associations could be terminated only by a court of law. The current Law "On Public Associations" (see *Sobranie*, No. 21, item 1930 (1995)) also provides that unconstitutional activities of public associations may be suspended or terminated only by a court of law (Arts. 42, 44).

If the Court was reasoning by analogy to the Law on Public Associations, why didn't it adopt that part of the Law that required a court order, not merely an executive order?

6. How did the Court approach the matter of the constitutionality of the Communist party? Why did the Court decline to consider the matter? Do

you think the Court's reasoning is persuasive? Do you know any prior cases in which a totalitarian party was declared a criminal or unconstitutional organization long after its dissolution? If you would agree to consider the matter, how would you handle the issues of retroactivity and mootness?

7. The *Communist Party Case* deals with one of the fundamental principles of the Russian constitutional order - the right to association. The Court noted that "according to Art. 7(2) of the [1978] Constitution, the activities of political parties and other public associations may be banned in order to curtail the unlawful activities described in this provision." It also noted that the presidential Decree suspending the activities of the Communist Party of the RSFSR "directly applied Article 7(2) of the [1978] Constitution. . . which prohibits the activities of parties, organizations and movements whose aims or actions are directed, in particular, at forcible alteration of the constitutional system and undermining of the security of the state."

Art. 13(5) of the current Constitution is similar to Art. 7(2) of the previous Constitution. Art. 13(5) of the 1993 Constitution provides that "the establishment and the activities of public associations, whose aims or actions are directed at forcible alteration of the fundamentals of the constitutional system and disruption of the integrity of the Russian Federation, undermining of the security of the state, the forming of armed units, the incitement of social, racial, national or religious strife shall be prohibited."

Do you agree that post-totalitarian states need restrictions on "unconstitutional" activities of certain political parties?

How would you interpret Art. 13(5)? Must the danger to the constitutional system be clear and present? Is it possible to invoke Art. 13(5) if a party is antidemocratic in its general philosophy? Is it possible to rely on Art. 13(5) if a party is generally antidemocratic, advocates systemic changes in the existing constitutional system but has no specific plans for the "forcible alteration of the fundamentals of the constitutional system?"

8. Some European countries impose special restrictions on the exercise of the freedoms of assembly and associations by civil servants. For example, in Germany members of certain extremist parties, including the German Communist Party, do not have access to the civil service on the ground that they do not uphold the free democratic constitutional system within the meaning of the 1949 German Basic Law. This practice is based on the notion of a "democracy capable of defending itself." It is considered to be of special importance to Germany because of that country's experience under the Weimar Republic and the nightmare of Nazism (See European Court of Human Rights: *Vogt v. Germany*, 21 European Human Rights Reports 205).

Similar restrictions have been imposed in some new Central and Eastern European democracies after the nightmare of communism. Russia did not follow this example. Do you think that was wise in the light of that country's experience under the Soviet regime?

9. Many commentators believe that this holding of the Court, which opened the door for the restoration of the Communist Party in Russia, was to that extent incorrect. Judge A.L. Kononov has stressed that "the compromise character of the ruling in that case resulted in the restoration of the structures, ideas and methods of operation, the constitutionality of which were not assessed by the [Constitutional] Court; by failing to do so, it did not fulfill its historical mission." (Statements of Constitutional Court Judge A.L. Kononov, in 5 *Gosudarstvo I Pravo* (State and Law) 10 (1997). See also A.L. Kononov, *Piatiletie Konstitutsionnogo suda v Rossii: Uroki* (The Five Year Anniversary of the Constitutional Court in Russia: Lessons), *VKS*, 1997, No. 2, p. 12, 13).

Indeed, Communist party membership has not been a liability for politicians. New parties of communist orientation were set up. The Russian Communist Party has become one of the strongest political parties in the country. It usually receives at least one-third of the popular votes in parliamentary elections. At the same time, the non-communist reformers have failed to establish a strong unified political organization. The absence of a strong and stable democratic organization to counter the Communist Party is a serious destabilizing factor in the Russian political environment.

10. Note that Art. 125 of the 1993 Constitution does not give the new Constitutional Court the power to determine the constitutionality of political parties. According to Art. 116 of the Civil Procedure Code, non-conformity with the Constitution of the aims or activities of the political parties or public associations is now adjudicated by the Supreme Court.

B. Legislative and Executive Agencies

The 1993 Constitution proclaims that state power in the Russian Federation is exercised on the basis of separation of powers between the legislative and executive branches. It also provides that these branches are independent.[22] While the Federal Assembly (the parliament) is described as "the representative and legislative organ",[23] the President is considered to be "the head of the state."[24]

[22] Constitution, Art. 10.
[23] Constitution, Art. 94.
[24] Constitution, Art. 80.

The allocation of governmental powers in Russia differs from that in the United States an a number of ways. The 1993 Constitution emphasizes the strong role of the President. The President has been granted very broad powers as head of state.[25] One might argue that the 1993 Constitution provides for one of the strongest presidencies in Europe. Although in some respects the Russian presidential model resembles the American system, in fact it is much closer to that developed in France. However, a careful analysis of the Russian Constitution indicates that the Russian president has even more power than the French President.[26]

The adoption of the model of "an imperial presidency"[27] is the result of popular dissatisfaction with the excesses and inadequacies of the preexisting parliament. One often repeated argument for wide presidential powers is that they will secure stable development for Russia while the country goes through a transitional period without established and well-functioning political parties. Whatever the justifications at this stage, the Constitution's difficult amendment process[28] makes it unlikely that there will be any far-reaching changes in the established governmental system. Given the traditional authoritarian political culture predisposed to acknowledging the predominance of the executive power, constitutional safeguards against the abuse of executive authority assume paramount political-legal significance.

One of these constitutional safeguards is legislative action by the Federal Assembly, which may impose serious limits on executive law-making.[29] A further guarantee is the division of executive power itself, in particular between the Administration of the President and the Government. Other important limitations are federalism, constitutional and judicial review, and human rights guarantees. These will be discussed in detail in Sections D, E, F and Chapter V *infra.*

1. The Executive Branch

The executive branch is represented by the President and the Government. The Government, which according to Art. 110(1) of the Constitution, exercises "executive power in the Russian Federation," is

---

[25] See Constitution, Arts. 80, 83-89.

[26] See B.N. Topornin ed., *Konstitutsiya Rossiiskoi Federatsii. Nauchno-prakticheskii Kommentarii* (Constitution of the Russian Federation. A Scientific-Practical Commentary) 469 (1997).

[27] Cf. A.M. Schlesinger, The Imperial Presidency (1973) (discussing the concept of the "imperial presidency" in the United States).

[28] See Constitution, Arts. 134-135.

[29] An example of legislative action in the sphere of treaty-making is discussed *infra* p. 168.

composed of the Chairman (Chairperson) of the Government of the Russian Federation, deputy chairmen and the federal ministers. The 1997 Constitutional Law on the Government of the Russian Federation[30] provides a detailed regulation of the functions of the federal Government.

Although the President may preside over meetings of the Government,[31] unlike the American President, he is not considered to be the head of the Government. The President, who is elected by general election for a term of four years,[32] is "the head of the state." Furthermore, under the 1993 Constitution, the President is "the guarantor of the Constitution" who is supposed to "ensure the coordinated functioning and interaction of the organs of state power."[33] He determines "guidelines for the domestic and foreign policy of the state."[34]

As "the guarantor of the Constitution" the President has even been granted certain quasi-judicial powers. Under Art. 85(1) of the Constitution the President may use conciliation to resolve disputes between the federal government and governments of the "subjects" of the Federation and disputes between the various "subjects" of the Federation. If the conciliation fails to resolve the dispute, the President may refer the dispute to "the appropriate court."[35]

---

[30] *Sobranie*, No. 51, item 5712 (1997) (as amended, *Sobranie*, No. 1, item 1 (1998)).

[31] Constitution, Art. 83 (b).

[32] Note that the 1993 Constitution allows one President to serve only two four-year terms.

[33] Constitution, Art. 80 (2).

[34] Constitution, Art. 80 (3).

[35] Under Art. 116 of the Civil Procedure Code, the Supreme Court has original jurisdiction over disputes between the federal government and governments of the "subjects" of the Russian Federation. Art. 125(3) of the Constitution also authorizes the Constitutional Court to resolve disputes between branches of the federal government, between the Federation and its subjects, and between the highest organs of state power of the subjects of the Federation over the limits of their respective powers. It is important to note, however, that Art. 93 of the Constitutional Law on the Constitutional Court establishes fairly restrictive rules concerning the admissibility of the relevant petitions. It states:

> An appeal to the Constitutional Court of the Russian Federation by an organ (organs) of state power shall be admissible, if:
> (2) the dispute does not concern questions of determining jurisdiction of courts;
> (3) the dispute has not been settled or cannot be settled by any other means;
> (4) the petitioner considers the normative act or any legally significant action, or the failure to issue a normative act or commit a legally significant action, to be a violation of the separation of competence between the organs of state power established by the Constitution of the Russian Federation;

Pending the decision of the Supreme (or Constitutional) Court, the President may suspend "the acts of organs of executive power of the subjects of the Russian Federation if such acts contravene the Constitution of the Russian Federation and federal laws, the international obligations of the Russian Federation, or violate the rights and freedoms of the human being and citizen."[36] It is clear that such suspension is conditional upon a temporary but quasi-judicial determination that the relevant acts of the "subjects" contravene the Constitution. This means that the Russian President not only governs and issues decrees but also "resolves disputes" among state bodies.[37] Although the Constitution does not place the President above the three main branches of government, some commentators argue that he may act (as the French President does) as "an arbiter" among the legislative, executive and judicial branches of government.[38]

As head of the state the President appoints the members of the Government (Chairman, Deputy Chairman and ministers) and directs its activities. While in general the presidential "direction" of the activities of the Government is limited to establishing guidelines, the President has a special authority over ministries dealing with defense, security, internal and foreign affairs. Under the 1997 Constitutional Law on the Government the President directly controls the activities of these ministries. The Government, on the other hand, only "coordinates" their activities.

In directing the activities of the Government, the President has the constitutional authority to rescind any governmental regulations that "contravene the Constitution."[39] The President has the power to dissolve or reorganize the Government at any time.[40]

---

(5) the petitioner has already addressed a written statement to organs of state power mentioned in Art. 125 (3) of the Constitution of the Russian Federation about violations of the petitioner's competence established by the Constitution of the Russian Federation and agreements defining the competence of the petitioner or about the failure by the said organs to fulfill duties within their competence. . .

(7) if the President of the Russian Federation has not initiated, within a month after the receipt of an appeal by the relevant organ, the conciliatory procedures envisioned by Art. 85 of the Constitution of the Russian Federation, or if the said procedures have not resulted in the settlement of the dispute.

[36] Constitution, Art. 85 (2).

[37] Cf. Topornin, *supra* note 26, at 470-471.

[38] See M.V. Baglai, *Konstitutsionnoe pravo Rossiiskoi Federatsii* (Constitutional Law of the Russian Federation) 394 (1997).

[39] Constitution, Art. 115 (3).

[40] Constitution, Arts. 83 (c, d), 117 (2).

While the appointment of the Chairman of the Government requires the consent of the State Duma,[41] other important governmental appointments are made without legislative participation. Thus, as Commander in Chief of the Armed Forces, the President appoints and removes the commanders of the armed forces of the country without the consent of the State Duma. The President also forms and heads the Security Council of the Russian Federation.[42] This important federal agency is not part of the Government (The Constitution says nothing about the structure and powers of this Council except that they are to be defined by federal law[43]).

The President exercises his powers through the office of the President called the Administration of the President. The Administration is formed without any participation of the legislature. Although under the Constitution the Administration of the President is not considered to be an organ of state power, in practice it is functioning as a state organ with wide-ranging responsibilities.[44]

One of the most important (and controversial) powers of the President is the power to issue normative decrees which are declared to be binding throughout the territory of the Russian Federation.[45] Although Art. 90 of the Constitution states that presidential decrees "may not contravene the Constitution of the Russian Federation and federal laws," it does not impose any subject-matter restrictions on the President's power to issue decrees. At the same time, the President is not supposed to interfere in various areas which, according to the Constitution, should be governed by federal statutes. Thus, President Yeltsin has issued several decrees on taxation. Although they have not been challenged in the Constitutional Court, it is clear that taxes may be

---

[41] Constitution, Art. 83 (a).

[42] Constitution, Art. 83 (g).

[43] Id.

[44] The exact legal status of the Presidential Administration became a controversial matter after the President issued regulations defining the status and responsibilities of the Administration. The 1996 Regulations defined the Administration as a "state organ." The State Duma challenged this aspect of the Regulations in the Constitutional Court. However, after the President modified certain provisions of the Regulations, the State Duma asked the Court to terminate the proceedings. However, the new version of the Regulations still defined the Administration as a "state organ." The Court noted in this connection, that this provisions is of a very general character and does not predetermine the real powers and functions of the Presidential Administration. See *Case Concerning the Decree of the President On Regulations Concerning the Administration of the President of the Russian Federation, Sobranie*, No. 22, item 2664 (1997). The closest equivalent in the US would be the White House staff of the President - if it were expanded to a considerable extent.

[45] Constitution, Art. 90.

imposed only by statutes. As the Constitutional Court stated in the *Case Concerning Some Normative Acts of the City of Moscow*,[46] "taxes and levies may be imposed only by statutes." The Court added that "taxes which are collected on the basis of a non-statutory law cannot be regarded as 'lawfully instituted taxes'."[47]

The on-going controversy concerning the presidential decrees is illustrated by the following case.

The Constitutional Court: *Case Concerning the Decree of the President "On Measures to Strengthen the Unified System of Executive Power in the Russian Federation"* (*VKS*, 1996, No. 3, p. 15)

The State Duma of the Federal Assembly submitted a request to determine the constitutionality of the Decree of the President of the Russia Federation of October 3, 1994 No. 1969 "On Measures to Strengthen the Unified System of Executive Power in the Russian Federation."

[The challenged Decree defined the legal status and organization of executive bodies of the "subjects" of the Russian Federation in the "unified system" of executive power of the Russian Federation. The President acted on the basis of Art. 77(2) of the Constitution according to which the federal organs of executive power and the organs of executive power of the subjects of the Russian Federation are supposed to form a "unified system" of executive power in the Russian Federation in areas of exclusive jurisdiction of the Russian Federation and joint jurisdiction of the Russian Federation and its "subjects." It also dealt with the procedure for the election of the heads of administration in the "subjects" of the Federation].

The State Duma believes that the question of the organization of the organs of the executive power of the subjects of the Russian Federation must be resolved on the basis of a federal statute, and not on the basis of other normative acts, including the decrees of the President of the Russian Federation. . .

According to Art. 72 (m) of the Constitution of the Russian Federation, establishing general principles for the organization of the system of organs of state power and local self-government falls within the joint jurisdiction of the Russian Federation and the subjects of the Russian Federation. On matters falling within their joint jurisdiction, federal statutes are adopted and, in accordance with them, statutes and other normative legal

---

[46] *VKS*, 1996, No. 2 p. 42.
[47] Id.

acts of the subjects of the Russian Federation are adopted (Art.72 (2) of the Constitution of the Russian Federation). The system of organs of state power of the subjects of the Russian Federation is established by the subjects independently, in accordance with the fundamentals of the constitutional system of the Russian Federation and the general principles for organizing the representative and executive organs of state power as envisioned by federal law (Art. 77(1) of the Constitution of the Russian Federation). According to Art. 77(2) of the Constitution of the Russian Federation, the federal organs of executive power and the organs of executive power of the subjects of the Russian Federation are supposed to form a unified system of executive power in the Russian Federation, within the jurisdiction of the Russian Federation and the powers of the Russian Federation on issues within the joint jurisdiction of the Russian Federation and its subjects.

It follows from these constitutional provisions that, in order to establish a single system of executive power in the Russian Federation, the federal legislative organ - the Federal Assembly (first of all the State Duma) and the legislative (representative) organs of the subjects of the federation must enact, within the limits of their jurisdiction, the relevant statutes. . .

However, at the time of the enactment of the challenged decree of the President of the Russian Federation, the required legislative foundation on this issue did not exist. Even now, the basic federal law on general principles for organizing the system of representative and executive organs of state power envisioned by Art. 77(1) of the Constitution of the Russian Federation has not been enacted. . .

In accordance with Art. 80 of the Constitution of the Russian Federation, the President of the Russian Federation is the guarantor of the Constitution of the Russian Federation; he is supposed to ensure the coordinated functioning and interaction of organs of state power. In view of this, the issuance of decrees to fill in gaps in legal regulation of issues calling for legislative resolution does not contradict the Constitution if the relevant decrees do not contravene the Constitution of the Russian Federation and federal laws and if their temporal sphere of validity is limited by the enactment of the relevant law-making acts. . .

Dissenting Opinion of Judge V.O. Luchin

[The law-making decrees of the President of the Russian Federation] are illegitimate because they are not envisioned by the Constitution of the Russian Federation. . . [They] are inconsistent with the principle of separation of powers and other values of a rule-of-law state. The President has no right to resolve any questions if their resolution does not follow from his powers envisioned by the Constitution. He cannot rely on the so-called "implied powers." In a situation where there is no stable constitutional order or legality, the use of "implied powers" leads to negative consequences: a weakening of the "checks and balances" mechanism, an increase in the power of one branch at the expense of another, and confrontation between them.

I cannot agree with the proposed interpretation of Art. 80(2) of the Constitution of the Russian Federation. . . The constitutional provision according to which the President, as the guarantor of the Constitution, "ensures the coordinated functioning and interaction of the organs of state power" (Art. 80) has led to much speculation and, in fact, is used to as a cover for his excesses. In my opinion, this provision does not imply that the President is not bound by the Constitution and that he can, on his own will, promulgate any decrees on any questions without any regard as to which branch of state power (organ of state power) has jurisdiction over the matter. . . It is an oversimplification to believe that the President, having determined, for example, that the Federal Assembly is not moving fast enough, has the right to issue decrees that take the place of statutes. . . A "temporary" decree in fact becomes a "temporary federal statute"; this proposition is absolutely beyond the scope of the constitutional framework for the law-making process. In my opinion, the temporary application of the Decree cannot justify presidential encroachment on the prerogatives of the legislative power and does not give him any right to fill in gaps in legal regulation of issues calling for a legislative solution. . . An exception is possible only in cases of the introduction of martial law or the proclamation of a state of emergency on the basis of federal constitutional law. . .

QUESTIONS AND COMMENTS

1. What is the Constitutional Court's opinion on the legal significance of presidential decrees? When can the President issue normative decrees that serve as temporary statutes?

2. Read the relevant constitutional provisions cited by the Court. With whom do you agree, the majority or the dissent?

3. In the *Case Concerning the Postponement of Elections of the Legislative Organs of Certain Subjects of the Federation* (*Sobranie*, No. 20, item 23 83 (1997)) the Constitutional Court once again confirmed that "the issuance by the President of the Russian Federation of decrees that fill in gaps in legal regulation on issues calling for a legislative resolution follows from his constitutional authority to ensure the enforcement of constitutional provisions and to ensure the coordinated functioning of the organs of state power (Art. 80)

and does not contradict the separation of powers between the federal organs of state power (at the federal horizontal level) established by the Constitution if the relevant decrees do not contravene the Constitution of the Russian Federation and federal laws and if their temporal sphere of validity is limited by the enactment of the relevant acts by the legislature." In that case, the State Duma challenged the Decree of the President which dealt with the extension of the terms of the legislatures in some of the "subjects" of the Federation.

4. The Government is also granted the power to issue directives that may have a "normative" character (Constitution, Art. 115). However, the Government cannot issue sub-statutory regulations in areas that require statutory enactments. In the *Case Concerning the Ruling of the Government On Duties for the Production of Alcoholic Beverages* (*VKS*, 1997, No. 1, p.43) the Constitutional Court emphasized that the Government has no power to enact regulations establishing taxes or duties because taxes can be imposed only by "statutes."

5. As noted earlier, the President may use conciliation to resolve disputes between the federal government and governments of the "subjects" of the Federation and disputes between the various subjects of the Federation. If conciliation fails to resolve the dispute, the President may refer the dispute to the Constitutional Court or to the Supreme Court. Pending the decision of the Constitutional Court, the President may suspend the enactments of organs of executive power of the "subjects." Because the suspension is conditional upon a determination that the relevant acts of the "subjects" contravene the Constitution, the President is thus granted at least temporary quasi-judicial functions. Do these powers of the President violate the notion of separation of executive and judicial power?

2. The Legislative Branch

(a) The Federal Assembly

The legislature - the Federal Assembly - consists of two separate chambers: the State Duma and the Federation Council. It is important to note that the 1993 Constitution does not place the State Duma on an equal footing with the Federation Council. Under Arts. 104 and 105 of the Constitution draft laws are introduced and adopted by the State Duma. They cannot be introduced in the Federation Council. The Federation Council only participates in the adoption of federal laws by giving its express or tacit consent to laws adopted by the State Duma.

The State Duma consists of 450 deputies who are elected for a term of four years. In conformity with the democratic principle of Art. 3 of the

Constitution, deputies of the State Duma are chosen in general, direct, free, equal and secret elections. The 1995 Federal Law "On the Elections of the Deputies of the State Duma"[48] defines the procedure for election of the deputies of State Duma. It provides for a dual system of representation in which each voter casts two ballots, one for an individual candidate, the other for a political party. Candidates receiving the highest number of votes in their districts are elected. The remaining seats are allocated in such a way that each political party's total representation is proportional to its total vote.

The 1995 Law tries to avoid the risk of ungovernability resulting from the dispersal of votes among a multitude of small political parties by excluding parties that attract less than five percent of the votes from the allotment of seats on the party ballot. The rule that political parties must obtain five percent of the national vote to get into the State Duma has been subject to much criticism because it may violate the principle of equal suffrage. Critics claim that the five percent threshold results in wasted votes if a minor party for which some citizens vote fails to surmount the five percent hurdle. These wasted votes may result in additional seats for stronger parties.

The five percent rule was challenged in the Constitutional Court by the State Duma during the parliamentary elections of 1995. However, the Constitutional Court refused to consider the petition. The Court held that the 1993 Constitution gave the responsibility for determining the specifics of the electoral procedure to the Federal Assembly. The Court also emphasized that the issues raised were "questions of political expediency" that were supposed to be resolved by the legislature.[49]

In contrast to the State Duma, the Federation Council consists of two representatives from each "subject" of the Russian Federation - one elected by the legislative organ of the "subject" and one appointed by the executive organ of the relevant "subject."[50] This means that there must be 178 "senators" (in reality there are only 176 representatives of the "subjects," because Chechnya considers itself an independent state and has declined to send any representatives ("senators")).

Because the members of the Federation Council are members of the legislature and the government of the "subjects," they are there as representatives of the "subjects." This arrangement ensures that the "subjects" participate through the Federation Council in the legislation and administration of

---

[48] *Sobranie,* No. 26, item 2398 (1995).

[49] See *Case Concerning the 1995 Federal Law On the Elections of the Deputies of the State Duma, Sobranie,* No. 49, item 4867 (1995).

[50] Constitution, Art. 95 (2).

the Federation. The "subjects" of the Federation thus play in important role in the enactment of federal legislation.

The composition of the Federation Council also affects the legislative process in another way. Because half of the "senators" represent the executive branch of the "subjects," the upper chamber of the Russian parliament tends to focus on practical questions of legislative proposals. While the State Duma is extremely politicized, the Federation Council acts as an important stabilizing force which injects a certain amount of reality into the legislative process.

(b) The President's Power to Dissolve the State Duma

The Federal Assembly is a permanently functioning body. However, in contrast to the United States where the President has no power to dissolve the Congress, the Russian President has been conferred the power to dissolve the lower chamber of the Federal Assembly - the State Duma. However, the President cannot dissolve the upper chamber of the Parliament - the Federation Council.

In the interests of parliamentary stability, the 1993 Constitution sharply limits the power of the President to dissolve the State Duma. This rather extreme weapon against an obstructive or destructive parliamentary majority may be used only in three situations envisioned by Arts. 111 and 117 of the Constitution. The President may dissolve the State Duma (1) if the State Duma rejects three successive candidates proposed by the President for Chairman of the Government, (2) if the State Duma adopts two no-confidence votes in the Government within three months of each other or if (3) the State Duma denies a vote of confidence requested by the Chairman of the Government. The third possibility is a particularly strong weapon in the hands of the executive branch, because the Government and the President are always able to request a confidence vote by the State Duma.

The Constitution includes several other important limitations on the President's power to dissolve the State Duma. Under Art. 109, the President cannot dissolve the State Duma for one year after its election for denial of a confidence vote requested by the Chairman of the Government or for two non-confidence votes within three months of each other. The President also has no power to dissolve if the State Duma has filed a criminal charge against him[51] or during a state of emergency or martial law.[52] Finally, the President cannot

[51] Constitution, Art. 109 (4).
[52] Constitution, Art. 109 (5).

dissolve the State Duma within the six months preceding the expiration of the President's term of office.[53]

(c) The Legislative Process

According to the Constitution, only the Federal Assembly may enact statutes. The right of legislative initiative - the right to introduce bills in the legislature - is vested in the President, the Federation Council, members of the Federation Council, deputies of the State Duma, the Government, the legislative bodies of the "subjects" of the Russian Federation, the Constitutional Court, the Supreme Court and the Supreme Arbitration Court.[54] Practice indicates that the President and the Government often initiate legislation.[55] The right of legislative initiative granted to the courts may appear strange, but it reflects the traditional attitudes that courts cannot make or change laws. Since courts may not make law, they must be given an opportunity to participate in the legislative process. However, this participation is restricted to issues within their sphere of activity.[56] This means that the Constitutional Court, the Supreme Court and the Supreme Arbitration Court can initiate only legislation concerning the organization and activities of the respective courts or court systems or legal problems which emerge in judicial practice and which require the attention of the legislature. For example, the current Constitutional Law on the Constitutional Court of the Russian Federation was enacted on the initiative of the Constitutional Court.[57]

Statues are first adopted by the State Duma if more than half of "all the deputies"[58] vote for it. Then they must be approved by the Federation Council in one of two ways. First, the Federation Council may consider and pass the law if more than half of "all its members"[59] vote for it. Second, with the exception of statutes listed in Art. 106 of the Constitution, the required Federation Council approval may be implied if the Federation Council fails to

---

[53] Id.

[54] Constitution, Art. 104 (1).

[55] See Topornin, *supra* note 26, at 545.

[56] Constitution, Art. 104 (1).

[57] See Topornin, *supra* note 26, 546.

[58] The Constitutional Court held that the phrase "all the deputies of the State Duma" means not all present and voting deputies but the total number of deputies envisioned by the Constitution, that is, 450 deputies. See *Case Concerning the Interpretation of Arts. 103(3), 105(2,5), 107(7), 108(2), 117(3) and 135 of the Constitution of the Russian Federation, VKS*, 1995, No. 2/3, p. 17.

[59] The Constitutional Court held that the phrase "all the members of the Federation Council" means the total number of members envisioned by the Constitution, that is 178 members. Id.

act on the draft law within 14 days.[60] Art. 106 of the Constitution provides for a compulsory examination by the Federation Council of certain most important laws, such as laws on the federal budget, federal taxes, ratification of international treaties or matters of war and peace. The Constitutional Court held that in principle the Federation Council must act upon the laws mentioned in Art. 106 within 14 days. However, if the Federation Council is not able to finalize the consideration of the law within this period, it then must make its decision during its following session.[61]

If the Federation Council rejects a federal law approved by the State Duma, both chambers "may set up a conciliation commission to settle the differences that have arisen, after which the federal law shall again be considered by the State Duma."[62] If the State Duma disagrees with the Federation Council's rejection of the law, "the federal law shall be considered adopted if, in the second voting, at least two-thirds of the total number of deputies of the State Duma vote for it."[63]

(d) Presidential Veto

The President also participates in the legislative process. A federal law adopted by the Federal Assembly is presented within five days by the Federation Council[64] or by the State Duma[65] to the President to be signed into law within 14 days. The President has the power to veto ordinary legislation.[66] The president has no right to veto constitutional laws.[67] If the President rejects the law, it must be reexamined by the State Duma and by the Federation Council. They may override the presidential veto if the original version of the law is approved by two-thirds of the total number of the deputies of the State Duma and the members of the Federation Council.

---

[60] Constitution, Art. 105 (4).

[61] See *Case Concerning the Interpretation of Arts. 105(4) and 106 of the Constitution of the Russian Federation*, *VKS*, 1995, No. 2/3, p. 3.

[62] Constitution, Art. 105 (4).

[63] Constitution, Art. 105 (5).

[64] The Constitutional Court held that the law must be submitted to the President by *the Federation Council* irrespective of whether the law has been approved by the Federation Council by way of a vote or implicitly. See *Case Concerning the Interpretation of Art. 107 of the Constitution of the Russian Federation*, *VKS*, 1996, No. 3, p. 5.

[65] The State Duma presents the adopted law to the President in cases when it, in accordance with Art. 105(5) of the Constitution, overrules a rejection of the law by the Federation Council.

[66] Constitution, Art. 107.

[67] Constitutional laws are discussed *supra* p. 13-14.

The President also has the right to determine whether a statute approved by the Federal Assembly was adopted in accordance with the procedural requirements of the Constitution. If the procedural requirements were violated, he may reject a statute on procedural grounds and refuse to publish it.[68] Practice indicates that the President often rejects laws "without consideration" of their merits on procedural grounds.[69] The Constitutional Court emphasized that, in that case, the procedurally rejected law is not considered "an adopted federal law." Consequently, the rejection on procedural grounds is not a veto.[70] While presidential veto may be overridden by qualified majorities of both chambers of the Federal Assembly,[71] disputes over procedural violations must be resolved by the Constitutional Court.[72]

(e) Parliamentary Control Over the Administration of Laws

Parliamentary control over the actual administration of laws is rather limited. The Federal Assembly's general control of policy is limited to passing laws, expressing a vote of "no confidence" in the Government and impeaching the President. Furthermore, both chambers of the Federal Assembly may form committees and commissions, and hold hearings on issues within their competence.[73] In addition, the 1993 Constitution provides for direct parliamentary control over the federal budget.[74] The Federation Council has also been granted important control functions with respect to war powers of the President.[75]

C. Foreign Relations

Under the 1993 Constitution, the foreign policy and international

---

[68] Out of populist sentiment, the State Duma often adopts laws on social programs affecting the state budget without the required preliminary assessment of such draft laws by the Government, as required by Art. 104(3) of the Constitution. Art. 104(3) states: "The draft laws on the imposition or elimination of taxes, tax exemption, the issue of state loans and changes in the financial obligations of the state and other draft laws providing for expenditures that are covered out of the federal budget may be introduced only if accompanied by a corresponding resolution by the Government of the Russian Federation." For details, see Topornin, *supra* note 26, at 547-548, 557.

[69] In 1995, the President vetoed 114 laws out of 368, and returned 24 laws without consideration because of procedural violations. Id., at 474.

[70] See *Case Concerning the Interpretation of Art. 107 of the Constitution of the Russian Federation*, *VKS*, 1996, No. 3, p. 5.

[71] Constitution, Art. 107 (3).

[72] Id.

[73] Constitution, Art. 101 (3).

[74] See Constitution, Art. 101.

[75] See Constitution, Art. 102.

relations of the Russian Federation, including foreign economic relations, are exclusively within the jurisdiction of the Federation.[76] At the same time, certain powers fall within the joint jurisdiction of the Federation and its "subjects." They include the coordination of the international and foreign economic relations of the "subjects" and the fulfillment of federal international treaties.[77]

The Constitution establishes the President's preeminence in foreign relations. The President determines the guidelines for the "foreign policy of the state"[78] and represents Russia "in international relations."[79] He forms and presides over the Security Council and approves the military doctrine of the country.[80] He also appoints, after consultation with the relevant committees of the chambers of the Federal Assembly, Russian diplomatic representatives abroad.[81] The federal Government also has enjoys broad powers in foreign policy. Under Art. 114 of the Constitution the Government carries out "measures aimed at ensuring the country's defense, state security and the implementation of the foreign policy of the Russian Federation." The most important federal agency in this field is the Ministry of Foreign Affairs of the Russian Federation.

While foreign relations fall mainly into the domain of executive responsibility, the Russian parliament is also involved in the foreign policy-making process. Foreign policy issues are often debated in the parliament. The State Duma has established several parliamentary committees on foreign affairs and defense. Federal ministers may be compelled to appear before the State Duma or its standing foreign affairs committees.

1. The Treaty-Making Procedure

(a) The Role of the President

The President negotiates and signs international treaties[82] (in practice, the President often delegates treaty-making powers to the federal Government or to a federal minister). The President also signs ratification documents after ratification action by the Federal Assembly.[83]

---

[76] Constitution, Art. 71 (j-m).
[77] Constitution, Art. 72 (1) (n).
[78] Constitution, Art. 80 (3).
[79] Constitution, Art. 80 (4).
[80] Constitution, Art. 83 (g,h).
[81] Constitution, Art. 83 (1).
[82] Constitution, Art. 86.
[83] Constitution, Art. 86.

(b) The Role of the Federal Assembly

The Constitution also contemplates an active role for the Federal Assembly in treaty-making. Although the President signs instruments of ratification, the parliament must first ratify the relevant treaty. Denunciation of treaties also requires the approval of the Federal Assembly.

The State Duma has the power to adopt federal laws pertaining to "the ratification and denunciation of international treaties of the Russian Federation." Art. 106 of the Constitution provides for a system of compulsory consideration of such laws by the Federation Council. While Art. 106 implies that the ratification of treaties must be carried out by both chambers of the Federal Assembly and that consent to treaties is given in the form of a federal statute, it is not clear which treaties require ratification. As a result, the Constitution, at least in principle, offers the President broad discretion to conclude executive agreements. By acting within their normal sphere of competence, the President and other federal organs may conclude such agreements without submitting them for parliamentary approval.

To restrict the potentially unlimited scope of executive agreements, the Federal Assembly enacted the 1995 Law "On International Treaties of the Russian Federation."[84] The 1995 Law assures Parliament's democratic participation in the treaty-making process by requiring ratification of a wide category of treaties. Art. 15 of the 1995 Law provides that the Federal Assembly must ratify the following categories of treaties:

a) the implementation of which requires modification of the existing federal laws or the adoption of new ones, as well as those treaties which set forth rules different from rules provided by a law;

b) the subject of which is the fundamental rights and freedoms of the person and the citizen;

c) concerning the territorial delimitation of the Russian Federation with other states, including treaties on the precise demarcation of the state boundary of the Russian Federation, as well as treaties on the delimitation of the exclusive economic zone and the continental shelf of the Russian Federation;

d) on the basic principles of inter-state relations, regarding questions affecting the defense capability of the Russian Federation, regarding questions of disarmament or international control over armaments, regarding questions of ensuring international peace

[84] *Sobranie*, No. 29, item 2757 (1995).

and security, as well as peace treaties and treaties on collective security;

e) on the participation of the Russian Federation in inter-state unions, international organizations and other inter-state associations, if such treaties provide for the transfer to them of part of the powers of the Russian Federation or establish that decisions of their organs are legally binding on the Russian Federation.

Under the 1995 Law, termination (including denunciation) of all these categories of treaties also requires the adoption of the relevant laws by both chambers of the Federal Assembly.

The Constitution implies that federal laws on the ratification of treaties will be considered in accordance with the normal legislative procedure. Thus, the Federation Council, which represents the "subjects" of the Russian Federation on the federal level, is entitled to exercise its normal powers under domestic procedural rules, including the power to veto the proposed law. This veto may be overruled only by a qualified majority of the State Duma.[85] The President has the power to veto the proposed laws, while the Federal Assembly may override presidential veto.

(c) Participation of the "Subjects" of the Federation in Treaty-Making

The normal treaty-making procedure allows the "subjects" of the Federation to participate in the treaty-making process only through their representatives in the Federation Council. The 1993 Constitution requires no formal consultations with the "subjects" of the Federation, even when the subject-matter of a federal treaty encompasses the legislative or administrative powers of the "subjects" and thus directly affects their rights or interests. However, Art. 4 of the 1995 Law on International Treaties provides that the conclusion of international treaties "affecting questions falling within the jurisdiction of a subject of the Russian Federation" requires the assent (*po soglasovaniiu*) of the relevant "subject."[86] This means that the affected "subjects" of the Federation have been granted the right to veto the conclusion of an international treaty of the Russian Federation. An authoritative commentary of the 1995 Law on International Treaties states that "an

[85] Constitution, Art. 105.

[86] A similar procedure has been established for "international treaties of the Russian Federation directly affecting the foreign trade interests of the subjects of the Russian Federation" by Art. 9 of the 1995 Law "On State Regulation of Foreign Trade Activity," *Sobranie*, No. 42, item 3923 (1995).

international treaty of the Russian Federation, affecting questions which fall within the jurisdiction of a subject, cannot be concluded without the assent of its organs of state power."[87]

If, on the other hand, a treaty affects matters falling within the *joint jurisdiction* of the Federation and its "subjects," the federal organs have the much softer obligation of communicating the treaty's basic provisions, or the draft, to the interested "subject." Proposals submitted by the "subject" must be considered when the draft treaty is prepared.

(d) Judicial Review of Treaties for Constitutionality

An important feature of the treaty-making process in Russia is the possible involvement of the Constitutional Court. If the constitutionality of the proposed treaty is challenged, the Court may be drawn into the ratification procedure.

The Constitution authorizes the Court to review the constitutionality of only those international treaties of the Russian Federation which have not entered into force.[88] The Constitutional Court may consider cases relating to treaties only before their ratification or after ratification, but before they enter into force for Russia. Certain treaties may be reviewed even after ratification because ratification of a treaty by the Russian parliament may not necessarily mean that the treaty would immediately enter into force. Furthermore, certain international treaties may not enter into force until a determined number of ratifications have been deposited, or the instruments of ratifications have been exchanged or certain formalities, defined by the treaty, completed.

While Art. 125(2) of the Constitution provides that the Constitutional Court has the power to review the constitutionality of "international treaties of the Russian Federation that have not entered into force," Art. 89(1) of the Constitutional Law on the Constitutional Court establishes an additional limitation according to which the Court may review only treaties that "are subject, in accordance with the Constitution and federal law, to ratification by the State Duma or subject to confirmation by other federal organ of state power." It follows that the Court would be unable to review the constitutionality of treaties concluded without parliamentary ratification, for example, executive agreements concluded by the President. Furthermore, the Court would not be able to review treaties which enter into force upon being signed.

---

[87] V.P. Zvekov, B.I. Osminin eds., *Kommentarii k Federal'nomu zakonu "O mezhdunarodnykh dogovorakh Rossiiskoi Federatsii"* (Commentary of the Federal Law "On International Treaties of the Russian Federation) 13 (1996). See also W.E. Butler, The Russian Law of Treaties 22 (1997).

[88] Constitution, Art. 125 (2).

The limitation imposed by the Constitutional Law on the Constitutional Court has become quite controversial. Some commentators believe that Art. 89(1) of the Constitutional Law on the Constitutional Court contravenes Art. 125(2) of the Constitution. The authors of an authoritative commentary of the Constitutional Law on the Constitutional Court emphasize that "the Constitution of the Russian Federation does not impose any limitation on [the Court's] powers according to the means by which consent to the binding force of a treaty is expressed. This is why the limitation in the Law on the Constitutional Court based on those means appears to contravene the goals of the Constitution: to grant to the applicants the right to initiate cases concerning the constitutionality of any international treaties of the Russian Federation which have not entered into force."[89] Under this interpretation, the Court should have the power to review the constitutionality of both executive agreements and treaties which enter into force without legislative approval.

As noted earlier, treaties are ratified by federal statutes. Because the Constitutional Court has jurisdiction to review the constitutionality of all federal statutes, there may be a separate basis for reviewing the constitutionality of federal laws ratifying treaties. Such a review may result in an indirect review of underlying international treaties, including treaties that have already entered into force. However, some commentators argue that judicial review of a treaty via a promulgating federal law is excluded by Art. 125 of the Constitution which allows only review of treaties which *have not entered into force*. They argue that an indirect review would violate this constitutional provision, which is based on the idea that domestic constitutional review cannot lead to any violations of Russia's international treaty obligations.[90] Any determination that a treaty in force is unconstitutional could cause Russia to be in violation of its treaty obligations. The commentary of the Constitutional Law on the Constitutional Court argues that in view of these considerations any indirect review of a treaty in force via review of the ratifying federal law is not within the competence of the Constitutional Court.[91]

Treaties that conflict with the Constitution are not to be given effect and are not applicable.[92] Art. 91(2) of the Constitutional Law on the

---

[89] N.B. Vitruk, L.B. Lazarev, B.S. Ebzeev eds., *Federal'nyi konstitutsionnyi zakon o Konstitsionnom sude Rossiiskoi Federatsii. Kommentarii* (Federal Constitutional law on the Constitutional Court of the Russian Federation. Commentary) 272 (1996). Cf. also A.N. Talalaev, *Konstitutsionnyi Sud Rossiiskoi Federatsii I nekotorye voprosy prava mezhdunarodnykh dogovorov* (Constitutional Court of the Russian Federation and Some Questions of the Law of International Treaties), *VKS*, 1997, No. 2, p. 25, 28-29.

[90] Id., at 276-277.

[91] Id., at 277.

[92] Constitution, Art. 125 (6).

Constitutional Court provides that from the moment the Constitutional Court declares a treaty unconstitutional or its individual provisions which have not entered into force, the treaty or the respective provisions "are not subject to introduction into operation and application, that is, may not be ratified, confirmed, and otherwise may not enter into force for the Russian Federation." This means, among other things, that if the Constitutional Court considers a treaty submitted for ratification to be unconstitutional, the only way it may be ratified is through a constitutional amendment.

(e) Independent Treaty-Making Power of the "Subjects"

Although the federal Government has primary competence over the conclusion of international treaties, the "subjects" of the Russian Federation also have the right to establish their own "international and external economic relations" with foreign state.[93] This implies that the "subjects" of the Federation are granted limited treaty-making power, at least for matters over which they have exclusive jurisdiction.

Because the Constitution requires the Federation and its "subjects" to coordinate their activities regarding "the international and external economic relations of the subjects of the Russian Federation",[94] one might argue that when concluding treaties, the "subjects" of the Federation must consult the federal Government. While there are many examples of treaties signed by the "subjects" of the Federation with foreign states, the exact scope of the "subjects" treaty-making power is unclear.[95] Nor is it clear whether the "subjects" need the federal Government's formal consent to their treaties.[96]

2. The War Power

The 1993 Constitution's provisions on the use of armed force are

---

[93] Constitution, Art. 72 (n).

[94] Constitution, Art. 72 (n).

[95] The 1995 Law "On State Regulation of Foreign Trade Activity" (*supra* note 86) mentions only the right of the subjects to "conclude treaties in the sphere of foreign trade relations with *the subjects of foreign federative states and administrative territorial subdivisions of foreign states*" (Art. 8(7)) (Emphasis added - eds.). The 1996 Decree of the President No. 375 "On the Coordinating Role of the Foreign Ministry of the Russian Federation in Conducting a Unified Foreign Policy of the Russian Federation" also mentions only treaties of "the subjects of the Russian Federation with the subjects of foreign federative states and administrative territorial subdivisions of foreign states." *Sobranie*, No. 12, item 1061 (1996).

[96] The 1996 Decree of the President "On the Coordinating Role of the Foreign Ministry in the Implementation of a Single Foreign Policy of the Russian Federation" (*supra* note 95) requires the submission of the relevant draft treaties of the subjects for the approval of the Foreign Ministry.

rather vague. "Matters of war and peace" as well as "defense and security" fall under the jurisdiction of the federal Government.[97] The President, who serves as Commander in Chief of the Armed Forces, is authorized to declare martial law in cases of aggression against the Russian Federation or in cases of an imminent threat of aggression.[98]

Upon declaring martial law, the President must immediately inform both chambers of the Federal Assembly.[99] However, only the upper chamber of the parliament - the Federation Council - has the competence to review and confirm or reject the President's declaration of martial law.[100] According to Art. 102 of the Constitution the Federation Council also resolves questions concerning the possibility of engaging the Armed Forces beyond the territory of the Russian Federation.[101] A strict interpretation of this clause means that the President has no power to send troops abroad without the Federation Council's prior approval (This includes the use of troops in the UN peace-keeping operations).

Finally, the Constitution provides that the Federation Council must consider all federal laws adopted by the State Duma that pertain to "war and peace." Thus, any formal declaration of war appears to require the assent of both chambers of the Federal Assembly.

D. Federalism

1. Introduction

The disintegration of the Soviet Union raised the question whether Russia, the largest multinational republic of the former Soviet Union, would be able to preserve its unity. During its Soviet period, Russia was formally defined as a federal republic. In reality, however, it remained a highly

---

[97] Constitution, Art. 71 (j).

[98] Constitution, Art. 87 (2).

[99] Id.

[100] Constitution, Art. 102.

[101] In contrast, the Federation Council has no control over the use of the Armed Forces on the territory of Russia. Thus, in the case of Chechnya, the President ordered troops to Chechnya without consulting with the Federation Council. In the case of Chechnya, it was unclear whether military force may be used only following a formal declaration of martial law or a state of emergency. In ordering the use of force in this domestic situation, the President declared neither. The relevant decrees were subsequently upheld by the Constitutional Court. The Court held that, in the absence of specific legislation, the President could act freely. See *Chechnya Case*, *VKS*, 1995, No. 5, p. 3 (We will study this case *infra* p. 192-199).

centralized, unitary state that granted only limited powers to its autonomous republics and regions. The rise of national movements in different parts of Russia became the most significant political factor shaping its constitutional developments. While dealing with the many daunting economic, social and political problems, the newly independent Russia also faced a challenging task of reforming its federal structure to accommodate the desire of its constituent republics and provinces for national statehood and more independence.

Russia's reformers realized that building a democratic state involved not only introducing a democratic form of government, but also modifying the preexisting excessively centralized federal structures to disperse at least some power to its political subdivisions.

2. The Federal Treaty

Of particular importance for the creation of a new Russian federalism was the signing, on March 31, 1992, of the Federal Treaty between the federal authorities and the constituent republics, territories, regions, autonomous territories and areas ("the Federal Treaty").[102] The Federal Treaty, which President Yeltsin described as "a guarantee" that Russia would not fall apart,[103] was approved by the Congress of People's Deputies in the spring of 1992.[104] Subsequently, the Congress amended virtually all the clauses of the 1978 Constitution pertaining to federal matters, and incorporated the Treaty itself into the then existing Constitution.

The 1992 Federal Treaty (or, more precisely, three independent agreements between the Federal authorities and different subjects of the Federation)[105] brought significant changes in the allocation of powers between the federal Government and the "subjects" of the Russian Federation. The Treaty was given greater legal force than the norms of the then existing Constitution. All three agreements contained clauses providing that they were superior to the existing Constitution. Under the 1992 Treaty, any modification of the federal arrangement was possible only with the consent of the "subjects" of the Federation.

Despite the Federal Treaty's superiority to the Soviet era constitution,

---

[102] Note that two "subjects" of the Russian Federation - Chechnya and Tatarstan - refused to sign the Federal Treaty.

[103] See the statement of President Yeltsin, in *Rossiiskaya Gazeta*, April 15, 1992, p. 4.

[104] See *O federativnom dogovore* (On the Federal Treaty), *Vedomosty RF,* No. 17, item 898 (1992).

[105] See Constitution, Part II, Art. 1.

it does not enjoy that status vis-a-vis the 1993 Constitution. The Constitution enacted in 1993 modified some of the preexisting federal arrangements.

From a broad political-legal perspective, the most important modification that the 1993 Constitution made to the 1992 federal arrangement was to recognize the principle of constitutional equality for all "subjects" of the Federation. The 1992 Treaty had given different powers to different "subjects." Thus, national republics, which traditionally enjoyed *de jure* autonomy even during the Soviet period, had received more rights and privileges than Russian populated provinces and regions. In the early 1990's, however, Russian ethno-territorial units also began to assert greater control over their own affairs. This movement resulted in "equal rights" guarantee for all "subjects" of the Federation.[106] What differences exist between them[107] are largely symbolic.

The 1993 Constitution also expanded the powers of the Federation. It gave the Federation the power to establish "general principles of the organization of the system of organs of state power and local self-government."[108] Furthermore, it included matters concerning "personnel of judiciary and law enforcement agencies" within the concurrent jurisdiction.[109]

The 1993 Constitution also asserts its superior legal force over inconsistent provisions of the Federal Treaty. The Constitution provides that if the provisions of the Federal Treaty contravene the Constitution "the provisions of the Constitution of the Russian Federation shall apply."[110] The Constitutional Court confirmed this principle in the *Case Concerning the Forest Code of the Russian Federation.*[111]

3. Russia as a Federal State

The 1993 Constitution defines Russia as a "federal" state[112] composed of 89 national states (republics), national-territorial units (an autono-

---

[106] See Constitution, Art. 5.

[107] See Constitution, Arts. 5(2), 66 (1,2).

[108] Constitution, Art. 72 (m).

[109] Constitution, Art. 72 (k).

[110] Constitution, Part II, Art. 1.

[111] *Sobranie,* No.3, item 429 (1998)(The case involved a dispute over ownership of Russian forests. The Forest Code defines all Russian forests to be federal property. By referring to Art. III(3) of the Federal Treaty the Republic of Karelia claimed that forests on its territory belonged to Karelia. The Constitutional Court refused to apply the Federal Treaty because the Constitution of the Russian Federation "has supreme legal force.")

[112] Constitution, Art. 1.

mous region and autonomous areas) and administrative-territorial units (regions, territories and two federal cities).[113]

As noted earlier, all "subjects" of the Federation have equal rights and responsibilities. The Constitutional Court confirmed this principle in the *Case Concerning the Law On Road Funds of the Russian Federation.*[114] The challenged law allowed all "subjects" of the Federation to establish road funds. However, it did not grant this right to two federal cities - Moscow and Saint Petersburg, which are also considered to be "subjects" of the Federation. The Court held the law unconstitutional because under the Constitution "all constituent elements of the Russian state - republics, regions, provinces, federal cities, the autonomous region and autonomous districts are equal subjects of the Russian federation."

Autonomous areas also raise the question of equality of the "subjects." Traditionally autonomous areas were constituent parts of another "subject," a larger territory or region.[115] As a result, the territory of autonomous regions is considered part of the territory of another "subject" - territory or region.[116] The population of autonomous regions is also considered to be a part of the population of the larger "subject." Such an arrangement raises difficult questions of equality between autonomous regions within a territory or region and the respective territory or region of which it is a part.

Art. 66(4) of the Constitution contains only a general provision to the effect that "relations of autonomous areas that form part of a territory or region may be governed by federal law and a treaty between the organs of state power of the autonomous area and, respectively, the organs of state power of the territory or region." The Constitutional Court was asked to clarify the meaning of Art. 66(4) in the *Case Concerning Interpretation of Art. 66(4) of the Constitution of the Russian Federation.*[117] One of the principal questions put before the Court was whether the organs of state power of the territories or regions exercise jurisdiction over autonomous areas within their borders.

---

[113] Constitution, Arts. 5, 65.

[114] See *VKS,* 1996, No. 4, p. 23.

[115] One of the autonomous areas - the Chukchi Autonomous Area- seceded from the Magadan province. The Magadan province challenged the secession in the Constitutional Court. The Court held that Chukchi's secession did not violate any constitutional provisions. See *Case Concerning the Law of the Russian Federation On the Direct Entry of the Chukchi Autonomous Area into the Russian Federation, VKS,* 1994, No. 2/3, p. 54.

[116] For example, the Charter of the Irkutsk Province provides that the Ust-Orda Buryat Autonomous Area is a part of the Irkutsk Province. See Topornin, *supra* note 26, at 396.

[117] *Sobranie,* No. 29, item 3581 (1997).

While territories and regions believe that they have jurisdiction over "their" autonomous areas, the autonomous areas claimed that the inclusion of their territories in the territory of another "subject" of the Federation did not mean that they were under the jurisdiction of the territory or region. Autonomous areas believe that as equal subjects of the Federation they have an equal power with the respective territories or regions. Therefore their jurisdictional relationship with the "parent" territory or region can be established only on the basis of mutual consent or agreement. In a carefully drafted opinion, the Court noted that the principle of equality of all "subjects" of the Federation should also govern the relations between the autonomous areas and the respective territories and regions. While territories and regions exercise jurisdiction over autonomous areas because they are considered part of their territory, jurisdictional relationships between these "subjects" must be established on the basis of mutual consent. If the parties fail to reach mutually acceptable solution, the exact scope of the jurisdictional relationship between two "subjects" may be defined by the federal legislature in accordance with Art. 66(4) of the Constitution.[118]

4. The Division of Power Between the Federation and its "Subjects"

The division of power between the Federation and its "subjects" is based on the fundamental principle that the "subjects" of the Federation "enjoy full state power" in all areas that have not been expressly delegated to the Federation or defined as spheres of joint competence.[119] Art. 71 of the Constitution enumerates the competencies of the federal government, which include such traditional federal powers as foreign affairs, national defense and security, establishment of a single market, federal banks, the currency and federal taxes and levies. Art. 72 of the Constitution defines the rather broad concurrent jurisdiction of the Federation and its "subjects."

The grants of authority to the federal government differ significantly from those in the United States. The Russian Federation retains very expansive legislative powers. For example, the Federation retains exclusive jurisdiction over criminal, criminal-procedural, civil, civil-procedural and arbitration-procedural legislation. As a result, much of the Russian law is federal law. As noted earlier in Chapter II, all the major Russian codes, such as the Civil Code, the Civil Procedural Code, the Criminal Code, and the Criminal Procedure Code, are federal law. Almost all commercial law is federal law. Joint stock companies and other business entities are also governed by federal law.

---

118 Id.

119 Constitution, Art. 73.

At the same time it should be kept in mind that the "subjects" of the Russian Federation, which have a direct representation in the Federation Council, play an important role in the enactment of federal legislation. While the "subjects" of the Federation do not have much autonomous power to formulate their own policy in comparison to the states in the United States, they compensate this by their direct influence on the federal state. Unlike the United States Senate, the Federation Council represents the "subjects" of the Russian Federation in their corporate capacities. The members of the Federation Council are appointed by the legislative and executive organs of the "subjects." As a result, the "subjects" participate through the Federation Council in the legislation and administration of the Federation. "Subject's" direct participation in the enactment of federal laws is an important safeguard for their interests. Furthermore, most federal laws are carried out not by federal organs but by the "subjects" of the Federation.

An analysis of Arts. 71 and 72 of the Constitution indicates that, despite progress in the development of federalism, many fundamental questions are still unresolved. The list of joint powers is very long and vague.[120] The framers of the new federalism failed to clearly define jurisdiction of the Federation and its "subjects."

Arts. 71 and 72 also contain some unfortunate contradictions that inevitably create serious jurisdictional conflicts. For example, Art. 71 of the Constitution lists "regulation and protection of the rights and freedoms of the human being and citizen" among the exclusive powers of the Federation. However, Art. 72, which defines the joint jurisdiction of the Federation and its subjects, also mentions "protection of the rights of the human being and citizen."

Art. 76 of the Constitution further defines the jurisdictional relationships when it sets out the legislative and executive competence of the Federation and its constituent parts. On issues within the jurisdiction of the Federation, the federal parliament enacts federal laws that are binding on the entire territory of the Russian Federation.[121] On matters within the joint

---

[120] See Constitution, Art. 72.

[121] The Constitutional Court stated in one of its rulings, that the constituent republics should not reproduce in their own laws the provisions of federal laws on matters of exclusive federal jurisdiction because the latter had direct effect on the entire territory of the country. The Court added that "the confirmation of the validity of federal laws with respect to the territory of republics by special legislative acts of the republics contravenes the nature of the exclusive federal competence; furthermore, it is redundant from the point of view of the economy of legislative efforts and legislative technique." *Case Concerning the Law of the Kabardin-Balkar Republic On the Status of Judges, VKS*, 1994, No. 6, p. 29, 31-32).

jurisdiction, the Federation enacts federal laws and the "subjects" enact laws and other normative acts that are in accord with federal laws. Laws and other normative legal acts of the "subjects" in areas within the exclusive jurisdiction of the Federation or joint jurisdiction may not contravene federal laws. In areas of their exclusive jurisdiction, the "subjects" adopt laws and other normative acts. In case of a conflict, federal law prevails in areas of exclusive federal jurisdiction and joint jurisdiction. In areas of the subject's exclusive jurisdiction, their own regulation should prevail over contrary federal laws.

Disputes over these issues are to be settled by the Constitutional Court.[122]

5. Elements of Asymmetrical Federalism

An important feature of the emerging Russian federalism is flexibility. The 1993 Constitution provides that "the jurisdiction and powers of the organs of state power of the Russian Federation and the organs of state power of the subjects of the Russian Federation shall be delineated by this Constitution, the Federal Treaty and *other treaties on the delineation of jurisdiction and powers*"[123] (Emphasis added - eds.). This provision of the Constitution, then, allows the creation of asymmetrical federal arrangements through special bilateral agreements between the Federation and its "subjects." According to the Constitution, the federal executive organs may delegate some of their powers to executive organs of the "subjects," while the "subjects," in turn, may delegate some of their powers to federal authorities.[124] As a result, the real jurisdictional relationships between the Federation and its "subjects" largely depend on bilateral agreements, the content of which is determined by various extra-legal factors, such as the relative strength of the negotiating parties.

It is important to note, however, that conclusion of bilateral arrangements between the executive organs of the Federation and the executive organs of its "subjects" does not mean that Russian Federation turns into a federal state based solely on treaties. As the Constitutional Court has emphasized in the *Tatarstan Case,*[125] "the relations between Russia and its constituent republics are established on a constitutional basis." Treaties between the Federation and its "subjects" cannot change the fundamental constitutional provisions concerning the legal status of the "subjects" of the Federation as constituent parts of the federal state. Nor can they change the essentially

---

[122] Constitution, Art. 125.
[123] Constitution, Art. 11 (3).
[124] Constitution, Art. 78 (2,3).
[125] *VKS*, 1993, No. 1, p. 43.

constitutional basis of the relationship between the Federation and its "subjects." As Judge B.S. Ebzeev has noted, "the Constitution proclaims the principle of equality of the subjects of the Federation in their relations to each other; it does not proclaim their equality with respect to the federal state."[126] Art. 78 of the Constitution contemplates only the transfer of competencies between the federal *executive organs* and *the executive organs* of the "subjects" of the Federation. It follows that in principle asymmetrical arrangements can only affect the jurisdiction and powers of these organs of state power of the Russian Federation and the relevant organs of state power of the "subjects" of the Russian Federation. The fundamental constitutional provisions concerning federalism remain intact. A confirmation of this principle may be found in Art. 1 of Part II of the Constitution which provides that "should the provisions of the Federal Treaty. . . and other treaties between the federal organs of state power of the Russian Federation and the organs of state power of the subjects of the Russian Federation and treaties between the organs of state power of the subjects of the Russian Federation - contravene the Provisions of the Constitution of the Russian Federation, the provisions of the Constitution of the Russian Federation shall apply."

While under this constitutional doctrine the bilateral arrangements between the Federation and its "subjects" do not change the fundamental principles of their mutual relations, practice indicates that the matter is not that simple. Bilateral treaties between the federal authorities and some of the constituent units go much further than simple transfers of competencies between the executive organs.

The first constitutional arrangement distributing state power was concluded with Tatarstan[127] (Tatarstan did not sign the 1992 Federal Treaty and, instead, held a referendum on independence).[128] The 1994 "Agreement of the Russian Federation and of the Republic of Tatarstan on the Delineation of Competencies and Mutual Delegation of Powers Between the State Organs of the Russian Federation and the State Organs of the Republic of Tatarstan" recognized Tatarstan as a "state" that is "united with the Russian Federation." It established a special status of Tatarstan within the Russian Federation.

Since 1994, the Russian Federation has signed bilateral agreements

---

[126] B.S. Ebzeev, *Rossiiskii federalism I edinstvo konstitutsionnogo prostranstva* (The Russian Federalism and the Unity of the Constitutional Area), *v Konstitutsionnyi sud Rossiiskoi Federatsii. Postanovleniya, Opredeleniya 1992-1996* (The Constitutional Court of the Russian Federation. Decisions and Opinions 1992-1996) 506, 515 (1997).

[127] *Rossiiskaya Gazeta*, February 17, 1994, p. 6.

[128] For details, see Tatarstan Case *infra* p. 184-192.

with many other "subjects" of the Federation.[129] The draft treaty proposed to Chechnya (another national republic that rejected the 1992 Federal Treaty and since then has been trying to secede from Russia) would leave to federal authorities limited powers in a very few areas, including defense and security, currency policy and the issuance of money. The Tatarstan and Chechnya examples show that, despite the preeminence of fundamental constitutional arrangements concerning federalism, a greater differentiation of ties is emerging between the "subjects" of the Federation and the federal authorities. The new relationships range from federative to confederative or semi-confederative systems.

6. Local Self-Government

An analysis of the Russian federalism must take into account a large degree of autonomy granted to local governments. While the US Constitution says nothing about the relation between state and local governments, which are regarded as mere instrumentalities of the states, the Russian Constitution expressly guarantees local self-government.[130] Under Art. 12 of the Constitution "organs of local self-government shall not be part of the system of the organs of state power." Art. 131 of the Constitution provides that "local self-government shall be exercised in urban and rural settlements and in other localities taking into account historical and other local traditions. The structure of the organs of local self-government shall be determined by the population independently." According to Art. 130 of the Constitution, "local self- government in the Russian Federation shall ensure independent solution of questions of local importance, possession, use and disposal of municipal property by the population."

These provisions on local autonomy provide an additional guarantee against the concentration of governmental power. The Constitution protects local governments against limitations of their authority on the part of the Federation or the "subjects" of the Federation. In particular, the Constitution establishes judicial guarantees against federal or regional infringements on the right to local self-government.[131]

At the same time, under Art. 72(m) of the Constitution the Federation has retained the power to establish general principles of the organization of organs of "local self-government." The general principles of the organization of local self-government are defined by the 1995 Law "On General Principles

[129] For the texts, see B.A. Strashun, *Federal'noe konstitutsionnoe pravo Rossii* (Federal Constitutional Law of Russia) 219ff (1996).

[130] Constitution, Art. 12.

[131] Constitution, Art. 133.

of Organization of the Local Self-Government in the Russian Federation."[132] The 1995 Law became controversial because it established, among other things, certain time limits for the election of organs of the local-self-government. The President of the Russian Federation and the Head of Komi Republic challenged this provision of the Law in the Constitutional Court. The Head of the Komi Republic argued that determination of time limits for the elections of organs of local self-government falls within the jurisdiction of the "subjects" of the Federation. The President stated that this question should be resolved by the organs of local self-government themselves. He claimed that federal intervention in the matter violated Arts. 12, 130, 131 and 133 of the Constitution.

In its first opinion on the subject,[133] the Constitutional Court defined limits to the authority of the Federation to invade the prerogatives of local self-government. The Court found that regulation of the election procedure for the organs of local self-government and the establishment of the system of such organs fall under the jurisdiction of the "subjects" of the Federation and of local-self-government. At the same time, the Federation has the right to establish a framework for the realization of the right of the "subjects" and of local self-government to determine a specific date for the elections. This right stems from the clauses of Constitution concerning human rights. In establishing a time framework for local elections, the federal legislature implemented electoral rights of citizens guaranteed by the Constitution, such as the right of citizens to exercise their power through organs of local self- government[134] and the right to elect and to be elected to organs of local self- government.[135] The Court emphasized that under Art. 71(c) of the Constitution "the regulation and protection of the rights and freedoms of the human being and the citizen" fall under the jurisdiction of the Federation, and under Art. 72 "the protection of the rights and freedoms of the human being and the citizen" falls under the joint jurisdiction of the Federation and its "subjects." As a result, the federal legislature has the right to enact a federal law on the matter.

The constitutional right to local self-governments was also confirmed by the Constitutional Court in the *Case Concerning the Law of the Udmurd Republic On the System of Organs of State Power in the Udmurd Republic.*[136] In that case, initiated by the Russian President, a group of deputies of the State

---

[132] See *Sobranie*, No. 35, item 3506 (1995) (as amended *Sobranie*, No. 17, item 1917 (1996)).

[133] *Case Concerning Arts. 58(1) and 59(2) of the Law On General Principles of Organization of the Local Self-Government, VKS,* 1996, No. 3, p. 37.

[134] Constitution, Art. 3 (2).

[135] Constitution, Art. 32 (2).

[136] *VKS,* 1997, No. 1, p. 2.

Duma and a group of citizens of the City of Izhevsk (Udmurd Republic), the Constitutional Court held that the Udmurd Republic had violated provisions of the 1993 Constitution on self-government by establishing its administration in small cities and towns which enjoy the right to self-governance.

Because local governments are not authorized to file complaints to remedy infringements of their right to self-government to the Constitutional Court, the Supreme Court emerged as their principal protector. In the leading case, *Citizens of Uglitch v. Vice-Governor and Governor of the Yaroslavl Region,*[137] the Supreme Court stated that "according to Art. 12 of the Constitution of the Russian Federation, local self-government operates independently within the limits of its authority. The bodies of local self-government are not part of the system of the organs of state power. The appointment of the head of local administration by the head of the administration of the subject of the Russian Federation violates the self-governance of the territory and is an attempt to establish a local organ of state power; this violates Art. 130 (1) of the Constitution of the Russian Federation which ensures that people will independently resolve questions of local importance. . ."

7. Federal Disputes in the Constitutional Court

The implementation of federal principles in Russia faces a double challenge from traditional centralism, on the one hand, and separatist movements on the other. While the establishment of a true federation characterized by both union and diffusion of power will largely depend on the general distribution of political power in the country, it is also assisted by the judiciary playing a greater role in resolving conflicts between the federation and its "subjects." The Constitutional Court has attempted to assert itself as the principal forum for conflict resolution in several cases concerning the development of federalism.

Rulings of the Constitutional Court reproduced below address several important areas of the emerging Russian federalism.

(a) The Issue of Separatism

Both Tatarstan and Chechnya refused to sign the Federal Treaty and both republics have been pressing for more independence from the federal authorities. Although Tatarstan asserted its sovereignty, it did not declare full independence from Russia. In contrast, Chechnya insisted on recognition of its full and formal independence. When negotiations failed, the federal authorities

[137] BVS, 1995, No. 9, p. 1 (the decision of the Supreme Court in this case is reproduced *supra* p. 92-94.

decided to use armed force against Chechen separatists. Both situations were reviewed by the Constitutional Court which had to deal with extremely delicate questions of self-determination, state sovereignty and territorial integrity.

The Constitutional Court: *Tatarstan Case* (*VKS*, 1993, No. 1. p. 43)[138]

The proceedings were initiated. . . by petitions filed by the Supreme Soviet of the Russian Federation and a group of People's Deputies of the Russian Federation who requested a review of the constitutionality of . . . normative acts promulgated by the Supreme Soviet of the Republic of Tatarstan. . .

1) Art. 5 of the "Declaration on State Sovereignty of the Tatar SSR" . . . stated that it would serve as the basis for the drafting of Tatarstan's constitution and the development of its own legislation. . . Unlike similar declarations by other constituent republics of the Russian Federation, the Declaration on state sovereignty of Tatarstan does not mention that Tatarstan is a constituent republic of the Russian Federation.

The Law of the Tatar SSR "On Amendments and Additions to the Constitution (Fundamental Law) of the Tatar SSR". . ., adopted on the basis of the Declaration, changed the preamble and the titles of Section 6 and Arts. 64 and 70 of the Republic's Constitution and removed provisions that provided that Tatarstan was a constituent republic of the Russian Federation and that the laws of the Russian Federation prevailed over the laws of Tatarstan.

The removal, from the Constitution of Tatarstan, of the provision stipulating that the republic is a constituent republic of the Russian Federation infringes upon the legal status of republics established by Art. 78 of the Constitution of the Russian Federation and is a violation of Art. 71 of the Constitution of the Russian Federation, which defines Russia as a federation.

The rejection of the principle of supremacy of federal laws over the laws of the federation subjects contradicts the republics' constitutional status in a federative state and is an obstacle impeding the creation of a law-based state. The proclamation of the supremacy of the Constitution and laws of Tatarstan on its territory contradicts Art. 78 of the Constitution of the Russian Federation, which requires that the constitutions of the constituent republics of the Russian Federation should be in strict accord with the Constitution of the Russian Federation and Art. 81, according to which all the laws of the

[138] Note that this ruling was rendered on the basis of the 1978 Constitution.

Russian Federation enacted within its sphere of jurisdiction are binding on all constituent republics and have equal legal force on their territory. . .

The provision of Art. 64(2) of the Constitution of the Republic of Tatarstan under which Tatarstan structures its relationship with Russia and other republics on the basis of treaties is inconsistent with Art. 78(3) of the Constitution of the Russian Federation. The latter provides that a constituent republic within Russia shall have a constitution corresponding to the Constitution of the Russian Federation. . . It follows from this article that the relations between Russia and its constituent republics are established on a constitutional basis. This does not exclude, however, the possibility of signing treaties between them consistent with the Constitution. . .

2) The petitions raise the issue of constitutionality of Arts. 1 and 33 of the Law of Tatarstan "On Referendum in the Tatar SSR," adopted on November 29, 1991.

Art. 1 of this Law envisions the possibility of holding referendums on the most important issues of the Republic's state and social life. A constituent republic of the Russian Federation may resolve issues that fall within its jurisdiction in accordance with the delineation of jurisdiction between the federation and its constituent republics. However, only issues within the republic's sole jurisdiction may be submitted to a republic-wide referendum. . .

In accordance with Art. 33 of the Law of Tatarstan "On Referendum," a referendum proposal is adopted if it is supported by more than half of the people of Tatarstan who participated in the vote and if more than half of the republic's registered voters voted. Thus, the decision on any issue put up for a referendum, including proposals concerning the adoption of the constitution of Tatarstan and constitutional changes and amendments, may be adopted by only a fourth of the Republic's registered voters. However, under Art. 35 of the Law of the Russian Federation "On Referendum in the Russian Federation," proposals concerning the adoption of the constitutional amendments or additions are adopted only if more than half of the registered voters have voted in favor. . .

This inconsistency between the Law of Tatarstan and the Law of the Russian Federation "On Referendum" provides no grounds to conclude that Art. 81 of the Constitution of the Russian Federation, according to which federal laws prevail over inconsistent republican laws, has been violated. The referendum laws of Tatarstan and the Russian Federation have different subjects of regulation. The Russian Federation Law establishes rules and procedures only with regard to an All-Russian referendum. It has no provisions on referendums in the Russian Federation's constituent republics. . . Republics are independent in regulating procedures for republican referendums on issues falling within their jurisdiction. Within their jurisdiction, the legislative bodies of a republic are not obliged to adopt laws that would completely coincide with federal laws. Thus, even if there are inconsistencies between Tatarstan's Law "On Referendum" and the Russian Federation's Law "On Referendum," there are no grounds for concluding that the latter should prevail.

3) The petitions assert that the Supreme Soviet of the Republic of Tatarstan has exceeded its authority by adopting the resolution "On Holding a Referendum on the Legal Status of the Republic of Tatarstan," according to which the following question should be submitted to popular vote to be held on March 21, 1992: "Do you agree that the Republic of Tatarstan is a sovereign state and a subject of international law, which builds its relations with the Russian Federation and other republics on the basis of equal agreements?" ("Yes" or "No").

In adopting the aforementioned resolution, the Supreme Soviet of Tatarstan has exercised its constitutional power to organize a referendum. However, the resolution also serves as a means to establish major legal consequences. . . Hence, the aforementioned resolution is not only a law-applying act but also an act of normative significance which presages the direction and meaning of the law-making process. The normative character of this resolution is also determined by the consequences of its implementation - the direct influence of the results of the referendum on the future constitutional process in the Republic and Russia as a whole.

In evaluating the constitutionality of the aforementioned resolution, it is necessary to keep in mind that the Republic of Tatarstan has the right to submit to a vote the issue of its legal status, because this right follows from the right of peoples to self-determination. . .

The modern international system includes the right to self-determination among norms governing human rights and freedoms (Art. 1 of the International Covenant on Economic, Social and Cultural Rights and Art. 1 of the International Covenant on Civil and Political Rights of December 16, 1966, ratified by the Presidium of the Supreme Soviet of the USSR on September 18, 1973). In accordance with these international documents, all peoples are entitled to the right of self-determination and may "freely determine their political status and freely pursue their economic, social and cultural development;" and all states are obliged "to promote the realization of the right of self-determination and shall respect this right." Pursuant to the Declaration on Principles of International Law Concerning Friendly Relations and Cooperation Between States in Accordance With the Charter of the United Nations, adopted by the UN General Assembly on October 24, 1970, the right of self-determination is one of the fundamental principles of international law. This right may be exercised by such means as "the establishment of a sovereign and independent state, the free association or integration with an independent state or the emergence into any other political status."

In addition, Art. 29 of the Universal Declaration of Human Rights proclaims that, in the exercise of one's rights and freedoms, it is necessary to ensure due recognition and respect for the rights and freedoms of others. In accordance with Resolution 41/117 adopted by the UN General Assembly on December 4, 1986, the promotion and protection of one category of rights may not be used as a pretext or justification for the failure of a state to promote and ensure other rights. Otherwise, the implementation of any right, including the right to self-determination, will constitute an abuse of rights rather than the exercise of one's rights.

International documents also emphasize the inadmissibility of using references to the principle of self-determination to undermine the integrity and national unity of any state.

In dealing with the principle of equal rights and self-determination of peoples, the Declaration on Principles of International Law Concerning Friendly Relations and Cooperation Between States in Accordance With the Charter of the United Nations provides that nothing in this principle should be

> construed as authorizing or encouraging any action which would dismember or impair, totally or in part, the territorial integrity or political unity of sovereign and independent states conducting themselves in compliance with the principle of equal rights and self-determination of peoples. . . and possessed of a government representing the whole people belonging to the territory without any distinction as to race, creed or color. Every state shall restrain from any action aimed at the partial or total disruption of the national unity and territorial integrity of any other state or country.

Similar principles have been codified in the documents of the Conference on Security and Cooperation in Europe - the Helsinki Final Act signed in 1975, the 1986 Final Document of the CSCE follow-up meeting in Paris, the 1990 Document of the Copenhagen Conference for the CSCE Human Dimension, and other international legal documents.

Therefore, without denying the right of peoples to self-determination exercised by the people's free will, it is necessary to proceed from the requirement of international law that this right be accompanied by respect for the principle of territorial integrity and respect for human rights. . .

The Constitution of the Russian Federation does not provide for the right of republics to secede from the federation. Nor is this right guaranteed by the Constitution of Tatarstan. The unilateral exercise of such a right by the Republic of Tatarstan would be tantamount to recognizing the legitimacy of a total or partial disruption of the territorial integrity of a sovereign federative state and of the national unity of its peoples. Any actions disrupting such unity damage the constitutional system of the Russian Federation and are incompatible with international standards concerning human and peoples rights. . .

As part of Russia, in managing its legal relations with Russia, the Republic of Tatarstan has no right to change its political status unilaterally in violation of the Constitution of the Russian Federation. It must be recognized that the only legitimate and just way of settling this problem is a law-based negotiating process that would include all interested subjects of the Federation.

By submitting for popular vote the proposal concerning the legal status of Tatarstan in the version contained in the February 1992 resolution of its Supreme Soviet, Tatarstan failed to observe the requirement that referendum proposals must be worded clearly and unambiguously. Understanding the meaning of the proposal is also difficult because the preamble to the aforementioned Supreme Soviet resolution does not contain a clear-cut definition of the aim of the referendum.

In fact, the referendum proposal contains several questions to which only one answer is expected. Unable to answer each of these questions separately, voters are thereby deprived of the right to express their free will. This constitutes a breach of the right to take part in the discussion and adoption of laws and decisions of national importance guaranteed by Art. 42 of the Constitution of Tatarstan and Art. 46 of the Constitution of the Russian Federation.

The proposal's wording, indicating that the Republic of Tatarstan is a subject of international law and that the legal nature of treaties and agreements signed between the Republic of Tatarstan and the Russian Federation and those signed between the Republic of Tatarstan and other republics and states is the same, contradicts both the Constitution of the Russian Federation and the Constitution of Tatarstan; Tatarstan's relations with the Russian Federation and other constituent republics of the Russian Federation can only be structured on the basis of the Constitution of the Russian Federation and treaties based on the Constitution. This does not rule out the possibility that the constituent republics of the Russian Federation may participate in international relations. . .

For these reasons . . . the Constitutional Court of the Russian Federation finds:

(1) Art. 5 . . . of the 1990 "Declaration on State Sovereignty of the Tatar SSR," which restricts the operation of the laws of the Russian Federation on the territory of the Republic of Tatarstan, contravenes the Constitution of the Russian Federation. . .

(4) Art. 4 of the Law of Tatarstan "On Amendments and Additions to the Constitution (Fundamental Law) of the Tatar SSR" according to which relations between the Tatar SSR . . . and the Russian Federation and other republics are built on the basis of treaties with the Russian Federation and other nation-republics, is inconsistent with the Constitution of the Russian Federation insofar as it ignores constitutional foundations for the relations between Tatarstan and the Federation as a whole, because it effects unilateral change of the Russian Federation's national-state structure and implies that the Republic of Tatarstan is not part of the Russian Federation.

(5) Arts. 1 and 33 of the 1991 Law of the Tatar SSR "On Referendum in the Tatar SSR" . . . are consistent with the Constitution of the Russian Federation.

(6) The 1992 resolution of the Supreme Soviet of Tatarstan "On Holding a Referendum on the Legal Status of the Republic of Tatarstan" is incompatible with the Constitution of the Russian Federation insofar as the referendum proposal provides that Tatarstan is a subject of international law and builds its relations with the Russian Federation and other republics on the basis of equal treaties, because it is tantamount to a unilateral change in the national-state structure of the Russian Federation and implies that the Republic of Tatarstan is not part of the Russian Federation. . .

QUESTIONS AND COMMENTS

1. Tatarstan claimed that it had the right to secede from Russia because this right followed from the right of peoples to self-determination. Note that the 1993 Constitution declares in its preamble that "We, the multinational people of the Russian Federation. . . proceeding from the universally recognized principles of equality and self-determination of peoples. . . approve the Constitution of the Russian Federation." Does the Russian Constitution implicitly recognize the right of its constituent "subjects" to secede from Russia despite what the Constitutional Court says?

2. The right to self-determination is recognized in two manifestations: internal and external. Internal self-determination deals with the right of a people to effective participation in the institutional and social mechanisms of the existing state. External self-determination has traditionally been defined as the right to secede from the existing state. How did the Constitutional Court interpret the right to self-determination? Are there any limitations on this right under international law? Does international law recognize the right to "external" self-determination, i.e. full secession? If the right to secession is not recognized, what is left of the right to self-determination?

3. What was the Court's view the proposed referendum on independence? What is the authority for the Court's observation that "referendum proposals must be worded clearly and unambiguously"? What was the Court's answer to the claim that Tatarstan's law "On Referendum" contravened the Law of the Russian Federation "On Referendum in the Russian Federation"?

4. Tatarstan did not appear before the Court and ignored the Court's rulings. The successful outcome of its referendum on independence[139] strengthened its position vis-a-vis Moscow. Federal authorities chose not to take full advantage of the Court's decision and agreed to a series of negotiations aimed at concluding a bilateral treaty granting Tatarstan special status.

As noted earlier, the 1994 "Agreement of the Russian Federation and of the Republic of Tatarstan on the Delineation of Competencies and Mutual Delegation of Powers Between the State Organs of the Russian Federation and the State Organs of the Republic of Tatarstan" recognized Tatarstan as a "state" that is "united with the Russian Federation."

The real significance of the 1994 Agreement is evidenced by Art. II defining the exclusive jurisdiction of Tatarstan. Art. II states that the Republic of Tatarstan will:

1) ensure protection of human and civil rights and freedoms;

2) form the republican budget, impose and collect republican taxes;

3) make decisions on issues related to the bar and the notary public service;

---

[139] Of the participants in the referendum, 61.4 per cent voted in favor of the proposal to declare the Republic independent. *Rossiiskaya Gazeta*, March 24, 1994, p. 1.

4) exercise legal regulation of administrative, family, housing and environmental relations, and relations arising from the use of natural resources;

5) grant amnesty for persons convicted by courts of the Republic of Tatarstan;

6) make decisions on issues related to ownership, use and disposal of land, subsurface resources, water, forest and other natural resources, and state enterprises, organizations or other movable or immovable state assets located on the territory of the Republic of Tatarstan and being exclusive assets and property of the people of the Republic of Tatarstan, with the exception of federal property. Delineation of government property shall be regulated by a separate agreement;

7) establish a system of state organs of the Republic of Tatarstan, their organization and procedure for their activities;

8) make decisions on issues of republican citizenship;

9) establish a procedure for an alternative civil service on the territory of the Republic of Tatarstan for citizens entitled by the federal law to an alternative arrangement to military service;

10) establish and maintain relations and conclude agreements and treaties with Russian Federation republics, territories, regions, the autonomous region and autonomous areas, the cities of Moscow and St. Petersburg, to the extent that they do not contradict the Constitutions of the Russian Federation and the Republic of Tatarstan, this Agreement or other agreements between the governmental organs of the Russian Federation and the governmental organs of the Republic of Tatarstan;

11) take part in international relations, establish relations with foreign states and conclude agreements with them which shall not contradict the Constitution and international commitments of the Russian Federation, the Constitution of the Republic of Tatarstan and this Agreement, and take part in the activities of corresponding international organizations;

12) create a National Bank in accordance with a separate agreement;

13) independently pursue foreign economic activities. The delineation of powers in the sphere of foreign economic activities shall be based on a separate agreement;

14) make decisions in accordance with a separate agreement on issues of conversion of state-owned enterprises of the Republic of Tatarstan;

15) establish state awards and honorary titles of the Republic of Tatarstan.

Why is Art. II so important? What contribution does it make to the clarification of the jurisdictional relationship between the Russian Federation and Tatarstan?

5. What is the legal basis for the relations between Russia and Tatarstan after the signature of the 1994 Agreement? Are the relations still based on the Constitution or are they exclusively built on the basis of the bilateral Agreement?

The Constitutional Court: *Chechnya Case* (*VKS*, 1995, No. 5, p. 3)

The proceedings were initiated. . . by petitions filed by a group of deputies of the State Duma. . ., the Federation Council. . . and a group of deputies of the Federation Council. . ., which requested a review of the constitutionality of [several Decrees of the President ordering troops to Chechnya].

2) In 1991-1994, an extraordinary situation arose on the territory of the Chechen Republic, a subject of the Russian Federation. The validity of the Constitution of the Russian Federation and federal laws was denied, the system of legitimate organs of power was destroyed, regular unlawful armed formations were created and armed with the latest weaponry; and widespread violations of the rights and freedoms of citizens took place.

In the autumn of 1991, the legitimately elected Supreme Soviet of the Republic was dissolved. The new elections to the supreme organ of state power and the election of the president of the Republic, held on October 27, 1991 were declared illegitimate on November 2, 1991 by the Fifth Congress of People's Deputies of RSFSR, which also held that enactments of the new organs were not to be implemented. The determination that these events were unconstitutional and entailed grave consequences was set out in the Declaration of the Seventh Congress of People's Deputies of the Russian Federation of December 10, 1992, addressed to the people, the organs of power and Government of the Chechen Republic, and in other documents of the federal authorities. The decisions of the Congress were confirmed by the State Duma of the Federal Assembly, on December 23, 1994, in a statement in connection with the resolution on the situation in the Chechen Republic adopted by the European Parliament. The statement said that no free elections or referendums had been held in the Chechen Republic and legitimate organs of state power had disintegrated.

Subsequently, the political situation in the Chechen Republic continued to worsen. In the autumn of 1994, armed conflicts took place between feuding groups on its territory, which threatened to develop into a civil war.

This extraordinary situation historically stems from the fact that, in the period of Stalin's repressions, the Chechen people had been deported and the consequences of that deportation had not been properly rectified. State power, first in the USSR and then in Russia, has failed to correctly assess the legitimate bitter feelings among the Chechens, the developments in the Republic and the forces behind them. The federal organs of power of the Russian Federation relaxed their law enforcement activities in the Chechen Republic, failed to ensure the protection of the state ammunition dumps on its territory, and, for several years, exhibited passivity in addressing the problems with that Republic as a subject of the Russian Federation.

The Constitution of the Russian Federation, like the previous Constitution of 1978, does not contemplate a unilateral resolution of the issue of changing the status of a subject of the Federation and its secession from the Russian Federation. Under Art. 66(5) of the Constitution of the Russian Federation, the status of a subject of the Russian Federation may only be changed by mutual agreement between the Russian Federation and the subject of the Russian Federation, in accordance with federal constitutional law.

Territorial integrity is one of the foundations of the constitutional system of the Russian Federation. It is enshrined in Arts. 4(3), 5 (3), 8, 65, 67 (1), 71 of the Constitution of the Russian Federation. The integrity of the state is an important precondition for the equal legal status of all citizens, irrespective of their place of residence; and it is essential for preservation of their constitutional rights and freedoms.

The constitutional goal of preserving the integrity of the Russian state accords with the generally recognized international rules concerning the right of nations to self-determination. It follows the Declaration on Principles of International Law Concerning Friendly Relations and Co-operation Among States in Accordance With the Charter of the United Nations, adopted on October 24, 1970, that the exercise of the right to self-determination "shall not be construed as authorizing or encouraging any action which would dismember or impair, totally or in part, the territorial integrity or political unity of sovereign and independent states conducting themselves in compliance with the principle of equal rights and self-determination of peoples."

Mindful of this, federal authorities, the President, the Government and the Federal Assembly made repeated attempts to overcome the crisis in the Chechen Republic. However, their attempts did not lead to a peaceful political solution.

The Decrees of the Russian President of November 30, 1994, No. 2137, of December 9, 1994, No. 2166, and the Resolution of the Government of the Russian Federation of December 9, 1994, No. 1360, challenged by the Federation Council, prescribed the use of measures of state coercion to ensure the state security and territorial integrity of the Russian Federation, and to disarm the illegal armed formations on the territory of the Chechen Republic.

Under Art. 3(2) of the Federal Constitutional Law "On the Constitutional Court of the Russian Federation," the Constitutional Court of the Russian Federation does not consider the political correctness of these decisions or the appropriateness of the actions carried out based on those decisions. . .

4) The Decree of the President of the Russian Federation of December 9, 1994 No. 1-26 "On Measures to Repress the Activity of the Illegal Armed Formations on the Territory of the Chechen Republic and in the Area of the Ingush-Ossetian Conflict" authorized the Russian Federation Government, in realization of its powers according to Art. 114(1) of the Constitution of the Russian Federation, to apply all means at the disposal of the State to ensure State security, legality, citizens' rights and freedoms, and public order protection; to combat crime; and to disarm all illegal armed formations.

This Decree was addressed to the Government of the Russian Federation, and, by virtue of Art. 90(2)of the Constitution, was binding. According to it, the Government, within the limits of its constitutional powers, was charged to eliminate violations of Art. 13(5) of the Russian Constitution in the Chechen Republic; Art. 13(5) prohibits the activity of public associations whose activities are aimed at changing, by violent means, the fundamentals of the constitutional system, violating the integrity of the Russian Federation, or undermining the security and establishing armed formations. The Decree did not grant the Government any new powers that did not follow from the Constitution of the Russian Federation.

The petition of the Federation Council challenges the powers of the President of the Russian Federation to instruct the Government to use special measures, including the use of the armed forces, to protect, in accordance with

Arts. 80 and 82 of the Constitution, the fundamentals of the constitutional order, sovereignty and state integrity, since the use of the armed forces of the Russian Federation on its territory in extraordinary circumstances is allowed only within the framework of a state of emergency or a state of martial law sanctioned by the Federation Council. It does not follow, however, from the Constitution of the Russian Federation, that state integrity and constitutional order in extraordinary situations can be ensured only by means of declaring a state of emergency or martial law.

The constitutional grounds for the Decree of the President of the Russian Federation of December 9, 1994, No. 2166 are Art. 71(m), Art. 78(4), Art. 80(2), Art. 82, Art. 87(1) and Art. 90(3) of the Constitution of the Russian Federation. It follows from these norms that the President is obliged to take measures to protect the sovereignty of the Russian Federation, its independence, security and state integrity.

The President and the Government of the Russian Federation are to ensure the implementation of the powers of the federal state power throughout the territory of the Russian Federation, including. . . defense and security.

The Constitution of the Russian Federation determines, at the same time, that the President of the Russian Federation shall act in accordance with the procedure established by the Constitution. In cases where this procedure is not stated in detail, and also in respect to the powers not listed in Arts. 83 - 89 of the Constitution of the Russian Federation, the general framework of this procedure is determined by the principle of the separation of powers (Art. 10 of the Constitution) and the requirements of Art. 90(3) of the Constitution, according to which decrees and orders of the President may not contradict the Constitution and the laws of the Russian Federation. In addition to this, the implementation by the President of his competence in the manner stipulated by the Constitution of the Russian Federation also presupposes charging the Government of the Russian Federation, in accordance with Art. 114(1) of the Constitution, with the task of carrying out the decrees of the President. . .

5) In accordance with the principles of a law-governed state laid down by the Constitution of the Russian Federation, the organs of power are bound in their activities both by internal and international law. The generally recognized principles and norms of international law and international treaties are, under Art. 15 para. 4 of the Constitution of the Russian Federation, an integral part of its legal system and must be observed in good faith, including being taken into account by domestic legislation.

The Supreme Soviet of the USSR, in ratifying on August 4, 1989, the Additional Protocol to the Geneva Conventions of August 12, 1949, pertaining to the protection of the victims of armed conflicts that are not international in character (Protocol II), directed the Council of Ministers of the USSR to prepare and submit to the Supreme Soviet proposals on making corresponding amendments in the legislation. However, that direction was not carried out. Nevertheless, the provisions of this Additional Protocol on humane treatment of all the persons who were not directly involved in or have ceased to take part in hostilities, on the wounded, on the sick, on the protection of civilians, of objects needed for the survival of the civilian population, of the installations and structures containing dangerous forces, and on the protection of cultural values and places of worship, should be respected by both parties of the armed conflict.

At the same time, improper consideration of these provisions in the domestic legislation became one of the reasons for non-compliance with the rules of the above-mentioned Additional Protocol, according to which the use of force must be commensurate with the goals to be accomplished and every effort must be made to avoid causing damage to civilians and their property. . .

For these reasons. . . the Constitutional Court of the Russian Federation finds:

(2) Decree No. 2166 of the President of the Russian Federation of 9 December 1994 on measures to neutralize the activities of the unlawful armed militia on the territory of the Chechen Republic and in the zone of the Ossetian-Ingush conflict was adopted within the limits of the constitutional powers of the President of the Russian Federation. . . and conforms to the Constitution of the Russian Federation. . .

(5) The examination of specific actions of the parties in the course of the armed conflict from the point of view of compliance with the Additional Protocol to the Geneva Conventions of 12 August 1949 concerning protection of the victims of non-international armed conflicts (Protocol II), in accordance with Article 125 of the Constitution of the Russian Federation and Art. 3 para. 1, 2 and 3 of the Federal Constitutional Law on the Constitutional Court, may not be a subject for consideration by the Constitutional Court of the Russian Federation and should be performed by other competent organs.

In accordance with Arts. 52 and 53 of the Constitution of the Russian Federation, and with the International Covenant on Civil and Political Rights (Art. 2 para. 3), victims of any violations, crimes and abuses of power must be granted effective means of legal protection and compensation for damages caused.

(6) The Federal Assembly of the Russian Federation must revise the

legislation on the use of armed forces of the Russian Federation, as well as on the regulation of issues arising out of extraordinary situations and conflicts, including those arising from the Additional Protocol to the Geneva Conventions of August 12, 1949, concerning protection of the victims of non-international armed conflicts (Protocol II). . .

Dissenting Opinion of Judge A.L. Kononov

6) The arguments, presented by the party that issued the enactments, that the measures taken were expedient and entirely indispensable, cannot be considered as convincing.

The decisions contained in the enactments are substantiated mainly by the necessity to protect the sovereignty, territorial integrity, constitutional order, state security and other state interests. Human rights are placed at the bottom of this list. But one should not think of these as belonging to the same order. Art. 2 of the Constitution of the Russian Federation unambiguously and explicitly considers the human being, his or her rights and freedoms to be of prime value. This basic distinctive principle of the present Constitution has been ignored in favor of state preferences.

The principle of territorial integrity cannot be an insurmountable obstacle for the right of the people to self-determination. Being one of the fundamental rights, and prefacing the 1966 International Covenant on Civil and Political Rights, the right of people to self-determination is not attended here with any provisos or restrictions; this right is actually implemented in international practice and reflects the progressive historical tendency; by virtue of Art. 15(4) of the Constitution of the Russian Federation it is incorporated into the system of fundamental constitutional rights. Both Art. 3, through the principle of democracy, and Art. 66, contemplating the possibility of changing - in due order - the status of a subject of the Russian Federation, directly express this right. It is reasonable to suggest that territorial integrity should not be established by force, contrary to the lawfully expressed desire of a people for self-determination, and that the conflict should be settled in a civilized manner and to the advantage of the people. . .

QUESTIONS AND COMMENTS

1. The *Chechnya Case* dealt with an extremely controversial decision to use military force to stop the Chechen rebellion against Russian Federation rule. Was it appropriate for the Constitutional Court to review the decision of the President to use force in view of the fact that the decision to send troops was made on purely political grounds?

2. What was the constitutional basis for the decision to use armed force in Chechnya? It is claimed that in domestic situations armed force may be used only following a declaration of martial law or a state of emergency. However, in the case of Chechnya, the President did neither. Why did the Court uphold the validity of the presidential Decree envisioning use of armed force?

How did the ruling of the Court affect the separation of powers in Russia?

3. What is the legal status of Chechnya according to the ruling of the Constitutional Court?

4. The Court acknowledged that the legal status of a subject of the Russian Federation may be changed. How might this be accomplished?

5. Although the Constitutional Court did not dismiss allegations about human rights violations in Chechnya, it refused to discuss them in any detail. According to the Constitutional Court, which courts have jurisdiction over these claims?

Note, however, that the Court did condemn violations of international humanitarian law. From a legal perspective, what was the major reason for numerous violations of humanitarian norms during the Chechen conflict? How might similar violations be avoided in the future?

6. What is Judge Kononov's point in dissent? Do you agree with it?

7. On August 31, 1996 the federal authorities and the Chechen leaders reached a peace accord. Russia withdrew its troops from the region in exchange for an agreement to postpone deciding the issue of independence until 2001. However, the Chechen leaders continue to press for the Chechen Republic of Ichkeria [the Chechen name for the region] to be recognized as a fully independent and sovereign state. Although the Russian leaders are ready to negotiate a long-term political deal with Chechnya, they made it clear that they would stop short of granting the region full formal independence. They would like to propose only an arrangement granting extensive autonomy. Chechen leaders counter that their demand for formal independence is merely a question of granting official recognition to the reality that the Chechen government is already fully in control of the territory.

8. Since Russian military withdrawal, federal laws have no force within the separatist republic. The Chechen Republic of Ichkeria has established "Islamic courts" which apply rules of traditional Muslim criminal law. These courts impose severe punishments, such as public executions by firing

squads. The Russian government strongly protested the first public execution. Some executions were canceled reportedly because of the possible negative reaction of the international community.

9. The reaction of the international community is an important factor in Chechnya's struggle for independence. However, traditionally states have refrained from recognizing separatist movements as independent states until their full victory has been assured. So far not a single foreign state has recognized Chechnya's independence from Russia.

(b) Governmental Structure of the "Subjects"

As noted earlier, the 1993 Constitution expanded the powers of the Federation. Among other things, it gave the Federation the power to establish by legislation "general principles of the organization of the system of organs of state power."[140] This extension of federal power was a political-legal reaction to certain negative developments in the constituent republics, some of which attempted to restore a Soviet system of government. Thus, in 1993, the communist-dominated parliament of the Mordovian SSR removed from office the popularly elected president of the Republic by introducing constitutional amendments that abolished the President's post. President Yeltsin intervened by claiming that the local parliament violated the principles of popular rule and the separation of powers. However, in the *Mordovian SSR Case*[141] the Constitutional Court held that Yeltsin's intervention violated the then existing federal arrangements. The Court stated that

> the Constitution of the Russian Federation in its April 21, 1992 edition and the [Federal] Treaty. . . do not assign the establishment of the system of governmental organs of the republics either to the jurisdiction of the Russian Federation or to the joint jurisdiction of the Russian Federation and its constituent republics. For this reason, the republics may independently resolve issues pertaining to the establishment or modification of the system of their organs of state power. . .

Despite its power to establish principles for organization of government in the constituent "subjects," the federal legislature never exercised that power through legislation. When the Altai Region made changes in its government structure, the question arose whether the 1993 Constitution itself imposed limits on the type of governmental structure a region could have. The following case deals with this question.

---

[140] Constitution, Art. 72 (m).

[141] See *VKS*, 1994, No. 4/5, p.21.

The Constitutional Court: ***Case Concerning the Charter (Fundamental Law) of the Altai Region*** (*VKS*, 1996, No. 1, p. 13)

5) The petitioner [the administration of the Altai Region] challenges the constitutionality of Art. 77 of the Charter, which provides that activities of the Legislative Assembly cannot be suspended or terminated by the decision of any organ of state power of the Russian Federation or of the Region; under the Charter, suspension of the activities of the Legislative Assembly, as well as of its permanent committees and commissions, is possible only on the basis of a decision adopted by the Legislative Assembly itself; termination of the powers of the Legislative Assembly is possible only upon expiration of the powers of its deputies or, in certain defined situations, on the basis of a decision adopted by the Legislative Assembly.

The petitioner believes that the provisions of this clause put the Legislative Assembly outside the jurisdiction of the Russian Federation. . .

However, the Constitution of the Russian Federation does not provide for the right of the federal organs of state power to terminate or disrupt the activities of the legitimately elected representative organs of the subjects of the Federation; there is a presumption that their activities conform to the Constitution and legislation of the Russian Federation. The Constitution of the Russian Federation and federal laws provide that disputes over competence between organs of legislative power of the Russian federation and its subjects are to be settled by the use of conciliation procedures, recourse to the relevant courts and other legal mechanisms. . .

6) The petitioner contends that Arts. 81(3), 82(1), 83(2), 84(2), 85 and 87(2) of the Charter contain provisions that upset the balance of powers in favor of the legislative branch by unlawfully restricting the powers of the executive branch. The petitioner mentions the following provisions: the head of the administration is elected by the Legislative Assembly; the Legislative Assembly determines the structure of the administration's Council, appoints principal executive officers of the administration and may express non-confidence in them, may remove from office not only the head of the administration but also many other executive officers of the administration, in particular the first deputy head of the administration and heads of regional organs of internal affairs, justice, finance, social security and state property management; every year the head of the administration must submit to the Legislative Assembly a report on his activities and activities of the executive power of the Region.

The constitutional principle of the unity of state power requires that the subjects of the Russian Federation in principle follow the federal scheme of the relationship between the executive and legislative power. Because, pursuant to the Constitution of the Russian Federation, legislative and executive branches of power are independent, it is inadmissable to go beyond the limits defined by the Constitution and adopt Charter rules that subordinate the executive power to the representative organ. That would violate Art. 77(2) of the Constitution of the Russian Federation because it hampers implementation of the requirement that, on certain matters within their competence, federal organs of executive power and the organs of executive power of the subjects of the Russian Federation form a single system of executive power.

The Constitution of the Russian Federation does not expressly determine the procedure for the election of the heads of the executive organs of state power of the subjects of the Russian Federation. However, it provides that the people exercise their power directly as well as through organs of state power (Art. 3(2)). It follows from the meaning this provision (taken in conjunction with Art. 32 of the Constitution, which guarantees the right of citizens to elect organs of state power) that the highest official who forms the organ of executive power must receive his mandate directly from the people and be responsible to them. Because the federal structure of the Russian Federation is based upon the uniform system of state power (Constitution, Art. 5(3)), organs of state power of the subjects of the Federation should be formed on the basis of the same principles as the federal organs. . .

The formation of the executive power of the subject of the Russian Federation on the basis of direct elections of the heads of administrations is envisioned by the majority of charters adopted by the subjects of the Russian Federation. The Charter of the Altai Region provides for a different procedure: the head of the administration is elected by the Legislative Assembly. . . As a result, the Legislative Assembly has been turned into a kind of electoral college, the decisions of which replace the direct manifestation of the will of the electorate. This procedure does not conform to the Constitution of the Russian Federation and existing legislation. The head of the administration elected in accordance with such a procedure cannot be considered a legitimate and independent representative of the executive power, because neither the legislative nor the executive power have the right to determine for each other their representatives, including representatives in federal organs. . .

For these reasons. . . the Constitutional Court finds:

(2) The following rules of the Charter (Fundamental Law) of the Altai Region do not conform to the Constitution of the Russian Federation: . . . 81(3), 82(1), 83(2). . .

QUESTIONS AND COMMENTS

1. By 1996 the Russian parliament failed to adopt a federal law on the general principles of the organization of the system of organs of state power in the constituent "subjects." As a result, the Constitutional Court had to base its ruling on certain general constitutional principles. Do you agree with the Court's reasoning that the principle of the uniform system of state power (Constitution, Art. 5 (3)) necessarily requires that "organs of state power of the subjects of the Federation should be formed on the basis of the same principles as the federal organs"? Does the Constitution require any particular form of government in the "subjects"?

2. What type of government structure was established in the Altai Region? How did it differ from the government structure of the Russian Federation?

3. Do you agree with the Court's reasoning that Arts. 3(2) and 32 of the Constitution require that the highest officials of the "subjects" (the head of administration or the governor) "must receive his mandate directly from the people"?

4. In the *Case Concerning the Charter (Fundamental Law) of the Tambov Region* (*Sobranie*, No. 51, item 5877 (1997)) the President of the Russian Federation challenged the constitutionality of a provision of the Charter of the Tambov Region which required the consent of the regional legislative assembly (Duma) for appointment of first deputies of the Head of the Administration of the region. The President argued that this procedure violated the principle of separation of legislative and executive powers. However, the Constitutional Court found that the challenged procedure did not "contravene the principle of separation of powers in the Russian Federation and independence of the legislative and executive organs" (Constitution, Art. 10).

5. The Constitutional Court had to deal with the electoral system in one of the "subjects" in the *Case Concerning Arts. 74 and 90 of the Constitution of the Republic of Khakasiya* (*Sobranie*, No. 26, item 3145 (1997)). The Constitution of the Republic of Khakasia established that a candidate for the position of deputy of the local legislature must reside in the republic for at least five years. The candidate for the post of the Chairman of the Government of the Republic of Khakasiya must have permanent residency in the republic for at least seven years. The President of the Russian Federation challenged these provisions in the Constitutional Court. He claimed that residency requirements violated several constitutional provisions, including the non-discrimination clause (Art. 19 (2)) and the right of citizens to

elect and to be elected to organs of state power (Art. 32 (2)). The Constitutional Court held that Khakasiya's residency requirements violated the principles of equality and non-discrimination.

(c) Delineation of Jurisdiction Between the Federation and its "Subjects"

The Constitutional Court: ***Case Concerning Temporary Regulations On Protecting the Activities of Deputies of the Kaliningrad Regional Duma*** (*VKS*, 1995, No. 6, p. 42)

1) Arts. 23 and 24 of the Temporary Regulations On Protecting the Activities of Deputies of the Kaliningrad Regional Duma, adopted by the ruling of the Kaliningrad Regional Duma of July 8, 1994, provide for immunity of the deputies of the Kaliningrad Regional Duma in the sphere of criminal, criminal-procedural, administrative and administrative-procedural law, and establish special prerequisites for bringing criminal and administrative charges, as well as other exceptions from the general rules of criminal, criminal-procedural, administrative and administrative-procedural legislation, including those concerning the procedure for detention, arrest, search, personal search and interrogation; according to the Regulations, all these measures with respect to deputies may be undertaken only with the consent of the Duma. . .

2) According to Art. 71(n) of the Constitution of the Russian Federation, criminal, criminal-procedural and criminal-executive legislation falls within the jurisdiction of the Russian Federation. Pursuant to Art. 76(1) of the Constitution of the Russian Federation, federal laws on matters within the jurisdiction of the Russian Federation are adopted which have direct effect throughout the entire territory of the Russian Federation. Art. 76(5) provides that laws and other normative legal acts of the subjects of the Russian Federation may not contravene federal laws adopted in areas falling within the jurisdiction of the Russian Federation; in the case of a conflict between a federal law and another act issued in the Russian Federation, the federal law must apply.

Because, in the above-mentioned areas, the subjects of the Federation can not enact their own law-making acts, the Kaliningrad Regional Duma had no right to alter the criminal legal status of its deputies. . .

3) According to Art. 72(1)(j) of the Constitution of the Russian Federation, administrative and administrative-procedural legislation falls within the joint jurisdictions of the Russian Federation and subjects of the Russian Federation. On these matters, federal laws are issued and, in

accordance with them, laws and other normative legal acts of the subjects of the Russian Federation are adopted (Constitution, Art. 76(2)). The establishment of general principles of the organization of the system of organs of state power and local self-government, including, therefore, principles concerning the status, rights and obligations of deputies of the legislative (representative) organ of the subjects of the Russian Federation, also fall within the joint jurisdiction of the Federation and its "subjects" (Constitution, Art. 72(1)(m)).

The absence of the relevant federal law on matters falling within this joint jurisdiction is not, in itself, a bar to the Kaliningrad Duma adopting its own normative act; this follows from the meaning of Arts. 72, 76(2) and 77(1) of the Constitution of the Russian Federation, as well as from the nature of joint jurisdiction.

However, legislation on questions of joint jurisdiction must be enacted in accordance with Chapter 1 of the Constitution of the Russian Federation, which defines the fundamentals of the constitutional system, as well as in accordance with other constitutional provisions and the system of federal legal acts that are based on the Constitution and develop and define its provisions.

The solution of the question of deputies' immunity in the field of administrative responsibility and other administrative measures contemplated by Arts. 23 and 34 of the Temporary Regulations affects not only the organization of the system of organs of state power of the subject of the Russian Federation, but also the principles, fundamental provisions and institutions of administrative law and administrative responsibility; in fact, these matters must be classified as foundations of administrative law established by existing federal legislation. Exceptions from these regulations in the above-mentioned areas cannot be established by an act of a subject of the Federation. Art. 76(2,5) of the Constitution provides that laws and other normative legal acts of the subjects of the Russian Federation adopted in areas of joint jurisdiction are to be issued in accordance with federal laws and may not contravene them.

Consequently, by contemplating for its deputies exceptions from the existing rules of federal legislation concerning administrative offenses and administrative responsibility, Arts. 23 and 24 of the Temporary Regulations contravene the delineation of jurisdiction and competencies between organs of state power of the Russian Federation and organs of state power of its subjects established by the Constitution. . .

For these reasons. . . the Constitutional Court finds:

(1) Arts. 23 and 24 of the Temporary Regulations On Ensuring the

Activities of Deputies of the Kaliningrad Regional Duma, adopted by the ruling of the Kaliningrad Regional Duma of July 8, 1994, do not conform to the Constitution of the Russian Federation. . .

QUESTIONS AND COMMENTS

1. What are the principal issues of the jurisdiction of the Federation and its "subjects" raised by this case?

2. What are the limits of the power of the constituent "subjects" to enact their own legislation in areas of joint jurisdiction?

3. Many disputes concerning allocation of jurisdiction arise in cases when a particular subject matter is not mentioned in Art. 71 of the Constitution, defining the exclusive powers of the Federation, or Art. 72, dealing with areas of joint jurisdiction. For example, neither Art. 71, nor Art. 72 mention regulations concerning advertising. One may therefore argue that this area falls within the jurisdiction of the "subjects" of the Federation.

In the *Case Concerning the Federal Law On Advertising* (*VKS*, 1997, No. 1, p. 54) the City of Moscow claimed that the federal law on advertising was unconstitutional because this area of activity falls within the jurisdiction of the "subjects" of the Federation. However, the Constitutional Court found that advertising activities are essentially entrepreneurial and therefore must be regulated by "civil legislation." The challenged federal law on advertising was found constitutional because under Art. 71(n) of the Constitution civil legislation falls within the exclusive jurisdiction of the Russian Federation.

The Constitutional Court: *Case Concerning Arts. 18(2) and 20 of the Law of the Russian Federation On the Fundamentals of the Tax System in the Russian Federation* (*Sobranie*, No. 13, item 1602 (1997))

[The 1991 Law of the Russian Federation "On the Fundamentals of the Tax System in the Russian Federation" establishes the general principles of taxation and levies in the Russian Federation. It also defines the tax powers of the federal government and the "subjects" of the Russian Federation. The Law is based on the principle that anything taxed by the Federation is exempt from further taxation by the "subjects." For example, because there is a federal value-added tax, the subjects may not impose any value-added taxes. Furthermore, the 1991 Law establishes an exhaustive list of all possible taxes. It provides that no governmental organ on any level may introduce taxes that are not provided for by the federal law. As a result, the Law imposes far-reaching restrictions on the tax power of the "subjects" of the Russian Federation. Several "subjects" challenged the Law in the Constitutional Court]

1. The petitioners [Komi Republic, Altai Region, Irkutsk, Vladimir and Volgograd provinces] believe that the provisions of Arts. 18 and 20 of the Law of the Russian Federation On the Fundamentals of the Tax System in the Russian Federation contravene Art. 72(I) of the Constitution of the Russian Federation (according to which the establishment of general principles of taxation and levies in the Russian Federation falls within the joint jurisdiction of the Russian Federation and its subjects) because the above Law does not provide for any powers of the organs of state power of the subjects of the Russian Federation to introduce taxes and levies. . .

2. In accordance with the Constitution of the Russian Federation the establishment of general principles of taxation and levies in the Russian Federation falls within the joint jurisdiction of the Russian Federation and its subjects (Art. 72(I)); the system of federal taxes and the general principles of taxation and imposition of levies in the Russian Federation are determined by the federal law (Art. 75(3)). At present this law is the Law of the Russian Federation On the Fundamentals of the Tax System in the Russian Federation. . . This Law defines the legal content of the constitutional provision concerning the general principles of taxation and levies. Under Art. 76(2) of the Constitution of the Russian Federation the laws of the subjects of the Russian Federation on this question of joint jurisdiction must be enacted in accordance with the above Law. . .

3. Those principles of taxation and levies which are determined by the provisions of the Constitution of the Russian Federation fall under the jurisdiction of the Russian Federation in accordance with Art. 71(a) of the Constitution. They include the insurance of a uniform financial policy, which includes a uniform tax policy, a uniform system of taxes, equal tax burden and the establishment of tax exemptions only on the basis of a statute.

The principle of a uniform financial policy, including a uniform tax policy, and the unity of the tax system is laid down in several clauses of the Constitution of the Russian Federation, first of all in Art. 114(1)(b) according to which the Government of the Russian Federation ensures the implementation in the Russian Federation of a uniform financial, credit and monetary policy.

These provisions implement one of the fundamental principles of the constitutional order of the Russian Federation - the unity of Russia as a single economic unit (Art. 8(1)), which, among other things, means that no customs frontiers, duties, levies or any other barriers for the free movement of goods, services and financial resources may be established on the territory of the Russian Federation (Art. 74(1)) and that restrictions on the movement of goods and services may be imposed in accordance with the federal law if this is necessary for ensuring security, the protection of lives and health of people, the protection of the environment and cultural values (Art. 74(2)).

It follows from these constitutional provisions that the imposition of taxes which would disrupt the unity of the Russian Federation as a single economic unit is not permissible. From this perspective, it is inadmissable to establish regional taxes which may directly or indirectly restrict free movement of goods, services and financial resources within the single economic unit; nor is it permissible to impose regional taxes which allow one region to form its budget at the expense of another or to impose the payment of taxes on the taxpayers of another region. . .

The principle of equal tax burdens follows from Arts. 8(2), 19 and 57 of the Constitution of the Russian Federation. In the sphere of tax relations it means that it is inadmissable to establish additional as well as increased taxes depending on the form of ownership, organizational forms of entrepreneurial activities, place of residence of the taxpayer or any other discriminatory basis.

The principle according to which taxes are introduced by statutes is laid down in Art. 57 of the Constitution of the Russian Federation. In the light of these constitutional provisions, "lawfully established" taxes of the subjects of the Russian Federation are only those taxes which are introduced by the legislative organs of the subjects of the Russian Federation in accordance with the general principles of taxation and levies defined by the federal law.

Consequently, it follows from the Constitution of the Russian Federation (in particular, from its provisions concerning equality of rights and freedoms of the human being and citizen, the prohibition of their restrictions except by the federal law, the single economic sphere, the guarantee of free movement of goods, services and financial resources, the recognition and protection by the state of all forms of ownership, freedom of economic activity, the principle of a uniform financial, including tax, policy and unity of the tax system, the introduction of taxes only by statute, and the equal tax burden principle) that the general principles of taxation and levies serve as one of the principal guarantees established by the law which ensure the realization and implementation of the fundamentals of the constitutional system, fundamental rights and freedoms of the human being and citizen and principles of federalism in the Russian Federation.

These constitutional principles form the basis for the delineation of powers in the tax sphere, which to that extent fall under the jurisdiction of the Federation.

4. It follows from Arts. 71(h), 73 and 132(1) that taxes and levies are introduced by the federal organs of state power, by the organs of state power of

the subjects of the Russian Federation and by the organs of local self-government. The federal legislature introduces federal taxes and levies in accordance with the Constitution of the Russian Federation and independently defines not only the list of taxes but also all elements of tax obligations.

With respect to the subject of the Russian Federation and organs of local self-government the notion "introduction of taxes and levies" assumes a different legal meaning. The question of the imposition of local taxes is beyond the scope of the present case. As far as the introduction of taxes and levies by the organs of state power of the subjects of the Russian Federation is concerned, it must be carried out in accordance with the Constitution of the Russian Federation, which has direct effect, and in accordance with the general principles of taxation and levies established by the federal statute. The right of the subjects of the Russian Federation to introduce taxes is always secondary because the subjects of the Russian Federation are bound by these general principles.

The right to introduce taxes granted to the organs of state power of the Russian Federation by the Constitution of the Russian Federation can be understood only by taking into account the fundamental rights of the human being and citizen set forth in Arts. 34 and 35 of the Constitution of the Russian Federation and the constitutional principle of the single economic unit. In view of the need to establish a balance between these constitutional values, tax policy always aims at equalization of taxes. This goal is also pursued by the general principle of taxation and levies which provides that the list of regional taxes introduced by the organs of state power of the subjects of the Russian Federation is exhaustive; this principle imposes limitations on the introduction of additional taxes and mandatory payments; it also limits the opportunities for increasing taxes and tax payments. In the current legislation this principle is set forth in the [challenged] Arts. 18(2) and 20(2) of the Law of the Russian Federation On the Fundamentals of the Tax System in the Russian Federation.

5. It follows from Arts. 5(2,3), 72(1)(I) and 76(2) of the Constitution of the Russian Federation, that the regulation of regional taxes established by federal laws creates a framework; the federal legislation must be further developed by the legislature of the relevant subject of the Russian Federation.

Because an exhaustive list of regional taxes creates only the right and not the obligation to introduce taxes, the right of the subject of the Russian Federation to introduce taxes means that it has the right to decide whether or not to introduce the relevant tax on its territory. The introduction of a regional tax also implies concrete definition of the general legal standards, including a detailed regulation on the subjects and objects of taxation, on the procedures and time limits for the payment of taxes, on tax privileges, methods for the calculation of specific tax payments (differentiated, progressive or regressive) etc.

Because the challenged provisions of Arts. 18(2) and 20(2) of the Law of the Russian Federation On the Fundamentals of the Tax System in the Russian Federation do not impose any restrictions on the right of the subjects of the Russian Federation to enact local laws in accordance with the general principles of taxation and levies, they conform to the Constitution of the Russian Federation. . .

QUESTIONS AND COMMENTS

1. The ruling of the Constitutional Court in the present case became a milestone in the Federation's struggle to put an end to the constituent "subject's" relentless pursuit of new revenues for local budgets. It expresses concern that divergent tax schemes in different "subjects" might disrupt the operation of the national market.

2. Although the Constitution expressly states that "the establishment of general principles of taxation and levies in the Russian Federation" falls within the joint jurisdiction of the Russian Federation and its "subjects" (Art. 72 (1)), the Constitutional Court held that certain fundamental questions concerning taxes fall within the exclusive jurisdiction of the Russian Federation. What were the principal legal-political arguments developed by the Court in support of this proposition?

Do you agree with these arguments? How does the ruling of the Court affect the tax power of the "subjects" of the Federation? What are the practical consequences of this ruling? In light of this case, what is an example of a permissible local tax? What is an example of an impermissible local tax?

What are the broader implications of the ruling for our understanding of the present federal arrangement in the Russian Federation?

3. Both the Constitutional Court and the Supreme Court had to deal with several specific cases of local taxes violating the general principles of taxation. In the *Case Concerning Art. 2 and 4 of the Law of the Moscow Region On Taxes On New Residents* (*Sobranie*, No. 27, item 3304 (1997)) the Constitutional Court declared unconstitutional local taxes imposed by the Moscow Region authorities on citizens who decided to take up residence in the area. These local taxes were unconstitutional because they were not envisioned by the list of admissible regional taxes included in the 1991 Law of the Russian Federation On the Fundamentals of the Tax System in the Russian Federation. The Court noted that "the legislative organs of the subjects of the Russian

Federation introducing their own taxes and levies must take into account that, according to Art. 75(3) of the Constitution of the Russian Federation, both the system of federal taxes and the general principles of taxation and levies in the Russian Federation are established by federal law; therefore, they have the right to introduce taxes and levies only within limits of the list of regional taxes and levies included in the Law of the Russian Federation On the Fundamentals of the Tax System in the Russian Federation."

The Supreme Court declared unlawful and therefore invalid local taxes introduced by the Altai Regional Legislative Assembly on all local companies "for the purposes of financial support of the agricultural production in the Region" (See *Joint-Stock Company Altai-Koks v. The Altai Regional Legislative Assembly*, *BVS*, 1997, No. 2, p. 1). The Supreme Court noted that the Altai Regional Legislative Assembly violated the federal law - the 1991 Law of the Russian Federation On the Fundamentals of the Tax System in the Russian Federation - according to which regional authorities "have no right to introduce additional taxes and levies not envisioned by the legislation of the Russian Federation."

4. In these cases both the Constitutional Court and the Supreme Court acted on the theory that an act of the "subject" of the Russian Federation that violates the requirements of a federal statute also violates the Constitution. This "indirect" review of constitutionality allows courts to annul a wide variety of local laws that are inconsistent with federal laws. For example, the Supreme Court declared unlawful the Law "On the Regulation of Sale and Advertisement of Erotic Materials on the Territory of the Belgorod Region" enacted of the Belgorod Regional Duma because it contemplated higher fines for violations of local regulations than of those established by federal administrative law (See *The Procurator v. The Belgorod Regional Duma, BVS,* 1996, No.5, p.1). In another case (*S.B.Nosov v. The Altai Regional Legislative Assembly , v Sudebnaya praktika po grazhdanskim delam 1993-1996* (Judicial Practice in Civil Law Matters 1993-1996), 84-86 (1997)) the Supreme Court declared unlawful Altai regional regulations which required a licence for entrepreneurs dealing in non-ferrous metals. The Supreme Court held the licence requirement unlawful because under Art. 49 of the Civil Code of the Russian Federation, the list of activities requiring licences may established only by a federal law.

E. The Process of Constitutional Review

1. Introduction

Art. 125 of the Constitution indicates that Russia is fully committed to constitutional review of both executive and legislative action as a legal means of assuring that these branches of government do not exceed the limits of their authority. Although the Constitutional Court has exclusive power to declare statutes unconstitutional, "ordinary" courts also have the power to review the constitutionality of laws or other normative acts that litigants seek to apply. Indeed, as we have already discovered in Chapter III, the limitations of Art. 125 of the Constitution open the door for a more active role of "ordinary" courts in constitutional litigation.

The concept of constitutional review by the Constitutional Court was already discussed in Chapter III. Chapter III outlined delineation of jurisdiction between the Constitutional Court, "ordinary" courts and arbitration courts. This section will focus on some procedural aspects of constitutional review.

Art. 118 of the Constitution provides that "judicial power shall be exercised by means of constitutional, civil, administrative and criminal judicial proceedings." While civil, administrative and criminal proceedings in the "ordinary" and arbitration courts are governed by the Civil Procedure Code, the Criminal Procedure Code and the Arbitration Procedure Code, there is no Constitutional Procedure Code. There is no need for such a Code, because the Constitutional Court is the only court that administers the constitutional proceedings. The relevant procedural norms have been included in the Constitutional Law on the Constitutional Court. The Court also adopted its rules of procedure which contains additional procedural norms.

An analysis of Art. 125 of the Constitution indicates that constitutional review proceedings before the Constitutional Court may be initiated in two ways. The first way is the so-called "abstract" review. The second is "incidental review." In addition, constitutionality of laws and other normative acts may by verified within a special procedure dealing with disputes over competence between different state organs.

2. Abstract Review

The "abstract" review may be initiated if one of the organs listed in Art 125(2) or one-fifth of the Deputies of the State Duma or the Federation Council believe that the relevant laws or acts are "inapplicable owing to their unconstitutionality or applicable despite the official refusal by the federal agencies of state power, the highest state agencies of the subjects of the Russian Federation or their officials to apply them because of their conflict with the Constitution of the Russian Federation."[142] The designated state organs or

[142] Federal Constitutional Law on the Constitutional Court, Art. 85.

groups of deputies may challenge the constitutionality of federal and local laws and other normative acts, including normative acts of the President.

The relevant acts are subject to constitutional review from the moment of their entry into legal force. The Russian concept of constitutional review does not recognize anticipatory review of draft laws. The only exception is international treaties which are reviewed after signing or ratifying but prior to their entry into force.

The organ challenging a law or a normative act does not need to prove any infringement on its rights or powers. In other words, there is no "case and controversy" or standing requirement for these cases. While "abstract" review is alien to American jurisprudence, it is similar to that accorded to the Federal Constitutional Court in Germany or several constitutional tribunals in other Eastern and Western European counties.

Because the abstract review procedure inevitably has political overtones, there is no political question doctrine to prevent review. Indeed, Art, 125(2) may put the Constitutional Court into the heart of the political or legislative processes. Two provisions of Art. 125(2) are particularly remarkable in this respect. First, the abstract constitutional review proceedings may be initiated by groups of deputies, for example by members of the the Federal Assembly who unsuccessfully opposed the statute being challenged. Second, Art. 125(2) expressly permits the State Duma or the Federation Council to challenge laws adopted by the Federal Assembly. As a result, one of the chambers of the parliament or a fraction within either chamber that loses in the legislative process may pursue the controversy before the Constitutional Court.

Although in principle all constitutional questions presented must be decided by the Constitutional Court, it has developed a concept that resembles the political question doctrine. In some cases the Court has rejected applications by referring to political considerations. As noted earlier,[143] during the parliamentary elections of 1995, the Constitutional Court refused to consider a request by State Duma Deputies who challenged several provisions of the 1995 Federal Law "On the Elections of the Deputies of the State Duma,"[144] including those imposing a five percent threshold required for parties in that election. The Court held that the 1993 Constitution gave the responsibility for determining the specifics of the electoral procedure to the Federal Assembly. The Court also emphasized that the issues raised were "questions of political

[143]See *supra* p. 162.

[144]*Sobranie*, No. 26, item 2398 (1995).

expediency" that were supposed to be resolved by the legislature.[145] In its ruling in the *Case Concerning Federal Law on the Procedure for the Formation of the Federation Council of the Federal Assembly of the Russian Federation*[146] the Court noted that Duma's application sought to change the direction of the parliamentary discussions on the challenged law. It stated that the "Constitutional Court cannot become a participant in the legislative process" and thus rejected the application.

The Constitution also allows the Constitutional Court to provide an interpretation of the Constitution. According to Art. 125(5) of the Constitution, the following organs may file petitions with the Court requesting an interpretation of the Constitution: the President, both chambers of the Federal Assembly, the Government and the legislatures of the "subjects" of the Federation. Again, the request for interpretation does not need to be connected to any actual case or controversy.

3. Incidental Review

The second way to initiate constitutional review is the so-called "incidental" review procedure. The constitutional complaint must be submitted in connection with a concrete case or controversy pending before a court or another state organ. The procedure deals primarily with the verification of the constitutionality of "laws."

Under Art. 125(4) of the Constitution "citizens" may submit complaints challenging the constitutionality of "laws."[147] However, in certain exceptional cases other normative acts can also be challenged. An important question is whether the term "law" under Art. 125(4) may be interpreted to include other normative acts, in particular sub-statutory regulations. The question is particularly important in the context of numerous sub-statutory regulations inherited from the pre-1993 Constitution period. These substautory regulations, including the remaining acts of the former USSR, often govern relations that under the 1993 Constitution are supposed to be governed by laws only. An authoritative commentary to the Constitutional Law on the Constitutional Court argues that in these cases the Constitutional Court may consider the constitutionality of such normative acts by way of individual complaint.[148]

---

[145] See *Case Concerning the 1995 Federal Law "On the Elections of the Deputies of the State Duma," Sobranie*, No. 49, item 4867 (1995).

[146] See *Sobranie*, No. 24, item 2804 (1997).

[147] To remind the reader, the term "law" (*zakon*) means a normative act enacted by the parliament.

[148] See Vitruk, Lazarev, Ebzeev, *supra* note 89, at 301.

Under Art. 125(4) of the Constitution the petitioners must show that (1) a particular law violates their constitutional rights and freedoms and (2) that the challenged law "has been applied or is due to be applied in a specific case." Two major issues arise in this connection. First, who may lodge constitutional complaints? The second deals with admissibility, in particular the correct interpretation of the phrase "specific case."

(a) Who May Initiate Review

According to Art. 125(4) of the Constitution, the individual complaint is filed by a "citizen." Furthermore, it is clear that the individual complaint procedure extends only to the vindication of certain specified rights and freedoms contained in the catalogue of fundamental rights. These rights, as the title of Chapter 2 of the Constitution makes perfectly clear, are "the rights and freedoms of the human being and citizen." As a result, two questions arise: first, does Art. 125 cover juridical persons and, second, does it cover foreign citizens and juridical persons on the Russian territory?

Art. 96 of the Law on the Constitutional Court clarified the issue by providing that not only "citizens" but also "citizens associations" may file complaints with the Constitutional Court. An important contribution to the clarification of the problem has been made by the *Case Concerning Art. 2 of the Law on Excise Duties.* Consider the following excerpt from the ruling of the Constitutional Court:

The Constitutional Court: *Case Concerning Art. 2 of the Law on Excise Duties* (*VKS*, 1996, No. 5, p. 2)

[The complaint was filed by the shareholders of the joint-stock company "Affa-Eko," by the limited partnerships "Titan" and "Kentavr" and limited liability company "Norok." They challenged Art. 2 of the Law on Excise Duties which had retroactive effect and, as a result, affected their rights and interests in a negative way]

2. Art. 125(4) of the Constitution of the Russian Federation does not define the subjects who have the right to submit complaints to the Constitutional Court of the Russian Federation; it leaves the resolution of this question to the law-maker. According to Art. 96(1) of the Federal Constitutional Court on the Constitutional Court of the Russian Federation, the right to submit individual or collective complaints about violations of constitutional rights and freedoms have been granted to citizens whose rights and freedoms have been violated by a law that has been applied or due to be applied in a specific case; this right has also been granted to associations of citizens.

It follows from the meaning of this rule that citizens and associations established by them have the right to submit constitutional complaints about violations of rights, including, inter alia, the rights of the association, in cases when the activities of the association are connected with the realization of the constitutional rights of those citizens who become their members (participants, founders). In this case, the joint-stock company, partnerships and the limited liability company who turned to the Constitutional Court, are associations - juridical persons, which have been created by citizens for joint realization of such constitutional rights as the right to freely use abilities and property for entrepreneurial or any other economic activity not prohibited by the law (Art. 34(1) of the Constitution of the Russian Federation). Consequently, the requirements of Art. 57 of the Constitution of the Russian Federation which prohibits retroactive force of laws worsening the situation of taxpayers are fully applicable to these associations as subjects of the right mentioned above.

Any violation of the constitutional rights and freedoms by laws provides a ground for a complaint to the Constitutional Court of the Russian Federation to protect these rights and freedoms. The petitioners in this case - partnerships, the limited liability company and shareholders of the joint-stock company have realized their right to complain.

It follows that in accordance with the requirements of the Federal Constitutional Law on the Constitutional Court of the Russian Federation the petitions under discussion are permitted. . .

QUESTIONS AND COMMENTS

1. The Supreme Court held in *Hublein, Inc. v. the Appellate Chamber of the Committee on Patents and Trademarks* (*VKS*, 1995, No. 1, p. 11)[149] that a foreign company can challenge administrative action in "ordinary" courts on the basis of Art. 46 of the Constitution. Do you think that foreign companies may also submit complaints to the Constitutional Court? What kind of argument can you advance in support of this proposition?

If a foreign company can file constitutional complaints, what other requirements should be imposed on it? Can you argue that standing should be restricted only to those foreign companies which are located on Russian territory and/or affected by the challenged law?

2. The question of whether foreign citizens can submit complaints to the Constitutional Court was the principal issue before the Constitutional Court in the *Case Concerning Art. 31 of the 1981 USSR Law "On the Legal*

---

[149] We will discuss this case *infra* p. 222-225.

Status of Foreign Citizens in the USSR" (*VKS*, 1998, No. 3, p. 35). In that case a stateless person who did not have any legal grounds to stay in Russia was detained and subsequently deported to Sweden. The petitioner challenged the constitutionality of Art. 31 of the 1981 USSR Law On the Legal Status of Foreign Citizens in the USSR which allowed detention of foreigners for more than 48 hours who cannot show a valid visa without a judicial order. The Constitutional Court held that under Arts. 17(2), 46, 62(3) and 125(4) of the Constitution "the right to protect the rights and freedoms by means of constitutional judicial proceedings must be granted to everyone, including foreign citizens and stateless persons, if a law violates their rights and freedoms guaranteed by the Constitution of the Russian Federation." As a result, the Court considered the petition and declared Art. 31 of the 1981 Law unconstitutional.

Before this ruling, an authoritative commentary to the Constitutional Law on the Constitutional Court argued that foreigners enjoyed the same right of appeal to the Constitutional Court as Russian citizens. See N.B.Vitruk, L.V. Lazarev, B.S. Ebzeev eds., *Federal'nyi konstitutsionnyi zakon o Konstitutsionnom sude Rossiiskoi Federatsii. Kommentarii* (Federal Constitutional Law on the Constitutional Court of the Russian Federation. Commentary) 297 (1996).

3. Note that in the *Case Concerning Art. 31 of the 1981 USSR Law "On the Legal Status of Foreign Citizens in the USSR"* the petitioner filed his petition from Sweden. Does this case affect the above question concerning the possible argument that standing should be restricted only to those foreign companies which are located on Russian territory and/or affected by the challenged law?

(b) Admissibility of Claims

As noted earlier, incidental review is possible only in "a specific case." The meaning of the phrase "specific case" has been clarified by the Constitutional Law on the Constitutional Court and by the Court's jurisprudence. The Federal Constitutional Law on the Constitutional Court provides that complaints about a law violating the constitutional rights and freedoms of citizens are admissible, not only when the law has been applied or may be applied in a concrete case by "a court" but also when applied by any "other agency applying the law."[150] This means that the term "specific case" does not relate only to court cases. "Other agencies applying the law" may, among other things, include law-enforcement agencies[151] and executive organs.[152]

[150] Federal Constitutional Law on the Constitutional Court, Art. 97.

[151] See *Case Concerning Arts. 1 and 21 of the Law on State Secrets (Sobranie,* No. 15, item 1768 (1996) (decisions of Procuracy and the Federal Security Service).

[152] See *Case Concerning Art. 1(3) of the Law on the Social Security of Citizens - Victims of the Nuclear Accident of 1957 (VKS,* 1996, No. 2, p. 26) (decision of the Administration of the Cheliabinsk Region).

Although the complainant must be directly affected by the challenged law, on a strict reading, Art. 125(4) of the Constitution does not require any actual or serious harm. Under Art. 125 (4) of the Constitution a complaint may be lodged even in cases when the controversial law is only "due to be applied in a specific case."[153] Certain cases have been considered by the Court when the proceedings affecting the complainant had been terminated.[154] Nor do Art. 125(4) or Art. 97 of the Law on the Constitutional Court require the exhaustion of ordinary legal remedies before a constitutional complaint is filed. Citizens and juridical persons have direct access to the Constitutional Court at any stage of the relevant proceedings.

Because Art. 125(4) of the Constitution and Art. 97 of the Law on the Constitutional Court established extremely liberal admissibility criteria, there is a serious danger that aggrieved citizens would flood the Court with individual complaints. Indeed, the Court is receiving hundred of complaints each month. The Court deals with the problem in three ways. First, the complaints are examined and sometimes rejected on procedural grounds by the Secretariat of the Court. Second, the flood of human rights cases is controlled by the use of two chamber each of which can render decisions. Third, the Court has started to developed a tendency to a rather strict interpretation of the notion of admissibility. The Court declines to exercise jurisdiction if it believes that the complaint is manifestly unfounded.[155]

(c) The Role of Courts and Procurators

Under Art. 125(4) of the Constitution "incidental" review may also be initiated by courts. On a strict reading of Art. 125(4), courts may request verification of any laws that have been applied or are due to be applied in a specific case. This means that the challenged laws may not necessarily involve actual violations of constitutional rights and freedoms of particular citizens.

---

[153] The Constitutional Court emphasized, however, that the mere possibility of application of a particular law is not enough. In the *Case Concerning Arts. 180, 181, 187(1) and 192 of the Arbitration Procedure Code* (*Sobranie*, No. 6, item 784 (1998)) the Constitutional Court refused to consider a request to review the constitutionality of one of the provisions of the Arbitration Procedure Code dealing with review of judgments by the Presidium of the Supreme Arbitration Court. A joint stock company which requested the constitutional review only intended to petition the Presidium of the Supreme Arbitration. The Constitutional Court noted that in that case "there was no specific case in which the challenged law had been applied or was due to be applied."

[154] See, e.g., *Case Concerning Arts. 220(1) and 220(2) of the Criminal Procedure Code* (*VKS*, 1995, No. 3, p. 39) (In this case the ruling ordering custody as a measure of suppression with respect to the complainant was repealed and the criminal investigation terminated prior to the petition to the Constitutional Court).

[155] Cf. Vitruk, Lazarev, Ebzeev, *supra* note 89, at 305-306..

Practice confirms this interpretation. For example, the *Case Concerning Art. 418 of the Criminal Procedure Code*,[156] (discussed in Chapter III) was initiated by a judge who was generally concerned about the proper administration of justice in criminal proceedings.

According to Art. 103 of the Law on the Constitutional Court, a petition for review in the Constitutional Court results in the suspension of the regular court's proceedings. The suspension lasts until the questions of the constitutionality is decided.

Recent legislation has expanded opportunities for "incidental" reviews. Under the 1995 Law "On the Procuracy of the Russian Federation"[157] the Procurator General has been granted the right to challenge in the Constitutional Court the constitutionality of any law that violates the constitutional rights and freedoms of citizens and that has been applied or due to be applied in a specific case.[158] Similar powers have been given to the Commissioner for Human Rights.[159]

4. Proceedings in the Constitutional Court

While the civil law procedure in Russia is still largely inquisitorial,[160] the procedure of the Constitutional Court is adversarial. At the same time, the Constitutional Court may play a more active role than would a US court.

During hearings, representatives of the organs which filed the petition or citizens who filed the complaint, as well as representatives of the organ that issued the challenged legislation, must be present. The parties appearing before the Court may present written evidence and make oral arguments. The Court itself may examine witnesses and experts. The Court also has the power to demand presentation of the relevant legal acts and documents, and to order their expert evaluation and request expert opinions.

5. The Effect and Enforcement of Constitutional Court Rulings

It is important to recall that decisions of the Constitutional Court are final. Acts or their individual provisions judged unconstitutional become null and void. Most importantly, "the legal force of a ruling rendered by the

---

[156] See *VKS*, 1996, No. 5, p. 15.

[157] *Sobranie*, No. 47, item 4472 (1995).

[158] 1995 Law on the Procuracy of the Russian Federation, Art. 35.

[159] See the Federal Constitutional Law on the Commissioner for Human Rights, Art. 29, *Sobranie*, No. 9, item 1011 (1997) (The powers of the Commissioner for Human Rights will be discussed *infra* p. 235-236).

[160] For details, see *infra* Chapter VII.

Constitutional Court of the Russian Federation declaring an act unconstitutional may not be overruled by the readoption of the same act."[161] While both the legislative and executive branches may try to develop different techniques to counteract decisions of the Constitutional Court, Art. 79 of the Law on the Constitutional Court makes it clear that the legislative branch cannot undermine constitutional review by enacting laws aimed at changing the Court's rulings.[162]

The Law on the Constitutional Court does not provide for any special mechanism for the enforcement of the Court's rulings. Nor does it set out any legal consequences for those who fail to obey the Court's rulings. The drafters of the Law obviously assumed that the rulings of the Court will be enforced as other sources of law are enforced in Russia, that is, by the whole legal system of the country. Not surprisingly, some of the rulings of the Constitutional Court have not been implemented. For example, the ruling in the *Tatarstan Case*, as noted earlier, was simply ignored by the Republic of Tatarstan. In Chapter III we also discussed problems concerning the implementation of some of the rulings of the Constitutional Court by the Supreme Court.[163] In 1996 the Constitutional Court declared Arts. 371, 347 and 384 of the Criminal Procedure Code unconstitutional because they contained a limited list of grounds for the Supreme Court to review or reopen criminal cases.[164] The Constitutional court ruled that criminal cases of several petitioners convicted by "ordinary" courts "must be reconsidered."[165] However, the Supreme Court refused to reconsider these cases. As a result, in June of 1997 the Constitutional Court issued an opinion in which it renewed its demand to reopen the cases.[166]

While the Court thus tries to monitor the implementation of its own rulings, in some cases it needs help from the executive branch. An example is the ruling of the Court in the *Case Concerning the Law of the Udmurd Republic*

---

[161] Law on the Constitutional Court, Art. 79.

[162] It should be noted that a new enactment of the same norm that was declared unconstitutional does not always violate Art. 79(2) of the Law on the Constitutional Court. In its ruling in the *Case Concerning Arts. 371, 374 and 384 of the Criminal Procedure Code*, the Court declared Art. 384 unconstitutional (see *VKS*, 1996, No. 2, p. 2). However, the Court noted that the law-maker may reintroduce Art. 384 if at the same time it adopts a new system of procedural norms allowing a broader review of previously adopted court decisions thus eliminating the defect identified by the Court in its ruling (Id.)

[163] See *supra* p. 75-76.

[164] See *Case Concerning Arts. 371, 374 and 384 of the Criminal Procedure Code*, *VKS*, 1996, No. 2, p. 2.

[165] Id.

[166] See *Sobranie*, No. 25, item 2950 (1997).

On the System of the Organs of State Power in the Udmurd Republic.[167] The Court declared some of the provisions of the challenged law unconstitutional because they violated constitutional provisions on local self-government. The administration of the Udmurd Republic was in no hurry to implement the far-reaching changes in the system of local self-government envisioned by the Court's ruling. The President of Russia had to issue a special Decree[168] in order to implement the ruling of the Court. The Decree restored the organs of local-self-government and suspended the relevant acts of the Government of the Udmurd Republic.

6. Proceedings in "Ordinary" Courts

Constitutional challenges to normative acts in ordinary courts are governed by Art. 46 of the Constitution and the 1993 Law "On Appealing in Court Actions and Decisions Violating the Rights and Freedoms of Citizens"[169] The 1993 Law on Appeals deals primarily with judicial review of administrative action. However, it also allows citizens to challenge normative acts. The Supreme Court has emphasized that, under the 1993 Law, acts of governmental organs or of officials of "a general normative character" may be appealed.[170] For example, regulations issued by federal ministries or local self-government may be challenged in ordinary courts. The procedure established by the 1993 Law on Appeals will be discussed *infra* p. 222-228.

7. Constitutional Review in Russia and the US: Differences and Similarities

Constitutional review in all countries that have it largely fulfills the same goals. It ensures the direct effect of constitutions. It protects fundamental rights and freedoms of individual against infringement by governmental authority or the legislature. It protects separation of powers. In federal states it also plays an important role in maintaining the balance between the federal government and political subdivisions of the country.

At the same time, the United States and many European countries, including Russia, differ in how they organize their systems of constitutional review. The American system is decentralized while European systems tend to be centralized. In the United States constitutional review is exercised by the

---

[167] See *VKS*, 1997, No. 1, p. 2.

[168] See *Sobranie*, No. 10, item 1130 (1997).

[169] *Vedomosty RF*, No. 19, item 685 (1993) (as amended in 1995, *Sobranie*, No. 51, item 4970 (1995)) (hereinafter "the 1993 Law on Appeals").

[170] See Ruling of the Plenary Session of the Supreme Court of the Russian Federation "On Judicial Consideration of Appeals Of Unlawful Actions Violating the Rights and Freedoms of Citizens," *BVS*, 1994, No. 3, p. 4.

judicial system at every level. In Germany and some other European countries, there is a special Constitutional Court that has the sole power to declare laws unconstitutional. Thus, constitutional review is centralized in one court. In Russia, constitutional review in the European style is lodged in the Constitutional Court which is separate from the courts of general jurisdiction and from arbitration courts. However, even if jurisdiction in constitutional matters is, at least in principle, reserved for the Constitutional Court, "ordinary" courts may also engage in constitutional adjudication. While Russian courts of general jurisdiction lack the power to declare statues unconstitutional with an *erga omnes* effect, they do have the power to ignore unconstitutional statutes and other normative acts that they determine unconstitutional. Furthermore, they always make an initial determination of constitutionality in cases before they decide to refer a constitutional issue to the Constitutional Court. These are elements of a decentralized system of judicial review. Thus, the Russian system of judicial review is somewhere between a centralized and a decentralized system.

On the other hand, the United States system has some centralized tendencies. Although the lower state and federal courts have the power of constitutional review, the US system tends to emphasize the special significance of the Supreme Court's opinions on constitutional matters. The United States Supreme Court tends to confine itself to the most significant, mostly constitutional, questions. In many cases it thus approaches the role of a specialized European-type constitutional court.[171]

The United States courts resolve all aspects of a case at hand and do not give any special treatment to constitutional matters found in the case. Constitutionality of laws is examined not in the abstract but in the context of specific cases. Although some constitutional litigation in Russia is incidental, the Constitution Court can also exercise abstract constitutional review.

While in the United States the generalized effect of the Supreme Court's opinions is ensured by the principle of *stare decisis*, the Russian Constitutional Court has an express power to annul the law with an *erga omnes* effect. In both countries, of course, the legal force of a ruling declaring a statute unconstitutional rendered by the Constitutional Court or the US Supreme Court may not be overruled by the adoption of the same provision or statute.

F. Judicial Review of Administrative Action

1. Introduction

Art. 46(2) of the Constitution guarantees judicial review of adminis-

[171] Cf. M. Cappelletti, The Judicial Process in Comparative Perspective 147 (1989).

trative action (or inaction) to anyone whose rights have been infringed by state organs, organs of local self-government, public associations and officials. The judicial review of administrative action is currently undertaken by courts of general jurisdiction and by arbitration courts, in accordance with the general principles governing their jurisdiction. As noted in Chapter III, the Concept of Judicial Reform envisions the creation of a separate system of administrative courts. It is expected that in the future these courts will have exclusive jurisdiction over all administrative matters, including appeals of administrative action.

Under the 1995 Arbitration Procedure Code,[172] judicial review of administrative action is governed by general procedural rules. Judicial review in courts of general jurisdiction is conducted in accordance with a set of special rules laid down by the 1993 Law "On Appealing in Court Actions and Decisions Violating the Rights and Freedoms of Citizens."[173]

2. The Right to Judicial Review as a Constitutional Right

The right to judicial review is a constitutional right. Courts tend to regard as unconstitutional all statutory restrictions on this right. Consider the following case:

The Supreme Court: *Hublein, Inc. v. the Appellate Chamber of the Committee on Patents and Trademarks* (*BVS*, 1995, No. 1, p. 11)

By two decisions of November 25, 1992, the Appellate Chamber of the Committee of the Russian Federation on Patents and Trademarks rejected the complaint of the firm "Hublein, Inc." (USA) regarding registration of the trademark No. 99074 "P.A. Smirnov and Descendants in Moscow" and of the trademark No. 99075 "Trading Company of Petr Smirnov and Descendants in Moscow."

The company "Hublein, Inc." (USA) sued in court to declare invalid the above mentioned decisions because the above trademarks are practically identical to the plaintiff's own trademarks "Smirnoff" and "Petr Smirnoff," which directly refer to the name and activities of the same person.

By a ruling of August 24, 1993, the Moscow City Court dismissed the claim; the ruling was confirmed by the Collegium for Civil Cases of the Supreme Court of the Russian Federation.

---

[172] *Sobranie*, No. 19, item 1709 (1995).
[173] See *supra* note 169.

The Deputy Chairman of the Supreme Court lodged a protest to vacate the rulings. The presidium of the Supreme Court sustained the protest for the following reasons:

The judge dismissed the claim by referring to Art. 28(3) of the Law of the Russian Federation "On Trademarks, Service Marks and Names of Origin of Goods;" according to Art. 28(3) the decisions of the Appellate Chamber [of the Committee on Patents and Trademarks] may be challenged only in the Supreme Patent Chamber, the decision of which shall be final; in other words, the Law does not contemplate any appeals in court of the decisions of the Appellate Chamber. The judge also stated that the reference of the plaintiff to Art. 63 of the Constitution of the Russian Federation (in the addition of April 21, 1992, which was in force at that time) is unfounded because this rule simply "declares" the protection of the rights of citizens in a court of law. These conclusions were confirmed by the Collegium for Civil Cases of the Supreme Court. However, they are wrong. . .

By relying on the Law [On Trademarks] the courts did not take into account the fact. . . that the Supreme Patent Chamber had not been established. In this case, the complainant believes that it has exhausted all means of legal protection within the administrative procedure, because the Appellate Chamber rejected its objections to the registration of trademarks and the Supreme Patent Chamber does not exist; therefore the company demands the realization of its right to protection in a court of law.

The complainant does have this right, notwithstanding the administrative (non-judicial) procedure for the protection of infringed rights established by a special law, because this right has been granted by an act of supreme legal force - the Constitution of the Russian Federation. In Accordance with Art. 63 of the Constitution of the Russian Federation (in the addition of April 21, 1992), which was in force at the time when the complaint was lodged and the above court rulings were rendered, everyone shall be guaranteed protection of his or her rights and freedoms in a court of law; the decisions and actions of officials, state organs and public associations violating the law or adopted ultra vires, as well as those infringing upon the rights of citizens, may be appealed in court.

An analogous provision is included in Art. 46 of the current Constitution of the Russian Federation adopted on December 12, 1993.

The argument advanced by the judge of the Moscow City Court that Art. 63 of the Constitution of the Russian Federation only "declares" the right to court protection is unfounded, because it contradicts the meaning of the norm, which expressly guarantees the right to court protection without any restrictions. Because the Constitution of the Russian Federation has supreme legal force, all legislative and other normative acts restricting the right to protection in a court of law, in particular, those establishing only an administrative procedure for the protection of rights, cannot be applied by courts because they contravene the Constitution of the Russian Federation.

Nor can we accept the argument of the judge that the above norm of the Constitution of the Russian Federation concerns only the rights and freedoms of the human being and citizen and that therefore the above complaint cannot be accepted by the court. This case concerns the protection of an intellectual property right. . . According to Art. 10(2) of the Constitution of the Russian Federation (in the addition that was in force at the time when the claim was submitted and the ruling were rendered), the state must ensure equal protection of all forms of ownership. An analogous norm is included in Art. 8(2) of the current Constitution of the Russian Federation. Therefore, court protection of property rights (in this case - intellectual property rights) must be equally guaranteed to both citizens and organizations; the rights of organizations are ensured by the courts of general jurisdiction or arbitration courts depending on the subjects of the relevant rights. Under Art. 25 of the Civil Procedure Code, cases involving foreign citizens, foreign enterprises and organizations are considered by courts of general jurisdiction. . .

QUESTIONS AND COMMENTS

1. What is the principal significance of this case?

2. What are the criteria for self-executing constitutional provisions formulated by the Court?

3. The Court noted that Hublein tried to exhaust all administrative remedies before turning to the court. Do you need to exhaust administrative remedies before filing a complaint against administrative action with a court?

4. The Supreme Court and the Supreme Arbitration Court confirmed the right of "everyone," that is, both citizens and juridical persons, to appeal unlawful actions or inactions in courts in a "Joint Explanation" (See the Joint Ruling of the Plenary Session of the Supreme Court and the Plenary Session of the Supreme Arbitration Court "*On Some Questions Concerning the Application of the First Part of the Civil Code of the Russian Federation*" (*BVS*, No. 9, p. 1 (1996)). The "Joint Explanation" also emphasized that this right is granted not only to Russian citizens and juridical persons but also to foreign citizens, stateless persons and foreign juridical persons.

5. Note that Art. 46 of the Constitution guarantees judicial review of both administrative action and "inaction." By relying on Art. 46 of the

Constitution, the Supreme Court emphasized in one of the recent cases that not only actions but also "inaction of organs of executive power" may be appealed in courts. See *Shupanko v. The Government of St.Petersburg* (*BVS*, 1996, No. 5, p. 2-3).

6. Note that the Supreme Court referred to Art. 25 of the Civil Procedure Code which grants jurisdiction over disputes involving foreign citizens and *foreign organizations* to "ordinary" courts. As we have discovered in Chapter III, the new Arbitration Procedure Code granted jurisdiction over disputes involving foreign juridical persons to arbitration courts.

7. Although Hublein has been waging a trademark battle with the Russian vodka distiller Smirnov since 1992, the outcome of the battle on the merits is still not clear. In 1997 the Circuit Arbitration Court for the Moscow Region rejected the cassational appeal of Hublein and ruled in favor of the domestic Smirnovskaya, upholding an earlier decision not to renew Smirnoff's registration in Russia (*Kommersant-Daily*, June 7, 1997, p. 2).

3. The Scope of Judicial Review

The scope of judicial review is very broad. It provides redress not only to victims of *executive action* but also to citizens whose rights were violated by "state organs," organs of self-government or officials.[174] Claimants aggrieved by action or inaction of these parties may lodge complaints in all cases when the action (decision) or inaction infringes upon their rights and freedoms, interferes with their exercise or imposes on them any responsibility or liability.[175] Exhaustion of administrative appeal procedures established by the relevant organ or agency is not mandatory. The 1993 Law on Appeals grants the aggrieved party the right to appeal directly to a court or to a superior governmental organ.[176]

The 1993 Law on Appeals provides that it does not cover complaints about actions violating citizens' rights and freedoms when verification of the complaints is assigned to the exclusive jurisdiction of the Constitutional Court.[177] Nor does it govern complaints about "actions (decisions) with respect to which the legislation provides a different judicial appeal procedure."[178] This means that court decisions in civil and criminal cases may be challenged only in the framework of the ordinary procedure established by

---

[174] 1993 Law on Appeals, Art. 1. Note that the 1993 Law on Appeals also covers actions of institutions, enterprises and public associations (Art. 1).

[175] 1993 Law on Appeals, Art. 2.

[176] 1993 Law on Appeals, Art. 4.

[177] 1993 Law on Appeals, Art.3.

[178] Id.

civil and criminal procedural law.[179] At the same time, review of administrative or other decisions by procurators does not fall into the category "of judicial appeal procedure." For example, under Art. 209 of the Criminal Procedure Code rulings of investigators terminating criminal proceedings could be appealed only to procurators. In the *Case Concerning Art. 209 of the Criminal Procedure Code*[180] the Constitutional Court ruled that under Art. 46 of the Constitution the complainants have the right to challenge the ruling of the investigator directly in courts.

In contrast to the traditional practice in the United States, the scope of Russian judicial review is very broad both as to law and fact. The drafters of the 1993 Law on Appeals apparently believed in the maxim that "the law ends where discretion begins." The administrative discretion conferred on executive organs and governmental agencies is very limited. Courts are not obliged to accept findings of fact or conclusions of law made by officials or state organs. Under the 1993 Law on Appeals, courts should review both findings of fact and conclusions of law made by executive organs or officials. The Law presupposes that otherwise courts cannot determine whether the complainant's rights have been violated. De novo examination of facts is strengthened by a clause that allows the citizen to challenge not just the decision itself, but also "information" that provided the factual basis for the decision.[181]

4. Procedural Aspects

The complaint for review must be filed within three months after the initial decision or one month after the decision of the superior body. However, if the period is missed for a valid reason, the right to file may be restored by a

---

[179] See Ruling of the Plenary Session of the Supreme Court of the Russian Federation "On Judicial Consideration of Appeals Of Unlawful Actions Violating the Rights and Freedoms of Citizens," *supra* note 170 ("The actions of a court, judge, procurator, interrogator, investigating officer, execution officers, and organs authorized to examine cases of administrative law violations, for which a different procedure for making an appeal has been provided for by the codes of criminal and civil procedure and the legislation on administrative law violations, may not be appealed in court in the manner established by the 1993 Law").

[180] VKS, 1995, No. 6, p. 18. During the consideration of the Case Concerning Art. 6 of the Criminal Procedure Code (VKS, 1996, No. 5, p. 11), which confirmed the ruling in the *Case Concerning Art. 209 of the Criminal Procedure Code*, the representative of the Supreme Court confirmed that courts have begun to consider complaints concerning rulings of investigators terminating criminal proceedings (Id.)

[181] 1993 Law on Appeals, Art. 2.

court. Difficulties in obtaining "information about the challenged actions and their consequences" is considered to be a "valid reason."[182]

Although the judicial review procedure is governed by the general rules of civil procedure,[183] the 1993 Law on Appeals introduced several important modifications that are supposed to help victims of administrative abuse. First, the complaint may be filed, not only at the place where the relevant organ or official is located or registered, but also at the place of the complainant's residence. Second, the court may, at the citizen's request or on its own initiative, suspend the implementation of the challenged action or decision while the case is pending. Third, the court may relieve the aggrieved citizen of the obligation to pay court costs or may reduce the amount of the court costs.[184] Last, but not least, the 1993 Law on Appeals (as amended in 1995) modifies the general rules concerning burden of proof. Art. 6 of the 1993 Law provides that the aggrieved citizen must prove only the fact that his or her rights have been violated. The citizen is not obliged to prove the unlawfulness of the challenged action or decision. Instead, the burden of proving the lawfulness of the challenged action is imposed on the defendant organ.[185]

Administrative complaints are generally not subject to the sovereign immunity defense. The 1993 Law provides that the courts are open to claims for money damages against executive organs or officials for injuries caused by violations of law. The 1993 Law is thus based on the liberal principle that the state, its organs and officials are liable to citizens for damages caused by the wrongdoing of state organs or public officials acting in the name of the state. However, this important guarantee of government liability is restricted by the reference to the Civil Code.[186] As a result, the state will pay only when the offending organ or official is liable under the Civil Code.[187]

5. Implementation of the 1993 Law on Appeals

While the 1993 Law on Appeals is clearly progressive, its implementation in actual practice is hampered by two major factors. The first is the low level of legal awareness of both authorities and the people, who often prefer to avoid the courts and to defend their interests through other channels. The second is the traditional attitudes of judges, many of whom still consider

---

[182] 1993 Law on Appeals, Art. 5.

[183] The applicability of the general rules of civil procedure is envisioned by Art. 6 of the 1993 Law on Appeals. Civil procedure will be discussed *infra* Chapter VII.

[184] 1993 Law on Appeals, Art. 4.

[185] 1993 Law on Appeals, Art. 6.

[186] 1993 Law on Appeals, Art. 7.

[187] The matter is governed by Arts. 1064, 1069, 1070 and 1100 of the Civil Code. For details, see Chapter VI.

themselves civil servants of the state and identify with the official defendants or agencies being sued. Although judges have been granted new broad powers, including the power to hold agency regulations illegal, in general, as legal experts of the Parliamentary Assembly of the Council of Europe noted, "the concept that it should in the first place be for the judiciary to protect the individuals has not become a reality in Russia."[188]

[188] Report on the Conformity of the Legal Order of the Russian Federation with the Council of Europe Standards. Doc. AS/Bur/Russia, at 32 (1994).

CHAPTER V

HUMAN RIGHTS

A. Introduction

One of the major goals of the constitutional reform in Russia is to create a strong system for protection of human rights. The Soviet legacy of mass human rights violations has made absolutely imperative the establishment of both legislative and institutional guarantees against disregard of fundamental human rights and freedoms.

Because Soviet domestic law lagged behind legal standards developed at the international level, it was first necessary to enact new laws to meet these standards. On November 22, 1991, the Supreme Soviet of the Russian Federation adopted the Declaration of the Rights and Freedoms of the Individual and Citizen.[1] This act had enormous political significance for it implemented all the basic provisions of international instruments on human rights and introduced positive changes in the preexisting human rights regime. It dramatically expanded the list of rights and freedoms. New norms were included, such as the right to life, the right to a clean environment, the right to freedom of movement, the right to choose one's place of residence, the right to equal access to jobs in state bodies, property rights and the right to perform entrepreneurial activity. The 1991 Declaration was subsequently incorporated into the then-existing 1978 Constitution.

The enactment of the 1993 Constitution was another important milestone in the establishment of legal and institutional guarantees for human rights. The 1993 Constitution's chapter on human rights includes an elaborate catalog of civil, political, economic, social and cultural rights, which are based on international human rights standards.

From a broad political-legal perspective, the 1993 Constitution signifies a complete departure from the communist theory of human rights. Communist doctrine rejects the idea of inherent human rights. Under the communist theory of human rights, human rights are granted to individuals by the state. As a result, individuals are always dependent on the state. The 1993 Constitution establishes a new relationship between the state and individuals by proclaiming that "fundamental human rights and freedoms shall be

[1] *Vedomosty RF*, No. 52, item 1865 (1991).

inalienable and shall belong to everyone from birth."[2] It also provides that "human beings and their rights and freedoms shall be of supreme value. Recognition of, respect for and protection of the rights and freedoms of the human being and citizen shall be the duty of the state."[3] This approach is in full accord with international human rights instruments which are based on the idea of inalienable rights.

B. The Issue of Aspirational Rights

Another principal feature of the 1993 Constitution is its attempt to provide legal guarantees for a wide variety of human rights. While the Constitution's chapter on human rights deals first with civil and political rights, it also contains an extensive catalogue of economic and social rights, including the right to work, house, education and health care. One might argue that the list of economic and social rights is a relic of the socialist past. Many lawyers would also argue that the presence of these essentially aspirational or programmatic rights in the Constitution undermines the credibility of the document and eventually may even serve to dilute political rights.

However, it is useful to keep in mind that it is not unusual for European countries to include economic and social rights in their constitutions. Furthermore, economic and social rights are recognized as human rights by such important international instruments as the 1948 Universal Declaration of Human Rights,[4] the 1966 Covenant on the Economic, Social and Cultural Rights[5] and, at the European regional level, by the 1961 European Social Charter.[6]

It is also useful to emphasize that the framers of the Russian Constitution were fairly cautious in their approach to economic and social rights. These rights are formulated in a programmatic way. As a result, there is no obligation for the governments to provide, for example, a particular job or house. Such a requirement would be absolutely unrealistic in a market-oriented system. The constitutional right to work and the constitutional right to housing limit state obligations to that of creating the conditions necessary to exercise the right to work or the right to housing.

The Constitution guarantees not only traditional civil and political rights (the "first generation" of human rights), social and economic rights (the

[2] Constitution, Art. 17 (2).
[3] Constitution, Art. 2.
[4] UN Doc. A/Res. 217 (1948).
[5] 993 UNTS 3.
[6] 529 UNTS 89.

"second generation" of human rights), but also several new human rights of the so-called "third generation." Among the "third generation" human rights, the right to a "favorable environment"[7] merits particular attention. The "constitutionalization" of the right to a favorable environment should serve to underscore environmental issues that emerged as a result of a series of environmental disasters caused by the former communist economic system.

While civil and political rights are conceived as safeguards afforded to individuals to protect them from the state, the economic and social rights, as well as the "third generation" of human rights, place upon the state an obligation to adopt positive measures to ensure the proclaimed rights. For example, the right to education[8] can be secured only if the state ensures positively and actively the operation of educational institutions. Furthermore, this positive obligation does not call only for the adoption of appropriate legislation. The implementation of the right to education has repercussions on the budget of the state.

The inclusion of the "second" and "third" generation of human rights raises serious concerns about the direct applicability of the relevant constitutional provisions. International practice demonstrates that the essentially programmatic nature of the "second" and "third" generation of human rights makes them largely unenforceable. Judges who are asked to decide cases based on the right to housing or the right to a favorable environment may find that the alleged right simply lacks any specific normative content capable of judicial enforcement. Yet, an analysis of the Constitution indicates that it is based on the idea of direct applicability of all human rights. The drafters of the Constitution embraced the idea of direct applicability because prior constitutions established only "paper rights." One of the lessons of the communist past is that constitutional provisions on human rights can be meaningless if the enforcement is not secured by direct applicability and strong and independent judiciary. As a result, the Constitution includes a special article that provides for the direct applicability of the Constitution.[9] Furthermore, Art. 18 states that "the rights and freedoms of the human being and citizen shall have direct effect" and that they "shall be enforced by the judiciary."

While the goal of direct applicability of human rights is thus recognized, it will be difficult to achieve it with respect to all rights guaranteed by the Constitution. However, practice indicates that courts may gradually develop certain standards that would make even programmatic rights more meaningful. Recent judicial practice with respect to the right to a favorable

[7] Constitution, Art. 42.
[8] Constitution, Art. 43.
[9] Constitution, Art. 15 (1).

environment is an interesting example of this trend. It indicates that the new entitlement to a favorable environment may be judicially enforceable. The right to a "favorable environment" has been interpreted by the courts[10] to allow citizens to judicially challenge conclusions of environmental impact assessment commissions. The Constitutional Court held that Art. 42 imposed on the state an obligation to "take adequate measures to protect the environment and the people from nuclear accidents and catastrophes."[11] The Court also noted that Art. 42, taken in conjunction with Art. 7, mandates the state to establish a "system of benefits and compensation" that would go beyond the limits of ordinary compensation of harm caused by environmental law violations.[12]

Although direct applicability of the constitutional provisions on human rights is an important constitutional principle, many political and especially socio-economic rights require implementing legislation. Constitutional rights have been further developed by new basic codes enacted in recent years. Of particular importance are the new Civil Code,[13] and the new Criminal Code.[14] Other basic codes, in particular a new Criminal Procedure Code and a number of specific laws concerning human rights, are still being debated by the Federal Assembly.

C. Holders of Rights

The Constitution differentiates between the rights of Russian citizens and rights of every human being. For example, only Russian citizens have equal access to state service.[15] On the other hand, "everyone" is guaranteed freedom of thought and speech.[16]

Most of the civil and political rights are guaranteed to each individual. In some cases, however, the Constitution imposes limitations linked to citizenship which are contrary to the generally recognizes human rights standards. Thus, the Covenant on Civil and Political Rights guarantees the

---

[10] See *Case Concerning State Ecological Examination of the Project to Rebuild Kuznetsk Metallurgical Works, BVS*, 1994, No. 8, p. 3.

[11] *Case Concerning Art. 1(3) of the Law on the Social Security of Citizens - Victims of the Nuclear Accident of 1957, VKS*, 1996, No. 2, p. 26.

[12] Id.

[13] *Sobranie*, No. 32, item 3301 (1994); Id., No. No. 5, item 410 (1996).

[14] *Sobranie*, No. 25, item 2954 (1996).

[15] Constitution, Art. 32.

[16] Constitution, Art. 29.

right of peaceful assembly to everyone.[17] In contrast, the 1993 Constitution guarantees this right only to citizens.[18]

Express limitations based on citizenship may not be as serious as they appear at first sight. Two factors must be taken into account. First, Art. 62(3) of the Constitution provides that "foreign citizens and stateless persons in the Russian Federation shall enjoy the rights of its citizens and bear responsibilities on an equal basis with the citizens of the Russian Federation, except in cases specified by federal law or an international treaty of the Russian Federation."

Second, broader international standards may affect the interpretation of constitutional provisions. For example, in the *Case Concerning Art. 31 of the 1981 USSR Law "On the Legal Status of Foreign Citizens in the USSR"*[19] the Constitutional Court held that Art. 22 of the Constitution (right to freedom and personal security) and Art. 46 of the Constitution (right to judicial protection) apply to foreigners because these clauses use the word "everyone." However, in addition to this argument the Court also relied on "the generally recognized principles and rules of international law." It noted that according to "the generally recognized principles and rules of international law the right to freedoms and personal security and the right to judicial protection are personal inalienable rights of every all beings irrespective of whether they have or do not have citizenship of a particular country and, therefore, must be guaranteed to foreign citizens and stateless persons on an equal basis with the citizens of the Russian Federation."

The Constitution also draws a distinction between natural and juridical persons. For example, Art. 36 states that "citizens and their associations shall have the right to have land in private ownership." Again, the absence of specific reference to juridical persons does not mean that they are excluded from those entitled to the proclaimed right. Of course, juridical persons will enjoy the proclaimed rights only to the extent consistent with the nature of the right. The right to life or the right to marriage can obviously be exercised only by individuals. On the other hand, the right of "everyone" to protection of "his or her rights in a court of law" applies not only to individuals but also to juridical persons.

D. Limitations of Rights

Another area of concern are possible limitations or restrictions on

---

[17] Covenant on Civil and Political Rights, Art. 21.
[18] Constitution, Art. 31.
[19] *VKS*, 1998, No. 3, p. 35.

constitutional rights. Under the new Constitution human rights are not absolute. The scope of human rights is limited by a general clause[20] which provides that

> The rights and freedoms of the human being and citizen may be restricted by the federal law only to the extent required for the protection of the fundamentals of the constitutional system, morality, health, rights and lawful interests of other persons, or for ensuring the defense of the country and the security of the state.

The general limitation clause in the Constitution raises serious problems. It appears that under Art. 55(3) even the most fundamental rights are not absolute. For example, it might be argued that restrictions are allowed even with respect to the right to be free from torture. Although no international human rights instrument provides for absolute human rights, international human rights treaties as a rule prevent restriction on the most fundamental rights by drawing a distinction between different categories of rights and allowing limitations only on certain rights.

However, a careful analysis of the Constitution indicates that it does not intend to allow inroads on the most important human rights and freedoms. Art. 56(3) contains an important list of non-derogable rights that cannot be restricted even when a state of emergency is proclaimed. The Constitution also provides other guarantees against infringement of fundamental rights.

First, under Art. 55 of the Constitution any limitation on human rights may be imposed only by "federal law." Because in Russia human right have been traditionally restricted primarily by agency regulations, Art. 55 serves as a guarantee that constitutional rights will not be limited by executive enactments or local legislation. By requiring parliamentary approval of human rights limitations, Art. 55(3) introduces an important element of both federalism and the separation of powers. An example of Art. 55's significance in this respect is the Ruling of the Constitutional Court on the unconstitutionality of the Moscow City regulations which reintroduced the infamous residence permit requirements at the regional level. One of the reasons for the Court's holding was the fact the local restrictive rules violating the constitutional provision on the right to choose place of residence were not imposed by "federal law."[21]

Second, a law limiting human rights cannot deny or diminish the

---

[20] Constitution, Art. 55 (3).

[21] See *Case Concerning Some Normative Acts of the City of Moscow, VKS*, 1996, No. 2, p. 42.

rights and freedoms of the human being,[22] diminish "the dignity of the individual"[23] or violate certain fundamental human rights principles, such as those prohibiting discrimination. Thus, a law that would diminish "the dignity of the individual" by singling out certain persons for unfavorable treatment would certainly be held unconstitutional.[24] Limitations, as the Constitutional Court has pointed out on several occasions, must also serve legitimate public interests and satisfy the general test of proportionality.[25]

E. Domestic Institutional Guarantees

One of the lessons of the communist past is that constitutional and legislative provisions on human rights can be meaningless if the enforcement of human rights is not secured by adequate institutional arrangements. One of the important tasks of the human rights reform in Russia has been the creation of institutions dealing with human rights violations. The Concept of Judicial Reform contemplates the creation of an independent judiciary that will be able to protect human rights. Procurators have been empowered to receive complaints about human rights violations. The Constitutional Court has emerged as a central guardian of fundamental human rights and freedoms.

Following the model of some European states, the 1993 Constitution also provides for the creation of a special agency that will exclusively deal with human rights violations - the Office of the Commissioner for Human Rights (Ombudsman). The powers of the Commissioner are defined by the 1997 Constitutional Law on the Commissioner for Human Rights.[26]

The Commissioner for Human Rights is an independent official who is appointed by the State Duma for a term of five years. The 1997 Law provides some protection to the Commissioner from politically motivated dismissals. Under the 1997 Law the State Duma is the only organ which can remove the Commissioner for Human Rights from office on limited grounds

---

[22] Constitution, Art. 55 (2).

[23] Constitution, Art. 21 (1).

[24] The Constitutional Court relied on these tests when it invalidated Art. 18 of the 1991 Law "On the Citizenship of the Russian Federation." Art. 18 of the 1991 Law imposed certain procedural restrictions on the citizenship right of former USSR citizens, who were born on Russian territory but lived in successor states of the former USSR. See *Case Concerning Art. 18 of the Law On the Citizenship of the Russian Federation*, *VKS*, 1996, No. 3, p. 29.

[25] See, in particular, *Case Concerning Some Normative Acts of the City of Moscow* (reproduced *infra*). See also p. 267. *Case Concerning Art. 560 of the RSFSR Civil Code* (reproduced *infra* p. 260).

[26] *Sobranie*, No. 29, item 1011 (1997).

specified by Art. 13 of the Law (such as partisan political activities, conviction in a criminal case or health reasons).

The primary task of the Commissioner is to receive complaints about human rights violations in the country and to remedy these violations. The aggrieved individuals may file human rights complaints with the Commissioner if they are not satisfied with the relevant decisions of courts or administrative agencies. As an independent officer functioning outside the judicial system, the Commissioner is empowered to examine complaints and take measures to remedy violations. These measures include petitions to courts, including petitions to reconsider decisions that have already entered into legal force, participation in court proceedings, petitions to state organs and petitions to the Constitutional Court. Under the Constitutional Law on the Commissioner for Human Rights, in cases of grave and massive violations of human rights, the Commissioner may react to human rights violations even in the absence of formal complaints. In such cases the Commissioner has the right to make reports to the State Duma which may establish a parliamentary commission to investigate.

Because the Commissioner for Human Rights has no power to issue decisions binding on state bodies, she or he must rely on the traditional weapons that are always at the disposal of human rights organizations: publicity and campaigns of shame. The Constitutional Law on the Commissioner for Human Rights guarantees the right of the Commissioner to publicize her or his work. The Commissioner has the right to publish both her or his findings in specific cases and annual reports of activities.

While the creation of new human rights institutions in Russia is extremely important, it must be kept in mind that further improvement of the human rights situation in Russian will largely depend on the development of a broad awareness and respect for rule of law and human rights. World experience demonstrates that an aggressive human rights culture and pressure groups, in particular non-governmental organizations, are indispensable elements for the effective implementation of constitutionally guaranteed human rights and liberties.

F. International Guarantees

Another lesson of the communist past is the importance of international guarantees for human rights. The drafters of the 1993 Constitution relied on international guarantees in two ways.

First, the domestic human rights regime is strengthened by direct incorporation of all applicable international human rights standards. Art. 15(4) of the 1993 Constitution provides that the generally recognized principles and norms of international law and the international treaties of the Russian Federation are "an integral part of its legal system" and that norms of international treaties take priority over domestic legislation.[27] In addition, Art. 17(1) states that "the rights and freedoms of the human being and citizen shall be recognized and guaranteed in the Russian Federation in conformity with the generally recognized principles and norms of international law."

Because comprehensive legislative reform aimed at eliminating restrictive rules inherited from the former Soviet Union will take several years, direct application of international standards is an indispensable ingredient for the genuine protection of human rights in Russia. Judicial practice shows that both the Constitutional Court and ordinary courts regularly rely on international human rights standards when resolving human rights disputes.

Second, the 1993 Constitution envisions recourse to international organs concerned with the protection of human rights. According to Art. 46(3) of the Constitution, all persons enjoy a constitutionally protected right to submit petitions to these organs. There are several international bodies that have the power to receive petitions from aggrieved Russian citizens. Russia is a party to the International Covenant on Civil and Political Rights and its Optional Protocol.[28] This means that, after the exhaustion of domestic remedies, all aggrieved persons may submit individual petitions to the Human Rights Committee established under these instruments.[29]

Russia's admission to the Council of Europe has lead to ratification of the European Convention for the Protection of Human Rights and Fundamental Freedoms[30] and the acceptance of the control mechanism established by the Convention, in particular the jurisdiction of the European Court of Human Rights. This will open access to the European Court to all persons whose fundamental rights have been violated by national authorities. In addition, there are attempts at establishing a new human rights system within the Commonwealth of Independent States.[31] Although the CIS Convention on Fundamental Rights and Freedoms does not provide for a strong regional implementation mechanism, it contemplates the establishment of the Human

[27] For details, see *supra*, p. 32-50.

[28] 999 UNTS 171.

[29] Russia has also accepted the complaint procedures under the Convention on Torture and Other Forms of Cruel and Inhuman Treatment and Punishment and under the Convention on the Abolition of All Forms of Racial Discrimination.

[30] 213 UNTS 221.

[31] See CIS Convention on Human Rights and Fundamental Freedoms, reprinted in 17 *Human Rights Law Journal* 159 (1996). Russia ratified the CIS Convention in 1995. See *Sobranie*, No. 45, item 4239 (1995).

Rights Commission of the CIS which will be monitoring the enforcement of the Convention. Regulations on the Human Rights Commission of the CIS[32] provide that the Commission may "examine individual and collective applications submitted by any person or non-governmental organization concerning matters connected with human rights violations by any of the parties."

It may be argued that the constitutional clause allowing recourse to all these international human rights bodies does not have any real significance because it simply affirms international obligations that Russia has already assumed in conformity with international treaties. However, the matter is not that simple.

There is at least one element of substance that will be of crucial importance for the future domestic implementation of the findings of international human rights bodies. In a recent case concerning the Criminal Procedure Code, Art. 46 has been interpreted by the Constitutional Court in a way that gives the clause concerning resort to international bodies real significance. The Constitutional Court has held that Art. 46(3) of the Constitution means that "decisions of inter-state organs may lead to the reconsideration of specific cases by the highest courts of the Russian Federation and, consequently, establish their competence with respect to the institution of new proceedings aimed at changing the previously rendered decisions, including decisions handed down by the highest domestic judicial instance."[33]

Experience indicates that if a country joins international institutions with jurisdiction to hear claims by individuals that the country is not complying with its treaty obligations, national authorities tend to take treaty obligations seriously. In Europe, the jurisprudence of the European Court of Human Rights exerts a strong influence on the attitude of domestic courts of the members of the Council of Europe. As soon as the domestic authorities, including judges, realize that the European Court has emerged as a kind of Pan-European Constitutional Court,[34] they start to pay much closer attention to the European Convention and to the Court's jurisprudence. As a result, there is much more willingness to apply the European Convention directly.

Although in practice only a small percentage of cases is likely to be

---

[32] Reprinted in 17 *Human Rights Law Journal* 163 (1996).

[33] *Case Concerning Arts. 371, 374 and 384 of the Criminal Procedure Code, VKS*, 1996, No. 2, p. 2.

[34] See A.H. Robertson, Human Rights in the World 299 (1989) ("Becoming a party to a treaty like the European Convention is rather like adopting a written constitution with judicial supervision").

appealed to the Human Rights Committee or to the European Court of Human Rights, Russian judges will know that there are international institutions which can review their interpretation of international human rights principles and norms. Russia's participation in the Council of Europe, in particular, is likely to make Russian courts more willing to look to European human rights standards. Thanks to the recent holding of the Constitutional Court just mentioned, they will also know that decisions of these international organs may lead to the domestic reexamination of previously decided cases.

G. Major Areas of Concern: Comments of the Human Rights Committee

Despite many positive legislative and institutional developments, much remains to be done to guarantee effective implementation of human rights standards in Russia. The majority of international observers agree that the current human rights situation in Russia is far from ideal.

The human rights situation in Russia has been reviewed by several international bodies. The most important UN human rights body - the Human Rights Committee established under the 1966 Covenant on Civil and Political Rights - had the opportunity to assess Russia's progress in the human rights field in 1995.The Committee, which acts as the guardian of the Covenant, has the right to receive and consider state reports on the human rights situation in the states that are parties to the Covenant. State parties to the Covenant are required to submit reports for consideration by the Committee "on measures they have adopted" which give effect to the rights recognized in the Covenant, and "on the progress made in the enjoyment of those rights."[35] Under Art. 40 of the Covenant, "reports shall indicate the factors and difficulties, if any, affecting the implementation of the present Covenant." Russia submitted its fourth periodic report in 1995.

Upon examining the state reports, the Human Rights Committee makes general comments on the human rights situation in the reporting country. The official Comments of the Human Rights Committee adopted in response to the 1995 Russian Report deal with many aspects of the human rights situation in Russia. Following are excerpts that reflect the Committee's primary critiques:

---

[35] Covenant on Civil and Political Rights, Art. 40.

Comments of the Human Rights Committee, UN Doc. CCPR/C/79/Add.2 (1995)

A. Introduction

2. The Committee welcomes the fourth periodic report of the Russian Federation and views with satisfaction its dialogue with the delegation, particularly the delegation's willingness to engage in a frank discussion with the Committee and the detail in which its written and additional oral questions were addressed. The Committee regrets that, while the report was mainly drafted on the basis of legal measures enacted or under consideration, insufficient information was provided regarding the actual enjoyment of some of the rights guaranteed in the Covenant. The Committee appreciates that this situation was partly remedied through the oral responses to the Committee's questions, which allowed it to obtain a clearer view of the overall situation in the State party.

B. Factors and Difficulties Affecting the Application of the Covenant

3. The Committee notes that it is necessary to overcome vestiges of the totalitarian past and that much remains to be done to strengthen democratic institutions and respect for the rule of law. This has created a legal vacuum in certain areas, in which the principles set forth in the Constitution are not implemented by corresponding laws and regulations. The Committee notes that the enactment of new laws is being undertaken by the Government but their consideration by two Chambers of the Federal Assembly prior to promulgation is generally a slow process.

4. The Committee is aware of economic difficulties facing the State party, which inevitably affect the application of the Covenant.

C. Positive Aspects

5. The Committee expresses its satisfaction as to the fundamental and positive changes which have recently taken place in the Russian Federation. These changes will create a better political, constitutional and legal framework for the full implementation of the rights enshrined in the Covenant.

6. The Committee welcomes the new Constitution of 1993, which gives legal recognition to the concept of human rights and freedoms of the individual. The Committee considers that chapter 2 of the Constitution, which

enumerates the rights and liberties of the individuals, conforms to many of the basic rights provided under the Covenant.

7. The Committee welcomes the provisions of article 15, paragraph 4, of the Constitution, which, together with the limiting provision of article 125, paragraph 6, establishes that international treaties, including the Covenant, are part of the Russian legal system and superior to domestic law. It further welcomes the inclusion of article 17, paragraph 1, which stipulates that the basic rights and liberties, in conformity with the commonly recognized principles and norms of international law, shall be recognized and guaranteed by the State party under the Constitution, the recognition in the Constitution of the right to apply to international bodies when domestic remedies are exhausted and the written and oral affirmations that the provisions of the Covenant are directly invocable in domestic courts of law.

8. In this context, the Committee also welcomes the fact that the Russian Federation is party to the Optional Protocol to the Covenant.

9. The Committee welcomes the progress made towards democracy since the consideration of the third periodic report. It also welcomes the promulgation of a number of legal instruments aimed at guaranteeing human rights for all persons in the territory of the State party, including the new Civil Code and Criminal Code. It further welcomes the draft law aimed at a comprehensive reform of the judicial process and the Code of Criminal Procedures currently in the drafting stage and notes with appreciation that the right of all persons whose rights are violated to have access to judicial recourse has been legally established.

10. The Committee welcomes the establishment of several bodies charged with the protection of human rights, including the Office of the Human Rights Commissioner under the State Duma and the Presidential Human Rights Commission, as well as the newly established Commission for Human Rights of the Commonwealth of Independent States.

11. The Committee welcomes the Government's assurances that a systematic review of persons placed in psychiatric facilities under previous regimes will be carried out and trusts that all those found to be placed in such facilities without due cause will be released. . .

4. Principal Subjects of Concern

13. The Committee is concerned that the profound legislative changes taking place within the State party have not been matched by the actual protection of human rights at the implementation level. Specifically, it regrets that many of the rights established under the Constitution have not been put

into effect through the enactment of implementing laws and regulations and that the relationship of the various bodies entrusted with the protection of human rights has not been clearly defined. . .

14. The Committee is concerned that, despite guarantees of equality in the Constitution and in labour legislation, the de facto situation of women is one of continuing inequality. The failure to ensure equal remuneration for work of comparable worth and the persistence of attitudes and practices which impose child-rearing and other domestic responsibilities entirely on women contribute to this inequality and to discrimination in the workplace. The Committee is especially alarmed at the extent of rape and domestic violence and the inadequate efforts made by the authorities to deal with this problem. It is also alarmed at the high incidence of unemployment among women.

15. Although the Committee notes that the draft Criminal Code before the Federal Assembly would reduce the number of crimes that may result in the imposition of the death penalty, it is still concerned at the wide range of crimes still punishable by such penalty. Moreover, the Committee notes that while the number of persons actually executed has declined dramatically since 1993, sentencing continues, which has resulted in a large and growing number of persons on death row.

16. The Committee expresses deep concern over the practice of pre-trial detention and over the fact that temporary detention has been extended from 10 to 30 days in certain cases. It is concerned by the extent of the Procurator's competence to decide on matters relating to arrest or detention which cannot be challenged by the person concerned before a court. Under article 9, paragraph 3, of the Covenant, the detention of persons before they are granted a trial should not be the norm and, when it occurs, persons so detained should be granted a trial within a reasonable time or be released. The Committee is concerned that pre-trial detention is practiced, not only in cases of serious criminal charges but more so on misdemeanour charges and frequently for unreasonably long periods of time, and that no effective mechanism exists for monitoring such detention.

17. The Committee further expresses grave concern over the lack of a monitoring mechanism for penitentiary facilities to ensure humane treatment of detainees and prisoners. In this regard, it deplores the cruel, inhumane and degrading conditions that persist in many detention centres and penitentiary facilities and condemns the use of food deprivation as punishment.

18. The Committee expresses concern about the lack of independence and efficiency of the judiciary and the long delays in the administration of justice, which do not conform with the requirements of both articles 9 and 14

of the Covenant, and notes in that regard that the judicial system in the Russian Federation cannot be effective to ensure protection of rights until there is a sufficient number of well-trained and qualified judges and lawyers.

19. The Committee is concerned that actions may continue which violate the right to protection from unlawful or arbitrary interference with privacy, family, home or correspondence. It is concerned that the mechanisms to intrude into private telephone communication continue to exist, without a clear legislation setting out the conditions for legitimate interferences with privacy and providing for safeguards against unlawful interferences.

20. Although federal law has provided for the abolition of the *propiska* (residence permit) system, the Committee is concerned that at regional and local levels, the system is still applied in practice, thus violating not only the Constitution, but also article 12 of the Covenant. It expresses further concern that the most important legal restriction on the right to leave the country is still cast in terms of a State secret. This does not correspond with the requirements of article 12, paragraph 3, of the Covenant and the Committee deplores, in that regard, the resistance to date in bringing the legislation in conformity with the Covenant. The Committee further regrets that all individuals not having yet performed their national service are excluded in principle from enjoying their right to leave the country.

21. The Committee is concerned that conscientious objection to military service, although recognized under article 59 of the Constitution, is not a practical option under Russian law and takes note in this regard of the draft law on alternative service before the Federal Assembly. It expresses its concern at the possibility that such alternative service may be made punitive, either in nature or in length of service. The Committee is also seriously concerned at the allegations of widespread cruelty and ill-treatment of young conscript-soldiers.

22. The Committee is concerned at reports of growing number of homeless and abandoned children in need of measures of protection. . .

25. The Committee expresses concern over the jurisdiction of the military courts in civil cases. Persons detained by members of the armed forces are said to be able to raise complaints before the Military Procurator's Office in charge of the detention centre where they were held. This would appear to create a situation in which the army is entrusted with the judgement and sentencing of the crimes committed by its own members. The Committee is concerned that such a situation may cause miscarriages of justice, particularly in the light of the Government's acknowledgment that the army, even at the

highest levels, is not familiar with international human rights law, including the Covenant. . .

27. With reference to the specific situation in Chechnya, the Committee expresses concern that article 4 of the Covenant, which specifies the provisions that are non-derogable even in times of public emergency, has not been complied with. It maintains that this article is applicable to the situation in Chechnya, where the use of weapons by combatants has led to the loss of life and deprivation of freedom of large numbers of persons, regardless of the fact that a state of emergency has not been formally declared.

28. The Committee deplores the excessive and disproportionate use of force by Russian forces in Chechnya, indicating grave violation of human rights. It further deplores the fact that no one has been made responsible for the inhumane treatment of prisoners and other detained persons, that investigations on charges of human rights violations by Russian forces, including killing of civilians, have so far been inadequate, that civilian installations such as schools and hospitals were destroyed by government forces, and that a large number of civilians have been killed or displaced as a consequence of the destruction of their homes.

29. The Committee expresses deep concern about the large number of reported cases of torture, ill treatment of the person and arbitrary detention in "reception centres" or "filtration camps," which were originally established to determine the identities of captured combatants but are reported to accommodate large numbers of civilians as well. It deplores the maltreatment of detainees in these centres and is concerned that the International Committee of the Red Cross (ICRC) has not been given access to all such camps. . .

E. Suggestions and Recommendations

31. The Committee recommends that the relationship between the various bodies charged with the protection of human rights be clearly defined and coordinated and that the existence and functions of these bodies be widely publicized. The Committee further recommends that a mechanism be clearly established to ensure conformity of all presidential decrees and laws with the provisions of the Covenant and other international human rights instruments to which the State is party. . .

33. The Committee recommends that greater efforts be made to collect information on the situation of women and the effects on them of the structural political, economic and social changes taking place. On this basis, the Government should initiate or strengthen programmes aimed at providing assistance to women in difficult circumstances, including unemployed women,

victims of domestic violence and victims of rape, with a view to ensuring their equality before the law and the equal protection of the law. In particular, it should consider allocating responsibility for that purpose to an appropriate high-level governmental body.

34. The Committee urges the Government to reduce substantially the number of crimes for which the death penalty may be imposed, in accordance with article 6 of the Covenant, with a view to its eventual elimination.

35. The Committee recommends that the treatment of persons deprived of their liberty, whether in detention centres or in penitentiary facilities, be effectively monitored. In this connection, it strongly recommends the adoption of new rules and regulations that comply fully with articles 7, 9, 10 and 14 of the Covenant and the United Nations Body of Principles for the Protection of All Persons under Any Form of Detention or Imprisonment and that the texts of all prison rules and orders and international norms on prison administration be made public and accessible. The Committee further recommends that priority be given to the establishment of the Visitors' Committee for the correctional institutions of the Federation and that legislation on the judicial review of arrest and detention be urgently passed in compliance with article 9, paragraph 3, of the Covenant, and article 22, paragraph 2, of the Constitution. It urges that the Government should refrain from placing first-time, non-violent and petty offenders in detention centres, and give consideration to various other practical measures designed to reduce the overcrowding of pre-trial detention centres, particularly the greater use of release pending trial. It also calls for an immediate end to the practice of food deprivation as punishment in prisons and encourages the Government's initiatives to institute alternative forms of punishment. . .

37. The Committee recommends that the abolition of the *propiska* system be carried out all over the country without exceptions. Further steps should be taken to bring the law concerning the right to leave the country in full line with the State party's obligations under article 12, paragraphs 2 and 3, of the Covenant and, in particular, to remove restrictions to knowledge of State secrets. The Committee urges that all regional and local authorities be made to comply with the Federal policy of abolishing the *propiska* system (i.e. the system of "internal passes" or "passports"). . .

39. The Committee urges that stringent measures be adopted to ensure an immediate end to mistreatment and abuse of army recruits by their officers and fellow soldiers. It further recommends that every effort be made to ensure that reasonable alternatives to military service be made available that are not punitive in nature or in length of service. It urges that all charges brought against conscientious objectors to military service be dropped.

40. The Committee recommends that national legislation be amended to reflect the broad concept of minorities contained in articles 2, 26 and 27 of the Covenant, which prohibit discrimination on the basis of race, colour, sex, opinion or other status, and further protect the rights not only of "national minorities" but also of ethnic, religious and linguistic minorities. . .

46. The Committee recommends that education in human rights be included in school and university curricula and that its comments be widely disseminated and incorporated into the curricula of all human rights training programmes organized for law-enforcement officers and administration officials.

QUESTIONS AND COMMENTS

1. What are the main areas of concern identified by the Committee?

2. What are the principal suggestions made by the Committee?

3. The Human Rights Committee was not the only international body to critique Russia's actions in Chechnya. The UN Commission on Human Rights condemned "grave violations of human rights as well as of international humanitarian law" in Chechnya (see the Statement of the Chairman of the Commission, reprinted in 17 *Human Rights Law Journal* 245 (1996)). At the European regional level, the human rights violations in Chechnya became the major obstacle to the acceptance of Russia in the Council of Europe. While Russia was admitted to the Council of Europe in 1996 as the 39th member state, the Parliamentary Assembly of the Council of Europe made it clear that one of the principal conditions for membership was a political solution of the Chechen conflict. The Political Affairs Committee of the Council of Europe also noted numerous human rights violations in Russia, including human rights violations in detention centers and in the armed forces. The Committee's Report on Russia's request for membership of the Council of Europe stated that the Russian legal system "is clearly not yet fully in line with the Council of Europe's standards" (Parliamentary Assembly of the Council of Europe, Report on Russia's Request for Membership of the Council of Europe, reprinted in 17 *Human Rights Law Journal* 187, 191 (1996)).

4. The 1996 Criminal Code retained the death penalty for most serious crimes. However, Russia's accession to the Council of Europe resulted in a moratorium on executions. One of the conditions for Russia's membership is adherence to the Protocol No. 6 to the European Convention on Human Rights on the abolition of the death penalty in time of peace. Although Russia has not yet ratified Protocol No. 6, the provisions of the Criminal Code on the death penalty are not enforced.

5. Note that the Human Rights Committee "deplores the cruel, inhumane and degrading conditions that persist in many detention centres and penitentiary facilities and condemns the use of food deprivation as punishment." Russian human rights organizations published well-documented studies indicating that three hundred thousand prisoners in Russian pre-trial detention facilities are kept in conditions that can be described as torture and inhuman treatment due mainly to horrible overcrowding in cells. For details, see Moscow Center for Prison Reform, In Search of a Solution. Crime, Criminal Policy and Prison Facilities in the Former Soviet Union (1996).

6. Note also that the Human Rights Committee "expresses deep concern over the practice of pre-trial detention and over the fact that temporary detention has been extended from 10 to 30 days in certain cases." Russian authorities improved procedures governing temporary detention. The current practice will be discussed in Chapter X.

7. The Human Rights Committee expressed its concern over conscientious objection to military service. It stated that "although recognized under article 59 of the Constitution, [it] is not a practical option under Russian law." Art. 59(3) states that "in cases where the performance of military service runs counter to a citizen's persuasions or religion, and also in other cases specified by federal law, a citizen of the Russian Federation shall have the right to substitute alternative civilian for military service."

Although Art. 59 contemplates adoption of a federal law for "other cases," the right to religious objections is a directly enforceable right. Recent judicial practice indicates that courts have begun to enforce this right. The Constitutional Court stated that the right to conscientious objection to military service for reasons of persuasion or religion has direct effect and "must be enforced irrespective of whether the relevant federal law has been enacted" (See *Konstitutsionnyi Sud Rossiiskoi Federatsii. Postanovlenia, opredelenia 1992-1996*, at 502 (1997)). The Supreme Court dismissed criminal charges against a conscientious objector who was of the Jehovah's Witness faith. The Supreme Court stated: "Under Art. 59(3) of the Constitution of the Russian Federation in cases where the performance of military service runs counter to a citizen's convictions or religion, and also in other cases specified by federal law, a citizen of the Russian Federation shall have the right to replace military service with alternative civilian service. The absence of a law on alternative civil service cannot serve as a ground for the enforcement of the Law of the Russian Federation of February 11, 1993 "On Military Duties and Military Service" with respect to persons who have the right to alternative service (*In Re Bakalin, BVS*, 1997, No. 3, p.8).

H. Human Rights in Judicial Practice

1. Introduction

Because the list of human rights guaranteed by the 1993 Constitution is extensive, the following discussion will focus on some selected areas that have been elucidated by the rulings of the Constitutional Court and the Supreme Court.

Note that human rights were discussed in previous chapters. Constitutional provisions on non-discrimination were the basis for the Constitutional Court's ruling in the *Labor Code Case.*[36] The principle of non-discrimination in matters of taxation was also one of the arguments advanced by the Constitutional Court in the *Case Concerning Arts. 18(2) and 20 of the Law of the Russian Federation on the Fundamentals of the Tax System in the Russian Federation.*[37] Freedom of association and the legal status of political parties were discussed by the Constitutional Court in the *Communist Party Case.*[38] Electoral rights of Russian citizens were the focus of discussion in *Potapov v. The Legislative Assembly of the Altai Region* and in *Citizens of Uglitch v. Vice-Governor and Governor of the Yaroslavl Region.*[39] The right to self- determination was an important element in both *Tatarstan Case* and *Chechnya Case.*[40] *Nuclear Fuel Cases*[41] involved the constitutional right to a favorable environment. The *Case Concerning Art 47 of the Criminal Procedure Code* dealing with the right to qualified legal assistance was summarized in Chapter III (F4). The right to judicial review as a constitutional right was discussed in Chapter IV(F).

Issues concerning the rights of individuals in criminal proceedings will be discussed in Chapter X.

2. Property Rights

Constitutional protection of property rights is extremely important in societies emerging from the socialist economic system. The right to property occupies a prominent position in Russian constitutional law. Art. 8 of the Constitution expressly recognizes and protects "private" property. According to Art. 35(2) of the Constitution "everyone shall have the right to own property

[36] See *supra* p. 34-41.
[37] See *supra* p. 205-210.
[38] See *supra* p. 141-153.
[39] See *supra* p. 91-94.
[40] See *supra* p. 184-199.
[41] See *supra* p. 18-22.

and to possess, use and dispose of it both individually and jointly with other persons." The right of inheritance is also guaranteed.[42]

The drafters of the 1993 Constitution also attempted to create legal guarantees against state interference with property rights. Art. 35(1) of the Constitution provides that "the right of private ownership shall be protected by law." While the Constitution recognizes the possibility of state intervention, it imposes limits on alienation of property. Art. 35(3) states: "No one may be deprived of his or her property except pursuant to a judicial decision. Property can be forcibly taken for state needs only on condition of prior and equal compensation."

The following cases illustrate several aspects of property right protection under the Constitution.

The Constitutional Court: *Case Concerning Art. 11 of the Law "On the Federal Organs of Tax Police"* (*VKS*, 1996, No. 5, p. 22)

[The proceedings were initiated by the founders of two limited liability partnerships - MKM LTD and 5M LTD - who claimed that Art. 11 of the federal Law "On the Federal Organs of Tax Police" violates their constitutional rights and liberties]

1. According to Art. 11 of the Law of the Russian Federation of June 24, 1993 "On the Federal Organs of Tax Police" (as amended on December 17, 1995) the federal organs of tax police have been granted powers . . . to investigate taxpayers and . . . impose sanctions.

Paragraphs 2 and 3 of Art. 11(1) of the Law dealing with sanctions imposed by the organs of tax police refer to other laws; as a result they must be considered in conjunction with Art. 13 of the Law of the Russian Federation of December 27, 1991 "On the Fundamentals of the Tax System in the Russian Federation" and Arts. 7(8,9) and 8 of the RSFSR Law of March 21, 1991 "On the State Tax Service of RSFSR." It follows from the literal meaning of the above acts, from the meaning attributed to them by the official interpretation (including interpretation by the Supreme Arbitration Court of the Russian Federation) and by the established legal practice, as well as from their place in the system of legal acts concerning the powers of tax officials, that the organs of tax police may collect from juridical persons tax arrears and fines and other penalties envisioned by the legislation in an uncontested procedure [summary administrative proceedings resulting in actual taking of tax arrears and fines].

[42] Constitution, Art. 35 (4).

The complaint challenges the constitutionality of this provision as enforced in specific cases. . .

2. The petitioners argue that the tax police power to collect the relevant payments from the juridical persons in an uncontested procedure as opposed to a judicial procedure (applied with respect to individuals only) violates the constitutional right to private property and contravenes Article 35 of the Constitution of the Russian Federation.

According to Art. 35 of the Constitution of the Russian Federation the right of private ownership shall be protected by law (paragraph 1); everyone shall have the right to have property in his or her ownership, to possess, use and dispose of it both individually and jointly with other persons (paragraph 2); no one may be arbitrarily deprived of his or her property except on the basis of a judicial decision. Property can be forcibly taken for state needs only on condition of prior and equal compensation (paragraph 3).

At the same time, the right of private ownership is not absolute; it does not belong to the category of rights which, according to Art. 56(3) of the Constitution of the Russian Federation, cannot be restricted in any circumstances. Therefore it may be restricted by federal law under Art. 55(3) of the Constitution of the Russian Federation but only to the extent required for the protection of the fundamentals of the constitutional system, morality, health, rights and lawful interests of other persons, for ensuring the defense of the country and the security of the state. This corresponds to the generally recognized principles and norms of international law, in particular the Universal Declaration of Human Rights of December 10, 1948, according to which everyone has duties to the community in which alone the free and full development of his personality is possible (Article 29(1)); in the exercise of his rights and freedoms, everyone shall be subject only to such limitations as are determined by law solely for the purpose of securing due recognition and respect for the rights and freedoms of others and of meeting the just requirements of morality, public order and the general welfare in a democratic society (Article 29(2)). An analogous provision allowing limitations of human rights is also included in the International Covenant on Economic, Social and Cultural Rights of December 19, 1966 (Article 4).

3. Under Art. 57 of the Constitution of the Russian Federation everyone shall pay lawfully instituted taxes and levies. This constitutional provision has a special public legal character (and not a private or civil law character) which results from the public legal character of state and state power under Articles 1(1), 3, 4 and 7 of the Constitution of the Russian Federation.

Taxes are a necessary condition for the existence of state; therefore all taxpayers have an absolute obligation to pay taxes in accordance with Article 57 of the Constitution of the Russian Federation. The taxpayer has no right to freely dispose of the part of his or her property which in the form of a certain amount of money must be payed to the state budget; the taxpayer must regularly transfer this sum to the state because nonpayment violates the rights and legally protected interests of other persons and of the state. The collection of taxes cannot be considered to be an arbitrary deprivation of property - it is a lawful taking of part of property based on the constitutional public legal obligation. . .

The demands of the tax organs and the tax obligation imposed on the taxpayer follow from the law and not from a contract. The statutory form of instituting taxes, the mandatory and compulsory procedure for their collection . . . result from the public legal nature of taxes and of the state budget and from the fiscal sovereignty of state. As a result, any dispute concerning non-payment of taxes is a public tax dispute and not a civil law dispute.

The powers of tax organs to enforce public obligations in an uncontested procedure for collecting taxes is legitimate to the extent that their actions, first, remain within the sphere of tax relations, and do not acquire the character of civil law, administrative law or criminal law sanctions, and, second, do not limit or diminish the rights and liberties of the human being and citizen. . .

According to Art. 46 of the Constitution of the Russian Federation, the taxpayer in any case has the right to challenge decisions and actions (inactions) of tax organs and their officials in a court of law. This right has been realized by the petitioners because the arbitration court has already resolved the dispute (including the question concerning the amount of tax arrears payment).

Under Art. 8(2) of the Constitution of the Russian Federation private, state, municipal and other forms of ownership shall be recognized and shall enjoy equal protection in the Russian Federation. The challenged provision envisions the enforcement of the same procedure - an uncontested procedure - for collecting tax payments, and, in cases of disagreement on the part of the taxpayer, the same dispute settlement procedure, namely petitions to higher tax authorities and (or) petitions to courts, with respect to all juridical persons irrespective of form of ownership (private or state owned). Consequently, all juridical persons enjoy a guarantee of judicial protection of their right to property. The difference in the application of judicial procedure with respect to juridical persons (subsequent judicial review) and individuals (prior judicial review) is determined not by the from of ownership but by the peculiarities of juridical persons as taxpayers. These differences apply with respect to the same form of property, namely private property, because the owners may be both individuals and juridical persons.

It follows that, if the rights of juridical persons are protected by subsequent judicial review, the uncontested procedure for collecting taxes does not contravene the requirements of the Constitution of the Russia Federation.

4. The constitutional right of the human being and citizen protected by Art. 35(2,3) of the Constitution of the Russian Federation applies to juridical persons to the extent that this right corresponds to the nature of juridical persons.

The materials of the case indicate that the petitioners to the Constitutional Court are limited liability partnerships (companies), that is, organizations governed by the rules concerning the activities of juridical persons operating as commercial entities. They were created by citizens for the purposes of joint enjoyment of certain constitutional rights, such as the right of everyone to freely use his or her abilities and property for entrepreneurial or any other economic activity not prohibited by the law (Constitution of the Russian Federation, Article 34(1)) and the right of everyone to have property in his or her ownership, to possess, use and dispose of it both individually and jointly with other persons (Constitution of the Russian Federation, Art. 35(2)).

In contrast to citizens - physical persons, juridical persons have separate property and are liable for its obligations with this property. As far as citizens are concerned, even in cases when they are individual entrepreneurs without the formation of a juridical person, they use their property not only for entrepreneurial activity but also as personal property necessary for the realization of inalienable rights and liberties. In this case the property of the citizen is not divided into different categories.

Different procedures for collecting taxes from individuals and from juridical persons has not been instituted for the purpose of creating inequality in the sphere of tax relations (the obligation to pay taxes); the purpose is to prevent administrative interference with individual rights and to ensure that the relevant questions would be resolved only in court. Collection of taxes in an uncontested procedure with respect to citizens would have gone beyond the framework of pure tax public legal relations and would have interfered with other relations, including civil law relations; in this sphere, the parties engaged in a legal relationship are not subordinated to each other; as a result, one of the parties cannot directly enforce its tax powers on the other. . .

5. It follows from the meaning of Art. 57 of the Constitution of the Russian Federation that a tax obligation is an obligation of the taxpayer to pay certain taxes established by law. Non-payment of taxes must be compensated

by the payment of tax arrears and full compensation of damages to the state resulting from the late payment of taxes. As a result, the law-maker has the right to demand the payment of not only tax arrears but additional payments aimed at compensating damages to the state budget resulting from non-payment of taxes or late payment of taxes. An uncontested procedure for the collection of these payments from the taxpayer - juridical person - results from the mandatory and compulsory character of taxes under the law.

Consequently, an uncontested procedure for collecting of tax arrears, as well as of forfeitures,[Forfeitures are defined by Art. 330 of the Civil Code as a monetary sum determined by a statute that a debtor must pay to the creditor in case of nonperformance or improper of an obligation, in particular in case of delay in performance] from juridical persons enforced by the organs of tax police and envisioned by Article 13 of the Law of the Russian Federation "On the Fundamentals of the Tax System in the Russian Federation" and Articles. 7(8,9) and 8 of the RSFSR Law "On the State Tax Service of RSFSR" does not contravene the Constitution of the Russian Federation.

Other measures envisioned by these clauses, namely the collection of all sums of concealed or understated revenues (profits) as well as of different categories of fines, by their character go beyond the framework of tax obligations as such. They are aimed not at restoring the prior obligation, but at penalizing tax law violations, that is, unlawful acts envisioned by the law, which may be committed intentionally or through negligence. When dealing with tax law violations the tax organs must prove not only the fact that these violations have been committed but also the degree of guilt. If a tax law violation occurs, the organs of tax police have the power to impose fines on juridical persons. Under Articles 45 and 46(1,2) of the Constitution of the Russian Federation this decision may be appealed by the juridical person in the established procedure to the higher tax organ and (or) court. If an appeal has been filed the fine may not be collected in an uncontested procedure; the execution must be postponed pending the decision of the court.

Consequently, in cases when the taxpayer disagrees with the decision made by the organ of tax police, an uncontested procedure for collecting fines envisioned by the challenged provision goes beyond the permissible limitation (Constitution, Articles 55(5) and 57) of the right protected by Article 35(3) of the Constitution of the Russian Federation according to which no one may be arbitrarily deprived of his or her property unless on the basis of decision by a court of law. . .

The Constitutional Court: ***Case Concerning Arts. 242(4,5) and 280 of the Customs Code of the Russian Federation*** (*Sobranie*, No. 21, item 2542 (1997))

1. On March 30, 1995, the head of the Novgorod customs office issued a ruling according to which a citizen A.B. Andreev was fined for violating customs regulations - non-declaration of a car VAZ-2109; in accordance with Article 280 of the Customs Code of the Russian Federation the car was confiscated. A.B. Andreev filed a petition with the Novgorod city court which, by its ruling of February 16, 1996, vacated that part of the ruling of the head of the Novgorod customs office that concerned confiscation of the car. The Procurator of the Novgorod province lodged a protest with the Novgorod provincial court. The Novgorod provincial court came to the conclusion that norms of the Customs Code concerning the right of customs organs to confiscate goods and transport vehicles, as applied in the case of A.B. Andreev, do not correspond to Article 35(3) of the Constitution of the Russian Federation; it then filed a request with the Constitutional Court of the Russian Federation to reveiw their constitutionality. . .

2. The object of review are norms of paragraphs 4 and 6 of Article 242 and Article 280 of the Customs Code of the Russian Federation which provide for the right of customs organs to confiscate goods and transport vehicles used in violation of customs regulations.

Confiscation of the above property is imposed by the customs organs for the purposes of protecting the economic security of the Russian Federation, as well as of the rights of citizens. The protection of the economic security of the Russian Federation as one of the bases of the sovereignty of the Russian Federation contemplates the establishment of a legal regime aimed at suppression of unlawful interference with the economic interests of the state. The resulting relations between the organs of the state, on the one hand, and juridical persons and individuals, on the other hand, have a public legal character. It explains the specific nature of the relationship between the state and persons who have violated rules established by the law; this relationship is quite different from the relations in the private sphere. It envisions, among other things, the definition in the Customs Code of the Russian Federation of certain wrongs and the corresponding sanctions, including confiscation of goods and transport vehicles from persons violating customs regulations.

3. The petitioner argues that the power of customs organs to confiscate property (goods and transport vehicles) of persons responsible for violating customs regulations in an administrative procedure contravenes Article 35(3) of the Constitution of the Russian Federation according to which "no one may be arbitrarily deprived of his or her property except on the basis of a judicial decision."

This provision must be considered in conjunction with Article 35(1) of the Constitution of the Russian Federation under which the right of private ownership shall be protected by law. This constitutional provision extends to all relations involving private property irrespective of whether they occur in the public or private legal sphere. . .

Taking of property by means of confiscation is a compulsory termination of the right to property. It follows from the meaning of Article 35(3) of the Constitution of the Russian Federation that confiscation of property may be imposed on the above persons - physical and juridical persons - only after the relevant court renders its decision. . . A court decision represents the final decision in matters concerning termination of property. Prior to the court decision the state organs may enforce administrative legal measures envisioned by the law (taking, confiscation etc.). If the interested person does not agree with the taking of property by means of administrative decision concerning confiscation, she or he has the right to challenge the decision in court. The possibility of challenging in court of decisions and actions of state organs and their officials is a general guarantee that follows from Article 46(2) of the Constitution of the Russian Federation. Persons who have violated customs regulations and who have been sanctioned by the competent state bodies for the violation still enjoy the constitutional guarantee to protect private property in court; however, this protection is guaranteed only by means of subsequent judicial review.

4. The law provides that one of the means of terminating the right of ownership over property is confiscation, i.e. taking of property by the state without compensation as a sanction for the commission of a crime or other violations of the law (Civil Code of the Russian Federation, Articles 235(2) and 243(1)). In the framework of this procedure, the taking of property and the adoption of a decisions by the competent agencies on confiscation does not in itself terminate the right of ownership. The right of ownership is terminated only as a result of actual enforcement of such a decision and actual transfer of title to the relevant property to the state. . .

The property which is subject to the relevant decision on confiscation becomes the property of the state only after the time period for challenging the decision in the higher customs organs or in court has lapsed (Article 370 of the Customs Code of the Russian Federation). A complaint postpones the enforcement of the decisions of the customs organ concerning sanctions for violations of customs regulations, including sanctions envisioning confiscation (Article 376 of the Customs Code of the Russian Federation). Under Article 378 of the Customs Code of the Russian Federation, if a complaint has been lodged, the ruling concerning confiscation of property may be enforced only after the court renders a decision dismissing the complaint and recognizing the lawfulness and legitimacy of the ruling.

Consequently, given the guarantee of subsequent judicial control as a means to protect the rights of the owner, the power of the customs organs to issue a ruling on confiscation of property as a sanction for customs law violations does not contravene the Constitution of the Russian Federation. . .

QUESTIONS AND COMMENTS

1. Are there any differences in the procedure for taking of property in cases of non-payment of taxes and in situations involving violations of customs regulations? How did these differences affect the reasoning of the Constitutional Court in the *Case Concerning Art. 11 of the Law "On the Federal Organs of Tax Police"* and in the *Case Concerning Arts. 242(4,5) and 280 of the Customs Code of the Russian Federation*?

2. What is the nature of the distinction between public law relations and private law relations emphasized by the Court in both cases?

3. Art. 35(3) of the Constitution clearly states that "no one may be arbitrarily deprived of his or her property except on the basis of a judicial decision." It means that only courts may render decisions on taking property. An administrative procedure for taking property envisioned by the Customs Code obviously violates the clear language of Art. 35(3). What was the opinion of the Constitutional Court on the matter? What arguments were used in support of the Court's holding? Do you agree with these arguments? What is the weakest point in the Court's position? Does this decision stand for the proposition that the government may take private property whenever it wants so long as the citizen has a right to sue in court to get it back?

4. Are these two cases consistent with each other? Note that in the *Case Concerning Art. 11 of the Law "On the Federal Organs of Tax Police"* the Court held that "the powers of tax organs to enforce public obligations in an uncontested procedure for collecting taxes is legitimate to the extent that their actions, first, *remain within the sphere of tax relations,* and do not acquire the character of civil law, administrative law or criminal law sanctions, and, second, do not limit or diminish the rights and liberties of the human being and citizen. . ." (Emphasis added - eds.). In that case the Court also held that if the relevant sanctions imposed by tax organs assume the character of administrative or criminal sanctions the question may be resolved only in a court of law. Did the Court change its position in the *Case Concerning Arts. 242(4,5) and 280 of the Customs Code of the Russian Federation*?

5. In explaining the sanctions envisioned by the Customs Code, the Court relied on the notions of public law and public interests. At the same time, the Court did not expressly rely on Art. 55(3) of the Constitution which

envisions several possibilities for imposing restrictions or limitations on human rights. What might be the reasons for the Court's reluctance to rely on Art. 55(3)?

6. Note that although the Court relied on the notions of public law when dealing with confiscation as a sanction for violations of customs regulations, at a later stage it stated that the constitutional provisions according to which "the right of private ownership shall be protected by law" (Constitution, Art. 35 (1)) "extends to all relations involving private property irrespective of whether they occur in the public or private legal sphere. . ." Is there any inconsistency in the Court's reasoning?

The Supreme Court: *Nevsorov v. State Traffic Inspectorate* (*BVS*, 1997, No. 6, p. 9)

Nevsorov filed a complaint with the court against actions of officers of the State Traffic Inspectorate [traffic police] of the Department of Internal Affairs of the Arkhangel'sk Province who, on September 22, 1995, towed his personal car "Moskvich-412" from the courtyard of a house on Popov Street in the City of Arkhangel'sk and put it on the "fine parking lot." He asked the court to declare the above actions of the officers of the State Traffic Inspectorate unlawful and order them to return the car.

The Oktiabrskiy district court of the City of Arkhangel'sk granted relief in Nevsorov's suit. The Judicial Collegium for Civil Case of the Arkhangel'sk Provincial Court affirmed the judgment. The Presidium of the Arkhangel'sk Regional Court vacated the judgment and rendered a new judgment dismissing Nevsorov's complaint. . .

The Deputy Chairman of the Supreme Court of the Russian Federation lodged a protest seeking to vacate the rulings of the Presidium of the Arkhangel'sk Provincial Court because the court incorrectly applied the norms of substantive law. On February 3, 1997, the Collegium for Civil Cases of the Supreme Court upheld the protest for the following reasons:

The materials of the case indicate that Nevsorov's car was parked on the lawn in the courtyard of a house and for this reasons was removed to the "fine parking lot." The representative of the State Traffic Inspectorate, who opposed the claim, argued that the officers acted lawfully because under Art. 4 of the Law of the Arkhangel'sk Province of May 25, 1995 "On the Administrative Liability for Violations of Rules Concerning Placing, Storage and Parking of Transport Vehicles on the Territory of the Arkhangel'sk Province," placing or parking of transport vehicles on lawns results in fines for drivers of these vehicles in the amount of one minimum monthly wage.

According to Art. 9 of the above Law, the organs of internal affairs and of the State Traffic Inspectorate have been granted the power to remove those transport vehicles which have been parked in violation of the rules established by the Law to a special parking lot or "fine parking lot."

In granting relief on the complaint the court referred to the fact that Art. 9 of the above Law contravenes Art. 35(3) of the Constitution of the Russian Federation according to which no one may be arbitrarily deprived of his or her property except on the basis of a judicial decision; as a result, the court declared the actions of the officers of the State Traffic Inspectorate unlawful. . .

The Presidium of the Provincial Court held that Nevsorov's car had been parked on a lawn in the courtyard of an apartment house; this violated the lawful interests of the inhabitants of the house; although the owner had the right to take, with respect to property belonging to him, any actions, he could not, under Art. 209(2) of the Civil Code of the Russian federation, violate the rights or legally protected interests of other persons; therefore, the actions of the officers of the State Traffic Inspectorate who towed the car to the "fine parking lot" were lawful because they were aimed at protecting the interests of these citizens.

This holding of the court of supervisory instance [the Presidium of the Provincial Court] does not correspond to the rules of substantive law. In accordance with Art. 55(3) of the Constitution of the Russian Federation, the rights and freedoms of the human being and citizen may be restricted by the federal law only to the extent required for the protection of the fundamentals of the constitutional system, morality, health, rights and lawful interests of other persons, for ensuring the defense of the country and the security of the state.

Although the Presidium of the Provincial Court made a reference to Art. 209(2) of the Civil Code of the Russian Federation, it is not possible to regard this reference as justified in light of the above constitutional norm; Art. 209(2) does not establish the right to take or detain property of the owner who violates, by his actions with respect to property belonging to him, the interests of other persons. The removal of the transport vehicle to the "fine parking lot" restricts the right of ownership; this follows from Arts. 9 and 11 of Temporary Regulations Concerning the Procedure for the Detention of Transport Vehicles enacted by the decision of the Soviet of Peoples Deputies of the City of Arkhangel'sk on April 6, 1993, according to which the detained transport vehicle is returned to the owner only upon the submission of a receipt confirming the payment of fines, as well as payment for the service of towing and storage; under these regulations, the transport vehicles which are not reclaimed from the "fine parking lots" within the period of one year, may be sold at auctions or used car dealerships after the appropriate decision of a court.

Removal of transport vehicles parked in violation of these rules is envisioned by the above Law of the Arkhangel'sk Province. Federal laws on administrative responsibility do not contemplate such a restriction of the right of ownership for similar violations. Thus, Arts. 114 and 242 of the RSFSR Code on Administrative Violations provides for the detention of transport vehicles, that is, prohibition of their use, and their storage in a special guarded area; however, this sanction is applied only in cases involving use of disabled vehicles that pose a threat to traffic safety.

It follows that the removal of Nevsorov's car in the circumstances established in the present proceedings is not envisioned by the federal law, violates his rights and is unlawful under Art. 55 of the Constitution of the Russian Federation. . .

QUESTIONS

1. What was the major argument used by the Supreme Court in support of its holding? Do you agree with it?

2. A similar case initiated by the International Confederation of Consumer Societies against the Moscow City Government was decided by the Supreme Court in 1998. In *International Confederation of Consumer Societies v. The Government of Moscow* (*BVS*, 1998, No. 2, p. 3) the Supreme Court vacated a judgment of the Moscow City Court which dismissed a suit challenging Moscow City regulations that allowed removal and towing of cars parked in violation of local rules. The Supreme Court noted that these regulations "impinged upon the right of private ownership."

3. Many European Constitutions expressly recognize the social content of ownership by limiting the owner's powers. Given the competing public and private interests in the use of private property, what kinds of balancing tests might have been applied by the Supreme Court in the present case?

4. As a review of jurisdiction, why is this case in the Supreme Court? It involves action taken pursuant to a local normative act that is challenged as violation of Constitution and federal law. Shouldn't such a case be decided by the Constitutional Court?

The Constitutional Court: *Case Concerning Art. 560 of the RSFSR Civil Code* (*VKS*, 1996, No. 1, p. 2)

1. The plaintiffs, A.B. Naumov and L.B. Kudasheva, brought suit in the Ramenski city court of the Moscow Region against N.B. Drozhina and V.B. Schetin to recognize their ownership right with respect to part of a house in the village of Niculino of the Ramenski district. The court rejected the suit because the house is part of the property of a collective-farm peasant household and, consequently, no inheritance of household property occurs, as envisioned by Art. 560(1) of the RSFSR Civil Code.

A.B. Naumov filed a complaint with the Constitutional Court of the Russian Federation and asked the Court to review the constitutionality of this norm because he believes that it violates his constitutional right of inheritance guaranteed by Art. 35(4) of the Constitution of the Russian Federation.

2. In civil law, the institution of the collective-farm peasant household represented a a special legal category of property which belonged to its members without demarcation of shares (joint ownership). Collective-farm peasant households owned production facilities on their land plots, houses, live-stocks and agricultural equipment. Part I of the 1994 Civil Code of the Russian Federation does not contain any reference to "collective farm peasant household." As a result, Art. 126 of the RSFSR Civil Code defining property of a collective-farm peasant household and, consequently, the recognition of its special regime in civil law, lost effect as of January 1, 1995 (Art. 2 of the federal Law of October 21, 1994 "On the Procedure for Putting into Effect of Part I of the Civil Code of the Russian Federation").

Although, from a formal point of view, Art. 560 of the RSFSR Civil Code is still in effect, it cannot apply because legislation adopted after the present Constitution became effective does not contemplate a special legal regime for collective-farm peasant households. However, as practice shows, the provisions of this article are still being applied; this affects the constitutional right of inheritance protected by the state. . .

4. The right of inheritance, envisioned by Art. 35(4) of the Constitution of the Russian Federation and governed in more detail by the civil legislation, ensures transfer of property belonging to the deceased (inheritance transferor) to other persons (heirs); this transfer is guaranteed by the state. This right includes both the right of the inheritance transferor to dispose of his or her property and the right of the heirs to receive it. These two entitlements of the right of inheritance also follow from Art. 35(2) of the Constitution of the Russian Federation, which provides that the owner may dispose of property

belonging to him or her; this is the foundation of the basic freedom of inheritance.

At the same time, Art. 35(4) of the Constitution does not proclaim an absolute freedom of inheritance. As some other rights and freedoms, this freedom may be restricted by the law-maker but only to the extent required for the protection of the fundamentals of the constitutional system, morality, health, rights and lawful interests of other persons, for ensuring the defense of the country and the security of the state (Art. 53(3) of the Constitution), i.e. on the condition that the relevant limitations are legitimate and proportionate.

5. Although the provisions of Art. 540 of the RSFSR Civil Code do not deny the right of inheritance, they allow the opening of a succession only upon termination of the collective-farm peasant household, inter alia, after the death of its last member. This special procedure for the succession in the collective-farm peasant household made the subjective right of inheritance dependent on certain conditions that had no relation to the individual (that is, dependent on the termination of the collective-farm peasant household as an entity), and which, by their nature, made the implementation of the subjective right practically impossible.

From a formal point of view, the right of a member of the collective-farm peasant household to write a will was preserved. However, if there were other members of the household after the death of the testator the succession would not begin and the will bequeathing part of the household property would be declared invalid. As a result, the law-maker introduced conditions that deprived the inheritance transferors and their heirs of the right to freely determine the succession and receive or renounce the inheritance. The imposition of these conditions distorted the basic content of the right of inheritance.

The above-mentioned restrictions, aimed at preventing the opening of a succession with respect to the property of the collective-farm peasant household, do not correlate to any of the goals listed in Art. 55(3) of the Constitution of the Russian Federation. . .

For these reasons . . . the Constitutional Court of the Russian Federation finds:

(1) Parts 1 and 2 of Art. 560 of the RSFSR Civil Code contravene the Constitution of the Russian Federation. . .

Dissenting Opinion of Judge N.V. Vitruk

Art. 560 of the 1964 RSFSR Civil Code establishes a special procedure of inheritance with respect to the collective-farm peasant household; however, it does not deny the fundamental provisions of the citizen's right of inheritance. . . It is also quite possible to establish special procedures of inheritance with respect to peasant (farmer) households. . . Thus, in accordance with Art. 258(2) of the 1994 Civil Code of the Russian Federation, the land plot and production facilities (houses are not included into this category) belonging to peasant (farmer) household are not divided if one of the members of the household wants to withdraw. In this case, the former member has the right to monetary compensation corresponding to his or her share in joint property. Because the succession contemplates the transfer of only such rights that the deceased member of the peasant (farmer) household actually had during his or her life, the special restrictive provisions of Art. 258(2) of the Civil Code of the Russian Federation must also determine the procedure of inheritance in the peasant (farmer) household. . . A special procedure of inheritance of the land plot and property of a peasant (farmer) household may be qualified as a certain restriction of the right of inheritance of a certain category of individuals imposed by the law in accordance with the permissible limitations and with an eye toward protecting the rights and interests of all members of peasant (farmer) household; these restrictions do not deny or diminish the right of inheritance and are in full accord with the requirements of Arts. 17(3 and 55(3) of the Constitution of the Russian Federation. . .

QUESTIONS

1. As Judge Vitruk has pointed out, the 1994 Civil Code contemplates a special restrictive regime for the division of property of the peasant (farmer) household with an eye toward protecting the rights and interests of all members of the peasant (farmer) household. It is quite possible to argue that lawful interests of the members of the peasant (farmer) household might also require certain restrictions on the right of inheritance. Why did the Constitutional Court come to the conclusion that Art. 560 of the old Civil Code contravenes the Constitution?

2. In the case at bar, the dispute arose prior to the adoption of the 1993 Constitution. Although the plaintiffs lost their case in ordinary courts, they succeeded in the Constitutional Court which declared the provisions of the old Civil Code unconstitutional. Will they be able to benefit form their success in the Constitutional Court?

3. What will have to happen in the future when a member of a peasant

(farmer) household dies and leaves a will bequeathing all his or her property to his or her nephew who lives in Moscow? If the nephew does not wish to live in the farm household, how can he get the property he was bequeathed?

3. Freedom of Movement

During the Soviet period the majority of big city residents lived in municipal housing which was heavily subsidized by the state.[43] In order to manage the available housing resources the Soviet government established an elaborate system of housing allocation. An important feature of this system were regulations concerning residence permits (*propiska*). Residence permits determined legal residency and the right to live in a particular apartment. Anyone who wanted to take up her or his new legal residence in an apartment or house had to obtain a residence permit from the local authorities.

As a general rule, citizens applying for residence permits had to prove that they had obtained housing on grounds specified by the housing law (such as moving in with relatives). In any case, however, local police authorities managing residence permits were granted broad powers to give or deny permission for residence. For example, residence permits could be refused if the addition of a new resident in an apartment resulted in overcrowding in excess of municipal norms. In this way, the local governments, which allocated municipal housing stock within their jurisdictions, were able to use the *propiska* system as a tool to control the flow of migration into metropolitan areas. While economic considerations played an important part in the system of regulated residence, it also provided a mechanism of state control over the movement of Russian citizens within the country. As a result, individuals were denied the right to freely choose their place of residence.

Although the 1993 Constitution proclaims that "everyone who is lawfully within the territory of the Russian Federation shall have the right to freedom of movement and the right to freely choose the place of temporary or permanent residence",[44] efforts to abolish the notorious *propiska* system encountered serious resistance, especially at the local level. Local governments wanted to retain residence permits as the traditional tool to manage the allocation of shrinking housing resources.

In 1993 the Russian parliament enacted the Law "On the Right of Citizens of the Russian Federation to Freedom of Movement and the Right to Freely Choose the Place of Temporary or Permanent Residence in the Russian

---

[43]In contrast, in rural areas and in small towns the majority of Russian citizens lived in their own private houses.

[44]Constitution, Art. 27.

Federation."[45] The 1993 Law replaced the old residence permit system with the registration system. However, in many respects the new system of registration resembles the traditional *propiska* system. The 1993 Law does not provide for a simple residence notification. Russian citizens who wish to change their place of residence are still required to register their place of residence with local governments. Registration can still be refused on essentially the same grounds as former *propiska*. Yet, even this restrictive law has met with serious opposition from several "subjects" of the Russian Federation which wanted to keep newcomers or immigrants out. For example, the City of Moscow enacted local regulations which introduced additional requirements for registration.

Various legal acts of the former USSR referring to residence permits and new local rules restricting the freedom of movement became the subject of several cases decided by the Constitutional Court. The *Case Concerning Art. 54 of the Housing Code* and the *Case Concerning Some Normative Acts of the City of Moscow* illustrate the principal legal issues that have arisen in this connection. These two cases are set out below.

Following them is *Case Concerning Art. 64(a) of the Criminal Code of the RSFSR*, which deals with another aspect of the right to freedom of movement: the right to freely leave the territory of the Russian Federation.

The Constitutional Court: *Case Concerning Art. 54 of the Housing Code* (*VKS*, 1995, No. 2/3, p. 32)[46]

[Ms. L.N. Sitalova lived for five years with Mr. V.N. Kaderkin and his parents in his apartment. After the death of Kaderkin's parents, she raised the question of obtaining a permit to reside in his apartment but failed to obtain his consent. Sitalova took the matter to court. While the court of first instance granted her request, the decision was vacated on cassational appeal. The court based its decision on the grounds that when moving into Kaderkin's apartment Sitalova had not complied with "the established procedure" in accordance with Art. 54 of the Housing Code. Art. 54 provides: "The lessee has the right by the established procedure to settle into housing premises occupied by him, his wife, children, parents, other relatives, dependants unable to work, and other persons, having received written permission for this of all adult members of his family."]

2) The subject of consideration in the present appeal are not the normative acts on residence permits (*propiska*). By a Decision of the

---

[45] *Vedomosty RF*, No. 32, item 1227 (1993).

[46] The first part of this ruling is reproduced *supra* Chapter 3, Section E(6).

Committee on Constitutional Supervision of the USSR of October 11, 1991, they were found invalid and as such are not subject to appeal. The legality of actions and decisions of law enforcement organs based on such acts is reviewed by the courts of general jurisdiction, which, in accordance with Art. 120(2) of the Constitution of the Russian Federation, having established during the consideration of a case, the inconsistency of an act of a government or any other organ with a law, must render a ruling in accordance with the law.

3) The complaint raises the question about the violation of Art. 40(1) of the Constitution of the Russian Federation, according to which everyone has the right to a home and no one may be arbitrarily deprived of a home. In effectuating the regulation of this constitutional right, the legislature must comply with the requirements of Art. 55 (2) of the Constitution of the Russian Federation on the inadmissability of any diminution of the rights and freedoms of individuals and citizens by laws. This directly relates to the procedure of taking up one's legal residence in a dwelling established by the Housing Code of the RSFSR.

Provisions of Art. 54(1) of the Housing Code of the RSFSR on the right of a tenant to allow other persons to take up legal residence in his or her dwelling "pursuant to the established procedure" refer to other legislative acts. In view of the resulting uncertainty of the legal content of Art. 54(1), it is not possible to answer the question of which governmental organ and by what kind of enactment this procedure is to be established; this leads to arbitrary understanding of its meaning.

The absence of any indication as to the kind of normative act that is supposed to "establish the procedure" for taking up one's legal residence in a dwelling allows the legislative and executive organs of state power of various subjects of the Russian Federation to establish this procedure at their discretion; this may result in violation of the constitutional right of citizens to a home and arbitrary deprivation of their dwelling. This does not meet the requirements of Art. 55 (3) of the Constitution of the Russian Federation, according to which the rights and freedoms of the human being and citizen may be restricted by the federal law only to the extent required for the protection of the fundamentals of the constitutional system, morality, health, rights and lawful interests of other persons, and for ensuring the defense of the country and the security of the state.

Judicial practice concerning the implementation of Art. 54(1) of the Housing Code of the RSFSR is inconsistent. Courts have rendered different decisions in legally similar circumstances; this results in different legal consequences for citizens.

The possibility of such an arbitrary application of the law violates the equality of all persons before the law and the court, which is proclaimed by the Constitution of the Russian Federation (Art. 19(1)).

4) According to Art. 74(2) of the Federal Constitutional Law "On the Constitutional Court of the Russian Federation," the Constitutional Court of the Russian Federation is supposed to assess both the literal meaning of the act under consideration and the meaning attributed to it by the official interpretation, other forms of interpretation and the prevailing practice of applying the law.

Judicial interpretation of the Housing Code of the RSFSR was formed as an acknowledgment of the fact that the realization of the right to a home depended on residence permits; the existence or absence of a residence permit had a direct legal impact on the relevant relations. Thus, paragraph 7 of the Ruling of the Plenary Session of the Supreme Court of the USSR of April 3, 1987, "*On the Judicial Practice Concerning Application of Housing Legislation*" contained an explanation that "taking up one's legal residence in the established procedure usually means taking possession of a dwelling place in accordance with the regulations concerning residence permits."

Although by its Ruling of April 22, 1992. . . the Plenary Session of the Supreme Court of the Russian Federation gave instructions that, pending the adoption of the relevant legislative acts of the Russian Federation, the laws and regulations of the former USSR and explanations concerning their application contained in the Rulings of the Plenary Session of the Supreme Court of the USSR may be applied by courts only in so far as they do not contradict the Constitution of the Russian Federation and the Treaty on the Creation of the Commonwealth of Independent States, law enforcement organs often relied on the invalid acts when resolving questions concerning the procedure for taking up one's legal residence in a dwelling. This violates the requirements of Art. 18 of the Constitution of the Russian Federation, according to which the rights and freedoms of human beings and citizens have direct effect and determine the meaning, content and application of the laws, and of Art. 27(1) of the Constitution of the Russian Federation, which proclaims the right to freely choose a place of temporary or permanent residence. . .

It follows from the Constitution of the Russian Federation and the Law of the Russian Federation "On the Right of Citizens of the Russian Federation to Freedom of Movement and the Right to Freely Choose the Place of Temporary or Permanent Residence in the Russian Federation" that the presence or absence of registration, which replaced residence permits, cannot provide grounds for the limitation of the rights and freedoms of citizens, including the right to a home, nor serve as a precondition for their realization (Art. 3 of the Law). However, until the present time "the established procedure" for taking up one's legal residence in a dwelling was understood in the practice of applying the law only in the sense of observance of rules concerning residence permits; (with reference to Art. 54 of the Housing Code of the RSFSR) this also happened during the consideration the case of the claimant in the present case – L.N. Sitalova.

It follows that provisions of Art. 54 of the Housing Code of the RSFSR, both in their literal interpretation and in terms of the prevailing practice of applying the law, lead to violations of Art. 18 and 19(1) as well as the fundamental rights and freedoms of citizens envisioned by Arts. 27 (1) and 40 (1), and do not conform to the grounds and conditions for their limitation laid down by Art. 55 of the Constitution of the Russian Federation. . .

For these reasons. . . the Constitutional Court of the Russian Federation finds:

(1) The provision on "the established procedure," as a procedure for taking up one's legal residence in a dwelling place under the condition of observance of the regime of residence permits contained in Art. 54(1) of the Housing Code of the RSFSR, contravenes the Constitution of the Russian Federation. . .

The Constitutional Court: *Case Concerning Some Normative Acts of the City of Moscow* (*VKS*, 1996, No. 2, p. 42)

1. Art. 2 of the Law of the City of Moscow of September 14, 1994 "On Taxes for Compensating the Expenses of the City Budget Concerning the Development of the City's Infrastructure and Provision of Everyday Necessities for Citizens Arriving in Moscow for Permanent Residence" provides that citizens of the Russian Federation who take up their permanent residence in Moscow in a dwelling owned by them must pay a tax in the amount of 500 times the monthly minimum wage. On the basis of the above Law, the Government of Moscow issued, by its Ruling No. 922 of October 11, 1994, Regulations Concerning the Procedure for the Consideration of Registration Requests Submitted by Citizens Arriving in Moscow for Permanent Residence From Other Regions. . . According to Art. 1 of these Regulations, only citizens who have paid the required tax may be registered in Moscow. . .

[The Head of the Komi Republic, U.A. Spiridonov, petitioned the Constitutional Court to recognize as unconstitutional the above normative acts of the City of Moscow; citizens V.I. Kutsillo and P.S. Kleba also filed individual complaints to review the constitutionality of Art. 2 of the above Law of the City of Moscow]

3. The rights and freedoms of human beings and citizens are recognized and guaranteed in the Russian Federation in conformity with the generally recognized principles and norms of international law and in accordance with the Constitution of the Russian Federation (Art. 17(1) of the Constitution). According to Art. 27(1) of the Constitution, everyone who is lawfully within the territory of the Russian Federation has the right to freedom of movement and the right to freely choose a place of temporary or permanent residence. Freedom of movement and the right to freely choose a place of temporary or permanent residence are also recognized by the International Covenant on Civil and Political Rights (Art. 12), other international and international legal acts, including Protocol No. 4 to the European Convention on Human Rights (Art. 2).

Freedom of movement and the right to freely choose a place of temporary or permanent residence are an important element of personal freedom and a necessary condition for the professional and intellectual development of the individual. As a social state, Russian Federation must pursue policies that would ensure such a development. . . The challenged normative acts directly affect the right to freely choose a place of permanent residence. . .

The right to freely choose a place of permanent residence belongs to citizens from birth and is, just as other fundamental rights and freedoms, inalienable (Art. 17(2) of the Constitution; Art. 150 of the Civil Code of the Russian Federation). At the same time, this right is not absolute; it is subject to legal regulation that must take into account that implementation of this right may result in violations of the rights and freedoms of other persons, which is not permitted under Art. 17(3) of the Constitution of the Russian Federation.

So the exercise of this right may be subject to justified restrictions imposed in accordance with Arts. 55(3) and 56 of the Constitution of the Russian Federation. Legal restrictions on the right to freely choose a place of residence may be imposed by the federal law only to the extent required for the protection of the fundamentals of the constitutional system, morality, health, rights and lawful interests of other persons, for ensuring the defense of the country and the security of the state (Art. 55(3) of the Constitution of the Russian Federation). Art. 12 of the International Covenant on Civil and Political Rights also provides that the right to liberty of movement and freedom to choose a place of residence are not subject to any restrictions except those which are provided by law and are necessary to protect national security, public order (ordre public), public health or morals or the rights and freedoms of others, and are consistent with the other rights recognized in the Covenant.

Consequently, both the Constitution of the Russian Federation and the international legal norms contain a requirement that restrictions on the freedom to choose a place of residence may be imposed only by a law. The Constitution of the Russian Federation specifies this requirement by stating that the rights and freedoms of the human being and citizen may be restricted only by a federal law. . .

Limitations on the right of citizens to freedom of movement and the right to choose a place of temporary or permanent residence. . . require the establishment of a balance between the public and private interests. . .

The Law of the Russian Federation ["On the Right of Citizens of the Russian Federation to Freedom of Movement and the Right to Freely Choose a Place of Temporary or Permanent Residence in the Russian Federation"] of June 25, 1993 governs this sphere of relations in the interests of creating the necessary conditions for the exercise of the citizen's rights and freedoms; it also ensures the fulfillment by citizens of their duties with respect to other citizens, the state and the society. The Law. . . introduces the system of registration which is based on a notification procedure; the presence or absence of registration is not intended to provide grounds for the limitation of other rights and freedoms of citizens (Art. 3).

The right to freely choose a place of residence is part of the freedom of personal self-determination. Organs of state power have only been granted the right to register the result of an act of free choice of the citizen of his or her place of residence. For this reason, the registration procedure cannot require any residence permits and serve as a ground for restricting the citizen's right to freely choose a place of residence. The notification procedure for registering the citizens of the Russian Federation at the place of their residence is a permissible restriction on the right to choose a place of residence; under Art. 6 of the 1993 Law, the only obligation imposed on citizens is the requirement that they apply to an official responsible for registration within seven days after the arrival to a new place of residence and submit their passport and a document that provides legal grounds for taking possession of their dwelling place. . .

The requirements concerning the payment of the above mentioned tax . . , which is considered as a precondition for registration, established by the [challenged] normative acts.., contravene the 1993 Law;. . . they introduce an entirely different legal regime for registration that presupposes the issuance of permits; this procedure contravenes the fundamental right of everyone who is lawfully staying on the territory of the Russian Federation to freely choose her or his place of residence. . .

These norms interfere with a number of fundamental rights and freedoms of citizens recognized and guaranteed by the Constitution of the Russian Federation, inter alia, the right to elect and be elected to organs of state power and to organs of local self-government, as well as to take part in a referendum, the right to freely use his or her abilities and property for entrepreneurial or any other economic activity not prohibited by the law, the right to freely and fully use and dispose of property, the right to freely move goods, services and financial resources, the right to social security, the right to health protection and medical assistance and the right to pre-school and secondary education.

The exercise of the constitutional right to choose a place of residence cannot depend on the payment or non-payment of taxes or levies because fundamental rights of citizens of the Russian Federation are guaranteed by the Constitution of the Russian Federation without any monetary preconditions. It follows that rejections of registration requests by reference to the non-fulfillment of duties concerning the payment of taxes or levies contravene the Constitution of the Russian Federation. . .

QUESTIONS AND COMMENTS

1. Note that in the *Case Concerning Art. 54 of the Housing Code* the Constitutional Court noted that "the subject of consideration in the present appeal is not the normative acts on residence permits (*propiska*). By a Decision of the Committee on Constitutional Supervision of the USSR of October 11, 1991, they were found invalid and as such are not subject to appeal." The USSR Committee on Constitutional Supervision held that "provisions regarding residence permits as approved by the USSR Council of Ministers, as well as other regulations by the USSR government on residence registration establishing an obligation for individuals to obtain permission from administrative bodies to reside, be employed or enrolled in educational establishments, sell residential houses, apartments, country houses, garages, as well as establishing responsibility for the breach of these obligations, are not consistent with the USSR Constitution, the Declaration on Human Rights and Freedoms or international acts on human rights" (*Vedomosty SSSR*, No. 46, item 1307 (1991)). The Committee declared invalid those provisions that "restrict the right of property owners to possess, manage and use at their discretion their residential houses, apartments and other property." In the *Case Concerning Art. 54 of the Housing Code* the Constitutional Court for the first time confirmed the continued validity of the USSR Committee's findings.

2. What were the major legal arguments for invalidating Art. 54(1) of the Housing Code?

3. What were the major legal arguments for invalidating the enactments of the City of Moscow concerning residence registration?

4. As noted earlier, the 1993 Law "On the Right of Citizens of the Russian Federation to Freedom of Movement and the Right to Freely Choose the Place of Temporary or Permanent Residence in the Russian Federation" replaced the old residence permit system with the registration system. Although the 1993 Law does not provide for a simple residence notification, it contains an exhaustive list of grounds to refuse registration. In 1995 the Government of Russia issued detailed Regulations on Registration which introduced additional grounds for registration refusals. The Constitution Court declared these provisions of the 1995 Regulations unconstitutional in the *Case Concerning Arts. 10, 12 and 21 of the Regulations on Registration* (*Sobranie*, No. 6, item 783 (1998)).

The Constitutional Court: *Case Concerning Art. 64(a) of the Criminal Code of the RSFSR* (*VKS*, 1995, No. 6, p. 48)

1. The Collegium for Criminal Cases of the Moscow City Court found, on October 26, 1982, that V.A. Smirnov was guilty of committing a crime under Art. 64(a) of the Criminal Code of the RSFSR ("High Treason"). The cassational and subsequent appeals filed by V.A. Smirnov were rejected. On June 19, 1991, the Presidium of the Supreme Court. . ., having considered the case on the protest of the First Deputy Procurator General, left the sentence intact and thus confirmed the conclusions concerning V.A. Smirnov's guilt which involved his refusal to return from abroad, transfer of state secrets to foreign states and assistance to foreign states in subversive activities. . .

3. In his complaint, citizen V.A. Smirnov asks the Court to recognize as unconstitutional the provision of Art. 64(a) of the RSFSR Criminal Code according to which an escape to foreign countries and a refusal to return from abroad is considered as one of the forms of high treason. . . The claimant contends that this provision contravenes Art. 27(2) of the Constitution of the Russian Federation.

According to Art. 27(2) of the Constitution of the Russian Federation, everyone is free to leave the boundaries of the Russian Federation; a citizen of the Russian Federation also has the right to freely return into the Russian Federation. The legal entitlement under this right, the procedure and conditions of its realization, are specified by the USSR Law "On Exit from the USSR and Entry into the USSR of the Citizens of the USSR" the validity of which with respect to the territory of the Russian Federation was recognized on December 22, 1992 by a Ruling of the Supreme Soviet of the Russian Federation. . . This Law allows restrictions on the right to travel for reasons of ensuring state security and other state protected interests; but these restrictions are of a temporary character and do not deny the right of the citizen himself to freely leave the country and return to it. This is in full accord with the provisions of Art. 12(2) of the International Covenant on Civil and Political Rights, which guarantee the right of everyone to freely leave any country, including his own and do not envision any obligation to return to this country.

As with any other constitutional right, the right to leave the boundaries of the Russian Federation may be restricted only for purposes defined by Art. 55(2) of the Constitution of the Russian Federation. These restrictions are not subject to expansive interpretation and must not diminish other civil, political and other rights guaranteed to citizens by the Constitution and laws of the Russian Federation; they must not lead to criminal responsibility for an escape to foreign countries and a refusal to return from abroad, which are considered by Art. 64(a) of the RSFSR Criminal Code to be high treason. Under the Constitution of the Russian Federation, as well as international treaties of the Russian Federation, an action contemplated by the challenged norm cannot be considered to be a crime infringing upon defense, sovereignty, territorial integrity, state security or defense and cannot serve as an independent basis for criminal responsibility for high treason. . .

For these reasons. . . the Constitutional Court finds:

(1) The provisions of Art. 64(a) of the Criminal Code of RSFSR, which qualifies an escape to foreign states or refusal to return from abroad as a form of high treason, do not conform to the Constitution of the Russian Federation, namely Arts. 27(2) and 55(3). . .[47]

Dissenting Opinion of Judge N.V. Vitruk

A determination of the constitutionality of certain provisions of Art. 64(a) of the RSFSR Criminal Code may be conducted only on the basis of a preliminary resolution of the general theoretical question about the content and limits of the realization of the constitutional rights of citizens and the possibility of their restriction. A constitutional right of a citizen is not limitless: its content and scope of realization depend on the relationship with other

[47] Art. 275 of the new 1996 Criminal Code of the Russian Federation (*supra* note 14) does not contain these provisions.

constitutional rights and freedoms of citizens and his or her constitutional duties. Furthermore, in accordance with Art. 55(3) of the Constitution of the Russian Federation, the rights and freedoms of the human being and citizen may be restricted by federal law to the extent required for the protection of the fundamentals of the constitutional system, morality, health, rights and lawful interests of other persons, and ensuring the defense of the country and the security of the state.

The law-maker, in the interests of a rational combination and harmonization of the interests of civil society, the state and the individual, establishes not only the content of the constitutional right but also the procedure for its exercise. The goal of the procedure for exercising a right is to ensure (guarantee) that the specific values that form the basis of the content of the right are being realized. The procedure for exercising the right may also restrict specific categories of citizens. Restrictions on the rights and freedoms of citizens may be effectuated by the exclusion of certain possibilities (entitlements) from the content of the right (freedom) as well as by establishing a special procedure for the right's exercise.

Let us now look at the constitutional right established by Art. 27(2) of the Constitution of the Russian Federation. . . The realization of this constitutional right may depend upon the fulfillment by the citizen of his or her legal duties. For example, a citizen who is serving a prison term. . . cannot freely leave the boundaries of the Russian Federation.

In accordance with Art. 55(3) of the Constitution of the Russian Federation, the constitutional right of everyone to freely leave the boundaries of the Russian Federation may be restricted for certain categories of citizens by establishing a special procedure for foreign travel that would require permission to travel and would contemplate the possibility of rejection of the request for travel by the competent organs in cases established by the law or that would provide that the permission to travel will be granted only if the citizen fulfills certain duties, for example, a duty to return home within the established period. . .

The complaint of citizen V.A. Smirnov challenges the constitutionality of the provision of Art. 64(a) of the RSFSR Criminal Code according to which an escape to foreign countries and a refusal to return from abroad. . . is considered as a separate and independent form of high treason. . . Only illegal means of the citizen leaving the country, i.e. crossing the border in violation of the rules concerning foreign travel, may be considered to be "an escape abroad;" in the criminal legal context, the refusal to return home may occur only if a citizen, for example a citizen who has access to state secrets, has a duty to return home within the established period; that period may be determined by the terms of the foreign business trip. If there is such a duty before the state, the law-maker may make violations of the established procedure for leaving the country and returning home an administrative or criminal offence. . .

Imposition of restrictions on the constitutional right to leave the boundaries of the Russian Federation is permissible if the relevant restrictions are in conformity with the requirements of Art. 55(3) of the Constitution of the Russian Federation. Consequently, special legal duties may also be imposed on citizens who are relying on the constitutional right to freely leave the country; the same applies to the imposition of a legal duty to return home for certain categories of individuals, for example, for those who have access to state secrets. The determination of specific kinds of offenses for violations of duties imposed on citizens in connection with the realization of their constitutional right to freely leave the country, including criminalization or decriminalization of the relevant offenses, is not a subject for constitutional regulation; this falls within the exclusive competence of the law-maker who resolves these questions through ordinary legislation. . .

QUESTION AND COMMENT

1. With whom do you agree, the majority or the dissent? According to the dissent, would the Court have the power to review legislation that claimed to be based on Art. 55(3) of the Constitution?

2. Note that the Constitutional Court stated that the 1992 USSR Law "On Exit from the USSR and Entry into the USSR of the Citizens of the USSR" "allows restrictions on the right to travel for reasons of ensuring state security and other state protected interests; but these restrictions are of a temporary character and do not deny the right of the citizen himself to freely leave the country and return to it." The Court also noted that "this is in full accord with the provisions of Art. 12(2) of the International Covenant on Civil and Political Rights." However, in its 1995 Comment on the fourth periodic reports of the Russian Federation, the Human Rights Committee expressed "concern that the most important legal restriction on the right to leave the country is still cast in terms of a State secret. This does not correspond with the requirements of article 12, paragraph 3, of the Covenant and the Committee deplores, in that regard, the resistance to date in bringing the legislation in conformity with the Covenant."

4. Access to Courts

The Constitutional Court: *Procuracy Officers Case* (*VKS*, 1994, No. 2/3, p. 24)[48]

The complainants, T.Kh. Gdlyan, N.V. Ivanov, S.I. Ilidjeva, N.P. Kanishcheva, A.Ye. Kiriyenko, V.A. Molochkov, S.N. Ovchinnikova and V.G. Yalovoi, who are former employees of the agencies of the Procuracy of the USSR, and R.V. Chistokhodova, who is an employee of the procurator's office of the city of Syktyvkar, complained to the Constitutional Court about the violation of their constitutional right to court protection in connection with disciplinary punishments, including dismissal, imposed against them by procurators of regions and territories of the Russian Federation and by the Procurator General of the USSR. . .

V.A. Molochkov and S.N. Ovchinnikova filed lawsuits with people's courts seeking restitution. However, their lawsuits were rejected for the reason that, in accordance with the norms of the Labor Code, disputes involving the dismissal of employees of procurator offices must be resolved not in court but by their superior authorities in the Procuracy. Other claimants testified in the Constitutional Court that they also appealed to courts seeking protection of their labor rights, but their lawsuits were rejected for the same reason.

The claimants believe that the established procedure for filing complaints against disciplinary punishments and dismissal with a superior agency of the Procuracy deprives the Procuracy officers, as citizens of the Russian Federation, of their constitutional right to court protection, including court protection of the constitutional right to work.

In rejecting the demands of the former employees of the Procuracy to restore them to their former jobs, the people's courts were guided by Art. 47 of the Law of the USSR "On the Procuracy of the USSR," which corresponds to Art. 40 of the current Law of the Russian Federation "On the Procuracy of the Russian Federation," as well as Art. 23 of the "Regulations on Rewards and Disciplinary Responsibility of Procurators and Investigators of the Agencies of the USSR Procuracy" and Art. 220 of the Labor Code, . . . which established a list of employees whose labor disputes over dismissal and disciplinary punishments were to be resolved by superior agencies. Procurators, their deputies, assistants and investigators were included in this category. . .

Neither the Law "On the Procuracy of the Russian Federation," nor the "Regulations on Rewards and Disciplinary Responsibility of Procurators

[48] Note that this ruling was rendered on the basis of the 1978 Constitution.

and Investigators of the Agencies of the USSR Procuracy" state directly that labor disputes of these categories of employees may not be resolved by courts. However, a controversial judicial practice developed with regard to labor legislation under which courts refused to hear the complaints of employees of the Procuracy against violations of their labor rights.

This practice. . . persisted after the approval of the Declaration of the Rights and Freedoms of the Individual and Citizen on November 22, 1991 and the relevant amendments to the Constitution of the Russian Federation according to which every citizen is guaranteed court protection of his or her rights and freedoms (Art. 32 of the Declaration and Art. 63 of the Constitution). The current practice of refusing to hear the labor disputes of employees of the Procuracy in courts contradicts the constitutional right to court protection guaranteed by the aforementioned norms. By dismissing complaints of employees of the Procuracy, courts failed to apply Art. 63 of the Constitution of the Russian Federation, which, according to the spirit of that article, should be applied directly. . .

Art. 34 of the Constitution provides that the state guarantees its citizens equal rights and freedoms irrespective of race, nationality, language, social origin, property, position, religion, convictions, affiliation with public associations, and other circumstances. This guarantee concerns the right to court protection as well. . .

In accordance with Art. 48 of the Constitution, "requirements for applicants seeking governmental employment shall depend exclusively on the nature of professional duties." However, the nature of professional duties of the employees of the Procuracy cannot serve as grounds for any discrimination against them in the sphere of constitutional rights, in particular, the right to court protection. A judicial practice which deprives people of the right to court protection violates the equal right to work guaranteed by Art. 53 of the Constitution, because other categories of employees are guaranteed unlimited court protection in labor disputes. Consequently, in resolving the labor disputes of employees of the Procuracy, courts have applied Arts. 220 and 218 of the Labor Code and thus violated the spirit of the Constitution of the Russian Federation.

This established practice of applying the law also contradicts the generally recognized international standards and norms on human rights, which, according to Art. 32 of the Constitution of the Russian Federation, prevail over the laws of the Russian Federation and directly establish civil rights and duties.

Art. 8 of the Universal Declaration of Human Rights, of December 10,

1948, provides that "everyone has the right to an effective remedy by the competent national tribunals for acts violating the fundamental rights granted him by the constitution or by law." Art. 14 of the International Covenant of Civil and Political Rights of December 19, 1966, ratified by the Presidium of the USSR Supreme Soviet on September 18, 1973, provides that "in determination of any criminal charges against him, or of his rights and obligations in a suit of law, everyone shall be entitled to a fair and public hearing by a competent, independent and impartial tribunal established by law." Art. 7 of the Declaration and Art. 26 of the Covenant guarantee the right to equal legal protection without any discrimination.

Art. 4 of the International Covenant on Economic, Social and Cultural Rights, of December 19, 1966, ratified by the Presidium of the USSR Supreme Soviet on September 18, 1973, provides that "the State may subject such rights only to such limitations as are determined by law only in so far as this may be compatible with the nature of these rights and solely for the purpose of promoting the general welfare in a democratic society." The limitation of the right of employees of the Procuracy to court protection on the basis of Art. 23 of the Regulations on Rewards and Disciplinary Responsibility of Procurators and Investigators of the Agencies of the USSR Procuracy contradicts the above conditions. . .

For these reasons. . . the Constitutional Court finds:

(1) The practice of applying the law that emerged as a result of the application of Art. 218 of the Labor Code, Art. 40 of the Law "On the Procuracy of the Russian Federation" and Art. 23 of the "Regulations on Rewards and Disciplinary Responsibility of Procurators and Investigators of the Agencies of the USSR Procuracy". . . contravenes the Constitution of the Russian Federation. . .

QUESTION AND COMMENT

1. Note the importance of the equal protection principles invoked by the Court in this case. What is the scope of "equal protection" as formulated by the Constitutional Court? How does it compare to US equal protection doctrine?

2. Procurators wear uniforms and have a quasi-military centralized structure. Would the Court hold that officers of the military who have disputes over how much they should be paid have the right to have the issue determined by a court? If so, would a special military court be sufficient, or do they have a right equal to everyone else to sue in an ordinary court?

5. The Right to Strike

The Constitutional Court: ***Case Concerning the USSR Law "On the Procedure for the Settlement of Collective Labor Disputes (Conflicts)"*** (*VKS*, 1995, No. 2/3, p. 45)

1. On May 18, 1994, on the initiative of the Trade Union of Aviation Workers of the Russian Federation, the flying personnel - members of this Trade Union - of aviation units and aviation enterprises went on strike. By their rulings, courts found this strike illegal by referring to Art. 12 of the Law of the USSR "On the Procedure for the Settlement of Collective Labor Disputes (Conflicts)."

The Trade Union of Aviation Workers of the Russian Federation filed a complaint with the Constitutional Court of the Russian Federation and asked the Court to determine the constitutionality of the above Law because, in its opinion, the ban on strikes contradicts the Constitution of the Russian Federation. . .

3. Art. 37(4) of the Constitution of the Russian Federation recognizes the right to individual and collective labor disputes with the employment of methods specified by federal law for their resolution, including the right to strike. Thus, the strike is considered as a means of dispute settlement; the legislator can determine when and in what circumstances such a means of dispute settlement can be used, and when it is inadmissible.

The regulation of the right to strike should establish the necessary balance between the protection of professional interests (a strike is one of the means for doing that) and public interests that may be harmed by the strike. . .

The possibility of restriction of the right to strike of some categories of workers, including those employed in civil aviation (taking into account the character of their activity and possible consequences of their walkout) follows from the provisions of Art. 17(3) of the Constitution of the Russian Federation; Art. 17(3) provides that the exercise of rights and freedoms of the human being and citizen may not infringe on the rights and freedoms of other persons. It also follows from Art. 55(3) of the Constitution of the Russian Federation. . .

Restrictions on the right to strike do not contradict the generally recognized principles and norms of international law. Thus, under the International Covenant on Economic, Social and Cultural Rights, the ban on strikes is admissible with regard to persons who are members of the armed forces, of the police or of the administration of the state (Art. 8(2)); restriction on the exercise of this right with regard to other persons are also possible if they are necessary in a democratic society in the interests of state security or public order or for the protection of the rights and freedoms of others (Art. 8(2 "c")). International legal instruments regard the regulation of the right to strike as falling within the sphere of domestic legislation. At the same time, domestic legislation should not contravene the limits of permissible restrictions established by these acts.

4. Art. 12(1) of the Law under consideration provides that walkouts, as a means of settlement of collective labor dispute (conflict), are not permitted at the enterprises and organizations of civil aviation. This wording means that the ban on strikes concerns all enterprises and organizations in the system of civil aviation without any exception; it also concerns all workers employed in it. It does not contemplate any differentiation between enterprises, subdivisions, services, categories of workers of civil aviation depending on the character of their activity or significance of the work performed by them.

As a result, restrictions are imposed on the right to strike of a considerably wider range of workers than it is necessary for achievement of the goals defined in Arts. 17(3) and 55(3) of the Constitution of the Russian Federation.

For these reasons. . . the Constitutional Court of the Russian Federation finds:

(1) The prohibition on strikes at enterprises and organizations of civil aviation established by Art. 12(1) of the Law of the USSR "On the Procedure for the Settlement of Collective Labor Disputes (Conflicts)" conforms to the Constitution of the Russian Federation to the extent that the right to strike of specific categories of workers may be restricted in accordance with Art. 55 (3) of the Constitution. . .

(2) The prohibition on strikes at enterprises and organizations of civil aviation on the only ground that they belong to a specific branch established by 12(1) of the Law of the USSR "On the Procedure for the Settlement of Collective Labor Disputes (Conflicts)" does not conform to Arts. 37(4) and 55(2,3) of the Constitution of the Russian Federation.

(3) The Federal Assembly of the Russian Federation should, pursuant to Art. 37(4) of the Constitution of the Russian Federation, determine the conditions and grounds of the restriction of the right to strike. . .; in this respect it should be guided by Art. 55 (2,3) of the Constitution of the Russian Federation and the generally recognized principles and norms of international law. . .

QUESTIONS

1. What kind of restrictions on the right to strike can be imposed by the national legislature? What are the impermissible restrictions?

2. In this yet another case based on the notion of the "proportionality" of the legislature's response to an admittedly legitimate state interest?

CHAPTER VI

CIVIL AND COMMERCIAL LAW

A. Introduction

One of the most challenging tasks of the on-going law reform in Russia is the reform of civil law. In the Soviet legal system, civil law was a branch of law regulating "property and personal non-property relations" in a socialist society for the object of creating the "material-technical base of communism."[1] Although many concepts of Soviet civil law had obvious roots in Romano-Germanic experience, the introduction of socialist ideas made it quite different from the civil law of other civil law countries. The general spirit of the Soviet civil law was largely determined by Lenin's demand that private law relations must be governed, not by "the *corpus iuris romani*, but our revolutionary concept of law." Under the influence of communist ideas, fundamental private law concepts were modified by the addition of public elements. As a result of far-reaching "socialization" and "publicization" of civil law, the Soviet civil law did not recognize private property, did not allow the creation of market-oriented legal entities and rejected the principle of freedom of contract. In general, civil law played only a limited role in the society dominated by command economy and state plan.

The reinstitution of the fundamental importance of civil law, the abolition of outdated socialist concepts and the general "privatization" of civil law became the major goals of the civil law reform that began with the enactment of special statutes on property and entrepreneurial activity. The systematic reformulation of civil legislation was first undertaken by the 1991 Fundamentals of Civil Legislation of the USSR and Union Republics.[2] Although the 1991 Fundamentals reintroduced many traditional concepts of civil law,[3] they only outlined the contours of the required reform.

---

[1] 1964 Civil Code, Art. 1, *Vedomosty RF,* No. 24, item 406 (1964).

[2] *Vedomosty SSSR,* No. 26, item 733 (1991).

[3] Commenting on the 1991 Fundamentals, A. Makovsky and E. Sukhanov emphasized that "to a certain degree the preparation of the 1991 Fundamentals was similar to the restoration of old paintings. Numerous norms and institutions lost in the thirties and sixties, norms indispensable to the functioning of a market economy, needed to be restored. The losses in particular concerned major actors of entrepreneurial activities - legal entities, such as commercial partnerships and societies. Layers of restrictive principles and norms which had been introduced into civil law by the administrative-command system had to be removed. In this connection, particular attention was paid to provisions concerning contracts and other obligations." A. Makovsky, E. Sukhanov, *Osnovy grazhdanskogo zakonodatel'stva I predpinimatel'skaya*

The codification of the basic principles and rules of the contemporary Russian civil law was accomplished in 1994 by the first part of the Civil Code.[4] Part One of the Code encompasses general principles of civil law, rights in property, and principles and rules governing obligations and contracts.[5] The second part of the Civil Code,[6] enacted in 1995, codified rules concerning specific types of contracts and tort.[7] The third and final part of the new Civil Code will deal with the remaining issues, including inheritance law, intellectual property and private international law. It is still under discussion.

The adoption of the new Civil Code became the fourth codification in the history of Russian civil legislation. The Draft Imperial Civil Code was submitted to the State Duma in 1913 but was never enacted due to the 1917 revolution. The 1922 Civil Code, which reflected the principles of a new economic program introduced by the communist leadership of the country, drew upon the Draft Imperial Russian Code and remained in force until the adoption of the 1964 Civil Code. Certain provisions of the 1964 Code, in particular those dealing with succession, will remain in force until the adoption of the third part of the new Civil Code.

Although as a formal matter the new Russian Civil Code rescinds all inconsistent prior civil legislation, it continues to use the traditional Russian civil law concepts. Many provisions of the Civil Code are based on the imperial Russian civil law legislation. At the same time, the drafters of the new Civil Code incorporated many modern foreign (particularly European) civil law principles and norms.

---

deayaetel'nost (Fundamentals of Civil Legislation and Entrepreneurial Activities), in *Osnovy grazhdanskogo zakonodatel'stva SSSR I souznykh respublik* (Fundamentals of Civil Legislation of the USSR and Union Republics) 5, 6 (1991).

[4] *Sobranie*, No. 32, item 3301 (1994).

[5] There are several widely used Russian-language commentaries to the first part of the Civil Code. See, in particular, M.I. Braginsky ed., *Kommentarii tchasti pervoi Grazhdanskogo kodeksa Rossiiskoi Federatsii* (Commentary to the First Part of the Civil Code of the Russian Federation) (1995) (This Commentary is particularly valuable because it was written mostly by scholars who served as members of the drafting group of the Civil Code).

[6] *Sobranie*, No. 5, item 410 (1996). For an English translation of the Civil Code see, The Civil Code of the Russian Federation (English translation by P.B. Maggs) (1997) (This publication also contains a useful introductory commentary to the Civil Code written by well-known Russian scholars A.L. Makovsky and S.A. Khokhlov). See also Civil Code of the Russian Federation (English translation by W.E. Butler) (1997).

[7] For a useful commentary to the second part of the Civil Code, see O.N. Sadikov ed., *Kommentarii k Grazhdanskomu kodeksu Rossiiskoi Federatsii (tchasti vtoroi)* (Commentary to the Civil Code of the Russian Federation (Second Part)) (1997).

1. The Concept of Private and Public Law

The new Civil Code, which is generally considered to be a "constitution" of the market economy, is designed to repeal all prior civil law and establish an entirely new system of market-oriented rules. It reinstated the traditional civil law separation between public law and private law. The essential difference between private and public law concerns the plane of the legal relations involved. Private law is based on the legal equality of its subjects, while public law establishes hierarchical relationships. The Civil Code regulates "property relations," that is, relations with respect to property or in connection with ownership among parties that operate on the basis of legal equality.[8] In private law relations equality of the participants is ensured even in cases where one of the parties is the state. In contrast, public law relations are not based on the principle of equality but on the principle of subordination of one party to another. For example, tax and customs relations are based on the public authority of the state. While relations of equality (horizontal relations) are the subject of private law, authority relations (or vertical relations) are governed by different branches of public law, such as constitutional or administrative law.

2. The Civil Code and Civil Legislation of the "Subjects"

The new Civil Code is enacted in accordance with Art. 71(n) of the 1993 Constitution, which provides that "civil" legislation falls within the exclusive jurisdiction of the Federation. All matters regulated by civil legislation, as defined by Art. 2 of the Civil Code, are supposed to be governed by the Civil Code itself and by the supplementary federal legislation.[9] Under Art. 71(n) of the Constitution and Art. 3 of the 1994 Civil Code, "subjects" of the Federation appear to have no right to enact their own civil legislation.

The matter is not that simple, however. Art. 72(c) of the Constitution allocates matters concerning "possession, use and disposal of the land, subsurface resources, water and other natural resources" to the joint jurisdiction of the Russian Federation and its "subjects." Furthermore, under Art. 72(j), "family, housing, land, water and forestry legislation," as well as "legislation on the sub-surface and environmental protection" also fall within the joint jurisdiction. As a result, "subjects" of the Federation do have the power to enact their own normative acts in at least certain areas of civil legislation. In case of a conflict between federal and local legislation on any of these "subjects," federal law will prevail.

---

[8] Civil Code, Art. 2.

[9] Civil Code, Art. 3.

3. The Civil Code and Other Rules of Civil Law

As the fundamental statute governing civil law relations, the 1994 Civil Code deals with a wide range of issues. It provides a normative foundation for all areas of private law.

At the same time, Russian legislature did not attempt to incorporate the entire body of private law into a single comprehensive act. For example, family law and land law are traditionally considered to be separate branches of law. Yet, the 1994 Civil Code does contain several clauses on private ownership of land and natural resources.[10] It also governs joint ownership of spouses.[11] Although the general provisions of the Code on these and other matters should be supplemented by specific statutes, they provide fundamental principles for other areas of law that continue to be governed in separate private law codes or statutes. As a rule, these codes and statutes contain express references to civil legislation. For example, Art. 4 of the new 1996 Family Code[12] provides that family relations which are not covered by the provisions of the Family Code are governed by the pertinent rules of civil legislation.

The Civil Code is based on the idea that it must be regarded as a pivotal act of civil legislation as a whole. This guarantees the unity and systematic integrity of Russian civil legislation. Art. 3 of the Civil Code provides that all legislative acts governing relations that are considered part of civil law must be adopted "in accordance" with the Civil Code. The idea of unity is further strengthened by the provision under which "rules of civil law laid down by other laws shall be consistent with the present Code."[13] Judicial practice indicates that courts have already started to emphasize the priority of the 1994 Civil Code over prior conflicting legislation.[14]

The situation is more complicated in cases where subsequent legislation contravenes the provisions of the Civil Code. Regrettably, the Russian parliament does not always follow the requirements of Art. 3 of the Civil Code just cited. For example, Arts. 100 and 103 of the Civil Code provide that increases in the charter capital of a joint stock company and the relevant changes in the charter of the company fall within the exclusive competence of the general meeting of shareholders. In contrast, under Arts. 12, 28 and 48 of

---

[10] Civil Code, Arts. 130, 261.

[11] Civil Code, Art. 256.

[12] *Sobranie*, No. 1, item 16 (1996).

[13] Civil Code, Art. 3.

[14] See, e.g., *Trukhina vs. UPP VOS (BVS*, 1995, No. 9, p. 3) (The Supreme Court held that the 1992 legislation concerning compensation of harm could not apply because it contravened Art. 208 of the new Civil Code).

the 1995 Law on Joint Stock Companies[15] these questions may be resolved by the company's Board of Directors. Although some Russian commentators claim that in this area of law the provisions of the Civil Code must be given priority,[16] it is not clear that will always be the case. Doubt about the formal priority of the Civil Code over subsequent inconsistent legislation result from the fact that Art. 3 of the Civil Code contains no express provision that contrary laws automatically become null and void. It may also be argued that the 1995 Law on Joint Stock Companies must govern the matter as *lex specialis.*

4. The System of the Civil Code

As many other continental codes, the Russian Civil Code is marked by a high degree of conceptual abstraction and legal formalism. It deals with the traditional topics of private law, in particular, persons, property and obligations. This way of subdividing private law can be traced back to Roman times when the famous threefold classification of *personae, res* and *actiones* was introduced. One of the central features of the Civil Code is the differentiation between the law of obligations and of property which represents the translation into substantive law of the dichotomy between the Roman *in personam* and *actiones in rem.* The concept of a law of obligations, embracing both contract and tort, is also of Roman origin.

The 1994 Civil Code (just as all prior Civil Codes, including the 1913 Draft Imperial Civil Code) follows the example of the German Civil Code (1900) which had, unlike codes that came into force earlier (in particular the French Code Napoleon of 1804), a "general part" dealing with a number of fundamental civil law concepts. These concepts provide a foundation for the interpretation and application of all other rules of the Code. The general part of the 1994 Civil Code is very extensive. It deals not only with the general principles of civil law but also with several other topics, including natural and juridical persons, capacity, property, agency, transactions and the statute of limitations.

This form of organization of the Code is not easy to work with. In some cases it is difficult to see the relevance of the general principles and rules until specific forms of legal transactions, contained in other parts of the Code, are studied. However, because the general part provides rules of general application, it is often necessary to refer back to them. As a result, many

---

[15] *Sobranie,* No. 1, item 1 (1996).

[16] See, e.g., G.S. Shapkina, *Arbitrazhno-sudebnaya praktika primeneniya federal'nogo zakona "Ob aktsionernykh obtshestvakh"* (Arbitration-Judicial Practice on the Application of the Federal Law "On Joint Stock Companies") 12 (1997).

sections of the Civil Code can be understood properly only when they are read in conjunction with other provisions in far-away chapters of the Code.

For example, if one is dealing with the sale of a house, one has to consult the special rule about the sale of housing premises ,[17] the more general rules concerning sale of immovables[18] and then even more general rules on contracts of purchase and sale.[19] However, the rules on purchase and sale must be read in conjunction with the general rules concerning all contacts.[20] These rules apply to all types of contracts and are essential if one, for example, wants to understand the procedure for concluding, amending or terminating contracts. Furthermore, one has to consult the general norms concerning obligations because the contract is just one of the types of civil legal obligations.[21] This part of the Code contains essential provisions concerning, among other things, performance of obligations and liability for violations of obligations. Finally, one has to turn to the chapter concerning transactions[22] (this chapter contains rules on the form of transactions, state registration of transactions and invalidity of transactions) and, as far as the transfer of ownership is concerned, the law of property.[23]

5. The Civil Code and Commercial Law

In principle the 1994 Civil Code establishes identical rules for all participants in private law relationships, regardless of whether they are companies or private citizens. Art. 2 of the Code states that "civil legislation regulates relations between persons involved in entrepreneurial activities or participating in them." This short clause brought to an end a very long discussion of the need to adopt a special entrepreneurial or commercial code that would regulate relations of professional entrepreneurs or companies outside the framework and institutions of the Civil Code. As a result, Russia joined the group of countries (such as Switzerland and Italy) which include the traditional principles and norms of civil law and principles and norms of commercial law into a single code.

Although commercial law is not considered separate from civil law, the 1994 Civil Code does contain a number of special rules for those who

---

[17] Civil Code, Art. 558.

[18] Civil Code, Arts. 549-557.

[19] Civil Code, Arts. 554-505.

[20] Civil Code, Arts. 420-453.

[21] Civil Code, Arts. 307-419.

[22] Civil Code, Arts. 153-181.

[23] Cf. A.L. Makovsky, S.A. Khokhlov, Introductory Commentary to the Civil Code, in The Civil Code of the Russian Federation (English translation by P.B. Maggs) lxix-lxx (1997).

engage in entrepreneurial activity. For instance, Art. 401 of the Code imposes a higher standard of care for entrepreneurs than that imposed on citizens participating in ordinary civil transactions.

The Civil Code also recognizes "commercial custom." This source of law may contain specific rules that could modify the general rules of the Code. For example, under Art. 438 of the Civil Code, silence does not constitute an acceptance of an offer. However, Art. 438 also provides that in transactions between entrepreneurs silence can be deemed to be an acceptance if it follows from "commercial custom."

While the 1994 Civil Code integrates the basic principles of commercial law into the general corpus of civil law, commercial activities require detailed legislation that develops the general principles of the Code. As a result, the Civil Code is gradually being supplemented by a host of specific statutes, an awareness and understanding of which are necessary to avoid being misled about Russian commercial law.

B. Persons

There are two categories of "persons" under Russian civil law: natural persons and juridical persons. Russian Federation, the "subjects" of the Federation and municipalities also may participate in civil legal relations.

1. Natural Persons

With respect to natural persons, the Civil Code differentiates between legal capacity and dispositive legal capacity. Legal capacity is the general capacity to bear civil rights and duties. It arises at birth and ceases upon death.[24] Legal capacity does not actually determine dispositive legal capacity, that is, the capacity to enter into biding contracts or liability for other actions. In general, the complete acquisition of the right to exercise legal capacity depends upon reaching legal age (18) or marriage (if earlier).

Individuals have the right to engage in entrepreneurial activity without forming a juridical person.[25] The only requirement for this kind of business activity is state registration that grants the citizens the status of citizen-entrepreneur. The procedure for state registration is very simple: it is necessary to file a statement and pay a registration fee.

The heads of peasant (farm) enterprises may also engage in business activities without forming a juridical person. They are recognized as individual

---

[24] Civil Code, Art. 17.
[25] Civil Code, Art. 23.

entrepreneurs from the moment of state registration of the peasant (farm) enterprise.

If a citizen carries on a commercial enterprise and acts as individual entrepreneur without the required state registration, she or he will still be considered as entrepreneurs as far as her or his transactions and liability for transactions are concerned. In cases where the Civil Code imposes a higher standard of care for entrepreneurs than that imposed on citizens participating in ordinary civil transactions, the rules concerning entrepreneurs will apply. This principle protects third parties who in good faith rely on persons who, either wilfully or negligently, make themselves out to be individual entrepreneurs.

Because no separate legal entity is formed, citizens-entrepreneurs are personally liable for all business debts out of their personal assets.[26]

2. Juridical Persons

Juridical persons are organizations that have in their ownership, economic management or operative management separate property, are liable for their own obligations and may in their own name acquire and exercise property and personal non-property rights, including constitutional rights, as well as bear duties and act as a plaintiff or defendant in court.[27]

The Civil Code provides that juridical persons may be established only pursuant to principal types defined by the Code. At the same time, the Code provides a wide variety of types to choose from.

According to Art. 50 of the Civil Code, there are two basic types of juridical persons: commercial and non-profit organizations. Commercial organizations seek profit as the main goal of their activity. They may only be set up in the form of economic partnerships, companies, production cooperatives or state and municipal enterprises.

Non-profit organizations do not seek profits and do not distribute the derived profits among their participants. In contrast to commercial organizations, they may be set up not only in forms determined by the Civil Code but also in other forms "envisioned by the law."[28] The Code itself mentions only consumer cooperatives, public and religious organizations (associations), and

---

[26] Civil Code, Art. 24.

[27] Civil Code, Art. 48. Juridical persons are protected by basic constitutional rights and have the right to file complaints in the Constitutional Court and sue in "ordinary" courts. For detailes, see Chapter IV.

[28] Civil Code, Art. 50.

charity and other funds. According to Art. 50 of the Civil Code, non-profit organizations may engage in business activities only insofar as it helps them to achieve their purposes as stated in their founding documents.[29]

The Civil Code distinguishes between three basic types of juridical persons depending on how their founders or participants relate to property controlled by the juridical person.

With respect to juridical persons of the first type, the participants have no property rights. The juridical persons themselves own the transferred or subsequently acquired property. However, the participants are still entitled to certain rights and privileges (defined as "the rights of obligation" or "the right to demand an obligated performance"[30]) such as the right to participate in the management or receive dividends. These are economic partnerships, companies and production and consumer cooperatives.

The founders may also establish a juridical person without transferring to it their property rights. The owner of the relevant property may convey to the juridical person only the right to possess, use and dispose of the property. In such a case, the juridical person will control or manage the property while the owner retains the legal title to the property. The transferred property may be controlled on the basis of the so-called "economic management" or "operative management."[31] As a rule, these arrangements are made with respect to state and municipal enterprises and also in cases of the establishment of certain institutions financed by the owner.

Finally, a juridical person may become a sole owner of the transferred property while the founders do not retain any property rights. Furthermore, in contrast to juridical persons of the first model, the founders would not be entitled to any other rights or privileges. These juridical persons are public and religious organizations, charity and other funds.

Differences between these models are important in several respects. In

---

[29] It is interesting to note under the 1995 Law on Non-Profit Organizations (*Sobranie*, No. 3, item 145 (1996)) "protection of the rights and interests of citizens and organizations" and "legal assistance" may be one of the goals of non-commercial organizations. "Colleges of Advocates" or Bar Associations are thus non-profit organizations. Regional "Colleges of Advocates" have their "legal consultation offices" providing legal services in all districts. Although "Colleges of Advocates" are thus engaged in business activity, their legal status as non-profit organizations helps them to avoid several important tax liabilities.

[30] The nature of "obligational relationships" is discussed *infra* p. 314-315.

[31] The concept of "economic management" and "operative management" is discussed *infra* p. 309-310.

the event of a liquidation, the participants in the juridical persons of the first model are entitled to the value of their interest in the organization. The founder of the juridical person of the second model is entitled to receive all the remaining assets, while the founders of the persons of the third model have no right to participate in the distribution of the net assets.

3. Legal Capacity of Juridical Persons

The legal capacity of juridical persons depends on their classification. As a general rule, commercial organizations may have all kinds of civil-law rights and bear civil-law duties necessary for conducting any types of activity not prohibited by a statute. At the same time, certain restrictions are imposed on the legal capacity of other types of juridical persons. The Civil Code has retained the traditional principle of special (purpose-oriented) formal legal capacity of certain juridical persons. Art. 49 of the Civil Code provides that a juridical person may have a limited number of civil-law rights corresponding to the purposes of activity provided in its founding documents and bear duties connected with this activity.

This restrictive definition of legal capacity concerns non-profit organizations and a special type of commercial organization - "unitary" enterprises. These enterprises are established and owned by a single ("unitary") owner - the state or municipalities. While on-going privatization has resulted in the emergence of many private companies, the "unitary" enterprises still constitute a substantial sector in the Russian economy. Restrictions on the legal capacity of "unitary" enterprises are imposed in the interests of the owner - the state.

The state establishes tight control over its property by restricting the property rights of "unitary" enterprises. "Unitary" enterprises do not own the relevant property. They receive a limited right of "economic management" or "operative management" over the relevant property. As a result, these enterprises may not alienate immovable property or general funds granted to the enterprise without the consent of the owner or a competent organ designated by the owner (state property administration committees).

The concept of special or restrictive legal capacity has important legal consequences. Under Arts. 168 and 173 of the Civil Code, transactions performed by a juridical person in violation of the purpose-oriented nature of its legal capacity may be invalidated by courts.

In contrast, as noted earlier, ordinary commercial organizations have no restrictions on their legal capacity. According to Art. 49 of the Civil Code, they have civil-law rights and duties necessary for the execution of all types of activity not prohibited by the law. Limitations on the legal capacity of these persons may be imposed only by the general rules governing business activity. For instance, certain activities, such as banking or transportation, require a special authorization or license.[32]

The founding documents of juridical persons may consist of a charter, a founding contract, or a founding contract and a charter. An exception are non-profit organizations. They may operate pursuant to general statutes for organizations of a given type.[33]

All juridical persons are subject to state registration. Registration of all business associations in Russia is a highly bureaucratic procedure governed by special legislation. Under existing legislation,[34] state registration requires presentation to the organs of the Ministry of Justice of several documents, including founding documents. All the relevant data are entered into the Unified State Register of Juridical Persons that is open to the general public. Legal capacity of a juridical person commences from the moment of its state registration and ceases at the moment of its dissolution.

The Civil Code provides the basic legal framework for all juridical persons. The rules of the Civil Code have been further developed by several statutes dealing with different types of juridical persons. The most important among these are the 1995 Law on Joint Stock Companies,[35] the 1995 Law on Non-Profit Organizations,[36] the 1995 Law on Agricultural Cooperatives[37] and the 1996 Law on Production Cooperatives[38] and the 1998 Law on Limited Liability Companies.[39]

---

[32] Under Art. 49 of the Civil Code a list of types of activities requiring special permission (or a licence) may be established only "by a statute." Although Art. 49 of the Civil Code does not provide that the licence requirement may be established only by a *federal* statute, the Supreme Court held that local regulations establishing licence requirements violate Art. 71 of the Constitution which establishes exclusive federal jurisdiction over "the establishment of the basic legal principles of a single market" and "civil . . . legislation." See *Ts. and Joint Stock Company "Trade-Industrial Company" "Vostok" v. The Head of the Administration of the Khabarovsk Region, BVS*, 1997, No. 10, p. 21-23 (The Head of the Administration of the Khabarovsk Region had no right to issue local regulations requiring a licence for trade activities in the Region).

[33] An example is a model statute for secondary schools providing vocational training. See *Sobranie*, No. 27, item 2893 (1994).

[34] See Regulations on the Procedure of State Registration of Subjects of Entrepreneurial Activity, *Sobranie*, No. 11, item 1194 (1994).

[35] See *supra* note 15.

[36] See *supra* note 29.

[37] *Sobranie*, No. 50, item 4870 (1995).

[38] *Sobranie*, No. 20, item 2321 (1996).

[39] *Sobranie*, No. 7, item 785 (1998).

C. Business Organizations

The law governing business organizations defines different forms that individuals can use for their entrepreneurial activities. It also determines rules that must be observed by business persons in their relationship with each other and vis-a-vis third parties. Although the 1993 Constitution guarantees "freedom of economic activity,"[40] overriding public concerns result in many limitations on the activities of business entities. An important element in the commercial law governing business organization is the desire to protect the emerging market economy from fraudulent or questionable business practices.

1. Partnerships and Companies

The Civil Code distinguishes between economic partnerships and companies. Partnerships are considered to be associations of persons, while companies are associations of capital. Partnerships are based on personal confidence which unites the partners. Because partnerships are associations of persons, there is a requirement of personal participation in the activities of the partnership. Furthermore, because partners are engaged in entrepreneurial activities, they must have the status of a commercial organization or citizen-entrepreneur. In contrast, associations of capital do not require any active participation in the conduct of the business of a company. Any person may become a shareholder in a company. In contrast to partners, shareholders usually look more for the financial returns on their shares than for active participation in the conduct of business.

2. Partnerships

There are two types of partnerships: the full partnership and the limited (commandite) partnership.

(a) Full Partnerships

The Civil Code defines the full partnership as a partnership whose participants are engaged in business activities on behalf of the partnership and are jointly and severally liable to creditors for the partnership's debts.[41] The full partnership is formed and operates on the basis of a written agreement. The Civil Code requires that the founding agreement contains several elements, including information on the amount and structure of the capital and capital contributions to be made by the partners.[42] In general, the

[40] Constitution, Art. 8.
[41] Civil Code, Art. 69.
[42] Civil Code, Art. 70.

operation of full partnerships is governed by rules agreed by the partners, in the absence of which the relevant provisions of the Civil Code apply.

The full partnership must carry at least one name of its partners indicating the existence of the partnership or carry the names of all partners. Because of the principle of full liability, a person may become a partner in only one full partnership.

Full partnerships are independent units. In contrast to contractual arrangements providing for joint entrepreneurial activities (simple partnership),[43] which do not create juridical persons, the full partnership has a legal personality. The individual partners have an interest in the partnership assets that is proportionate to their share in the partnership.

As a rule, full partnerships are operated on the basis of consensus of all partners. However, the founding document may also provide for a majority vote. Unless otherwise agreed, each partner is entitled to one vote on management matters.

Each partner may act on behalf of the partnership and the act of any partner in the name of the partnership binds the partnership. Partners can also agree in the partnership agreement that no partner can do business with third parties without the approval of all others or that all decision-making authority in external relations will be granted to only one or several partners.

In the absence of an agreement to the contrary, all partners share in the profits and losses of the partnership proportionate with the amount of capital contribution of each partner.[44]

Each partner has the right to withdraw from the partnership. However, the withdrawal of a partner does not cause dissolution. Automatic dissolution does occur, however, if there is only one remaining partner.

All the partners are jointly and severally liable to third parties and cannot limit their liability. Even a partner who enters at a later date is liable for all previous claims by third parties. Actions by the creditors should be taken against the partnership and all partners or an individual partner as co-defendants.

Full partnerships are not a very popular form of association because of the unlimited liability of all members. Because solidarity and trust between the

---

[43] Civil Code, Arts. 1041-1054.

[44] Civil Code, Art. 74.

partners are an important element of full partnerships, they are usually used in family business.

(b) Limited (Commandite) Partnerships

A limited (commandite) partnership has two groups of participants. Partners (citizen-entrepreneurs or juridical persons) create the limited partnership by a written agreement and are engaged in entrepreneurial activity on behalf of the limited partnership. Just as full partners in full partnerships, they are jointly and severally liable to creditors for the partnership's debts.[45] The rules concerning management, representation and dissolution of the partnership are the same as for the full partnership.

Participant-investors (commanditaires) are investors who are not subject to unlimited liability for the debts of the limited partnership. The limited partners risk only the loss of their initial capital contribution to the limited partnership. Participant-investors may be citizens or juridical persons. While full partners operate the limited partnership, the participant-investors have no power to manage or represent the limited partnership. However, they have rights of information and are entitled to share in the profits of the limited partnership as specified in the partnership agreement.

There is no upper limit on the number of participant-investors. This means, that, in principle, a large number of participant-investors may join as members and a considerable capital fund can be established.

Because the limited partnership is created on the basis of a written agreement between partners, at least two partners are required for its establishment. Participant-investors may become partners. A simple addition of the name of the investor in the trade name of the commandite partnership is enough.

This form of commercial association is popular for small and medium-sized business.

3. Companies

In contrast to partnerships, participants of companies are not personally liable for the companies' debts. The principle of limited liability is the principal advantage of the company form of doing business. This feature of companies requires stronger protection of third parties. The Civil Code provides this protection in many ways. An important requirement is that the charter capital must not be mere "starting capital." There must be a certain

[45] Civil Code, Art. 82.

minimal capital (as defined by the supplementary legislation) that will guarantee the interests of the creditors of the company.[46] This principle is further strengthened by the requirement that capital contributions to companies (and partnerships) must consist of property realistically capable of being used to satisfy claims of potential creditors. An initial contribution to companies must be in the form of cash, property, property rights or other rights that may be evaluated in money.[47] These requirements are designed to prevent the creation of "paper companies" devoid of any asset. Additional protection is provided by restrictions on the payment of dividends, personal responsibility of managers and regulations governing securities.[48]

The Civil Code envisions three types of companies: the limited liability company, the additional liability company and the joint stock company.

(a) Limited Liability Companies

The limited liability company is a popular form of business organization that provides its members with limited liability. The participants risk only the loss of their initial capital contribution to the company. The legal status and operation of limited liability companies are governed by the general rules of the Civil Code and the 1998 Law on Limited Liability Companies.[49]

Limited liability companies may be formed by several persons or just by one person. Under Art. 7 of the 1998 Law on Limited Liability Companies the maximum number of investors cannot exceed fifty. As a general rule, limited liability companies are formed by participants who have close association to the common enterprise. A limited liability company cannot have as a sole investor another company founded by a single person (This rule also applies to joint stock companies discussed below).

The limited liability company is founded on the basis of a written contract signed by the founders. The founding documents of a limited liability company are a founding contract and a charter approved by the founders. If the company is established by a single person, the founding document is a charter approved by that person. The Civil Code and the 1998 Law on Limited Liability Companies provide that the founding documents must contain several elements, including information on the amount of the capital and

---

[46] Civil Code, Arts. 90 (1), 99 (1).

[47] Civil Code, Art. 66 (6).

[48] Federal regulation of securities is based on the 1996 Law "On the Securities Market" (*Sobranie*, No. 17, item 1918 (1996)).

[49] See *supra* note 39.

membership interests of every participant. The founding documents are subject to state registration.

According to Art. 14 of the 1998 Law on Limited Liability Companies, the nominal capital of a limited liability company must be not less that the amount of 100 times the monthly minimum wage established by federal law. The minimal amount of capital may be increased or reduced (upon notification of all creditors). These changes are effected by an amendment to the founding documents which are subject to a new state registration.

An important characteristic feature of limited liability companies is organization of their capital. The charter capital of these companies is divided into membership interests. The amount of interest of each investor is determined by the charter of the company. The charter may prohibit any changes in the allotment of membership interests of each participant. In the absence of an agreement to the contrary, interests in the limited liability companies may be transferred to third persons. However, other participants have the right to acquire membership interests of any member who wishes to sell on a priority basis.[50]

The advantage of this form of doing company business is the absence of any general requirement to publish information on the company's business or finance.[51] Another advantage is relative flexibility. Although the Civil Code and the 1998 Law on Limited Liability Companies provide for the establishment of certain governing bodies (such as the general meeting of the participants and an executive body), in general the participants themselves determine the procedures to operate the company. They can choose to manage the company directly or indirectly through managers. At the same time, the limited liability company is not a suitable company form to invite the general public to subscribe to its shares. As a result, these companies have no access to the public capital markets.

(b) Additional Liability Companies

In order to improve the credit rating of their company, the investors may provide in the founding documents of a company (a founding contract and a charter) for additional liability proportional to their initial capital contribution to the company.[52] This form of business is called the additional

[50] Civil Code, Art. 93; 1998 Law on Limited Liability Companies, Art. 21.

[51] Under Art. 49 of the 1998 Law on Limited Liability Companies, these companies have to publish annual reports and balance sheets if they issue securities or bonds to the general public.

[52] Civil Code, Art. 95.

liability company. In other respects it is formed and operated according to the same rules as a limited liability company.

(c) Joint Stock Companies

The joint stock company also provides limited liability for investors. It is the most complex business form in Russia. The legal status and operation of joint stock companies are governed by the general rules of the Civil Code and by the 1995 Law on Joint Stock Companies.[53] The emerging judicial practice in the field has been consolidated in the Joint Ruling of the Plenary Session of the Supreme Court and the Plenary Session of the Supreme Arbitration Court "*On Some Questions Concerning the Application of the Law On Joint-Stock Companies.*"[54]

The 1995 Law on Joint Stock Companies provides a comprehensive set of detailed regulations for this form of business association. The 1995 Law also contains numerous clauses on the rights and obligations of the shareholders and on the protection of their rights and interests. As noted earlier, some of the provisions of the 1995 Law are inconsistent with the Civil Code. It is not entirely clear how these inconsistencies will be resolved. It may be argued, however, that the 1995 Law could prevail as *lex specialis.*

The Civil Code and the 1995 Law distinguish between two types of joint stock companies: open and closed companies.

Shareholders of an open company may alienate their shares without approval of other shareholders. The number of shareholders of an open joint stock company is not limited. Although all shares are issued only in the name of the registered shareholder (as apposed to shares issued for the bearer),[55] they can be freely traded by the general public. Limited liability and free exchange of shares allows joint stock companies to raise considerable capital.

The company whose shares are distributed only among its founders or participants is a closed company. These companies do not have the right to freely trade shares. The number of shareholders of a closed company may not

---

[53] See *supra* note 15. For English-language commentaries on the Russian joint stock company law, see O. Sirodoeva, The New Russian Joint Stock Company Law, 3 *The Parker School Journal of East European Law* 85 (1996); W. Frenkel, Overview of the New Russian Corporation Law, Id., at 101. For more detailed analysis, see W. Frenkel, Commercial Law of Russia: A Legal Treatise III.D (1997). For a comparative analysis, see W.E. Butler, The Russian Open Joint-Stock Society and the American Corporation: The Principal Attributes Compared, 2 *Sudebnik* 565 (1997).

[54] *BVS*, 1997, No. 6, p. 1.

[55] As a result, companies must keep a ledger listing the shareholders.

exceed fifty. In many respects the closed joint stock companies resemble limited liability companies. However, joint-stock companies have a different organization of capital: all membership interests are confirmed by shares, all of which must be of equal value. Furthermore, closed joint stock companies lack the limited liability company's flexibility and must comply with many restrictions imposed by the joint stock company law.

Joint stock companies are formed on the basis of a written agreement signed by their founders. However, the agreement is not considered to be a founding document of the joint stock company. The founding document is the charter of the company.[56] If the company is created by a single person (who cannot be another company founded by a single person), the founding document is also a charter. The charter must comply with numerous requirements of the 1995 Law. The charter must, among other things, include the name of the company and its location, and specify the number, nominal value, class (ordinary or preference) of shares and type of preference shares, if any, issued by the company, rights of shareholders, amount of charter capital, the structure and the powers of the company management organs, the procedure for decision-making, the procedure for the preparation and holding of the general shareholders meeting, and information on subsidiaries and representative offices of the company.[57] Companies are subject to state registration. Amendments to the company's charter are also subject to state registration.[58]

According to the 1995 Law, the nominal capital of an open joint stock company must be not less that the amount of 1000 minimal monthly wages established by the federal law. The nominal capital of a closed joint stock company must be not less that the amount of 100 minimal monthly wages.[59] The company's charter capital may be increased through the increase of the nominal value of the shares or through issuance of additional shares. The charter capital may also be decreased through the decrees of the nominal value of the shares or through the decrease of the total number of shares. While both changes require state registration,[60] creditors must be notified of the decrease of the company's' charter capital.[61]

Joint stock companies may issue two categories of shares: ordinary shares and preferred shares. Ordinary shares confer upon the holders the right

---

[56] 1995 Law on Joint Stock Companies, Art. 11.
[57] 1995 Law on Joint Stock Companies, Art. 11.
[58] 1995 Law on Joint Stock Companies, Art. 12.
[59] 1995 Law on Joint Stock Companies, Art. 26.
[60] 1995 Law on Joint Stock Companies, Art. 12.
[61] 1995 Law on Joint Stock Companies, Art. 30.

to participate in the shareholders general meeting, the right to vote on all issues within its jurisdiction, and the right to the net assets of the company upon its dissolution. The holders of ordinary shares may also receive dividends.

Joint stock companies may issue different types of preferred shares. These may grant their holders different rights and privileges. The most important privilege is a dividend preference over ordinary shares and a priority over other stockholders in the event of a dissolution of the company. As a rule, the holders of preferred shares have no right to vote at a shareholders general meeting. However, they have the statutory right to participate in general meetings and the right to vote on issues of reorganization and liquidation of the company.[62] Company charters may expand voting rights of the holders of preferred shares depending on their class. In any case, however, the proportion of the preferred shares in the total volume of the charter capital cannot exceed 25 percent.[63]

In addition to shares, the joint stock companies may also issue securities or bonds. The nominal value of all the bonds issued by the company cannot exceed the amount of the charter capital or the amount of the security provided to the company by third parties for the purpose of the bond issue.[64]

The essential elements of the management structures of a joint stock company are defined by its charter. The supreme organ of the company is the general shareholders meeting. Under the 1995 Law, general meetings must have exclusive jurisdiction over the most important matters, including amendments to the charter, reorganizations, liquidation, election of the company's board of directors, election of executive officers, annual dividends and conclusions of the most important transactions related to the acquisition and transfer of company's property. The general meeting of the shareholders also elects an inspection commission (inspector) of the company and approves an auditor. Both the inspector and the auditor supervise the company's financial and economic performance.

The majority rule applies to decision-making of the shareholders meeting. Resolutions are usually adopted by a simple majority. However, on certain fundamental issues the 1995 Law requires that decisions be adopted by a three-quarters majority of the participants in the meeting. Special rights are granted to minorities owning no less than two percent of the company's voting stock. Minorities have the right to introduce proposals for the agenda of the

---

[62] 1995 Law on Joint Stock Companies, Art. 32.
[63] Civil Code, Art. 102.
[64] 1995 Law on Joint Stock Companies, Art. 33.

annual general meeting of shareholders and the right to nominate candidates to the company's board of directors and inspection commission (inspector).[65]

Boards of directors (supervisory boards) are usually responsible for the general management of the company. These bodies are elected in companies with more than fifty participants. Russia has adopted the so-called dual principle, according to which the supervisory organ and the management organ are two separate bodies. According to this principle, day-to-day operations of the company are managed by the company's executive organ. It may be an individual officer (director or general director) or a collective executive organ (management board or directorate). The management may be selected and removed by the board of directors or by the general meeting of the shareholders. The two-tier structure of the management of the joint stock company is the feature that most strikingly distinguishes Russian joint stock companies from American corporations.

The company's individual executive (director or general director) is the legal representative of the company. Although restrictions may be imposed internally on the managing director by the shareholders, they must respect the validity of normal business transactions conducted by the managing director externally. Third parties, who conclude normal business transactions with the managing director, can rely on the director's power of representation and the effectiveness of the relevant contracts.[66] However, they must also know that conclusion of major transactions related to the company acquisition and alienation of its property may fall within the jurisdiction of the board of directors or the general meeting of shareholders. Under Art. 79 of the 1995 Law, the decision to conclude a major transaction the subject of which constitutes property with a value ranging from 25 to 50 percent of the book value of the company assets must be approved by the company's board of directors. Major transactions with respect to property with a value exceeding 50 percent of the book value of the company's assets require the approval of the general meeting of shareholders. If the managing director concludes a major transaction without the required authorization from the board of directors or from the general meeting of shareholders, the transaction may be declared null and void. However, it would be enforced by courts if it was subsequently approved by the board of directors or the general meeting of shareholders.[67]

---

[65] 1995 Law on Joint Stock Companies, Art. 53.

[66] Cf. The Joint Ruling of the Plenary Session of the Supreme Court and the Plenary Session of the Supreme Arbitration Court "*On Some Questions Concerning the Application of the Law On Joint-Stock Companies,*" *supra* note 54.

[67] Id.

Internal control over the company's operations is exercised by the shareholders who have the right to inspect the company documents.[68] While there is no general right to inspect the originals of accounting documents and the minutes of meetings of the company's executive body, the company must provide copies of these documents.[69]

Shareholders' rights may be protected in court. The 1995 Law provides, in particular, that shareholders have the right to appeal a decision adopted by the general meeting of shareholders that violates legislation, the company's charter and their rights and interests.[70] Shareholders may also challenge decisions of the board of directors and company's executive organs in court "if the decision contravenes the requirements of the [1995] Law and other normative acts and violates the rights and legally protected interests of the shareholder."[71]

Every open joint stock company is obliged to publish every year in the mass media available to all shareholders of the company the most important information concerning the company. This information includes an annual report, balance sheet, profit and loss account and the list of company's affiliated persons with the number and class of shares owned by them.[72] A closed company is obliged to disclose appropriate information only if it offers bonds or other securities to the general public.[73]

The Civil Code and the 1995 Law contain important provisions on liability of parent companies for obligations of subsidiary or dependent companies. Both the Civil Code and the 1995 Law state that a principal company incurs joint liability for transactions of a subsidiary if the principal company has the power to give mandatory instructions to the subsidiary. The Civil Code did not tie the origin of the right to give mandatory instructions to specific documents.[74] The 1995 Law clarifies the matter by providing that the parent company is deemed entitled to issue mandatory instructions to the subsidiary only if the right is provided for by a contract with the subsidiary or by its charter.[75]

---

[68] 1995 Law on Joint Stock Companies, Arts. 89, 91.

[69] Id.

[70] 1995 Law on Joint Stock Companies, Art. 49.

[71] The Joint Ruling of the Plenary Session of the Supreme Court and the Plenary Session of the Supreme Arbitration Court "*On Some Questions Concerning the Application of the Law On Joint-Stock Companies,*" *supra* note 54.

[72] 1995 Law on Joint Stock Companies, Art. 92.

[73] Id.

[74] Civil Code, Art. 105.

[75] 1995 Law on Joint Stock Companies, Art. 6.

4. Cooperatives

Cooperatives give persons engaged in trade and farmers the possibility to secure for themselves the advantages of large-scale enterprises by joining forces. The Civil Code defines production cooperatives as associations of citizens for the purpose of joint production or any other kind of economic activity based on their personal labor and capital contribution.[76] Detailed regulation of agricultural and production cooperatives is provided by the 1995 Law on Agricultural Cooperatives[77] and 1996 Law on Production Cooperatives.[78] The distinctive feature of cooperatives is that they are associations of citizens who are not entrepreneurs. All members of the cooperative have an equal voice in the management of the cooperative regardless of the amount of cash or property contribution.[79] While capital or property contribution may be a factor affecting the sharing of profits, personal labor contribution is listed as the first element to be taken into account.[80]

The Civil Code provides that there must be at least five members of a production cooperative. The founding document is a charter, which must be registered.

Cooperatives are governed by their members. The supreme organ is always the general meeting of the cooperative. Members of the cooperative also exercise control through a supervisory board and management. Members of the supervisory board and managers of a cooperative must always be members of that cooperative.

In contrast to partnerships and companies, cooperatives do not have fixed capital. The cooperative share of the members of the cooperative consists of their initial contribution as well as the credited profit share. The interest of the individual member of the cooperative, which may be reclaimed in the event of the resignation, is not a prerequisite (as in partnerships) but a consequence of membership. In other words, some members may join a cooperative without any cash or property contribution and gradually acquire the relevant interest if cooperative profits are reinvested.

Although the Civil Code proclaims the principle that members of the production cooperative may be held personally liable for all of the cooperative's debts out of their personal assets, detailed regulation of the issue is

---

[76] Civil Code, Art. 107.
[77] See *supra* note 37.
[78] See *supra* note 18.
[79] Civil Code, Art. 110.
[80] 1996 Law on Production Cooperatives, Art. 12.

referred to in supplementary legislation.[81] So far this principle has not found strong support. The 1996 Law on Production Cooperatives provides, for example, that members of the cooperative bear subsidiary liability for the cooperative's debts "according to the procedure defined by the charter of the cooperative."[82] This may mean that members of the cooperative could, by charter, limit their liability.

5. State "Unitary" Enterprises

As noted earlier, in the majority of cases these enterprises are owned by the state or municipalities and fully controlled by it. The state or the municipality retains broad supervisory rights over the activities of "unitary" enterprises. At the same time, these enterprises are separate legal entities. Because their legal capacity is purpose-oriented, they cannot engage in activities not directly specified in their charters. Nor can they conclude major transactions concerning the alienation of property without the consent of the state. If a "unitary" enterprise has been granted only limited rights of "operative management,"[83] the state control over their activities becomes even tighter. The lack of independence for these type of enterprises is accompanied by the acceptance by the state of secondary liability for their debts.[84] As a result, these enterprises are practically immune from bankruptcy.

PROBLEM

An American businessman, John Dunn, who is the sole owner of a company "John Dunn, Inc." asks you to give him advice about the best form of organizing his business in Russia. He is looking for a way to establish a company that would satisfy the following basic requirements:

1. The company must be able to engage in any form of entrepreneurial activity;

2. Mr. Dunn would like to have full control over the activities of the company's management;

3. He would like to keep all the information concerning financial operations of the company confidential;

4. He would like to limit his liability by his contribution to the company's capital.

---

[81] Civil Code, Art. 107.
[82] 1996 Law on Production Cooperatives, Art. 13.
[83] The concept of "operative management" is discussed *infra* p. 309-310.
[84] Civil Code, Art. 115.

He also asks you to give him information on the basic formalities concerning the establishment of a company in Russia.

D. The State as a Subject of Civil Law

Prior to the 1994 Civil Code, Russian legislation did not define the legal position of the state or municipalities as participants in commerce. The Civil Code is based on the idea that if a state or a municipal formation enters into civil law relations, it cannot rely on its public authority (imperium) to exercise its civil-law rights. Art. 124 of the Code provides that the Russian Federation, the "subjects" of the Russian Federation, as well as cities and municipal formations enter into relations regulated by civil legislation on equal bases with other participants in these relations - citizens and juridical persons. General principles and norms of civil law apply to these special subjects of civil law unless otherwise follows from a statute or the peculiarities of the given subjects.

Another important innovation of the 1994 Civil Code is the principle of full state liability for harm caused to persons and entities. General rules of the Code concerning compensation for harm are also applicable to the state. The Civil Code contains several clauses in which unlawful actions of state organs that cause harm to property or personal rights of citizens and legal persons are defined as violations of civil-law rights. Under Arts. 16 and 1069 of the Code damage caused to a citizen or legal person as a result of illegal actions (or inaction) of state organs, organs of local self-government or officials are compensated by the Russian Federation, the respective "subject" of the Federation or the municipality.

E. Property

As we have already discovered in Chapter V, the Constitution guarantees the right of private ownership. According to Art. 35(2) of the Constitution "everyone shall have the right to have property in his or her ownership, to possess, use and dispose of it both individually and jointly with other persons." The right of inheritance is also guaranteed.[85] Under Art. 8 of the Constitution, Russia recognizes and protects private, state, municipal and other forms of ownership.

The drafters of the 1993 Constitution attempted to create strong legal guarantees against state interference with property rights. Art. 35(1) of the

[85] Constitution, Art. 35 (4).

Constitution provides that "the right of private ownership shall be protected by law." While the Constitution recognizes the possibility of state intervention, it imposes clear limits on alienation of property. Art. 35(3) states: "No one may be deprived of his or her property except pursuant to a judicial decision. Property can be forcibly taken for state needs only on condition of prior and equal compensation." The fact that ownership is a constitutional right means that it is protected against the Russian state. As Chapter V indicates, this is important not only in cases of expropriations but also in other situations infringing upon property rights.[86]

On the level of civil law, the fundamental principle of the inviolability of property is proclaimed by Art. 1 of the Civil Code. The Civil Code also establishes additional guarantees against state alienation of property. For example, with respect to nationalization, Arts. 235 and 306 of the Civil Code require not only compensation for alienated property but also compensation for economic losses.

The Civil Code provides additional protection of property rights by means of a list of the sole grounds for their forcible termination. This list includes the termination of the right of ownership with respect to objects that cannot be privately owned or that require special permission (for example, weapons),[87] the mandatory purchase of immovables in cases when the land has been taken for public use,[88] the mandatory purchase of certain cultural objects protected by the state in cases when the owner has not been taking proper care of them,[89] mandatory purchase of animals in cases of inhumane treatment,[90] commandeering property in an emergency[91] and confiscation as a sanction for crimes or administrative violations.[92]

1. The Concept of Property

Traditionally the civil law concept of property is very broad. It includes not only the right to a thing but also the right of quiet enjoyment of that thing. Consistent with this broad concept, Art. 209 of the Civil Code provides that an owner has the right to possess, use and dispose of property. The owner has the right to do anything with her or his property if it does not violate the law or other legal acts and the tights and interests of other persons. Public law limitations include such things as rules for the protection of the

[86] For details, see p. 248-263.
[87] Civil Code, Art. 238.
[88] Civil Code, Art. 239.
[89] Civil Code, Art. 240.
[90] Civil Code, Art. 241.
[91] Civil Code, Art. 242.
[92] Civil Code, Art. 243.

environment. In private law, the interests of other persons, in particular, neighbors must be taken into account.

2. Protection of Property and Property Rights

As noted earlier, ownership is protected as a fundamental constitutional right. Both the Constitution and the Civil Code provide strong guarantees for property owners against expropriation or other public taking without compensation. Constitutional law allows recourse against unlawful state interference pursuant to a federal statute by means of an individual complaint to the Constitutional Court. Any unlawful or unfounded interference by officials may be challenged in the "ordinary" courts under the law concerning judicial review of administrative action. In addition, claims for compensation arising from state interference are provided by tort law.[93] Protection against private interference is also given under tort law.[94]

Two specific claims in property law patterned on Roman models serve to protect the ownership of an object: the claim for the return of property when the property has been removed (the *rei vindicatio*)[95] and the claim to compel someone to refrain from an activity that interferes with ownership or use of property (the *actio negatoria*).[96] In addition, the owner may request the court to render a declaratory judgment defining the petitioner's rights with respect to property.

Property law also protects lawful possession of property. The Civil Code distinguishes between proprietary possession (possession as owner) and factual possession. Factual possession may be created through the establishment of a relationship allowing factual power over an object. An example is a lease or tenancy where a person is allowed possession for a certain period of time. The Civil Code protects the possessor against the loss of possession or disturbance of the control over an object, including unlawful interference by the owner.[97]

Russian property law specifically provides protection for several other "property rights" of non-owners. According to Art. 216 of the Civil Code, these "property rights" include: "economic management," "operative management," right of "perpetual use," inheritable possession for life and servitudes.

[93] Civil Code, Art. 1069.
[94] Civil Code, Art. 1064.
[95] Civil Code, Art. 301.
[96] Civil Code, Art. 304.
[97] Civil Code, Art. 305.

3. Movable and Immovable Property

Property law is divided into two main subject areas - movables and immovables. These terms correspond roughly with the division of property in common law into personal property and real property. Immovables are land and the structures built on it. Natural objects, such as forests, are also immovables. Aircraft, spacecraft and ships are classified as immovables as well. The Civil Code also contains a special clause on "enterprises." An enterprise is defined as "a property complex used for the performance of business activities." An enterprise is classified as an immovable notwithstanding the fact that the concept of "an enterprise" includes not only land plots and buildings but also raw materials, products, debts and intellectual property, such as trademarks.[98] The definition of immovables may also include other things specifically designated as such by the law.[99] Movables are all things that are not classified as immovables.

The distinction between movables and immovables is important to the way they are transferred or sold. While the transfer of movables is generally not subject to any registration, any transfer of immovables requires state registration.[100] Other norms governing transactions may also contemplate different regimes for movables and immovables. In addition, the Civil Code establishes different requirements for adverse possession. This subsidiary way to obtain ownership of property requires the passage of a certain period of time. Acquisition of title over immovables requires a bona fide, open and continuous possession for at least fifteen years. Movables require only five years.[101]

4. The Issue of Land Ownership

Arts. 9 and 36(1) of the 1993 Constitution and the Civil Code expressly recognize the right to private ownership of land. Although the right to private ownership of land is recognized in principle, many specific issues of land ownership remain unresolved. The anti-reform forces continue to resist the very idea of unlimited private ownership of land. Their representatives in the State Duma are delaying the enactment of a new Land Code. They have also managed to block the implementation of Chapter 17 of the Civil Code, which deals with the rights pertaining to land ownership. Although the Civil

---

[98] Civil Code, Art. 132.

[99] Civil Code, Art. 130.

[100] Civil Code, Arts. 131 and 551. State registration of immovables is governed by the 1997 Law on the State Registration of Rights and Transactions Concerning Immovable Property, *Sobranie*, No. 30, item 3594 (1997).

[101] Civil Code, Art. 234.

Code entered into force on January 1, 1995, Chapter 17 will become effective simultaneously with the entry into effect of the a Land Code, an important and extremely controversial piece of legislation that has not yet been passed.[102]

President Yeltsin has enacted several decrees confirming private ownership of land.[103] However, the legal situation remains unstable. Three factors will explain why this is so.

First, the presidential decrees will remain in effect only until the new Land Code (or any other federal law concerning land) is approved by the parliament.[104]

Second, the draft Land Code contains numerous restrictions on the right to own land. For example, according to the draft, a private land owner is obliged to use the land strictly for a fixed purpose (lands may be specifically designated for agricultural or for other purposes). If the land owner does not use his or her plot for agricultural purposes within one year, his or her rights to the property may be forfeited. As to plots for non-agricultural purposes, owners may be deprived of their rights if they violate the fixed time limit for construction. Forfeiture can be effected without compensation if the owner changes the purpose of the plot fixed in the "Certificate of the Ownership Right."[105]

Third, the absence of federal laws governing "the terms and procedures for land use" (envisioned by Art. 36(3) of the Constitution) allows the "subjects" of the Russian Federation to adopt their own laws on land use on

---

[102] The suspension of the application of Chapter 17 of the Civil Code runs counter to the principle that it must be regarded as the pivotal legal act governing private law relationships. The decision of the Federal Assembly not to apply the provisions of the Civil Code concerning ownership of land directly makes it secondary to the envisioned Land Code.

[103] The Decree No. 1767 "On the Regulation of Land Relations and the Development of Agrarian Reform in Russia" (*Sobranie aktov*, No. 44, item 4191 (1993)) was one of the first decrees confirming the right of Russian citizens and legal entities to own land and to buy, sell, lease, donate, bequeath, mortgage it or transfer the land or part of it as a contribution to the capital fund of joint stock companies, partnerships and cooperatives. Decree No. 337 "On the Implementation of the Constitutional Right of Citizens to Land" (*Sobranie*, No. 11, item 1026 (1996)) again confirmed the right of citizens to own land and to use it at their pleasure.

[104] The power of the President to legislate by decree in the absence of a statute on the subject was discussed in Chapters II and IV.

[105] It should be emphasized that the Civil Code itself takes a fairly conservative approach to land ownership. It also envisages limitations on usage of the land based on fixed purposes. Land plots may be forcibly seized if not used in accordance with the fixed purpose (Civil Code, Arts. 284, 285).

the basis of Art. 72(c) of the Constitution. While some "subjects" of the Federation have enacted local laws allowing private ownership of land, others refuse to recognize this right. To the extent that "subjects" enact such laws, the unity of the legal structure for land ownership in Russia is undermined.

5. Forms of Ownership

There are a number of forms of ownership. Sole ownership relates to ownership by one person. Joint ownership can be either of a precise fraction of a particular object in which each individual has a divisible interest in the object or joint collective ownership where the individual interests are undivided.[106] All joint ownership, except as otherwise provided for by the law, is considered to be held in shares. The owners determine the size of participatory shares by agreement. If there is no agreement, the shares are presumed to be equal. The Civil Code provides for joint collective ownership in two instances: property of spouses and property of a peasant (farmers) enterprise. They are considered as joint collective ownership unless otherwise established by a contract.[107] In both cases of joint ownership, transfer of property rights is subject to special rules. Thus, the share-owners of the joint property have a preferential right of purchase.[108]

Each co-owner has the right to partition her or his share in kind. In cases where partition in kind is prohibited by the law or is impossible without excessive damage to the property, the co-owner is entitled only to payment equivalent of the value of her or his share. The Civil Code specifically prohibits the partition of land plots and other "means of production" belonging to peasant (farm) enterprises.[109]

6. The Concept of Economic and Operative Management

Under the Civil Code, an owner of the property may convey to another person almost all property rights. While another person controls and manages the property, the owner may still retain the legal title.

One arrangement that provides a non-owner with a significant bundle of property rights is the right of "economic management." Although "economic management" stops short of full title to property, an enterprise or person who has this right is authorized to possess, use and even dispose of movable property as it sees fit. As noted earlier, this concept applies, among other things, to cases of the transfer of property rights from the state to certain state

---

[106] Civil Code, Art. 244.
[107] Civil Code, Arts. 256, 257.
[108] Civil Code, Art. 250.
[109] Civil Code, Art. 258.

enterprises.[110] The concept of "economic management" thus serves an important function: it defines the means by which the state owns or controls public property. It is difficult to find a comparative concept in the US law. It may, however, be argued that the concept of "economic management" parallels the trust or investor relationship.

A much narrower concept is that of "operative management." This concept was first developed under the Soviet civil law when it was used with state enterprises owned by the state. It usually comprises only two rights of the property triad - the right to possess and to use property, but not the right to dispose of the property. The right to operative management of state property is usually given to state "treasury" enterprises wholly controlled by the state and to many social service establishments (such as educational and health care institutions) financed by the state budget.

Under the Civil Code, the owner of the right of "economic management" may freely dispose of movables. Restrictions are imposed only with respect to immovables: the owner of this right cannot sell the relevant immovables, lease them or pledge them as a security, contribute them to the capital fund of joint stock companies or partnerships or otherwise conclude a transaction which may alienate the property without the consent of the owner.[111] In contrast, the owner of the right of "operative management" may not, as a rule, dispose of any object without the consent of the owner.[112]

7. The Concept of Perpetual Use

Under the Civil Code, plots of land may be held in "perpetual use."[113] The concept of "perpetual use" is also applied to situations where an individual or a legal entity owns immovable property (for example, a building) upon land owned by another. Under this concept, the immovable property owner has the right of perpetual use with respect to the land.[114] In this case, the right of perpetual use runs with the immovable property. If the immovable property is sold or transferred, the right of perpetual use is transferred with it.

8. Inheritable Possession for Life

Individuals and legal entities may have a special kind of property right in land called "inheritable possession for life." The owner of a right of inheritable possession for life enjoys the rights of possession and use. Upon her

---

[110] See *supra* p. 303.
[111] Civil Code, Art. 295.
[112] Civil Code, Art. 296.
[113] Civil Code, Arts. 268-270.
[114] Civil Code, Art. 271.

or his death, the property passes to the heirs in inheritable possession for life. Although the owner of this right may lease the property, he or she cannot sell it or pledge it as a security or otherwise conclude a transaction which may alienate the property.[115]

9. Servitudes

Servitudes may impose serious limitations on ownership. The concept of servitude is very broad and includes the common-law devices of easements, servitudes and restrictive covenants.

It is important to emphasize that servitudes are not based on any express agreement, prior practice or implied consent. Under the Civil Code, an owner of a land plot may demand a servitude against another plot. The owner must show sufficient need which may include the laying of a water pipeline or telephone wire.[116] The owner of the burdened propriety has a right to payment commensurate with the burden imposed by the servitude, but servitude runs with the land.[117]

10. Consensual Limitations on Ownership

The Civil Code also allows consensual limitations on ownership. Privatization, which leads to the general reassignment of property rights from the state to private individuals and legal entities, has resulted in many consensual limitations on property rights. Thus, many enterprises were privatized on the condition that the new private owner honors obligations to produce specific products, maintains social services or keeps the privatized enterprise operating for a fixed period.[118]

11. Acquisition and Transfer of Ownership

Property may be acquired or lost by operation of a statute or through a transaction. Statute-based reasons include found objects and adverse possession. Legal transactions may be bilateral (agreement) or unilateral (wills or acts aimed at relinquishing the ownership).

The freedom of contract in property law is limited and property rights can only be established in the way provided by the Civil Code. Public policy requirements of certainty are the main reason for stricter rules for transactions concerning immovables. As noted earlier, these transactions are subject to

---

[115] Civil Code, Art. 267.
[116] Civil Code, Art. 274.
[117] Civil Code, Art. 275.
[118] Cf. *infra* p. 336-343.

state registration. Without registration the legal transaction is not legally valid and the acquirer of the registered property does not become the new owner. According to Art. 223 of the Civil Code, the right of ownership arises only at the time of registration.

In contrast, the transfer of ownership of movables is usually much simpler. The transfer of ownership requires an agreement that ownership pass and that delivery of possession to the acquirer take place. As a general rule, the right of ownership arises at the time of the transfer or delivery of the property to the transferee, unless the contract or applicable legislation provides otherwise. Under Art. 224 of the Civil Code, not only actual delivery to the acquirer but also delivery to the common carrier or post office for delivery to the acquirer constitute a transfer of property.

F. Legal Acts

As noted earlier, the 1994 Civil Code follows the German model of a civil code. A distinctive characteristic of this model is the tendency to present the whole body of civil law in a highly systematic manner. Systematic presentation requires formulation of certain fundamental principles and concepts applicable to all civil law relations. One of these concepts, contained in the general part of the Civil Code, is the concept of a legal "act" or "transaction."

Legal acts are actions of citizens and juridical persons aimed at the establishment, modification or termination of civil-law rights and obligations.[119] Legal acts may be unilateral and bi- or multilateral. A unilateral act is an act that can be effectuated by the expression of the will of only one party.[120] The expression of the will of only one party may be deemed sufficient under the existing law or agreement between the parties. For example, a will is regarded as a unilateral act under the Civil Code. A notice to terminate a contract may be sufficient if the contract contemplates such a procedure.

The Civil Code establishes a fundamental principle that unilateral acts create legal duties for persons who have undertaken them.[121] For example, a promise to hold an auction is regarded as a unilateral act that creates enforceable legal obligations for the actor. At the same time, unilateral acts cannot establish duties for persons other than the actor. They may create

---

[119] Civil Code, Art. 153.
[120] Civil Code, Art. 154.
[121] Civil Code, Art. 155.

duties for them only in cases established by the law or by an agreement between the parties.[122]

Bi- or multilateral legal acts usually contain the expressions of will of two or more persons. Contract is the most common legal act. It requires "the expression of the mutual will of two parties (bilateral transaction) or three or more parties (multilateral transaction)."[123]

An expression of will (or declaration of intent) is a necessary prerequisite of any legal act. In Russian law, two aspects of intent are considered: the external or objective aspect, which is the expressed will, and the internal or subjective aspect, which is what the person actually intended or desired. This, among other things, affects the rules of contract interpretation.[124]

The expression of intent may be written or spoken and may also include forms of meaningful conduct. Silence would not normally constitute an objective expression of intent except where it is recognized as such by the law or by an agreement of the parties.[125]

The Civil Code provides that legal transactions may be undertaken orally or in writing. If the law imposes no written form, legal transactions may be concluded orally. As a general rule, all transactions that are executed at the moment of their performance may be concluded orally.[126] Oral acts are considered to be performed if the will to do so is manifest from the conduct of the person.[127] For example, the selection of goods in a supermarket and taking them to the cashier makes it clear that the buyer has expressed the intention to purchase.

Except for the oral transactions mentioned above, all other transactions between juridical persons *inter se* and with natural persons must be performed in writing. The same requirement applies to transactions between citizens in excess of ten times minimum monthly wage established by federal law.[128] The failure to observe the required written form deprives the parties of the right (in the event of a dispute) to rely on witness testimony regarding the content of the agreement. At the same time, parties may submit written and

---

[122] Id.
[123] Civil Code, Art. 154.
[124] See *infra* p. 322.
[125] Civil Code, Art. 158.
[126] Civil Code, Art. 159.
[127] Civil Code, Art. 158.
[128] Civil Code, Art. 161.

other evidence.[129] In cases envisioned by the law, such a failure may make the transaction void. The Civil Code states, in particular, that the failure to observe the required written form in foreign economic transactions invalidates the transaction.[130]

Certain transactions, such as wills, must be notarially certified. As a rule, the failure to observe this form invalidates the transaction. As noted earlier, transactions concerning immovables also require state registration.

The general part the Civil Code[131] governs all kinds of legal acts or transactions. Therefore, the formal requirements just described also apply to the most common legal act - the contract. Other important provisions contained in this part of the Civil Code deal with grounds for invalidity of transactions. These will be discussed *infra* Section H.

G. The Law of Obligations

Another rather abstract part of the Civil Code that reflects the desire to present a systematically arranged body of law is the general part of the law of obligations. The law of obligation lays the foundations for all aspects of legal relations in civil law and all proprietary rights. In particular, it covers contracts, torts and unjustified enrichment.

The law of obligations is based on the concept of an obligational relationship. The obligational relationship exists between the creditor and the debtor. The term "creditor" means anyone who has the right to demand an obligated performance from another. "Debtor" is any person who is obliged to comply with a demand to perform. Art. 307 of the Civil Code provides that by virtue of an obligation, the debtor is required to do a certain act - e.g., transfer property, perform work, pay money, etc. - or to refrain from doing a certain act, and the creditor has a right to demand from the debtor the performance of such duty.

Art. 307 is a very abstract clause. To make sense, it must be applied to particular types of obligations which appear in the second part of the Civil Code. Thus, in a contract of sale[132] the creditor, as purchaser, may demand the delivery of the goods and the transfer of ownership from the debtor, as seller. And the seller as creditor has the right to demand payment from the buyer as debtor.

---

[129] Civil Code, Art. 162.
[130] Id.
[131] Civil Code, Arts. 153-181.
[132] Civil Code, Art. 454.

The general part of the law of obligations contains all fundamental principles and rules governing all types of obligational relationships. In particular, it contains principles and rules concerning performance duty, performance guarantees, liability for performance irregularities or non-performance and termination of obligations. Some of these principles and norms will be discussed in the following Section.

H. Contracts

The first part of the Civil Code contains general rules concerning all types of obligations, including contracts, and more specific rules regulating formation, change and termination of contracts. The second part of the Civil Code includes numerous and detailed rules governing individual types of contracts (such as contract of sale, barter, gift, rent, lease, loan and credit etc.). While in the United States practical problems relating to different types of contracts are usually solved by recourse to general principles of the law of contracts, in Russia (and in some other civil law countries) specific practical questions concerning individual types of contracts require a careful study of special rules governing individual contracts. The rules of the second part of the Civil Code deal with specific practical problems presented in the context of individual types of contracts. The present Section will focus only on general principles governing all types of contracts in Russia.

1. Freedom of Contract

The new Russian law of contracts governs contract relations of individuals and legal entities in accordance with the fundamental principle of freedom of contract. Freedom of contract, which has an important ideological connection with the free or mixed market economy, means freedom to conclude contracts, freedom to decide the content of contracts and freedom to choose the form of the contract.

While Art. 1 of the Civil Code proclaims the principle of freedom of contract, Art. 421 deals with specific aspects of this freedom. It provides that mandatory conclusion of contracts is inadmissable. This means that the parties are generally free to decide whether and with whom a contract can be concluded. At the same time, Art. 421 allows exceptions from the general rule in cases when the duty to conclude the contact has been imposed by the law (for example, if deliveries of goods to the regions of the Far North are involved) or by a voluntarily assumed obligation (for example, in the framework of a preliminary contract[133]).

[133]"Preliminary contracts" are discussed *infra* p. 321.

The Civil Code also envisions mandatory conclusion of public contracts. Public contracts are various contracts between commercial entities serving the general public and consumers. An example of a public contract would be a public utility contract or a banking services contract. Under Art. 426 of the Civil Code, a commercial organization serving the general public may not refuse to conclude a public contract with customers if it is possible to provide the necessary goods or services to the consumer. Thus, a supplier of electricity in a particular town has a legal monopoly for the supply of electricity to customers. Therefore, it is obliged to conclude contracts with them.

The freedom to decide the content of the contract gives the parties the right to determine the terms of the contract. Two restrictions may be imposed on this freedom. First, the Civil Code and the supplementary legislation may contain mandatory provisions for certain types of contacts. Secondly, this right can only exist within the general limits imposed by the Civil Code. Thus, contacts violating statutory provisions or fundamentals of the legal order are void (for example, contracts to supply drugs).

The freedom to determine the form of the contract gives the parties the right to deviate from the prescribed forms of contracts and to choose novel forms or combine types of legal relations and types of specific contracts listed in the second part of the Civil Code. Because the second part of the Civil Code does not attempt an exhaustive listing of contracts, there is no requirement that only contracts corresponding to a type of contract listed in the Civil Code is valid. As a result, the parties are entirely free to conclude a non-typical contract, for example a contract that would combine elements of different types of specific contracts. This does not mean, however, that in exercising this freedom parties may disregard mandatory requirements of form. Thus, contracts for the purchase of immovables are subject to the adoption of a particular form. They must be written and registered in the State Register by the competent organ of the Ministry of Justice.[134]

2. The Concept of Contract

A contract requires "the expression of the mutual will" of two or more parties. According to Art. 420 of the Civil Code, "contract" means *an agreement* concluded by two or several persons aimed at the establishment, modification or termination of civil rights and duties. Thus, it is an agreement (not a "promise"!) that is the root of an enforceable obligation.

[134]Civil Code, Arts. 131, 550, 551.

3. Formation of Contract

An agreement is formed if there are two or more declarations of intent, both corresponding with one another. As everywhere else, these declarations are termed "offer" and "acceptance." A contract is completed on the acceptance of an offer. As in all other civil law systems, a contract under Russian law does not need to be supported by consideration. Because the doctrine of consideration is not familiar to Russian contract law, a party may, without consideration, enter into a purely unilateral contractual obligation which will be enforceable in courts.

(a) Offer

The offer is a declaration of intent to conclude a contract which must be received by the other party. The offer must be sufficiently definite. In particular, it must "contain the essential terms of the contract."[135] According to Art. 435 of the Civil Code, an offer becomes effective when received by the other party.

While under common law the offeror remains basically free to withdraw the offer at any time before it has been accepted by the offeree, the civil law systems emphasize the binding nature of offers. Under Art. 436 of the Civil Code, the offeror is bound by the offer for the time of the offer unless otherwise specified by the offer itself, by the substance of the proposal or by the general setting in which it has been made. The rule according to which every offer is in principle irrevocable protects the offeree who can act with assurance in the knowledge that her or his acceptance will bring about a contract. Because the offeror takes the initiative, it is assumed that the risk of any changes in supplies and prices is placed on the offeror rather than on the offeree.

An offer is not generally open to acceptance except by those to whom it is made. Advertisements and other proposals addressed to the general public are regarded as an invitation to make offers. A proposal containing all the essential terms of the contract and manifesting intent to conclude a contract with anyone who would respond is treated as a public offer.

The offer is extinguished if it has been turned down, if the acceptance is not received in time or if there is a counter-offer.

(b) Acceptance

Acceptance must be unreserved and unconditional. An answer indi-

---

[135] Civil Code, Art. 435.

cating willingness to conclude the contract on terms other than those indicated in the offer is not regarded as acceptance. According to Art. 443 of the Civil Code, such an answer is treated as counter-offer, which extinguishes the offer. Silence or inaction usually carries no legal consequences. However, there are circumstances in which silence can be taken as a valid manifestation of intent. A contract may arise by the acceptance of an offer without notification of acceptance where such notification is not required by the law, commercial customs or previous commercial practice of the parties.[136] If the person who has received the offer starts to comply with the terms of the offer within the indicated period of time, for example, dispatches goods, renders a service, performs a work or pays the required amount of money, the relevant actions would normally be regarded as acceptance.

If the offer specifies the amount of time in which the offer may be accepted, the contract is concluded if the acceptance is received by the offeror within that period of time. If no period is specified in the offer, the acceptance must be received within the "normally required" period of time.[137] The duration of a "normally required" time is a question of fact, dependent upon the nature of the contract, commercial practice and other factors.

While common law follows the rule that the contract is formed when the offeree dispatches the acceptance (the "mailbox" rule), under the civil law systems acceptance becomes effective only upon receipt. Under Art. 439 of the Civil Code, an acceptance will not be effective if a revocation reaches the offeree before or at the same time that the acceptance reaches the offeror. Therefore, if an acceptance is to be effectively revoked, the revocation must arrive sooner than, or at least simultaneously with, the original.

Because, as a general rule, the contract is considered concluded at the moment when the offeror receives the acceptance, the place of residence of the citizen or the place of business of the juridical person who has made the offer is recognized as the place of the conclusion of the contract (if no place is specified in the contract itself).

(c) Essential Terms

The contract is concluded if there is agreement on all its essential terms. The goal of this requirement is to make contracts sufficiently definite and therefore enforceable. It is also based on the concept that there is a close relationship between certainty of terms and external manifestation of intent to be bound.

[136] Civil Code, Art. 438.
[137] Civil Code, Art. 441.

According to Art. 432 of the Civil Code, the essential terms of a contract are those which relate to the subject matter of the contract, as well as those which are recognized as essential and indispensable for contracts of the given type by the applicable statutes or other normative acts. This means that the essential terms will vary from transaction to transaction. Thus, under Art. 455 of the Civil Code, in a contract of sale the subject matter (specific object) is the only essential condition. The terms of a contract of sale are considered complete if the contract indicates the goods and determines their quantity. If the parties fail to fix the price, the goods are deemed to be sold for a price that is customary for similar goods under comparable circumstances at the time the agreement was made.

Under Art. 432 of the Civil Code, all the terms upon which one of the parties has indicated that agreement must be reached are also essential.

Judicial practice indicates that if parties fail to reach agreement on essential terms of a contract the courts will not enforce them. Thus, in *Titan-Transit v. Bashneftgeofisika*[138] the Supreme Arbitration Court found that the plaintiff and the defendant had not concluded a contract of sale because the defendant signed the contract with a significant modification. Instead of payment after the delivery of crude oil, it proposed prior payment. The Supreme Arbitration Court held that "because the amendments to the contract concerned the change in the method of payment for the goods, this contract term must be considered as essential. In view of the fact that the parties failed to reach an agreement on this essential term, no contract . . . was formed."[139]

4. Formal Requirements for Contracts

The form of a contract is governed by the general rules concerning transactions.[140] Under Russian civil law certain contracts must take special form if they are to receive legal recognition. The purpose of formal requirements established by the Civil Code is to facilitate proof and to confirm seriousness of intention.

When the contract value exceeds a certain sum (for example, contracts between citizens in excess of an amount ten times the minimum monthly wage established by federal law[141]) or when a particular material object is the subject matter of the contract (such as immovables), the contract must be in writing. Certain types of contracts must be in writing whatever the subject

[138] *VVAS*, 1997, No. 1, p. 51.
[139] Id., at 53.
[140] See *supra* p. 313-314.
[141] Civil Code, Art. 161.

matter of the contract (for example, all transactions between juridical persons *inter se* and with citizens that are not executed at the moment of their performance).

Some contracts must be certified by a notary before they become valid. For example, the Civil Code requires a notary certification of mortgage contracts.[142] In practice many parties seek notarial certification even in cases not required by the law. The reason is simple and is the same as the reason why some contracts are required to be notarized. First, a certified contract constitutes irrefutable evidence that the contract has been formed. Second, it may help to counter possible claims of one of the parties concerning incapacity, fraud or duress. Third, notarial certification is to ensure seriousness of intention. Under the 1993 Fundamental Principles of Legislation on the Notariat[143] notaries must explain to citizens and organizations "their rights and duties and inform them about the consequences of notarial activities performed so that lack of legal information can not be used to their detriment."[144] The notary who certifies a contract must "explain to the parties the meaning and consequences of the draft contract submitted by the parties."[145]

Failure to observe the requisite form does not always result in the substantive invalidity of the contract. For example, as a general rule failure to observe the written form requirement does not invalidate contracts. However, there is a procedural sanction: a contract defective in form is "unprovable" by means of witnesses. At the same time, certain contracts are invalid if they fail to observe the required form. For example, under the Civil Code the failure to observe the written form requirement concerning foreign trade transactions makes the relevant contract void.[146] In addition, preliminary contracts (discussed below) are enforceable only if concluded in writing.[147]

---

[142] Civil Code, Art. 339.

[143] See *Vedomosty RF*, No. 10, item 357 (1993).

[144] 1993 Fundamental Principles of Legislation on the Notariat, Art. 16.

[145] 1993 Fundamental Principles of Legislation on the Notariat, Art. 54.

[146] Civil Code, Art. 162. As a successor state of the former Soviet Union, Russia continues to adhere to a reservation concerning oral transactions formulated by the USSR with respect to the UN Convention on Contracts for the International Sale of Goods. The reservation states, among other things, that an offer, acceptance or any other expression of intent, which are not in writing, are not applicable to contracts for the international sales of goods (See UN Doc. A/CN.9/416 (1995)). Art. 11 of the Convention provides: "A contract of sale need not be concluded in or evidenced by writing and is not subject to any other requirement as to form. It may be proved by any means, including witness."

[147] Civil Code, Art. 429.

Some contracts, such as contracts concerning the sale of immovables, require state registration. Contracts that are subject to state registration are regarded as concluded from the moment of registration.[148] As a rule, violation of this form requirement makes the contract unenforceable.

If the contract is in writing, it does not have to be in any particular form. It may be concluded by the parties signing one document or by way of exchanging documents by mail, telegraph, teletype, telephone, by the electronic or any other means of communication which makes it possible to establish that the document comes from the contract party.[149] Under Art. 434 of the Civil Code, the written form of the contract is regarded as observed if the written offer to conclude the contract has been accepted by performance (for example, by a shipment of goods).[150]

5. Preliminary Contract

In order to achieve a certain stability and predictability in their mutual relations, the parties may reach a preliminary agreement to conclude a more detailed contract in the future. Art. 429 of the Civil Code defines the preliminary contract as a contract by which the parties assume an obligation to conclude in the future a contract on the transfer of property, on the performance of work or on rendering services on the terms defined by the preliminary contract. The preliminary contract must contain the essential terms of the basic contract. It also must specify the time period for the conclusion of the basic contract. If no time is specified, the basic contract must be concluded within one year. Preliminary contracts must be concluded in writing.

It is important to emphasize that preliminary contracts are not "soft." They create enforceable obligations. If one of the paries avoids concluding the basic contract, the other party has the right to turn to a court with "a claim to compel conclusion of a contract." [151] Furthermore, the party who enters into a preliminary contract and avoids concluding the basic contract without any valid reason is obliged to compensate the other party for losses.[152]

---

[148] Civil Code, Art. 432.

[149] Civil Code, Art. 434.

[150] It appears that this method of acceptance is also possible in foreign trade contracts despite the general rule that they must be written. In *Electrim v. Kosmos* (*VVAS*, 1997, No. 6, p. 100, 101) the Supreme Arbitration Court held that "the buyer's acceptance of the change in contract [of sale] is confirmed by sending the ship for loading and payments made for the freight."

[151] Civil Code, Art. 448.

[152] Id.

6. Interpretation of Contracts

The Civil Code seeks to apply an objective standard as the first step in contract interpretation. An analysis of the external expression of the parties' intent is the first step in contract interpretation. The principles of interpretation proceed from the literal meaning of the terms contained in the contract. If the terms are vague or unclear, the literal meaning is determined by comparison of the relevant term with other terms of the contract and the meaning of the contract as a whole.[153]

If this method of establishing the content of the contract is unsuccessful, "the true common will of the parties" must be ascertained by taking into account the goals and purposes of the contract. Although the Civil Code stresses the importance of ascertaining "the true common will of the parties," it again applies objective standards and requires that the intention of the parties be ascertained on the basis of a set of objective criteria. All the relevant circumstances, including negotiations and correspondence relating to the contract, prior practice of the parties and their subsequent behavior, as well as commercial customs, may be taken into account.[154]

7. Invalidity

The Civil Code draws a distinction between void legal transactions and voidable transactions. Void transactions, including contracts, are automatically invalid *ab initio*. Voidable transactions, including contracts, are not void automatically; the grounds of invalidity must be invoked by an interested person or organ. While the claim for the application of the consequences of a void transaction may be submitted by any interested person or enforced by the court on its own initiative, the claim for the recognition of the voidable transaction to be invalid may be filed only by persons specifically designated by the Civil Code.[155] For example, contracts concluded by juridical persons in violation of their special purpose-oriented legal capacity (such as state "unitary" enterprises)[156] may be invalidated by the court upon the submission of the relevant claim by the juridical person, its founder or state control organ.[157]

At the same time, there are cases where the Civil Code does not specify "interested persons" who may contest the validity of a contract. For

---

[153] Civil Code, Art. 431.
[154] Id.
[155] Civil Code, Art. 166.
[156] See *supra* p. 290, 303.
[157] Civil Code, Art. 173.

example, under Art. 449 of the Civil Code auctions that violate the auction rules established by the law may be declared invalid by the court upon the claim of "an interested person." Although such an action may lead to very serious consequences (invalidation of the results of an action automatically invalidates the sales contract concluded with the successful bidder), Art. 449 fails to indicate who may be the relevant "interested person."[158]

The Civil Code establishes several grounds for invalidity. As noted earlier, in certain cases the non-observance of formal requirements may result in the transaction being void. The general rule on the matter is contained in Art. 168 of the Civil Code, which states that a legal transaction not conforming to the requirement of the law is void. Art. 442 of the Code also provides that contracts must conform to mandatory rules established by the law or other normative acts. In addition, some statutes prohibit certain conduct and expressly provide that contracts made in violation of the statute are void.[159]

Compelling public policy reasons must also be taken into account. Under Art. 169 of the Civil Code, a legal transaction performed for a purpose deliberately contrary to the foundations of the legal order and public morals is void.

In addition, the Civil Code provides that courts may declare invalid all transactions performed by persons who lack the legal capacity (minority or mental incompetence). As noted earlier, courts may also hold invalid transactions violating the purpose-oriented legal capacity of certain juridical persons. These provisions may be used not only in situations in which the legal capacity of a juridical person is expressly restricted by its founding documents, but also in cases where contracts are made in violation of laws imposing licensing requirements for a particular type of activity.

Other grounds for invalidity of a legal transaction, including contracts, are: sham or pretense, restrictions on authority of a representative, error, fraud, coercion, threats, collusion and extreme necessity. In addition, the Civil

---

[158] Some controversial issues in this area have already been clarified by the courts. For instance, the Supreme Arbitration Court held that any person who was not allowed to participate in a publicly announced action or tender had the right to challenge the validity of the resulting contract of sale (See *VVAS*, 1993, No. 9, p. 83).

[159] Thus, Art. 17 of the 1995 Law "On State Regulation of Foreign Trade Activity" (*Sobranie*, No. 42, item 3923 91995) provides that transactions concerning export or import of certain goods that may be exported or imported only by the state are void.

Code specifically declares certain contracts void.[160] Supplementary legislation may establish additional grounds for invalidity.[161]

Although generally the entire transaction, including the contract, is rendered void, Art. 180 of the Civil Code allows partial nullity if the parties would have agreed to conclude the contract without the affected parts.

Art. 167 of the Civil Code states that an invalid transaction does not entail any legal consequences beyond those directly connected with its invalidity. According to Art. 167 of the Code, in the event of invalidity each of the parties is obliged to return to the other party everything it has received under the transaction. If the restitution in kind is not possible, the party who benefitted from the transaction must provide compensation to the aggrieved party.

The Civil Code creates a special regime for contracts performed for a purpose deliberately contrary to the foundations of the legal order and public morals. If both parties knowingly and intentionally made such an agreement and the contract has been executed by both parties, everything received by them under the contract is forfeited to the state. If there is improper intent on the part of only one of the parties, everything received by it under the contract must be returned to the other party while that received by the latter or due it in compensation for the performance is recovered for the state.[162]

***

The following case illustrates some of the legal issues discussed above in a contracts of sale.

The Supreme Court: *Shepin v. Kurbatov* (*BVS*, 1994, No. 2, c. 2)[163]

Shepin filed suit in court against Kurbatov to declare void a contract of October 20, 1988, for the sale of a house situated in the village of Krasnoe, Pereslav district of the Yaroslavl Region and to evict Kurbatov from the house on the ground that he, as the owner of the house, did not conclude the contract with Kurbatov nor did he sign it. Kurbatov, for his part, filed suit against

---

[160] For example, any agreement among the partners of a full partnership imposing limitations on the principle that they are personally and jointly liable for all of the partnership's debts is void (Civil Code, Art. 75).

[161] An example is Art. 30 of the 1991 Law "On the Privatization of State-Owned and Municipal Enterprises in the Russian Federation" (See *infra* p. 339-341.

[162] Civil Code, Art. 169.

[163] Note that this decision was rendered on the basis of the 1964 Civil Code.

Shepin to recognize a contract of June 30, 1987, for the sale of the house as valid.

The Pereslav district people's court of the Yaroslavl Region granted Shepin's claim in part: the contract of October 20, 1988, was declared invalid; the request to evict Kurbatov was rejected (this decision was left intact by the Judicial Collegium for Civil Cases of the Yaroslavl Regional Court). Kurbatov's claim seeking to recognize the contract of June 30, 1987, for the sale of the house valid was granted. . .

[The ruling was affirmed by the Presidium of the Yaroslavl Regional Court and the Judicial Collegium for Civil Cases of the Supreme Court. The Deputy Procurator General brought a protest to vacate the rulings. The Presidium of the Supreme Court affirmed the rulings on the following grounds]:

The materials of the case indicate that on June 30, 1987, Shepin and Kurbatov concluded a transaction concerning a house belonging to Shepin by right of ownership and situated in the village of Krasnoe, Pereslav district of the Yaroslavl Region. Shepin claimed that he concluded a rent contract with Kurbatov while Kurbatov, for his part, claimed that they made a contract for the sale of the house which, however, was not formalized and registered with the executive committee of the village Council of People's Deputies, as required by Art. 239(2) of the Civil Code because the then existing normative acts did not allow the sale of village houses to citizens living in cities.

In recognizing the transaction of June 30, 1987, for the sale of the house valid, the Pereslav district people's court found that the conclusion of the contract for the sale of the house was confirmed by a receipt of June 30, 1987, signed by Shepin and attested to by his wife Belyeva and his son S. Shepin, which stated that he had received from Kurbatov 2500 roubles for the house, by an admission of Shepin made on June 30, 1987, bequeathing his house to Kurbatov, by the fact that for four years Kurbatov had made all the insurance payments for the house as well as by the actual use of the house and the land plot by Kurbatov since 1988. This conclusion of the court does not contradict Art. 47(2) of the Civil Code which provides that if one of the parties has fully or partially executed the legal transaction requiring notarial certification, and the other party avoids notarial formalization of the legal transaction, the court has the right, on the demand of the party who has executed the legal transaction, to recognize the legal transaction as valid so long as it does not contain anything contrary to law. . .

Because the court established that the owner of the house was

Kurbatov it had good reasons to deny the suit to evict the owner from his own house. . .

The protest [of the Deputy Procurator General] expresses doubt as to whether Shepin and Kurbatov concluded a contract for the sale of the house on June 30, 1987, because one of the essential conditions of such a contract is the price which, as the protest claims, was not determined by the parties. However, this statement contradicts the materials of the case. The receipt signed by Shepin on June 30, 1987, and the explanations of the parties during the judicial consideration of the case confirm that Shepin had received from Kurbatov 2500 roubles for his house. True, on the day of the transaction the insurance value of the house was 6182 roubles; however, this fact does not indicate the absence of a price in the contract for sale of June 30, 1987. According to Art. 92 of the Civil Code, an owner has the right to possess, use and dispose of property within the limits prescribed by law. Therefore, the owner has the right to freely determine the price of the property for sale. Shepin himself determined the price of the house he wanted to sell on June 30, 1987 to be the amount of 2500 roubles.

The protest [of the Deputy Procurator General] contends that it is not possible to rely on witness testimony of E., because she, as a secretary of the village Council, certified the fictitious contract of October 20, 1988, for the sale of the house. Although the court referred to this testimony in its decision, this cannot serve as a ground for vacating the decision. The materials of the case contain written evidence confirming the conclusion of the transaction of contract on June 30, 1987, concerning the sale of the house; nothing in the case contradicts this evidence. . .

The protest also refers to Shepin's serious health problems on the day the contract for the sale of the house was concluded. However, Shepin did not refer to his serious health problems as a factor that could have negatively affected his actions during the conclusion of the transaction in the statement of claim; nor did he refer to this fact in the judicial session, nor in his appeals. Furthermore, his wife and his son were present when the deal was made; by their signatures they acknowledged that Shepin realized what he was doing.

As regards the contract for the sale of the house which was concluded on October 20, 1988, and certified by the secretary of the village Council, it was recognized by the court as null and void for good reasons because it had been formalized in the absence of Shepin whose signature had been written by Kurbatov. These facts were confirmed in the judicial session by Kurbatov and witness E. . .

QUESTIONS

1. Although Russian law imposes strict requirements of form with respect to certain types of contract, does this decision support the view that in certain situations the requirements of form may be ignored? What are the justifications for this approach?

2. Does this decision support the doctrine that the presumption that a written contract is accurate and complete may be rebutted by the testimony of witnesses?

3. Note that the case came before the Supreme Court on the protest of the Deputy Procurator General and not at the request of either party. What accounts for this?

8. Remedies for Breaches of Contracts

The Civil Code contains a complicated set of rules for determining when compensation should be provided in the case of a breach of obligations, including contract obligations. Under Art. 393 of the Code, the debtor is obliged to compensate the creditor for all the losses caused by the failure to fulfil an obligation or its improper fulfillment.

In contrast to American law, the Russian law of contracts requires the presence of fault in cases of contract breach by private individuals. Art. 401 of the Civil Code provides that a breaching party is financially liable only if there is fault (intent or negligence), except for instances provided for by the law or by a contract. The debtors may be found not to be at fault if they prove that they have taken all measures within their powers in order to secure the proper fulfillment of the obligation.

At the same time, Art. 401 of the Civil Code establishes a stricter standard for entrepreneurs: persons engaged in entrepreneurial activities will be held liable for the failure to fulfill the obligation or its improper fulfillment in all cases unless they prove that the proper fulfillment was impossible due to force majeure. Force majeure is defined as "an extraordinary and overwhelming event under the given circumstances." The Civil Code makes it clear that such events do not include the non-fulfillment of obligations on the part of debtor's contractors or absence of goods needed for the fulfillment of the obligation on the market.

Although as a general principle the Civil Code introduces strict liability for breach of contract by entrepreneurs, this general rule may be subject to certain modifications. The Civil Code expressly allows statutory or contractual limitations on liability.[164] Indeed, the Civil Code itself establishes different types of liability for special types of contracts. For example, in contracts of sale the seller is not liable for defects of goods which occurred as a result of a failure by the purchaser to observe "the rules for the use of goods, or the storage or preservation thereof, acts of third parties, or force majeure."[165] A fault-based liability has been established by the Civil Code for contracts concerning research and development projects.[166] A lesser form of liability of entrepreneurs has also been established by transport charters and codes.

The definition of losses includes all expenditures that the aggrieved party has made or will incur to compensate for the loss of or damage to his or her property (compensatory damages), as well as profits not received by the aggrieved party which he or she would have received under normal circumstance if the obligation had not been violated (lost profits).[167] It follows that the amount of compensation is the amount it would take to put the injured party in the position that party would have been had the damage not taken place. An aggrieved party who claims lost profits must prove the expected profits. Under Art. 393 of the Civil Code, when determining lost profits the courts may take into account all the measures (in particular, the relevant preparations) taken by the creditor to realize the expected profits.

The Civil Code does not say expressly that only direct and foreseeable losses must be compensated. However, the Code does state that only "damages that have been incurred" are to be compensated. This may mean that only damages that have a direct casual link to the breach of the contract will be compensated.

If a party fails to fulfil an obligation to pay money, the other party is entitled to interest on the sum that is in arrears without prejudice to any claim for damages.[168] Losses beyond interest must be compensated as well.

The parties may also protect themselves against uncertain or unmeasurable losses by agreeing that the party in breach will forfeit a particular amount of money. Forfeitures are generally used to compel performance, to compensate for uncertain or incalculable damages and sometimes to punish the guilty party. To a certain extent, forfeitures operate as a combination of liquidated damages and penalty clause.

Art. 330 of the Civil Code defines forfeitures as sums of money

---

[164] Civil Code, Art. 400.
[165] Civil Code, Art. 476.
[166] Civil Code, Art. 777.
[167] Civil Code, Art. 15.
[168] Civil Code, Art. 395.

determined by law or by contract which the debtor is required to pay to the creditor in the event of nonperformance or defective performance of an obligation, in particular, in the event of delay in performance. The creditor has the right to demand the payment of a forfeiture without any proof of losses. At the same time, the court may reduce the amount of forfeiture if it finds that it is disproportionately large when compared to the consequences of the violation of the relevant obligation.[169] If the parties agree on a forfeiture, the losses in excess of the forfeiture amount are usually compensated.[170] The parties may also agree that losses may be recovered in the full amount independently of the payment of forfeiture.[171] Of course, such a serious penalty for nonperformance or improper performance of an obligation must be expressly provided for in the contract.

9. Specific Performance

In contrast to common law which grants specific performance only in exceptional cases, the Civil Code is based on the concept that specific performance is the essence of the obligation. However, there are limits. The Civil Code makes a distinction between non-fulfilment and improper fulfilment of obligation. In cases of non-fulfillment the payment of a forfeiture and compensation of losses releases the debtor from the duty to perform the obligation. However, in cases of an improper fulfillment of the obligation the payment of a forfeiture and compensation of losses does not release the debtor from the duty to perform the obligation.[172] As a result, in these cases the creditor may sue for specific performance.

Specific performance is particularly important in cases where the subject matter of the contract is unique. For example, the Civil Code expressly requires specific performance for contracts concerning the transfer of unique property.[173] Specific performance may also be granted in situations in which the contracting party could not obtain a comparable contract on the open market. Of course, a judgment ordering the debtor to perform a contractual obligation in kind can be issued only if performance by the debtor is still objectively possible. For example, a judgment for performance cannot be issued if the unique property, such as a picture, has been destroyed after sale. Furthermore, as a practical matter, parties are not likely to sue for specific

[169] Civil Code, Art. 333. Judicial practice indicates that courts often use their power to reduce disproportionally large forfeitures. See, e.g., *VVAS*, 1997, No. 9, at 75-76.

[170] Civil Code, Art. 394.

[171] Id.

[172] Civil Code, Art. 396.

[173] Civil Code, Art. 398.

performance when the failure to receive the promised performance can be made good by the payment of monetary compensation. This is particularly true of parties to commercial transactions who would typically sue only for monetary compensation. As a result, the differences between American and Russian law in this area may be less important in practice than in theory.

Specific enforcement rulings may be granted by both ordinary and arbitration courts. Judgments ordering the debtor to perform are enforced according to the general rules of civil procedure governing execution of judgments.

10. Amendment and Termination of Contracts

The amendment and termination of contracts depend on the consent of the parties. Any contract may be modified or terminated by the agreement of the parties. The basic requirements for modification or termination of a contract are no different from those required to create a contract. As a rule, agreements on the modification or on the termination of contracts must satisfy the same formal requirements as the basic contract itself.[174] As a general rule, written contracts require a writing to modify them, although in certain cases modifications may result from an implied agreement.

There are situations in which a contract may be modified or terminated on the initiative of only one party. One such situation is the case of adhesion contracts or contracts concluded after one party proposed a standardized contract to the other without any opportunity for negotiation or modification. The Civil Code establishes a simplified procedure for the amendment or termination of these contracts, which often exploit the weaker party. Art. 428 of the Code provides that in adhesion contracts the weaker party (often an individual consumer) has the right to demand amendment or termination, not only when such contracts violate the law, but also when they contain clearly burdensome conditions to which that party would not have acceded had there been an opportunity to participate in their formulation.

Another situation is that contemplated by Art. 450 of the Civil Code. Under that Article, if one party commits a major breach of the contract, the other party may seek amendment or termination in court. This option by the aggrieved party is accepted as a sanction to encourage parties not to breach contracts. A major breach is defined as a violation of the contract by one of the parties which results in losses that, to a considerable extent, deprive the other party of the principal value of its bargain.[175]

---

[174] Civil Code, Art. 452.
[175] Civil Code, Art. 450.

In the event of the amendment or termination of a contract, the parties have no right to claim the return of what has been performed by them in accordance with the contract terms prior to the amendment or termination.[176] However, if the contract has been amended or terminated because of a major breach of the contract by one of the parties, the other has the right to claim damages.[177]

11. Termination of Contracts Through Impossibility of Performance

Termination of contacts through impossibility of performance is governed by the general rules concerning obligations. If performance becomes impossible after the conclusion of the contract because of circumstances for which the debtor is not responsible, the debtor is excused from his or her obligation to perform. Art. 416 of the Civil Code provides that "an obligation is terminated through impossibility of performance if the impossibility was caused by a circumstance for which none of the parties is responsible."

While under this general rule the debtors who fail to perform are not liable if they prove that they are not answerable for the obstacle to performance, in practice it may difficult to determine who is to blame for the obstacle. The following case illustrates these difficulties.

The Supreme Arbitration Court: *KAPO S.P. Gorbunova v. GTK "Rossia"* (*VVAS*, 1997, No. 6, p. 62)

The Kazan aviation production association S.P. Gorbunova (KAPO S.P. Gorbunova) brought a suit in the Arbitration Court of the Republic of Tatarstan against the State Transportation Company "Rossia" (GTK "Rossia") to terminate the contract and recover damages resulting from the nonfulfillment of the terms of a contract.

In a decision dated 27.07.95, the relief on the claim was granted. Neither appellate nor cassational instances reviewed the decision. A protest was lodged to vacate the decision and dismiss the suit. The Presidium [of the Supreme Arbitration Court] holds that the protest must be sustained for the following reasons:

Under the contract of 25.05.94 No. 321-6/25 KAPO S.P. Gorbunova assumed an obligation to produce and deliver in the fourth quarter of 1994 an airplane IL-62M "Salon"; GTK "Rossia," for its part, assumed an obligation

---

[176] Civil Code, Art. 453.
[177] Id.

to receive the product and make an advance payment in 1994 in the amount of 80 percent of the cost of the airplane. . .

However, in August of 1994 the Government of the Russian Federation made a decision not to produce airplanes of the model IL-62M "Salon." As a result, the respondent [State Transportation Company GKT "Rossia"] did not receive any money from the state budget and failed to make the advance payment. . .

In granting the relief on the claim the court held that non-payment of the advance payment by GTK "Rossia" constituted a major breach of the terms of the contract; therefore it held that the plaintiff had the right to terminate the contract and demand compensation for damages. . .

Under Art. 416 of the Civil Code of the Russian Federation and Art. 73 of the Fundamentals of Civil Legislation in effect at the time of the conclusion of the contract, an obligation is terminated by impossibility of performance if the impossibility was caused by a circumstance for which none of the parties is responsible. The defendant was not able to perform its obligation because it did not receive money from the state budget. Therefore the contract obligations must be deemed terminated on August 31, 1994. . .

QUESTIONS

1. If the State Transportation Company "Rossia" acted as an independent contracting party, why should it be excused for non-performance of a contact obligation even if the Government of the Russian Federation failed to finance the production of airplanes Il-62M "Salon"?

2. KAPO S.P. Gorbunova sought to recover damages for nonfulfillment of the contract, in addition to termination. Should it receive damages? What would those damages be? Should the court instead have upheld the contract and simply substituted an equivalent airplane?

12. Fundamental Change of Circumstances

Art. 451 of the Civil Code introduces a new doctrine of fundamental change of circumstances. The doctrine deals with cases involving the collapse of the foundations of the contract frustrating its objectives and expectations of the parties. It involves implying an additional contract term that the obligations of a contract would end if there has been a change of circumstances. Note that this doctrine is different from the impossibility of performing a contract, which, in the majority of cases (at least as far as entrepreneurs are concerned), terminates the obligational relationship due to an irresistible force[178] or governmental action.[179]

While in the case of impossibility, performance is physically or literally impossible, the doctrine of fundamental change of circumstances deals with situations in which the contract may be performed but unforeseeable circumstances have made performance extremely burdensome or grossly unfair to one party. Fundamental change must concern facts of such importance to the achievement of the objectives of the contract that the parties would not have intended the obligations to be applicable under the changed circumstances.

Art. 451 of the Civil Code deals with the matter with as much precision as can be reasonably expected:

1. A fundamental change of circumstances, from which the parties have proceeded when concluding the contract, shall be the ground for its amendment or termination except for instances when such an amendment or termination is excluded by the terms of the contract or by its nature.

   The change of circumstances shall be recognized as fundamental if the circumstances have changed to such an extent that, if the parties could have reasonably foreseen it, they would not have concluded the contract or would have concluded it on essentially different terms.

2. If the parties fail to reach an agreement on the modification of the contract so as to bring it in conformity with the fundamentally changed circumstances, or upon its termination, the contract may be terminated, and amended by a court on the grounds set forth in by paragraph 4 of the present Article upon the claim of the interested party if all of the following conditions are present:

   1) at the moment of the conclusion of the contract, the parties assumed that no such change of circumstances would take place;

   2) the change of circumstances resulted from circumstances which the interested party was not able to control through the exercise of the degree of care that could be expected from it by the nature of the contract and by the conditions of trade;

178 Civil Code, Arts. 416, 401.
179 Civil Code, Art. 417.

3) the enforcement of the contract without amendment of its provisions would upset the balance of the property interests of the parties to the contract to such an extent and thus would entail such a loss for the interested party that it would, to a substantial degree, be deprived of what it expected when concluding the contract;

4) it does not follow from commercial customs or from the nature of the contract that the risk of the changed circumstances must be borne by the interested party.

3. In the event of the termination of the contract based on fundamentally changed circumstances, the court shall, upon the claim of any of the parties, determine the consequences of the termination of the contract; the court shall allocate the expenses of the parties in connection with the execution of this contract in a fair manner.

4. The amendment of the contract in connection with a fundamental change of circumstances shall be granted by a court only in extraordinary cases when the termination of the contract is against the public interests or if it would cause losses for the parties that would considerably exceed the expenses required for the execution of the contract on the amended terms as determined by the court.

The doctrine of fundamental change of circumstances remains controversial: some jurists dislike it, regarding it as a primary source of insecurity of contract obligations. The following case illustrates some elements of the doctrine.

The Supreme Arbitration Court: *Krup v. Komfort-Service* (*VVAS*, 1997, No. 6, p. 44)

The open joint-stock company "Krup" brought a suit in the Arbitration Court of the Krasnoiarsk Region to change conditions concerning lease payment in a lease contract between "Krup" and the closed joint- stock company "Komfort-Service."

Relying on Art. 451 of the Civil Code of the Russian Federation, the court, in its decision of 05.12.95, introduced changes in the contract under which the lessee had to pay to the lessor a new lease payment the amount of which is determined according to a special formula which takes into account the market value of the leased property and the interest rate of the Central Bank of the Russian Federation. . .

The appellate instance of the Arbitration Court of the Krasnoiarsk

Region of 31.01.96 and the Federal Arbitration Court of the Vostochno-Sibirskogo Circuit of 28.03.96 affirmed the decision.

A protest was lodged to vacate all the above rulings and remand the case for new consideration.

The Presidium [of the Supreme Arbitration Court] holds that the protest must be granted for the following reasons:

On August 31, 1992, the open joint-stock company "Krup" and the closed joint-stock company "Komfort-Service" entered into a contract of lease under which "Krup" provided the lessee an office space of 4205 square meters until December 31, 2000. Under Annex I to the contract the lease payment was defined in the amount of 200 roubles for each square meter monthly.

Because the costs for maintenance of office space have risen dramatically, the lease payments defined by the contract no longer cover them; as a result, the lessor is suffering substantial damage. The lessor proposed to the lessee that the lease payments be increased. However, the proposal was rejected.

In rendering its decision on changes in the contract, the court assumed that the contract of 31.08.92 determined lease payments without foreseeing any possibility for their change; at the same time, the circumstances, on which the parties had relied when concluding the contract, had fundamentally changed. The court also held that article 2.4 of the contract which contemplated an increase in the payment depending on energy price increases dealt only with the issue of payment increases for energy.

Under Art. 431 of the Civil Code of the Russian Federation, in the interpretation of the terms of a contract a court must take into account the literal meaning of the words and expressions contained in it. Chapter 2 of the contract has the title "Amount of the lease payment and procedure for payment." The meaning of the words and expressions contained in this chapter provide a basis for concluding that, under article 2.4 of the contract, the parties have established a mechanism for the increase not only of payments for energy, but also of lease payments. . .

Because the contract foresaw the possibility of change in lease payments taking into account the very circumstances which were referred to by the plaintiff, the court's conclusion concerning the fundamental change of circumstances calling for application of Art. 451 of the Civil Code of the Russian Federation is not justified. . .

QUESTIONS

1. Why did the court reject the claim for the application of the doctrine of fundamental change of circumstances?

2. The court held that lease payments, like payments for energy, are subject to negotiation upward based on increased costs. If the lessee rejects the proposal to increase the lease payments, what are the legal options available to the lessor? Would Art. 451 of the Civil Code be applicable now?

3. Effective January 1998, the Russian Government changed rouble denomination by striking the last three zeros. So 10,000 roubles became 10 roubles. Would a court allow the parties to a fixed price contract to demand payment in new roubles in the old rouble amount?

I. Legal Issues of Privatization

1. Introduction

The transition from a command economy to a market economy requires large-sale conversion and privatization of state-owned enterprises. Conversion means that socialist enterprises which used to rely on the state as the decision-maker are transformed into commercial entities under private law. As a result, sub-units of the state are transformed into companies that are largely independent of the state (although the state may emerge as the sole proprietor of the company).

While commercialization transforms state-owned enterprises into market-driven and self-sufficient business entities, privatization allows individual citizens and juridical persons to acquire ownership in state-owned enterprises. Privatization means that the state transfers its equity stake in the state-owned companies to private actors. Initially the transfer of certain state property to Russian citizens was made without any payment. The contemporary phase of privatization is conducted through cash sales of state equity interests.

2. The Legal Basis for Privatization

The fundamental principles of privatization were defined by the 1991 Law on the Privatization of State-Owned and Municipal Enterprises in the Russian Federation.[180] The current privatization process is governed by the

---

[180] *Vedomosty RF*, No. 27, item 927 (1991) (as amended, see *Vedomosty RF*, No. 28, item 1966 (1992)).

1997 Law on The Privatization of State Property and the Fundamentals of Privatization of Municipal Property in the Russian Federation.[181] The 1991 and the 1997 Laws on privatization establish basic legal principles and procedures for selling off state and municipal enterprises. These Laws also define the powers of governmental bodies supervising and conducting privatization. The actual process of privatization takes place in accordance with privatization programs approved by the Russian President.[182] Privatization programs not only establish the general goals of privatization at a particular stage of privatization, but also define enterprises and assets subject to privatization, preferred means of privatization and payment, privileges for labor collectives and restrictions on the participation of foreign citizens or organizations.[183]

3. Privatization Authorities

Privatization is carried out by special organs - state property committees and property funds. The highest-level property committee is the State Committee on Administration of State Property. Similar committees have been established at all levels of government. The highest level property fund is the Russian Fund of Federal Property which is paralleled by similar funds at all levels of government.

The State Committee on Administration of State Property is the principal organ responsible for carrying out privatization and administering the process. While property committees make decisions on privatization of specific state enterprises, property funds act as sellers of property earmarked for privatization.

4. Privatization Procedures

The 1991 Law on Privatization defined privatization as acquisition of property (including enterprises, shares and tangible and intangible assets) from federal state and local governments by private individuals and juridical persons.

Until 1994 the main form of privatization was the sale of state property at special auctions for vouchers issued to every Russian citizen free of

[181] *Sobranie,* No. 30, item 3595 (1997).

[182] For the 1993 Program, see *Sobranie aktov*, 1994, No. 1, item 2 (1994); for the 1994 Program, see *Sobranie*, No. 13, item 1478 (1994).

[183] Restrictions on the participation of foreign citizens or organizations in the privatization will be discussed in Chapter IX.

charge (one per citizen).[184] Although the voucher program allowed all Russian citizens to take part in the privatization process,[185] it had serious negative economic consequences. A major drawback of the procedure based on payment with vouchers was that neither the privatized company nor the state received any money from the "voucher buyers." By contrast, contemporary cash auction sales of state property involve capital transfers to the state. The 1997 Law on Privatization emphasizes that acquisition of state and municipal property is possible only for monetary compensation. Another method of sale of state property used in Russia is investment tender. Contemporary investment tenders also infuse cash or other assets into the company in addition to the purchase price.

Under the 1991 Law on Privatization state-owned and municipal enterprises were offered for sale through auctions in cases when the buyer was not obligated to fulfill any additional terms of acquisition. Under such an arrangement, the right of ownership was granted to the bidder offering the highest price. In contrast, tenders contemplated additional obligations of buyers. Art. 20 of the 1991 Law provided that state and municipal enterprises were offered for sale by tender in cases when "the buyers must fulfill certain conditions determined by the appropriate Property Administration Committee." In both cases the process was supervised by the State Committee on Administration of State Property or its local branches. The 1997 Law on Privatization also contemplates auctions and investment tenders.

5. Contracts of Sale

Whatever method of privatization is chosen, the seller and the buyer of a state-owned or municipal enterprise conclude a contract of sale. The seller is always represented by the State Property Fund. Art. 28 of the 1997 Law provides that the sale contract must, among other things, contain information on the composition and the price of the assets of the enterprise, conditions concerning the use of land plots, the number and the price of shares, payment

[184] Foreign nationals and juridical persons were able to participate in voucher sales by paying with vouchers bought or received from Russian citizens.

[185] The voucher method of privatization was used by the Russian authorities to enhance the legitimacy of the "mass privatization" of state property created by generations of Soviet/Russian citizens. Practice indicates, however, that few Russian citizens have become owners of new private companies. Ordinary Russian citizens had no idea about stock markets. As a result, they turned to voucher investment funds the majority of which collapsed in the early 1990s. In contrast, managers of state enterprises and former Communist *apparatchiks* who had all the necessary information about the assets offered for voucher sale were able to acquire valuable assets or stocks of former state enterprises, often for an insider price. For details on *nomenklatura* privatization in Russia, see A. Aslund, How Russia Became A Market Economy 268-69 (1995).

procedures as well as "obligations of the buyer with regard to the further use of property" and "investment and (or) social conditions according to which the relevant property has been acquired by the buyer." The 1991 Law on Privatization contained similar provisions.

Art. 30 of the 1991 Law established several grounds for the invalidity of transactions concerning acquisitions of state-owned or municipal enterprises. Such transactions could be declared invalid if:

- the privatization of the enterprise has not been approved by the State Committee of Russia on Administration of State Property, a territorial agency thereof or the respective property administration committee of the national-state or administrative- territorial entity concerned;

- the rules of the tender or auction have been blatantly violated;

- the purchaser has refused to pay for the acquired enterprise or for his or her stake (holding, shares) in the capital of a joint stock company (partnership);

- the enterprise or a stake (holding, shares) in the capital of a joint stock company (partnership) has been acquired by a party having no right to do so;

- illegal methods of payment have been used in the acquisition;

- there has been an arrangement between the seller and the purchaser concerning an unlawful division of the property or reduction of the price of the enterprise (holding, shares);

- the purchaser has been granted illegal privileges and advantages over other buyers;

- the terms on which the enterprise had been acquired by tender have been violated;

- the requirements of the antimonopoly legislation of the Russian Federation have been violated;

- for other reasons as stipulated by the Civil Code of the Russian Federation.

Art. 30 of the 1991 Law had given rise to much controversy because some of its provisions were too broad and dealt with grounds for the termination of the contract as provided for in Art. 450 of the 1994 Civil

Code.[186] For example, Art. 30 provided that transactions concerning acquisitions of state-owned or municipal enterprises could be declared invalid if "the purchaser has refused to pay for the acquired enterprise or for his or her stake (holding, shares) in the capital of a joint stock company (partnership)." However, under the general rules of the Civil Code, if the purchaser has refused to pay for the acquired enterprise or if he or she has violated the terms on which the enterprise had been acquired the seller is not supposed to initiate an action to invalidate the contract; rather, he or she is entitled to invoke "the fundamental breach of the contract" as a ground of termination under Art. 450 of the Civil Code. In view of this, the Supreme Court and the Supreme Arbitration Court ruled that such actions must be regarded as a ground for the termination of contracts of privatization and not as a ground for their invalidity.[187] At the same time, courts were instructed not to apply general rules concerning the consequences of the termination of the contract[188] because Art. 453 of the Civil Code provides that application of these rules may be excluded by "the law." In this case, the 1991 Law contemplated only general restitution.

Art. 29 of the new 1997 Law on Privatization dealing with invalidity of transactions concerning privatization no longer contravenes the provisions of the Civil Code. It provides that privatization transactions may be declared invalid if:

- there were violations of the present Federal Law, other normative legal acts establishing procedure for privatization of state or municipal property;

- state or municipal property has been acquired by a party having no right to do so;

- illegal methods of payment have been used during privatization of state or municipal property;

- there has been an arrangement between the seller and the purchaser, including an arrangement concerning reduction of the price of the relevant property;

[186] See *supra* p. 330-332.

[187] See the Joint Ruling of the Plenary Session of the Supreme Court and the Plenary Session of the Supreme Arbitration Court "*On Some Questions Concerning the Application of the First Part of the Civil Code of the Russian Federation*" (*BVS*, No. 9, p. 1 (1996)).

[188] The general rules concerning the consequences of the termination of the contract were discussed *supra* p. 331.

- the purchaser has been granted privileges and advantages over other buyers;

- there are other reasons envisioned by the legislation of the Russian Federation.

While under Art. 449 of the Civil Code the results of an auction or tender may be challenged by any "interested person,"[189] under both the 1991 and the 1997 Law only specifically designates persons or organs have the right to challenge privatization transactions.

Art. 30 of the 1991 Law provided that "disputes concerning the recognition of privatization transactions as invalid shall be heard by an [ordinary] court or by an arbitration court in a suit brought by the seller, the purchaser, an intermediary, a procurator, a People's Deputy, the State Committee of the Russian Federation on Administration of State Property, territorial agencies thereof, the property administration committee of the national-state or administrative-territorial entity concerned." Under Art. 29 of the 1997 Law on Privatization transactions may be challenged in court by "the Government of the Russian Federation, organs of state power of the subjects of the Russian Federation, organs of local self-government, the relevant state property administration committees, sellers, buyers and organs of Procuracy of the Russian Federation."

Note that the privatized enterprise was regarded by the 1991 Law and is still regarded by the 1997 Law as a property complex. As such, it is treated as a subject matter of the relevant legal relations. As a result, it cannot have the right to challenge privatization transactions.

The following case illustrates several issues of privatization.

The Supreme Arbitration Court: *Obergan v. Moscow Property Fund* (*Zakon*, 1995, No. 11, p. 119)

Small enterprise "Obergan" filed suit in the Moscow City Arbitration Court against Moscow Property Fund to recognize a privatization transaction invalid. . . The enterprise requested:

- to invalidate the protocol of the tender commission concerning the sale of shares of the joint stock company "Bolshevitchka";

- to declare the small enterprise "Obergan" the winner of the tender;

---

[189] See *supra* p. 322-323.

- to compel the Moscow Property Fund to sign a contract on the sale of shares of the joint stock company "Bolshevitchka" with "Obergan". . .

[The Moscow City Arbitration Court granted the suit in part. In particular, it declared the protocol of the tender commission invalid. Cassational and supervisory instances left this part of the decision intact].

The Chairman of the Supreme Arbitration Court brought a protest and requested that all the previous decisions be vacated and the case be sent for new consideration. The Presidium of the Supreme Arbitration Court finds that the protest must be granted. It also finds that it may render a new decision on the merits of the case and reject the suit for the following reasons:

According to Art. 5.6(5) of the State Program for Privatization of State-Owned and Municipal Enterprises in the Russian Federation, state and municipal enterprises are sold by investment tenders (investment sales) if the purchaser is required to implement investment programs. In that case, the ownership right is transferred to the purchaser whose proposal satisfies the criteria established by the privatization plan. . . On April 29, 1993, the State Committee on Administration of State Property endorsed the privatization plan for the Moscow garment factory "Bolshevitchka" and approved the conditions of the investment tender for the sale of shares of the joint stock company "Bolshevitchka." One of the conditions of the investment tender was guarantees of investments in "Bolshevitchka" and their use in accordance with the investment program. The approved conditions also provided that another criterion for the determination of the winner would be the proposed price for the shares. This condition conforms to Art. 3 of the Temporary Regulations on the Investment Tenders (Investment Sales) For the Sale of State-Owned and Municipal Objects of Privatization. According to Art. 3, privatization of state-owned and municipal enterprises by way of a tender results in the acquisition for private ownership of objects of privatization, including shares (sets of shares), by citizens and juridical persons, who are recognized as buyers under Art. 9 of the Law on the Privatization of State-Owned and Municipal Enterprises in the Russian Federation, when the purchaser is required to provide investments in the privatized enterprise in accordance with the investment program defined by the privatization plan, and to fulfil certain conditions concerning:

- price of the privatized object, including the price of its shares (sets of shares);

- obligation to produce specific goods, provide specific services or perform work in the established amount within one or two years;

- maintenance of the existing work-force or a certain percentage of the work-force;
- maintenance and use of social facilities within the property complex on sale;
- prohibition to perform certain acts with respect to the object of the tender. . .

The materials of the case indicate that the tender commission studied the documents submitted by the bidders before the tender. It found that the small enterprise "Obergan" did not fulfill several conditions of the tender and failed to provide real guarantees that it would be able to carry out the investment program. While the investment program required investments in the amount of $5 million, the amount of the charter capital of the small enterprise did not support the conclusion that the enterprise was really able to provide the required investment and, therefore, meet tender requirements. . .

In view of these circumstances, the court had no grounds to declare the results of the tender void. . .

QUESTIONS

1. What is the difference between sales by action and investment tenders (sales)?

2. What are the aims of special conditions imposed on the buyer of a state enterprise sold through the investment tender (sale)?

3. How did the tender commission determine that the small enterprise "Obergan" did not fulfill conditions of the tender? What kind of "real guarantees" that it would be able to carry out the investment program would have satisfied the commission and the Supreme Arbitration Court?

J. General Principles of Tort Liability

While in common law countries the law of torts consists of a bundle of relatively independent remedies (negligence, conversion, nuisance etc.) envisioned by a large number of separate rules which apply to different kinds of harmful activity, the law of tort in civil law countries is largely unified. Consistent with this tradition, the Civil Code includes several general clauses and more specific rules that apply to all kinds of harmful activity.

These principles and rules are largely based on the traditional principles and rules concerning tort liability codified by the 1964 Civil Code. Because the traditional rules were rather general, judicial practice became an important vehicle for their clarification and development. The more detailed rules of the new Civil Code incorporated these developments. This area of law is also based on supplementary statutes which contain additional rules establishing liability for torts. Thus, the 1992 "Law on Protection of the Rights of Consumers"[190] is the main source of the law on products liability.

In the Russian legal system, tort liability is a form of obligational relationship between persons which establishes the right of the victim to claim damages against the wrongdoer. Because tort liability is based on the concept of obligational relationship, it is not treated as a separate area of law. It is always considered to be a constituent part of a larger area of law - the law of obligations. However, in contrast to contracts, where obligational relationships, including the contractual obligation not to breach contractual duties, result from a contract created by the parties themselves, the duty to refrain from committing torts is imposed by the general Russian law independently of the wishes of the plaintiff and the defendant. Russian law of torts is based on the idea that the wrongdoer violates a general duty to refrain from behavior that causes harm to other persons. The goal of the law of tort is to shift, where possible, the cost of harm to those responsible for causing it.

It is important to note that because in Russia the state may be subject to the rules of private law, civil liability for torts concerns not only relations between private individuals but also between individuals and the state.

1. Basis of Liability

Art. 1064 of the Civil Code provides that harm caused to the person or property of a person as well as harm caused to property of a juridical person is subject to compensation in full by the person who has caused the harm. The Civil Code presupposes an unlawful act or omission which has been wilfully or negligently committed by the wrongdoer and which has caused damage to another person. The basic elements of liability include damage, unlawful act or omission, adequate or legally relevant casual connection between the wrongful act or omission and the damage, and fault. While the burden of proving the first three elements of a wrongful act rests on the injured party, the burden of proof shifts to the defendant with respect to fault. Plaintiffs are not obligated to prove fault. The burden of proof that there has been no fault is imposed on the defendant.

---

[190] *Vedomosty RF*, No. 15, item 766 (1992) (as amended in 1995, see *Sobranie*, No. 3, item 140 (1996)).

Art. 1064 of the Civil Code states that a person who has caused harm is relieved from compensating it if she proves that the harm was not caused by her fault. The concept of fault includes intentional and negligent actions. Intent implies willingness to commit a wrongful act accompanied by the desire to cause harm or by an indifference toward the possibility of causing harm. Negligence is the failure to observe the standard of care required by specific circumstances. Gross negligence is a variant of negligence characterized by a high degree of reckless disregard for elementary and obvious standards of care.

Under Art. 1064 of the Civil Code, the law may provide for compensation of harm even "in the event the wrongdoer is not at fault." In areas where the risk and potential damage to the public is very serious, the law imposes strict liability even for lawful activities. Strict liability has traditionally been applied to extra-hazardous activity.[191] Strict liability is also imposed on manufacturers and sellers of consumer products.[192]

2. Compensation

Under Art. 1064 of the Civil Code damages may be awarded for both economic and non-economic losses. Compensation is determined by Art. 1082 of the Civil Code. It states that a court, in accordance with the circumstances of the case, may require the person liable for the harm either to compensate in kind (provide a thing of the same kind and quality, repair the damaged thing, etc.) or to compensate for losses. Judicial practice indicates that monetary compensation of losses is used in the overwhelming majority of cases. The general concept of losses defined by Art. 15 of the Civil Code[193] is also applicable to torts. Compensation is supposed to cover all the losses the injured party has incurred.

3. Compensation of Moral Harm

While under Art. 1064 of the Civil Code damages may be awarded for both economic and non-economic losses, compensation of "moral harm" is governed by special rules. The Civil Code seeks to impose certain limitations on compensation of moral harm. Art. 151 of the Civil Code defines moral harm as "physical or mental suffering." It provides that, as a general rule, monetary compensation for moral harm is possible only in cases where it has been caused by actions violating citizen's "non-property rights" or infringing upon their "non-material values." "Non-property rights" concern intangible

---

[191] Civil Code, Art. 1079.
[192] Civil Code, Art. 1095.
[193] See *supra* p. 328.

values, such as life, health, dignity, personal inviolability, honor and good name, business reputation, privacy.[194]

Under Art. 1099 of the Civil Code, moral harm caused by actions or inactions violating "property rights" of citizens is subject to compensation only in cases provided for by specific statutes.[195]

Many commentators believe, however, that in practice it is difficult to draw a clear line between "mental suffering" caused by violation of "non-property" rights and the same suffering caused by violations of "property rights." For example, a car damaged in a traffic accident often causes "mental suffering" that may be detrimental to the "health" of the owner, i.e. one of the "non-property rights" protected by Art. 151 of the Civil Code.[196]

In some cases, compensation for moral harm does not depend on the presence of fault. For example, under Art. 1100 of the Civil Code, moral harm is subject to compensation regardless of fault if the harm has resulted from dissemination of defamatory information discrediting the individual's honor, dignity or business reputation.

An important innovation introduced by the new Civil Code is the principle of absolute liability for the moral harm caused by unlawful conviction, unlawful prosecution, unlawful imprisonment or detention or unlawful imposition of an administrative penalty by organs of enquiry, preliminary investigation, the Procuracy or courts.[197] Such compensation was not available before the entry of the second part of the new Civil Code in force (March 1, 1996).[198] Unlike the situation in the United States,[199] sovereign or governmental immunity is no barrier to suits for damages directly against state organs.

---

[194] Civil Code, Art. 150.

[195] An example is the 1992 "Law on Protection of the Rights of Consumers" (*supra* note 190) which imposes fault-based liability for moral harm caused by actions or inactions of manufacturers and sellers violating property rights of citizens (1992 Law on Protection of the Rights of consumers, Art. 15).

[196] For details, see A.M. Edelevsky, *Moral'nyi vred I kompensatsiya za stradaniya* (Moral Harm and Compensation for Suffering) (1997).

[197] Civil Code, Art. 1100.

[198] The pre-existing law did not envision compensation of moral harm in cases of unlawful imprisonment or detention by state authorities. Such claims were routinely rejected by the courts. See, for example, *Stepanovskaya vs. Astrakhan Regional Procuracy* (*BVS*, 1995, No. 1, p. 13); *Polusitov vs. Department of Justice of the Krasnodar Territorial Administration* (*BVS*, 1995, No. 6, p. 2).

[199] See W. Burnham, Introduction to the Law and Legal System of the United States 229-234 (1995).

The Civil Code provides that the amount of compensation for moral harm depends on the nature of the physical and mental suffering caused to the victim. Under Art. 1101 of the Code, the courts must assess the nature of the physical and mental suffering by taking into account the actual circumstances under which the harm has been caused, and the injured individual's characteristics. In cases where fault constitutes the grounds for compensation, courts are also obliged to take into account the degree of fault of the tortfeasor. In all cases, courts must be guided by the requirements of reasonableness and justice.

In practice, courts pay particular attention to "the financial status of the person who has caused the harm."[200] In order to prevent unreasonably high awards, the Supreme Court has emphasized that the courts must always provide explanations justifying their rulings on the amount of compensation for moral harm.[201]

4. Strict Liability

Strict liability is independent of any fault by the tortfeasor. It is based only on her or his control of a particularly dangerous activity. In Russia, strict liability has traditionally been imposed on owners of all "sources" of harm classified as presenting "excessive" or "increased" danger, such as trains, aircraft and automobiles. Rules imposing strict liability for failure to control operations which create a serious or unusual risk of harm to others are based, in part at least, upon principles of loss distribution.

The traditional rules concerning strict liability codified in the 1964 Civil Code were rather general. As a result, judicial practice became an important vehicle for their clarification and development. The judicial decisions reproduced below provide illustration of the traditional approach. These decisions also show how Russian courts develop and clarify the general provisions of the Civil Code.

The Supreme Court: *Nikolaev v. Ruzaevskii Division of the Kuibyshev Railway* (*BVS*, 1970, No. 6, p. 1)[202]

Nikolaev brought suit against the Ruzaevskii Division of the Kuibyshev Railway for compensation of loss caused by mutilation. In justification of his claims Nikolaev pointed out that on November 27, 1965 he boarded a train

---

[200] See the Ruling of the Plenary Session of the Supreme Court "*On Judicial Practice Concerning Suits for Compensation of Harm to Health*" (*BVS*, 1994, No. 7, p. 3, 8).

[201] Id.

[202] Note that this decision was rendered on the basis of the 1964 Civil Code.

in the city of Orenburg. At Sura Station of the Kuibyshev Railway he left the car during the train stop, and when getting back on the car of the already moving train he slipped and fell under the wheels, as a result of which he received injuries. After treatment he at first was deemed a first group invalid, and subsequently a second group with loss of 100% general and professional capacity to work. A pension has been assigned to him at present and is paid in the amount of 51.26 roubles per month. His average earning before the accident amounted to 166 roubles per month.

[The Pskov City Court granted relief and awarded Nikolaev 54.47 roubles monthly. Both the Judicial Collegium for Civil Cases of the Pskov Regional Court and its Presidium rejected the procurator's protest of the decision. The Judicial Collegium for Civil Cases of the RSFSR Supreme Court granted the procuratorial protest and vacated all previous decisions, remanding the case for reconsideration. In its ruling of November 20, 1969, the Court stated]:

In accordance with Art. 458 of the RSFSR Civil Code, if the gross negligence of the victim himself facilitated the origin or the aggravation of the harm, then depending on the extent of the victim's fault the amount of compensation should be reduced or compensation of the harm should be refused.

The people's court, in deciding the dispute, did not discuss the question of the presence or absence of gross negligence in the actions of the victim himself. The Judicial Collegium for Civil Cases and the Presidium of the regional court did not see gross negligence in Nikolaev's actions. It is clear from the materials of the case that Nikolaev, in riding on the railway train and leaving the car during the stop at Sura Station, endeavored to get back on the car of a train already moving but slipped and fell under the wheels. His endeavor to board a moving train cannot be anything other than gross negligence. Therefore, the reference of the Judicial Collegium and Presidium of the Regional Court to the fact that there was no gross negligence in Nikolaev's actions, but was simply imprudence is not in accord with the data in the file of the case concerning the occurrence of the accident.

In the new consideration of the suit the court shall take proper account of the foregoing and investigate more carefully the materials of the case. Depending on the information established in the case, the court should discuss the question of the extent of Nikolaev's fault in causing the accident, and the application of comparative fault. . .

The Supreme Court: *Drozov v. Gorky Railway Administration* (*BVS*, 1972, No. 6, p. 6)[203]

Drozdov brought suit against the Gorky Railway Administration for compensation of harm causing mutilation, basing his claim on the fact that on April 3, 1970, he was knocked down by an electric train while crossing the right-of-way, as a result of which he lost both feet, was deemed a second group invalid, and had loss of earnings. The Moscow Railway Administration and the Moscow-Kursk Division of the Moscow Railway were joined as co-defendants during the trail.

The Vladimir Regional Court granted the plaintiff compensation for harm from the Moscow Railway Administration.

The Judicial Collegium for Civil Cases of the RSFSR Supreme Court, having considered the case by way of cassation, vacated the decision by a ruling of February 17, 1972, and remanded the case for reconsideration on the following grounds.

In accordance with Art. 454 of the RSFSR Civil Code organization and citizens whose activity is connected with an increased danger for surrounding persons (transport organizations, industrial enterprises, construction sites, owners of motor vehicles, etc.) shall be obliged to compensate for harm caused by a source of increased danger, unless it is proved that the harm arose as a consequence of force majeure or an intentional act of the victim.

The court, in releasing the Gorky Railway Administration from liability for the harm caused, referred to the fact that the harm was caused to the plaintiff as a result of the action of a source of increased danger: electric locomotive No. 2355 belonging to the Orekhovo-Zuevo Depot of the Moscow-Kursk Division of the Moscow Railway. The fact that the plaintiff's accident occurred on the railway lines of the Gorky Railway Administration could not serve [in the lower court's view] as a basis for imposing liability for harm on this railway administration, inasmuch as the railway line, as well as the platform, are not a source of increased danger. The Supreme Court cannot concur with this argument.

The Plenary Session of the USSR Supreme Court explained in paragraph 5 of its Ruling No. 16 of October 23, 1963 "*On Judicial Practice Concerning Suits for Compensation of Harm*" that the phrase "possessor of a source of increased danger" should be understood to be an organization or citizen using the source of increased danger either by virtue of its belonging to

[203] Note that this decision was rendered on the basis of the 1964 Civil Code.

him by right of ownership or right of operative management, or also on other grounds (for example, by contract of lease, hire, or by arrangement), as well as by virtue of regulations of competent agencies concerning the transfer to organizations of a source of increased danger for temporary use.

It follows from the copy of a letter of the legal department of the USSR Ministry of Railways No. TsIu-25 of April 7, 1971, attached to the cassational appeal, that in railway transport the possessor of a source of increased danger is considered to be the railway which is using trains as sources of increased danger at the time of the accident. . . Because at the moment of the accident with the plaintiff, the electric locomotive No. 2355 was in the operative management of the Gorky Railway Administration and was used by it, it is of no significance that the owner of the electric locomotive is the Orekhovo-Zuevo Depot of the Moscow-Kursk Division of the Moscow Railway. There are no grounds for imposing liability for the harm caused to the plaintiff on the Moscow Railway Administration. . .

The Supreme Court: *Igonina v. Glazunov* (*BVS*, 1970, No. 1, p. 10)[204]

While driving a Moskvich-407 automobile, Glazunov struck Igonin who died from injuries received. The spouse of the deceased Igonina brought suit in court against the owner organization of the source of increased danger and Glazunov, who was sentenced under Art. 211(2) of the RSFSR Criminal Code to six years deprivation of freedom, for compensation of damage in connection with the loss of the breadwinner. Two small children were dependent on the deceased breadwinner.

The Kamenskii District People's Court of the Sverdlov Region granted relief in Igonina's suit and she recovered to her benefit from the owner organization of the source of increased danger a single payment of 118 roubles and 23 roubles for each child monthly.

By a ruling of the Sverdlov Regional Court upon the cassational protest of the Procurator of the Kamenskii District, the decision of the people's court was vacated and the case tried de novo by the regional court at first instance.

Igonina offered evidence in support of her suit in the trial. The representative of the owner organization of the source of increased danger opposed the suit, asserting that the driver Glazunov, taking advantage of the absence of any guard at the garage, took the vehicle from the garage at midnight and at 4:00 a.m. on August 28, 1968 struck Igonin. Inasmuch as the

[204] Note that this decision was rendered on the basis of the 1964 Civil Code.

source of increased danger had left the possession of its owner as a result of the unlawful actions of Glazunov, liability for compensation of harm to the plaintiff should be imposed on Glazunov.

The Sverdlovsk Regional Court ordered Glazunov to pay 17 roubles monthly for each child of the deceased and a single payment of 242 roubles for the benefit of the plaintiff. The suit against the owner organization of the source of increased danger was rejected by decision of the court.

In a cassational appeal Glazunov requested that the decision of the court be vacated since he took the motor vehicle from the garage, not unlawfully but by arrangement with the administration, which permitted him to take the car from the garage at any time in his discretion. The travel sheet was written out to him for a week or a month and when finishing work neither the travel sheet nor the key from the garage were taken from him.

The Judicial Collegium for Civil Cases of the RSFSR Supreme Court by its ruling of July 25, 1969 vacated the decision of the regional court and remanded the case for new consideration, stating the following:

According to Art. 454 of the RSFSR Civil Code, organizations and citizens whose activity is connected with an increased danger for surrounding persons (transport organizations, industrial enterprises, construction sites, owners of motor vehicles, etc.) shall be required to compensate for harm caused by a source of increased danger, unless it is proved that the harm arose as a consequence of insuperable force or the intentional act of the victim.

Paragraph 5 of the Ruling of the Plenary Session of the USSR Supreme Court of October 23, 1963, "*On Judicial Practice Concerning Suits For Compensation of Harm*" provides that the owner of a source of increased danger shall not be liable for harm caused by the action of this source if it is proved that the latter left the possession of the owner, not by his fault, but as the result of unlawful actions of third persons.

The materials of the case indicate that the garage in which the motor vehicle was located was not guarded, that the driver Glazunov had the key from the garage, and that he had access to the vehicle at any time. Consequently, Glazunov's trip in the car about the city early on the morning of August 28, 1968, when he struck Igonin, became possible due to the owner's failure to ensure proper protection of the vehicle in the garage during non-working hours.

Glazunov's assertion in the cassational appeal that the travel sheet was issued to him for a week or a month and that, when finishing work neither the travel sheet nor the garage key nor the ignition key for the vehicle were taken from him nor handed in for keeping to an appropriate official, were not verified by the court in the judicial session. These facts have material significance for the correct resolution of the case. . .

QUESTIONS

1. What kind of compensation was awarded in the above cases?

2. How does the contributory fault of the victim affect the regime of strict liability? Would the mere negligence on the part of the victim be taken into account?

***

The foregoing cases were based on the rather general provisions of the 1964 Civil Code. Art. 1079 of the new Civil Code states the modern version of the law:

> 1. Juridical persons and citizens whose activity is connected with increased danger for the community (use of transport vehicles, mechanisms, high voltage electric energy, nuclear energy, explosives, strong poisons, etc., construction and other activity related to it, etc.) shall be obligated to compensate harm caused by a source of increased danger, unless they prove that the harm arose as a consequence of force majeure or the intentional act of the victim. The possessor of a source of increased danger may be relieved of liability by the court either in full or in part on the grounds provided for by paragraphs 2 and 3 of Article 1083 of the present Code.[205]

---

[205] Art. 1083 of the Civil Code states:

"2. Should the gross negligence of the victim facilitate the cause or the aggravation of the harm, the amount of compensation shall be decreased depending on the degree of the fault of the victim and the tortfeasor.

In the event of gross negligence on the part of the victim, and absence of fault of the tortfeasor in instances when liability ensues irrespective of the fault, the amount of compensation shall be decreased, or compensation of harm may be refused, unless provided otherwise by a statute. Should the harm be caused to the life or the health of a citizen, refusal to compensate for harm shall not be allowed.

The fault of the victim shall not be taken into account in the event of compensation for extra expenses (paragraph 1 of Article 1085), compensation for harm in connection with the death of the breadwinner (Article 1089), and in the event of compensation for burial costs (Article 1094).

3. The court may decrease the amount of compensation for harm caused by a citizen taking into account his financial status, with the exception of instances when harm was caused by intentional actions."

The obligation to compensate for harm shall be imposed on the juridical person or individual who controls the source of increased danger by the right of ownership, right of economic management or right of operative management, or on any other legal ground (contract of lease, permission to operate a transport vehicle, instruction of the relevant organ concerning the transfer of the source of increased danger, etc.).

2. The possessor of the source of increased danger shall not be liable for harm caused by the source if it proves that the source has been removed from its possession by unlawful actions of other persons. Liability for harm caused by the source of increased danger shall be borne in such instances by the persons who have unlawfully taken possession of the source. Should the possessor of the source be at fault for the unlawful taking of the source from its possession, liability may be imposed both on the possessor and the person who has taken unlawful possession of the source of increased danger.

3. The possessors of sources of increased danger shall bear joint and several responsibility for harm caused as the result of interaction of such sources (transport vehicle collision, etc.) to third persons on the grounds provided for by paragraph 1 of the present Article.

Harm caused as the result of interaction of sources of increased danger to their possessors shall be compensated on general grounds (Article 1064).

QUESTION

Which elements of the prior judicial practice concerning strict liability were codified in the 1994 Civil Code?

5. Strict Liability for Environmentally Harmful Activities

The concept of strict liability has been applied to a great variety of dangerous activities. Of particular interest is the operation of the concept in respect to environmentally harmful activities. The Supreme Arbitration Court has ruled that

> All enterprises, agencies and organizations whose activities present a risk of harm to the environment shall compensate for all the harm caused to the environment and public health. . . Arbitration courts shall decide in each case whether a particular enterprise, agency or organization may be classified as an entity

> presenting an increased environmental risk of danger. In this connection, arbitration courts shall bear in mind that industrial enterprises discharging toxic and other harmful substances into the environment and using transport vehicles for their operation may be classified as presenting increased environmental danger.
>
> Enterprises, agencies and organizations presenting increased environmental danger shall be exempt from liability only if they prove that the harm was caused by force majeure circumstances. . .[206]

This means that courts may impose strict liability on the operators of environmentally dangerous installations, in particular "industrial enterprises discharging toxic and other harmful substances into the environment," for damage to the environment caused by them.

[206]The Ruling of the Plenary Session of the Supreme Arbitration Court "*On Some Questions Concerning the Application of the Law" "On the Protection of the Natural Environment*" *Zakon*, 1993, No. 4, p. 64).

CHAPTER VII

CIVIL AND ARBITRATION PROCEDURE

A. Introduction

As noted earlier,[1] during the Soviet period civil law played only a limited role in the society dominated by command economy and state plan. The same is true of civil procedure. The majority of economic transactions were performed by state-owned enterprises. Disputes between these entities were settled not by courts but by *State Arbitrazh*, a system of quasi-judicial bodies that applied simplified rules of procedure. "Ordinary" Russian courts applied more elaborate rules of the Civil Procedure Code. However, these rules governed proceedings in only a limited number of cases, primarily those initiated by private citizens. The reinstitution of the fundamental importance of civil law in a market economy has been accompanied by a growing importance of principles and rules of civil procedure. The increasing complexity of economic relations among private citizens and Russian and foreign companies results in numerous suits brought to "ordinary" and arbitration (commercial) courts.[2] As a result, there is a greater awareness that principles and rules of civil procedure are of paramount importance for the smooth functioning of the Russian legal system.

The 1993 Constitution outlines several fundamental principles of Russian civil procedure. First, the Constitution guarantees the right of everyone to protect her or his rights in a court of law.[3] Second, the Constitution provides that "judicial proceedings shall be conducted based on adversarial principles and equality of the parties."[4] Third, "in the administration of justice evidence obtained in violation of federal law shall not be admissible."[5] Finally, under the Constitution questions concerning "civil procedural and arbitration-procedural legislation" fall under the exclusive jurisdiction of the Russian Federation.[6] As a result, all rules of civil and

[1] See p. 281.

[2] The system and structure of "ordinary" and arbitration (commercial) courts were discussed in Chapter III.

[3] Constitution, Art. 46.

[4] Constitution, Art. 123.

[5] Constitution, Art. 50.

[6] Constitution, Art. 71 (n).

arbitration procedure are uniform for all courts in all the "subjects" of the Federation.

The 1964 Civil Procedure Code (as amended in 1995),[7] which governs proceedings in "ordinary" courts, codified traditional principles and rules of civil procedure. Although the Civil Procedure Code was amended in 1995, there is a consensus that the country needs an entirely new civil procedure code. A draft of the new Civil Procedure Code was published in 1997.[8] It is still under discussion. Proceedings in arbitration (commercial) courts are governed by the 1995 Arbitration Procedure Code.[9] There are several important differences between the two set of procedural rules which will be discussed in Section C. Because Russia has not yet established separate administrative courts, the law of civil procedure applies not only to the process of judicial enforcement of rights and duties arising under civil legislation but also to enforcement of administrative law.

As in any other civil law country, the most distinguishing characteristic of civil procedure in Russia results from the traditional absence of a jury. While the existence of a jury in the common law countries requires a concentrated presentation of everything that bears on the dispute, civil law countries, including Russia, do not have a trial in that sense. Instead, there is a main hearing which may take place in one uninterrupted audience but may also be adjourned several times. As a result, there may be a series of connected yet separate hearings and written communications between the parties or their counsel and the judge, in which evidence is introduced, testimony given, motions and rulings on procedure made, and areas of agreement and disagreement gradually marked out.

Another characteristic feature of Russian civil procedure is broad powers of judges. Although the parties have considerable power to determine what will take place in the proceedings, judges play a very active role in the process. They have the power to determine which issues are supposed to be discussed and what evidence must be introduced. Furthermore, judges are given power to go beyond the limits of the claim filed by the plaintiff if they find it necessary to protect his or her interests. In contrast, the investigative power of the parties and their lawyers is rather limited.

The third distinguishing feature of Russian civil procedure is the

---

[7] *Vedomosty RF*, No. 24, item 407 (1964), (as amended, *Sobranie*, No. 49, item 4696 (1995)).

[8] *Grazhdanskii protsessual'nyi kodeks Rossiiskoi Federatsii (Proekt)* (Draft Civil Procedure Code of the Russian Federation) (1997) (hereafter 1997 Draft Civil Procedure Code).

[9] *Sobranie* No. 19, item 1709 (1995).

absence of any rigid rules concerning the evaluation of evidence. Because of the absence of a jury in civil actions, rules concerning evidence are not of an exclusionary nature.

B. Proceedings in Ordinary Courts

1. Initiation of Civil Proceedings

A civil action begins when an "interested person" files a suit with a competent court. The Russian Code of Civil Procedure provides that "any interested person" has the right to apply within the procedure established by law to a court for the protection of a violated right or interest protected by law.

The term "person" refers to both natural and juridical persons. Every natural person and every juridical person may file suits if they are capable of holding rights under the law. With respect to natural persons there is a distinction between the capacity to be a party to a suit and the capacity to conduct litigation in one's name. The latter is granted only to persons enjoying full legal capacity, i.e. generally to all persons above the age of eighteen with the exception of those who have been declared incapable of handling their affairs by a judicial decision (for example, those who are mentally incompetent). Parties not capable of conducting litigation in their own name as well as all juridical persons have to act through their legal representatives. By their nature, juridical persons always have the legal capacity to sue. Under Art. 49 of the Civil Code the legal capacity of a juridical person arises at the time of its state registration and terminates at the time of completion of its liquidation.

The 1964 Civil Procedure Code in principle grants standing to sue only to persons whose rights were violated. It does not allow thirds persons having only an indirect or remote interest to initiate civil proceedings. As a result, neither the *actio popularis* nor American class actions are known to Russian law. However, the 1997 Draft Civil Procedure Code seeks to introduce a major change in this respect. Under Art. 4(2) of the Draft in certain cases civil action may be initiated by persons protecting the interests of other persons or "rights, liberties and interests of a group of people." Under the existing law, a limited version of class action is permitted only in consumer protection cases, as well as in antitrust and environmental cases.

Traditionally public interests or interests of aggrieved groups of people have been protected by civil actions initiated by procurators. The Procuracy has been granted broad powers to file civil suits. Under the socialist concept of law many essentially private relationships were considered to be public. Moreover, there was a strong emphasis on the social significance and ramifications of any "private" dispute which required judicial intervention for resolution. As a result, the concept of "interest," especially of public "interest," was interpreted in a very broad manner. The power to initiate actions and seek a remedy was given not only to "an interested person" but also to the procurator who could initiate civil proceedings or intervene in a case where there was a violation of state, social or citizens' interests or when there was an abuse of rights (such as unlawful legal transaction).

This socialist concept is still considered useful in a number of important areas where the distinction between public rights (which are the responsibility of the procurator) and private rights (where the party disposition principle is supposed to reign supreme) has become difficult to maintain. The constitutional right to "a favorable environment," for example, defies characterization as one or the other.

Another consideration favoring the active role of the Procuracy relates to the fact that aggrieved individuals may have meritorious claims, but may not have the ability or the resources to prosecute them. In such cases, the Procuracy assumes the role of a public plaintiff representing the aggrieved party. Under the 1964 Civil Procedure Code the procurator has been granted very broad powers to initiate civil actions on behalf of aggrieved individuals. Art. 41 of the Code simply states that the procurator has the right to initiate an action or intervene in a case at any stage of the proceedings, if this is required to protect "the rights or legally protected interests of citizens." The 1997 Draft Civil Procedure Code seeks to place certain restrictions on the power of procurators to initiate actions on behalf of individuals. Under Art. 47 of the Draft Code the procurator has the right to initiate civil actions only "upon the request of the interested person" and only "if for valid reasons this person cannot apply to the court himself or herself."

Because in cases initiated by procurators the Procuracy is not a party to the dispute, it becomes a plaintiff only from a procedural point of view. A person in whose interests a case has been initiated by the procurator takes part in the proceedings as a plaintiff.[10] The rights of the aggrieved party under the substantive law remain unaffected. Thus, if the Procuracy decides to withdraw

---

[10] In *Procurator v. ZSK "Babushkinskii"* (*BVS*, 1994, No. 10, p. 3) the Supreme Court vacated judgments of lower courts because they defined the procurator who initiated the proceedings as plaintiff and the interested persons as third parties. The Supreme Court noted that "the procurator who initiates court proceedings in accordance with Art. 41 of the Civil Procedure Code is not a party to the case. . . Under Art. 33(2) of the Civil Procedure Code a person in whose interests a case has been initiated by the procurator takes part in the proceedings as a plaintiff."

its suit, the aggrieved party may still demand consideration of the case.[11] The Procuracy may not settle the case. For the same reason, counterclaims against the Procuracy are not possible.

2. Legal Representation

Although interested parties in complicated suit always hire lawyers, representation by a lawyer is not mandatory in Russian courts, including the Supreme Court. As noted in Chapter III, Russian lawyers do not have a monopoly in the representation of litigants before the courts. Any person may represent any other person before any court.

Legal aid in civil cases is generally not available. However, members of the Colleges of Advocates are supposed to give free legal advice in some cases, in particular in labor disputes. Parties who cannot afford the legal costs of a civil lawsuit often turn to the Procuracy which may initiate civil law actions on their behalf.

3. Jurisdiction

The statement of claim must be filed in the appropriate court. Jurisdiction of the Russian courts is governed by the rules concerning allocation of jurisdiction between different court systems, subject matter jurisdiction of courts within different court structures and rules of territorial jurisdiction. Allocation of jurisdiction between different court systems was considered in Chapter III.

As far as the subject matter jurisdiction in the "ordinary" court system is concerned, district courts have original jurisdiction with respect to the overwhelming majority of civil actions. At the same time, the supreme courts of the constituent republics or courts of other "subjects" of the Russian Federation and even the Supreme Court may have original jurisdiction over some disputes. Thus, courts of the "subjects" of the Russian Federation have original jurisdiction over cases involving state secrets. Art. 6 of the 1993 Law on International Commercial Arbitration[12] provides that international arbitration awards rendered in Russia may be challenged only in the courts of the second level, that is, in the supreme courts of the constituent republics or courts of other "subjects" of the Federation. According to Art. 116 of the Civil Procedure Code the Supreme Court has original jurisdiction over appeals challenging the legality of non-normative acts of the President and the Government of the Russian Federation.

[11] Civil Procedure Code, Art. 41.

[12] *Vedomosty RF*, No. 32, item 1240 (1993).

In addition, in complex cases second-level "ordinary" courts may, upon request of the parties, assert original jurisdiction over cases that would normally fall under jurisdiction of district courts.[13]

4. Territorial Jurisdiction and Venue

If a case falls within the jurisdiction of the "ordinary" courts, the principles of territorial division of jurisdiction would govern venue. These principles are fairly simple. Under Art. 117 of the Civil Procedure Code, suits are to be filed at "the place of residence of the defendant." If the place of residence of the defendant is not known, suit may be filed at the place where his or her property is located.[14] Suits against juridical persons are to be "filed at the place where an organ or property of the latter is located."[15] In all these cases, however, territorial jurisdiction may be changed "by the agreement of the parties."[16]

At the same time, Art. 119 of the Civil Procedure Code establishes several cases of "exclusive jurisdiction" which cannot be changed by the agreement of the parties. For example, disputes concerning immovables are under the jurisdiction of the court at the place where the immovables are located.

It must be noted that in the Russian legal system issues of personal jurisdiction over the defendant do not arise because all the federal courts constitute one unitary system with jurisdiction over all defendants within the territory of the Russian Federation.[17]

Russian courts will always accept jurisdiction if the rules of the Civil

---

[13]Under the original version of the 1964 Civil Procedure Code all higher courts had the power to assert original jurisdiction over cases which were considered complex or important. However, this traditional approach is in conflict with Art. 47 of the 1993 Constitution according to which "no one may be denied the right to having his or her case examined by the court and by the judge under whose jurisdiction the given case falls under the law." In view of this, the latest amendments to the Civil Procedure Code require "the consent of the parties" for any change in the original jurisdiction. In 1996 the Supreme Court also issued an "Explanation" according to which "a superior court shall not examine at first instance a case that falls under the jurisdiction of an inferior court without a motion or consent of the parties." See Ruling of the Plenary Session of the Supreme Court "*On Some Questions Concerning the Application of the Constitution of the Russian Federation by Courts.*" (*BVS*, 1996, No. 1, p. 3).

[14]Civil Procedure Code, Art. 118.

[15]Civil Procedure Code, Art. 117.

[16]Civil Procedure Code, Art. 120.

[17]International jurisdiction of Russian courts will be discussed in Chapter VIII.

Procedure Code provide for at least one basis for jurisdiction. Plaintiffs basically have the right to litigate in the forum designated by the law. Unlike in the United States, in Russia there is no doctrine of *forum non conveniens* which would enable courts to refuse to hear and resolve a case if it does not appear to have the closest connection to the forum. Although some forum shopping may occur, there is a reluctance among lawyers to wage battles about a court's jurisdiction. An explanation for this probably lies in the fact that the same federal law will be applied in all courts and that it is generally applied in a uniform way.

5. Forms of Actions

Russian procedural law divides actions into three categories: actions for performance, actions for declaratory judgment and actions for judicial modification of legal relationships.

A plaintiff who wants the defendant to be ordered by the court to do or not to do something, will file an action for performance. This type of action is available in all cases where the plaintiff seeks to compel performance of a contractual obligation (for example, delivery of goods) or a legal duty (for example, payment of alimony). The performance may be specific, or it may involve the payment of money. While declaratory judgments are not enforceable by execution (as discussed later), the judgement for the performance may be executed against the defendant.

Declaratory judgments are sought in situations where the plaintiff wants a judicial determination of a legal relationship that will bind the parties. The plaintiff seeks a declaratory judgment that an alleged relationship does or does not exist. Judicial determination of a legal relationship is possible only in concrete circumstances involving a specific legal relationship and a legal interest on plaintiff's part worthy of protection. For example, the plaintiff may wish to establish that a particular person is the father of her child. Although such a declaratory judgment does not order that the defendant, for example, pay child support, the plaintiff will always have the right to bring a subsequent action if the defendant does not fulfil his obligations resulting from the declaratory judgment. Actions for a declaratory judgment may thus be the first step in clarifying the legal relations between the parties. Recourse to such actions is easier because they are not subject to much higher court fees levied on the trial of an action for performance (which usually are a percentage of the amount in controversy).[18] At the same time, they send a very strong signal to the defendant that subsequent litigation for performance is possible.

---

[18] Court fees are governed by a special federal Law "On State Fees." See, *Sobranie*, 1996, No. 1, item 19 (1996).

Actions for a modification of legal relationships aim at an immediate modification by the court of an established right or legal relationship. Examples of such action are actions to rescind a contract based on fraud or actions for a divorce.

6. Form and Contents of the Complaint

The complaint must be submitted in writing and contain information specified in the Civil Procedure Code. Every complaint must specify the parties and the court applied to. It also must indicate the grounds upon which the plaintiff bases his or her claims and a demand for the relief that the plaintiff seeks.[19] Although the plaintiff has the general duty to "prove those circumstances on which he relies as the basis of his claim",[20] there is no duty to formulate legal arguments in support of the complaint.

A properly drafted complaint must be accepted by the judge unless it falls under certain specified criteria for rejection (not triable by a court, failure to exhaust preliminary extra-judicial procedures, *res judicata*, same case already pending in court, parties had agreed to settle their disputes by private arbitration, lack of jurisdiction and others).[21]

7. Defense by the Defendant

Once the defendant has been served with the complaint, he or she may respond on the merits of the case or assert procedural defense. However, there is no general duty to defend. The defendant may choose not to respond to the allegations made by the plaintiff and may even fail to appear in court. The defendant's failure to appear in court may lead to a default judgment (as discussed later). The defendant may also choose to admit the plaintiff's factual allegations and acknowledge the claim.

In addition, the defendant may respond to the claim with a counterclaim. The counterclaim must be related to the transaction or event which gave rise to the original claim. Under Art. 132 of the Civil Procedure Code a judge will accept a counterclaim if (1) the counterclaim is to be set off against the original claim; (2) granting relief in the counterclaim would wholly or partly defeat the original claim or (3) there is a mutual connection between the original claim and counterclaim and the disputes would be more expeditiously and properly tried if they were tried together.[22]

---

[19] Civil Procedure Code, Art. 126.

[20] Civil Procedure Code, Art. 50.

[21] Civil Procedure Code, Art. 129.

[22] For an illustration of a counterclaim, see *Shepin v. Kurbatov*, reproduced *supra*, p. 324-326.

8. Pre-Trial Proceedings

The section of the Russian Civil Procedure Code regarding pre-trial proceedings and activities emphasizes the need for a comprehensive and timely preparation for trial. While both plaintiff and defendant must present everything in support of their claims or defenses, the court also has an obligation to prepare for trial. The prime function of the pre-trial stage is to determine the nature of the dispute between the parties. Pre-trial proceedings also seek to identify and obtain evidence that the parties will need at trial. The purpose of pre-trial proceedings is to clarify further the legal grounds relied upon by the parties and the nature of relief sought. Finally, the court may attempt to guide the parties to a settlement.

After a statement of claim or petition is accepted, a judge acting alone takes several actions to prepare for trial. The powers of the judge during the preparation stage are very extensive. They include the power to determine the time limits for taking procedural steps and the power to call the parties in for questioning. The judge usually questions the plaintiff about the substance of the case and requests additional evidence when necessary. The defendant, who always receives a copy of the statement of claim from the court, may be summoned for the same purpose. The judge usually proposes to submit evidence supporting possible objections within an established time limit. The defendant may also be requested to file a written answer to the claim. As a rule, counterclaims are also submitted at this stage.

The judge also decides the issue of joinder or intervention if there are co-defendants or third parties. He or she also resolves which witnesses are to be summoned, at the request of the parties orders the citizens or organizations to submit documentary or real evidence, resolves whether expert evidence must be obtained and appoints an expert and orders interim measures for protection. All materials obtained during the pre-trial stage make up the basis of the official court file which is open to inspection by the parties and their attorneys.

Court's supervision of the pre-trial stage includes the duty of the court to help parties to identify factual and legal issues of the dispute and to obtain any necessary evidence. Although judges are supposed to help the parties, they also must remain impartial. In practice the extensive powers of judges during the preparation stage often allow them to determine in what direction the investigation of the facts will go.

At this stage the facts of the case may also be investigated by the lawyers independently of the court through informal means. However, in contrast to the American civil procedure, there is no "discovery process."

Under the Civil Procedure Code, only the judge can order one of the parties or a third person to produce documents or other evidence deemed to be relevant to the proceedings. The absence of pre-trial discovery is also explained by the absence of a single and concentrated trial. As a rule, factual and legal issues are defined gradually as the case proceeds. The spreading of the trial over several sessions makes the element of surprise less important, since a party can simply respond to new evidence by presenting contrary evidence at a later hearing. As a result, Russian lawyers do not feel pressure to forearm themselves with information and arguments on every fact or claim that might possibly arise and prove relevant.

Russian lawyers usually obtain additional evidence by petitioning the judge to order the presentation of documents, appoint an expert and so on. Although the Civil Procedure Code does not preclude interrogation of witnesses by the lawyers of the opposing party, there are no procedural devices to compel any member of the public who has knowledge of the facts of the case to divulge his or her knowledge to the parties before the trial.

9. The Trial

Although some important cases may be heard at first instance by superior courts, the overwhelming majority of cases are heard and decided initially by the district courts. In these courts cases are usually heard by a single professional judge. At the same time, certain cases may be heard by a judge and two people's assessors (lay judges), if requested by any person participating in the case.

An important principle of the Russian civil procedure is the requirement of oral hearing. Oral hearing allows all parties to follow the proceedings and control the activities of the court. The parties are required to submit their motions and present the facts before the court orally even if the relevant motions or facts are also submitted to the court in writing. The court may base its decision only on those facts which were presented by the parties during oral hearings.

The principle of orality is closely linked to the principle according to which judicial proceedings must be conducted in public. Public proceedings make it possible for the general population to observe trials. Although as a general principle hearings on the case are open to the public, *in camera* hearings may be held in order to protect individual rights or trade and state secrets.

Another important requirement is that the proceedings must be uninterrupted. This does not mean that Russian courts cannot adjourn. In fact, they adjourn quite frequently for various reasons, for example, in order to obtain new evidence. The above requirement simply means that the court must consider the case only with the usual recesses until it is finished and before hearing another case or until it has adjourned the case for reasons specified in the Civil Procedure Code. Simultaneous consideration of several cases is prohibited because the drafters of the Civil Procedure Code believed that would not allow the judge to give her or his full attention to the case at hand.[23] If an adjournment occurs, the part of the oral hearing which has already taken place must be repeated. However, witness testimony given at the first session and recorded in the file of the case may be used in subsequent sessions.

The usual procedure involves the oral explanations of the parties and other persons participating in the case, testimony of witnesses and statements of experts, examination of other evidence and judicial pleadings. During the judicial examination of a case judges are usually active in asking questions to the parties, witnesses and experts and play an important role in introducing testimony and evidence.

As in other civil law countries, there are no court stenographers who take down verbatim all the testimony and everything else said in the proceedings. As a rule, the record would reflect only the main points of the proceedings or testimony. Because the records are not full verbatim transcripts, the parties may make a motion to record a particular testimony or statement verbatim.[24] Furthermore, within three days after the record is signed by the presiding judge and the secretary the parties may submit corrections or additions to the record which the presiding judge or, in case of a dispute, the whole bench must verify and add to the file of the case.[25]

10. Evidence

The Russian Civil Procedure Code does not contain exclusionary rules of evidence in the American sense. The highly complicated rules of the common law concerning the exclusion of various kinds of evidence are intended to prevent the jury from being misled by untrustworthy or inflammatory evidence. Because in Russian civil procedure the evidence is evaluated by professional judges (and, in some cases, by lay assessors) rules concerning admissability of evidence are more flexible than in the American Law. For example, there is no prohibition against hearsay evidence. However, the judge has been granted broad powers to decide how much weight to give to different

---

[23] Cf. M.K.Treushnikov, *Uchebnik grazhdanskogo protsessa* (Manual of Civil Procedure) 49 (1996).

[24] Civil Procedure Code, Art. 228.

[25] Civil Procedure Code, Arts. 229, 230.

types of evidence and in general hearsay is given little weight unless it is supported by other evidence.

At the same time, the Civil Procedure Code includes an exhaustive list of admissible means of proof. Means of proof are: explanations of the parties and third persons, the testimony of witnesses, documentary evidence, real evidence and the conclusions of experts.[26]

(a) Burden of Proof

As a general rule, each party bears the burden of proving the facts supporting her or his claim or defense. However, substantive law or procedural law may include special rules on the allocation of the burden of proof. For example, under the 1993 Law "On Appealing to Court the Actions and Decisions Violating the Rights and Freedoms of Citizens"[27] the aggrieved party must prove only the fact that action was taken or decision made infringing upon his or her interests or rights. The petitioner is not obliged to prove the unlawfulness of the challenged action or decision. Instead, the burden of proving the lawfulness of the challenged action is imposed on the defendant organ.[28]

Under Art. 55 of Civil Procedure Code parties do not need to prove facts that are manifest and well-known (such as the accident at Chernobyl). They also need not prove facts established by a judgment of a court in a previous civil case in which the same parties took part. Similarly, there is no need to prove facts established by judgments in prior criminal cases.

The judgment of a court in a criminal case is binding on a court trying a civil case involving the actions of the criminal defendant.[29] However, the effect of a criminal court judgment is limited only to the question whether the relevant acts took place and whether the person involved committed them.[30] All other issues, including the amount of compensation, are decided by the new

---

[26] Civil procedure Code, Art. 49.

[27] *Vedomosty RF*, No. 19, item 685 (1993) (as amended in 1995, *Sobranie*, No. 51, item 4970).

[28] Cf. *SP "Kamsing" v. Petropavlovsk-Kamchatsky Customs Administration*, *BVS*, 1996, No. 5, p. 4 ("The burden of proof that there was a legal ground for using administrative sanctions is imposed on the Petropavlovsk-Kamchatsky Customs Administration, [but it] failed to submit any proof justifying the imposition of administrative sanctions").

[29] Russian criminal procedure law also allows submission of civil law claims as part of the criminal case. As a result, a judgment in a criminal case may also deal with the civil law matters raised by the parties.

[30] Civil Procedure Code, Art. 55.

court independently. If, for example, a driver of a car was convicted by a criminal court for traffic rules violations, victims of the accident may rely in the criminal court judgment to prove that damage or death was caused by actions of the convicted driver. At the same time, victims need to provide additional proof concerning their damage claim. If, on the other hand, the criminal proceedings against the driver have been dismissed because another car was involved in the accident, the acquittal in the criminal case would preclude any separate civil law action against the person declared innocent in the criminal law case. However, if the acquittal in the criminal case is based on another ground, for example, because a minor traffic rule violation is not considered to be a crime under the Criminal Code, the acquittal in criminal proceedings will not preclude a separate civil action against the wrongdoer.[31]

(b) The Quest for the "Objective" Truth

Although under the revised Civil Procedure Code Russian courts are no longer required to establish "objective" truth,[32] an analysis of the current law of evidence reveals the continuing desire to establish "objective" truth.

Rules concerning facts admitted by the defendant may be a good illustration of this trend. In contrast to civil procedure rules of many Western European civil law countries which are based on the idea that facts admitted by the defendant are not subject to further evidentiary hearing and have to be treated by the court as true, the Russian Civil Procedure Code provides that such admissions "do not bind the court." The court must evaluate such admissions together with the other evidence collected in the case. The court may consider an admitted fact established only if it "has no doubt that the admission corresponds to the circumstances of the case and was not made by the party under the influence of fraud, force, threats, mistake or with the object of concealing the truth."[33]

(c) Explanations of the Parties

As noted earlier, the Civil Procedure Code regards explanations of the parties as possible means of proof. However, under the Civil Procedure Code explanations of the parties are not considered to be witness testimony. Unlike in the American civil procedure, where a party may testify as a witness in her or his own case, Russian Civil Procedure Code does not consider parties to be

---

[31] Cf. *In Re Alferov, BVS*, 1997, No. 9, p. 19.

[32] For details, see I.V. Reshetnikova, *Dokazatel'stvennoe pravo v grazhdanskom sudoproizvodstve* (Law of Evidence in Civil Procedure) 34-35 (1997).

[33] Civil Procedure Code, Art. 60. The 1997 Draft Civil Procedure Code codifies the same rule based on the idea of an active court (1997 Draft Civil Procedure Code, Art. 70).

witnesses. This view, shared by the majority of other civil law countries, is based on the realistic (or, as some may claim, cynical) assumption that although parties are usually best aware of the events leading to the litigation, they have an interest in its outcome. Because parties would always pursue their interests, they cannot give unbiased testimony. Thus, if the only evidence in the case are the conflicting statements of the parties, the plaintiff's complaint will be dismissed.

(d) Expert Opinion

As in many other civil law countries, experts in Russia are not considered to be witnesses. They are appointed by the court, act under the court's instruction and owe the court a duty of impartiality. The courts are free to designate any expert they choose, but experts are generally chosen from official state institutions having varying specializations. In contrast to American civil procedure where one often sees head-on clashes between experts called and paid by the parties, Russian experts are supposed to act as impartial advisors to the court on various technical matters.

The court-appointed experts always submit written reports to the court. But they rarely testify at trial. Although the expert's report is not binding upon the judges, judges usually give considerable weight to the expert's findings. If there is doubt about the expert's conclusions, the court can always order a second expert evaluation.

(e) Witness Testimony

As a general rule, witness testimony consists of statements made at trial under penalty of perjury. In Russian civil procedure there are no pre-trial discovery procedures for witnesses, such as depositions. At the same time, under Art. 57 of the Civil Procedure Code parties "having grounds to apprehend that it may later become impossible or difficult to produce evidence which they need may request the court to take action to preserve such evidence." This means that the judge may take witness testimony before the trial. Under Art. 57 of the Civil Procedure Code, before an action is brought in court, witness testimony may also be given before notaries.

Witnesses who are summoned by the court to appear in the judicial session are under a general duty to testify unless they claim an exemption from the obligation to give evidence.

Art. 51 of the Constitution proclaims that "no one shall be obliged to testify against himself or herself, or against his or her spouse and close relatives as specified by federal law." Spouses of the parties and persons related to the parties by blood or marriage may refuse to testify. The Civil Procedure Code also grants a privilege to legal representatives in civil proceedings and defense attorneys in criminal proceedings (including non-lawyer legal representatives).[34] It should be noted, however, that as a general principle privilege does not cover confidential relations between persons other than those specified by the Civil Procedure Code. Thus, Russian courts will not recognize claims to privilege based on the trade secret exemption.

Although Russian civil procedure does not recognize the concept of contempt of court, witnesses may be prosecuted for refusal to testify or perjury under the Criminal Code. Before taking testimony judges always warn witnesses about possible criminal responsibility for refusal to testify and false testimony. However, witnesses are not required to take an oath to tell the truth.

During the evidence-taking session the judge usually asks the witness to give her or his narrative account of the facts relating to the subject matter of the dispute. The judge may then ask supplemental questions. The parties and their attorneys are then permitted to ask additional questions of the witness.

(f) The Principle of Free Evaluation of Evidence

As noted earlier, Russian civil litigation is governed by the principle of free evaluation of evidence. Judges are supposed to evaluate evidence according to their inner conviction based on an objective, comprehensive and full consideration of evidence available in the case viewed as a whole. No particular type of evidence is accorded any a priori established weight.[35] However, in some instances there are statutory requirements about what type of evidence is necessary. For example, failure to observe the written form of a legal transaction deprives the parties of the right to refer to witness testimony.[36] Furthermore, the 1995 revision of Civil Procedure Code introduced a new clause which provides that evidence obtained in violation of law would not be valid and could not form the basis of the court's decision.[37] The new clause is a reflection of the constitutional requirement according to which "in the administration of justice no evidence obtained in violation of the federal law shall be admissible."[38]

While the general principle in the evaluation of evidence is "free evaluation by the judge," in practice there is a tendency to attribute particular

[34] Under the 1997 Draft Civil Procedure Code the list of persons who may refuse to testify has been expanded. For example, the new Civil Procedure Code will grant a privilege to clergymen.

[35] Civil Procedure Code, Art. 56.

[36] 1994 Civil Procedure Code, Art. 162.

[37] Civil Procedure Code, Art. 49.

[38] Constitution, Art. 50.

importance to documentary evidence.[39] Opinions of court-appointed experts may also carry far greater weight than, for example, witness testimony. And, as noted earlier, party testimony is looked at with some suspicion.

The following case illustrates the importance of new constitutional rules concerning admissibility of evidence.

The Kurgansk Regional Court: *V. v. The Procuracy of Kurgansk Region* (*Sudebnaya praktika po grazhdanskim delam 1993-1996* 327 (1997))

V. filed suit in court against the Procuracy of Kurgansk Region requesting reinstatement in his job and compensation for the time when he was not able to perform his duties. . . The plaintiff served as senior assistant procurator of the City of Kurgan and on 7.10.94 was dismissed from his job and from the organs of the Procuracy by the Procurator of the Region on the ground of committing an act involving moral turpitude, which the plaintiff claims he did not commit. . .

In a judgment of 15.11.94 the Kurgansk City Peoples Court dismissed the claim; the decision was affirmed on 6.12.94 by the Collegium for Civil Cases of the Kurgansk Regional Court.

The Presidium of the Kurgansk Regional Court, which considered the case on the protest of the Deputy Chairman of the Supreme Court of the Russian Federation, finds that both the judgment and the cassational ruling must be vacated and the case remanded for a new trial in the Kurgansk City Court for the following reasons:

The court dismissed V.'s claim because it believed that it had established that V. had personal relationships with several directors of commercial companies and participated in commercial activities concerning purchase and sale of alcoholic beverages; these personal relationships undermined V.'s credibility as a Procuracy officer; his dismissal was therefore justified under Arts. 10, 12 and 13 of the Regulations on Rewards and Disciplinary Responsibility of Procurators and Investigators of the Agencies of Procuracy. The court based its judgment on materials of search and operational activities which involved tapping of V.'s telephones.

However, under Art. 23 of the Constitution of the Russian Federation everyone has the right to privacy of telephone communications; this right may

---

[39] Note, however, that Russian commentators usually assert that "written evidence has no priority over other means of proof." See K.I. Komissarov, Yu.K. Osipov eds., *Grazhdanskii protsess* (Civil Procedure) 201 (1996).

be restricted only on the basis of a judicial decision. The materials of the case do not contain any reliable evidence that a court authorized the tapping of V.'s telephones.

According to Art. 50 of the Constitution of the Russian Federation in the administration of justice no evidence obtained in violation of the federal law is admissible; in view of this, the opinion of the court that the materials seized in the search and operational activities involving V. may be considered as evidence under Art. 49 of the Civil Procedure Code can be justified only if these materials were obtained in accordance with the requirements of the Constitution of the Russian Federation and other federal laws. The Procuracy of the Kurgansk Province submitted to the Presidium [of the Kurgansk Provincial Court] copies of rulings on tapping of telephones approved by the court; however, these documents were not considered by the court of first instance. In these circumstances the relevant judicial decisions cannot be considered as lawful; they must be vacated and remanded for a new trial in the court of first instance. . .

11. Active Role of the Court

The Civil Procedure Code proclaims the general rule that parties should each prove those facts on which they rely. At the same time, the Civil Procedure Code provides that if the evidence submitted by the parties is inadequate, the court may propose that the parties submit additional evidence. If the parties cannot obtain the necessary additional evidence, the court, at the request of the parties, may assist the parties in assembling the evidence.[40]

An active role of the court is further illustrated by the judicial interrogation of witnesses. While in common law procedure the questioning of witnesses is mainly conducted by the attorneys for the parties through the technique of oral examination and cross-examination, in Russia the judge generally directs the questioning.

The Civil Procedure Code also contains several important provisions imposing constraints on party disposition of cases. A court may refuse to allow the defendant to concede a claim, or the parties to settle a claim, if these actions would be contrary to law or violate the rights and the legally protected interests of any person.[41] Furthermore, a court may go beyond the limits of the claim filed by the plaintiff and award higher compensation if it finds it necessary to protect the rights and the legally protected interests of the

[40] Civil Procedure Code, Art. 50.
[41] Civil Procedure Code, Art. 34.

plaintiff.[42] Still another area of civil procedure where Russian courts traditionally play an active role is when they exercise their power and duty to ascertain the applicable foreign law *ex officio.*[43]

These constraints on party control of proceedings were retained in the Civil Procedure Code even after extensive revisions of the Code in 1995, which eliminated even broader powers of the court, in particular the power to assemble evidence on its own motion and the power to assert the public interest in court decisions concerning disputes between private parties. Under the prior version of the Code the courts were obliged to explore all the facts of a case *ex officio;* in particular, the courts were supposed to collect all the additional evidence at their own initiative. They were "required, without restricting themselves to the materials and explanations produced by the parties, to take all steps provided by law for the all-round, full and objective elucidation of the true facts of the case and of the rights and duties of the parties."[44] In addition, the courts were instructed to go beyond the limits of the claim filed by the plaintiff, not only in cases where they would find it necessary to protect the rights and the legally protected interests of the plaintiff, but also to protect the interests of "state institutions, enterprises, collective farms, and other cooperative and social organizations or citizens".

The 1997 Draft Civil Procedure Code makes additional attempts to assert the principle of party control of proceedings in an adversary system. It no longer imposes on the court any duty to take independent steps for the "objective elucidation of the true facts of the case and of the rights and duties of the parties." Parties have more freedom to independently formulate their claims and determine the course of the proceedings. This approach is based on the recognition of the importance of the principle of party control of proceedings in an adversary system. However, even under the 1997 Draft Civil Procedure Code Russian courts will still play an active role in civil proceedings.

Although Russian judges traditionally play an unusually active role in civil proceedings, it should be noted that similar forms of judicial activism are also recognized in many other civil law countries. For example, under the German Code of Civil Procedure the court is required to clarify the issues and help the parties to present their positions fully. German courts are under a statutory duty to "help if a party fails to present all facts through oversight, inadvertence or mistake."[45] Among other things, courts help the parties to

---

[42] Civil Procedure Code, Art. 195.

[43] See *infra* p. 410.

[44] Civil Procedure Code, Art. 14 (no longer in effect).

[45] See, W.F. Ebke, M.W. Finkin, Introduction to German Law 364 (1996).

make the applications necessary to assert their claims in the correct legal form. German judges also dominate the evidence-taking sessions.[46] Judicial activism in civil law countries has been traditionally justified by the need to increase the efficiency of judicial administration and the desire to establish not merely formal but also real equality of the parties.[47]

12. Judgments

Judgments are given "in the name of the Russian Federation." Courts must pronounce judgments immediately after the trial of cases. In exceptional circumstances (in especially complicated cases) the formulation of a full judgment may be postponed for a period of not more than three days.[48] However, even in these cases the operative part of the judgment must be given at the same session at which the trial was concluded.

The final decision of the court in the case must be based on evidence considered in the judicial session. Where cases are considered by a panel of a professional judge and lay assessors, judgments are adopted by simple majority vote. The deliberations and the vote are secret. Any member of the court who holds a dissenting opinion may set it out in writing. However, the dissent is not disclosed when the decision is pronounced in a public hearing. It is attached to the file of the case, where it may be considered by a higher court during an appeal or review.

The Civil Procedure Code does not contain any provision on the right of the parties to review the dissent. However, this right may follow from a general provision of Art. 30 of the Code according to which "parties taking part in a case have the right to familiarize themselves with the materials of the case." At the same time, some experts deny the existence of this right because under Art. 193 of the Code "judges may not reveal the opinions expressed at the time of their deliberations." The proponents of this view argue that disclosure of dissenting opinions may violate the requirements of Art. 193.[49]

The Civil Procedure Code defines the form and content of a court

---

[46] See N. Horn, H. Kotz, H.G. Leser, German Private and Commercial Law: An Introduction 47 (1982) ("A common lawyer who attended one of the conferences in a German civil suit would think the judge rather vocal and dominant and the attorneys relatively subdued").

[47] See M. Cappelletti, The Judicial Process in Comparative Perspective 252 (1989).

[48] Civil Procedure Code, Art. 203.

[49] See, e.g., Komissarov, Osipov, *supra* note 39, at 288.

judgment.[50] The introductory part recites the court pronouncing the judgment and the composition of the court, the parties, the subject-matter of the dispute as well as the date and place of judgment. The descriptive part of the judgment must contain an indication of the plaintiff's claim, the defendant's defenses as well as the explanations of other persons taking part in the case. The main part of the judgment gives the findings of fact and the legal reasons for the decision. The operative part of the judgment gives the final ruling in the case.

The form of the judgment corresponds to the form of the action initiated by the plaintiff. For example, judgments granting performance order the defendant to do or refrain from doing something. In contrast, declaratory judgments simply pronounce that a legal relationship does or does not exist.

Judgments must also contain a decision on the costs of proceedings. Court costs, including state duties and compensation for the witnesses and experts, are paid by the losing party. In addition, the loser usually pays the winner's counsel fees but only "within reasonable limits, taking into account specific circumstances" of the case.[51] In cases where the court finds only in part against one of the parties, he or she would be ordered to cover only some of the costs. The rest will be assumed by the other party. The principle that costs are borne by the losing party is viewed as an important barrier to frivolous suits.

Russian judicial opinions, compared to American ones, are rather short. They never contain references to scholarly work or case law. However, courts often cite "Explanations" issued by the Supreme Court.

Judgments become effective upon the expiration of the term for cassational appeal or protest if they have not been made the subject of an appeal or protest. If a cassational appeal or protest is made, but the judgment is upheld, the judgment acquires legal effect at the end of the hearing by the higher court. Judgments of the Supreme Court acquire legal effect immediately after they are pronounced.[52]

13. Effect of Judgments

Once the judgment has entered into legal effect, it binds all state institutions, officials and citizens, including the court and the parties. Parties or any other persons who took part in the case (or their legal successors) may not file any new action concerning the same subject and on the same grounds. Nor is it possible for the parties or any other person who took part in the case

[50] Civil Procedure Code, Art. 197.
[51] Civil Procedure Code, Art. 91.
[52] Civil Procedure Code, Art. 208.

(or their legal successors) to dispute in any other proceedings the facts and legal relations established by the judgment.[53]

It is important to emphasize that judgments establish facts only for the parties and other persons who took part in the case (or their legal successors). If new proceedings concerning the same set of facts involve new parties, the court must again establish the relevant facts according to the general rules of proof-taking. This means, for example, that if one of the victims of a helicopter crash sues the owner for damages and there is already a judgment against the same owner in a suit brought by a different victim of the same crash that establishes that the helicopter crashed because of motor malfunction, the defendant can relitigate the issue.

New proceedings on the same subject, between the same parties and on the same grounds are precluded by the principle of *res judicata.* At the same time, it is still possible to initiate a new action if the later dispute is not absolutely identical to the previous one. Under Art. 13 of the Civil Procedure Code the binding force of a judgment "in no way deprives interested persons of the possibility of applying to the court for the protection of any rights and legally protected interests, disputes about which were not considered and decided by the court in the earlier case." The following case illustrates this point:

The Supreme Court: *Shiverski v. Avtokhosiaistvo* (*BVS*, 1993, No. 11, p. 8)

Shiverski brought suit against the transport enterprise of the Council of Ministers of the Republic of Buratia for compensation of harm. He based his claim on the fact that on August 9, 1992, his car was damaged in an accident which resulted from violations of traffic rules by a driver by the name of Simushkin who was driving a car belonging to the defendant. By its judgment of September 10, 1992, the people's court entered a judgment against the transport enterprise in the amount of 58 245 rubles for the benefit of Shiverski. However, the awarded sum was not paid until January 19, 1993. Because of the delay in the payment, Shiverski was not able to repair the car since the cost of repairs had risen. In view of that Sheverski brought a new suit for compensation of the difference in repair costs.

By its judgment of March 23, 1993 the Zhelesnodorozhnii district peoples' court granted relief in Shiverski's suit and awarded him 297 350 rubles.

---

[53] Civil Procedure Code, Art. 208.

The Presidium of the Supreme Court of the Republic of Buratia vacated the judgment and terminated the proceedings.

The Deputy Chairman of the Supreme Court of the Russian Federation lodged a protest and asked to vacate the ruling of the Presidium of the Supreme Court of the Republic of Buratia and to affirm the judgment of the Zhelesnodorozhnii district peoples' court.

The Judicial Collegium for Civil Cases of the RF Supreme Court granted the protest for the following reasons.

The Presidium of the Supreme Court of the Republic of Buratia vacated the judgment of the Zhelesnodorozhnii district peoples' court and terminated the proceedings by referring to the fact that the district court had issued two judgments in a dispute between the same parties on the same subject and on the same grounds. This was not admissible because under Art. 219 (3) of the Civil Procedure Code in such a situation the court was obliged to terminate proceedings.

The Judicial Collegium cannot agree with such a conclusion.

Indeed, Shiverski brought suit against the transport enterprise of the Council of Ministers of the Republic of Buratia for compensation of harm caused by an accident. However, the new dispute resulted from a different ground: it resulted from the delay in the payment of the awarded sum in a situation where the cost of repairs of the damaged car had risen. The Court argued that the law did not envision any increase in the compensation for damage in cases of delays in the execution of judgments. However, this argument is not correct.

Under Art. 444 of the Civil Code, harm caused to the person or property of a citizen, as well as harm caused to an organization, is subject to compensation in full by the person who has caused such harm. Because during the time of the non-fulfillment of the judgment of the court of September 10, 1993 the prices for spare parts and repairs had risen, the district court correctly concluded that harm inflicted on Shiverski was not compensated in full and therefore was justified in granting relief in the suit. . .

QUESTION

The Civil Procedure Code provides that a court will terminate proceedings if there is a prior judgment by a Russian court, provided that such was rendered in a dispute (1) between the same parties; (2) on the same subject, and (3) on the same grounds. This means that the Civil Procedure Code may permit relitigation of a dispute on the same facts in cases where plaintiffs assert a new legal theory of action. How does this concept of *res judicata* differ from practice in the US?

14. Appeal

Russian civil procedure law offers two forms of appeal: cassational appeal and protests by way of supervision. Cassational appeals are directed against judgments that have not acquired legally binding effect. The filing of a cassational appeal suspends the execution of the original judgment. Review by way of supervision may be characterized as extraordinary because it deals with judgments that have become final and because only certain designated officers of the Procuracy or higher court judges have been granted the power to lodge protests by way of supervision. The filing of a protest by way of supervision does not suspend the execution of the challenged judgment.

(a) Cassational Appeal

A losing party has the right to initiate cassational review by lodging a cassational appeal to a higher court. However, not only the parties enjoy the right of appeal. A judicial decision may also be contested by the Procuracy which has the right to lodge cassational protests even with respect to cases tried at first instance without Procuracy's participation. The right of the representative of state to appeal judgments has been traditionally justified by requirements of public policy. The same justification has been advanced in several other civil law countries where specially designated state officials have the right to challenge court judgments.[54]

While considerations of procedural economy favor appeals only of final judgments, the right of appeal is also granted with respect to various non-final orders entered by the court throughout the course of the case. However, separate appeals of orders are allowed only with respect to major procedural decisions of the judge "specified" by the Civil Procedure Code or in cases when the relevant order "prevents the possibility of further consideration of the case."[55] An example of the first situation is Art. 139 of the Code which expressly allows separate appeals of any decision on questions of taking security for an action. An example of the second situation is a decision to terminate proceedings in the case.

---

[54] For example, in France the attorney general may appeal a judgment before the *Cour de Cassation* if he or she considers that a lower court has violated the law. In Italy cassational review may be initiated by the *Publico Ministero* if the review application has not been made by the aggrieved party. In Spain the cassation appeal may be initiated not only by the parties but also by the attorney general. For details, see C. Platto ed., Civil Appeal Procedures Worldwide 164, 188, 212 (1992).

[55] Civil Procedure Code, Art. 315.

The cassational appeal is initiated by the submission of a written complaint to the court which rendered the original judgment or directly to a higher court. The complaint must set out the object of the review and the factual and legal arguments supporting the request for review. A copy of the complaint is served upon the other party who is summoned to appear in court on a given date. Parties and their attorneys have the right to participate in the cassational court review of the case. In particular, the may present new evidence and make oral arguments. However, if no appearance is made by the parties or by a party, the court of cassation will render an ex-paztei opinion.

It is important to emphasize that the right of cassational appeal includes the right to the reconsideration of factual as well as legal issues. Consequently, the cassational instance, which is always composed of three professional judges, reviews both errors of law and fact. Although the higher court would generally rely on the record prepared by the court of first instance as the factual basis for reconsideration of the case, in certain situations the parties have the right to introduce new evidence at the cassational level. Submission of new evidence is permitted if the court finds that the parties were not able to present the relevant evidence to the court of first instance.[56] The cassational instance may reconsider the facts of the case only if it receives new evidence. As a rule, parties submit new documents. Although court of cassational instance usually do not take witness testimony directly, it is possible to submit written testimony of new witnesses secured by notaries.[57]

As a general rule, the cassational instance reviews "the legality and justification" of the decision of the court of first instance only to the extent indicated by the appeal. However, "in the interests of legality" the higher court may also review the decision as a whole.[58] This means that the case may be reviewed both in the appealed and non-appealed parts as well as in relation to persons who have not appealed.

The powers of cassational instance are defined by Art. 305 of the Civil Procedure Code:

> The court, having considered the case by way of cassation, shall have the right by its ruling:
>
> 1) to leave the judgment unchanged and to dismiss the appeal or protest;
>
> 2) to vacate the judgment wholly or in part and remand the

---

[56] Civil Procedure Code, Art. 286.
[57] See Komissarov, Osipov, *supra* note 39, at 387.
[58] Civil Procedure Code, Art. 294.

case for a new trial in the court of first instance by a court composed of the same or different judges.

3) to vacate the judgment wholly or in part and to dismiss or discontinue the case;

4) to modify the judgment or render a new judgment without ordering a new trial, if the material facts of the case have been established on the basis of the available, as well as additionally submitted materials, which have been examined by the parties.

Grounds for vacating a court judgment by way of cassation are defined by Art. 306 of the Civil Procedure Code:

The grounds for vacating a judgment of a court of first instance and remanding the case for a new trial in the court of first instance shall be:

1) incomplete elucidation of the material facts of the case;

2) inadequate proof of material facts which the court considered to have been established;

3) a discrepancy between the court's conclusions, as set forth in the judgment, and the circumstances of the case;

4) violation or incorrect application of the rules of substantive law or procedure.

(b) Review by Way of Supervision

The decision of the court of cassation is not subject to further ordinary appeal and enters into legal force as soon as it is pronounced. Thereafter, review of a civil judgment is possible only on the basis of a protest of a procurator or a higher court chairperson (or their deputies) by way of judicial supervision. Procurators and court chairpersons may lodge protests on the basis of their own analysis of lower court decisions or by virtue of representations from interested parties. Although the parties cannot institute the judicial supervision proceedings, they have the right to ask the appropriate official to initiate such proceedings.

Supervisory review may be conducted by different courts. Cases originating in district courts may be reviewed by way of supervision by the presidiums of the supreme courts of the republics or regional courts of other "subjects" of the Russian Federation. After that they may again be reviewed by the Judicial Collegium for Civil Cases of the Supreme Court. Judgments of the

Judicial Collegium for Civil Cases of the Supreme Court may be reviewed by way of supervision by the Presidium of the Supreme Court.

When reviewing a case by way of supervision, the court considers only questions of law on the basis of materials available in the case. Although the supervisory instance may refuse to accept lower courts findings of fact, it has no power to establish new facts or take new evidence. As a general rule, the court verifies "the correctness of the application and interpretation of norms of material law and norms of procedural law by the courts of first and cassational instance" only within the limits of arguments contained in the protest. However, "in the interests of legality" the higher court may also go beyond the limits of the protest.[59]

The powers of the court considering a case by way of supervision in general are similar to those of the cassational court. Decisions, rulings or orders of any lower court may be vacated by way of supervision if the higher court establishes "incorrect application or interpretation of norms of material law" or "serious violations of norms of procedural law."[60] The court of supervisory instance may render a new judgment if there is no need to establish new facts or take new evidence.

An additional form of appeal is the appeal to review judgments that have entered into legal force upon discovery of new circumstances.[61] Circumstances which may lead to review of a judgment include, for example, criminal acts committed by the parties or judges during the proceedings and discovery of new material evidence. The Constitutional Court has indicated in a case concerning the Criminal Procedure Code that decisions of "inter-state organs concerned with the protection of human rights and freedoms" mentioned in Art. 46 of the Constitution may lead to domestic reexamination of previously decided cases.[62] It may well be argued that decisions of these organs concerning civil law cases may also lead to their domestic reexamination. A decision of "inter-state organs" may be considered as "a new circumstance" under the Civil Procedure Code.

***

The following case illustrates some of the procedural principles and rules discussed above.

[59] Civil Procedure Code, Art. 327.
[60] Civil Procedure Code, Art. 330.
[61] Civil Procedure Code, Arts. 333-337.
[62] See *Sobranie*, No. 7, item 701 (1996).

The Supreme Court: *XMX Hamburger Metall Handel GMBX v. Severo-Zapadnoe Customs Administration* (*BVS*, 1996, No. 1, p. 7)

The company "XMX Hamburger Metall Handel GMBX" brought suit in court against Severo-Zapadnoe Customs Administration requesting return of 100 tons of nickel and 25 tons of copper which the latter acquired under a sales contract with the closed joint-stock company "Riad" and which were detained by the customs officials.

The Procurator of the Northwest Regional Transport Procuracy intervened with a petition to declare the sale contract of the above metal goods null and void because it violates the requirements of the statute.

The Judicial Collegium for Civil Cases of the St. Petersburg City Court, having considered the case at first instance, dismissed the Procurator's petition and granted relief in the suit. On September 20, 1995, the Collegium for Civil Cases of the Supreme Court of the Russian Federation, having considered the case on the cassational appeal of the Customs Administration and the cassational protest of the Procurator of the Northwest Regional Customs Procuracy, vacated the judgment for the following reasons:

According to Art. 168 of the 1994 Civil Procedure Code of the Russian Federation a transaction not corresponding to the requirements of a statute or of other legal acts is void, unless the statute provides other consequences for the violation. . . The materials of the case indicate that on August 24, 1994 the representatives of the closed joint-stock company "Riad" and the German company "XMX Hamburger Metall Handel GMBX" entered into a contract for sale of 100 tons of nickel and 25 tons of copper. Art. 4 of Regulations "On Measures to Improve State Regulation of Export of Goods and Services," adopted by the Government of the Russian Federation on July 1, 1994, introduced a system of registration of contracts involving export of goods listed in the Annex to the Regulations with a view toward ensuring state control over the export of strategic materials. These goods may pass through customs only on the basis of registered contracts.

The customs officials have detained the shipment because they believe that the above metal goods fell under the category of strategic materials which could be shipped abroad only on the basis of registered contracts and because there was no proof that the contract in question had been registered. The Saint Petersburg City Court dismissed the Procurator's petition and granted relief in the suit requesting return of metal goods detained by the customs officials by pointing out that the contract under discussion was not a foreign trade contract envisioning export of materials; the representatives of the [German] company testified that they did not intend to export nickel and copper abroad; rather, they intended to use it on the territory of Russia.

However, the conclusions of the City Court cannot be considered as justified. During the hearing in the Collegium for Civil Cases of the Supreme Court of the Russian Federation, the representatives of the [German] company admitted that they had no contacts with enterprises or companies in the Russian Federation envisioning processing, transfer or use of the above nickel and copper on the Russian territory.

The materials in the casefile do not contain any admissible evidence. The court admitted as evidence photocopies of documents, including the contract of sale, and did not establish during the hearing the identity of the copies and the originals; the translation of documents from German into Russian was made by a person who was not warned of his responsibility under Art. 181 of the RSFSR Criminal Procedure Code,[63] for knowingly giving a false translation (as envisioned by Art. 152 of the Civil Procedure Code).

The court did not investigate whether the persons who signed the sales contract had the power to conclude the transaction, what was the price of the goods and whether the German buyer paid the relevant sum to the seller - the closed joint-stock company "Riad." Conclusions of the court concerning these matters are based on materials that have not been fully examined. The court accepted as evidence copies of documents confirming payment of money under the contract; these copies were not certified in the established procedure. The record of the hearing does not contain any evidence that the Court examined the originals of these documents. The parties to the contract submitted contradictory explanations as to the method of payment.

Because the court violated Arts. 14,[64] . . . 50, [65] 54[66] and 152[67]

[63] Under 1996 Criminal Code the responsibility for false translation is envisioned by Art. 307.

[64] Art. 14 provides: "While maintaining impartiality, the court shall ensure necessary conditions for the all- round and full elucidation of the facts of the case: explain their rights and duties to the persons taking part in the case, warn them of the consequences of taking or failing to take any procedural steps and assist them in enforcing their rights in cases envisioned by the present Code."

[65] Art. 50 provides: "Each party must prove those circumstances on which she relies as the basis of her claims or defenses. The court determines which circumstances have significance for the case, which party must prove them and proposes to discuss these circumstances even if the parties fail to mention them. Evidence is presented by the parties and other persons taking part in the case. If the evidence presented is insufficient, the court shall direct the parties and other persons taking part in the case to supply additional evidence or it shall collect such evidence on its own initiative."

[66] Art. 54 provides: "Circumstances of a case which according to statute must be proved by specified types of evidence may not be proved by any other means of proof whatsoever."

of the RSFSR Civil Procedure Code the judgment is vacated and remanded for a new trial.

QUESTIONS

1. The case was initiated by "XMX Hamburger Metall Handel GMBX." What was the purpose of the intervention petition filed by the Procurator of the Northwest Regional Transport Procuracy? Why was the Procurator able to intervene in a private law suit?

2. The court of first instance was the Judicial Collegium for Civil Cases of the St. Petersburg City Court - a second level court (St. Petersburg is a "subject" of the Russian Federation). Why would this court, and not one of the district courts in the city of St. Petersburg, have original jurisdiction over the dispute?

3. Who initiated cassational review of the case? The Procurator of the Northwest Regional Customs Procuracy was not a party to the trial court proceedings. Why was she or he able to lodge the cassational protest? What may be the justification for this intervention?

4. What does the case tell us about the cassational review proceedings in the Supreme Court?

5. Why did the Collegium for Civil Cases of the Supreme Court dismiss the evidence contained in the casefile?

6. What were the grounds for vacating the judgment in this case?

7. Under Art. 305(4) of the Civil Procedure Code, a court of cassation has the power "to modify the judgment or render a new judgment without ordering a new trial, if the material facts of the case have been established on the basis of the available, as well as additionally submitted materials, which have been examined by the parties." The Collegium for Civil Cases of the Supreme Court apparently took new evidence (statement of the representatives of the German company). Could the Collegium have rendered a new judgment instead of remanding the challenged judgment for a new trial?

15. Reopening of Default Judgments

Under Art. 157 of the Civil Procedure Code the court may render a

[67] Art. 152 provides: "The presiding judge shall warn the interpreter of his responsibility under Article 181 of the Criminal Code of the RSFSR for knowingly giving a false translation."

default judgment against the defendant if the defendant has been duly served, fails to appear and there is no information as to the causes of non-appearance or if the court considers the causes of non-appearance inadequate.

Default judgments handed down in the absence of the defendant may be reopened if the defaulting party proves within fifteen days that non-appearance was caused by circumstances beyond her or his control (such as *force majeure* or illness). The petition to reopen the default judgment must be submitted to the court which considered the case in the first hearing. The defendant may also submit all arguments supporting her or his position. If the court finds the causes of non-appearance adequate and if the defendant submits new evidence supporting his or her position, the court will set aside the default judgment and reopen the proceedings. In addition to a petition that a default judgments be set aside, the defaulting party also has the right to file a cassational appeal to a higher court.

16. Summary Proceedings

The Russian Civil Procedure Code provides for a kind of summary proceeding restricted to certain types of undisputed claims confirmed by documentary evidence. In cases where claims are based on certain written documents (such as notarized contracts or promissory notes) creditors may obtain an enforceable court order (which is not considered to be a formal judgment) within a short period of time. Summary proceedings leading to a court order do not resolve disputes about questions of law. The court simply confirms the existing substantive law obligations between the creditor and the debtor. As a result, there are no plaintiffs and defendants; the parties are still considered to be creditors and debtors. The judge issues the order on the basis of the available documentary evidence without any court hearing. As a result, the debtor has no opportunity to present her or his objections.

However, once the court order has been issued, the debtor has the opportunity to challenge it in the same court.[68] If valid objections are submitted, the court will vacate the order. After that, the aggrieved party may still initiate normal proceedings by filing a suit with the same court.

17. Special Proceedings

The Civil Procedure Code draws a distinction between contested or adversary and special proceedings. Contested proceedings involve a civil or administrative dispute between at least two parties. By contrast, special proceedings do not refer to relationships between different parties; they

[68] Civil Procedure Code, Art. 125.10.

involve only one person and that person's legal situation. Parties may seek a judicial determination of their legal situation in anticipation of future needs.

Under the Civil Procedure Code special proceedings may be initiated by the interested party in several categories of cases. These include cases concerning the establishment of facts having legal relevance (for example, the fact of being in *de facto* marital relation, the fact of the death of a person or the fact of acceptance of an estate in cases of inheritance), declaration of a person as missing or dead or restoration of rights under lost bearer documents.[69]

There are no opposing parties in special proceedings; there is only the person introducing the request. As a result, the proceedings tend to be rather simple. If the court discovers that there is an actual dispute, it discontinues the hearing and explains to the interested parties that they have the right to bring an action according to the general rules of civil procedure.[70]

18. Provisional Relief

Provisional relief ordered by the court is an important means of protecting the interests of the parties to an action. The court may issue a provisional relief upon the request of an interested party or on its own initiative[71] in all cases where it is necessary to assure the future enforcement of an eventual judgment in the party's favor. Provisional relief is particularly important in view of possible delays in the proceedings.

Relief can include the imposition of an attachment of money or property in the possession of the defendant or a prohibition on the defendant doing certain acts.[72] Provisional relief orders are executed by the same procedure established for the execution of judgments. The defendant has the right to file separate appeals of any decision on questions of taking security for an action.[73] If the claim is dismissed, the defendant is entitled to compensation from the plaintiff for the losses caused the defendant by the provisional relief.[74]

---

[69] Civil Procedure Code, Art. 245.

[70] Civil Procedure Code, Art. 246.

[71] Under the 1997 Draft Civil Procedure Code the court takes measures to secure an action only on the application of persons taking part in a case. There is no provision allowing the court to take preliminary measures on its own initiative.

[72] Civil Procedure Code, Art. 134.

[73] Civil Procedure Code, Art. 139.

[74] Civil Procedure Code, Art. 140.

19. Execution of Judgments

Traditionally judgments were executed by "execution officers" attached to "ordinary" courts. The traditional system proved to be absolutely unsatisfactory in the new political and economic environment. The "execution officers" lacked the power and expertise to enforce judgments against powerful private entities. As a result, the enforcement of judgments became one of the most serious problems for the Russian judiciary.

In 1997 the Russian parliament enacted two important laws aimed at facilitating the execution of court judgments. The 1997 Law on Enforcement Procedure[75] provides for a comprehensive set of rules governing the enforcement of court decisions. The 1997 Law on Court Bailiffs[76] establishes a new paramilitary enforcement agency within the Ministry of Justice. The 1997 Law on Court Bailiffs grants the "execution bailiffs" broad powers to enforce courts judgments.

If a losing party fails to satisfy a judgment voluntarily, the winner may take action to enforce it. Judgments are executed by the "execution bailiffs" upon receiving a "writ of execution" issued by the court. Money judgments are usually executed by withdrawing the amount due from the bank account of the losing party. Employed persons may be ordered by the court to pay a percentage of their wages to the winner until the judgment is satisfied. If the loser has property, the "execution bailiffs" may seize nonexempt property and sell it in order to satisfy the judgment. Property taken in execution may be sold in special shops or by public auction. Proceeds form public sales are given to the winner in order to satisfy the claim. The defendant has the right to claim any surplus. If the defendant fails to meet an obligation to perform a certain act, enforcement may become indirect: the winner may have the act performed at the loser's expense.

If a judgment for the recovery of property has been rendered, the defendant may be ordered by the judge to deliver movables to the plaintiff or vacate immovables. If the defendant fails to do so, the property may be forcibly taken by the "execution bailiff."

A person who disobeys a judgment may be liable to a party for damages. Judges may impose fines on citizens or officials for failure to comply with a judgment. Criminal prosecution of officials for failure to comply with the judgment is also possible.

---

[75] See *Sobranie*, No. 30, item 3591 (1997).
[76] See *Sobranie*, No. 30, item 3590 (1997).

C. Proceedings in Arbitration (Commercial) Courts

The adoption of the 1995 Arbitration Procedure Code[77] resulted in the official recognition that proceedings in arbitration (commercial) courts[78] require a separate set of procedural rules. There is some disagreement among Russian commentators as to whether civil procedure and arbitration procedure are entirely independent of each other. While some Russian commentators contend that civil procedure encompasses both traditional civil procedure and arbitration procedure,[79] the majority appears to believe that arbitration procedure constitutes an independent area of procedural law.[80]

The most important differences between "ordinary" court procedure and arbitration (commercial) court procedure are as follows:

1) In arbitration courts of first instance cases are heard by a single judge or three professional judges. In some arbitration courts cases may be tried at first instance by panels composed of one professional judge and two arbitration assessors. In contrast to lay assessors in "ordinary" courts arbitration assessors are required to possess specialized knowledge and experience in the sphere of business and commerce.

2) The Procuracy may file suits in the arbitration court only if it is necessary to protect "state and public interests."[81] Procuracy representation of individual aggrieved parties is allowed only if the respondent's actions infringed upon state and public interests.

3) While in ordinary courts there is a division between the "contested procedure," which is initiated by a statement of claim, and the "special" procedure, initiated by a petition, arbitration procedure is unified. Although the establishment of certain facts having legal significance may be within the jurisdiction of arbitration courts, all arbitration proceedings are initiated by a statement of claim.

4) Neither the Civil Procedure Code nor the Arbitration Procedure Code requires representation of parties by professional attorneys. However, in contrast to civil proceedings in ordinary courts, where there is no general duty for the plaintiff to formulate legal arguments in support of the claim when

[77] See *supra* note 9.

[78] The system of arbitration (commercial) courts was discussed in Chapter III.

[79] See, e.g., *Grazhdanskii protsess* (Civil Procedure) 14 (1993).

[80] See R.E. Gukasian, V.F. Tarasenko eds., *Arbitrazhnyi protsess* (Arbitration Procedure) 7 (1996); Komissarov, Osipov, *supra* note 39, at 13.

[81] Arbitration Procedure Code, Arts. 4, 32 and 41.

filing the suit, statements of claims submitted to arbitration courts must set forth not only factual but also legal grounds for the claim.[82]

5) In general, arbitration court proceedings are less formal than "ordinary" court proceedings. This is largely due to the fact that the arbitration courts are the descendants of the former *State Arbitrazh*, a system of quasi-judicial bodies that settled economic disputes between state enterprises in accordance with simplified rules of procedure.

Although the 1995 Arbitration Procedure Code introduced many standard rules of civil procedure, some of them were adopted in a simplified form. Thus, in ordinary courts a court secretary keeps a record of the judicial session. According to Art. 123 of the Arbitration Procedure Code the record is kept by the judge or one of the judges on the bench.[83] The record itself would be even shorter than the record of an ordinary court. According to Art. 123 the record is supposed to reflect only the most important developments or procedural steps, such as statements of the parties, testimony of witnesses and experts, and rulings of the court on procedural motions made in the courtroom.

6) The principle of orality in court proceedings is applied in arbitration procedure less distinctly than in ordinary court proceedings. Arbitration procedure is dominated by written communications. Procedural motions are usually submitted in writing. Under Arts. 69 and 70 of the Arbitration Procedure Code, a judge may propose that the parties or witnesses submit their statements in writing. Although such written statements do not replace oral examination, Arts. 69 and 70 provide a good illustration of the general emphasis on written communications.

7) In certain cases established by federal law, a petition to the arbitration court is possible only if "an interested person" has first made an

---

[82] Arbitration Procedure Code, Art. 102.

[83] The introduction of the arbitration court record has been hailed as a new guarantee of the rights of the parties to arbitration proceedings. See V.F. Yakovlev, M.K. Yukov, *Vstupitel'naya statia* (Introductory Article), *v Kommentarii k Arbitrazhnomu Protsessual'nomu Kodeksu Rossiiskoi Federatsii* (Commentary to the Arbitration Procedure Code of the Russian Federation) XXVI (1995). However, the procedure envisioned by the Arbitration Procedure Code has been subject to much criticism. Critics point out that a judge who keeps notes of the proceedings is not able also to fully concentrate on the legal aspects of the case. Furthermore, the content of the record of the hearing may reflect the preferences of the judge acting as a court clerk. See V.M. Shestuk, *Novye polozheniya Arbitrazhnogo Protsessual'nogo Kodeksa Rossiiskoi Federatsii* (New Provisions of the Arbitration Procedure Code of the Russian Federation) 64 (1996).

attempt to resolve the dispute by using "preliminary extra-judicial procedures." Preliminary extra-judicial settlement of a dispute in the form of direct presentation of the claim to the debtor is envisioned by several codes, including the Merchant Shipping Code, Air Code and Railway Charter. The Arbitration Procedure Code imposes serious sanctions on parties who fail to resort to the preliminary dispute settlement procedures: the arbitration judge has the right to return the statement of claim without considering it on the merits or to dismiss it.[84]

8) In general, arbitration judges are not as active as their "ordinary" court counterparts. While preparing a case for hearing, it is only in the most complex of cases that the arbitration judge will summon the parties and question them in detail about their positions and the available evidence. Arbitration courts have no express power to go beyond the limits of the claim filed by the plaintiff.

At the same time, arbitration courts have been granted the power to deny a party the right to withdraw the suit, reduce the amount claimed or settle it where doing so would "contradict the law or other normative legal acts or violate the rights and lawful interests of other persons."[85]

9) The appeal procedure in the arbitration court system differs from that in the "ordinary" court system. There is a right to appeal in the form of an appellate complaint to appellate panel of the same arbitration court that considered the case at first instance. This arrangements raises questions about the objectivity and impartiality of the appellate panel judges. Both first instance arbitration judges and appellate judges are members of the same court and work closely together. It may therefore be difficult for at least some of them to remain impartial.

Because appellate judges are members of the same arbitration court that considered the case at first instance, an appellate arbitration court always reconsiders the case as a whole and renders a new decision. It has no power to send the case for reconsideration.

An appellate court may receive new evidence on the factual issues in the case if the interested party proves that it was not able to present it to the

---

[84] Arbitration Procedure Code, Arts. 87, 108.

[85] There are cases confirming that arbitration courts rely on these powers. See, for example, *SU-180 v. Aeroflot -Russian International Airlines, VVAS*, 1997, No. 11, p. 73 (The Supreme Arbitration Court rejected a voluntary settlement between the parties because it violated property rights of a third party).

court of first instance.[86] However, the appellate court cannot consider new demands which have not been submitted to the trial-level arbitration court.

10) Additional right of appeal by way of cassation to arbitration courts of the circuits is also available. A panel of three or more professional judges reviews decisions of lower courts which have entered into legal force. Proceedings at this stage are not de novo. In principle, federal arbitration courts of the circuits are supposed to decide only questions of law. However, they often reexamine the whole written record of the file. The circuit court may always refuse to accept lower courts findings of fact and substitute their own fact-finding under the guise of law finding by determining that the lower court decision is "unfounded."[87]

Circuit courts may not only send the case back to the lower court if the ruling is "unfounded," but also may issue a new judgment. Thus, they enjoy extremely broad supervisory powers.

11) In the arbitration court system, review by way of supervision is considered to be exceptional. The right to lodge protests against decisions of lower courts has been granted only to the Chairman of the Supreme Arbitration Court, the Procurator General and their deputies.

Cases on supervisory review are reviewed by the Presidium of the Supreme Arbitration Court. As the court of supervisory instance, the Supreme Arbitration Court has the right to review the case as a whole, i.e. to reconsider not only legal but also factual issues. However, review of factual issues of the case is limited to facts already established by the lower court judgments. Although the Supreme Arbitration Court may refuse to accept lower courts findings of fact, it has no power to establish new facts or take new evidence.

---

[86]The Supreme Arbitration Court ruled that the appellate instance must always review the reasons for non-submission of evidence to the court of first instance. New evidence will not be accepted by the appellate court if it establishes that the interested party acted in bad faith. See *Ruling of the Plenary Session of the Supreme Arbitration Court On the Application of the Arbitration Procedure Code of the Russian Federation During Consideration of Cases by the Appellate Instances, VVAS*, 1997, No. 12, p. 12, 15.

[87]Judicial practice indicates that arbitration courts do substitute their own fact-finding under the guise of law finding. Thus, in *Firma "STEK" v. Tcheliabmashopttorg (VVAS*, 1997, No. 5, p. 109) the Supreme Arbitration Court upheld the judgment of the federal arbitration court of the Ural circuit which vacated a judgment of the lower arbitration court because the file of the case did not contain any evidence on damages claimed by the plaintiff. The Supreme Arbitration Court noted that judicial action that is not supported by sufficient evidence is illegal.

The Presidium of the Supreme Court has the power to vacate the judgments of lower courts and send the case for new consideration and the power to vacate the judgments and render new judgments. New judgments are rendered only in cases where there is no need to assemble new evidence.

13) Prior to the enactment of the 1997 Law on Enforcement Procedure[88] and the 1997 Law on Court Bailiffs[89] the arbitration courts experienced the same problems with respect to execution of judgments as "ordinary" courts.[90] The enactment of comprehensive legislation on the enforcement of court decisions will facilitate execution of arbitration court judgments.

Arbitration court decisions are subject to execution in the same manner as "ordinary" court judgments. With the exception of money judgments, arbitration decisions are executed by the "execution bailiffs." The execution is governed by the general rules of the Civil Procedure Code and the 1997 Law on the Enforcement Procedure.

Money judgments of arbitration courts are commonly enforced through garnishment of bank accounts. Arbitration courts issue orders directing a bank holding the losing party's monetary assets to pay that money to the winning party directly. Upon receiving the order banks are obliged to withdraw the amount due from the bank account of the debtor. This procedure is fairly effective because banks which fail to comply with an arbitration court order are subject to heavy monetary penalties. Nonperforming banks may also lose their licences.

D. Resolving Disputes By Private Arbitration

Russian civil procedure provides for private arbitration as a less time-consuming and often less expensive alternative method of dispute resolution. The general right to private commercial arbitration is recognized by both the 1964 Civil Procedure Code and the 1995 Arbitration Procedure Code. Thus, Art. 23 of the 1995 Arbitration Procedure Code provides that "a dispute falling within the jurisdiction of the arbitration court that has arisen or one that might arise from civil law relations may be transferred to an arbitration

[88] See *supra* note 74.

[89] See *supra* note 75.

[90] See Program to Increase the Effectiveness of the Activities of the Arbitration Courts in the Russian Federation For the Years 1997-2000, *VVAS*, 1997, No. 11, at 7, 10 ("At this stage the execution of judgments of arbitration courts represents the weakest aspect of their activity").

tribunal for resolution by agreement between the parties at any time prior to the adoption of the decision by the arbitration court."

Domestic private arbitration is governed by two normative acts: Rules on Arbitration Tribunals (Annex 3 to the 1964 Civil Procedure Code) and the 1992 Temporary Regulation on Commercial Arbitration for the Resolution of Economic Disputes.[91] These acts govern different types of private arbitration and often conflict with each other. A comprehensive law that would establish a unified set of rules for all types of domestic private arbitration is still under discussion.[92] A separate set of procedural rules governs international commercial arbitration.[93]

Under Art. 1 of the Rules on Arbitration Tribunals[94] parties may submit any dispute arising between them to arbitration except disputes arising out of labor or family relations. An agreement to submit a dispute to private arbitration (arbitration clause) must be concluded in writing. The agreement to arbitrate can be concluded either before any dispute has arisen or after it has arisen. The scope of the agreement and the procedure for arbitration depends entirely on the parties' will. However, Annex 3 to the 1964 Civil Procedure Code contains certain basic rules concerning the nomination of arbitrators and the procedure to be followed. If parties have agreed to submit their dispute to arbitration, the "ordinary" court will refuse to accept any claim regarding that dispute.[95]

Arbitration awards in arbitration between private citizens are executed on the basis of a writ of execution issued by "ordinary" courts. Courts issuing the writ of execution have rather broad powers to review a dispute that has been settled by arbitration. Courts have the power to review both questions of law and fact and may set aside an award which contravenes substantive or procedural law.

The 1992 Temporary Regulation on Commercial Arbitration for the Resolution of Economic Disputes governs private arbitration of economic disputes that would normally fall within the jurisdiction of state arbitration (commercial) courts. Under the 1992 Temporary Regulation, parties may submit any dispute arising between them to private arbitration except disputes

---

[91] See *Vedomosty RF*, No. 30, item 1790 (1992).

[92] For details, see E.A. Vinogradova, *Treteiskii sud* (Commercial Arbitration) 327-328 (1997).

[93] International commercial arbitration will be discussed in Chapter VIII.

[94] 1964 Civil Procedure Code, Annex 3.

[95] Civil Procedure Code, Art. 129.

arising out of administrative relations.[96] If parties have agreed to submit their dispute to private arbitration, the state arbitration court will terminate or dismiss proceedings in a case.[97]

Private arbitration awards in economic disputes involving companies and businesspeople are enforced by arbitration courts. State arbitration courts issuing execution orders have also been granted broad powers to review the awards of private arbitration tribunals. Under Art. 26 of the 1992 Temporary Regulation, an arbitration (commercial) court may refuse to issue an order for the enforcement of a private arbitration decision in the following cases:

> If the paries did not reach agreement on the submission of the dispute to arbitration;
>
> if the composition of the arbitration tribunal or the procedure for resolving the dispute was not in accordance with the parties' agreement to arbitrate;
>
> if the party against whom an arbitration award was rendered was not given proper notice of the date for arbitration proceedings or for another reason was not able to present his case;
>
> if the dispute arose in the sphere of administration and was not capable of settlement by arbitration.

It is important to note that one of the possible objections may be the claim of the losing party that "the composition of the arbitration tribunal. . . was not in accordance with the parties' agreement to arbitrate." This provisions is often misused in cases of ad hoc arbitration because under Art. 5 of the 1992 Temporary Regulation, failure of one of the parties to appoint an arbitrator may serve as a ground for terminating the arbitration agreement. Practice indicates that these and other procedural grounds are often raised by the losing parties at the enforcement stage.[98]

The power of state arbitration courts, however, is not restricted to procedural aspects of the case. Although at first sight it appears that the state

---

[96] 1992 Temporary Regulation, Art. 26.

[97] Arbitration Procedure Code, Arts. 85, 87.

[98] See, for example, *Vostokburvod v. Sibneftegeofizika, VVAS,* 1997, No. 7, p. 7 (The Supreme Arbitration Court quashed the ruling of the Arbitration Court of Novosibirsk Region which issued a writ of execution because the casefile did not contain any materials indicating that the private commercial arbitration tribunal "observed the requirements concerning the formation of the tribunal, equality of the parties during the consideration of the case or took into account the interests of the plaintiff who did not participate in the proceedings").

arbitration courts have no power to review private arbitration awards on the merits,[99] a closer analysis of Art. 26 of the 1992 Temporary Regulation indicates that it allows state arbitration courts to conduct substantive review of private arbitration decisions. Art. 26 expressly provides that the state arbitration court may remand the case for reconsideration by the private arbitration tribunal that rendered the award if it establishes that "the award is not in accordance with legislation or was issued on the basis of unexamined material." Substantive review of private arbitration awards by state arbitration courts may thus deal with questions of both law and fact. Such an extensive involvement of state arbitration courts in the private arbitration process discourages private arbitration since the main reason for resorting to arbitration is to avoid the problems associated with courts.

Notwithstanding these procedural drawbacks, practice indicates that many business organizations prefer to turn to private arbitration to resolve their economic disputes.[100] There are several important permanent private arbitration tribunals, such as an arbitration tribunal established by the Association of Russian Banks,[101] an arbitration tribunal sponsored by the Russian Union of Lawyers[102] and an arbitration commission at the Moscow Interbank Currency Exchange.[103]

In contrast, private Russian citizens almost never utilize the institution of private arbitration.[104] Major reasons for this are the lack of information about the advantages of private arbitration and the absence of permanent arbitration institutions for arbitration among citizens. These institutions have not been established because under Art. 8 the Rules on Arbitration Tribunals (Annex 3 to the 1964 Civil Procedure Code) private arbiters resolving disputes

---

[99] Some writers claim that Art. 26 of the 1992 Temporary Regulation is based on the principle that "revisions of the decisions of private arbitration tribunals by state arbitration courts are not allowed." See M.K. Treushnikov ed., *Arbitrazhnyi protsess* (Arbitration Procedure) 337 (1995).

[100] For details, see E.A. Vinogradova, *Al'ternativnoe razreshenie sporov* (Alternative Dispute Resolution), *VVAS,* 1997, No. 8, p. 89.

[101] See *Regulation on Arbitration Tribunal of the Association of Russian Banks,* reprinted in Vinogradova, *supra* note 92, at 214. The Arbitration Tribunal sponsored by the Association of Russian Banks appears to be the most active and successful private arbitration tribunal. For details, see L. Balaian, *Treteiiski sud Assotsiatsii Rossiiskikh Bankov: Itogi pervogo goda raboty* (Arbitration Tribunal of the Association of Russian Banks: Results of the First Year of Operation), *VVAS,* 1994, No. 10, at 117.

[102] See *Rules of the Commercial Court at the Union of Lawyers,* reprinted in Vinogradova, *supra* note 92, at 248.

[103] See *Rules of the Arbitration Commission of the Moscow Interbank Currency Exchange,* reprinted in Id., at 284.

[104] See Treushnikov, *supra* note 23, at 455.

between citizens cannot charge arbitration fees.[105] Russian commentators agree that one of the major goals of the proposed new legislation on domestic private arbitration is to change these outdated rules and procedures.[106]

QUESTION

How does the private arbitration in Russia differ from practice of arbitration in the US?

---

[105] Id., at 455-456.
[106] Id., at 456.

CHAPTER VIII

PRIVATE INTERNATIONAL LAW

A. Introduction

The internationalization of markets leads to numerous contacts, international transactions and transnational litigation among parties coming from different countries. As a result, lawyers have to deal with numerous cases involving issues of private international law.

The Russian concept of private international law includes several areas of law dealing with cases involving parties, transactions or litigation that concern more than one country. The first broad area of the law deals with international conflict of laws. The second area is the law dealing with international civil procedure. It includes questions concerning jurisdiction of Russian courts over disputes involving foreign parties, determination of the content of foreign law, recognition and enforcement of foreign judgments and arbitration awards, and international commercial arbitration. This Chapter will therefore cover basic principles relating to international conflict of laws, issues concerning application and determination of foreign law in Russian courts, jurisdiction of Russian courts over disputes involving foreign parties and recognition and enforcement of foreign judgments and arbitration awards. The last section will deal with international commercial arbitration in Russia.

Rules concerning international conflict of laws in different areas of law may be found in several major codes (for example, the Family Code). Codification of the basic principles of international conflict of laws is expected to be completed by the third part of the new Civil Code which is still under discussion. In the meantime, the most important applicable principles are to be found in the Fundamentals of Civil Legislation of the USSR and Union Republics of May 31, 1991[1] which continue to be the main source of law on international conflict of laws. In general, the 1991 Fundamentals reflect contemporary trends in private international law among European countries, many of which had enacted special codifying acts on private international law. The third part of the new Civil Code is expected to reflect the same trends and tendencies. We will discuss some of the proposed new rules by relying on the

[1] See *Vedomosty SSSR*, No. 26, item 733 (1991) (hereafter 1991 Fundamentals).

1996 Model Civil Code (Part III) adopted by the Inter-Parliamentary Assembly of the Commonwealth of Independent States.[2]

The law on international civil procedure has not been codified in any single act. Rules concerning recognition and enforcement of foreign court judgments and arbitration awards are contained in the 1964 Civil Procedure Code and the 1993 Law on International Commercial Arbitration.[3] This Chapter will also rely on the 1997 Draft Civil Procedure Code[4] as an indication of the proposed changes in the rules governing international civil procedure.

It is important to note that Russia is party to several multilateral conventions on private international law, including the 1980 United Nations Convention on Contracts for the International Sale of Goods,[5] the 1958 New York Convention on the Recognition and Enforcement of Foreign Arbitral Awards[6] and the 1961 European Convention on International Commercial Arbitration.[7] Between member states of the Commonwealth of Independent States, an important international source of applicable rules is the 1992 Agreement on the Procedure for Resolving Disputes Relating to Economic Activities.[8] Russia also concluded numerous bilateral conventions with other states which contain rules of private international law. These international treaties constitute an important source of Russian law, which may override contrary domestic regulations. This follows from Art. 15 (4) of the 1993 Constitution which provides that "the international treaties of the Russian Federation shall constitute an integral part of its legal system. If an international treaty of the Russian Federation establishes other rules than those stipulated by the law, the rules of the international treaty shall apply."

B. International Conflict of Laws

International choice of law rules form the core element of private international law in Russia. As noted earlier, rules governing the matter may

---

[2] See *Grazhdanskii kodeks. Tschast' tret'ia. Model'* (Civil Code. Third Part. Model), *Iformatsionnyi bulleten'* (Informational Bulletin), 1996, No. 10, p. 72 (hereafter 1996 Model Civil Code (Part III)).

[3] See *Vedomosty RF*, No. 32, item 1240 (1993).

[4] *Grazhdanskii protsessual'nyi kodeks Rossiiskoi Federatsii (Proekt)* (Draft Civil Procedure Code of the Russian Federation) (1997) (hereafter 1997 Draft Civil Procedure Code).

[5] UN Doc. A/CONF. 97/18 (1980).

[6] See 330 UNTS 38.

[7] See 484 UNTS 364.

[8] See *VVAS*, 1992, No. 1, p. 114.

be found in international conventions on international choice of law and domestic Russian law. There are also several international conventions providing uniform substantive rules governing international transactions. The most important example is the 1980 United Nations Convention on Contracts for the International Sale of Goods.[9] The 1980 Convention provides uniform substantive law governing many sales contracts between parties doing business in participating states. Where it applies, the 1980 Convention makes choice of law by and large irrelevant.

However, it is important to keep in mind that multilateral efforts to unify the law of international transactions have so far failed to produce substantive rules in many traditional areas of private law. A lawyer dealing with private international cases involving Russian parties must also keep in mind that Russia may not be a party to a particular convention. This means that in areas not covered by international conventions one still needs to turn to Russian domestic sources containing choice of law rules.

As in other civil law countries, the principal objective of the Russian choice of law rules is to determine what law is most appropriate to determine the status or rights of private litigants. The traditional territorial criteria - nationality and domicile - are often used to achieve this result even in cases where the choice of law does not appear to provide the best substantive solution in the individual case. This approach differs from the predominantly "value oriented" American approach which emphasizes considerations like state interests or "better law" in terms of substantive results.[10]

1. Natural Persons

Russian private international law applies to foreigners the same body of law applicable to Russians. Art. 160 of the 1991 Fundamentals states that foreign citizens and stateless persons enjoy civil law capacity in Russia equally with Russian citizens. At the same time, the 1991 Fundamentals envision the possibility of certain exceptions that may be established by statutes. Limitations may be imposed by way of retaliation against citizens of those states that restrict the rights and freedoms of Russian citizens (this rule also applies to juridical persons).

The national regime granted to foreigners means that as a rule they enjoy the same legal capacity as Russian citizens. Under Art. 160 of the 1991 Fundamentals, civil dispositive legal capacity of foreign citizens and stateless persons with respect to legal transactions performed in Russia and obligations

---

[9] *Supra* note 5.
[10] See generally Restatement (Second) of Conflict of Laws (1971).

arising as a consequence of causing harm in Russia are determined according to Russian law. Thus a person who lacks civil dispositive legal capacity under the law of the country of which she is a national is still regarded as having such capacity in Russia with respect to transactions performed in Russia. The recognition of a person as lacking legal capacity or having limited legal capacity in Russia is also subject to Russian law.

For all other purposes the 1991 Fundamentals apply the nationality principle: the civil dispositive legal capacity of a foreign citizen is determined in accordance with the law of the country of which she or he is a citizen. The 1991 Fundamentals emphasize the nationality criterion because it connects a person with a particular national legal system and therefore justifies a presumption that subjecting an individual to its power is highly appropriate. The civil dispositive legal capacity of a stateless person is determined by the law of the country in which she or he has a permanent place of residence.

Nationality or domicile are determined according to the law of the country the nationality or domicile of which is claimed by the party.

2. Juridical Persons

While many European countries insist on applying the law of the "real seat" of management of legal entities, the 1991 Fundamentals adopt a formalistic approach based on the principle of incorporation. Under Art. 161 of the 1991 Fundamentals the civil legal capacity of foreign juridical persons is determined in accordance with "the law of the country where the juridical person is founded." Under the principle of incorporation, a juridical person, such as corporation, formed under foreign law and having its registered seat abroad is recognized as such even if its "real seat" is in Russia. This principle also means that the corporate structure and the rights and duties of governing bodies within the company are governed by the law of the country where it is incorporated. Another important consequence of this rule is that certain types of legal entities may be recognized in Russia even if some of them are unknown to Russian law.

It should also be noted that although under the 1991 Fundamentals legal capacity of foreign juridical entities is governed by the law of the country where they are incorporated, foreign juridical persons may not invoke the limitations of the powers of representation of its organ or representative that are unknown to the law of the country where the organ or representative of the foreign juridical person is performing the transaction. This principle protects the interests of domestic juridical persons entering into transactions with foreign parties in Russia.

3. Property

Under Art. 164 of the 1991 Fundamentals property rights in movable and immovable property are subject to the law of the place where the property is located. Property rights with respect to vehicles subject to state registration in the relevant registers is determined by the law of the country where the vehicle is registered. The creation and termination of the right of ownership in property is generally governed by the law of the country where the property is located at the time when the act or other circumstance serving as the basis for the creation and termination of the right of ownership took place. This means that under the Russian law the principle of *lex rei sitae* determines which things may be the object of the right of ownership, the scope and content of the rights and the creation, transfer and termination of the right of ownership.

At the same time, questions of property law may be distinguished from the underlying contractual relationships. Under the 1991 Fundamentals the creation and termination of the right of ownership in a property serving as an object of a legal transaction is determined in accordance with the law of the place where the transaction was performed unless otherwise established by agreement of the parties. This means that if the parties to a contract involving transfer of property fail to agree which law will apply, the principle *lex loci contractus* will govern the choice of law. For instance, the contract for the sale of a house in Germany between two Russian nationals domiciled in Russia would be governed by Russian law as the law applicable to the contractual relations. However, the transfer of the house will still be governed by the *lex rei sitae*. This is due to the fact that legal status of immovable property is usually recorded in written documents and land registers of the country where it is located.

Because formal requirements for the transfer of immovable property have a public policy component, contracts concerning immovable property have to meet the mandatory requirements of the *les rei sitae*. The 1996 Model Civil Code (Part III) takes this factor into account in a separate clause concerning the form of transactions concerning immovable property. Under Art. 1216 of the 1996 Model Civil Code (Part III) the form of a transaction concerning immovable property must meet the formal requirements of the law of the country where immovables are located.

International practice indicates that many difficult questions arise in situations where the subject of a legal transaction are goods in transit. It is a matter of daily practice in international trade that transactions are made with regard to goods in transit from one country to another. Because at the moment of the conclusion of the transaction the parties do not know the actual *situs* of goods, which may be carried, for example, from Saint Petersburg to London, they cannot apply the law of the *situs*. In view of this, Russian law provides that the rights of ownership in property in transit under a foreign economic transaction is determined by the law of the country from which it was shipped unless otherwise established by agreement of the parties. This means that the parties may still select, for example, either the law of the country of destination or the law applicable to the underlying legal transaction.

If the owner files a claim for the protection of proprietary right her rights are determined, at her choice, either in accordance with the law of the country where the property is located, by the law of the country where the claim is filed in court, or by the law of the country where the vehicle is registered.

The 1996 Model Civil Code (Part III) contains a separate clause dealing with intellectual property.[11] It follows the territoriality doctrine for intellectual property. Intellectual property rights are governed by the law of the country where protection of these rights is sought. Contracts involving intellectual property rights are subject to the law determined in accordance with the choice of law rules governing contracts.

4. Contracts

Russian law concerning international conflict of laws recognizes broad party autonomy in determining the applicable law. In general, the parties are completely free to choose the country's law they want to be applied. No connection is required between the contract, the parties or the dispute and the law they have chosen or are going to choose. In addition, there is no time limit for the choice of law agreement: the parties are free to make their choice until the time of judgment.

It is important to keep in mind, however, that in certain situations, including those affecting foreign investment, the application of Russian law may be mandatory. Mandatory rules embody important and imperative principles or policies that cannot be displaced by any other law chosen by the parties. Many rules of public law, such as rules governing export or import controls, are mandatory. In these areas, a contractual clause providing for the applicability of foreign laws may be declared invalid by a Russian court resolving the dispute.

(a) The Concept of a Foreign Economic Transaction

Under Art. 166 of the 1991 Fundamentals, only parties to a "foreign

[11] 1996 Model Civil Code (Part III), Art. 1232.

economic transaction" have the right to choose applicable foreign law and, by choosing foreign law, exclude the application of Russian law. However, Russian law does not contain any definition of a "foreign economic transaction" or of a "foreign trade transaction." While there are different doctrinal opinions on the matter,[12] practice tends to rely on one basic criterion, contained, among other places, in Art. 1 of the 1980 United Nations Convention on Contracts for the International Sale of Goods:[13] when the places of business of the parties are in different states. Under this approach, different *nationalities* of the parties do not automatically make a contract concluded between them a "foreign economic transaction." As a result, the applicability of foreign law, even in cases where the pertinent clauses to that effect have been included in the contract, may be excluded. In cases, where a party has more than one place of business, "the place of business" for these purposes would be that which has the closest relationship to the contract and its performance.[14]

(b) Applicable Law

If the parties fail to agree on the choice of law, Art. 166 of the 1991 Fundamentals defines the applicable law for certain types of contracts. In determining the applicable law Russia follows the doctrine of "characteristic performance" as the connecting factor. "Characteristic performance" means the performance that is characteristic of a particular type of contract. Because of the different specific content of different types of contracts, this key element cannot be the same in each type. For a large group of contracts the 1991 Fundamentals uses a common key element: where the person or company who, as obligor, carries out "the characteristic performance," is founded, domiciled or carries out its main activity.

In other cases, where the residence of the performing party is not relevant enough from the point of view of "characteristic performance," the 1991 Fundamentals rely on other connecting factors. Thus, contracts on

---

[12] For details see I.S. Zykin, *Vneshneekonomitcheskie operatsii: Pravo I praktika* (Foreign Economic Transactions: Law and Practice) 63-74 (1994).

[13] See *supra* note 5.

[14] Cf. Art. 10 of the 1980 United Nations Convention on Contracts for the International Sale of Goods (*supra* note 5) which states:

"For the purposes of this Convention:

(a) if a party has more than one place of business, the place of business is that which has the closest relationship to the contract and its performance, having regard to the circumstances known to or contemplated by the parties at any time before or at the conclusion of the contract;

(b) if a party does not have a place of business, reference is to be made to his habitual residence."

production cooperation are governed by the law of the country where the relevant activity is carried out or the results envisioned by the contract are achieved.

The 1991 Fundamentals also establish an auxiliary norm for complex contracts that do not fall under any of the categories listed in Art. 166. Such contracts are governed by the law of the country where the party, whose execution is of decisive importance for the terms of contract, is founded, domiciled or where it carries out its main activity.

(c) Statutory Provisions: The 1991 Fundamentals of Civil Legislation

Art. 166. Obligations Under Foreign Economic Transactions

1. The rights and duties of the parties under foreign economic transactions shall be determined by the law of the country chosen by the parties when performing a transaction or pursuant to subsequent agreement.

If there is no agreement between the parties as regards applicable law, the laws of the country shall apply where the party is founded, domiciled or carries out its main activity, acting as:

1) the seller - in a purchase and sale contract;

2) the lessor - in a contract for the lease of property;

3) the licensor - in a license contract on exclusive or analogous rights;

4) the keeper - in a storage contract;

5) the commission agent - in a contract of commission;

6) the agent - in a contracts of agency;

7) the carrier - in a contract of carriage;

8) the forwarding agent - in a forwarding contract;

9) the insurer - in a contract of insurance;

10) the creditor - in a contract of credit;

11) the donor - in a contract of donation;

12) the guarantor - in a contracts of guarantee;

13) the depositor - in a contract of security.

2. Contracts on production cooperation, specialization and cooperation, on construction, assembly and other works in capital construction shall be subject to the law of the country where such activity is carried out or the results envisioned by the contract are achieved unless otherwise established by agreement of the parties.

3. A contract concerning the establishment of a joint venture involving foreign juridical persons or citizens shall be subject to the law of the country where the joint venture is founded.

4. A contract concluded at the action, tender or exchange shall be subject to the law of the country where the auction or tender is held, exchange is located.

5. The rights and duties under contacts not listed in paragraphs 1-4 of this article shall be subject to the law of the country where the party, whose execution is of decisive importance for the terms of contract, is founded, domiciled or where it carries out its main activity.

Art. 1225 of the 1996 Model Civil Code (Part III) is largely based on the same principles. However, it allows choice of law with respect to contracts on production cooperation and construction. It does not expressly deal with the choice of law with respect to contracts involving joint ventures. It also includes an additional provision concerning immovables. If there is no agreement between the parties regarding applicable law, contracts on immovables are subject to the law of the country where the property involved is located.

(d) Formal Requirements for Contracts

Formal requirements for contracts is governed by general rules concerning transactions. Under Art. 165 of the 1991 Fundamentals the form of a legal transaction is subject to the law of the place where it is executed. However, in modern international commerce the place where contracts are concluded is often fortuitous (for example, an airport conference room). In view of this, the 1991 Fundamentals allow the parties to disregard the formal requirements of the place where the contract is concluded if the contract will be performed in Russia. Under Art. 165 of the 1991 Fundamentals a contract concluded abroad shall be valid as to form as soon as it meets the formal requirements of Russian law.

On the other hand, the form of foreign economic transactions performed by Russian juridical persons and citizens, irrespective of the place where they are executed, is governed by Russian legislation. The form of transactions concerning buildings and other immovable property in Russia is subject to Russian law. This means that in these two situations Russian law requirements concerning contract form will always govern the matter.

As noted in Chapter VI, under the Civil Code, the failure to observe the requirement that the contract concerning foreign trade transactions be in writing makes the relevant contract void.[15] Under Art. 434 of the Civil Code a contract in written form may be concluded by reducing it to a single document signed by the parties and also by "the exchange of documents by mail, telegraph, teletype, telephone, electronic or other communications that allow the reliable establishment that the document proceeds from a party to the contract." According to Art. 434 of the Civil Code, the written form of a contract is considered observed if a written proposal to conclude a contract has been accepted by beginning performance of the contract (shipment of goods, provision of services, performance of work, payment of the appropriate amount, etc.)

It is important to keep in mind that as a successor state of the former Soviet Union, Russia continues to adhere to a reservation concerning oral transactions formulated by the USSR with respect to the United Nations Convention on Contracts for the International Sale of Goods.[16] The reservation states that an offer, acceptance or any other expression of intent, which is not in writing, are not applicable to contracts for the international sales of goods.[17] In *Electrim v. Kosmos,*[18] a case involving a dispute between a Polish and a Russian company over a contract of sale, the Supreme Arbitration Court confirmed that, as a successor state to the former USSR, Russia is bound by the reservation concerning the form of international contracts of sale. The Court noted that international contracts of sale may be formed and modified only "in writing."

At the same time, in this case the Supreme Arbitration Court also confirmed that the written form of a contract is considered observed if a written proposal to modify the terms of a contract has been accepted by beginning performance of the new terms of the contract. The Polish company "Electrim" sent to the Russian company "Kosmos" a fax letter that contained

---

[15] Civil Code, Art. 162.

[16] See *supra* note 5.

[17] See UN Doc. A/CN.9/416 (1995). Art. 11 of the Convention provides: "A contract of sale need not be concluded in or evidenced by writing and is not subject to any other requirement as to form. It may be proved by any means, including witness."

[18] *VVAS*, 1997, No. 6, p. 100.

a proposal to change the port of delivery of goods and their price. The Court held that although there was no further exchange of documents the contract was modified "in writing" because the consent of the buyer to contract modification was confirmed by its actions. The Supreme Arbitration Court noted that "the buyer's acceptance of the change in the contract [of sale] was confirmed by sending the ship for loading and by making payments made for the freight."[19]

The place where a legal transaction is executed is determined according to Russian law. This means that the contract is formed at the place where the offeror receives acceptance. If an international contract is concluded by exchange of letters the place of conclusion will thus be the country of the offeror.

PROBLEM

A German shoe manufacturer (SAL AG) has found a Russian partner who was interested in producing shoes in Russia under the SAL AG license.

SAL AG and its Russian partner - a Saint Petersburg company AO Tufel - concluded several contracts, one of which was subsequently amended by an "understanding."

The framework contract, signed in Saint Petersburg, dealt with the basic principles of cooperation between the partes. Another contract (contract of sale) involved sale of the unique SAL AG equipment. Under a licence contract SAL AG granted to AO Tufel the right to produce the famous SAL shoes.

The parties also founded a new Russian company, AO SAL-TUFEL, whose principal task was export of Russian-made shoes to foreign markets. Although AO SAL-TUFEL has been granted the right to sell shoes produced under the SAL AG license worldwide (under a contract between SAL AG, AO Tufel and AO SAL-TUFEL), this right was subsequently modified by a "mutual understanding" of the parties that AO SAL-TUFEL would not export SAL shoes to Poland and Hungry. The "mutual understanding" was reached by the presidents of SAL AG, AO Tufel and AO SAL-TUFEL during a press conference in Saint Petersburg. The parties agreed that there was no need to sign any documents confirming this "understanding."

Surprisingly, all the transactions mentioned did not mention choice of law. In case of dispute, which law will govern these contracts?

---

[19] Id., at 101.

5. Torts

The basic conflicts criterion in this field is the principle of the law of the place of the tort (*lex loci delicti*). Art. 167 of the 1991 Fundamentals provides that the rights and duties of parties in obligations arising as a consequence of causing harm are determined according to the law of the country where the action or other circumstance serving as a basis for an action concerning compensation of harm took place. This broad clause may cover both the place of the wrong and the place where the consequences of the wrong are felt.

At the same time, the 1991 Fundamentals make an exception from the *lex loci delicti* principle in cases where a Russian citizen or a Russian company abroad inflicts harm on other Russian citizens or companies. Art. 167 of the 1991 Fundamentals provides that the rights and duties of parties in obligations arising as a consequence of causing harm abroad, if the parties are Russian citizens and juridical persons, are determined according to Russian law. The 1996 Model Civil Code (Part III) extends this principle to all parties having the same nationality. Under Art. 1229 of the 1996 Model Civil Code (Part III), in cases when the wrongdoer and the injured party are nationals of the same country, liability in tort is always governed by the law of that country.

If an action is brought in Russian courts, Russian judges will not apply foreign law if the action or other circumstance serving as a basis for an action concerning compensation of harm is not unlawful according to Russian legislation.

In product liability cases the conflict of laws is usually very complicated. The tortious act may be connected with several states. Art. 1230 of the 1996 Model Civil Code (Part III) contains a special clause dealing with product liability. Art. 1230 is based on the modern "principle of most favorable law." This means that in this area the choice of law issues must be settled by applying the law which is most favorable to the plaintiff. Victims will be allowed to choose (1) the law of the country where the victim resides, (2) the law of the country where the producer resides or has his or her place of business or (3) the law of the country where the product was acquired by the person suffering damage. This approach may create problems for the producers who always want to calculate and insure their risks. Nonetheless, the victims may choose the most favorable law, either that which offers the strictest standard of liability or that which guarantees the greatest recovery of damages.

PROBLEM

RUS-Air, an air-carrier company, was founded in Moscow, but

operated primarily in the Middle East. In 1997, a cargo plane belonging to RUS-Air crashed into a Russian-owned vessel passing through the territorial sea of Israel.

The owners of the vessel sued RUS-Air in the Moscow Arbitration Court. On the basis of the available information, is it possible to determine which body of law will be applied by the Arbitration Court?

6. *Renvoi*

Renvoi occurs when Russian conflict law points toward the law of a foreign country, but the conflicts law of that country refers back to Russian law. *Renvoi* is one of the most complex problems relating to the application of conflicts rules. Conflicts rules on personal legal capacity may provide an illustration of the problem. In some countries personal legal capacity is governed by the law of a person's nationality. Other countries apply the law of domicile. The conflict rules of the country of domicile may designate as governing law that of nationality, but the law of a person's nationality may contain a contrary rule according to which the matter of personal legal capacity must be governed by the law of domicile. In more complicated situations, *renvoi* can present itself not only in the form of a reference back to the law of the forum but also in the form of a reference to the law of a third country.

The 1991 Fundamentals do not contain any provisions concerning *renvoi*.[20] Russian commentators have traditionally used *renvoi* as an additional argument to apply Russian law. It has been argued that if Russian law refers to foreign law but the foreign law itself fails to regulate the specific relationship and refers the matter back to Russian law or to law of a third state, then Russian law should apply.[21]

International practice indicates that the circle created by *renvoi* may be eliminated if the reference to foreign law by the forum's conflicts rule means reference only to foreign *substantive* law and not to foreign *conflicts* rules. The 1996 Model Civil Code (Part III) adopts this approach. It provides that, in principle, a Russian choice of law rule refers only to substantive foreign law, not to foreign choice of law rules.[22] As a result, if a Russian choice of law rule refers to the law of a particular state and the choice of law rules of that state refer the issue in question back to Russian law or to the law of a third state, the

---

[20] In the United States *renvoi* is rejected as a general matter. See Restatement (Second) of Conflict of Laws (§ 8) (1971).

[21] See M.M. Boguslavski, *Mezhdunarodnoe chastnoe pravo* (Private International Law) 91 (1994).

[22] 1996 Model Civil Code (Part III), Art. 1197.

law of the legal system referred to by the Russian choice of law rules applies, and the foreign country's choice of law rules are ignored.

Under the 1996 Model Civil Code (Part III) *renvoi* is accepted only in four specific cases dealing with the personal law of natural persons, legal capacity of natural persons, the name of natural persons and guardianship.

C. Application of Foreign Law

Russian courts apply rules of foreign law in all cases where such application is required by Russian law, norms of international law or contract. The 1964 Civil Procedure Code provides that "the court shall apply norms of foreign law in accordance with the law."[23] The 1995 Arbitration Procedure Code also states that "the arbitration court shall apply norms of law of other states in accordance with the law or a treaty of the Russian Federation."[24] The duty of the Russian court to apply foreign law extends not only to legislative enactments, but also to customary rules and judicial precedents of foreign states to the extent that the latter are recognized as sources of law in these states.

The friendly attitude towards foreign law is confirmed by the procedure for its determination. While knowledge of foreign law is not to be imputed to a Russian judge, the parties are under no obligation to prove the content of foreign law. The court must determine the content of applicable foreign law *ex officio*.[25] The duty of the court to ascertain foreign law is enforced by a sanction: according to the general principles of civil procedure the incorrect application of norms of foreign law may be considered as one of the possible grounds for vacating the decision of the court.[26]

Art. 157 of the 1991 Fundamentals defines the method for determining the content of foreign law. It provides that, in applying foreign law, courts "shall determine the content of its norms in accordance with their official interpretation, their application in practice and the doctrine in the relevant foreign country." Courts may resort to the Ministry of Justice of Russia or other competent agencies or institutions in Russia and abroad for assistance

[23] 1964 Civil Procedure Code, Art. 10.

[24] 1995 Arbitration Procedure Code, Art. 11.

[25] 1991 Fundamentals, Art. 157.

[26] Cf. Art. 306 of the Civil Procedure Code reproduced in Chapter VII(14). Commentators are unanimous that the incorrect application of norms of foreign law is one of the grounds for vacating the decision of the court. See, e.g., M.S. Shakarian ed., *Grazhdanskoe protsessual'noe pravo Rossii* (Russian Civil Procedure Law) 340 (1996); Boguslavski, *supra* note 18, at 374.

and interpretation or may turn to experts. Persons participating in the case have the right to present documents confirming the content of the pertinent norms of foreign law. Art. 158 of the 1991 Fundamentals also provides that if the content of norms of foreign law cannot be established despite the measures taken, Russian law is to be applied to the case at hand.

It is well recognized that circumstances may arise in which the law of the forum (*lex fori*) must be preferred to foreign law that would normally be applicable to the case. The most important example of this is the doctrine of public order (*ordre publique*) or public policy under which certain basic principles of domestic law designed to protect the public welfare must prevail over an inconsistent foreign rule. An extensive interpretation of this rather vague doctrine may provide an easy excuse for the forum state to apply its own law and thus defeat the underlying purpose of private international law.

Art. 158 of the 1991 Fundamentals provides that foreign law is not applied in cases where its application would be contrary to the foundations of the Russian legal order (public order). Art. 158 also provides that in such cases the Russian law applies. Art. 158 seeks to clarify the doctrine of public order (policy) by stating that refusal to apply foreign law may not be based only on the difference between the political or economic system of the relevant foreign country and the political or economic system of Russia.

Under Art. 158 of the 1991 Fundamentals, the concept of public order has both "negative" and "active" functions. In its "negative" aspect, the concept precludes the application of rules of foreign law and thus protects "the foundations" of the Russian legal order. The "active" aspect of the concept ensures that Russian substantive rules apply irrespective of the content of foreign law.

Traditionally, the concept of public order is interpreted in a narrow sense. There must be exceptionally serious reasons to apply the concept in each particular instance. In practice, there have been very few cases where public order has been invoked under Russian law. Courts rely on the concept only in the most exceptional of cases.[27]

D. International Jurisdiction of Russian Courts

In private international law, international jurisdiction means the

---

[27] See M.M. Boguslavski ed., *Mezhdunarodnoe chastnoe pravo: Sovremennye problemy* (Private International Law: Contemporary Problems) 473 (1994); D.K. Moss, *Avtonomia voli v praktike mezhdunarodnogo kommercheskogo arbitrazha* (Party Autonomy in the Practice of International Commercial Arbitration) 31-32 (1996).

power of the courts of a particular country to decide civil law cases that have a foreign defendant. This concept is called "personal jurisdiction" in the US. The international jurisdiction of Russian courts in cases involving foreign persons is governed by the 1964 Civil Procedure Code and the 1995 Arbitration Procedure Code.

The Civil Procedure Code contains very few specific rules governing the matter. Arts. 433(1) and 434 of the Civil Procedure Code provides that foreign citizens and stateless persons have the same right of access to the courts and enjoy the same civil procedural rights as Russian citizens.[28] Restrictions on these rights of foreign citizens, enterprises and organizations are possible only in cases of retaliations against procedural restrictions imposed on Russian citizens or organizations in their respective countries. Art. 435 of the 1964 Code also proclaims the principle of absolute sovereign immunity by stating that suits against foreign states are permissible only if those states consent to the jurisdiction of Russian courts.[29] Suits against diplomatic personnel are permissible only "within limits laid down by the rules of international law or by conventions."[30]

As far as the international jurisdiction of Russian courts is concerned, the 1964 Code simply states that it will be determined by the general rules for territorial jurisdiction.[31] As a result, provisions of the Civil Procedure Code on jurisdiction aimed at internal situations have to be extended or applied by analogy[32] to cover international situations.

---

[28] This is illustrated by a recent case involving a German citizen. The Supreme Court pointed out that the rights guaranteed by Art. 433 of the Civil Procedure Code do not depend on any international treaty (such as treaty on legal assistance) between Russia and Germany (*BVS*, 1994, No. 7, p. 16).

[29] The principle of absolute sovereign immunity is also proclaimed by the 1995 Arbitration Procedure Code (Art. 213). This doctrine is clearly outdated and must be replaced by a restrictive principle of immunity denying immunity in respect of commercial transactions. At this stage there is no indication of a trend toward a restrictive principle. However, it might be adopted in the future: Art. 127 of the 1994 Civil Code states that "the peculiarities of the responsibility of the Russian Federation and of the subjects of the Russian Federation in relations with foreign judicial persons, citizens and states governed by civil legislation shall be determined by the law on the immunity of the state and its property." The law envisioned by the Civil Code is still under debate.

[30] Id.

[31] Civil Procedure Code, Art. 434.1.

[32] The need for the application of the relevant general principles by analogy in this case is emphasized by some commentators. See, e.g., Shakarian, *supra* note 26, at 334.

General jurisdictional rules of the Civil Procedure Code provide that in general jurisdiction depends upon the presence of the defendant or his or her property in Russia. Under Art. 117 of the Civil Procedure Code suits are to be filed at "the place of residence of the defendant." "Place of residence" connotes a presence that has a greater degree of permanence than that which is occasional or temporary. Thus, a mere transient presence of a person in Russia would not suffice to render him or her amenable to the jurisdiction of the Russian court under this test. If the place of residence of the defendant is not known, suit may be filed at the place where his or her property is located.[33]

The same rule applies to suits against defendants who do not reside in Russia.[34] Suits against juridical persons are to be "filed at the place where an organ or property of the latter is located."[35] Suits concerning the activities of a branch of a judicial person may be filed at the place where the relevant branch is located.[36]

The Civil Procedure Code establishes several additional criteria that could be used by the Russian courts as grounds for asserting wider jurisdiction over defendants located in other countries. These are based on the fact that the dispute has some connection to the territory of Russia. If the place of residence of the defendant is not known, suit may be filed at the place of his or her last known place of residence in Russia.[37] The same rule applies to suits against defendants who do not reside in Russia.[38] In addition, suits resulting from contracts or torts may be filed at the place where the contract is performed or where harm was caused.[39]

Of particular importance is Art. 119 of the Civil Procedure Code which establishes "exclusive jurisdiction" of Russian courts. Art. 119 states that "actions concerning rights to a building, for the release of property from arrest and to establish the manner of use of plots of land shall be under the jurisdiction of the court at the place where the property or plot of land is located." Under Art. 119 "actions of creditors of a deceased person brought before the estate has been accepted by the successors shall be under the jurisdiction of the court at the place where the estate of the deceased or the main part of it is located." Furthermore, "actions against carriers arising out of contracts of carriage of goods, passengers or luggage shall be brought at the

[33] Civil Procedure Code, Art. 118.
[34] Id.
[35] Civil Procedure Code, Art. 117.
[36] Civil Procedure Code, Art. 118.
[37] Civil Procedure Code, Art. 118.
[38] Id.
[39] Id.

place where the administration of the transport organization, to which the claim has been presented in the established manner, is situated."

In contrast to the 1964 Civil Procedure Code, which, for purposes of adjudicative jurisdiction, treats both domestic and international cases in the same manner, the 1997 Draft Civil Procedure Code contains a special chapter dealing with questions of international civil procedure. Under Art. 381 of the 1997 Draft Civil Procedure Code Russian ordinary courts will have jurisdiction to consider different kinds of disputes if one of the elements of the disputed relationship is located in Russia. The principal rule is location or place of residence of the defendant on Russian territory. Other major elements include representation, property, contract performance and tort. Art. 383 of the Draft Civil Procedure Code defines the exclusive international jurisdiction of Russian courts. Under Art. 383 Russian courts will have exclusive jurisdiction with respect to immovables located in Russia, actions against carriers arising out of contracts of carriage, actions for divorce involving Russian citizens and foreigners if both parties reside in Russia, actions concerning electoral rights and actions involving judicial review of normative acts and administrative action.

Rapid expansion of foreign trade requires a more detailed determination of the international jurisdiction of Russian arbitration courts. The 1995 Arbitration Procedure Code Russian has granted arbitration courts authority to consider different kinds of disputes if one of the elements of the disputed relationship is located in Russia. Art. 212 of the 1995 Arbitration Procedure Code provides:

> 1. Arbitration courts of the Russian Federation shall resolve disputes in which foreign persons participate, if the respondent is located and the citizen resides on the territory of the Russian Federation.
>
> 2. Arbitration courts of the Russian Federation also have the right to resolve disputes in which foreign persons participate, if:
>
>   1) a subsidiary or representation of a foreign person is located on the territory of the Russian Federation;
>
>   2) the respondent has property on the territory of the Russian Federation;
>
>   3) the statement of claim results from a contract that is supposed to be performed or has been performed on the territory of the Russian Federation;

4) in a dispute concerning compensation for harm to property where the action or other circumstance serving as the basis for the claim took place on the territory of the Russian Federation;

5) the statement of claim results from unjust enrichment that took place on the territory of the Russian Federation;

6) the plaintiff in a suit concerning the protection of honor, dignity and business image is located on the territory of the Russian Federation;

7) there is an agreement conferring jurisdiction to arbitration courts between an organization or citizen of the Russian Federation and a foreign person.

3. Disputes concerning the recognition of the right of ownership to buildings, installations, plots of land or a claim for the return of buildings, installations, plots of land from unlawful possession by another party, or the elimination of violations of the rights of the owner or lawful possessor not associated with dispossession shall be considered at the place where the building, installation, plot of land are located.

4. Disputes arising from contracts for transportation, including cases where the carrier is one of the respondents, shall be considered at the place where the organ of transportation is located.

5. If the case has been accepted by the arbitration court for consideration in accordance with the rules established by the present Article, it shall be resolved by the said court even if at a later stage in the proceedings it may fall within the jurisdiction of the court of another state due to the relocation of the participants or other circumstances.

Art. 212 indicates that the Russian law of jurisdiction rests on a number of traditional civil law bases. Thus, Art. 212(1) establishes the widely accepted principle that Russian courts will have general jurisdiction over individuals and companies located on the Russian territory in all cases, that is irrespective whether they are relayed to forum activities or not. Additional forms of specific jurisdiction require some kind of connection to the forum, such as the operation of a branch, ownership of property, performance of a contract or the commission of a wrongful act.

In contrast to the United States and other common law countries there is no transient jurisdiction by service of process. On the other hand, from an

American perspective, Art. 212 appears to contain certain elements of exorbitant jurisdiction. An example is Art. 212(6) which allows exercise of jurisdiction over foreign defendant having no connection with Russia in suits concerning the protection of honor, dignity and business image if the plaintiff is located on the territory of the Russian Federation. Furthermore, Art. 212(2) allows jurisdiction based solely on the presence of property unrelated to the litigation.

Because Russian civil procedure rejects *forum non conveniens*,[40] Russian courts will hear every case over which they have jurisdiction. As a result, an often employed common law argument for dismissal on the grounds that the Russian forum is grossly inconvenient and there is a better place to litigate will not be accepted.

At the same time, parties to a "foreign economic transaction" in principle have the right to exclude, by an agreement in writing, the jurisdiction of Russian state arbitration (commercial) courts by submitting their disputes under a contract to the jurisdiction of foreign commercial arbitration tribunal. As noted earlier,[41] if parties have agreed to submit their arbitrable dispute to arbitration, the "ordinary" court will refuse to accept the statement of claim[42] and the state arbitration court will terminate or dismiss proceedings in a case.[43] Arbitrability of international transactions is defined be the 1993 Law on International Commercial Arbitration.[44]

Submission of disputes to foreign courts may cause more serious problems. In situations where Russian courts have exclusive jurisdiction, they may disregard even express foreign jurisdiction clause. Decisions of a foreign court or arbitration tribunal will be respected in Russia only if they have not been rendered in a case exclusively reserved for the jurisdiction of a Russian court as defined by Art. 119 of the 1964 Civil Procedure Code and Art. 212 of the 1995 Arbitration Procedure Code.

---

[40]See *supra*, p. 361.

[41]See *supra*, p. 391-392.

[42]Civil Procedure Code, Art. 129.

[43]Arbitration Procedure Code, Arts. 85, 87. See, for example, "*B&R*" *v.* "*Golunov&Taigai, PLLV,*" *BVAS*, 1997, No. 9, p. 66 (The Supreme Arbitration Court upheld the ruling of the Volgograd Regional Arbitration Court dismissing proceedings in the case because the parties to the dispute agreed to submit their contractual disputes to the Arbitration Institute in Stockholm, Sweden).

[44]Arbitrability of international commercial disputes is discussed *infra* p. 425-426.

E. Recognition and Enforcement of Foreign Court Judgments and Foreign Arbitration Tribunal Awards

Recognition and enforcement of foreign judgments and foreign arbitration awards are the key elements of transboundary litigation. The party who succeeds in a foreign court often has to turn to courts of another country for recognition and enforcement. Because international arbitration is an essentially private procedure, international arbitration tribunals, unlike national courts of law, cannot enforce their decisions. If the losing party refuses to carry out the award voluntarily, the winning party has to turn to national courts of a country where the losing party's assets are located with a request to recognize and enforce the award.

Recognition and enforcement touch upon different concerns of the parties. Recognition means that a given country will treat a foreign court judgment or arbitration award as *res judicata* in the respective dispute between the parties. Recognition is used to block any attempt to raise, in fresh proceedings, issues which have already been decided by the judgment or the award. Enforcement goes a step further than recognition. Enforcement requires a country to take action to execute the judgment or award. Although enforcement appears to be more important than recognition, in Russia both are granted under essentially the same conditions.

1. Foreign Court Judgments

Because of the principle of territorial sovereignty, a judgment delivered in one country cannot have direct effect in another. Nevertheless, Russian law permits enforcement of foreign judgment within certain defined limits. As a general rule, recognition and enforcement of judgments of foreign courts in Russia is possible only if such recognition and enforcement is provided for by a bilateral or multilateral international treaty (at present there is no world-wide on the recognition of judgments). Such treaties are always based on the principle of reciprocity.[45]

The successful party to proceedings in a foreign country is supposed to file a petition for the recognitions and enforcement of the judgment in an "ordinary" court. Under Art. 437 of the Civil Procedure Code "a decision of a foreign court or arbitration tribunal may be submitted for compulsory

[45] Member states of the Commonwealth of Independent States concluded a special multilateral Agreement on the Procedure for Resolving Disputes Relating to Economic Activities (see *supra* note 7). Art. 7 of the 1992 Agreement provides that CIS states "shall mutually recognize and enforce decisions rendered by the competent courts which have entered into legal force."

execution within three years from the moment the decision entered into legal force."

The 1988 Decree of the Presidium of the Supreme Soviet of the USSR "On Recognition and Execution in the USSR of Decisions of Foreign Courts and Arbitration Tribunals"[46] provides that the relevant petition is to be filed with the Supreme Court of the republic, regional, provincial or city court where the debtor resides or, if the debtor has no place of residence or his place of residence is unknown, at the place where his or her property is located.[47]

Art. 5 of the 1988 Decree enumerates six requirements for recognition and enforcement of foreign court judgment in Russia. It provides:

Petition to enforce a judgment of a foreign court may be rejected in cases, when:

1. The judgment has not entered into legal force according to the law of the country where it was rendered.

2. The party against which the judgment was rendered did not participate in the proceedings because it did not receive proper notice of the proceedings in sufficient time.

3. The judgment was rendered in a dispute which falls under the exclusive jurisdiction of the Russian courts or other organs.

4. There is a judgment of a Russian court in a case between the same parties, concerning the same subject, and on the same grounds, which has entered into legal force, or a Russian court is considering the case of a dispute between the same parties, concerning the same subject, and on the same grounds which was accepted for consideration before the submission of the suit to a foreign court.

5. The time limit for the submission of the judgment for enforcement has expired.

6. The execution of the judgment would be contrary to the sovereignty of the Russian Federation or basic principles of the Russian legislation.

An important feature of Art. 5 is the requirement that the judgment

---

[46] *Vedomosty SSSR*, No. 29, item 427 (1988).

[47] 1988 Decree of the Presidium of the Supreme Soviet of the USSR "On Recognition and Execution in the USSR of Decisions of Foreign Courts and Arbitration Tribunals," Art. 2.

not violate "the sovereignty of the Russian Federation or basic principles of the Russian legislation." This is the standard public policy exception. The instances in which this clause may be used are extremely rare. As a general rule, Russian courts will not review the substance of foreign judgments.

Another important requirement under Art. 5 is that the rendering court must have proper jurisdiction over the matter. Russian courts will measure the rendering court's jurisdiction by applying Russian domestic rules. Courts will always refuse recognition and enforcement in cases where they can claim exclusive jurisdiction, for example, in cases involving immovable property located in Russia.

It is expected that all these requirements will be codified in a new Civil Procedure Code. The 1997 Draft Civil Procedure Code contains provisions analogous to Art. 5 of the 1988 Decree.

2. Foreign Arbitration Awards

While a foreign arbitral award in principle is on a similar footing to a foreign judgment, recognition and enforcement of foreign arbitration awards is facilitated by several important multilateral conventions to which Russia is a party. The most important among these is the 1958 New York Convention on the Recognition and Enforcement of Foreign Arbitral Awards.[48] Bilateral treaties concluded with foreign countries may also contain provisions on arbitration.

The Russian parliament also enacted a special domestic statute governing recognition and enforcement of international arbitration awards. The 1993 Law on International Commercial Arbitration[49] establishes a liberal regime for the recognition and enforcement of foreign arbitration awards. Art. 35 of the 1993 Law provides that "an arbitration decision, irrespective of the country in which it was rendered, shall be binding and shall, upon the submission of a written petition to the competent court, be enforced pursuant to the provisions of this Article and Article 36." Art. 35 also provides that the party relying on an arbitration decision or petitioning for its enforcement must supply the duly authenticated original arbitration decision or a duly certified copy thereof and the original of the arbitration agreement or a duly certified copy thereof. If the arbitration decision or agreement is made in a foreign language, the party must also supply a duly certified translation of these documents into Russian.

---

[48] See *supra* note 6.
[49] See *supra* note 3.

Art. 35 of the 1993 Law does not specify which courts have jurisdiction over enforcement and recognition of foreign arbitration awards. It simply states that the relevant petition must be submitted "to a competent court." As a result, the issue of jurisdiction continues to be governed by the 1988 Decree "On Recognition and Execution in the USSR of Decisions of Foreign Courts and Arbitration Tribunals."[50] Under the 1988 Decree an application for the enforcement of a foreign arbitration award must be submitted to the second level of "ordinary" courts - the Supreme Court of the republic, regional, provincial or city court where the debtor resides or, if the debtor has no place of residence or his place of residence is unknown, at the place where his or her property is located.

It is important to emphasize that the 1993 Law does allow for domestic judicial review of foreign arbitration awards. However, the scope of such review is strictly limited. Art. 36 of the 1993 Law, which is modeled on Art. V of the the 1958 New York Convention on the Recognition and Enforcement of Foreign Arbitral Awards,[51] defines the limited grounds for

[50] *Supra* note 46.

[51] Art. V the 1958 New York Convention on the Recognition and Enforcement of Foreign Arbitral Awards provides:

> 1.Recognition and enforcement of the award may be refused, at the request of the party against whom it is invoked, only if that party furnishes to the competent authority where the recognition and enforcement is sought, proof that:
>
> a) the parties to the agreement referred to in article II were, under the law applicable to them, under some incapacity, or the said agreement is not valid under the law to which the parties have subjected it or, failing any indication thereon, under the law of the country where the award was made; or
>
> b) the party against whom the award is invoked was not given proper notice of the appointment of the arbitrator or of the arbitration proceedings or was otherwise unable to present his case; or
>
> c) the award deals with a difference not contemplated by or not falling within the terms of the submission to arbitration, or it contains decisions on matters beyond the scope of the submission to arbitration, provided that, if the decision on matters submitted to arbitration can be separated from those not so submitted, that part of the award which contains decisions on matters submitted to the arbitration may be recognized and enforced; or
>
> d)the composition of the arbitral authority or the arbitral procedure was not in accordance with the agreement of the parties, or, failing such agreement, was not in accordance with the law of the country where the arbitration took place; or
>
> e) the award has not yet become binding on the parties, or has been set aside or suspended by a competent authority of the country in which, or under the law of which, that award was made.
>
> 2.Recognition and enforcement of an arbitral award may also be refused if the

refusing recognition or enforcement of international arbitration awards. It states:

1. Recognition or enforcement of an arbitration decision, irrespective of the country in which it was rendered, may be refused only:

1) at the request of the party against whom it is invoked, if that party furnishes to the competent court where the recognition and enforcement is sought, proof that:

- a party to the arbitration agreement referred to in Article 7 lacked legal dispositive capacity to some extent; or the said agreement is not valid under the law to which the parties have subjected it or, failing any indication thereon, under the law of the country where the decision was rendered; or

- the party against whom the decision was rendered was not given proper notice of the appointment of the arbitrator or of the arbitration proceedings or was unable to present its explanations for other reasons; or

- the decision was rendered in a dispute not envisioned by the arbitration agreement or not falling within its terms, or it contains rulings on matters beyond the scope of the arbitration agreement, provided, however, that if the rulings on matters within the scope of the arbitration agreement can be separated from those not envisioned by this agreement, that part of the arbitration decision which contains rulings on matters covered by the arbitration agreement may be recognized and enforced; or

- the composition of the arbitration court or the arbitration procedure was not in accordance with the agreement of the parties, or, in the absence of such an agreement, was not in accordance with the law of the country where the arbitration took place; or

- the decision has not yet become binding on the parties, or has been set aside or suspended by a court of the country in which , or under the law of which, that decision was rendered; or

---

competent authority in the country where recognition and enforcement is sought finds that:
a) the subject matter of the difference is not capable of settlement by arbitration under the law of that country; or
b) the recognition or enforcement of the award would be contrary to the public policy of that country.

2) if the court finds that:

- the subject matter of the dispute cannot be settled by arbitration under the law of the Russian Federation; or

- the recognition and enforcement of the said arbitration decision would be contrary to the public policy of the Russian Federation.

Art. 36 demonstrates how minimal judicial control over foreign arbitration awards is. There is no review on the merits of an award and recognition can be refused of only those foreign awards that contain blatant procedural irregularities. The only substantive requirement is that recognition or enforcement would not be "contrary to the public policy of the Russian Federation" and the public policy exception is used sparingly by the Russian courts.

The above analysis indicates that Russia has succeeded in establishing an effective legal framework to assure recognition and enforcement of foreign arbitration awards on its territory. Judicial practice also indicates that Russian courts recognize and enforce foreign arbitration awards. In an authoritative book on the subject K. Hober describes several enforcement proceedings in the Moscow City Court involving foreign companies that won arbitration proceedings against Russian entities in London and Stockholm and sought recognition and enforcement in Russia.[52] It is interesting to note that in one of the cases the defendant raised an objection concerning the merits of the dispute. The Moscow City Court rejected this argument because it did not deal with procedural objections.[53] The Moscow City Court and the Russian Supreme Court have adopted the approach of both the 1958 New York Convention on the Recognition and Enforcement of Foreign Arbitral Awards[54] and domestic Russian law, that objections touching on the merits of the dispute are excluded.[55] Hober concludes that Russian courts have adopted "a pro-enforcement approach that would be consistent with case law in most other jurisdictions."[56]

---

[52] K. Hober, Enforcing Foreign Arbitral Awards Against Russian Entities p. 52-54 (1994).

[53] Id., at 54.

[54] See *supra*, note 6.

[55] Id., at 57-58.

[56] Id., at. 58. Hober's study reproduces several judgments rendered by Russian courts, including the Supreme Court, in enforcement cases at 171-191.

PROBLEM

AA is a Russian exporter of medical equipment that includes certain nuclear components. In September of 1996 it contracted for the delivery of the equipment to an Indian company BB. The contract has two clauses of interest:

"1. All claims and disputes arising out of and in relation to this contract shall be arbitrated through the International Arbitration in Stockholm, Sweden.

2. This contract shall be governed by Swedish law."

In November of 1996, the Russian Government began a new policy of tighter control over the export of nuclear materials. A new law governing foreign trade required a special licence for the export of all nuclear-related goods. Because AA did not have any special export licence, it failed to deliver the equipment in time. BB initiated arbitration proceedings in Sweden.

The Arbitration Court in Stockholm ruled in favor of BB because neither the contract's *force majeure* clause nor Swedish law excuse AA's timely performance. AA was ordered to pay $ 1.000.000 in damages.

BB petitioned the Moscow City Court to recognize and enforce the award. Does AA have any defense?

F. International Commercial Arbitration in Russia

1. Introduction

Arbitration has become one of the most important instruments for the settlement of disputes in international commercial relations. The reasons for this development are well-known. Parties to transnational contracts often try to avoid the courts of the home state of another party because otherwise they would have to deal with unfamiliar institutions and legal procedures and may fear bias in favor of the other party. The claimant may find that the language of the national court is not that of the contract or local courts are not accustomed to international commercial transactions. International businessmen usually expect a better knowledge of the facts and usages of international commerce from arbitrators. Moreover, they can select their own arbitrators, while the judge they will get is unknown until the case is filed. In addition, arbitration rules are generally more flexible than domestic civil procedure. Confidentiality of arbitration proceedings is also considered an advantage. Finally, thanks to the 1958 New York Convention on the Recognition and Enforcement of

Foreign Arbitral Awards[57] enforcement of arbitration awards is assured in a much higher number of states throughout the world than is the enforcement of court judgments.

In view of this, it is not surprising that the majority of contracts between Russian enterprises and foreign partners contain arbitration clauses providing for international commercial arbitration. Parties entering the Russian market must take into account the basic rules governing commercial arbitration in Russia.

2. General Legal Framework

Russian law recognizes that parties to commercial transactions may agree to refer their disputes in international trade matters that would otherwise be within the jurisdiction of the courts to international commercial arbitration. Specific issues of international commercial arbitration in Russia are governed by a comprehensive international arbitration act - the 1993 Law on International Commercial Arbitration.[58] The 1993 Law is based on the 1985 Model Law on International Commercial Arbitration adopted by the UN Commission on International Trade Law (UNCITRAL) and endorsed by the UN General Assembly.[59] A careful analysis of the 1993 Law indicates that Russia has established the basic legal framework promoting and facilitating international arbitration. The 1993 Law incorporated the generally recognized international standards into the Russian domestic law.

3. The Arbitration Agreement

According to the 1993 Law, an arbitration agreement must be concluded in writing. Art. 7 of the 1993 Law defines "an agreement in writing" in the following manner:

> An agreement shall be considered concluded in writing, if it is contained in a document signed by the parties or contained in an exchange of letters, teletype or telegraph messages, or with the aid of other electrical communications facilities which fix the said agreement, or by an exchange of the claim and response to the claim, whereby one party alleges the existence of an agreement and the other party does not object to this allegation. A reference in a contract to the document containing an arbitration clause shall be an arbitration agreement, provided that the

---

[57] See *supra* note 6.

[58] See *supra* note 3.

[59] See UNCITRAL Model Law on International Commercial Arbitration, UN Doc. A/40/17 (1995) (reprinted in 24 ILM 1302 (1985)).

contract was concluded in writing and that the reference incorporates the above-mentioned clause into the contract.

The agreement may mean an arbitration clause in the contract or a separate arbitration agreement signed by the parties.

The 1993 Law is based on the concept that an arbitration clause in a contract is an independent contract that is severable from the other provisions of the contract. As a result, challenges to the validity of the transaction as a whole do not, in principle, call into question the validity of the arbitration clause. This permits issues concerning the validity of the transaction as a whole, such as fraud or illegality to be determined by arbitration.

If the parties have agreed on what body of law will govern an arbitration agreement providing for arbitration in Russia, the arbitration court will accept the choice. However, if the parties fail to reach such an agreement, the validity of the agreement will always be determined by the law of the forum (*lex fori*).[60] This means that Russian private international law will govern the issue of what law applies. To the extent international conventions to which Russia is a signatory contain different conflict rules, the provisions of those conventions will prevail.

The doctrine of severability is supplemented by the endorsement of the *Kompetenz-Kompetenz* principle. The 1993 Law empowers arbitrators to rule on their own jurisdiction, including the issue of the existence or validity of the arbitration agreement. A commercial arbitration court has the power to rule on the extent of its adjudicatory authority. Ultimately, of course, a Russian or foreign national court may reach a different conclusion in cases concerning challenges to the award or its recognition and enforcement.

4. Arbitrability of Transactions

The issue of arbitrability is settled by Art. 1 of the 1993 Law. According to Art. 1, parties engaged in international economic transactions may make various kinds of disputes subject to international commercial arbitration. Included are "contractual and other civil law disputes arising from the conduct of foreign trade and other international economic relations, if the commercial enterprise of at least one party is located abroad, as well as disputes between enterprises with foreign investments and international

---

[60] Cf. V.S. Posdniakov, *Mezhdunarodnyi kommercheskii arbitrazh v Rossiiskoy Federatsii* (International Commercial Arbitration in the Russian Federation) 23 (1996); M.G. Rosenberg, *Kontrakt mezhdunarodnoi kupli-prodazhy* (Contracts for the International Sale) 43-44 (1996).

associations and organizations set up on the territory of the Russian Federation, disputes between their participants and also their disputes with other subjects of the law of the Russian Federation."

An analysis of Art. 1 indicates that it gives a wide interpretation to terms "foreign trade and other international economic relations." It allows international commercial arbitration between companies incorporated in Russia. If, for example, the subsidiary of a foreign company doing business in Russia is incorporated in Russia, any arbitration between that company and a Russian company would be classified as a foreign trade dispute. Moreover, Art. 1 allows international arbitration even between two Russian-controlled companies if they have "foreign investments." As a result, Russian companies "with foreign investments" may avoid the more stringent rules of domestic arbitration[61] whenever the underlaying transaction does not relate to domestic trade.

5. Applicable Law

The 1993 Law recognizes that the parties have considerable control over the law governing substantive issues. Art. 28 of the Law provides that "the arbitral tribunal shall resolve the dispute in accordance with the rules of law designated by the parties as applicable to the substance of the dispute." In the absence of any indication of the parties as to the applicable law, "the arbitral tribunal shall apply the law determined by the conflict of laws rules which it considers applicable."

The phrase "rules of law designated by the parties" enables the parties to pick and choose among different national laws. In addition, the parties may choose principles and rules of public international law. It is not clear, however, whether the term "rules of law" would cover principles of international commercial practice or customs and usages of international trade, known as *lex mercatoria.*[62] Although the reference to "rules of law," rather than to "law" or "a system of law" appears to embrace even *lex mercatoria,* it may be useful to keep in mind that many Russian lawyers traditionally regard these rules as having doubtful validity. Russian experts on private international law argue that rules of *lex mercatoria* lack any ties to any national legal system and do not represent an established or autonomous system of law, so they are not "rules of law."[63]

---

[61] These rules were discussed *supra*, p. 391-395.

[62] See generally, T. Carbonneau ed., *Lex Mercatoria* and Arbitration. A Discussion of the New Law Merchant (1990).

[63] Cf. M.M. Boguslavski ed., *Mezhdunarodnoe chastnoe pravo: Sovremennye problemy* (Private International Law: Contemporary Problems 402 (1994).

6. Procedural Rules

Under the 1993 Law, the parties enjoy broad autonomy in shaping procedural rules that will govern the arbitration. The parties are free to select the applicable procedural rules they desire. In the majority of cases the parties will choose the applicable rules by reference to a set of standard procedural rules, such as the 1976 UNCITRAL Arbitration Rules.[64] Despite broad party autonomy as to procedural rules, it would be unwise to ignore certain mandatory provisions of the 1993 Law.

The requirements and limitations that the Russian law imposes on the international commercial arbitration process are that judges be impartial,[65] that both parties are afforded an appropriate hearing[66] and that generally recognized procedural grounds for setting aside arbitral awards and reasons for denial of recognition and enforcement of awards be observed.[67] These provisions may become crucial when the arbitration process or its result comes before Russian national courts in any challenge to the award or its recognition and enforcement.

7. The Role of Russian Courts

As noted earlier, an arbitration agreement generally excludes recourse to Russian courts. According to the 1993 Law, a court, when seized of a matter in which the parties made an arbitration agreement, must (if one of the parties so requests before addressing the merits of the case) terminate the court proceedings and refer the parties to arbitration. The court may, however, consider the case on the merits if it finds that the arbitration agreement is invalid, inoperative or unenforceable.

Arbitral awards rendered by arbitral tribunals in Russia are final and generally there is no possibility of appeal to domestic courts. An award may be challenged in courts only if there was a violation of mandatory requirements established by the 1993 Law. This may raise issues of the arbitrability of the subject matter of the dispute as well as setting aside of the arbitral award.

Under the 1993 Law international arbitration awards rendered in Russia must be challenged in the second-level "ordinary" courts. Art. 6 of the 1993 Law provides that applications to set aside the award must be submitted to "the Supreme Court of a republic forming part of the Russian Federation,

[64] See 2 Yearbook Commercial Arbitration 161 (1977).
[65] 1993 Law on International Commercial Arbitration, Arts. 12-13.
[66] 1993 Law on International Commercial Arbitration, Art. 18.
[67] 1993 Law on International Commercial Arbitration, Arts. 34-36.

the provincial, regional or city court, or the court of the autonomous region or autonomous area where the arbitration takes place."

The list of grounds for setting aside arbitral awards rendered in Russia are almost identical to the reasons for denial of recognition and enforcement of foreign arbitral awards.[68] Art. 34 of the 1993 Law dealing with grounds for setting aside arbitral awards provides:

> 1. Recourse to a court against an arbitral award may be made only by an application for setting aside in accordance with paragraphs 2 and 3 of this article.
>
> 2. An arbitral award may be set aside by the court specified in article 6(2) only if:
>
> 1) the party making the application for setting aside furnishes proof that:
>
> - a party to the arbitration agreement referred to in article 7 was under some incapacity, or the said agreement is not valid under the law to which the parties have subjected it or, failing any indication thereon, under the law of the Russian Federation; or
>
> - she was not given proper notice of the appointment of an arbitrator or of the arbitral proceedings or was otherwise unable to present her case; or
>
> - the award was made ergarding a dispute not contemplated by or not falling within the terms of the submission to arbitration, or contains decisions on matters beyond the scope of the submission to arbitration, provided that, if the decisions on matters submitted to arbitration can be separated from those not so submitted, only that part of the award which contains decisions on matters not submitted to arbitration may be set aside; or
>
> - the composition of the arbitral tribunal or the arbitral procedure was not in accordance with the agreement of the parties, unless such agreement was in conflict with a provision of this Law from which the parties cannot derogate, or, failing such agreement, was not in accordance with this Law; or
>
> 2) the court finds that:

---

[68] See *supra* p. 421-422.

- the subject-matter of the dispute is not capable of settlement by arbitration under the law of the Russian Federation; or

- the award is in conflict with the public policy of the Russian Federation.

Similar to the treatment of foreign arbitral awards, Art. 34 provides for strict limits on judicial review of international arbitration awards rendered in Russia. No review on the merits is permitted. While judges may set aside an award contravening "the public policy of the Russian Federation," this provision is interpreted narrowly.

***

In general, the 1993 Law seeks to ensure the effective functioning of the arbitration process. At the same time, certain issues still remain unresolved. An important issue is the availability of interim security measures. Art. 9 of the 1993 Law provides that "it is not incompatible with an arbitration agreement for a party to request a court, before or during arbitration proceedings, to order interim measures for protection and for a court to make a decision granting such measures." However, under Arts. 133 and 136 of the Civil Procedure Code an application for interim security measure must be considered "by the court or a judge trying the case." This provision has been interpreted in practice to mean that an interim security measure is possible only in a case pending before the court hearing the dispute on the merits.[69] Art. 75 of the 1995 Arbitration Procedure Code contains a similar rule. It provides: "Upon request of a party participating in the case, arbitration court may order interim measures of protection. . . The request for interim measures of protection shall be considered by the arbitration court considering the case not later than one day after its submission." References to "a party participating in the case" and to "the arbitration court considering the case" indicate that an order concerning interim security measures may be issued only by the court hearing the disputes on the merits. As a result, under the existing procedural law neither ordinary nor arbitration courts in Russia have the power to take security measures because the case is pending before an international arbitration court and not before these domestic courts.

The 1997 Draft Civil Procedure Code may have incorporated the rule authorizing security measures that is proclaimed in Art. 9 of the 1993 Law. Under Art. 128 of the Draft "the court, on request of persons taking part in a case, may take measures to secure an action." Art. 130 of the Draft provides

[69] Cf. M.K.Treushnikov, *Utchebnik grazhdanskogo protsessa* (Manual of Civil Procedure) 466 (1996). Cf. also Hober, *supra* note 52, at 51.

that "an application to the court to secure an action is decided on the same day without notifying the defendant and other persons taking part in the case." The 1997 Draft Civil Procedure Code still contains references to "persons taking part in the case." However, it omits the key phrase "by the court trying the case." Although the significance of this omission is still not clear, it is possible to argue that the court may order interim measures of protection even with respect to cases that are being considered by international arbitration tribunals.

8. The Moscow International Commercial Arbitration Court

Although foreign partners of Russian companies often prefer arbitration in neutral venues, they may also consider the advisability of arbitration in Russia. The best known permanent arbitration institution in Russia is the International Commercial Arbitration Court of the Russian Chamber of Commerce and Industry.[70] The activities of the Court are governed by its 1993 Charter[71] and 1995 Rules of Procedure.[72]

The International Commercial Arbitration Court has managed to establish a general reputation as an impartial and trustworthy institution. It is composed of a panel of arbitrators who are appointed by the Presidium of the Russian Chamber of Commerce and Industry. Arbitrators are required to possess specialized knowledge in resolving foreign trade disputes. The impartiality of the International Commercial Arbitration was generally recognized even before enactment of the 1993 Law and adoption of the 1995 Rules of Procedure.[73] The 1993 Law and the 1995 Rules of Procedure provide additional guarantees of impartiality by allowing parties to a dispute to choose arbitrators from outside the Chamber's list of qualified Russian or foreign arbitrators. As a result, parties have the right to select arbitrators of any nationality.

---

[70] According to Art. 1 of the 1993 Law "On Chambers of Commerce and Industry in the Russian Federation" (*Vedomosty RF*, No. 33, item 1309 (1993)), the Chamber of Commerce and Industry of the Russian Federation is "a private non-commercial organization composed of Russian enterprises and Russian businessmen."

[71] The Charter of the International Commercial Arbitration Court is contained in Annex I to the 1993 Law on International Commercial Arbitration, see *supra* note 3.

[72] Rules of the International Commercial Arbitration Court at the Chamber of Commerce and Industry of the Russian Federation (1995). The 1995 Rules are reproduced (In English) in E.A. Vinogradova, *Treteiskii sud* (Commercial Arbitration) 318 (1997).

[73] Cf., *Filanto v. Chilevich International*, 789 F.Supp. 1229, 1242 (1992) ("[T]here is no reason to believe that the Chamber of Commerce in Moscow cannot provide fair and impartial justice to these litigants").

Arbitration in Moscow may become particularly attractive to parties to commercial agreements that are governed by Russian substantive law. Parties to such agreements (for example, those concerning foreign investment in Russia) may find it more efficient to arbitrate in Russia, since the International Arbitration Court in Moscow is certainly the most competent body to apply Russian law. Another consideration may be the possibility of expeditious enforcement of the awards.

Awards rendered by the International Arbitration Court may be challenged in "ordinary" courts. Under Art. 6 of the 1993 Law applications for setting aside the award must be submitted to the Moscow City Court. Awards may be set aside only on procedural grounds defined by Art. 34 of the 1993 Law.[74]

Art. 34 of the 1993 Law has been tested in several proceedings initiated by the losing parties in the Moscow City Court. One judgment of the Moscow City Court on the subject has been reproduced in an authoritative book on commercial arbitration.[75] The case involved a Swiss company which entered into a contract of sale with a Lithuanian company. The contract included an arbitration clause which provided that all disputes under the contract were to be settled by the International Commercial Arbitration Court of the Russian Chamber of Commerce. Because the Swiss company failed to fulfill certain contractual obligations, the Lithuanian company filed suit in the International Commercial Arbitration Court which granted relief.

The Swiss company filed a petition in the Moscow City Court to set aside the arbitration award. The petitioner based its claim on Art. 34 of the 1993 Law according to which a Russian court may set aside an award if "the subject matter of the dispute cannot be settled by arbitration under the law of the Russian Federation" or "the recognition and enforcement of the said arbitration decision would be contrary to the public policy of the Russian Federation." The Moscow City Court dismissed the petition because the Swiss company "failed to furnish proof supporting its request."[76]

The Court noted in particular, that the arbitration clause in the contract did "not contravene Art. 1(2) of the Law of the Russian Federation 'On International Commercial Arbitration,' which provides that the International Commercial Court may settle contractual and other civil law disputes arising from foreign trade contracts. Therefore the argument that the subject matter of the dispute is not capable of settlement by arbitration is not justified.

---

[74] See *supra* p. 427-429.
[75] Vinogradova, *supra* note 72, at 318.
[76] Id., at 320.

Because in the present case the subject matter of the dispute as a foreign trade contract of sale, it may be resolved by arbitration."[77] The petitioner argued that the Moscow International Commercial Arbitration Court violated procedural rules. However, these allegations were not substantiated by any proof. The Moscow City Court noted, among other things, that "the company was given proper notice and it was able to participate in the appointment of arbitrators."[78] The Court also found that "the argument that the arbitration award contravenes the public policy of Russia has not been supported by any proof during the hearing. Procedural violations in the International Arbitration Court do not constitute violations of 'the public policy'."[79]

Awards rendered by the International Arbitration Court are enforceable in the same way as judgments of domestic Russian courts.[80] The execution procedure commences with the issuance of the writ of execution upon the petition of the interested party to an "ordinary" district court.[81]

[77] Id.
[78] Id.
[79] Id.
[80] Civil Procedure Code, Art. 338 (7).
[81] Civil Procedure Code, Art. 339 (1).

CHAPTER IX

LEGAL ISSUES OF FOREIGN INVESTMENT

A. Introduction

While foreign investment regimes exist in all countries of the world, not all countries have specific legislation on foreign investment. In developed market economy countries the rights of foreign investors are usually defined by domestic laws of general applicability. However, the newly emerged market economies, particularly those of Eastern Europe, have tried to establish a favorable foreign investment regime by adopting special laws on foreign investment. In order to attract foreign capital, technology and know-how, Russia also enacted a special law on foreign investment. The 1991 Law on Foreign Investment[1] envisions a liberal regime for direct foreign investment in Russia.

The drafters of the 1991 Law made an attempt to establish a comprehensive legal regime for foreign investment. However, in many respects the 1991 Law is little more than a broad statement of principles. In practice it is applied in conjunction with other Russian laws of general application, in particular the Civil Code and specific statutes dealing with land and natural resources, stock companies, banking, taxation, privatization, environmental protection and labor. International investment treaties may provide additional rules governing the matter. Russia concluded a series of bilateral investment treaties that lend greater predictability to Russia's foreign investment regime. American investments in Russia are protected by the 1992 Russian-US Treaty Concerning the Encouragement and Reciprocal Protection of Investment.[2]

The 1991 Law establishes a number of important foreign investment principles and incentives. Under the 1991 Law, foreign investors are allowed to acquire full or partial ownership of enterprises, either directly or through shares of stocks, bonds and other securities. The 1991 Law also confers the right to use land and other natural resources. It grants "national treatment" to foreign investment, permits profit repatriation in foreign currencies and

[1] See *Vedomosty RF*, No. 29, item 1008 (1991).

[2] *Biulleten' mezhdnarodnykh dogovorov*, No. 9, p. 43 (1993). The English language version of the treaty was published in 31 *International Legal Materaila* 794 (1992).

reinvestment of rouble profits in Russia and provides strong guarantees against state expropriation or nationalization.

It should be noted, however, that in many respects the 1991 Law no longer corresponds to contemporary political and legal realities in Russia. A new version of the Russian law on foreign investment is expected shortly to fill in the gaps and to conform the law to the new economic, political and legal conditions in the Russian Federation.[3]

It is also important to keep in mind that under the 1993 Constitution the "subjects" of the Russian Federation may enact their own laws affecting foreign investment. Of particular importance is the power of the "subjects" of the Federation to promulgate laws governing investments in natural resources exploration and exploitation. For example, the 1992 Law on Subsoil[4] expressly acknowledges the role of the constituent units of the Russian Federation in establishing natural resources regulations. In fact, several constituent republics have already enacted their own laws relevant to natural resources development. This means that a successful investment project requires a careful examination of both federal and local laws.

B. The Concept of Foreign Investment

Trans-border transfers of payments and of capital differ from each other in that the former serve to satisfy short term monetary obligations that result from traffic in goods, services and other forms of trans-border commerce, whereas the latter are intended for long-term capital investment. Foreign direct investment usually refers to the creation or acquisition of enterprises or assets in the host country through ownership of an enterprise or a substantial portion of it. Direct investments are usually made with a view to acquiring a lasting interest in an enterprise. Participation in the management of an enterprise is often the result of the direct control of either assets or a whole enterprise in a foreign country. Short-term equity investments without entrepreneurial commitment placed through the capital markets constitute portfolio investments.

The 1991 Law defines "foreign investment" in a very broad manner to include even commercial lending activity. At the same time, the 1991 Law uses the criterion of the intended purpose. While the 1991 Law does not specifically

[3]The Government submitted the new draft law on foreign investment to the Federal Assembly in 1995. The new draft contains more than 60 amendments to 42 articles of the 1991 Law. For details, see A.V. Kirin, *Pravovoi rezhim inostrannykh investitsii* (The Legal Regime of Foreign Investments) 29-33 (1996).

[4]As amended in 1995, *Sobranie*, No. 10, item 823 (1995).

require that the investment be "long-term," a transfer of capital is qualified as an investment if the purpose of the transfer is the placement of assets "into the objects of entrepreneurial and other for-profit business activities."[5] The 1991 Law does not introduce the criterion of control of an enterprise and thus covers both direct and portfolio investments. However, mere portfolio investments in various securities placed for the sake of capital yield are governed by specific securities regulations. In addition, this kind of international capital movement is subject to the provisions and restrictions of foreign exchange regulations.

According to Art. 1 of the 1991 Law, foreign investors may be "foreign legal entities, including all companies, firms, enterprises, organizations or associations created under the law of their domicile and authorized to make investments in accordance with that law," foreign citizens, stateless citizens and Russian citizens permanently residing abroad, provided that they are duly registered to conduct business in their domicile, foreign states and international organizations. In contrast to the 1991 Fundamentals of Civil Legislation of the USSR and Union Republics,[6] which, as we have established in Chapter VIII, looks to the law of place of incorporation in determining the legal capacity of foreign juridical persons,[7] the 1991 Law on Foreign Investment relies on "domicile." Russian experts explain this discrepancy as simply careless drafting. The principle of incorporation proclaimed in the 1991 Fundamentals still governs the capacity of foreign entities to invest in Russia.[8]

C. Business Forms for Foreign Investment

Art. 13 of the 1991 Law deals with the forms of enterprises with foreign investment. It provides that "an enterprise with foreign investment may be created through the formation of a new entity, through the acquisition of an ownership interest or shares of stock in an existing domestic enterprise, or through the purchase of a domestic enterprise outright."

Art. 12 lists the following types of enterprises: (1) enterprises in which foreign investors hold partial ownership (shareholding) interests, or joint enterprises (ventures), and their subsidiaries and branches; (2) enterprises wholly owned by foreign investors and their subsidiaries and branches; and (3) branches of foreign legal entities.

The details of the procedure for the creation of enterprises with

---

[5] 1991 Law on Foreign Investment, Art. 2.

[6] See *Vedomosty SSSR*, No. 26, item 733 (1991).

[7] See *supra*, p. 400.

[8] Cf. M.M. Boguslavskii, *Inostrannye investitsii: Pravovoe regulirovanie* (Foreign Investments: Legal Regulation) 66 (1996).

foreign investment and the conduct of investment transactions in Russia is subject to a host of laws and regulations of general application. For example, a foreign corporation that intends to set up its wholly owned subsidiary in Russia may do so by following the incorporation procedures established by the 1994 Civil Code and supplementary legislation. However, the 1991 Law contains several additional requirements for the formation of companies by foreign investors. For example, the Ministry of Justice registers all joint stock companies. However, under the 1991 Law, companies with foreign investment exceeding 100 million roubles and companies doing business in the area of petroleum, natural gas and coal extraction and processing must register with the Ministry of the Economy.[9]

In some cases foreign investors (just as Russian juridical persons and citizens) must receive special authorization to engage in particular types of activity. For example, the Russian Central Bank grants authorization (licenses) for banking and certain types of foreign exchange transactions. The Ministry of the Economy grants authorizations for insurance transactions as well as for trading in securities.

D. National Regime for Foreign Investors

The 1991 Law proclaims the principle of "national treatment" of foreign investors. Art. 6 of the 1991 Law provides that as a matter of principle "the legal regime applicable to foreign investments and activity of foreign investors may not be less beneficial than the regime applicable to the property, property rights and investment activity of juridical entities and citizens" of Russia.

At the same time, existing Russian legislation introduces numerous exceptions from the principle of "national treatment." Under the 1991 Law, a foreign investor may engage in any activity except where expressly prohibited by the Russian legislation. There are extensive restrictions on foreign private investment in the armaments industry. Limitations on exploration and exploitation of certain natural resources, transportation and ownership of land are further examples.

Laws governing privatization of state and municipal enterprises also place important restrictions on foreign participation in the privatization process. Although foreign participation in the privatization process is allowed, there are various restrictions on how foreign companies or citizens may

[9] See *infra* p. 442.

acquire assets of Russian state and municipal enterprises undergoing privatization. The following case illustrates this point.

The Supreme Arbitration Court: *Deputy Procurator General v. The Moscow Property Fund, The Joint Stock Company "Military-Industrial Investment Company," The Closed Joint Stock Company "Financial Center 'Capitol'," The Limited Liability Company "Denek" and "Nick and C Corporation"* (*VVAS*, 1997, No. 7, p. 86)

The Deputy Procurator General brought suit in the Moscow City Arbitration Court to protect state and public interests against the Moscow Property Fund, the Joint Stock Company "Military-Industrial Investment Company," the Closed Joint Stock Company "Financial Center 'Capitol'," the Limited Liability Company "Denek" and "Nick and C Corporation" to recognize as null and void the contract of delegation No. 36 of 05.30.94, the contract of commission agency No. 18mc of 06.23.94 and the protocol of the voucher auction No. 4828 of 08.31.94 concerning the purchase of the shares of the Open Joint Stock Company "MNPK Avionika" by the Closed Joint Stock Company "Financial Center 'Capitol'.". . .

In a ruling dated 06.05.96, the Moscow City Arbitration Court dismissed the suit. In a ruling of 09.11.96, the Federal Arbitration Court of the Moscow Circuit affirmed the trial court. A protest was lodged to vacate the above rulings and grant relief in the suit.

The Presidium [of the Supreme Arbitration Court] finds that the protest must be granted for the following reasons:

On 05.30.94 "Nick and C Corporation" and Limited Liability Company "Denek" entered into a contract of delegation No. 36. Under this contract the Corporation (the delegant) gave the Company (the delegate) the power to. . . purchase 200 000 privatization vouchers and use these vouchers in the All-Russian voucher auctions for the purchase of shares of joint stock companies designated by the delegant. Once all transactions required to perform the contract of delegation had been concluded, all the acquired shares were transferred to the delegant and became the property of "Nick and C Corporation."

On 06.23.94 the Limited Liability Company "Denek" entered into a contract of commission agency No. 18mc with the Closed Joint Stock Company "Financial Center 'Capitol'." Under Art. 1 of this contract "Capitol" assumed an obligation to submit an application to the All-Russian voucher privatization auction and purchase shares of 19 joint stock companies listed in the Annex to the contract, including the shares of the Open Joint

Stock Company "MNPK Avionika," for 200 000 privatization vouchers. The shares purchased by the commission agent become the property of the commission principal.

According to the terms of this contract the Closed Joint Stock Company "Financial Center 'Capitol'" submitted an application to participate in the auction and on 08.31.94, on the basis of the protocol of the voucher auction, purchased 30 000 shares of the Open Joint Stock Company "MNPK Avionika" for 10 000 privatization vouchers. On the directions of the Limited Liability Company "Denek" No. 4/04-1 of 09.26.94, the Closed Joint Stock Company "Financial Center 'Capitol'" transferred the acquired shares to the "Nick and C Corporation." As a result of all these transactions "Nick and C Corporation," a company incorporated in California (USA) and acting as a foreign investor, became the owner of the above shares.

According to Art. 10.1 of the State Program for Privatization of State-Owned and Municipal Enterprises in the Russian Federation approved by the Decree of the President of the Russian Federation No. 2284 of 12.24.93, decisions sanctioning participation of foreign investors in the privatization of enterprises whose defense contracts constitute more than 30 percent of their orders must be approved by the Government of the Russian Federation at the same time when the decision concerning privatization of these enterprises is issued.

The Open Joint Stock Company "MNPK Avionika" is an enterprise whose defense contracts at the time of privatization constituted more than 30 percent of its orders. The Government of the Russian Federation did not sanction participation of foreign investors in the privatization of the Open Joint Stock Company "MNPK Avionika."

According to Art. 10.1 of the State Program for Privatization of State-Owned and Municipal Enterprises in the Russian Federation, the organizers of the voucher auction were supposed to submit to the Government of the Russian Federation and to the Federal Security Service of the Russian Federation information concerning foreign investors - winners of the auction. This requirement was not fulfilled.

As a result, by using intermediaries "Nick and C Corporation" acquired shares of the Open Joint Stock Company "MNPK Avionika". . . in violation of Art. 10.1 of the State Program for Privatization. In accordance with Art. 168 of the Civil Code of the Russian Federation this transaction is null and void. . . The contract of delegation and the contract of commission agent envisioned acquisition of shares by a party having no legal right to do so; in other words, they were made with the purpose of concluding an illegal transaction; according to Art. 168 of the Civil Code they are also null and void. . .

E. Major Areas of Concern

The scope of the "national treatment" proclaimed by the 1991 Law remains controversial. It is accepted that the "national treatment" principle does not exclude the possibility that certain areas will be off-limits for foreign participation.[10] There is also a consensus that the new version of the law on foreign investment must clearly define the spheres of the national economy where foreign investments are not allowed. The proposals of the Government concerning the revision of the 1991 Law envision restrictions on foreign investment in the interests of national security. Restrictions may be imposed not only in the form of licensing but also by establishing maximum limits of foreign participation.[11]

Another controversial issue is a stabilization or grandfathering clause providing foreign investors with immunity from changes in the existing legislation. The 1991 Law does not envision such an immunity. However, a three year immunity from legislative changes to "foreign and joint enterprises" operating in Russia was granted by the Presidential Decree of September 27, 1993.[12] While the need for a grandfathering clause in the current conditions of far-reaching and rapid changes in Russian legislation is generally recognized, there is no unity with respect to its scope. Critics of the 1993 Presidential Decree point out that a broad application of the grandfathering clause could lead to undesirable discrimination against Russian investors.[13]

There appears to be a general agreement among Russian experts that any future grandfathering clause must apply only to special legislation defining the relationships between foreign investors and the Russian state. It cannot affect "horizontal" relations between domestic and mixed economic entities because otherwise the unity of the civil law regime and, in particular, the principle of equality of all participants of civil law relations proclaimed by the 1994 Civil Code, would be undermined. Experts also believe that the future

[10] Cf. I.S. Zykin, *Vneshneekonomitcheskie operatsii: Pravo I praktika* (Foreign Economic Transactions: Law and Practice) 36-37 (1994).

[11] Kirin, *supra* note 3, at 32.

[12] Presidential Decree "On Improving Operations With Foreign Investment", *Sobranie aktov*, No. 40, item 3740 (1993). The 1993 Decree provides that "newly issued normative acts regulating foreign and joint enterprises' operating conditions on Russian Federation territory shall not operate for three years in respect to enterprises in existence at the time these acts come into force."

[13] Cf. Zykin, *supra* note 10, at 38.

grandfathering clause must guarantee immunity only to large investors or to enterprises fully owned by foreign investors and joint ventures with more than a 30 percent foreign involvement.[14] Furthermore it will probably not apply to legislative changes concerning defense, security, public order, environmental protection, consumer protection and taxation.[15]

While the debates about the grandfathering clause continue, the Civil Code has already provided for certain stability in all contractual relations in Russia. Art. 422 of the Civil Code states: "If after the conclusion of a contract a statute is adopted establishing mandatory rules for the parties which differ from those in effect at the time when the contract was concluded, the provisions of the contract shall remain in force except in cases when the statute provides that its effect extends to relations arising from previously concluded contracts."

Russian commentators also agree that the future regime of foreign investment must clarify foreign rights in real property.[16] The 1991 Law on Foreign Investment does not resolve the issue of land ownership. The 1991 Land Code[17] does not allow foreign ownership of land. Art. 7 of the 1991 Land Code states: "Foreign citizens shall have no right to have land in their private ownership or lifetime use and inheritance."[18] The draft of the new Land Code indicates that Russian lawmakers are not ready to grant foreigners the right to own land.[19] According to the prevailing opinion foreign juridical persons and individuals may only be allowed the right to lease land.[20] At the same time, the 1991 Law on Foreign Investment guarantees to foreign investors the right to

---

[14]See M.M. Boguslavskii, *Problemy stabil'nosti pravovogo regulirovaniya* (Problems of the Stability of Legal Regulation), in *Pravovoe regulirovanie inostrannykh investitsii v Rossii* (Legal Regulation of Foreign Investment in Russia) 45, 51 (1995); Id., *Inostrannye investitsii: Pravovoe regulirovanie* (Foreign Investments: Legal Regulation) 45- 48 (1996).

[15]These far-reaching exceptions are contained in the proposals of the Government concerning the envisioned revision of the 1991 Law. See Kirin, *supra* note 3, at 31.

[16]Cf. I.A. Ikonitskaya, *Inostrannye investitsii I zemel'nye otnosheniya* (Foreign Investment and Land Relationships), in *Pravovoe regulirovanie inostrannykh investitsii v Rossii* (Legal Regulation of Foreign Investment in Russia) 58-65 (1995).

[17]See *Vedomosty RF*, No. 22, item 768 (1991).

[18]The legal status of the 1991 Land Code is a matter of controversy. After the adoption of the 1993 Constitution many clauses of the 1991 Land Code , including Art. 7, were declared invalid by the Decree of the President of December 24, 1993 *(Sobranie aktov,* No. 52, item 5085 (1993)).

[19]See I.A. Ikonitskaya, *Osnovy zemel'nogo prava Rossiiskoi Federatsii* (Fundamentals of Land Law of the Russian Federation) 35-37 (1997).

[20]Id.

hold shares, establish wholly-owned enterprises and acquire enterprises and buildings. Yet, Art. 3 of the same Law grants to foreign investors only the right to *use* land and other natural resources.

Restrictions on foreign investors become particularly confusing when a foreign investor buys an enterprise with extensive holdings, including land plots. Under the existing Russian law, the foreigner's ownership of the land tracts is not clear. Nor is the situation any clearer when the foreign investors participate in a joint venture formed with a Russian enterprise which owns land and contributes it to the joint enterprise. Although under the 1994 Civil Code a joint venture would become the owner of the land,[21] the rights of foreign participants with respect to the land are not clear. One can only hope that the issue of land ownership will be clarified with the adoption of the new version of the Law on Foreign Investment and of a new Land Code.

F. Guarantees Against Expropriation

The 1991 Law on Foreign Investment establishes strong guarantees against expropriation of foreign investments. Art. 7 of the 1991 Law provides that foreign investments in Russia "are not subject to nationalization and may not be requisitioned or confiscated except as provided by legislative acts adopted in the face of extraordinary circumstances which require that such measures be taken in the public interest. In the event of a nationalization or requisition, the foreign investor is entitled to the payment of swift, adequate and effective compensation." Decisions of the governmental bodies on expropriation of foreign investments may be appealed to Russian courts.

Under Art. 8 of the 1991 Law "compensation payable to the foreign investor must correspond to the value the nationalized or requisitioned investments had immediately prior to the time the decision on the nationalization or requisition was made officially known. Compensation must be paid without unreasonable delays in such currency as the one in which the investment was first made or in such foreign currency acceptable to the foreign investor." Until such compensation is actually paid, the principal amount of the compensation is to earn interest at the official rate in effect in Russia.

Furthermore, Art. 7 of the 1991 Law provides foreign investors with the right to be compensated for their losses, including lost profits, incurred as a

[21] Art. 213 of the Civil Code provides that commercial organizations "are the owners of property transferred to them as investments (or contributions) of their founders (participants or members) and also of property obtained by these juridical persons on other bases."

result of the acts by the Russian governmental bodies or their officials in contravention of the law in force in Russia.

Art. III of the 1992 Russian-US Treaty Concerning the Encouragement and Reciprocal Protection of Investment[22] provides additional guarantees. Under Art. III of the 1992 Treaty "investments" shall not be expropriated or nationalized either directly or indirectly through measures tantamount to expropriation or nationalization ("expropriation") except for a public purpose; in a nondiscriminatory manner; upon payment of prompt, adequate and effective compensation; and in accordance with due process of law. It also states that "compensation shall be equivalent to the fair market value of the expropriated investment immediately before the expropriatory action was taken or became known, whichever is earlier; be paid without delay; include interest from the date of expropriation at a commercial rate established on a market basis; be fully realizable; and be freely transferable at the market rate of exchange existing on the date of expropriation."

G. Registration of Foreign Investment

The 1991 Law provides for the registration of enterprises with foreign investment. Although in principle the procedure may result in the denial of registration, the measure serves control purposes aimed at supervising and not hindering foreign investment projects. Denial of registration may be appealed in court.

State registration of enterprises with foreign investment is carried out by the governments of the republics and by the administrations of other "subjects" of the Russian Federation. However, state registration of all enterprises with foreign investment in oil exploration and petroleum refinement as well as in all other areas where the amount of foreign investment exceeds 100 million roubles is carried out by the Ministry of Economy. Certain companies may require additional approvals. For instance, large construction or renovation projects require a state-conducted expert evaluation. Some enterprises may require ecological approvals. In addition, some "subjects" of the Russian Federation, such as the City of Moscow, have enacted their own regulations governing registration which may impose some additional registration and franchise tax requirements.[23]

---

[22] See *supra* note 2.

[23] See *Polozhenie o poriadke registratsii predpriyatii v Moskve* (Regulations on the Procedure of Registration of Enterprises in the City of Moscow), reprinted in *Inostrannye Investitsii* (Foreign Investments) 160 (1994).

H. Free Economic Zones

The 1991 Law envisions the possibility of establishing a preferential procedure for setting up and operating enterprises with foreign investment in "free economic zones." A "free economic zone" is a specially administered territory established for the purpose of attracting foreign investment on the most favorable of terms and conditions. Under the 1991 Law, these special terms may include additional benefits regarding taxation, a lower rate of payment for land plots, a more lenient customs policy, including a lower customs duty, special customs exemptions, more lenient procedures for import and export, and a simplified visa regime (including the possibility of a complete waiver of visa requirements).

These general provisions on free economic zones will be further developed by a special law on free economic zones which is still under debate. A specific package of benefits for each particular zone is defined in separate laws designed for each individual zone. An example is the federal Law "On the Special Economic Zone in Kaliningrad Region."[24] This Law, among other things, establishes a duty-free regime, grants certain exceptions from foreign exchange regulations and allows the local authorities to establish a favorable tax regime.[25]

I. Concessions

The 1991 Law contains an important clause concerning concessions. Concessions are a special form of investment which were used in Russia in the 1920s. In accordance with agreements concluded between foreign investors and the Russian Government, the Government granted the concessionaire the right to exploit mineral resources or to operate an enterprise, and the concessionaire, in return, was obliged to provide capital and equipment in the quantity and within the time-frame provided by the agreement. The concessionaire acquired the right of ownership of the resulting product (for example, extracted natural resources) which it could export at its own discretion after transferring to the Russian Government a specified share of the product or profits.

The 1991 Law includes only the most general provisions concerning concession agreements. It provides, in particular, that such agreements may only be concluded for the development and management of renewable and

---

[24] See *Sobranie*, No. 4, item 224 (1996).

[25] For details, see V. Ignatov, V. Butov, *Svobodnye ekonomitcheskie zony* (Free Economic Zones) 50-61 (1997).

nonrenewable natural resources, as well as for doing business related to the utilization of state property that has not been transferred to private enterprises, organizations or agencies. The Government of the Russian Federation or other agency duly authorized by it is the contracting party with the concessionaire. Fifty years have been established as the maximum period for a concession. During this period, any unilateral modification of the terms of a concession agreement is permitted only where directly envisioned by the agreement itself. Of particular importance is the clause according to which concession agreements may include provisions which deviate from the existing Russian legislation. However, such provisions acquire legal force only when they are approved by the Russian parliament.

J. Production Sharing Agreements

While special legislation on concessions is still under discussion, in 1995 the Russian parliament enacted the Law on Production-Sharing Agreements[26] which governs concessions with respect to certain natural resources, in particular Russia's immense oil and gas wealth.

The 1995 Law establishes the basic parameters for foreign investment in the gas and oil sectors of the Russian economy. In general, the 1995 Law creates a legal structure for long-term and significant capital commitments which is generally familiar to potential investors. The 1995 Law provides that production sharing agreements establish a contractual relationship between the foreign investor and the Russian Federation. It also contemplates important tax exemptions, assures tax stability and grants investors unrestricted export rights, exceptions from currency conversion requirements and the right to settle disputes through commercial arbitration.

An important innovation under the 1995 Law is that it considers production-sharing agreements to be civil law contracts. As a party to a commercial contract governed by the general principles of civil law, Russia will be bound by the contractual terms and in principle will not be able to change or amend the contract unilaterally. Art. 2 of the Law defines the production-sharing agreements in the following manner:

> A production-sharing agreement is an agreement under which the Russian Federation shall grant the subject of entrepreneurial activity (hereinafter referred to as "investor") an exclusive right to explore, develop and exploit mineral resources on the subsoil area defined in the agreement and for conducting operations related thereto for a price and for a certain period of

[26] See *Sobranie*, No.1, item 18 (1996).

> time, while the investor shall undertake to finance and perform the said operations at his own risk. The agreement shall provide for all necessary terms and conditions concerning the use of the subsoil, including terms and procedures for sharing the product between the parties to the agreement in accordance with the provisions of this federal law.

The 1995 Law provides that the parties to a production-sharing agreement are the Russian Federation (the state) and the investor. The Russian Government and the executive organs of the relevant "subject" of the Federation represent the state. The investors may be Russian citizens, foreigners, legal entities and associations of legal entities established under the joint venture contract. A foreign investor may designate an operator to carry out the recourse activities. The investor may use its own branch registered in Russia, a Russian subsidiary, Russian contractors or foreign contractors.

Because the Russian state becomes a party to a commercial contract, Art. 23 of the 1995 Law provides that "agreements concluded with foreign citizens and foreign judicial persons" may contain a waiver of sovereign immunity with respect to court proceedings, security for the claim and enforcement of court judgments or arbitration awards. As a result, a foreign party to the production-sharing agreement may sue the Russian state in courts. Russia will not be able to rely on the defense of sovereign immunity from jurisdiction of courts and execution of judgments and arbitration awards.

Art. 1 of the 1995 Law provides that production-sharing agreements are governed by the 1995 Law itself as well as by "the civil legislation of the Russian Federation." According to Art. 6 of the 1995 Law agreements must always be "concluded in accordance with the legislation of the Russian Federation." This means that parties to production-sharing agreements cannot choose foreign law to govern the transaction.[27]

Under the 1995 Law, a production-sharing agreement is the primary document which contains the grant of exclusive mineral rights. This means that the 1995 Law introduces a major change in the restrictive approach to resource development established by the 1992 Law on Subsoil.[28] Under the 1992 Law on Subsoil, the primary document was a license to carry out resource operations. The issuance of licenses depended on the discretion of Russian federal and local administrative organs. Furthermore, in exercising its state

[27] Some commentators claim that the mandatory application of Russian law "may present great difficulties for foreign investors and even discourage them from such investments in Russia." O.V. Radaeva, Production Sharing Agreements: The Investor and the State, 2 *Sudebnik* 265, 290 (1997).

[28] See *supra* note 4.

authority Russian was always able to unilaterally change or modify the license.[29] In contrast, under the 1995 Law the license is of secondary importance: the issuance of a licence becomes a pure formality because it must be issued automatically if a production-sharing agreement is signed. As a result, foreign investors will be able to avoid the burdensome requirements of the 1992 Law on Subsoil and enjoy a much more secure position vis-a-vis Russian federal and local recourse management agencies.

As a general rule, rights to extract minerals from the subsoil are granted as a result of a contest or auction. The 1995 Law provides that contests or auctions are conducted "in a manner established by legislation of the Russian Federation."[30] The 1995 Law also provides that agreements signed without contests or auctions must be confirmed by a federal statute. The same requirement applies to agreements concerning the continental shelf, the exclusive economic zone and areas of strategic importance.

The major incentive under the 1995 Law are tax advantages and safeguards. Instead of different taxes, the 1995 Law provides for three kinds of deductions: a payment for the use of the subsoil, the Government's share of the extracted minerals and a profit tax. Payments for the use of the land and the profit tax rate are fixed as of the date of the signing of the agreement.

Under the 1995 Law, all production is divided into portions which are either compensatory or profit bearing. The former remains the property of the investor and is used to reimburse it for production costs. The latter represents profit in kind and is subject to division between the state and the investor. The compensatory portion, as well as the portion which remains with the investor after sharing with the state, is fully owned by the investor.[31] The product may be exported without any restrictions. However, in exceptional cases restrictions may be imposed in accordance with the Law on State Regulation of Foreign Trade.[32]

---

[29] See S.A. Sosna, *Kommentarii k federal'nomu zakonu o soglasheniyakh o razdele produktsii* (Commentary to the Federal Law on Production-Sharing Agreements) 28 (1997).

[30] Under Art. 448 of the 1994 Civil Code auctions by bidding and competitions may be open or closed. Any person may participate in an open auction by bidding or in an open competition. Only persons specially invited for this purpose may participate in a closed auction by bidding or a closed competition.

[31] For details, see Sosna, *supra* note 28, at 80-98.

[32] Under Art. 15 of the Law on State Regulation of Foreign Trade (*Sobranie*, No. 42, item 3923 (1995)) restrictions on export may be imposed only in cases where it is necessary to insure the interests of national security or to fulfil international obligations of the Russian Federation.

The 1995 Law proclaims the principle of stability of production-sharing agreements. The terms and conditions of a production-sharing agreement are supposed to "retain validity for the entire period of its operation." According to Art. 17 of the 1995 Law amendments to an agreement can be made only by the consent of the parties. In addition, the investor is not subject to normative acts promulgated by the federal organs of executive power, "subjects" of the Federation or municipalities, if these acts "impose restrictions on the investor's rights acquired and exercised by him under the agreement."[33]

The 1995 Law also provides guarantees against changes in the legislation. If the legislation establishes conditions which negatively affect the commercial outcome of the investor's activity, the agreement must be amended to include conditions which would allow the investor to receive the commercial results which he or she would have obtained according to the legislation in force at the time of the conclusion of the agreement.[34]

While this general framework appears to be familiar and attractive to foreign investors, several important provisions of the 1995 Law disappointed the foreign investment community.[35] Many potential investors are unhappy about references to the restrictive 1992 Law on Subsoil. The 1995 Law states, in particular, that the terms and conditions for the use of the subsoil under production-sharing agreements cannot conflict with the provisions of the 1992 Law on Subsoil. Furthermore, there is a possibility of the termination of obligations with regard to the use of the license on several grounds listed in the 1992 Law on Subsoil. Under the 1992 Law on Subsoil a license may be terminated by the licensing agency in a wide range of situations.[36] As a result,

---

[33] 1995 Law on Production-Sharing Agreements, Art. 18(2).

[34] 1995 Law on Production-Sharing Agreements, Art. 17(2).

[35] Cf. V. Khrenov, J. Sheedy, Production Sharing in Russia: Investors Share Hope, 3 *The Parker School Journal of East European Law* 71-77 (1996); M.Y. Galyatin, A Hazy Future for the Law on Production-Sharing Agreements, Id., at 79-84.

[36] According to Art. 20 of the 1992 Law on Subsoil, licenses may be terminated upon the occurrence of any of the following events, some of which are beyond the licensee's control:

> "1) a direct threat to the life or health of the people working or living in the area where the work is carried out, arising in connection with the use of the subsoil;
> 2) the licensee's violation of the essential terms of the license;
> 3) the licensee's systematic violation of the established rules for use of the subsoil;
> 4) extraordinary circumstances (disasters, military operations and others);
> 5) the licensee's failure to obtain the envisaged production volumes within the period defined by the license;
> 6) liquidation of the enterprise or other subject of entrepreneurial activity which had been granted the right to use the subsoil."

foreign investors may feel that there no sufficient security, stability or predictability.

Many observers also believe that the 1995 Law does not provide sufficient protection for investors because the principle of stability of production-sharing agreements is undermined by three important exceptions. First, the 1995 Law allows amendments to agreements "by demand of one of the parties in case of a fundamental change in circumstances in accordance with the Civil Code of the Russian Federation."[37] Second, the investor cannot demand modifications of the agreements in cases of new legislation adversely affecting his or her interests if the relevant legislation introduces changes in standards of safety, protection of the subsoil, protection of the environment or health of the population. Third, while new restrictive normative acts are generally not applicable to investors, they would not be immune from administrative rules concerning safety, protection of the subsoil, protection of the environment, public health, as well as "public and state security."

Furthermore, the 1995 Law envisions an extremely complicated procedure for concluding production-sharing agreements. The need for parliamentary approval of certain agreements is particularly burdensome. The 1995 Law provides that not all areas of subsoil may be exploited under the production-sharing agreements. The relevant areas must first be determined by a special federal law.

Communists and nationalist legislators have fought the proposed legislation for years, arguing that it amounts to a sell-out of Russia's national wealth to foreigners. However, in 1997 the Federal Assembly finally approved a list of mineral and energy projects open to outside investment under production-sharing rules (the first seven deposits eligible for the deals included five oil fields, a goldfield and an iron ore deposit).[38]

K. Dispute Settlement

Under Art. 9 of the 1991 Law, disputes among foreign investors and enterprises with foreign investment and Russian governmental bodies or juridical entities are heard by Russian courts. In cases agreed by the parties, private law disputes may be submitted to international arbitration.

Art. 9 of the 1991 Law also deals with disputes concerning the

---

[37] 1995 Law on Production-Sharing Agreements, Art. 17. The fundamental change of circumstances may be the ground for the modification or termination of contract under Art. 451 of the 1994 Civil Code. See *supra* p. 332-336.

[38] See *Sobranie*, No. 30, item 3584 (1997).

amount, conditions or procedure for the payment of compensation in cases of expropriation. These disputes are to be resolved by the Supreme Court or Supreme Arbitration Court.

It is well known, however, that in cases of expropriation foreign investors often consider lawsuits in host state's courts as futile. They prefer international arbitration. Traditionally international arbitration plays an important role in resolving disputes involving expropriation. The right to arbitrate may derive from either a contract between an investor and Russia or a treaty between the investor's home state and Russia.

The 1992 Russian-US Treaty Concerning the Encouragement and Reciprocal Protection of Investment[39] contains a special clause on dispute settlement which provides for arbitration. Under Art. VI of the 1992 Treaty at any time after six months from the date on which the dispute arose, a national or company of a state party may choose to consent in writing to the submission of an investment dispute to the International Centre for the Settlement of Investment Disputes established in accordance with the 1965 Convention on the Settlement of Investment Disputes Between States and Nationals of Other States[40] or to the Additional Facility of the Centre or pursuant to the Arbitration Rules of the United Nations Commission on International Trade Law ("UNCITRAL Rules") or pursuant to the arbitration rules of any arbitral institution mutually agreed between the parties to the dispute.

PROBLEM

In September of 1993 the State Committee on Administration of State Property endorsed the privatization plan for the Moscow furniture factory "Garant" and approved the conditions of the investment tender for the sale of the shares of the joint stock company AO "Garant." One of the conditions of the investment tender was a guarantee of investments in "Garant" and application of investment money in accordance with the investment program.

The tender commission studied the documents submitted by five bidders before the tender. On January 4, 1994 the State Committee on Administration of State Property declared that the winner of the investment tender for a 49 percent stake in "Garant" was Berber Berber (BB), one of Germany's largest furniture manufacturers. On April 1, 1994 the Moscow Property Fund signed with BB a contract of sale according to which BB acquired 49 percent of the "Garant's" shares. The contract dealt only with the sale of shares (Art. 1). Art. 2 of the contract also provided that "within two

---

[39] See *supra* note 2.
[40] See 575 UNTS 159.

months" AO "Garant" and BB would sign a separate investment contract that would specify the investment obligations of BB.

The investment contract was signed on June 10, 1994. BB agreed to invest $8 million in the Moscow factory. The parties to the investment contract agreed that the contract "shall be governed by, and construed in accordance with the laws of Sweden, without regard to Swedish conflict of law rules." The contract also contained another clause of interest: "All claims and disputes arising under and in relation to this contract shall be arbitrated through the International Commercial Arbitration Institute in Stockholm, Sweden. No court shall have jurisdiction with regard to any such claims or disputes unless parties voluntarily submit to such jurisdiction."

Although the deal started amicably, relations between the parties deteriorated rapidly. One of the problems was the investment contract, which contained several preconditions for the investment. One of the conditions envisioned far-reaching changes in "Garant's" charter to allow the representatives of BB to sit on the company's board of directors. The general director of AO "Garant" also learned that BB wanted to establish full control of the company before making any investment. Another bone of contention concerned trademarks which BB promised to provide under the investment contract. AO "Garant" was not happy about many restrictions which BB sought to impose in the proposed license contract. As a result, the envisioned license contract was never signed.

By 1998 no money has been invested in the company, and each side blames the other. The director of AO "Garant" says that their German partners do not want to hand over a promised $8 million, while the German side says that the Russians do not want to change the charter and thus are preventing investment.

Mr. Sessel, chairman of BB, announced that he plans to file suit in the International Commercial Arbitration Institute in Stockholm for what he contends are contract violations by the firm in which he owns a minority share.

You have been hired by AO "Garant." Mr. Stol, chairman of AO "Garant," indicates that he "wants to get rid of BB." He also says that when he signed the investment contract he did not realize that the promised investment would be made only under certain conditions, which he describes as "extremely burdensome." Mr. Stol says that he does not really need any of BB's money any more. Although the company is ready to arbitrate in Stockholm, he would prefer to resolve the issue in Russia. He asks you to prepare a memorandum that discusses possible solution of the problem.

Your client asks your opinion on the following questions:

1. Are there any legal mechanisms that would allow AO "Garant" "to get rid of BB"?

2. What are the substantive law provisions governing the matter?

3. Which remedies are available under the Russian law? "What kind of proceedings do we have to initiate"?

4. "Do we have to arbitrate in Stockholm? Can we somehow prevent this arbitration"?

5. "If we cannot avoid arbitration in Stockholm, and Mr. Sessel wins, what can we do to prevent recognition and enforcement of the award in Russia"?

L. Effectiveness of the Foreign Investment Regime

Although Russia has made an effort to establish the basic elements of a relatively liberal foreign investment regime, large-scale direct investments are still rare. Besides political risks, shortcomings of the transitional economic system and risks resulting from the general instability of the legal environment, progress in attracting the much needed foreign capital is hampered by many restrictions imposed by the current legislation. Restrictive policies result from the widely-shared fear that foreigners will acquire all major Russian assets at the time of economic crisis.

Economic nationalism has made some of the provisions of the 1991 Law on Foreign Investment inoperative. A good example is Art. 28 which envisions "certain benefits in taxation matters." Incentives such as tax holidays and lower tax rates were first implemented but subsequently abolished. Current Russian tax legislation contains very few "benefits" or inducements for foreign investors. Only enterprises that are engaged in material production have been granted a two-year tax holiday. Certain additional benefits have been granted to foreign enterprises in free economic zones. However, in general the existing Russian tax law, which still lacks any degree of stability, establishes a single legal regime for both domestic enterprises and enterprises with foreign investment.

From a broader perspective, an important factor which impedes the flow of foreign capital into Russia is the absence of a clear foreign investment policy. Policy uncertainty and bureaucratic obstacles and inaction stand as continuing barriers to the effective use of law to regulate foreign investment. Furthermore, the existing institutional arrangements for foreign investments are unsatisfactory. In Russia there is no single federal entity responsible for implementing the relevant laws and regulations and attracting foreign investment. The creation of such an entity is envisioned only by the proposed revision of the 1991 Law.

Another major problem is ineffective enforcement of existing laws, in particular laws protecting property and other rights of private parties. While Russia has established the basic elements of an independent and impartial judiciary, many judges lack expertise in commercial matters.[41] Experience indicates, however, that the success of market-oriented legislation which favors private sector domestic and foreign investment depends on efficient and experienced judiciary. Like other Eastern European judges, Russian judges lack training and experience to handle complex investment disputes.[42] It is not surprising that foreign observers find administration of investment laws in Russia "substantially deficient."[43]

All this suggests that Russia needs greater emphasis on the strengthening of the institutions, including courts, responsible for the enforcement of foreign investment legislation.

---

[41] For details, see *supra*, p. 116-117.

[42] For details, see J.L. Taylor, F. April, Foreign Investment Law in Transitional Economies: A Case for Refocusing Institutional Reform, 4 *The Parker School Journal of East European Law* 1 (1997).

[43] Id., at 39.

CHAPTER X

CRIMINAL PROCEDURE

A. Introduction

1. The Checkered Past and Uncertain Future of Criminal Procedure in Russia

Soviet criminal justice was generally known in the West for the "show trials" of Stalin's enemies in the 1930s, the political trials of dissidents that took place in the 1960s, 70s and 80s, and the "gulag" system of prisons written about by Solzhenitsyn. But political cases tell us little about the ordinary criminal case. For lack of information to the contrary, many Western commentators assumed that, except for political cases—which no legal system handles well—the Soviet system of criminal procedure worked quite well in the ordinary criminal case. True, the conviction rate high,[1] but this was the case in many Western European systems as well.

There is evidence that Soviet criminal procedure made some colossal blunders in ordinary criminal cases, some as chilling as the blunders it made in the political cases. And it is no accident that those blunders favored the state rather than the criminal defendant. In more than one case, a person was convicted and sentenced, and sometimes executed only to discover later that someone else was responsible for the crime. Many such instances came to light in the "Perestroika" era in both newspaper accounts and discussions in the Supreme Court of the USSR.[2]

In post-Soviet Russia, difficulties have increased because of a phenomenal increase in crime. As a recent textbook on criminal procedure states:

[1] Actually, the conviction rate varied substantially over time with a gradual increase in the last years of Soviet power. However, this was less a result of acquittals on the merits in serious cases than of dismissals for lack of evidence in trivial cases. *See infra* p. 527.

[2] *See* Aloys Hastrich, *Die Diskussion ber 'Perestroika' in der sovjetischen Rechtspflege*, 34 Ost Europa Recht 205 (1988) and Ruling of the Plenum of the USSR Supreme Court,'O dal'neishem ukreplenii zakonodatel'stva pri osushestvlenii pravosudiya (On Further Strengthening of Legislation in the Administration of Criminal Justice), 1 BVS SSSR (1988).

> In the years 1981-1985, 6 million cases were filed, while in the years 1991-1995, there were over 13 million filed. In comparison with 1986, the rate of growth of serious crime has increased three times. The last five years have seen a great increase not just in numbers, but in the degree of armed violence and cruelty and the level of organization and professionalism of criminal elements.
>
> In addition, the Ministry of Internal Affairs estimates that for each reported crime that results in a case being filed, there are 2 that are not filed. Considering the rate of crime that remains completely unreported, the number of crimes that took place in 1995 was more like 10 million (and not the 2,755,700 filed that year). Criminologists estimate that as the year 2000 approaches, the number of filed cases will increase by 2 and a half times.[3]

The greater burden on the criminal justice system cannot help but place strains on it at every level. This presents a heightened danger both of the guilty going free and of the innocent being convicted. In addition, the political pressure to "do something" about the crime problem will undoubtedly put pressure on criminal justice organs to cut corners, thereby placing civil liberties in jeopardy. This cannot be good for society or for those accused of crime.

---

[3] B.S. Teterin and Ye.Z. Troshkin, *Vozbuzhdenie i rassledovanie ugolovnykh del* (Initiation and Investigation of Criminal Cases) 3 (1997). Other recent editions of textbooks that are useful sources for understanding Russian Criminal Procedure law are P.A. Lupinskaya, ed., *Ugolovno-protsessual'noye pravo Rossiiskoi Federatsii, izdanie vtoroye* (Criminal Procedure Law of the Russian Federation, 2d ed.) (1997); K.F. Gutsenko, ed. *Ugolovnyi protsess* (Criminal Procedure) (1997) and A.P Ryzhkov, *Sledstvennye deystvia i inye sposoby sobirania dokazatel'tsv* (Investigative Techniques and Other Methods of Gathering Evidence) (1997). Complete texts of the Criminal Procedure Code abound. One that also contains a description of the changes made most recently to conform to the new Criminal Code is V.N. Grigoriev and A.P Guliaev, ed., *Ugolovno-protsessual'nyi kodeks RSFSR: Obshchaya kommentarij i postateynaia tablitsa izmenenii i dopolnenii* (Criminal Procedure Code of the RSFSR: General Commentary and Table of Changes and Additions) (1997). A more complete article-by-article commentary edited by a justice of the Russian Supreme Court is V.M. Lebedev, *Nauchno-prakticheskij commentarij k Ugolovnomu- protsessua'nomu kodeksu RSFSR* (Academic and Practical Commentary to the Criminal Procedure Code of the RSFSR) (1995). A useful compendium of examples of documents used in the criminal process is V.I, Baskov, *Protsessual'nye akty ugolovnogo protsessa* (Official Acts in Criminal Procedure) (1996). A useful copy of all the various laws regarding criminal procedure as well as important guiding explanations of the Supreme Court compiled by a prominent defense attorney is N.M. Kipnis, *Ugolovno-portsessual'nyj kodeks RSFSR* (Criminal Procedure Code of the RSFSR) (1996).

2. The Law Applied in Criminal Cases

In Russia, all criminal procedure law and criminal law is federal, governed by the 1960 Criminal Procedure Code of the RSFSR[4] (cited here as CrPC) and the 1996 Criminal Code of the Russian Federation[5] (cited here as CrC). These are laws of nationwide applicability in all "subjects" of the Russian Federation.[6]

One might wonder why there is a new Criminal Code of the Russian Federation, but an old Criminal Procedure Code of the RSFSR. After Soviet power was abolished in 1991, work began almost immediately on both and, while this work continued, the old codes were amended as necessary to implement particular reforms. Agreement was reached on a new Criminal Code, but it was thought appropriate that both Codes should take effect at the same time. However, by 1996 it was clear that there were still major disagreements on the new Criminal Procedure Code. Consequently, it was decided that the Criminal Code would be enacted without further delay. Transitional amendments were made in the Criminal Procedure Code to make it correspond with the new Criminal Code and work on ironing out remaining disagreements continues.

As of this writing, a final version of the bill has gone through a first reading in the State Duma and a second reading is scheduled for June 1998. However, virtually no one is happy with it, including the Council of Judges of the Russian Federation, a organization of all Russian judges, an important interest group. Among other things, the Council criticized the new draft for its failure to simplify procedures and to introduce some form of plea bargaining. Currently, it is reported that the drafting group is working well and is making compromises, especially in the direction of simplifications urged by the judges, including abbreviated trials in cases of confessions.[7]

Despite the fact that all criminal and criminal procedural law is federal, there are some geographical variations in procedure at the trial stage. Part of the reason for this is that the right to trial by jury, with its more adversarial procedural rules, has been implemented in only 9 "subjects" of the

---

[4] Vedomosty RF, No. 40, item 592 (1960), (as amended through 1997).

[5] Sobranie, No. 25, item 2954 (1996)(effective January 1, 1997).

[6] A new Criminal Procedure Code of the Russian Federation remains to be passed.

[7] Letter from Professor Peter Solomon, University of Toronto, July 2, 1998, on file with the authors. A copy of the version of the proposed Criminal Procedure Code that passed the first reading is on file with the authors. Also, it may be viewed on the Russian computerized legal information data-base "Garant" in the Proposed Legislation Library (in Russian).

county. But even in non-jury trials, there are differences in the degree of adversarialness present. This results from the conflict between the current inquisitorial trial procedures of the RSFSR Criminal Procedure Code and the Constitution's command in Article 123(3) that "all judicial proceedings shall be conducted based on adversarial principles and equality of all parties." Most trial judges are waiting for the new Criminal Procedure Code to show them the way, but other judges—many spurred on by their jury trial experience — have taken the constitutional command to heart and have begun to conduct non-jury trials in a more adversarial manner.

3. Russian Criminal Procedure in Comparative Context: The Civil Law Tradition with Russian Modifications

Two great traditions make up the Western legal world: the common-law tradition and the civil-law tradition. Correspondingly, there are two great criminal procedure traditions: common law countries follow adversarial-accusatorial principles and civil law countries generally follow inquisitorial principles. Because the word inquisitorial sounds sinister to the English-speaking ear—calling up visions of the Spanish Inquisition and torture—the term "investigative" is sometime substituted.[8]

Russia's legal system falls into the civil law category and its criminal procedure system has traditionally been and remains today overwhelmingly investigative or inquisitorial, though it has some adversarial aspects, particularly when it comes to jury trials. The Russian term for its criminal procedure system is *rozysknaya*, which essentially means "investigative."

Because the Russian criminal justice system still follows essentially the continental inquisitorial tradition, it is important to examine the specifics of the Russian system with one eye on practices and institutions in Western Europe. Without this context, it will be impossible for the U.S. reader to tell what differences are truly Russian and what differences are simply continental European.

The need to examine the Russian system in the context of the continental tradition is not reduced by the fact that the new Criminal Procedure Code will presumably conform Russian criminal procedure to the Constitutional requirement of "adversarial principles and equality of all parties." First, the constitution's requirement applies only to "judicial proceedings." There are presently no proposals to eliminate inquisitorial *pre-trial* procedures. As we will soon see, an important stage in civil law countries

---

[8]For some reason the word "inquisitorial" is associated with "inquisition" rather than the more benign word with the same root "inquisitive."

and in Russia, is an extensive quasi-judicial pre-trial investigation. Second, "adversarial principles and equality of all parties" is a phrase with some room for different interpretations. Continental eyes will likely view it differently than American lawyers might understand it. Despite the constitutional command, the new Criminal Procedure Code will undoubtedly have more in common with continental European legal systems than with the Anglo-American tradition.[9]

B. Pre-Trial Procedure

1. Initiation of the Criminal Case and Police Inquiry

There are three distinct stages of Russian criminal procedure before trial: (1) initiation of the criminal case following police or other observation of evidence of a crime (*vozbuzhdenie ugolovnogo dela)*; (2) inquiry conducted by police or other law enforcement organs authorized to do so (*doznanie*); and (3) a formal quasi-judicial "preliminary investigation" (*predvaritel'noye rassledovanie*) of the full circumstances of the case.

The first two stages include both the taking and investigating of citizen complaints or other information and pursuit and investigation of facts that come directly to the attention of police officers. As such, the first two are not that different from the initial work that the police do in most countries. The distinctive stage for pre-trial Russian criminal procedure is the third stage of preliminary investigation, so we will spend some time describing it.[10]

2. The Criminal Investigator

The preliminary investigation is conducted by a "criminal investigator" (*sledovatel' po ugolovnym delam*). Criminal investigators are generally based in the Ministry of Internal Affairs or, on lower levels, subordinate to

---

[9] *See* Lupinskaya, *supra* note 1, pp. 14-17 for widely shared Russian views of the various types of criminal procedure, pp. 25-29 for a statement of what changes in the Criminal Procedure Code are needed and pp. 123-127 for an explanation of what "adversarial principles and equality of parties" means.

[10] Some petty crimes do not require a preliminary investigation and may be prosecuted in court after being investigated simply by a police inquiry. In such cases the police inquiry is more extensive than it is in cases where the system relies on the criminal investigator to conduct the investigation. When the police inquiry will be the only pre-trial investigation, the police inquirer generally may use the same techniques of evidence gathering that are described here as being used by the criminal investigator. A list of the crimes for which a full preliminary investigation is not required is contained in Art. 126, CrPC.

police chiefs. Such investigators also work for the Federal Security Bureau, the tax police and soon will be working in the customs agency. The name "criminal investigator" may fool the American lawyer, who may think that this is someone on par with a police detective who must charm and cajole witnesses to talk to him. This is hardly the case. The Russian Criminal Investigator has subpoena power to call witnesses and issue orders for the conduct of searches and seizures, production of documents, medical examinations and the like.

Officially, Russia's pre-trial investigation system seeks to be like that of continental Western European tradition with the criminal investigator as the Russian equivalent of the French "juge d'instruction" or the French, Italian or German public prosecutor. These traditional civil-law-system officials conduct the investigation of a crime and are often empowered to take action that in a common-law country could only be taken by a judge. But in return for that power, they exercise protective functions and act quasi-judicially. Thus, they are expected to investigate not just incriminating evidence, but evidence of innocence as well and to assure that the rights of the suspect are protected. Much of the actual hands-on investigative work is done by the police, but it is done at the direction and under the supervision of the investigating official.[11]

Russian criminal investigators are supervised by procurators and together they are also empowered to take actions which in the Anglo-American tradition generally can only be done through a judicial order.[12] Russian law similarly charges the criminal investigator to engage in a "complete and objective investigation of all sides" of the case.[13] However, in terms of education, pay and inclination, the Russian criminal investigator varies considerably from the continental ideal. Unlike their Western European counterparts, while Russian investigators generally have some legal education, only a few have graduated from the standard 4 or 5 year curriculum that practicing lawyers have. Often criminal investigators are law students studying in the evening divisions of law schools who are paid less than $200 a month.[14] Clearly, it is not a job that is at the top of the list of potential career

---

[11] An excellent and readable summary and commentary from the adversarial perspective on French and German criminal pre-trial procedure can be found in Leonard H. Leigh and Lucia Zedner, Report to the Royal Commission on the Administration of Criminal Justice in the Pre-Trial Phase in France and Germany (HMSO, London 1992).

[12] The procuracy was discussed in Chapter III, pp. 117-123.

[13] Art. 213(3), CrPC.

[14] Todd Foglesong, *Habeas Corpus* or Who Has the Body? Judicial Review of Arrest and Pre-Trial Detention in Russia, 14 Wis. Int'l L.Rev. 541, 552 (1996), citing conversations with the Deputy Procurator of the Intermunicipal Borough in Moscow, and the Deputy Procurator of Moscow.

opportunities for graduates of quality law schools. In addition, both criminal investigators and their supervising procurators tend to be "law and order" types, often being former police officers.

There is also evidence of relatively lax supervision by lawyer-procurators. As in other parts of the criminal justice system, there are too many cases and too few underpaid investigators.[15]

Thus, despite their charge to engage in full and objective investigation of all sides of the case, there are few criminal investigators who act as if their job is anything other than finding and compiling as much evidence against the defendant as possible. While this is not objectionable in a system in which investigators of crime have no quasi-judicial powers and the evidence they gather is not filed with the court, it is problematic when they are entrusted with such powers and, as discussed below, their findings become part of the official court record at trial.

3. The Preliminary Investigation Casefile

As in continental Western European systems, the pre-trial investigation dominates Russian criminal procedure. During this investigation, evidence is collected and evaluated for the purpose of making a recommendation to the supervising procurator as to what formal charges should be brought against the defendant. The supporting evidence is collected in a dossier or casefile. In most cases, the casefile consists primarily of witness testimony made under penalty of perjury and relevant documents. This casefile is used for two purposes. First, it is sent to the supervising procurator who uses it as the basis for deciding whether the formal charges recommended by the criminal investigator should be approved. Second, if formal charges are authorized, the casefile is filed in court and becomes the official court record.

Western European continental systems differ in terms of the degree to which the written contents of the case file can, without more, be used directly as evidence of guilt. In some, there is no live testimony and guilt is determined based on the written record compiled during the pre-trial investigation, while in others there is a full trial with live witnesses. The Russian system falls at the latter "live trial" end of the spectrum: the Criminal Procedure Code declares that all trials are based on the principles of "immediacy" and "orality" of the

[15] *Id.*, p. 552: "When asked in September 1995, to assess the quality of procuratorial supervision [of investigators], the Deputy Procurator of the Tver Intermunicipal Borough in Moscow, replied with a wry smile: 'right about average' (*gde-to na posredstvenno*). And one should not expect anything better than that, he said, since on average, one procurator supervises between fifteen and twenty investigators, each managing approximately fifteen cases."

evidence.[16] Under these concepts, a conviction must be based solely on the evidence produced at trial in open court and that evidence must generally be first-hand witness testimony or other primary evidence.

Despite these requirements, Russian law permits statements in the casefile to be used against the defendant at trial under some circumstances. First, some statements are automatically admissible at trial—medical and other expert conclusions, and official descriptions (protocols) of examinations of the crime scene, searches and seizures, line-ups and experiments.[17] Second, ordinary witnesses' statements may be used at trial as proof if the witness is "absent from court for reasons that prevent his or her appearance in court" or if the defendant's and any witness's trial testimony varies in a substantial way from their pre-trial testimony.[18] The permissible reasons for unavailability are not set out in the statute. One commentator suggests they are "death, serious illness, travel to another country either permanently or on business for a long period of time, relocation to a place of abode that is far away, long absence from home for other valid reasons, etc."[19]

Despite the clarity and strictness of these requirements, when witnesses fail to show up at trial—regardless of the reason—the temptation is great for the judge to simply reach for the casefile and read the witnesses' statements into the record. The following two cases deal with the question of the circumstances under which witness statements contained in the case file can be used at trial.

Supreme Court: *In re Komarov et al.* (*BVS*, 1997, No. 4, p. 9)

Komarov [and others] were convicted by the Kirov Regional Court [of banditism, extortion, kidnaping and other violent crimes] . . .

The Collegium for Criminal Cases of the RF Supreme Court reversed the convictions and remanded the case for a new trial. . . .

As the Collegium saw it, the regional court . . . violated the principle of immediacy of trials.

The trial record reflected that the testimony of many witnesses was read in order to remove ambiguities, even though testimony given at the preliminary investigation is properly admitted at trial only if there are substantial contradictions between it and the trial testimony.

---

[16] Art. 240, CrPC (the Russian words are "neposredstvennost" and "ustnost").
[17] Art. 87, CrPC.
[18] Art. 286, CrPC.
[19] Commentary, *supra* note 4, p. 364.

In violation of Art. 286 CrPC RSFSR[[20]] the testimony of the victim Krutikhin, witnesses K., M. and others who were absent from the trial was read, even though the court did not set out any reasons why they did not attend the trial.

The Deputy Chair of the RF Supreme Court lodged a protest raising the issue of whether the appeal panel's decision should be reversed and the case remanded for appellate reexamination.

The Presidium of the RF Supreme Court on September 26, 1996, sustained the protest, stating the following:

As is apparent from the record, the defendants were prosecuted for banditism, extortion, kidnaping and other serious violent crimes.

In the process of the preliminary investigation, the victim and many other witnesses were threatened with retaliation and for that reason the trial court took several security measures to protect the victim and witnesses and to assure that the case could be tried on the merits and the real truth of the case could be established. These circumstances were not sufficiently taken into account by the appeals court and this failure affected the correctness of its decision [reversing the convictions]. . . .

The trial court, relying on Art. 286 CrPC RSFSR, read the testimony of the victim Krutikhin and witnesses K., N., Zh. and Sh.

However, before reading this testimony, the court issued 16 warrants requiring that the victim and witnesses be brought before the court. In connection with this, as shown by police reports of the officers seeking to execute the warrants and the explanations of the witnesses' and victim's relatives, it is clear that victim K. was not living at his house and that his current address was unknown. Similar information is in the file regarding the witnesses Sh., Zh. and M-kh. Witnesses M-na was in the hospital and N. was on maternity leave. As for witness M., a republic-wide search was being conducted. Witness K. was a convict and as of the trial date it had not been established in what correctional facility he was being held.

Moreover, the testimony of M and M-kh were not relied on as evidence in the court's decision.

Nowhere in the appeals court's decision is it indicated why the stated actions taken by the trial court at trial in pursuit of a complete, even-handed and objective examination of all the circumstances of the case, resulted or

[20] See text accompanying note 18 for the content of Art. 286.

could have resulted in anything other than a legal and properly reasoned decision.

In light of such information, the decision of the appeals court reversing the convictions cannot be said to be properly reasoned. . . .

Notes and Questions

1. Why do you think that the intermediate appeals court reversed on this basis if the record made clear the reasons why witnesses were not there and what efforts had been made to procure the presence of the witnesses at trial? Would the author of the commentary quoted just before the case agree with the Supreme Court's decision?

2. In what contexts might an analogous issue come up in a U.S. court? How would the U.S. resolution of the issue differ from that here?

3. One problem with compelling attendance of witnesses is that witnesses suffer little if any consequences for failure to appear in response to a subpoena. One reason is that subpoenas are mailed and registered mail is no longer used, so there is no proof the witness actually received the subpoena.

4. The Draft Criminal Procedure Code, which has survived a first reading in the Duma, provides even greater protections for witnesses. The combination of Arts. 176(8) and 324(5) of the bill would seem to allow witnesses to testify anonymously where that is necessary to protect them or those close to them. When giving testimony during the preliminary investigation, their statement would not reflect their identity. They would then testify at trial, but they would not be seen by the other participants and would not give their names. How would this sort arrangement work out in the U.S.?

* * * *

Supreme Court: *In re Zavialov* (BVS, 1995, No. 11, p. 9)

Zavialov, who has a record of one previous conviction, was convicted and sentenced to prison for 2 years for [theft] and, combining that with the unserved portion of his earlier sentence . . . , to three years of imprisonment.

His sentence was affirmed by the appeals court.

He was found guilty of breaking and entering the apartment of one Bissenov and stealing property valued at 54,600 rubles pursuant to a prior conspiracy.

The Deputy Procurator-General of the RF lodged a protest asserting that the conviction should be reversed and the case remanded for a new trial in view of the fact that the court did not fulfill the requirements of Art. 20 [requiring a full and objective examination of the facts of the case] and Art. 286 CrPC RSFSR.[[21]]

The Collegium for Criminal Cases of the RF Supreme Court on September 15, 1995 sustained the protest, stating the following: . . .

As the record indicates, not a single witness specified on the witness list attached to the procurator's indictment appeared at trial.

The conviction was based on the testimony of Zavialov himself, who had admitted during the preliminary investigation that he was guilty of the theft that took place in Bissenov's apartment, but later changed his testimony, asserting that he took responsibility for the crime falsely because of the application of improper investigation methods.

The admission of guilt by a defendant may form the basis for a conviction only if it is supported by the totality of all the other evidence.

In the present case, no such other evidence was presented at trial. Instead prior testimony was read in violation of Art. 286 CrPC RSFSR.

It has been demonstrated that neither the victim nor witnesses were present at trial and there is no indication of the reasons for their absence. But the court, finding that their absence was for good cause, read the prior testimony of the witness Kuksov and relied on it as proof of Zavialov's guilt.

As is obvious from the record, sweat suits that were taken from a friend of Zavialov's were made by the same firm as that stolen from the victim. A significant number of them were seized by the police officers from Shmagin, who was selling them at the market.

However, the seized sweat suits were not presented for the victim to identify and their location is not known. There is no information either of their return to Bissenov or to their being admitted into evidence. . . .

The conviction is based on evidence that was not presented at trial and in substantial violation of the criminal procedural norms. Therefore, the conviction and appeals decision are reversed and the case remanded for a new trial.

---

[21] See text accompanying note 18 for the content of Art. 286.

NOTES AND QUESTIONS

1. The court treats this case as a simple one filled with less-than-subtle violations of criminal procedure norms. However, it is clear that one appeals court approved the conviction before the case got to this stage. What might account for that?

2. What situations analogous to the situation in this case might arise in the U.S. legal system? How would they be dealt with by the U.S. system?

3. An interesting aspect of this case is that the protest that resulted in the reversal of the defendant's conviction came from the Deputy Procurator-General of the RF. How can that be? How does this role of the Russian procurator compare with the role of the prosecutor in criminal litigation in the U.S.?[22]

* * * *

Even when witnesses appear at trial, they are often simply shown their preliminary investigation testimony and either asked to read it or otherwise affirm what they said in it. In other cases, the slightest hesitation on the part of the witness will result in the witness's entire preliminary investigation statement being read into the record. A suggestion that this happened in the *Komarov* case above is the court's comment when it described the decision below: "The trial record reflected that the testimony of many witnesses was read in order to remove ambiguities, even though testimony given at the preliminary investigation is properly admitted at trial only if there are substantial contradictions between it and the trial testimony." However, the Supreme Court did not address that point specifically in its decision. These practices and others give the impression that, despite the requirement of immediacy and orality of trials, the Russian criminal trial is often more a review of the preliminary investigation than a separate public proceeding in its own right.

Perhaps the greatest effect of the Russian case file on determinations of guilt lies in the fact that it is filed in court for the presiding judge to read and remains with the court for reference during deliberations. Even in cases in which there is a substantial amount of live testimony at trial, judges clearly "fill in" from the case file what might be omitted or unclear from the trial testimony.

From the standpoint of the American observer, there are two basic

---

[22] Procurator protests are discussed in greater detail *infra* p. 540.

problems with using the products of the preliminary investigation to prove guilt at trial. The first is the fact that the witness was not subject to cross-examination when the preliminary investigation statements were made nor is the witness available at trial to be cross-examined regarding the statement. While a substitute might be the opportunity for cross examination of the witness by defense counsel at the preliminary investigation, that is generally not permitted, as discussed below.[23] A second problem with using preliminary investigation testimony is that it is not given in a public proceeding.[24] Not only is the preliminary investigation closed to the public, it is largely secret. Art. 139 of the Criminal Procedure Code prohibits any participant at any stage of the preliminary investigation from disclosing any information about the preliminary investigation without the permission of the criminal investigator.

4. Arrest and Detention of Suspects

a. The Two Routes to Arrest and Initiation of a Criminal Case

There are two ways that criminal cases get started in most countries: (1) an investigation takes place first, then charges are filed and an arrest takes place; and (2) an arrest takes place first, charges are initiated, then further investigation takes place to find further evidence to substantiate those charges. An example of (1) in the U.S. is where the police have some evidence of wrongdoing, but they have not themselves observed facts sufficient for an immediate arrest. In such a case, they must gather sufficient evidence for an arrest through further investigation and then file charges and seek an arrest warrant. An example of (2) is where the police themselves witness the suspect committing the crime or in "hot pursuit" make a warrantless arrest. A similar situation obtains in Russia—making allowances for differences in institutions.

In situation (1)—investigation first, then arrest — information about a crime comes to the attention of the police or criminal investigator by means of a citizen complaint, discovery of a body or other such information, but there is either insufficient evidence to determine who the perpetrator is or the evidence is not solid enough for an arrest. After a brief police inquiry (*doznanie*), a preliminary investigation begins and a criminal investigator collects evidence. When the criminal investigator has collected "sufficient

[23] In the U.S. system, written statements of witnesses unavailable for trial would be inadmissible hearsay. *Cf.* FRE 803(8). Only if the statement is sworn and given in a prior trial, hearing or deposition at which the declarant was subject to cross examination can it be used as substantive evidence. FRE 801(b)(4).

[24] The Russian Constitution's guarantee in Art. 123(1) that *court proceedings* be open to the public does not apply to the preliminary investigation. Gutsenko, *supra* note 3 p. 55.

evidence to support an accusation that someone has committed a crime, the investigator is to issue an order requiring that person to appear [before the investigator] as an accused" (*obviniaemyi*), and an arrest follows.[25]

In situation (2)—arrest first, then investigation—there is sufficient evidence for an immediate arrest. Under Russian law, this can occur in three situations: whenever "1) the person is caught in the act of committing the crime or shortly thereafter, 2) eyewitnesses (including victims) immediately point out the person as the one who committed the crime and 3) when contraband or other products of the crime are visible on the person's clothing or in the person's home." Immediate arrest and detention are also possible when "the existence of *other information* provides a basis for suspecting the person of committing a crime," but "only if the person is attempting to flee, has no permanent residence or cannot establish his or her identity."[26]

A person detained under these circumstances is a "suspect" (*podozrevaemyi*). A suspect can be interrogated and searched and other investigation can be done, but within 72 hours, either a criminal investigator must determine that there is enough evidence to declare that the "suspect" is an "accused" or the suspect must be released. This period cannot be extended. Moreover, after 24 hours, the police must notify the procurator in writing about the detention. The procurator then has 48 hours to decide whether detention is proper and to order the suspect freed or held in continued detention.[27] If a formal accusation cannot be issued by the criminal investigator within the 72-hour period, in "exceptional situations" the suspect can be held for up to 10 days while the criminal investigator determines whether there is enough evidence to charge the suspect as an accused.[28]

b. Other Detention for Investigation

The growth of crime and particularly of organized crime has brought political pressure to apply extraordinary measures that would allow arrest and detention in situations and for periods of time beyond those outlined above. Many have felt that the 72 hour detention (or even the 10-day detention provided for in extraordinary cases) is insufficient to "check out" the detainee to see if he or she is involved in crime, especially in organized crime. An attempt to respond to this pressure was President Yeltsin's 1994 Decree

---

[25] Art. 143, CrPC. This order states that the person is being charged with a crime. It must be supported with a recitation of the crime the person is accused of and the facts of the crime.

[26] Art. 122, CrPC.

[27] *Id.*, p. 138.

[28] Art. 90, CrPC. This eliminated in the Draft CrPC.

allowing detention for investigation for up to 30 days of persons suspected of engaging in "banditism." This decree was rarely used and was quietly withdrawn by the President in June of 1997.[29]

However, local authorities also got into the act with detention laws. The following Constitutional Court case reviews a statute of the Republic of Mordovia allowing authorities to hold people without charge for up to a month if they were members of an "organized crime gang."

The Constitutional Court: *Case on the Constitutionality of the Statute of Mordovia of January 20, 1996 "On Temporary Emergency Measures in the Fight against Crime"*, Sobranie, 1997, No. 28, item 3498

On June 18, 1996, citizen R.K. Khayrov, who worked as the assistant director of the company "Tonus-Extra," was detained and placed in a temporary lockup pursuant to the administrative detention procedures set out in point b of Art. 1 of the Law of the Mordovian Republic, "On temporary emergency measures in the fight against crime." On June 24, 1996, he was freed on the order of the procurator of the city of Saransk. Neither before his detention nor after it was any criminal case initiated against R.K. Khayrov or any charges brought. Believing that his good name and business reputation had been injured by his detention, Khayrov filed suit in the Lenin district court of Saransk against the MVD [Ministry of Internal Affairs] of the Republic of Mordovia seeking damages for such injury. The court, dismissed his suit based on the fact that the police officer had acted within the scope of the Law of the Mordovian Republic "On temporary emergency measures in the fight against crime." . . .

2. Point b of Art. 1 of the law "On temporary emergency measures in the fight against crime" gave the Mordovian Ministry of Internal Affairs the right to administratively detain members of organized crime groups for a period of up to 30 days on the approval of the procurator. . . .

[The Court reviewed the means contemplated for determining whether a person is a member of an organized crime group, which ranged from actual witness testimony to "sources of mass information."]

4. A whole complex of criminal law, criminal procedure and prison laws provided for in the Constitution of the Russian Federation and federal statutes guarantees compliance with the constitutional rights and liberties of citizens when government organs exercise their power in the struggle against crime. These laws permit the detention only of persons charged with

---

[29] *Sobranie*, No. 25, item 2898 (1997).

committing a particular crime, and further determine the bases, duration and means of employing immediate detention measures and incarceration before charges are brought and regulate both the rights and obligations of law enforcement officers and the legal rights of a person subject to such coercive actions.

At the same time, the disputed provision of the law . . . permits a finding that a person belongs to an organized crime group (is participating in its activities) through the use of methods and evidence not contemplated by either the Constitution of the Russian Federation or federal criminal procedural statutes, i.e., effectively branding that person a criminal and applying coercive measures to him in the form of "administrative" detention for up to 30 days. This violates article 49 (part 1) of the Constitution of the Russian Federation, under which every person charged with a crime is considered innocent until his guilt is proven in accordance with the procedures provided in federal law and is established by valid judgment of a court.

5. Pursuant to article 22 of the Constitution of the Russian Federation, every person has the right to liberty and to personal inviolability (part 1); detention, confinement or imprisonment are permitted only pursuant to a judicial decision; before a judicial decision, a person may be detained for no longer than 48 hours (part 2).

The effect of this article at the present time is affected by provisions of point 6 of the second section of the Constitution of the Russian Federation, which describes "Final and Transitional Provisions," in accordance with which the procedures for arrest and detention of criminal suspects that existed before the Constitution was ratified are preserved. However, the sense of this provision as it relates to article 22 of the Constitution of the Russian Federation is that detention of a criminal character may be employed only when it is provided for by criminal procedural laws then in effect. Detention on any other basis may be effectuated only in compliance with the requirements of article 22 (part 2) of the Constitution of the Russian Federation.

The disputed provision of the Law of the Republic of Mordovia vesting a right in the Ministry of Internal Affairs with agreement of the procurator to detain administratively members of an organized crime group (persons participating in organized crime activities) for up to 30 days, violates article 22 and point 6 of the second section of the Constitution of the Russian Federation. . . .

6. . . . Detention as a measure to be taken in the fight against crime and as a means to suppress crime in reality is not "administrative" as it is labeled by the legislature of the Republic of Mordovia, i.e. it is not a form of

administrative procedure, but criminal procedure. Consequently, the relationships regulated by point "b" of part 1 of Art. 1 of the statute do not fall into the category of administrative (administrative procedure). Therefore, the argument of the party that passed the challenged statute that it acted pursuant to Art. 72 (point "k" of part 1) of the Constitution of the Russian Federation, which provides that administrative and administrative procedure legislation fall within the concurrent jurisdiction of the Russian Federation and the subjects of the Russian Federation, and that in the absence of Federal law on the subject it has the right to enact an appropriate law under Art. 76 of the Constitution of the Russian Federation, is groundless.

7. Under Art. 71 (point "o") of the Constitution of the Russian Federation, laws on crime and criminal procedure and the law of correctional facilities fall under the jurisdiction of the Russian Federation. In accord with Art. 76 . . . , on the subjects of its jurisdiction the Russian Federation is authorized to pass federal constitutional laws and federal laws that have direct application on the entire territory of the Russian Federation (part 1); laws and other normative acts of the subjects of the Russian Federation may not contradict federal law passed pursuant to the exclusive jurisdiction of the Russian Federation or the concurrent jurisdiction of the Russian Federation and its subjects. In the event of a conflict between federal law and any other statute passed in the Russian Federation, the federal law prevails (part 5).

By regulating relationships which are subject solely to regulation by criminal law or criminal procedure law or the law of correctional facilities, the Legislature of the Republic of Mordovia has tread upon an area within the exclusive competence of the federal legislature.

On the basis of the foregoing and the [statutes on the Constitutional Court], the Constitutional Court rules: . . .

That . . . the Law of the Republic of Mordovia "On Temporary Emergency Measures in the Fight against Crime" is unconstitutional . . . .

NOTES AND QUESTIONS

1. As the Court notes in point 5 of its opinion, Art. 22(2) of the Constitution provides that, in absence of judicial order, a person may not be detained for more than 48 hours. If so, how can the Criminal Procedure Code allow detention for up to 72 hours and in some situations for up to 10 days? The answer is found in point 6 of section 2 of the Constitution, entitled "Final and Transitional Provisions." It provides that "[u]ntil the introduction of a criminal procedure code of the Russian Federation that accords with the

provisions of this Constitution, the former process of arrest, pre-trial detention and custody of persons charged with crimes is preserved."

One basis for the decision of the Court is that the local law violated Art. 22(2) of the Constitution. Why wasn't the Mordovian law saved by the transitional provisions of the Constitution just cited?

2. Before condemning the Russians for allowing arrest and detention without probable cause or a judicial warrant, consider that France (like many other Western European countries) allows the police to detain anyone without a warrant or probable cause for 24 hours and the period can be extended to 48 hours by a prosecutor (called *gardé vue*).[30] How does U.S. law on the subject compare? How would the Russian or the French regime "play" in the United States?[31]

3. If Russian federal law permits detention based on suspicion for up to 72 hours and in "extraordinary circumstances" for up to 10 days, why would the Mordovian authorities not consider those measure sufficient to deal with organized crime? Note that the petitioner in the case was released after just a week.

* * * *

5. Preliminary Investigation Procedures

The person subject to investigation, then, may be an "accused" or just a "suspect" and may be free or under arrest. Whatever the situation, the law provides the criminal investigator with procedural devices that can be used to carry out the investigation of the circumstances of the commission of the crime.

a. Witness and Victim Testimony

The taking of witness and victim testimony is by far the most common activity of the criminal investigator.[32] All citizens have the duty to give

---

[30] Leigh and Zedner, *supra* note 11, p. 9, citing Art. 145-2 of the French CrPC. France requires a medical examination and report for any suspect held more than 24 hours.

[31] The purpose of the study cited in the last footnote was to determine whether any aspects of German or French pre-trial procedure should be adopted in England and Wales. The report observed on p. 22: "We do not think that French procedure concerning the interrogation of suspects in *garde a vue* by the police would be regarded as tolerable in this country."

[32] *See generally* CrPC, Art. 155-161.

evidence before the criminal investigator. Witnesses are summoned to attend through use of a subpoena. Generally the criminal investigator's examination of the witness is conducted at the investigator's office, although the investigator may do it where the witness is located, such as at the witness's place of work, a hospital, etc.

Before giving testimony, witnesses are warned that refusal to give testimony and the giving of false testimony subject them to criminal liability,[33] and the investigator obtains their signature indicating that they understand the warning.[34] Witnesses are then asked to state everything they know relevant to the crime being investigated. Following this, the investigator may ask questions, although leading questions are not permitted.[35] After the witness gives testimony, it is written up in a document called a "protocol" and signed by the witness. Much of the casefile is made up of witness protocols.

A problem with respect to witness testimony is the failure of the criminal investigator to advise witnesses regarding their right not to testify against their spouse or close relatives.[36] This is important, as Russia uses a strict version of the exclusionary rule. Art. 69 states: "Evidence obtained in violation of law shall have no legal effect and may not be used as the basis for criminal charges nor to prove the factual circumstances [of a crime]."[37] If warnings are not given, the judge must free them of their obligation to testify at trial and must exclude from trial any testimony given during the preliminary investigation.[38]

b. Testimony of the Suspect or Accused Before the Criminal Investigator

The subject of a criminal investigation or arrest may start out as a

[33] Art. 307-308, CrC.

[34] Art.158 CrPC.

[35] Art. 158(5), CrPC.

[36] Those relatives are spouses, parents and children (natural and adopted), brothers, sisters, grandparents, and grandchildren. Art. 34(9), CrPC.

[37] Art. 69, pt. 3, CrPC. Russia's exclusionary rule is enshrined in Art. 50(2) of the Constitution. The Russian exclusionary rule is "strict" in the sense that there are no exceptions for "good faith," Leon v. United States, 468 U.S. 897 (1984), "inevitable discovery," Nix v. Williams, 467 U.S. 431 (1984), "impeachment use," Walder v. United States, 347 U.S. 62 (1954) (4th Amendment violations); Harris v. New York, 401 U.S. 222 (1971) (*Miranda* violations), or others. The Draft Russian CrPC, in Art. 71(3), would radically change this by requiring exclusion only when the evidence was obtained through violation of law that are of a type that could affect the trustworthiness of the evidence.

[38] *See, e.g.*, jury trial cases described in Stephen Thaman, The Resurrection of Trial by Jury in Russia, 32 Stanford Journal of International Law 61, 91 at note 190 (1995).

"suspect" or an "accused." A "suspect" is a person who is being held on suspicion of committing a crime pending being charged as an "accused." An "accused" is a person as to whom the criminal investigator has declared that there is sufficient evidence for a formal charge.[39]

The designation of a person as a "suspect" or an "accused" has special significance because of the rights that accrue upon that person being called to give testimony before the criminal investigator. The most important of these rights are the right to counsel and the right against self-incrimination. The right to counsel is secured by Art. 48(2) of the Constitution, which states: "Every person detained in custody and the accused in a criminal case have the right to assistance of a lawyer (defense counsel) from the moment of arrest, detention or charge, whichever comes first." The right against self-incrimination is set out in Art. 51 of the Constitution, which provides: "No one is required to testify against oneself, one's spouse or close relatives . . .".

Article 48(2) makes it clear when the right to counsel attaches and the Criminal Procedure Code clearly requires the criminal investigator to inform an accused or suspect of that right.[40] The Code is not so clear regarding the right against self-incrimination. It prohibits compelling the accused to testify through the application of violence or threats or other illegal means.[41] However, it does not clearly state when or whether a warning about the right against self-incrimination is to be given.[42]

This lack of clarity has special significance because of the overlap of the definitions of "witness" and "suspect." Art. 73 and 74 of the Code define a "witness" as anyone having knowledge of a crime—a definition that includes a "suspect" or an "accused." As noted in the last section, if the person is called as a "witness," the criminal investigator warns that person that he or she is subject to criminal charges for refusing to testify. If the person is called as a "suspect" or "accused," the warning that should be given is a radically different one—a warning against self-incrimination. Thus, someone who is interrogated as a "witness" who should be interrogated as an "accused" or a "suspect" will be advised that they must testify on pain of criminal liability. In other words, the situation is worse than the "accused" or "suspect" simply not

[39] *See supra* pp. 465-466.

[40] Art. 47(1), 46(3), 149, CrPC.

[41] Art. 20, CrPC. Strangely, the Draft CrPC doesn't resolve this problem either. See Art. 203, Draft CrPC.

[42] Lupinskaya, *supra* note 3, does not include the right against self-incrimination among the rights that must be disclosed to the accused (p.295) or the suspect (p. 257). Gutsenko, *supra* note 3, is not so clear on informing the accused (p. 123), but very clear that the suspect must be advised of the right before interrogation begins (p. 83).

being advised of his or her constitutional right not to testify. The "accused" or "suspect" is told erroneously that he or she is *required* to testify.

Determining who is an "accused" is relatively simple. Art. 46 defines an "accused" as a "person who has been charged with a crime" by way of the criminal investigator's written declaration that there is sufficient evidence against him or her. Determining who is a "suspect" is a little more slippery. Art. 52 includes as a suspect any "person detained on suspicion of committing a crime." Persons appearing as witnesses and warned that they must testify could easily cross the line at some point and become "suspects"—perhaps based on testimony they were compelled to give as "witnesses."

The following case touches on both the right to be warned about self-incrimination and the right to counsel during pre-trial stages of a case. It illustrates how criminal investigators sometimes take advantage of the lack of a clear line between a "witness" and a "suspect."

Supreme Court: *In re Kamenev*, BVS, 1996, No. 8, p. 10[43]

Preliminary investigation organs charged Kamenev with bribe-taking and illegal acquisition and possession of firearms and ammunition (part 3, Art. 173 and part 1, Art. 218 CrC of the RSFSR).

A jury of the Moscow Regional Court acquitted Kamenev.

In a cassational protest, the procurator sought reversal of the judgment[[44]] based on substantial violations of the standards set forth in the CrPC of the RSFSR, which in his opinion were the following: 1) at the preliminary hearing [[45]] the judge improperly excluded . . . the protocols of the examination of Kamenev [taken before the criminal investigator] . . .

The Collegium for Criminal Cases of the RF Supreme Court on February 13, 1996, affirmed the acquittal, stating the following:

---

[43] The case is also discussed approvingly in a Supreme Court report on jury trials written by Judge Shurygin, President of the Collegium for Criminal Cases. A.P. Shurygin, *Pravoprimenitetl'naia praktika rassmotrenia del s uchastiem kollegii prisiazhnykh zasedatelei* (Application of the Law in Practice in Jury Trial Cases), *BVS*, 1997, No. 2, p. 18.

[44] The prosecution can appeal an acquittal in Russia on grounds of legal errors, though it may not appeal an acquittal on grounds of disagreement with the jury's determination of guilt. *See infra* p. 542 [Footnote by eds.]

[45] A preliminary hearing is a hearing, provided for when there is a jury trial, at which motions to suppress evidence and other motions *in limine* may be determined before trial. *See infra* pp. 531-532 [Footnote by eds.]

In accord with Art. 459 CrPC RSFSR, a jury verdict of acquittal is binding on the presiding judge and requires that the judge enter a judgment of acquittal.

In Kamenev's case, the jury decided that the charges were not proven and therefore the trial judge entered a judgment of acquittal in accord with the jury verdict.

The arguments of the procurator set out in the cassational protest that the judge improperly excluded some of the evidence from the trial contradict existing legislation.

The judge properly excluded from evidence the protocol of the examination of Kamenev in the capacity of witness, since a criminal complaint had already been initiated against him and the organs of preliminary investigation had every indication that he should be examined as an accused observing the criminal procedural laws and the requirements set out in Art. 51 of the Constitution of the Russian Federation, that no one may be compelled to testify against himself or herself.

In violation of the stated requirements of the Constitution, Kamenev was warned by the criminal investigator that he would be criminally liable if he declined to give testimony or if he gave false testimony [the standard warnings given to a witness—eds.].

Also, the judge properly excluded the protocols of the examination of Kamenev that were done without the participation of his lawyer, as this violated his right to counsel. Attached to the casefile was a notice from lawyer K. of her appearance in all planned investigatory actions, but the investigator did not inform the lawyer and upon questioning Kamenev failed to explain to him his right under Art. 51 of the CRF. . . .

The trial judge did not commit any procedural errors during the trial that would lead to reversing the judgment.

The ruling of the Collegium for Criminal Cases was affirmed by a decree of the Presidium of the Supreme Court of the RF on May 15, 1996.

NOTES AND QUESTIONS

1. Is there an obligation on citizens witnessing a crime to provide information to investigators in the U.S.? Under what circumstances?

2. Anecdotal reporting and examination of appellate cases suggest that

questioning suspects as witnesses happens quite often in Russia.[46] Given the inclination of judges to suppress defendant statements for this reason, why would criminal investigators continue the practice? Reconsider your answer to this question after you read the next few paragraphs of the text.

* * * *

Even when given the requisite warnings, the overwhelming majority of suspects and accuseds give testimony before the criminal investigator unless a lawyer is there and specifically advises them not to talk (and sometimes even then). The same seems to be true in Western European continental countries and the explanations given for this phenomenon there are generally applicable to Russian criminal procedure.

Several things about continental criminal procedure "encourage" defendants to talk.[47] First, to a greater or lesser degree in most continental countries, a defendant's silence in the face of accusations can be used to infer guilt.[48] Second, taking responsibility for one's transgressions early in the process will be looked upon favorably when it comes to sentencing. Third, in civil law countries the defendant cannot be prosecuted for perjury for lying either to the investigating magistrate or to the judges at trial. Fourth, the widespread use of pre-trial detention in some civil law countries, especially France and Italy, seems to have its effect in "coaxing" defendants to talk. In addition, a tradition of giving testimony in a particular culture can be a self-propelled phenomenon: to the extent that defendants are expected to talk, the rare refusal to talk will seem all the more strong evidence of guilt to the investigator and the trial judges—and to the accused.

The same kinds of "encouragements" apply to Russian defendants, although officially no inference from silence is permitted to be drawn in jury

---

[46] Thaman found that in six out of 114 jury trial cases he observed, the trial courts suppressed defendants' testimony before criminal investigators for this reason. *See* Thaman, *supra* note 38, p. 91 at note 188.

[47] *See generally* Rudolf B. Schlesinger, Comparing Criminal Procedure: A Plea for Utilizing Foreign Experience, 26 Buffalo L.Rev. 361, 337-81 (1977).

[48] A distinction is made between the right to remain silent and the right not to be directly compelled to give testimony against oneself. Drawing an inference from silence is thus not thought to constitute a prohibited compulsion. In 1995, the English began to draw this distinction by retaining the right against self-incrimination generally, but allowing the prosecutor to comment on the defendant's failure to testify. *See* George W. O'Reilly, England Limits the Right to Silence and Moves Toward and Inquisitorial System of Justice, 85 *Journal of Criminal Law & Criminology* 402 (1994).

trials at least.[49] The widespread use of pre-trial detention is certainly a major factor for Russian defendants. And probably the horrible conditions of pre-trial confinement in some parts of Russia provide even greater "encouragement." That makes it appropriate to discuss it here.

6. Pre-Trial Detention

a. Basic Procedure and Practice

The Criminal Procedure Code provides an entire menu of possible measures to assure the attendance of the defendant at trial or other proceedings, and several factors to be considered in choosing among them. They include release on recognizance, confinement to home, payment of bail, release under the supervision of a social organization (not often used any more) and detention.[50] The Code requires the criminal investigator, procurator or judge involved to take into account "the seriousness of the crime, the personal attributes of the defendant, line of work he or she is in, age, condition of health, family situation and other factors."[51] However, the measure of choice for serious crimes is pre-trial detention.

One commentator doing his own research and extrapolating from official data worked out a detention rate for all non-petty offenses of 52.8%. In one Moscow district, a spot check for eight months in 1995 disclosed a rate of 61.4%. He compared these rates with those of the United States, which detains in between 8% and 20% of all crimes, and France—the highest pre-trial detainer in Western Europe—which detains in 10% of non-petty crimes. He concluded that "the rate of detention in Russia appears unusually high."[52]

The reasons for this are various. First, only in a few limited circumstances is detention completely prohibited, such as when the crime charged is punishable by less than a year in prison, and even then there are exceptions if the defendant is particularly dangerous. Second, despite the range of factors to be considered in deciding which method of assuring attendance should be adopted, the Code provides a list of several crimes for which dangerousness of the alleged offense alone is sufficient for pre-trial deten-

---

[49] *See* Art. 451, CrPC, which requires the judge to instruct the jury to this effect. The Criminal Procedure Code contains no similar provision for non-jury trials. *Cf.* Art. 49(2) of the Constitution ("the accused is not required to prove his or her innocence,") The Draft CrPC, in Art. 388(1), continues this distinction.

[50] *See* Art. 92-96, CrPC.

[51] Art. 91, CrPC.

[52] Foglesong, *supra* note 15, pp. 548-549.

tion.[53] Finally, pre-trial detention is decided upon and ordered by the procurator rather than by a court, and arguments about the presumption of innocence tend to be lost on procurators. As one major law enforcement official is reported to have said, "I'm all for the violation of human rights if the human in question is a bandit or a criminal."[54]

b. Judicial Review of the Propriety of Pre-Trial Detention

In 1992 the legislature passed a law setting up a mechanism for gaining judicial review of procurators' orders of detention—an act sometimes referred to as a "habeas corpus" remedy.[55] This statute represents a radical departure from the traditional lack of any judicial supervision of the procuracy detention decisions. Practice under the statute has not been without difficulties.[56]

This legislation was motivated by several things. One was the feeling that the widespread use of pre-trial detention was often not necessary to assure the accused's attendance at trial. Another was the general notion that it was a massive violation of human rights and the presumption of innocence not to have meaningful judicial review of procurators' orders of detention. The Courts have been relatively sympathetic to prisoners' petitions. As a Supreme Court study reports, 34,294 petitions were filed in the first half of 1994, of which 19.4% were granted.[57]

A petition may be filed at any time by the detainee, defense counsel or other legal representative. If the petition is submitted by the detainee, it must be transmitted to the warden of the detention facility, the criminal investigator

---

[53] *See* Art. 96 (2), CrPC. It is interesting that the standard is the dangerousness of the *offense* rather than the offender. Among the crimes are murder, assaults resulting in serious injury and rape of a minor, forcible sodomy, kidnaping, robbery, fraud, extortion, arson, vandalism, price-fixing, sale of dangerous goods, theft of weapons and drug trafficking.

[54] John Lloyd, "Anti-Crime Measures Split Russians," Financial Times, June 27, 1994, quoting the head of the Federal Counter-Intelligence Service, successor to the KGB, as reported in Foglesong, *supra* note 15, p. 550.

[55] *See* Art. 220(1)-220(2), CrPC.

[56] An excellent summary of practices under the act is Foglesong, *supra* note 15.

[57] Ruling of the Plenum of the Supreme Court Russian Federation "*O vypolnenii sudami postanovlenie Plenuma Verkhovovo Suda RF ot 27 aprelia 1993 No. 3 'O Praktike sudebnoi proverki zakonnosti i obosnovannosti aresta ili prodleniq sroka soderzhania pod strazhei'" (s izmeneniem ot 25 oktiabria 1996)* ("On the Implementation by Courts of the Ruling of the Plenum of the Supreme Court of the RF of April 27, 1993 no. 3 'On the Practice of Judicial Review of Legality and Bases for Pre-trial Detention and Extensions of Terms of Pre-trial Detention" (with changes from October 25, 1996), Garant Criminal Procedure Library (1994).

or police inquiry officer, who is obliged to forward it to the court and give notice of it to the procurator within 24 hours. Then the procurator or criminal investigator or inquiry official must respond within 24 hours of receiving notice of the petition by sending to the court materials "confirming the legality and proper grounds justifying the application of detention."[58] If the procurator fails to produce the required materials for the hearing, the judge is to release the petitioner. The detainee must be produced for the hearing and may be absent only under exceptional circumstances.

The Plenum of the Supreme Court has noted that courts are handling the petitions "correctly in general," but that some errors have been made. The ruling lists such things as judges failing to follow the short time limits imposed for deciding such petitions, some judges handling petitions in a summary fashion, a few isolated cases of judges going beyond the issues raised in the petition to other matters, such as the guilt or innocence of the detainee, failures of judges to engage in more than a superficial examination of the materials submitted and thus not fully considering all the factors, including the character of the accused, failure of the procurator to submit in a timely fashion the necessary materials, as well as the procurator's failure to appear at the hearing, and in some cases failure of the authorities to release defendants from detention when ordered by the court.[59]

There has been considerable political backlash against the law by the public and law enforcement officials based in large part on the belief that it results in releasing probably guilty criminals who will use their release as an opportunity to hide. However, the rate of released detainees who do not show up for later court dates is quite low—2.6% — especially when compared to the rate of 12% of bailed defendants in U.S. state courts who do not appear.[60] Perhaps in part because of the political backlash, there has been a lack of leadership by the Supreme Court.[61]

An issue that arose recently involving the 1992 act was the question of who can challenge an order for pre-trial detention. The case also gave the Court the opportunity to develop the meaning of yet another important provision of the Constitution.

The Constitutional Court: *Case on the Constitutionality of Articles 220(1) and 220(2) Criminal Procedure Code*, VKS, 1995, No. 2/3, p. 39.

---

[58] Art. 220(1), pt.3, CrPC.

[59] Plenum Ruling, *supra* note 57.

[60] *See* Foglesong, *supra* note 15, p. 563 n.88.

[61] Both the politics of the law's implementation and the Supreme Court's reaction are set out in detail in Foglesong, *supra* note 15.

1. Criminal prosecutions for violations of Art. 122 (intentional non-payment of support) and Art. 130 (criminal libel) of the Criminal Code of the RSFSR were brought against V.A. Avetian and an order for pretrial detention was issued to be executed on him, but it was not executed. This order, dated August 16, 1990, remained unchanged right up to the time that the criminal case was dismissed on April 16, 1994. Thus, the order for Avetian's arrest and detention was in effect for a period of four years; in connection with that order, he was listed as wanted by the police and this was reported in the local newspaper.

Mr. Avetian filed a complaint in the local court of general jurisdiction challenging the legality of the order and seeking its reversal. However, the complaint was dismissed on the ground that under Art. 220(1) and 220(2), such complaints may be brought only by persons who are actually in custody and that those complaints are heard by a court of the place where the person is detained.

2. In his complaint to the Constitutional Court, the petitioner asserts that the provisions of Art. 220(1) and 220(2) CrPC RSFSR [the 1992 law] applied in his case limit his right to freedom and personal inviolability and his right to judicial protection, violate the declarations of the Constitution of the Russian Federation regarding equality of all before the law and courts and therefore is not in accord with Art. 19, 22, 45, and 47 of the Constitution of the Russian Federation. . . .

. . . Art. 220(1) and 220(2) CrPC RSFSR set out the procedure for . . . complaints and in this way—the realization of the constitutional right of access to judicial protection secured by Art. 46 of the Constitution of the Russian Federation.

According to the Constitution of the Russian Federation, this right may not be limited. The legislature may enact limitations in accord with Art. 55 (part 3) of the Constitution of the Russian Federation only for the purposes of protecting the constitutional structure, morals, health, rights and interests of other persons, national security and sedition. The right to judicial protection does not in any manner conflict with these goals and therefore is exempt from limitation. It is for this reason that the right to judicial protection under Art. 56 (part 3) belongs to the categories of rights and freedoms that may not be limited under any circumstances. Art. 220(1) and 220(2) CrPC RSFSR, by diverging from this provision, limit the right to file suit in court for several categories of criminal defendants and suspects. . . .

6. The limitation of the categories of persons who have the right to file suit under Art. 220(1) and 220(2) CrPC RSFSR solely to those who are actually

confined violates Art. 19 of the Constitution of the Russian Federation guaranteeing equality of all before the law and the courts.

Equality before the law and the courts does not prohibit factual distinctions or the necessity for the legislature taking them into account. However, these distinctions may not result in limiting rights and freedoms, in which case the distinctions are impermissible under the Constitution of the Russian Federation. Moreover, the factual difference between persons who are only supposed to be detained and those who are already subject to preventive detention has nothing to do with the issue of their right to seek and the duty of a court to review of the legality of their detention order. . . .

Questions for Discussion

1. This challenge was brought after the fact when Avetian was no longer wanted by the police. What about someone who *is* wanted? Does this case give well-heeled criminals a way to avoid even one day in jail by having their lawyer contest the legality of their pre-trial detention while they remain hidden? After all, they may be more willing to give themselves up if they know they won't have to sit in pre-trial detention.

2. The Art. 46 right to judicial protection would seem to enshrine the old common-law judicial maxim of *ubi jus ibi remedium* (for every right there is a remedy). What is the status of this maxim in the U.S. system?

3. What are the broader implications of this case for constitutional doctrine as it relates to the Art. 46 right to judicial protection of rights? Would statutes of limitations for lawsuits violate Art. 46? What about requiring exhaustion of administrative remedies before suit can be filed? What about requiring a filing fee? Does the case contain any limiting principle by which the kinds of limits involved in this case would be struck down, but these other suggested "limits" would not?

4. Look at the section of the opinion on "equality before the law and the courts" dicsussed under point 6 of the opinion. What aspects of it appear similar to U.S. doctrine of equal protection of the laws?

5. What would happen if a similar case were brought in a United States federal court? Would the plaintiff have standing?

* * * *

c. The Duration of Pre-Trial Detention

The length of pre-trial detention is not supposed to exceed two months. However, it may be extended to 3 months by the local procurator and to 6 months by a "subject" procurator in light of the "specially complicated nature" of the case. Then it may be extended up to a year and a half in cases of serious crimes if there are "exceptional circumstances."[62] However, delays in trials have resulted in massive violations of these limits.

As will be discussed below, after the preliminary investigation is completed, the case is sent to the procurator for a decision on whether to file the case in court. Generally, the trial must then be scheduled within 28 days after filing.[63] To the extent that there are delays in scheduling and holding trials, there is the danger that pre-trial detainee defendants will be held beyond the standard 2-month detention period. A recent study conducted by the Supreme Court's Chamber of Criminal Appeals demonstrates that these limits are being exceeded in many cases and that the problem is getting worse.[64] In some courts in Moscow, there were defendants who had been in detention waiting for trial for three years or more. In more ordinary cases, 25% of the Moscow cases in 1996 were tried within 3 to 6 months (compared to 10.7% in 1992) and 35.8% were tried more that 6 months after being initiated (compared to 6.9% in 1992). In the St. Petersburg area, 23% of the trials scheduled as of April 1, 1997 were scheduled in apparent violation of the required time limits and cases filed in 1996 were being given trial dates in the second half of 1997. In the Chitinski Region in March 1997, of 578 defendants in detention, 114 waited more than a year for trial. In Kamchatka Region, of 527 criminal cases involving detainees, 235 took longer than 5 months to reach trial and 31 took over a year.

Delays in getting to trial also have an effect on the conditions of pre-trial confinement, as detention centers become more crowded. The study reported that "in many places, the number of persons held in detention centers exceeds the maximum permitted number by 2 to 3 times, which causes social-psychological stress in those places of detention. In Volgograd, in Detention Center No. 1, where there is a limit of 1800 persons, each month over 3,000 are confined there."

Recently, the Constitutional Court stepped into the fray surrounding the length of pretrial detention. The issue it addressed is admittedly not the

---

[62] Art. 97 (1), (2), CrPC.

[63] *See infra* p. 508.

[64] *Obzor sudebnoi praktiki Verkhovnogo suda Rossiiskoi Federatsii o sobliudenii srokov rassmotreniq ugolovnykh del sudami Rossiiskoi Federatsii* (Judicial Practice Report of the Supreme Court of the Russian Federation Regarding Compliance by Russian Federation Courts with Time Limits for Trying Criminal Cases), BVS, 1998, No. 2, p. 18.

most important issue in the area. It involved a challenge to the constitutionality of a provision of the Criminal Procedure Code that stated that the time spent by the accused and defense counsel examining the materials in the preliminary investigation case file are not to be counted toward the time limits on pre-trial detention discussed above. However, the case gave the Court the opportunity to discuss the nature of the constitutional limits on pre-trial detention. Given the difficulties that are taking place in observing the limits on pre-trial detention, the Court's views as stated in this case could prove important.

The Constitutional Court: *Case Concerning the Constitutionality of Art. 97(5) of the Criminal Procedure Code of the RSFSR*, VKS, 1996, No. 4, p. 2

1. In March of 1995 a criminal case was filed against Mr. Schelukhin regarding a number of crimes and on April 20, 1995 pre-trial detention was ordered.

Upon the expiration of the term of his detention that had been set, he filed a complaint with the Kuntevskij inter-municipal (regional) court of the Western Administrative District of the City of Moscow in accord with the provision of Art. 220(2) of the Criminal Code of the RSFSR regarding illegal and unreasonable arrests [the 1992 law]. The court refused to grant relief on the complaint of V.V. Schelukin, referring to the fact that the requirements of Art. 201 of the Criminal Code . . . (familiarization with the materials in the criminal case file) were being fulfilled with regard to him and his fellow defendants in the case, and in connection with that, in accord with Art. 97(5), the term of both the investigation and detention had expired.

[Art. 97(4) and (5) provided as follows: "[4] The materials from a completed investigation of a criminal case must be presented to the accused and his or her defender not later than a month before expiration of the term of pre-trial detention . . . [5] The time for the accused and his or her defender to familiarize themselves with the materials of the criminal case file is not counted as part of the term of pre-trial detention."]

4. Combining Art. 22(1) of the Constitution of the Russian Federation, which protects the right of freedom from confinement, with point 1 of Art. 9 of the International Covenant on Civil and Political Rights, which sets out the conditions for limiting this right, the rule emerges that no one may be subjected to arbitrary arrest or detention or otherwise deprived of his or her freedom, except on the basis of good cause and in accordance with procedures established by law.

Art. 97(5) . . . fosters the use of pre-trial detention without the necessary cause, the necessary procedures and for a period that has no limit or other control, all of which make it an arbitrary violation of the right of freedom from arrest: the confinement of the accused on the basis of this law beyond the limits of the term ordered does not contemplate the issuance of any necessary order by competent authorities. As a result, the accused can remain in custody after the earlier order of detention or order extending detention have expired, have ceased to have any force and, consequently, when the legal basis for incarceration of the accused has disappeared. . . .

5. The rule of Art. 97(5) . . . , like the entire institution of pre-trial custody, is intended above all to prevent the accused from avoiding investigation and interfering with the investigation, but moreover to prevent the accused and defense counsel from dragging out the time for their examination of the file without formally limiting them to a particular time period.

At the same time, the state, having the goal of avoiding abuse of the law so that the exercise of the accused's constitutional rights do not interfere with the rights and freedoms of others, may not employ excessive means to do so, but only measures that are essential and narrowly tailored to serve its goal. This principle of proportionality in the limiting of rights and freedoms embodied in Art. 55(3) of the Constitution of the Russian Federation means that the public interests listed in this constitutional provision may justify legal limitations on constitutional rights and freedoms, but only such limits as are sufficient to vindicate the state's legitimate goals. The rule set out in Art. 97(5) . . . , is not proportionate to the stated goals. . . .

Any problem of the accused and his or her counsel clearly delaying matters by engaging in an extended examination of the case file materials can be accommodated by the application of Art. 201(6) CrPC RSFSR, which permits limiting the time for examination of the file if such behavior is taking place. Therefore, attaining the stated goal by means of applying the challenged law does not satisfy the requirement that the government use means that are proportionate to its goals. . . .

6. . . . In effect, the application of Art. 97(5) CrPC RSFSR renders a nullity the law establishing a direct right to a judicial remedy at any point in the criminal process for improper detention, to be applied by the Constitutional Court of the Russian Federation and by the courts of general jurisdiction, which right is not subject to any limitation according to articles 55(3) and 56(3) of the Constitution of the Russian Federation.

An accused to whom the materials from the finished investigation have been provided for examination may contest his continued detention in court on the ground that the period of detention ordered has expired. However, the literal meaning of Art. 97(5) CrPC RSFSR means that upon the investigator's notice that the investigation has ended the court will have to decide whether there is a need for the accused and his lawyer to examine the material in the case file. If there is, this will be a sufficient reason for continuation of the petitioner's detention . . . . In this way, the challenged law violates the right to judicial protection from unjustified detention. . . .

7. [The Court suspended the operation of its ruling to allow the legislature time to react to it to prevent "negative social consequences" of wholesale release of pre-trial detainees. The legislature must] adopt measures that will preserve a balance of the interests of justice and rights to freedom and personal security as well as avoiding the possibility of arbitrary detention, including assistance in shoring up the procedure for judicial review of the legality and justifications for detention at all stages of the criminal process.

NOTES AND QUESTIONS

1. Why was the accused in this case taking so long to familiarize himself with the file? Did he like staying in pre-trial detention? If his strategy was to take his time reading the file so that his term of pre-trial detention would expire, this was thwarted by Art. 97(5). But the Court held Art. 97(5) unconstitutional. Why wasn't he released from custody? What would have happened if a similar case had been brought in the U.S.?

2. The Court in part justifies its conclusion that the continued imprisonment of the petitioner is unconstitutional because it is not "in accordance with procedures established by law" since "the legal basis for incarceration of the accused has disappeared" when the original term of the pre-trial detention order expires. If the Court is correct about the meaning of Art. 97(5), how is continued detention "not in accordance with procedures established by law"? If the Court is saying this because the "procedures established by law" are invalid, isn't this circular?

3. In reaction to the Constitutional Court ruling, the Russian legislature passed an amendment to Art. 97 (effective December 31, 1996) providing that, if it is impossible for the casefile to be examined by the defendant and defense counsel by the end of the term of pre-trial detention, further detention may be ordered. The Procurator-General of the Russian Federation and the procurator of a subject of the Russian Federation may, no later than 5 days before the expiration of the term of pre-trial detention, make a motion before a judge of the appropriate regional, territorial or similar level

court to extend the term.[65] Judges then must, within 5 days after receiving the motion, either "1) extend the term of pre-trial detention until the time when the defendant and defense counsel are finished examining the case file and the case is referred for trial by the procurator, but for not more than 6 months; or 2) deny the procurator's motion and release the person from detention."[66]

Does the law passed in reaction to the Court's decision comply with it? Does it comport with the principle on which the decision is based? Is the new law consistent with Art. 22(2) of the Constitution? Does it need to be? If the Court's purpose in deciding this case as it did was to move criminal procedure closer to the ideal of Art. 22(2) of the Constitution without waiting for a new Criminal Procedure Code, did it succeed?

4. Does the "ends-means" aspect of the "proportionality" principle the Court adopts remind you of any constitutional doctrines in U.S. law?[67]

5. Before one criticizes the Russian system too severely for its pre-trial detention practices, it should be pointed out that in the French system the basic maximum term for pre-trial detention is one year, and even this period of time may be extended by a judge.[68]

* * * *

7. Other Preliminary Investigation Procedures Employed by the Criminal Investigator

Aside from interrogating witnesses and suspects or accuseds, criminal investigators have several other investigative tools at their disposal.

a. Expert Analysis and Testimony

The criminal investigator may order expert analysis of evidence in the case. In accord with the continental tradition, experts are selected by the court and are supposed to be neutral. Experts rarely testify in person at trial. Instead, they submit written reports, which are included in the case file that goes to the

---

[65] *See* current Art. 97(4) (added effective December 31, 1996).

[66] *See* current Art. 97(5) (added effective December 31, 1996).

[67] Proportionality is a doctrine drawn from German law which was first incorporated into European law by the European Court. It has since been inserted into the European Community treaty by the Maastricht Agreement as follows: "Any action by the Community shall not go beyond what is necessary to achieve the objectives of this Treaty." *See* T.C. Hartley, The Foundations of European Community Law, 3rd ed. 155-156 (1994).

[68] Leigh and Zedner, *supra*, p. 11, citing Art. 145-2 of the French CrPC.

trial judges and these reports (usually entitled "Expert Findings") are deemed admissible at trial without any need to call their author-analyst.[69]

b. Examination of the Crime Scene

As necessary, the criminal investigator can make an inspection of the crime scene or other relevant place.[70] Photographs and videos may be taken and diagrams made and any evidence found catalogued and seized. A protocol is prepared and signed by the criminal investigator. As with experts, the CI is not called at trial to testify about what he or she did and saw there. The written report of the examination of the scene as part of the casefile is simply admissible at trial. In recent years, videotape records have been used to supplement the written descriptions.

c. Line-Ups

Line-ups (*predyavlenie dlya opoznania*) are essentially the same in Russia as in the U.S. However, as with other investigatory action taken once the preliminary investigation gets under way, the police are not the ones who arrange the line-up. Instead, it is ordered by the criminal investigator and an official protocol is made of it that is automatically admissible in evidence.[71] Moreover, the way a line-up must be conducted is specified in the federal Criminal Procedure Code, so there is no variation from place to place as in the United States. This provides some set standards for determining the propriety of a line-up rather than the vague "totality of the circumstances" test used in the United States.[72] The witness must first be questioned about the occasion for viewing the person involved and particularly about what characteristics were distinguishing. Then the line-up must have no less than three people in it and the witness will be asked whether they see the person among those in the line-up.

Despite the presence of clear standards, difficulties nonetheless arise, as the following intermediate appellate case illustrates in the context of a car-jacking.

Voronezh Regional Court: *In re Sviridov* (1992) (Garant Criminal Procedure Library)[[73]]

---

[69] *See* Art. 184-194, CrPC.

[70] *See* Art. 141-142, 178-179, CrPC and Lupinskaya, *supra* note 3, pp. 286-287.

[71] Art. 164-166, CrPC.

[72] *Stovall v. Denno*, 388 U.S. 293 (1967).

[73] Garant is one of the Russian computer-based legal research services.

Sviridov was convicted by the Kominternovski District Court of the city of Voronezh of [armed robbery].

The panel of the Voronezh Regional Court affirmed the conviction.

The Deputy Chairman of the Supreme Court of the RF lodged a protest asserting that the conviction should be reversed and the case sent back for a new trial.

The Presidium of the Voronezh Regional Court upheld the protest, stating the following:

As is clear from the record, Sviridov was convicted of two robberies in attacks on Kruk and Antsiferov, owners of automobiles.

As the basis for holding Sviridov guilty, the trial court relied on the testimony of Kruk and Antsiferov who identified him as the person who attacked them, and on the testimony of one Lazarev.

However, the identification of Sviridov by the victims and witnesses was conducted in violation of Art. 164 - 166 CrPC.

Before Sviridov was arrested on November 5, 1991, he was identified by the victim Antsiferov by photograph No. 2 as the person who attacked him. The victim pointed out the features on which he relied in making the identification.

However, as is clear from the protocol, the labeled photographs identified by the victim were not attached with an official seal. Although the three photographs have the same format, the image of Sviridov is larger than the other two men.

The next identification of Sviridov by Antsiferov took place on November 21, 1991, from among two other men named Aliev and Vinokurov. However, in the protocol of the line-up there is a complete lack of any description of their appearance nor are there photographs, and the birth date of Vinokurov does not appear.

At a line-up on November 14, 1991 for victim Kruk, Sviridov was presented together with Omarov, born in 1966, and Takhirov, who was younger than Sviridov by 11 years, and there is no description in the protocol of the appearance of Omarov and Takhirov.

At the line-up, the victim Kruk stated that he recognized Sviridov by his age and appearance. But in the protocol there is no description of the men appearing in the line-up even though the difference in age is significant.

Moreover, Kruk was not questioned extensively about the characteristics and aspects of the appearances of the criminals who attacked him. While giving testimony about the facts of the crime, he pointed to characteristics of one of the robbers that hardly correspond to the appearance of Sviridov (whom he identified) and that differ from those recited by the victim Antsiferov in his description of the criminal. The trial court did not evaluate this. . . .

The witness Lazarev, when shown three photographs, identified Sviridov as the person who drove up to him in the car that belonged to the victim Kruk. But the photograph in the record is of Sviridov when he was 16 years old, although at the time of his arrest he was 31.

The trial court did not clarify and analyze any of these circumstances in its decision. . . .

No actions were taken during the preliminary investigation to search for, examine and arrange for a comparative line-up of the clothes allegedly worn by Sviridov, despite the fact that the victims Kruk and Antsiferov described them.

Neither during the preliminary investigation nor at trial did Sviridov admit being guilty of any of these crimes and categorically denied any participation in the crimes. He proffered the defense of alibi, which was supported by the witnesses L. Sviridov, Lesnikvo, V. Sviridov, Kryukov, Vovchenko and Demidenkov. The trial court simply rejected the testimony of these witnesses. pointing out that they were all relatives or friends of Sviridov who were interested in the outcome of the case.

In view of this, the trial court's finding of Sviridov's guilt in [the armed robberies] is based on an insufficient examination of the evidence (some of which was obtained in violation of the law) that needs additional examination. Therefore, the judgment is vacated and the case remanded for a new investigation.

NOTES AND QUESTIONS

1. The court remands to the trial court for a new preliminary investigation. What is the criminal investigator supposed to do? At this point, will this cure the problem in the case? Reading between the line in the case, how does the appellate court think the trial court should have decided the case?

2. Toward the end of the opinion, the court suggests that there should

have been a "line-up" of the defendant's clothes for the victims to view. One peculiarity about line-ups in Russia is their use for things as well as people. For example, in one burglary trial, the victim's identification of his television set during the investigation was suppressed because the television had not been properly displayed to the victim along with other similar television sets.[74]

* * * *

d. Confrontation of Witnesses

Confrontation (*ochnaya stavka*) is an interesting device used when there are conflicts in testimony among witnesses and defendants.[75] The general idea is to bring together the two whose testimony is at odds to try to resolve the contradictions or, if that is not possible, to have the two confront each other regarding their differing accounts. The sessions starts out with the criminal investigator essentially conducting a dual examination of the participants. The criminal investigator asks them whether they know each other, and what kind of relationship it is. Then the criminal investigator elicits from each his or her version of the events and gets the reaction of the other person. With the CI's permission, the witnesses can ask each other questions and this is most often done by each in an effort to impeach the other person. The criminal investigator can also read or play a tape of the participants' earlier testimony to try clarify things. The result of the session is that the criminal investigator either resolves the contradictions or, if no one account can be agreed upon, is able to clarify exactly what the differences are and become informed by the participants of reasons why the criminal investigator should believe one or the other version. A protocol of the confrontation is written up just as for other testimony and has the same evidentiary status as a protocol of any other witness or accused testimony.

e. Searches and Seizures

Russian Criminal Procedure Code provides that the criminal investigator has the power to order seizures of documents or real evidence in the possession of any person or organization and, with the approval of a procurator, to issue search warrants to search for such evidence.[76] In addition,

---

[74] Thaman, *supra* note 38, Moscow-1 trial, preliminary draft before editing (on file with the authors). For another line-up with numerous errors, including presentation of the defendant in a line-up that included only him and two uniformed police officers, *see In re Mikheev*, BVS, 1998, No. 2, p. 6.

[75] Art. 162-163, CrPC. *See* Lupinskaya, *supra* note 3, p. 280.

[76] Art. 168. *See generally* Art. 167-177 and Lupinskaya, *supra* note 3.

warrantless searches are possible "in situations that do not permit delay" with notification being given to the procurator within 24 hours afterward.[77]

However, since 1993 Art. 23 of the Constitution provides: "Everyone has the right to privacy of correspondence, telephone conversations, mail, telegram and other communications. Limits on this right are permitted only on the basis of a judicial decision." Art. 25 of the Constitution provides: "The home is inviolate. No one has the right to enter a home against the will of the occupant except under circumstances established by federal law or pursuant to a judicial decision." Because of the disjunctive "or" in Art. 25 and the provisions of the Criminal Procedure Code, searches of and seizures that are not within dwellings are permitted without judicial authorization, though searches of and seizures within dwellings need judicial authorization. Under Art. 23 judicial authorization is needed for intercepting all telephone calls, mail or other means of communication.[78]

Unlike the U.S., for a search to be conducted, there is no need to know the exact object of the search or its location.[79] However, the criminal investigator's order for a search and any court authorization must state the grounds for the search and what types of articles are sought.[80]

8. The Role of Civilian Attesting Witnesses

Many of the above devices used by the criminal investigator require the presence of "*poniatye*" or non-police attesting witnesses for the use of that device or procedure to be valid—a practice unknown to the Anglo-American tradition. Any citizen who has no interest in the case can be called on by the criminal investigator or the police acting for the investigator to perform the role of an attesting witness. Art. 135 of the Criminal Procedure Code requires the presence of at least two attesting witnesses during the execution of searches, examination of the crime scene and other items, line-ups, confrontation of witnesses and many other such actions. The task of attesting witnesses

[77] Art. 168. *See* Lebedev Commentary, *supra* note 3, p. 242 for examples of circumstances justifying warrantless searches.

[78] Lebedev Commentary, *supra* note 3, pp. 240-241. *See also* Ruling of the Plenum of the Supreme Court, "*O nekotorykh voprosakh primenenia sudami Konstitutsii RF v osushchestvlenii pravosudia*" ("On Some Questions Concerning the Application of the Constitution of the RF in the Administration of Justice"), *BVS* 1995, No. 1, p. 3, point 14.

[79] *Id.* p. 241.

[80] *See* Gutsenko, *supra* note 3, pp. 204-205 for a sample form for a criminal investigator order and judicial approval of a search of all mail or other correspondence received by the live-in companion of a fugitive in effort in to determine the fugitive's whereabouts.

is to observe the particular procedure so that they can later testify as to what happened, what was observed, seized or done, and the like. When the protocol of the particular action is drawn up by the police or criminal investigator, the attesting witnesses must sign.

As one might imagine, being an attesting witness is not popular among Russian citizens, especially in large cities, where they are almost as reluctant as New Yorkers to get involved in anything that does not directly concern them. The police and criminal investigators are inclined to fudge the requirement, sometimes having police officers sign as attesting witnesses. This is risky, however, as the lack of attesting witnesses can invalidate the action taken or ordered by the criminal investigator and thus render the evidence obtained inadmissible at trial.[81]

9. Defense Counsel and the Preliminary Investigation

a. The Role of Defense Counsel

As noted earlier, suspects and accuseds have a right to counsel during the preliminary investigation. Art. 48(2) of the Constitution provides: "Every person detained in custody and the accused in a criminal case have the right to assistance of a lawyer (defense counsel) from the moment of arrest, detention or charge, whichever comes first."[82] It was not always the case that the right to counsel extended to the preliminary investigation stage. This lack of counsel from the moment of arrest was a sore point between the government and prominent academics even in Soviet times and it became one of the first reforms to be discussed once Soviet power began to fade. As we saw in the *Kamenev* case (p. 473), absent a waiver from the accused or suspect, the criminal investigator must include counsel in any further investigative activities on pain of exclusion of the gathered evidence at trial.

Because the right to counsel at preliminary investigation sessions is a relatively recent phenomenon, the precise role defense counsel is to play in the preliminary investigation is still being worked out. Some have argued that the greatest contribution of counsel is simply to be there, as the mere presence of counsel prevents the worst kinds of abuses of defendants' and witnesses' rights. Counsel does have the right to question any of the witnesses, subject to approval by the criminal investigator.[83] Although defense counsel cannot directly call witnesses as might be true in the U.S.-style preliminary hearing, a criminal investigator who refuses a defense request that a particular witness be

---

[81] *See* Art. 69, pt. 3, CrPC, quoted *supra* p. 471 and note 37.
[82] *See also* Art. 47, CrPC.
[83] Art. 51(3), (4), CrPC.

called runs the risk of a judicial remand of the case for supplemental investigation if the nature of the witness's testimony is clearly relevant to the case. Defense counsel can attach written objections to any illegal or improper investigatory actions of the criminal investigator and point out avenues of investigation that the criminal investigator declined to explore and other ways in which the preliminary investigation is not a complete investigation into all the relevant facts of the case. Defense counsel is not permitted to appear at any investigatory actions that the accused does not have the right to attend. These actions may include examination of the crime scene, witness confrontations, executions of search warrants and the like, unless the accused is invited to attend. Any more involved role for defense counsel at the preliminary investigation is subject to the discretion of the criminal investigator.

In practice, in cases where the accused or suspect is factually innocent or there are clear circumstances reducing the seriousness of the initial charges, vigorous representation at the preliminary investigation stage provides the best opportunity for defense counsel to get the charges dismissed or reduced. This can be done by all the methods outlined above, as well as by informal contacts with the criminal investigator.

Representation both at the investigation stage and at trial is complicated by the fact that the defense is not expected to do its own independent investigation of the facts of the case. Prepared defense lawyers in the U.S. will interview all the defense witnesses and as many of the prosecution's witnesses as will talk to them. The reasons why Russian defense counsel do not do this is not entirely clear. They generally explain that they do not seek out and interview exculpatory witnesses because neither the judge at trial nor the criminal investigator will believe such witnesses once defense counsel has contacted and interviewed them. As for trying to interview incriminating witnesses, the response usually is that this is because contacting prosecution witnesses would be unethical or would be considered witness tampering. The Russian practice in this respect is consistent with the practice in other civil law countries.[84]

b. Who Is Permitted to Appear as Defense Counsel

A basic issue regarding the right to counsel during the preliminary investigation that has arisen and which occupied the attention of the Constitutional Court is the question of who can represent an accused or suspect at this stage. There are two types of lawyers in Russia who represent individual clients: those who are members of the official city or regional

---

[84]Art. 82(3) of the Draft CrPC gives defense counsel the right to gather evidence independently.

College of Advocates and "private" lawyers who run their own firms who are simply licensed by the Ministry of Justice. Both have the right to render legal services to clients for a fee.[85] As earlier discussed, Art. 48(2) of the Constitution provides that a person detained in custody and the accused in a criminal case "have the right to assistance of a lawyer (defender) from the moment of arrest, detention or charge, whichever comes first." The word in the original Russian that is translated here as "lawyer" is "*advokat*" (advocate) and the term of "defender" is "*zashchitnik*." The question of exactly who is an "advocate" or "defender" arose before the Constitutional Court.

The Constitutional Court: *Case Concerning the Constitutionality of Art. 47(4) of the Criminal Procedure Code of the RSFSR* (VKS, 1997, No. 1, p. 25)

[Petitioners were prosecuted for criminal offenses and sought to have certain lawyers represent them in the criminal proceedings. Permission was denied on the ground that Art. 47(4) CrPC limited representation solely to advocates who are from an official legal consultation office of the college of advocates. They petitioned the Constitutional Court arguing that this law violated their right to counsel and other rights set out in the Constitution.]

2. Art. 47(4) provides that the following are permitted to appear as defenders in criminal cases: an advocate on order from a legal consultation office or a representative from a union or other social organization appearing as a defender, upon presentation of an appropriate client authorization and identification. In accord with art 47(5), close relatives and legal representatives of the accused and other persons may appear on behalf of the defendant if the court so determines and orders. From this it follows that the law challenged by the petitioners, in establishing who will be permitted to appear as a defender in the criminal process, determines the groups of people who may be permitted to appear in the capacity of defender at the stages of police inquiry and preliminary investigations, including in that group only advocates and representatives from unions or other social organizations.

According to Art. 48(2) of the Constitution of the Russian Federation every person who is detained or charged with a crime has the right to the services of defense counsel from the moment of being taken into custody or being charged with a crime. Art. 14f of the International Covenant on Civil and Political Rights provides that every person charged with a crime has the right to consult with a lawyer of his own choosing and to have the assistance of such lawyer for his defense. The right of a citizen to independent choice of a

---

[85] Advocates and colleges of advocates were discussed in Chapter III, pp. 123-129.

defense lawyer is supported by the declaration of the Constitutional Court of the Russian Federation from March 27, 1996 in the case reviewing the constitutionality of arts. 1 and 21 of the July 21, 1993 Law of the Russian Federal "On State Secrets"[[86]] . . .

However, the right of independent choice of defense counsel does not mean that any person may be chosen in the unfettered discretion of the suspect or accused and does not contemplate the possibility of the participation of just any person as defense counsel. The right to the assistance of counsel contained in Art. 28 (2) of the Constitution of the Russian Federation is just one of the manifestations of the more general right guaranteed to every person by Art. 48 (1) of the Constitution . . . the right to receive competent legal services. Consequently, the provisions of Art. 48(2) . . . cannot be interpreted in a vacuum and without consideration of the provisions of part (1) of the same article.

3. In guaranteeing the right to receive competent legal services, the state must first, establish the conditions necessary for preparing qualified lawyers who can provide citizens with various types of legal services, among them representation in criminal cases, and, second, to establish other requirements and criteria of competence to achieve this goal. . . .

The criteria for competent legal assistance in a criminal case, informed by the need to observe adversarial principles and equal rights of the parties guaranteed by Art. 123 (3) of the Constitution . . . , are established by the legislature through determination of the appropriate conditions for permitting persons to appear in the capacity of defense counsel.

4. At the present time, the legal-organizational form for the work of advocates is the college of advocates founded on the basis of the Law on the Advokatura of the RSFSR established by the Law of the RSFSR of November 20, 1980, and the procedures set out therein. This law also specifies certain professional qualifications for advocates designed to assure that they render competent assistance in light of the great importance of decisions made in criminal cases for the individual and society in general.

In view of the foregoing, the provision of Art. 47(4) of the Criminal Procedure Code of the RSFSR, which permits only an advocate with an official order from a legal consultation office to appear in the capacity of defense counsel in a criminal case, does not violate the Constitution . . . .

---

[86] This case is reprinted below pp. 515-517.

The Constitution . . . does not contain any indication of what qualifications are required for a person to provide legal services to citizens.

The determination of such criteria for permitting someone to render legal services to the suspect or accused in a criminal case is the province of the legislature. Only the legislature has the right to determine, consistent with the need to preserve the right of every accused (suspect) to receive competent legal assistance in the interests of justice, the extent to which it will permit persons chosen by the accused, besides advocates, to fulfill the role of defense counsel, including those who are licensed to represent clients for a fee.

5. Art. 47(4) of the Criminal Procedure Code . . . provides that not only advocates, but representatives from unions and other social organizations which present the appropriate authorization and proper identification, are permitted to serve as defense counsel. Under this provision, there is no requirement that this representative have any legal education or any kind of professional knowledge or experience. This might seem to cast doubt on the possibility of securing to the accused or suspect the right to receive competent legal assistance in those situations in which the defense counsel in the preliminary investigation is not a lawyer, but a representative of a union or other social organization. However, since the petitioners' situations do not present this question, this Court does not have the right to determine the constitutionality of this provision . . . based on Art. 74(3) of the law "On the Constitutional Court of the Russian Federation." . . .

The question of whether the decision of the [criminal] investigator excluding the petitioners' lawyers from the criminal proceedings was well-founded and the extent to which reliance on Art. 47(4) of the Criminal Procedure Code of the RSFSR was proper cannot be decided by the Constitutional Court . . . , since by virtue of Art. 3(2) and (3) of the Federal Constitutional Law "On the Constitutional Court of the Russian Federation," the establishment and sifting of the facts of a violation of the right to counsel brought about through improper application of Art. 47(4) . . . in the course of hearing the cases of the petitioners is not within the jurisdiction of the Constitutional Court . . . .

. . . [T]he Constitutional Court of the Russian Federation rules:

1. That the provisions of the article 47(4) of the Criminal Procedure Code of the RSFSR, according to which an advocate is permitted to appear in the capacity of a defender upon presentation of an order of a legal consultation office, do not violate the Constitution of the Russian Federation.

The other conditions, professional criteria and legal-organizational form that will assure the provision of competent legal services in criminal cases are determined by the legislature. . . .

Dissenting Opinion of Judge E.M. Ametistov

1. The basic question which has to be resolved in the present case is the following: does Art. 48 of the Constitution . . . permit the assistance of not only advocates, but also private practitioner lawyers who are not members of the college of advocates? . . .

This leads to the question that must be resolved: does the Constitution use the words "advocate" and "defender" in Art. 48(2) as synonyms or does it suppose that one term is broader than the other?

If they are used as synonyms, that is, that they have exactly the same meaning, then it follows that the term "defender" in parentheses has as its sole purpose clarifying the term "advocate."

It is extremely doubtful that this is the case considering the fact that the term "advocate" from time out of mind has been used in the Russian lexicon and the contemporary reader is hardly in need of clarification of its meaning.

Consulting the dictionary meaning of "advocate" and "defender" set forth in authoritative dictionaries of contemporary Russian literary language demonstrates that the word "advocate" in ordinary usage refers only to the work of professional lawyers. The term "defender" is broader and refers to any person performing the functions of defending or otherwise representing the interests of someone in court, in litigation. From this, we can conclude that in using this word in art 48(2), the Constitution grants citizens the right to legal assistance, not just of advocates, that is, a member of the college of advocates, but also of other defense counsel.

The actual intent of the framers of the Constitution in this connection can be confirmed by examining the materials of the 1993 Constitutional Convention at which the draft of the Constitution was hammered out and discussed.

During the process of the Constitutional Convention, there was more than one attempt to amend Art. 48 to narrow the types of persons who could render legal services solely to members of a college of advocates. All the amendments were defeated because their passage would lead to the establishment of a "closed shop" for advocates, which would deprive all non-member lawyers of their practices and which would establish a "right of monopoly" for advocates to offer legal services. In light of this, the participants at the constitutional convention emphasized that allowing only representative of the colleges of advocates to participate in the preliminary investigation would substantially encroach on citizens' rights and that, to the contrary, the proposed language used in the article under discussion (permitting at that stage the participation of others) responds to the principle of free choice of counsel. [Citations to Constitutional Convention materials omitted.] Said one of the representatives of the governments of the "subject" of the Russian Federation at the Convention, "The main thing is that the person, in exercising his right to counsel, would have a choice of an independent defender according to his choice. The existing college of advocate structure is not always independent of governmental power and therefore the person is given a choice: go to the college of advocates, to the Union of Lawyers or to a private lawyer or defender—that is complete realization of the right to be defended." [Citation to Constitutional Convention materials omitted.]

All the above permits us to come to the conclusion that the founders of the current Constitution of the Russian Federation in the final text of its art 48 had the intention of establishing and securing **the right of a person who is arrested and the person accused of crime to the independent and the widest range of choice of defenders.** [bold type in original] . . .

[As for art 48(1) requiring the government to assure the right to qualified legal services] . . . this does not mean that the citizen is always required to use services on that level, assuming of course that there is no constitutional principle regarding litigation or the rights and interests of other people. . . .

Dissenting opinion of Judge V.O. Luchin

Having examined the constitutionality of Art. 47(4) of the CrPC of the RSFSR . . . the Constitutional Court of the Russian Federation has held the provisions permitting advocates presenting an order from a legal consultation office to represent suspects or the accused in a criminal case to be constitutional.

This observation in not in itself objectionable . . .

[However] not one of the citizens who petitioned the Constitutional Court asked that we hold the authorization of advocates to appear as defenders to be unconstitutional, nor did they object that an advocate would have to present an order from a legal consultation office. They have all challenged something else—the consistent and persistent practice of interpreting the provisions of Art. 47(4) . . . to exclude from appearing as defenders anyone other than advocates and representatives of social organizations, even those who have a license to render paid legal services. However, the requests for relief not only did not get resolved in the decree portion of the decision; they were barely analyzed in the opinion portion of the decision.

2. The Constitutional Court . . . then, coming to the conclusion that the right to counsel of an accused (suspect) guaranteed by Art. 48(2) of the Constitution of the Russian Federation is part of the more general constitutional right that is guaranteed to everyone under part 1 of that same article—the right to receive qualified legal services, recognizes the right and obligation of the legislature to determine the conditions for permitting particular persons to appear as defenders (among them and relevant to the professional characteristics such persons must have, members of the colleges of advocates).

However, this generally correct observation does not provide any basis for determining that Art. 47(4) . . . is such a law—one which currently determines the professional criteria for rendering legal services—and as such is constitutional. There is nothing in the text of this article about legal and professional qualifications of a defender, only an indication of the person's membership either in a college of advocates or to a social organization. Currently, there is no federal law that determines any criteria for what are considered qualified legal services to be rendered to an accused or a suspect. Accordingly, in the area of criminal justice the general requirements for people rendering legal services should apply. Therefore, there is no basis for not allowing persons to appear as defenders who have a license issued by the government attesting to their necessary legal qualifications to render paid legal services to citizens. The authorization for licensed lawyers to render legal services comes from [citations to various statutes omitted]. These statutes do not contain any kind of limitation on providing legal services in the criminal law area, including appearing in the capacity of a defender. . . .

NOTES AND QUESTIONS

1. If you were puzzled when you read the final decree part of the majority decision, you were reading it correctly. As Judge Luchin's dissent points out, the majority decision answers a question that no one disputes and that was not presented by the petitioners: whether the statute's authorization of a member of the *college of advocates* to represent defendants in criminal cases is constitutional? *See* the paragraph number 1 in the last part of the majority opinion (p. 495). What is going on? The first reaction upon reading this is that it is a misprint—that the Court meant to write that the authorization *only* of advocates to represent defendants is constitutional. But the dissents points out the mistake and there is no response from the majority. Can you figure out what the majority is doing?

2. Another reason not to view the decree portion as a misprint is the paragraph just before the decree portion. In that paragraph the majority observes: "The question of whether the decision of the [criminal] investigator excluding the petitioners' lawyers from the criminal proceedings was well-founded and the extent to which reliance on part 4 of Art. 47 of the Criminal Procedure Code of the RSFSR was proper cannot be decided by the Constitutional Court." Assume a case comes before the Russian Supreme Court in which the criminal investigator excluded participation of non-advocate lawyers, interpreting Art. 47(4) as prohibiting participation by any lawyers other than advocates. Is it open for the Supreme Court now to interpret Art. 47 as not providing an exclusive list of possible defense counsel, i.e. as not impliedly excluding private practitioner defense counsel?[87]

3. Assume that the majority opinion really answered the question presented by the petitioner, i.e. that Court really decided that Art. 47(4) permits *only* members of a college of advocates and social organizations to appear as defense counsel and that it does not violate the right to counsel set out in Art. 48(2) of the Constitution. If this is really the majority's holding, who has the better of the arguments on the meaning of Art. 48(2) of the Constitution, the majority or Judges Ametistov and Luchin in dissent?

4. It is important to emphasize what the decision does *not* do. As the majority notes in passing, the very next subsection of Art. 47 states: "On order of a court or ruling of a judge, close relatives and legal representatives *and other persons* may be permitted to appear as counsel." Art. 47(5). This subsection—which would clearly include not just private lawyers, but any non-law-trained person—was apparently not deemed controlling on the question in the case because the reference to "court" and "judge" implied that it only applied to the trial stage of criminal procedure, not the preliminary investigation stage. Thus, the only issue in the case was who has the right to appear to represent the defendant at the *pre-trial stages* of a criminal case. The proposition that anyone can represent the defendant *at trial* with court permission is not affected.[88] Does Art. 47(5) support the majority's or the dissents' interpretation of Art. 47(4)?

The degree to which trial judges permit "private" non-advocate lawyers to appear and represent clients in criminal trials varies from judge to

[87] In fact, the Supreme Court recently considered the issue and interpreted Art. 47 the same way the Constitutional Court did without citing or referring to the Constitutional Court's earlier decision. *See In re Voronin and Artiorev*, *BVS*, 1998, No 3, p. 15.

[88] Lupinskaya, *supra* note 3, at 270, citing BVS 1993, No. 6, s. 6 and No. 1, s. 14

judge and from lawyer to lawyer. Some judges question the qualifications of some of these "private" lawyers, especially those who are graduates of one of the new crop of public and private profit-making law schools that have sprung up in recent years. Other non-advocate lawyers are experienced and well qualified and are often former members of traditional colleges of advocates who for one reason or another have struck out on their own.

5. What is at stake in this case as a practical economic matter for advocates and "private" lawyers? Before you answer, consider that advocates represent not just paying criminal defense clients, but must also represent free those unable to pay. Non-advocate private lawyers have no such duty. In addition, as in the U.S., the overwhelming majority of criminals in Russia—at least the ones the police catch—are poor.

6. Note 2 above suggests a broader problem with the whole idea of a separate Constitutional Court. Challenges to laws as unconstitutional on their face clearly fall within the court's competence. However, not all challenges take this form. Some will be challenges to laws as applied — where one interpretation would make the law subject to constitutional challenge, while another would eliminate the constitutional problem. Doesn't the Court have to be able to determine first what the law means before it turns to the issue of constitutionality? Or at the very least, if the Constitutional Court cannot interpret the law, shouldn't there be a requirement that the meaning of the law be authoritatively determined by the ordinary courts before the Constitutional Court passes on its validity? Otherwise, a constitutional ruling is based on no more than a "guess" as to what the law means. An analogous problem arises in the U.S. federal courts when they are asked to declare a state law unconstitutional. How is this problem in the U.S. dealt with?

* * * *

10. Time Limits on Preliminary Investigations

The backlog of cases to be investigated is long and the growth of crime and the lack of sufficient number of criminal investigators to conduct investigations have resulted in delays in investigations of criminal cases. The maximum limit on preliminary investigations parallel those imposed on pre-trial detention. The basic limit is 2 months, extendable to 3 months by a local procurator, then in cases of "unusual complexity" extendable to 6 months by a "subject" procurator, with further extensions possible from the Procurator-General of the Russian Federation or his assistant, though only in "exceptional circumstances."[89] However, the Code does not specify any consequences for failing to comply with these time limits. Anecdotal evidence suggests that the limits are commonly violated or avoided in one way or another and are no better observed than the time limits on pre-trial confinement or for setting trial dates.[90]

11. Formulation and Approval of the Indictment Against the Defendant

If a criminal investigator, following completion of the preliminary investigation, finds sufficient evidence of guilt to require a trial, the next step is the filing of formal charges. The criminal investigator must decide what charges should be brought.[91] These proposed charges are written up in a document called "accusatory conclusions" (*obvinitel'nye zakliuchenia*) in what is the last major task of the criminal investigator. This document is sometimes referred to in English as an "indictment" to reflect that the charges have been screened and deemed sufficient to warrant a trial, and that term will be used here. Generally, prosecutorial discretion does not exist, at least not to the extent that it does in the Anglo-American tradition. Consequently, all cases in which the criminal investigator properly concludes that there are sufficient grounds to proceed on particular charges, an indictment should be issued. Exceptions are provided for cases in which administrative penalties might be more appropriate.

In form, the Russian indictment is a considerably more prolix document than its U.S. version. Before concluding what the legal basis for the charges should be in the final or "conclusions" portion of the indictment, there is a summary of the entire body of evidence collected in the process of the preliminary investigation. If the accused denies his guilt, there must be a recitation of the evidence supporting the criminal investigator's contrary conclusion. This summary of the evidence is supposed to give the defendant notice of what the prosecution will rely on at trial. However, the defendant and his lawyer have full access to the entire case file compiled by the criminal investigator and are likely to rely on it in preparing for trial rather than just on the criminal investigator's summary.[92]

---

[89] *See* art 133, CrPC. *Compare* with the limits on pretrial detention discussed *supra* pp. 480-481. However, unlike pre-trial detention, there is no absolute maximum limit on extensions ordered by the Procurator-General.

[90] *See supra* p. 481 and *infra* p. 508.

[91] *See* Art. 205-207, CrPC.

[92] For an example of the Supreme Court criticizing a relatively detailed statement as not sufficiently reciting evidence, *see In re Khairullin*, BVS, 1998, No. 2, p. 12.

The final part of the indictment is where the defendant is charged with violating a particular criminal statute.[93] Attached to the indictment is a list of the witnesses that should be subpoenaed for trial along with information about pre-trial detention, how long the preliminary investigation took to complete, real evidence to be presented and the civil suit.

When the procurator receives the case file and the recommended indictment, he or she is supposed to examine all the evidence in the case file carefully to assure that a proper offense has been charged and can be supported by the evidence at trial. The procurator must also examine the file to determine whether the preliminary investigation and the police inquiry before it were properly conducted and were "complete and objective."[94] The procurator can approve the charges, change them or dismiss them, or send the case back for supplemental investigation. The procurator is also supposed to review the pre-trial detention status of the accused. If the procurator is convinced the proposed indictment is proper, he has 5 days to sign it and send it on to the court. There must be an indication whether the procurator considers it necessary for a procurator to appear at trial. The notice of what court the matter has been sent to is then served on the defendant.

If the criminal investigator or procurator orders that the charges against the accused be dismissed, the question has arisen whether the victim of crime has any recourse. The Constitutional Court dealt with that issue in the following case.

The Constitutional Court: *Case on the Constitutionality of Art. 209(5) of the Criminal Procedure Code* (VKS, 1995, No. 6, p. 18

1. R.N. Sammigullina, the victim in a criminal case arising out of the death of her brother, O.N. Sammigullina, made a timely complaint to the office of the procurator contesting the order of the investigator dismissing the case for lack of evidence. The Lenin District Court of the City of Ekaterinburg, the Collegium for Civil Cases of the Sverdlovsk region, and the presiding judge of the Sverdlovsk Regional Court and the Deputy Chair of the Supreme Court of the Russian Federation denied her relief, relying on the fact that Art. 209(5) of the Criminal Procedure Code of the RSFSR provides that an order of dismissal of a criminal case entered in the process of a preliminary investigation may be appealed only to the procurator and that there is no right of judicial review.

[93] Lupinskaya, *supra* note 3, p. 302-304. The offense charged in the indictment is not supposed to be more severe than the one charged in the initial charges formulated against and served on the accused by the criminal investigator.

[94] Art. 213(3), CrPC.

In her complaint addressed to the Constitutional Court of the Russian Federation, Sammigullina requests that we declare the provision of Art. 209(5) unconstitutional to the extent that it allows law enforcement organs to limit the constitutional right of a victim to court access and to justice. . . .

[Art. 209(5) states: "The decision to dismiss a case may be appealed to the procurator within five days of notice of the order of dismissal."—ed.]

[T]his provision of Art. 209(5) . . . has been understood by courts and other law enforcement organs not just as granting rights to interested persons to appeal dismissals to the procurator, but also as a prohibition on filing a similar appeal in court. As made clear by research in the course of this case, this approach has been consistently adopted as a matter of judicial interpretation in the country for many years. This view was that adopted by the courts mentioned above in their examination of the complaint of Sammigullina . . .

3. According to Art. 46 (1) and (2) of the Constitution of the Russian Federation, everyone is guaranteed the right to judicial protection of rights and freedoms, and the right of access to courts for the redress of all decisions and actions (or omissions) of government agencies and officials is secured.

The right of citizens to judicial protection of their rights falls into the category of rights which may not be limited under any circumstances by virtue of Art. 56(3) of the Constitution of the Russian Federation.[95] At the same time, according to the meaning given to the provisions of Art. 209(5) of the CrPC through interpretation, a party in a criminal case whose rights and legal interests are affected by the dismissal of a criminal case is deprived of his rights to gain access to the courts for relief.

In this way, the rule of part 5 . . . , interpreted as the sole law to establish a procedure for appealing a dismissal of a criminal case, causes a significant number of decisions affecting citizens' basic rights and freedoms to be excluded from judicial review despite the commands of Art. 46 of the Constitution of the Russian Federation.

4. The criminal procedure law under review, as interpreted, also does not conform to the provisions of Art. 52 of the Constitution of the Russian

---

[95] Art. 56(1) of the Constitution provides: "In the event of an emergency, specific limitations on rights and freedoms may be adopted through passage of a constitutional law with limits specified with regard to their scope and time period if needed for the protection of the security of citizens and the constitutional structure." However, part 3 states that the rights set out in particular articles including the right to judicial protection set out in Art. 46 "are not subject to limitation" under part 1. [Footnote by the editors.]

Federation which guarantees victims of crime and abuses of official power the right to seek justice. Parties to cases which are unlawfully dismissed at the stage of the preliminary investigation — whether victim, suspects or defendants—are deprived of this right. . . .

In accordance with the foregoing and [legislation on the Constitutional Court], the Constitutional Court of the Russian Federation rules:

1. That Art. 209(5) of the Criminal Procedure Code of the RSFSR is unconstitutional to the extent that it limits, in accord with long-established judicial interpretation, the authorization of judicial review of an order of dismissal of a criminal case, in violation of Art. 46 (parts 1 and 2) of the Constitution of the Russian Federation.

The provisions of Art. 209(5) of the CrPC of the RSFSR may not be used as a basis for denying judicial review of an order dismissing a criminal case. . . .

Questions and Notes

1. What has Ms. Sammigullina won? Even if she wins her appeal and the decision to dismiss is reversed, what further obstacles does she face? Reconsider your answer after reviewing the materials below on the victim's role at trial, *infra* pp. 523, 535-536.

Another possibility for a victim thwarted by procurators unwilling to proceed in a criminal case is a "private" prosecution. This procedure permits a private person to file and prosecute criminal charges against someone. However, Ms. Sammigulina could not resort to a private prosecution because the crime involved was not one of the crimes specified as qualifying for private prosecution—simple assaults, simple defamation and insult. Prosecutions can be initiated by the victim and can end upon the parties agreeing to an appropriate settlement. Also possible are the so-called "private-public" prosecutions for simple rape and copyright and patent infringement.[96] These differ from purely private prosecutions in that they will not be dismissed upon agreement of the parties. If the victim wins, in addition to any criminal punishment, damages may be awarded and other appropriate orders entered, such as a requirement that any newspaper publishing the defamation publish a retraction. In either kind of case the procurator can appear to support the charges if it is deemed appropriate.

2. How does the Court know that Art. 209(5) prohibits a judicial appeal of a dismissal at the preliminary investigation stage? Is another

---

[96] Art. 27, CrPC. *See generally* Lupinskaya, *supra* note 3, pp. 507-511.

interpretation of the statute possible? If the Court's reading of Art. 209(5) is correct, is it inconsistent with its reading of Art. 47(4) on on who can represent defendants in criminal cases (see pp. 493-498)? What is the principle of statutory interpretation involved here?

3. There is currently a Victims' Rights movement afoot in the United States to lobby for laws giving victims of crime more rights. It has even been suggested that the U.S. should pass and ratify a Victims' Rights Amendment for the U.S. Constitution. Are there difficulties with the U.S. system going as far as the Russian system has in terms of allowing victims standing to appeal dismissals of criminal charges or to file "private" prosecutions?

4. In another interesting case, the Constitutional Court—citing the present case—held that the *accused* can appeal the dismissal of criminal charges.[97] The Court observed that the dismissal did not remove the allegations in the case file gathered during the preliminary investigation that the accused committed the crime and thus did not amount to a "rehabilitation" of the accused. Consequently, the accused was entitled to insist on a trial to clear his name.

* * * *

12. An Alternative Procedure: The "Protocol" Form of Proceeding in a Criminal Case

There is an alternative method of proceeding in criminal cases that does not involve a full preliminary investigation followed by procurator indictment. This is the "protocol" form of proceeding. It is used for certain uncomplicated, relatively minor offenses in which the perpetrator is known. The upper limit for offenses prosecutable by this simplified procedure is fine and/or imprisonment for up to four years. Some examples of the kinds of offenses that qualify will give a flavor of what kinds of cases they are: assault and battery, non-payment of support, slander, malicious destruction of property, petty theft, petty fraud, running an unlicensed business, refusal to testify, unlawful disclosure of information from a preliminary investigation, insulting government officials and desecrating the seal or flag of the Russian Federation. If the perpetrator is unknown or other complications arise, the case can be converted into a normal criminal case with a full preliminary investigation.[98]

---

[97] *Case Concerning the Constitutionality of Art. 6 of the Criminal Procedure Code of the RSFSR*, VKS, 1996, No. 5, p. 11.

[98] Art. 414-419, CrPC.*See generally* Lupinskaya, *supra* note 3, at 535-546 .

The cases in this category are generally investigated by the uniformed police. They take statements from all the witnesses and the suspects. These statements and other evidence are then compiled and sent to the court with the procurator's approval. The court is supposed to formulate the correct charges and try the defendant within 14 days of receiving the material.

Since there has been no full preliminary investigation by a criminal investigator in "protocol" prosecutions, no in-depth examination of the facts has been made by a legally-trained person to determine what charges are proper. The solution to this problem is to give that task to the trial court. However, the Constitutional Court found constitutional difficulties with this. In the *Case Concerning the Constitutionality of Art. 418 of the Criminal Procedure Code of the RSFSR,*[99] a regional court judge referred the issue of the constitutionality of this arrangement to the Constitutional Court.

The Court held that the procedure violated separation of powers, since the function of initiating and formulating criminal charges is an executive function that was being thrust on judicial organs. It further noted that "a judge who has decided that a criminal case should be initiated and has formulated the charge against the defendant has an interest in these determinations. This complicates the judge's task of objectively deciding the facts of the case, all the more if acquitting the defendant or rendering some other decision in the defendant's favor can be construed as an admission of a mistake in the judge's earlier view of the case." Consequently, the Court held that the protocol form of proceeding, "which places on the court the power to initiate a criminal case and formulate the charges against the defendant, violates Art. 123(3) of the Constitution . . . guaranteeing the principle of adversarialness in court proceedings." Noting that the court "may not take upon itself what are the special procedural functions of the parties," it continued:

> In the criminal judicial process, adversarial principles dictate that there be a strict separation of the functions of the court in its decision of the case and the function of the prosecution and defense, each of which is allocated to its respective role in the process. In initiating a criminal case against a person and particularly in determining what charges will be brought, the court is unavoidably siding with the prosecution and begins to perform two functions — prosecution and adjudication of the case, which results in inequality of the parties before the court in the criminal case and violates adversarial principles.

The legislature reacted to the case by passing an amendment to the Criminal Procedure Code. It provides that, upon completion of the police

---

[99] VKS, 1996, No. 5, p. 15.

inquiry, the head of the organ of police inquiry is to "formulate the charges with cites to the appropriate articles of the Criminal Code" and forward the file to the procurator. Then the procurator has the option of sending it to court, sending it for a formal preliminary investigation or dismissing it.[100]

13. Placing the Case on the Trial Docket

Except for the possible episodic need to intervene at the request of the accused or the procurator, the trial court will not get involved in a case until the stage of placing the case on the docket (*naznachenie sudebnogo zasedania*). The name of this stage is more modest than its content. Many preliminary issues must be determined at this time, somewhat similar to what is done in pre-trial conferences in cases in the U.S. The presiding trial judge decides these issues sitting alone and without any other judges, lay or professional. The judge, in addition to setting the date, time and place of trial, must also decide such things whether the court has jurisdiction and venue, whether sufficient evidence has been collected to proceed to trial, whether the procurator's formal charges are proper and whether changes should be made in the defendant's pre-trial detention status. The judge must also decide whether any motions filed by the procurator, defense or victim should be granted, what witnesses and experts should be called and whether an interpreter is needed. The judge needs to decide as well whether there is any need to send the case back to the criminal investigator for supplemental investigation or if the investigation was complete, but the evidence is weak, whether the charges should be dismissed.[101] Clearly, the questions to be decided will require that the judge become intimately familiar with the case file compiled during the preliminary investigation.

The admonition that the judge is to determine whether there is sufficient evidence to proceed to trial should not be confused with the preliminary hearing in the typical U.S. felony case. The judge's knowledge of the case is not gained from the prosecutor presenting live evidence. All the

---

[100] *Rossiskaya Gazeta* (November 19, 1997). p. 3. It is interesting to note that at least one noted commentator maintains that the protocol with all the facts compiled in the police inquiry certified by the head of the police inquiry organ and approved for filing by the procurator *in fact is* a decision initiating a criminal case made by the requisite prosecutorial authorities. *See* Lupinskaya, *supra*, note 3 pp.545-546. However, this is not the Constitutional Court's view. Interestingly, the academic editor of Lupinskaya's book went to the trouble of penning a footnote reminding the reader that, contrary to her suggestion, the Court did in fact hold the protocol procedure unconstitutional. *See id*, p. 546 n. 1.

[101] *See generally* chapter 20, CrPC, Lupinskaya, *supra* note 3, pp. 319-330, and Gutsenko, pp. 271-297.

judge has is the preliminary investigation case file compiled by the criminal investigator.

There is one aspect of Russian criminal procedure that could reduce the degree of rigor that judges employ in reviewing the casefile: a case can be sent back for supplemental investigation (*dosledovanie*) at any time, even during the trial. Thus, if the trial reveals that insufficient evidence was collected or errors were committed during the preliminary investigation, the judge can send the case back for supplemental investigation at that time. Once that supplemental investigation is complete, if the procurator believes the evidence has improved or errors have been corrected, another trial can be had.[102]

Trials must begin within 14 days of the date of the case docketing session. A 1996 Ruling of the Plenum of the Supreme Court indicates that 20% of the regional-level court trials in 1995 were held in violation of this time limit. But this does not tell the entire story. The docketing session at which the trial date is set is supposed to be held within 14 days (for those in pre-trial detention) after the procurator files the formal charges and casefile with the court.[103] The ruling notes that "apparent violations of the time period for holding case docketing sessions are widespread" and such sessions are "sometimes being held several months after the case is filed in court, including cases in which the defendant is in pre-trial detention."[104] One can suppose that judges are delaying holding their case docketing sessions in order to start the clock later on the time limits for setting the trial date.

C. The Trial

1. Trial Courts and Decision-Makers

The first-level trial courts are District Courts, which are the lowest level federal courts. They are usually organized as city courts and have jurisdiction over all criminal cases in which the maximum punishment is less than 5 years in prison. As noted in Chapter III, the second-level trial courts, most of them Regional Courts, are organized on the "subject" level of a region,

---

[102] Art. 258, 232, CrPC. More discussion of sending a case back for supplemental investigation after the trial has started is set out below where trial procedure is discussed. See *infra* p. 529.

[103] Art. 223.1, 239, CrPC.

[104] Ruling of the Plenum of the Supreme Court, *"Ob ogranicenii vremei slushaniia ugolovnykh i granzhdanskikh del sudami Rossiiskoi Federatsii"* ("On the Time Limits for Trying Criminal and Civil Cases by Courts of the Russian Federation") BVS, 1996, No. 8, p. 3.

territory, autonomous republic and autonomous region and on the city level in Moscow and St. Petersburg. These courts have jurisdiction over the more serious criminal cases, the maximum punishments for which are from 5 years up to life imprisonment and the death penalty.

Decision-makers in these courts are of various types.

a. Single-Professional-Judge Courts

Criminal cases in which the maximum punishment does not exceed 5 years of incarceration are heard by a single professional judge.[105] In such a case, the judge resolves all matters of fact and law and pronounces sentence. However, the principle of collegiality is strong in judging criminal cases, so most other cases are adjudicated by different arrangements of professional judges or a professional judge and lay persons.

b. The Mixed Professional and Lay Judge Court

Criminal cases involving juveniles and cases involving a maximum punishment that is greater than 5 years are generally heard by courts made up of one professional judge and two lay assessors.[106] The lay assessors have a vote equal to the professional judge and could theoretically overrule the professional judge were they inclined to take a different view of the case. In Soviet times, this never happened. In part, this was because of the natural advantage the professional lawyer-judge would have over lay persons in any deliberations on the case. But the experience in Soviet times was further affected by the fact that lay assessors were screened for their political reliability first and foremost.[107] Typical were "workers of the month" who long ago learned the benefits of bending whichever way the official winds were blowing. Undoubtedly, anyone with an independent streak was screened out by this process.[108]

---

[105] Art. 35, pt. 2, CrPC.

[106] Art. 35, pt. 3, CrPC.

[107] Even without the factor of political liability, the level of disagreement between lay and professional judges is low. The German *Schoffengericht* has the same composition and the level of disagreement in that system is 1.4%.*See* Gerhard Casper and Hans Zeisel, Lay Judges in the German Criminal Courts, Journal of Legal Studies 135 (1972).

[108] Among the non-lawyer populace at least, lay assessors were referred to derisively as "kivalki" or "the nodders," thus describing their constant nodding agreement with everything the presiding professional judge said or suggested. The Concept of Judicial Reform opposed an increase in the number of lay assessors as a way to make them more independent, referring to it as nothing more than "a mechanical increase of heads, nodding in unison to the words of the presiding judge." Concept of Judicial Reform, p. 32.

Today in most areas, courts have had to resort to semi-permanent "professional" lay assessors from different, but equally non-diverse groups—the unemployed and retirees—the only people whose lives would not be disrupted by service as a lay assessor.[109] Not only does diversity suffer in such a system, but there is additional pressure on these "professional" assessors to conform, because they develop relationships with the professional judges and want to keep their "jobs" for whatever reasons attracted them to become lay assessors in the first place. At various times reformers have suggested improvements in the system of lay assessors that would seek to get more diversity in their ranks. Others have suggested that they be elected by legislative assemblies, while yet others believe they should simply be eliminated. The Constitutional Law on the Judicial System[110] contemplates the continuation of the system, makes such service, along with jury service, a "civic duty" and requires that assessors be paid from the federal budget.[111] However, the details of selection and tenure are to be dealt with in a separate law on lay assessors. Pending enactment of that law the terms of existing lay assessors have been extended by presidential decree.[112]

In Soviet times, the professional judges did not wear robes, nor did the lay assessors. Today, in keeping with the greater status and increased powers of judges, professional judges wear black robes and, with the exception of the feature of a collar (some have called it an "Elvis collar"), look much like judges in the United States. Lay assessors continue to sit without robes.

c. Courts of Three Professional Judges

All cases except those heard in the city district courts, may be heard by a court composed of three professional judges if the court decides to do so and the defendant consents. This option has not been implemented in many regions because of the shortage of judges. In addition, the most serious criminal cases—those punishable by more than 15 years of imprisonment, life in prison or the death penalty—may only be heard by a panel of three professional judges or by a jury.[113]

---

[109] "*Predlagaet iustitsiia Rossii*," *Rossiiskaia iustitisiia*, 1994, No. 4, p. 4.

[110] *Sobranie*, No. 1, p. 1 (1997).

[111] *Id.*, Art. 8(2), (4).

[112] *Ukaz Presidenta RF*, No. 41, January 23, 1997 "On continuation of the terms of lay assessors of republican supreme courts, regional and territorial courts, the city courts of Moscow and St. Petersburg, courts of autonomous regions, autonomous areas, district and military courts."

[113] Art. 15, CrPC.

d. The Russian Jury

More promising than lay assessors in terms of providing independent lay participation in criminal trials is the recently reintroduced Russian jury. Trial by jury was one of the major emphases of the Concept of Judicial Reform and the Russian Constitution of 1993 provides a right to trial by jury.[114] However, the constitutional right exists only to the extent that it is implemented by legislation. After considerable acrimonious debate and political compromising in the State Duma, legislation was passed in July of 1993 implementing the right, but only for a narrow category of extremely serious criminal offenses heard by second-level trial courts.[115] Most of these crimes have the potential for the death penalty. Because jury trial procedure differs from non-jury trial procedure, it is separately discussed later on pp. 429-539. Consequently, the description that follows in the next two sections is of the more typical non-jury trial.

2. The Actors and Setting of the Trial

a. The Presiding Judge

Whatever the makeup of the decision-making body, there is a presiding judge whose job it is to run the trial. The tradition in Soviet times, consistent with continental Western European practice, was that the presiding judge was active in eliciting the facts of the case at trial. Few changes in this respect have been made in the old RSFSR Criminal Procedure Code that continues in force. Indeed, the phrase from that Code that has so far in this book been freely translated as "trial," is really "judicial examination" (*sudebnoe razbiratel'stvo*) and the title of the Code chapter devoted to trials is dubbed "Judicial Investigation" (*sudebnoe sledstvie*). The Criminal Procedure Code charges the judge in a non-jury case to actively seek the objective truth of the matter—"to employ all measures to assure a complete and objective investigation of the facts of the case from all sides."[116] This usually has meant that the presiding judge calls all the witnesses and actively questions them and attaches to the record such other evidence as is needed.

The Constitution, however, speaks of "adversary principles and equality of the parties" in "all judicial proceedings."[117] As a result, at least some presiding judges have begun to insist that the parties take a more active

[114]Russian Constitution, Art. 47(2).

[115]*See* Chapter III, pp. 77-79 where second-level trial courts are discussed.

[116]Art. 20, CrPC (emphasis added). *Compare* Art. 429, quoted *infra* p. 531, text at note 180, which is applicable to jury trials.

[117]Art. 123(3), Constitution of the Russian Federation.

role in presenting the evidence and have themselves assumed a more passive role. The majority of judges, however, are waiting for the new Criminal Procedure Code to show them the way and continue largely as before.[118]

b. The Prosecutor

The tradition of the presiding judge actively exploring the evidence has made the presence of a state prosecutor largely unnecessary. Consistent with this, in Soviet times procurators did not show up at many trials.[119] Given the procurator's role as guardian of legality, the procuracy has resisted the notion of turning them into "mere" participants in trials who are inferior to the judge. As one commentator phrased it, it is more comfortable and much less work "to not participate in a trial . . . , to make no objections to the way the trial is handled, and yet to protest the judgment if dissatisfied with it."[120] However, while many of the traditional supervisory functions of procurators have remained, the 1995 Law "On the Procurary of the Russian Federation,"[121] flatly states that "the procurator performs the role of government prosecutor."[122]

Yet, nothing in the Criminal Procedure Code has been changed regarding their new duties. As a result, in some areas of the country, the combination of procurators resistant to change, judges comfortable with their old active ways and the lack of direction from a new Criminal Procedure Code have resulted in the "prosecutor" and the presiding judge making few changes in how they perform. Thus, the procurator, if he or she attends at all, does not engage in much questioning of witnesses. And their participation in the most advocacy-oriented aspect of the trial — closing arguments—tends to be less an

---

[118] Some of the informal changes over to more adversarial procedure can be ascribed to sections of the Criminal Procedure Code and judges' experience in jury trials. *See infra* pp. 429-439, where jury trial procedure is discussed.

[119] One of the issues that the presiding judge must decide in setting the case for trial is whether a procurator should appear as prosecutor at the trial. Art. 228(3), CrPC.

[120] Steven Thaman, Reform of the Procuracy and Bar in Russia, 3 Parker School Journal of East European Law 1, 7 (1996). This article traces the developments that led to the 1995 Law "On the Procuracy of the Russian Federation."

[121] Sobranie zakonodatel'stva, 1995, No. 47, p. 4472.

[122] *Id.*, Art. 35. The new law still preserves the right of procurators to initiate appeals of convictions by way of the procurator's right to "protest" perceived illegalities that occurred at trial or in the pre-trial investigation, and this power is exercised regularly. However, the 1995 law draws a distinction between head procurators and their deputies on the one hand and the various assistant procurators (*pomoshchniki prokurora*) who appear as state prosecutors in court. The latter are allowed to appeal or protest only decisions in cases in which they participated at trial. *Id.* Art. 36(1). The right to protest is discussed *infra* p. 540 when appellate remedies are discussed.

exercise in persuasion than a delivery of the prosecutor's conclusions regarding the law and the facts.

c. Court Secretary

There is no verbatim transcript kept of the trial. Instead the court secretary takes notes and writes up summaries of testimony. It is not unusual for the judge to interrupt the trial to dictate a particular part of a summary deemed important, or for the lawyers to turn to the secretary and make sure a telling part of the testimony of some witness has been included in the summary. As with most other characteristics of Russian trials that shock U.S. lawyers, this characteristic is common to most modern Western European civil law legal systems. Because of the way the record of testimony is kept, good trial lawyers must always be aware of whether the court secretary is paying attention and writing at crucial points during witness examinations or arguments. However, the problem of an incomplete record is somewhat alleviated by the fact that the parties have 3 days after trial to make corrections and additions to the record and even during trial may make a motion to have testimony recorded verbatim.[123]

d. The Victim

In the non-homicide case, the victim (*poterpevshii*, literally "one who has suffered") is the person who was directly affected by the crime, while in homicide cases, it is the nearest relative of the deceased. As in other civil law systems and as we saw when we read the case allowing victims to appeal dismissals of criminal charges, Russia's victim of crime has a much greater status and many more legal rights in criminal cases than in the U.S. The victim may join a claim for money damages to the criminal charges and the result of the trial determining that the defendant is guilty will be not just a criminal sentence, but also a civil judgment for damages.

Russian criminal procedure accords the victim the status of a party. As such, victims have the right to appear at trial and state their positions as to any issues that arise in the trial and to question witnesses and offer evidence. They have the right to bring a lawyer to represent them, though this is not often done even in serious cases, since the lawyer's work would largely duplicate that of the judge or prosecutor. Consequently, most victims defer to the prosecutor or court in questioning witnesses. Victims generally may not participate in closing arguments at least in non-jury trials.[124]

---

[123] Art. 264-265, CrPC.

[124] Exceptions are simple assaults, criminal defamation and insult. *See* Art. 295. CrPC. The draft CrPC gives the victim the right to participate in closing arguments in all cases. Art. 46(6), Draft CrPC.

e. The Defendant

In some Russian criminal courts, the defendant is located in a "prisoner's dock," as in the English system. In others, there is a barred cage in the courtroom for the defendant, as in the Italian system. When in the dock, the defendant is usually flanked by two machine-gun toting guards.[125] The cage and even the dock are sometimes a shock to the American observer who is used to defendants sitting next to their lawyers at the counsel table. Whether in the dock or cage, the defendant is usually several feet or, in a large courtroom, several yards away from his or her lawyer. This arrangement sometimes makes consultation with one's client difficult and the need for consultation a public affair, since defense counsel must make their way over to the client while the everyone watches and waits.

f. Defense Counsel

The physical separation of the defendant and defense counsel is symbolic of their legal separation. In the U.S. trial, the defense attorney fully "represents" the defendant in every way in the sense that defense counsel *acts for* the defendant. Indeed, it is possible for the defendants in U.S. trials to go all the way through trial without ever being required to address the judge or other participants directly in front of the jury, unless they choose to testify.[126] What is striking to the American trial lawyer witnessing a Russian jury trial is the way the defendant and the defendant's lawyer are treated as if they were separate parties. Whenever input from the parties is required on any matter, the defendant and the defense lawyer are asked separately what their position is. If there is a conflict between the two, then the defendant's position prevails. But in most cases, defendants, upon inquiry by the judge, simply state that they agree with their counsel's position.

One could argue that this kind of separate treatment tends to devalue the role of defense counsel. In any event, it sometimes needlessly and unfairly displays the defendant in a poor light. In one Russian jury trial, an issue arose of whether to admit particular evidence. The defense attorney had raised what seemed to be a valid objection to that evidence. The judge nonetheless asked the defendant personally what his position was. When the defendant said he

---

[125] These have been troops of the Ministry of Internal Affairs. Now, under Art. 11 of the new Law "On Court Bailiffs" provides that court bailiffs will now be responsible for all court security. It is anticipated that the new bailiffs will guard defendants somewhat more subtly. *Zakon o sudebnykh pristavakh* (Law on Court Bailiffs), *Sobranie*, No. 118-FZ (1997).

[126] Perhaps significantly, in English, "[a]ttorney literally means 'one who is designated by another to transact business for him." Garner, A Dictionary of Modern Legal Usage 74 (1987).

did not know, the judge asked him pointedly "do you support your lawyer's position on this question or not." The defendant clearly did not understand the issue (which was rather technical), but the judge's inquiry was so pointed that he wasn't sure what he should say. His stammering and the judge's impatience with him did not create a good impression before the jury even though his reaction was the completely understandable.[127]

As noted in the discussion of preliminary investigations, defense counsel generally do not conduct any independent investigation of the case before or during the preliminary investigation. This is also true with regard to preparing for trial. Lawyers generally do not prepare their own witnesses for trial, other than the defendant and perhaps defendant's family members, if they are testifying. As a result, many witness examinations do not go as smoothly as they often do in U.S. trials.

An interesting issue about who—among otherwise qualified lawyer-advocates—may appear as defense counsel in a case arose recently in a case involving government secrets. The case gave the Constitutional Court the opportunity to give some shape to the constitutional provision guaranteeing the right to counsel.

The Constitutional Court: *Case Concerning the Constitutionality of Art. 1 and 21 of the Law of the of June 21, 1993 "On State Secrets" (VKS,* 1996, No. 2, p. 34)

1. The military court of the Moscow Military District, in trying a case against V.M. Gurdzhianets for a violation of Art. 64 of the CrPC RSFSR [treason], refused to permit the advocate D.D. Shteinberg to appear as counsel for the defendant. The basis for the refusal was Shteinberg's lack of the special security clearance required of people who will have access to state secrets, as provided in Art. 21 of the Law of the Russian Federation "On state secrets." . . .

2. The Constitution of the Russian Federation, while guaranteeing to everyone the right of to freely seek, receive, communicate and produce and distribute information by any legal method, at the same time provides that legislation may list types of information that are state secrets (Art. 29, part 4). This decision is necessary for the defense of the sovereignty of Russia, the protection of its defense and security and complies with the prescription of Art. 55 (part 3) of the Constitution of the Russian Federation, which allows limitations to be imposed by federal law on rights and freedoms of citizens and persons, including the right to information, in pursuit of the purposes set out in

[127] Burnham *et* al., *infra* note 188, p. 126.

Art. 55. Based on this, the legislature has the right to establish a list of types of information that are state secrets, to regulate matters related to their declassification and protection and to determine the procedures for access of citizens to such information. . . .

4. . . . Art. 48 of the Constitution of the Russian Federation protects the right of everyone to receive qualified legal services and the right to use the services of an advocate (defender) at all stages of the criminal process. In accordance with Art. 14 of the International Covenant on Civil and Political Rights, which is a constituent part of the legal system of the Russian Federation, everyone who is faced with a criminal charge has the right to communicate with counsel of his choice and to defend himself by counsel.

Therefore, the refusal to permit the accused (suspect) to use the lawyer of his choice based on the lack of a security clearance for that lawyer and the suggestion that the accused (suspect) choose a defender from a list of advocates who have a security clearance . . . improperly infringes on the constitutional right of a citizen to receive qualified legal services and the right to free choice of counsel. . . . This constitutional right, under Art. 56 (part 3) of the Constitution of the Russian Federation, may not be limited under any circumstances.

5. The fact that the defendant's choice of counsel depends on counsel's security clearance status also violates the adversarial principles and equality of parties in litigation secured by Art. 123(part 3) of the Constitution of the Russian Federation.

The investigation of the majority of criminal cases in which there is secret information is vested in the Federal Security Service. These same organs perform security investigations to determine whether to grant security clearances, pursuant to . . . the Law of the Russian Federation "On state secrets." Under these circumstances, the advocate in reality is dependent on the same organs conducting the criminal prosecution, which places the defense and the prosecution in unequal positions.

6. . . . From these constitutional provisions, the legislature in determining the means and methods for protecting state secrets must use only such measures and methods as will eliminate the possibility of unwarranted limitations on the rights and freedoms of citizens and persons. In the context of criminal procedure, such measures may in part include closed court sessions, warning to the participants in the trial not to communicate any state secrets they learn in connection with their participation on the case and criminal prosecution of those who do communicate them. The preservation of state secrets in criminal cases is secured as well by the Provisions on the

Advokatura of the RSFSR, contained in the Law of the RSFSR of November 20, 1980, which impose a duty on the advocate to keep professional secrets, not to commit any improper conduct that is inconsistent with membership in the bar and to be an example of irreproachable behavior (Art. 13, 16). . . .

NOTES AND QUESTIONS

1. An interesting contrast to the solicitude for the right to counsel in this case is the system of special "access" which advocates had to receive in Soviet times to represent dissidents in court (or any other case investigated by the KGB). No law provided for it; it was just implemented by the KGB.[128]

2. Do you notice at least a rhetorical conflict between what the Court says in this case about the right to counsel and what it said in the case on whether non-advocates could represent defendants in pre-trial proceedings (p. 493)?

3. The Court makes a point of the right of defendants to have counsel *of their own choice.* Is this realistic? How does this compare to the right to counsel in the United States?

* * * *

As Note 3 suggests, the defendant's right to counsel is taken seriously in Russia. The appellate court reports are replete with reversals of trial courts for failing to allow the defendant his own choice of counsel.[129] If there is a financial problem, the government is required to pay.[130] Both trial[131] and appeals decisions[132] will be reversed if defense counsel does not appear and

---

[128] For an account of this phenomenon by the defense attorney for Natan Scharanski and other dissidents until revocation of her "access" rights, *see* Dina Kaminskaya, Final Judgment, pp. 31-32 (1982).

[129] *See, e.g., In re Efimov*, Supreme Court, BVS, 1995, No. 2, p. 8 (when there is an agreement that a particular advocate would participate in the preliminary investigation, the participation of a different one is a violation of Art. 48).

[130] *See, e.g., In re Rezukhin*, Presidium of the Volgograd Regional Court, BVS 1995, No. 9, p. 10 (when defendant declines counsel, the judge or criminal investigator must determine whether it is for lack of money and, if so, must provide money for defense counsel; conviction reversed).

[131] *In re Kravchuk*, Supreme Court, 1997, BVS, No. 4, p. 5 (defense counsel failed to show up at trial; trial went on with prosecutor's participation; conviction reversed).

[132] *In re Ubaichin*, Supreme Court (Presidium), Supreme Court, Garant Criminal Procedure Library (1993) (collegia requested that appeal hearing not be set in a month when advocate was at a health resort; it was set then anyway, the advocate did not appear, but the hearing was held; reversed).

the case is heard and decided. However, if it appears that counsel of choice will not be available to handle the case for an extended period of time, the defendant will have to choose another lawyer.[133]

A related right is the right of the defense to examine all the evidence collected against the defendant in the case file. This must be allowed both to the defendant and defense counsel and to them together. In one case, a defendant's conviction was reversed in part because the defendant and defense counsel had separate opportunities to view the file, but not together.[134] In another case, video and audio tapes which were supposed to be part of the casefile were not shown to the defendant or his lawyer. The conviction was vacated and the case sent back for a new investigation.[135] This right of the defense to examine the entire evidence collected during the pre-trial investigation is typical of civil law systems and considerably different from the situation of the defense in the United States, which has a right only to exculpatory evidence in the hands of the prosecution.

3. Trial Procedure

a. The Opening of the Trial

All trials open with the reading of the indictment.[136] This would not be so bad except for the fact that, as discussed earlier, the indictment summarizes all the evidence against the defendant. It is common for the indictment to go on for several pages even in a relatively simple case. In some more complex trials, the reading of the complete charges takes days.

In the authors' view, no satisfactory answer has ever been given why it is necessary to read the entire charging paper. Under the Criminal Procedure Code, the defendant must be given a copy of the indictment. As just discussed, both the defendant and defense counsel have a full opportunity to review the entire case file.[137] It would not seem necessary in the interest of informing the public, since all the evidence is required in any event to be presented in open court during the rest of the trial. There would seem to be no good reason why

---

[133] Art. 48, CrPC; *In re Zaporozhets and Dubinin*, Supreme Court, 1992 (Garant Criminal Procedure Libarary) (right to counsel not violated by assigning counsel other that defendant's choice, since defendant's preferred counsel was to be on leave and that would delay trial).

[134] *In re Kir'ianov*, Supreme Court, BVS 1996, No. 11, p. 8.

[135] *In re Soloviev*, Supreme Court, BVS 1996, No. 5, p. 14. There was even some indication that the defendant and his counsel had declined to examine the tapes, but there was no written record of their declining to do so in the case file.

[136] Art. 278, CrPC.

[137] *See* Art. 236-237, CrPC.

on trial day the court could not get more quickly to more substantive matters.[138]

In jury trials, it is the prosecutor who must read the charges against the defendant, not the judge. This is more consistent with the notion of an adversarial proceeding. Inspired by this and sensitive to the constitutional admonition that criminal litigation is based on adversarial principles, some judges have been requiring that the prosecutor read the charges even in non-jury trials.[139]

b. Testimony of the Defendant

After the reading of the charges, the judge asks the defendant whether he or she understands the indictment and whether he or she pleads guilty to it or not. The defendant must respond personally and not through counsel. The Criminal Procedure Code provides that the defendant has the opportunity to explain his or her plea (*motivirovat'*), but most do not take advantage of this right.[140] If the defendant pleads guilty in response to the indictment, this does not avoid a full trial. Consistent with the continental tradition, there is no institution in the Russian system similar to the Anglo-American guilty plea, whereby the defendant waives the right to a trial, nor is there any plea bargaining in the Russian system.

The defendant is next is informed of the right against self-incrimination and the right to testify if he or she wishes. Then the defendant is invited testify. If the defendant so wishes, it is with the defendant's testimony that the trial usually starts. The defendant testifies first in the vast majority of trials.[141]

To the American observer, the way in which the Russian trial typically begins does much to vitiate the presumption of innocence. There is an exhaustive summary of all the prosecutor's evidence at the beginning (often read by a judge). Then the presiding judge calls on the defendant essentially to

---

[138] Art. 310 of theDraft CrPC mercifully puts an end to this. The court is simply required to assure that the defendant was given a copy of the indictment and has had it for at least 3 days before the trial. Then the trial begins "with a description by prosecutor of the essence of the charges against the defendant." The defense is then permitted to respond in kind with the defendant's position. *See* Art. 319.

[139] Conversation with Judge Yevgennyj Druzin, Saratov, Russia, June 17, 1997. The Criminal Procedure Code provides only that the trial begins "with the reading of the charges" and does not specify who does the reading. Art. 278.

[140] Art. 278, CrPC.

[141] Art. 280. CrPC. Actually, Art. 279 provides that the court is supposed to hear the suggestions of the parties about the order in which the evidence will be presented, but in most cases the defendant testifies first.

explain himself. This seems to shift the entire focus of the case from the question "Can the prosecution prove any of these allegations?" to the question "What explanation does the defendant have for his or her behavior?" While it may make sense to look to the defendant for an explanation at some point in the proceedings, looking to the defendant for testimony at the very beginning of the trial—when no competent and admissible evidence of guilt whatsoever has yet been presented—seems in effect to presume guilt.

When the preliminary investigation was discussed, it was noted that the overwhelming majority of defendants give testimony at the preliminary investigation despite their right to remain silent.[142] In part, talking at the pre-trial stage and talking at trial go together, since defendants at trial will have to explain incriminating statements made during the preliminary investigation on pain of their being accepted as true. But there are additional "encouragements" for defendants to testify at trial.

The first is the way in which the trial begins. It is a common police interrogation tactic in the U.S. to try to convince the defendant that he might as well confess because the evidence against him is overwhelming. One can suppose that the tactic works even better when it is judges rather than the police who solemnly explain just how much evidence they have against you and then pointedly ask you what you have to say for yourself. Second, as in other continental countries, there is no separate sentencing proceeding and both guilt and punishment in Russia are determined at the trial. Thus, defendants who wish to have a say about their punishment will have to speak up at some point in the trial. Finally, if pre-trial detention has any effect of encouraging suspects to talk at the preliminary investigation stage, the additional time in detention pending trial will make them all the more willing to talk. The facts that this may be a considerable period of time and that Russian pre-trial conditions are quite bad only adds to the "persuasive" effect of detention.[143]

The defendant testifies while standing in the prisoner's dock or cage. The defendant's testimony, like that of witnesses, is given in narrative form, followed by any necessary clarifying questions. Interestingly, as is the case with other civil law systems, the defendant even at trial does not take an oath or otherwise incur a legal obligation to tell the truth, as do other witnesses giving testimony later. Indeed, it is improper to refer to the defendant as a "witness" when testifying. The term "witness" applies only to those who are testifying who are not parties. However, what the defendant says both at trial and before

---

[142] *See supra* pp. 475-476.

[143] *See supra* p. 508, where the extent of non-compliance with time limits for docketing and trial is discussed.

the criminal investigator is called "testimony" and is evidence on which a decision in the case can be based.

Following the defendant's narrative statement, he or she is then questioned in the following order: by the Judge, then by the Procurator, then by the victim and finally by defense counsel.

c. Testimony of Witnesses

Before testifying, witnesses are asked to identify themselves and approach a table in the courtroom where there is form (*raspiska*) for the witnesses to sign that acknowledges that the testimony is being given under penalty of perjury. Witnesses then go to the podium in front of the bench and give testimony while standing there. The first question the judge asks is: "Tell me everything that you know that is relevant to this case." The answer is usually a long narrative. Following this, the same order of supplemental questioning is followed, with the addition of the defendant to the list: judge(s), prosecutor, victim, defendant, and then defense counsel. Questioning by the judge, prosecutor and defense lawyer are generally done while they are seated. All others must stand to ask a question.

Witnesses are mandatorily sequestered before they give testimony so that they cannot hear the testimony given by other witnesses. However, after giving testimony they must stay in the court room and may be asked supplemental questions at any time, even during the testimony of another witness.[144] Unless those supplemental questions are numerous, witnesses in the audience simply stand and answer from their place in the hall. Likewise, the defendant can be asked a question at any time and, with the permission of the presiding judge, may give testimony at any time.[145] In cases in which there is a great deal of switching between witnesses or between witnesses and the defendant, the trial takes on a somewhat disorderly appearance. This is especially so when there are conflicts in testimony and one or more of the witnesses is seated in the hall. It is not unusual that, in the heat of the moment, witnesses or the defendant reply to each other without being prompted by a question. On occasion, members of the audience supporting one side or the other chime in, encouraged by what appears to be an open forum.

In general, like other continental trials, there are fewer "advocacy opportunities" for the lawyers participating in the Russian trial. Certainly, any attempt to do an adversarial "cross examination" is seriously obstructed by the

---

[144] Art. 283, CrPC.
[145] Art. 280, CrPC.

fact that no leading questions are permitted to be asked at all.[146] The only possibility for leading questions are the so-called "clarifying questions" (*utochniaiushchie voprosy*). These are narrow and leading questions permitted to be asked only after the examiner has asked an open question on the topic. Some judges, however, will permit a clarifying question without the examiner first asking an open question if the topic was touched upon in an earlier examination by the judge, prosecutor or victim. Whether under the rubric of "clarifying questions" or not, it is not uncommon to see several instances of what an American trial lawyer would call leading questions pass without objection or intervention by the court.[147]

Another obstacle to advocacy is the fact that the presiding judge takes more control over the trial. In a typical trial, many if not most of the questions asked of witnesses and the defendant are asked by the judge. Also, while the adversary trial leaves to the parties the responsibility of objecting to inadmissible evidence or improper questions, the presiding judge enforces these rules *sua sponte* in the Russian trial. For example, the ban on leading questions is almost exclusively enforced by the judge, who stops the lawyer even before the opposing side has a chance to object. In any system, it is difficult for lawyers at trial to object to questions asked by the judge. It is equally difficult when the "objections" to counsel's questions come from the judge.

Having said all this, one must remember what was said earlier — that there is some variation in the adversarialness of trial procedure among regions of the country and even among judges in the same region. The switch to adversarial principles, when it occurs, is most profoundly felt in witness examination and other presentation of evidence in the case. Thus, some judges

---

[146] Traditional advice on cross examination technique for U.S. lawyers is that every question on cross examination should be a leading question.

[147] One could argue that the Criminal Procedure Code contains no prohibition against leading questions at trial. The only provision of the Code that prohibits them is Art. 158 (5), but this provision appears in an article that governs pre-trial investigation. *See supra* text at note 35. In the chapter dealing with trial procedure, chapter 30 of Part 3 of the Code, there is no such prohibition. If Art. 158 is being applied by analogy, the analogy would seem inapt. A criminal investigator, who is supposed to be gathering evidence on all sides of the case in the investigation stage, should not be permitted to lead witnesses. The parties at trial are in a different position, especially if the trial is truly based on adversarial principles. *Cf.* Art. 446(4) (permitting the *jury* at trial to submit questions to the judge to be asked of witnesses, but prohibiting the asking of leading questions). There is some support for this view from Russian academics. *See* L.B. Alekseeva, S.Ye. Vitsin, E.F. Kutsova, I.B. Mikhailovskaya, *Sud prisyazhnykh: Posobie dlia sudey* (Jury Trials: A Handbook for Judges) p. 92 (Joint Project of the Russian Legal Academy of the Ministry Justice and the American Bar Association 1994).

require that a procurator attend all trials and present the case for the prosecution and allow greater latitude to all counsel in "cross-examining" witnesses and to defense counsel in calling and interrogating their own witnesses at trial.[148]

d. Testimony and Rights of the Victim

Victims have the right to testify. This is so even if they have no knowledge of the circumstances of the crime. Their testimony usually consists of statements of the impact the crime has had on their lives. But since everyone testifies in narrative form and victims are rarely interrupted by the judge, the victim's testimony often includes statements about the case and the defendant that are not strictly relevant to determining guilt. It is fair to say that victims generally use their right to appear and testify to obvious profound negative effect on the defendant's case.[149] In all cases, the judges will explicitly consult victims on the issue of punishment. As to this, Russian victims are on occasion quite forgiving and often request that the defendant not be sentenced to a prison term.

Sometimes victims actually seek to help the defendant. In one murder case, following the defendant's admission that he beat and strangled the victim's husband, the widow-victim testified to all the horrible things that her husband had done to the family when he was alive, including attacking her to get her pension money to buy vodka, trying to strangle one daughter to death and beating another so badly that she suffers from epilepsy. She reported that all her sister could say when she visited his grave was "Thank God!" She yelled at the prosecutor: "You said my husband was a human being. He was not a human being! He was an animal! They should have hanged him twice and shot him three times!" Then she bowed to the defendant and thanked him for murdering her husband.[150]

e. Expert Evidence

The Russian and continental European tradition's belief in a single objective truth of a matter carries over to experts. Indeed, the belief is stronger with experts, since their conclusions must have an objective scientific basis. Consequently, when issues in a case require expert examination, analysis and conclusions, there is only one expert and that expert is a "neutral" one

---

[148] The Draft CrPC requires that the prosecutor and defense present the evidence from "their" witnesses and contains other elements of adversary-style witness examination. *See* Draft CrPC, Arts. 320, 321, 324.

[149] Thaman, *supra* note 38, pp. 107-108, 112.

[150] *Id.* p. 107 n. 289. The jury acquitted the defendant on this count, but it convicted him and his co-defendant on a second count of murder. *Id.*, pp. 173-174.

employed by the court or the criminal investigator.[151] Also, while *non-expert* witnesses must testify at trial, expert witnesses need not do so. Their written report obtained during the preliminary investigation automatically qualifies as evidence.

The defense can suggest that a second expert be engaged by the investigator or the court and this request is sometime granted, especially if the defense can point to flaws or unclarity in the original expert's report.[152] However, many investigators routinely deny such requests. Even less often granted are defense motions that the expert be required to testify in person at trial and answer defense questions. More likely, upon being informed of substantial defects in the expert's report, the judge will return the case for supplemental investigation. It perhaps follows from the above that defense lawyers generally have no right to employ and present their own expert witnesses (at government expense or otherwise) to contradict the analysis and report of the "court's" expert, as is done in the United States.

Similar but not identical to an expert is a "specialist." Specialists, like the expert, have some form of specialized knowledge of subject matter involved in the case.[153] However, their purpose is to assist the criminal investigator, court or jury understand specialized materials or phenomena. They generally do not submit conclusions to the court as experts do.

f. Final Arguments

The Tsarist criminal law bar on both the defense and the prosecution side had a rich history when it came to the art of the closing argument.[154] This tradition is being continued by Russian lawyers today. One is not as likely to see the flamboyance one can see in U.S. courtrooms, perhaps for cultural rather than legal reasons. But final arguments are probably the part of the Russian trial that are most like the U.S. trial and the observer will find a great deal in terms of argument structure and technique that is familiar.

---

[151] *See generally* Art. 78-82, CrPC.

[152] Where experts disagree with each other, they may be ordered to meet together to see if they can reach agreement. If they cannot, then they render their conclusions separately. *See* Art. 80, CrPC.

[153] *See* Art. 133, CrPC.

[154] With the renewal of interest in the jury came the publication of books collecting famous closing arguments by Tsarist-era prosecutors and defense counsel in jury trial cases. An excellent example of one such book is S.M. Kazantev, ed., *Sud prisiazhnykh v Rossii: Gromkie ugolovnyie protsessy* 1864-1917 (Trial by Jury: Famous Criminal Cases 1864-1917) (1991). The book includes not only famous closing arguments, but biographical sketches of famous trial lawyers and an article on jury trials by the most famous Russian lawyer in history, A.F. Koni.

Because guilt and sentence are decided in one trial, the Russian defense lawyer's job can be complicated. At least in cases where there is an argument that the defendant is not guilty, it is difficult to avoid some rhetorical inconsistency in arguing both that the defendant did not commit the offense and that, if he did, he is sorry and should not be punished too severely. However, in most trials the defendant's guilt is a foregone conclusion—remember that a plea of guilty will not avoid a trial—so a great deal or most of the final argument in most cases is devoted to factors related to sentencing, including issues of the defendant's remorse and his or her character and background.

Russian law considers closing arguments very important even when they are given by defendants representing themselves. In one case, the defendant, a police inspector with some legal education was prosecuted for police brutality and represented himself at trial. After the closing argument of the prosecutor, he made a motion requesting that the court give him until the next morning to prepare his closing argument. Instead, the court gave him only an hour. As result, Borisov declined to participate in closing arguments, explaining that he was given too little time to prepare. The Supreme Court reversed the constitution and held that the district court "effectively deprived Borisov of any real opportunity to participate in closing arguments which violated his right to defend himself."[155]

g. Final Word of the Accused

Even for defendants whose lawyers make closing arguments for them, the final stage of the trial affords something like the opportunity for a *pro se* final argument. This is the defendant's right to the "final word" (*poslednoie slovo*) in the trial.[156] Consistent with other continental legal systems, Russian law provides that no one may ask questions of the defendant during the final word, the judge may not limit its length and the law does not specify any particular content.[157] It must be the last event in the trial and, once the defendant finishes, the judges immediately leave to deliberate.[158] The right to a last word is a right and not a requirement. And the right is important enough that, if the defendant has not exercised his right in a given case, the conviction

---

[155] *In re Borisov*, BVS, 1996, No. 9, p. 8.

[156] *See generally* Art. 297, CrPC and Lupinskaya, *supra* note 3, pp. 392-393.

[157] These aspects of the right to a final word were used to some advantage by dissidents during anti-Soviet activity trials as a podium for them to set out their political views.

[158] If the final word of the defendant contains new evidence, then the case can be sent back for a supplemental investigation. Art. 297(3), CrPC.

will be reversed unless it appears clearly from the record that the defendant affirmatively waived the right.

In cases where guilt is a foregone conclusion, the final word is important as an occasion for the defendant to express sincere remorse. Sincerity is the key; a mechanically-voiced token apology is probably worse than saying nothing. In cases where guilt is an issue, the defendant will have already testified and fully gone into why he or she is innocent, so the final word will generally be a final appeal to believe that testimony. Rarely are final words an organized marshaling of the evidence in the defendant's favor.

h. Deliberation and the Process of Weighing the Evidence

As with the standard continental trial, no great efforts are made to define precisely the applicable standard of proof, and Russian lawyers share the incredulity of their fellow continental lawyers about Anglo-American proof standards. One feels the full weight of the legal cultural differences between Anglo-American and continental legal systems when one tries to explain to the continental legal mind how a criminal case is determined by "proof beyond a reasonable doubt," while civil cases are proven by a "preponderance of the evidence" and occasionally by "clear and convincing evidence." The Anglo-American mind thinks of proof in terms of degrees of probability. The continental lawyer is likely to view proof in more absolute terms. A case, whether criminal or civil, is either proven or it is not. It cannot be half proven anymore than a woman can be "half-pregnant."

What the Russian law says about proof is that there is "free" evaluation of the evidence, i.e., no particular type of evidence has any predetermined strength or effect. Also, the Criminal Procedure Code provides that "[t]he court, procurator, investigator, inquiry official are to evaluate evidence *according to an inner conviction*, based on a complete and objective examination of all the facts from all sides."[159] In addition, the presumption of innocence in the Russian Constitution requires that "remaining doubts about guilt shall be resolved in favor of the accused."[160] Putting together "inner conviction" and the presumption of innocence, this would seem to be equivalent to the U.S. standard of "beyond a reasonable doubt."

[159] Art. 71, CrPC. Actually Art. 71 (still) goes on to say "guided by the law and socialist consciousness." Art. 437(1) provides the same standard for jurors. The jurors' oath states that the juror will decide the case "according to my inner conviction and conscience as befits a free and fair citizen." Art. 443, CrPC.

[160] Constitution, Art. 49(3). "Remaining doubts" is a translation of *neustranimye somnenia* or doubts that have not been eliminated.

i. Judgment and Sentence of the Court

As in other continental systems, the final judgment of the court, if it finds the defendant guilty, contains both a judgment of conviction and the defendant's sentence.[161] There is no pre-sentence investigation done or separate sentencing hearing held. It is considered that all the facts relevant to the severity of sentence, including the defendant's character and previous criminal record, will have been explored at the trial. Further, the defendant's opportunity to have the final word at the end of the trial affords the defendant a sufficient opportunity to be heard on the issue of punishment.

(1) The Determination of Guilt or Innocence and Its Justification

The Constitution provides that a person may be punished for a crime only by means of a judicial decision.[162] Both the finding of guilt and the sentence must be justified by written reasons contained in the court's decision. The Criminal Procedure Code sets out a list of questions that must be answered in the decision relating to guilt and punishment[163] and each answer must be justified by a description of the evidence upon which the court relied. An acquittal must be justified in similar terms.[164]

At several points, provisions in the appeals section of the Criminal Procedure Codes provide for rather searching scrutiny of the decision, which can be read as additional instruction to trial judges on how to write their decisions and make factual findings. These provisions as they are applied to trial court decisions raise the issue of the scope of appellate review of factual determinations of trial courts. That issue is discussed in the section on appeals, *infra* pp. 539-542.

Statistics on conviction rates disclose that they fell by a substantial amount from 1980 to 1990. In 1980, approximately 94% of defendants were convicted. This gradually decreased over ten years to a rate of approximately 84% in 1990.[165] However, this was largely the result of an increase in

---

[161] *See generally* Art. 300-322, CrPC, and Lupinskaya, *supra* note 3. It is interesting that the Russian word for the court's judgment "*prigovor*" can be used to refer either to the judgment of guilt or to the sentence.

[162] Art. 10, Constitution.

[163] Art. 303, CrPC. Each question and what is involved in answering it are discussed in Lupinskaya, *supra* note 3, pp. 400-404.

[164] Art. 314, CrPC.

[165] *See* Todd Foglesong, The Reform of Criminal Justice and Evolution of Judicial Dependence in Late Soviet Russia, in Peter Solomon, ed. Reforming Justice in Russia, 1864-1996 (1997). p. 282.

dismissals at an early stage of cases of trivial import, and is therefore not very significant.[166]

(2) Disposition of the Victim's Civil Suit

As noted earlier, where a civil claim has been made by the victim, the court will also rule on the disposition of that claim and the amount of any damages to be paid by the defendant. However, in exceptional circumstances where the issue of damages is difficult and resolution of it is not important to determining questions in the criminal cases, such as what offense the defendant has committed or the punishment the defendant should receive, the civil claim can be postponed while the criminal case is disposed of and then placed on the civil docket for later trial.

What happens to the victim's civil claim in the event the court determines that the defendant is not guilty depends on the grounds for the acquittal. If the acquittal is because no crime was proven or the defendant was not proven to have participated in the crime, then the civil suit is dismissed. If the acquittal was because some element of the crime was not proven, then the civil suit is simply left unresolved so that it can be decided as a normal civil case.[167]

Interestingly, the same proof standard—which as discussed above is probably close to the Anglo-American criminal standard—is applied to the civil claim as well. For some, this seems a high standard indeed for proof of a civil claim for damages.[168]

(3) Determination of and Justification for the Sentence

The other task of the trial court in its decision is to determine the defendant's sentence. Questions of the propriety of and justification for particular sentences are subject to the same requirement of justification as the determination of guilt. The decision must discuss both the mitigating and the aggravating circumstances of the case and the reasons why the particular punishment was chosen. The issues of what types of punishments are possible

---

[166] Letter from Peter Solomon, University of Toronto, July 2, 1998.

[167] Art. 310, CrPC.

[168] Similar difficulties result in Western European continental countries. Thus, in an auto accident in France witnessed by no one other than the parties where the parties' accounts contradict each other, a decision in favor of the plaintiff would be impossible. One commentator has suggested that this is the reason why there has been the widespread move to strict liability in many civil cases. *See* Martin Shapiro, Courts: A Comparative and Political Analysis, pp. 139-143 (1981) (discussing strict liability for automobile accidents in France).

and the propriety of each type are discussed in the chapter on Criminal Law.[169]

j. An Alternative Trial Disposition: Return of the Case for Supplemental Investigation

As mentioned earlier, a case can be sent back for supplemental investigation even during the trial.[170] After that supplemental investigation is completed, there can then be a second trial of the defendant on the same or different charges. While American observers concerned about defendant's rights against double jeopardy are quick to criticize this practice, it is often the defense that moves to send the case back for supplemental investigation. This is because a return of the case to the criminal investigator often results in dismissal of the case when the criminal investigator takes a look at any supplemental evidence and, along with that, a more careful look at the evidence collected earlier.

There are limits on sending a case back for supplemental investigation because of defects in the facts. Incompleteness of the preliminary investigation can be a reason only if the defect in the case cannot be cured at trial, e.g. through bringing additional witnesses or other evidence on issues that were not sufficiently explored during the preliminary investigation.[171] Further, the judge is required, in sending the case back to the procurator, to state precisely what factual circumstances need to be reinvestigated. In practice, however, judges who have better-prepared cases waiting in the wings to be tried are often inclined not to try to salvage the case, but simply to send it back with a general order to investigate it better.[172]

---

[169] See chapter XI, pp. 582-592. Also sometimes issued along with the judgment is a "separate finding" (*chastnoie opredelenie*) of the judge. This finding may refer to appropriate law enforcement organs particular organizations or persons (other than the defendant) whom the court believes have violated the law. It may also find violations by officials involved in the criminal case, such as the improper conduct of the criminal investigator or any participant in the trial. This is one possible way the trial court can criticize the prosecutor or defense counsel for improper conduct during the trial. *See* Art. 21.2, CrPC.

[170] Art. 308, 258, 232, CrPC.

[171] Art. 232(1), referenced in Art. 258, CrPC.

[172] Cases can also be sent back because of legal errors by the criminal investigator, to change the charges set out in the indictment to a more severe or entirely different charge and to deal with issues of joinder of multiple defendants. Art. 232, CrPC. It should be mentioned that the drafting group for the new Criminal Procedure Code has agreed to drastically reduce the grounds for returning a case for supplemental investigation. Simple insufficiency of the evidence will no longer suffice. Even the normally "law and order" Ministry of Internal Affairs (where most criminal investigators are based) wants supplemental investigation abolished entirely. Letter from Professor Peter Solomon, University of Toronto, July 2, 1998.

4. Special Procedures in Jury Trials

Articles 47 and 123(4) of the 1993 Constitution contemplate the potential of juries in all criminal and civil cases if provided for by legislation. Appropriate legislation was passed on July 16, 1993[173] and the first Russian jury trial in over 75 years was held in Saratov in December of 1993.[174] However, there are two principle limits on the jury trial right. First, the law provides for the option of a jury trial only for defendants in the most serious of criminal cases prosecuted in the second-level trial courts.[175] Second, the law has been implemented only in 9 regions of the country.[176] Plans were made to extend the right to 3 other regions in July, 1996, but money was not forthcoming to allow for the transition.[177]

On a scale of the degree of independent decision-making, Russian juries rank high. In this respect, the Russian jury is more similar to the Anglo-American jury than to the mixed-judge tribunals of Germany or even the French jury. As such, it shares the three signal features of the traditional common law jury: (1) 12 members chosen at random from the community (2) who deliberate independently from the judge and (3) who are not required to provide any reasons for their decision.[178] Current statistics indicate the

---

[173]The jury trial law is set out primarily in Articles 414-466 of the Criminal Procedure Code. A good Russian-language source on the Russian jury trial that includes citations to other sources is M.V. Nemytina, Rossiiskij sud prisiazhnykh (The Russian Jury Trial) (1995).

[174]One of the authors was sent by the American Bar Association to be an official American observer at this trial. Russia had a jury trial system in criminal cases during the period 1865-1917. A good book on this era that describes the tsarist jury trial is Samuel Kucherov, Courts, Lawyers and Trials Under the Last Three Tsars (1953). An excellent and comprehensive article dealing with both the legislation and jury trial practice that draws on examples from recent jury trials held under the new law is Thaman, *supra* note 38. For a journalist's report of the first trial and the impact of the new legislation, *see* Deborah Stead, "The Jury is Back," Los Angeles Times Magazine, p. 38 (April 24, 1994).

[175]These offenses are primarily various forms of aggravated murder, *See* Art. 36, CrPC.

[176]Those regions are Altai Territory, Ivanovo Region, Krasnodar Region, Moscow Region (suburbs of Moscow, not including the city itself), Riazan Region, Rostov-on-Don Region, Saratov Region, Stavropol Region, Stavropol Territory and Ul'yanovsk Region.

[177]The City of St. Petersburg is nonetheless proceeding on its own and has outfitted courtrooms for juries and conducted training for judges and lawyers. E-mail from Vassily Vlasikhin, ABA consultant at its Moscow office, on file with the author.

[178]In the German mixed-judge courts, lay judges deliberate in the company of professional judges and the court must render a written decision justifying its conclusions. The French jury, at nine members might be inclined to "gang" up on the three professional judges, but they must deliberate with the professional judges and the court's decision must be justified in writing.

independent bent of the modern Russian jury, which acquits in around 20% of the cases it decides.[179]

The Criminal Procedure Code describes the judge's responsibilities in jury trial cases quite differently than it does in non-jury cases. In wording somewhat similar to the constitutional command, the Code states that jury trials are to be "based on adversarial principles" under which "*equal rights are assured* all the parties and the judge, while maintaining objectivity and impartiality, is to *create the conditions necessary* for an objective and complete investigation of the facts of the case from all sides."[180]

While jury independence and the adversarial approach of jury trial procedure are radical departures from the inquisitorial tradition, there are limits to the changes that jury trials introduce. First, the law provides that when the jury trial law does not otherwise provide, the non-jury trial procedure already outlined is to be applied. Since the jury trial law is somewhat sparse in its requirements for trial procedure, there is a tendency in practice in to revert to non-adversarial non-jury procedure. Second, the jury trial law does nothing to change the inquisitorial preliminary investigation stage. The only change in the preliminary investigation stage is the requirement that the criminal investigator advise the accused at this time of the right to a jury trial if that is available for the offense with which the defendant is charged and has been established in that region of the country.[181]

a. Pre-Trial Stages

One pre-trial stage is added in jury cases after the indictment has been approved and filed with the court: the "preliminary hearing."[182] Despite the name, this hearing is nothing like the hearing of the same name in U.S. criminal procedure. It is more like a U.S. pre-trial hearing on issues of the admissibility of evidence. This step had to be added to deal with the new problem of avoiding jury exposure to inadmissible evidence during the trial.

As is the case in other civil law countries, however, there are few evidentiary limitations on otherwise relevant evidence. Hearsay evidence, for example, is freely admissible. However, evidence that has been illegally obtained can be contested.

As a means of limiting illegally obtained evidence, the preliminary

---

[179] Thaman, *supra* note 38, pp. 270-271.

[180] Art. 429, CrPC (emphasis added). *Compare* the language of Art. 20, quoted *supra* text at note 116.

[181] Art.423-424, CrPC.

[182] Art. 432, CrPC.

hearing as structured by the jury trial law has one major defect: the judge is limited to the factual record made by the criminal investigator as set out in the casefile when deciding motions to suppress. Since it is not likely that the case file will include evidence of such things as police beatings of the defendant or illegal search procedures, this is a substantial limit on the ability to establish the factual predicate for exclusion of evidence. Motions can be made at trial, when the testimony of the defendant and other witnesses and other evidence may be offered in support. However, the procedure is cumbersome on the day set for trial when there is a jury waiting in the wings. The result is that it is often the case that neither the prosecution nor the defense knows when they show up for trial whether some key piece of evidence will be admitted.[183]

The evidence can also be contested at trial in front of the jury. Few U.S. defense attorneys would find comfort in this option. However, many Russian defense lawyers do not hesitate to save for the jury's consideration at trial such things as the defendant's claim that the police beat and threatened the defendant to get a confession. Unlike jurors in most parts of the U.S., Russian jurors are inclined to believe a defendant's allegations the confession was coerced and to ignore it.[184]

The preliminary hearing is also the occasion for the trial court to confirm the defendant's wish for a trial by jury. The defendant's decision at this stage is irrevocable.[185]

b. Trial Procedure

1) The Beginning of the Trial

The reading of the indictment at the beginning of a jury trial is limited to the prosecutor reading only the concluding paragraphs where the offenses are listed and only a few basic facts are set out. In addition, in recognition of the danger that impressionable jurors might misuse the information, any prior convictions the defendant has or his status as a recidivist may not be mentioned. However, the same procedure is followed of asking the defendant to plead and forcing him to decline to testify in open court and in the presence

---

[183] Art. 270 of the Draft CrPC creates the prliminary hearing stage for all cases and allows witnesses to be called to testify on matters related to the admissibility of evidence.

[184] Burnham *et al., supra* note 187, p. 129: "The foreperson of the jury in the first jury trial in Saratov" was a "solid-citizen" manager of a factory, but he fully believed the defendants' story that the police beat them severely and their confession was the result of that beating. As he explained to a newspaper reporter after the trial, 'I got in trouble a lot as a kid and every time the police caught me, I got a beating.'"

[185] Art. 432(9), CrPC.

of the jury.[186] If, as suspected, this method of opening the trial conveys the impression of presuming guilt in a non-jury trial,[187] that impression is all the more strong for jurors. If it is really necessary to begin the trial this way, there would seem to be no reason why the jury should observe it. Instead, the judge could inform jurors in short what crimes the prosecution has charged the defendant with, remind them that these are only allegations and inform them that the defendant pleads not guilty to them.[188]

No opening statements to the jury are permitted for either the prosecution or defense. But what seems like an even-handed, if ill-advised, prohibition applicable to both sides in fact results in inequality of the parties. In fact, the prosecution *has* the right to make an "opening statement" by reading the summary of the indictment, while the defense has no similar right. A defense opening statement would give the jury a similarly coherent introduction to the defense's response to the charges. Instead, the jury usually gets its first exposure to the defendant's legal position in the case—whether it is self-defense, insanity, coercion or alibi—in the worst way imaginable. Instead of a coherent statement of the defendant's legal position by counsel, the jury has to figure out on its own what that position is by listening to the often-rambling, nervous narrative testimony of the defendant (recall that the defendant usually testifies first) and through the defendant's answers to the prosecutor's often hostile questions (recall that the prosecutor questions all witnesses first). And if the defendant chooses not to testify first, the jury will hear nothing at all about what the defense's position is. The result is that the jury at the very beginning of the case has a quite clear idea of the prosecutor's contentions, but no such clear understanding of the defense case.[189]

This inequality between prosecution and defense is not as much a problem in non-jury trials. In non-jury trials the judges and lay assessors have access to the entire indictment, which includes references to the defense contentions, or to the case file compiled during the preliminary investigation and can inform themselves before the trial starts as to the defendant's likely defenses.

---

[186] Art. 446, 278, 280, CrPC.

[187] *See* discussion *supra* pp. 519-520.

[188] *See* "*Rossiiskii i amerikanskii sudy prisyazhnykh: Sravnitel'no-pravovoi analiz*" ("Russian and American Jury Trials: A Comparative Legal Analysis") in William Burnham, Irina Reshetnikova, Alexei Proshlakov, *Sudebnaya Advokatura* (Trial Advocacy) (St. Petersburg U. Press 1996), pp. 122-124.

[189] Burnham, *et al.*, *supra* note 188, pp. 123-124. Perhaps for these reasons, Art. 383 of the Draft CrPC provides for opening statements from both the prosecution and the defense in jury trials. In non-jury trials, something opening statements are provided for, but different language is used, suggesting that these statements would be shorter in non-jury trials. *See and compare* Art. 319, Draft CrPC.

A unique effort to get away from the continental notion that everyone should have a full trial is introduced in the jury trial law. If the defendant, in response to the indictment, pleads guilty, the court may ask the defendant to testify as to what he did. Then, if the court is satisfied that there is no doubt that the defendant is guilty and the parties consent, the court can shorten the trial or proceed directly to closing arguments. The jury then deliberates to a decision just as they would in a full contested trial.[190]

2) Presentation of the Evidence

The prosecutor's attendance and participation are required in all jury trials and judges more or less require that the prosecutor perform the function of presenting the evidence. However, this does not mean that evidence is presented by way of questions and answers between lawyers and witnesses. Witnesses and victims give their initial testimony in narrative form in jury trials just as in non-jury trials.

Narrative testimony has led to problems when it comes to dealing with inadmissible evidence. The question-and-answer format gives opposing counsel time to determine from the question asked whether inadmissible evidence is called for, so that an objection can be interposed before the jury hears the answer. Because of the narrative format in Russian jury trials, there have been several cases in which witnesses have blurted out inadmissible evidence, usually violations of the ban on the admissibility of the defendant's prior convictions or evidence of the defendant's bad character.[191] In one jury trial any efforts to avoid jury exposure to the defendant's prior record were dashed when a witness sitting in the audience shouted to the jury: "It's the second person he's killed and he says he didn't kill!"[192] The Supreme Court has

---

[190] Art. 446(2), CrPC.

[191] *Id.*, p. 128. There is no direct prohibition on character evidence in the jury trial law. However, a recent decision of the Russian Supreme Court has made it clear that no evidence of defendant's character (lichnost') can be admitted at trial. Ruling of the Plenum of the Supreme Court "*O nekotorykh voprosakh primeneniq sudami ugolovno-prtsessual'nykh norm, relgamentiruiushchikh proizvodsvtvo v sude prisiazhnykh*" ("On Several Questions Regarding Application of the Criminal Procedural Law in Jury Trials"), BVS, 1995, no. 9, p. 54, point 16. This is not a complete boon for the defense. Though many jury trial cases involve rather unsavory characters, most murders (as in most countries) are committed by "ordinary" people against relatives and close friends. There is often evidence that the defendant otherwise led an exemplary life.

[192] Thaman, *supra* note 38, p. 107. Thaman collects several other examples of witnesses blurting out inadmissible evidence.

instructed trial judges in such situations to instruct the jury to disregard the improper evidence.[193]

A different problem with the use of narrative testimony before juries is that the relevant facts of that narrative go by very fast. "Professional listeners," as judges are, may not have much of a problem with this. And, in any event, the judges can read the witnesses' statements in the case file if they miss something in the testimony. But the Russian jury often has only a vague impression of what happened after hearing quickly spoken, rambling or collapsed narratives from witnesses. The almost universal practice of never using a diagram to explain testimony contributes to the incompleteness and vagueness of the picture the jury sometimes gets. In general, judges and the lawyers in Russian jury trial are not yet used to the idea that the evidence in a jury trial must be *presented* to a body of *lay people* who have *no prior knowledge of the case.* Instead, they treat the jury trial as they often do the non-jury trial—as a *review* of the evidence with a *professional judge* who is already familiar with it from reading the case file.

The Plenum of the Supreme Court has instructed that the jury trial law's requirements of "adversarial principles and equality of the parties" require that "the examination of the defendant, victim, witnesses and experts will be conducted by the parties. The presiding judge and the jury through the judge may ask questions after they have been questioned by the parties."[194] However, this does not necessarily get rid of narratives. In Russian law, "examination" or "questioning" of a witness or party are the follow-up questions that come after they give their "testimony" by way of a narrative. In addition, there is no change in the remaining order of questioning. Thus, it is still the case that, even if the defendant is the one testifying, the procurator goes first, then the victim and only then does defense counsel have the right to ask questions.

3) Enhanced Rights of the Victim

If there are evidence problems connected with the narrative form of testimony, it is certainly asking for trouble to give victims the right to make closing arguments. Yet, despite the fact that victims do not generally have this right in non-jury cases, they are given the right in jury trial cases.[195] After analyzing the first 114 jury trials held in post-Soviet Russia, Thaman called the right of the victim to make closing arguments "disastrous."[196]

---

[193] *See* point 7 of Plenum Ruling, *supra* note 191.
[194] *See* Plenum Ruling, *supra* note 191.
[195] Art. 447, CrPC. *Compare* Art. 295.
[196] Thaman, *supra* note 38, p. 112.

A second disturbing prerogative of the victim unique to jury trials is that the victim in a jury trial can prevent dismissal of the case by the prosecutor.[197] Perhaps it would depend on why the prosecutor wanted to dismiss the case, but if it is on the ground that the prosecutor has determined that there is not enough evidence for conviction, then this would seem to be unwarranted oppression of the defendant.

4) The Judge's Charge to the Jury

At the end of the evidence, the judge must give instructions to the jurors just before they retire to consider their verdict. This stage, which keeps the terminology from the tsarist jury trial law — "parting words" (*naputstvennoie slovo*)—contains more than instruction on the law and how to weigh the evidence.[198] The Russian judge—like the English judge and unlike the U.S. judge — helpfully sums up all the evidence that has been presented on both sides of the case. In the authors' experience, most judges do this quite skillfully and objectively and, when so done, the summary is probably quite helpful to the jury. The negative side of the summary is that it provides the opportunity for the loser to comb it for signs of bias and use that as a basis for appeal. The issue of non-objectivity of the charge to the jury, however, must be raised in a contemporaneous objection, not after the trial is over.[199]

An innovation that might be useful in U.S. jury trials is that Russian jurors have the right to ask the judge questions and receive further clarification of any part of the instructions they did not understand.[200]

c. Deliberations and Decision

1) Jury Nullification

U.S. jurors are told that they must accept the law as given to them by the judge and, if they find beyond a reasonable doubt that the defendant did the acts charged in the indictment, they must find the defendant guilty. However, since a jury acquittal in a criminal case is not reviewable on appeal or otherwise in the U.S., juries in this one situation have the power of

[197] Art. 430(2), CrPC. Thaman relates an interesting case in which the victim's assertiveness of her right to return the case for supplemental investigation led ultimately to the conviction of the defendant. Thaman, *supra* note 38, p. 100 and note 248.

[198] Art. 451, CrPC.

[199] Art. 451(9), CrPC. The likelihood of close scrutiny of the summary is all the more likely for the fact that the Supreme Court requires that, unlike any other part of the trial, it must be "set out in detail" or recorded verbatim for appellate review. *See Plenum* Ruling on Juries, *supra* note 191, point 21, p. 59.

[200] Art. 451(8), CrPC.

"nullification"—the power to ignore the law and acquit a criminal defendant despite clear evidence of guilt. Thus, it is said U.S. jurors have the *de facto power* to nullify, though they do *not* have the *legal right* to do so. The importance of the distinction is that the lack of *legal right* to nullify means that neither the judge nor the lawyers appearing in the case may tell the jury of their power to nullify, nor may defense counsel argue nullification to the jury.[201] Since jurors would have to violate the judge's instructions to engage in nullification, the U.S. approach assures that it will be invoked relatively rarely.[202]

By contrast, nullification seems to be built into the Russian jury trial system. Set forth in the statute are three separate questions the jury is to answer: "(1) was it proven that the acts charged took place; (2) was it proven that the defendant committed those acts; [and] (3) is the defendant guilty of committing those acts."[203] It is fully contemplated that there may well be "yes, yes, no" verdicts. By separating the questions of whether the defendant "did it" from the question of whether the defendant is guilty, the law emphasizes the need for the verdict to be a true "verdict of conscience."[204]

There have been several acquittals by Russian juries in the face of strong prosecution evidence. Most have involved murder victims who one might say in a moral sense "deserved" to be killed by the defendant under the

---

[201] In *United States v. Krzyske*, 836 F.2d 1013, 1121 (6th Cir. 1988), jurors specifically asked the trial judge to explain nullification to them after an unrepresented defendant, a tax protester, mentioned it in his closing argument. The trial judge's decision to be less than candid in answer to the jury's question was upheld on appeal. *But see* Todd Barnet, *New York Considers Jury Nullification: Informing the Jury of Its Common-Law Right to Decide Both Facts and Law*, 65 N.Y. S. Bar J. 40 (1993).

[202] There are no statistics on jury nullification since no reason for the verdict need be given and the question whether the evidence of guilt was overwhelming is a matter of judgment. The frequency of nullification probably seems higher than it actually is since the non-legal aspects of the case that can lead to nullification have often long ago attracted the attention of the press.

[203] *See* Art. 449(1) CrPC. The judge has the option of submitting just one question, but it must be a combination of all three questions. *See* Plenum Ruling, *supra* note 191, point 17.

[204] This practice is consistent with the tsarist jury trial law. *See* Kucherov, *supra* note 174, at 65-71. The most notable instance of nullification in tsarist times was the acquittal of the revolutionary Vera Zasulich. The jury acquitted her of shooting and wounding a general who had ordered that a political prisoner be flogged severely for not taking off his hat when the general inspected a prison, despite the fact that she admitted the shooting. *See id.* at 214-225.

circumstances. Many such cases, to the authors' view, would have resulted in a guilty verdict before most U.S. juries.[205]

A major pitfall for Russian jury trials is the option of submitting questions in addition to those provided for in the statute. The obvious intent of the framers was the same as the intent of the proponents of special verdicts in civil cases in the U.S.—to try to channel and rationalize the jury decision-making process. If the history of the special verdict in civil cases in the U.S. is "a rocky road strewn with innumerable wrecks,"[206] the same can be said of the use of jury interrogatories in criminal verdicts in Russia.[207] The Supreme Court has addressed the issue, but to no one's satisfaction.[208]

2) Leniency and Special Leniency

The Russian jury has another means of expressing its not-strictly-legal opinion of the prosecution's case: it may find that the defendant deserves leniency or special leniency. If the jury elects leniency, the judge may not impose the death penalty or life imprisonment, and the defendant's sentence can be no higher than the two-thirds the maximum sentence provided. If the jury elects special leniency, then the judge may not sentence the defendant to more than the minimum sentence.[209] To facilitate an informed decision on leniency, the judge informs the jury of the possible range of sentences (including the death penalty). This is unlike the Anglo-American jury, which generally does not decide the appropriateness of punishment except in a separate "penalty phase" of the trial in death penalty cases in some states. In addition, jurors in the U.S. are not permitted to hear information about

---

[205] It is interesting to note that similar questions are posed for the decision-maker in non-jury cases: "3) whether the defendant committed the act [he is charged with committing, and] 4) whether the defendant is guilty of committing that crime." Art. 303, CrPC. As explained by commentators, this separate question 4) has to do with the question whether the defendant acted with the requisite *mens rea*, i.e. either intentionally or negligently. Lupinskaya, *supra* note 3, p. 401. This seems strange, however, since the issue of whether the elements of the offenses are present is covered by an earlier question.

[206] Sunderland, Verdicts, General and Special, 29 Yale Law Journal 253, 261 (1920).

[207] *See* Thaman, *supra* note 38, pp. 116-123.

[208] *See* Ruling of the Plenum, *supra* note 191, p. 58, point 18. The Court required that the questions to the jury avoid the language of the statute defining the offense even if that language is the best way to explain the concept to a lay person. For a general discussion of the problem in the wake of the Plenum's Ruling, *see* Steven Thaman, *Postanovka voprosov pered kollegiiei prisiazhnykh* (Framing Questions for the Jury Panel), Gosudarstvo i Pravo, No. 10, p. 8 (1995).

[209] Art. 445, 449, CrPC.

possible punishment because of the fear that it will improperly influence their performing their job of determining guilt or innocence.

3) Non-Unanimous Verdicts

The Russian jury is supposed to try for 3 hours to reach a unanimous verdict, but if that is impossible then a majority verdict is sufficient (the jury is told this).[210] This is unlike the U.S., where unanimous verdicts are required in federal courts and in all but five states. Given that most of the jury-qualified crimes involve the possibility of the death penalty, the fact that after three hours of discussion there are still 5 jurors who insist the defendant is not guilty would seem to be a thin basis for a sentence of death. Also, the leniency option seems to provide more "bargaining room" for jurors in a close case. For example, 5 jurors convinced of the need for conviction and the death penalty might well persuade 2 others leaning toward "not guilty" to go along and vote guilty if the first 5 promise to vote for leniency instead of death. However, while a majority vote makes conviction more likely in some cases, Russian law also makes acquittal more likely if that is the way at least half the jury is inclined. The statute provides that the defendant is not guilty if 6 of 12 jurors give a "no" answer to any one of the three statutory questions discussed above.

d. The Future of the Russian Jury

The rate of acquittals by Russian juries varies widely, but averages around 20%.[211] Considering the horrific nature of most of the crimes that juries hear, Russian juries have been remarkably compassionate toward defendants, particularly in their extension of leniency. If judged by these factors alone, given the concern about crime among Russian voters and the added costs of jury administration, the Russian jury may not seem to have a very healthy future. However, the Draft Criminal Procedure Code would continue the jury trial right and, as of this writing, St. Petersburg, which will be the first really large city to participate, plans to begin jury trials soon.

D. Appeals

1. Appellate Courts

The two basic trial courts for criminal cases are the district court (*raionnyi sud*) and the second-level courts (Regional Courts, Supreme Courts

---

[210] Art. 435, CrPC. A majority verdict reached in less than three hours will be rejected by the judge. *See* Report, *supra* note 43, p. 20.

[211] *See* statistics cited in Thaman, *supra* note 38, pp. 270-271. *See also* pp. 135-138 for a discussion of the results in the 114 cases Thaman studied.

of Republics or, in Moscow and St. Petersburg, City Courts). Judgments of the District Court are appealed to the second-level courts and then to the Russian Supreme Court. When these second-level courts act as trial courts (as in the case of extremely serious felonies), the appeal is to the Russian Supreme Court.

2. Cassation and Supervisory Review

Unlike the U.S. Constitution, the Russian Constitution clearly provides that "[a]ll persons convicted of a crime have the right to review of their conviction in a higher court, in accordance with a process established by federal law . . .".[212] Federal law currently provides two ways that the judgments of courts are reviewed by higher courts: by appeal (called "cassation") or by a supervisory "protest." The standard of review of the two types of review is the same. The difference lies in who instigates the review and when that review can be initiated.

Cassational appeals are the normal appeal that is taken by losing parties. They must be filed within 7 days of the entry of judgment in the trial court.[213] Thus, cassational appeals are against judgments that have "not yet entered into force." Supervisory review is by a "protest" filed by the chairpersons of a higher court or by a procurator. These may be filed at any time and are usually filed after the judgment has entered into force and often after the case has been decided on cassational appeal.

The fact that the judges of higher courts or procurators institute supervisory review by a protest does not mean that higher courts and procurator's offices comb all the decisions of the courts looking for legal errors. Instead, the protest is in most cases filed at the behest of the losing party. But there is still the element of discretion whether to agree to file the protest or not, thus making review of a case on a supervisory protest somewhat more likely to meet with success than a normal appeal brought by a party.

In general, the court on cassational review may address and correct whatever errors occurred in the proceedings below regardless of whether they are raised by the parties. This is based on the principle of "revision" of decisions—the notion that the higher court is to check every aspect of the decision to assure that it is legal and properly justified.[214] However, a procedural device to avoid burdening a defendant's right to appeal is the principle of not permitting certain appeals filed by the accused to take "a turn

[212] *See*, Art. 50(3), Constitution of the Russian Federation.

[213] Art. 328, CrPC. This period may be extended for "good cause." Art. 329, CrPC.

[214] Art. 332, CrPC.

for the worse" (*povorot k khudshemu*). Under this principle, an appellate court cannot increase the severity of the offense or the defendant's punishment if the case came to it on the defendant's appeal. To do so, it must come to the court on supervisory review or on normal review at the behest of the prosecutor or the victim when they have assigned excessive leniency of charge or sentence as the error for which they seek review.[215] Similarly, upon reversal and remand the trial court may not make things worse for the defendant either unless that was the basis for the reversal. However, if the case has been sent back for a new supplemental preliminary investigation and that investigation reveals new facts showing that the defendant is guilty of a more serious offense, a "turn for the worse" is permitted.[216]

An acquittal may be appealed by the prosecution even when the result will be retrial of the defendant. Art. 50(1) of the Constitution, the Russian "double jeopardy" clause, provides: "No one may be *convicted* twice for the same crime."

3. The Scope of Review on Appeal or Supervisory Review

As explained in Chapter III, review on cassation in Russian is much broader than cassation in Western Europe. In Western Europe, cassation is a review for legal errors alone. If one desires review of factual findings, that is done by way of a normal appeal. Cassation in Russia combines aspects of Western European cassation and appeal and involves an in-depth review of both law and fact. However, Russian cassation does not go as far as appeal in some other civil law countries. In some civil law countries, additional evidence can be submitted and considered by the appellate court directly and used as a basis for reversal of the trial court, somewhat like a new trial in the appellate court. Any factual review on Russian cassation is confined to the written record made in the trial court.[217]

---

[215] Art. 340, CrPC. The same is true of review of acquittals: following reversal, the defendant cannot be tried for any higher offense. Interestingly enough, the acquitted defendant can also appeal the acquittal if the defendant disagrees with the basis for the acquittal. Art. 325, 341, CrPC.

[216] Art. 353, CrPC.

[217] Tsarist Russia shared the classic Western European organization of appeals and cassation. Cassation was made the sole basis for review in the very first law No. 1, "On Courts." However, from 1917 until the 1960 Criminal Procedure Code, cassation evolved to take on many elements of the classic civil law appeal. *See* Lupinskaya, *supra* note 3, pp. 446-447. The Draft CrPC makes radical changes in the current law, reviving the division between appeal and cassation and allowing in many ways almost a complete retrial of the case in the appellate court, complete with presentation of live witness testimony. *See* Arts. 410, 417, Draft CrPC.

New issues of fact that might come to light in a cassational appeal by submission of new evidence must be sent back to the trial court for a supplemental hearing. Only where the facts raised on appeal clearly show that dismissal is necessary may the higher court decide the case on the merits.[218] As one commentator stated, the cassational court "on the basis of [review of the written] record cannot and should not determine the facts that are either established or not established by the judgment below; it may not and should not turn itself into a trial court and try the case over again on the merits."[219]

Other than the legal issues of misapplication of substantive criminal law or code of criminal procedure, there are two bases for challenging a trial court judgment: that the parsing of the evidence at trial was "incomplete or one-sided"[220] or that there was a "non-correspondence" of the trial court's factual conclusions with the circumstances of the case.[221] Similarly, reversal of a sentence is possible if there is "non-correspondence of the sentence imposed by the court with the seriousness of the crime or the personality of the defendant."[222]

4. The Limited Scope of Appellate Review in Jury Cases

Jury verdicts, even verdicts of acquittal, may be appealed in the Russian system. By law, they are appealed only to a cassational panel of the Supreme Court.[223] Especially given the broad scope of appellate review on issues of fact in criminal cases, the framers of the Jury Trial Law sought to limit the scope of that review so that the cassational panel could not reverse a judgment in a jury trial based on disagreement with factual findings of the jury. As a result, appeals are generally possible only to correct legal errors committed during the trial: improper admission or exclusion of evidence that could have affected the verdict, violations of the Criminal Procedure Code, improper application of the law by the court to the facts as found by the jury, and imposition of an unfair sentence.[224]

---

[218] *See In re Ibragimov*, BVS, 1997, No. 1, p. 20 (submission on appeal of document of expert on the question of whether a particular knife was a deadly weapon is not a sufficient reason for the appeals court to order dismissal when the trial court relied on an expert at trial who came to the opposite conclusion).

[219] Lupinskaya, *supra* note 3, p. 450.

[220] Art. 343, CrPC.

[221] Art. 344, CrPC.

[222] Art. 347, CrPC.

[223] Art. 464, CrPC.

[224] Art. 465, CrPC.

5. Further Collateral Attacks on Convictions that are Final

As noted earlier, the Russian Constitution clearly provides for a constitutional right to appeal a criminal case. It also provides a broader right that may be invoked even when all appeals have been exhausted.

In the following case, the Constitutional Court deals with issues of the finality of convictions and the grounds on which challenges to their validity can be made in a collateral attack. In the process, it explains the bases provided for addition collateral attacks on convictions set out in the Criminal Procedure Code.

The Constitutional Court: *Case Concerning the Constitutionality of Article 371(2) point 5, Article 374(3) and Article 384(2)(4) of the Criminal Procedure Code RSFSR* (VKS, 1996, No. 2, p. 2)

[The petitioners were convicted and sentenced to incarceration some time ago and had over a long period of time challenged the legality and bases of their convictions, arguing that the courts in trying their cases "failed to take into account substantial exculpatory circumstances that bore on the correct decision of their cases, and also committed errors in the application of the criminal law." They appealed all the way to the Presidium of the Russian Supreme Court of the Russian Federation and some errors were corrected in these direct appeals. Later petitions to the Supreme Court and to the Procurator-General of the Russian Federation were denied on the ground that the applicable provisions of the criminal procedure code do not provide the opportunity for review of judicial decisions in such situations. They sued in the Constitutional Court alleging that such denial of review violated articles 45, 46 (part 1) and 50 (part 3) of the Constitution.]

5. Review of a final judgment, order or decree of a court by means of reopening the case based on newly discovered evidence, in accord with Art. 384 CrPC RSFSR, is possible only on the basis of establishing that the judgment was the result of the criminal actions of participants in the case resulting in an unjust result (point 1-3), or because other facts unknown to the court at the point of decision that would, along with other facts in the case, establish the innocence of the defendant, or guilt with regard to a different crime other than the one he was convicted of, or prove the guilt of a person who has been exonerated or who was dismissed from the case (point 4).

As is clear from part 2 of Art. 384 CrPC RSFSR, and particularly point 4 therein, it is not a basis for reopening a case that the decision was unjust or that it was the result either of ignoring the evidence presented or erroneous evaluation of evidence or that the law was improperly applied.

Excluding bases for possible reopening of a criminal case that could result in review of illegal or unsubstantiated judicial decisions that are unreviewable by any other means, including supervisory review, makes impossible the correction of many judicial errors and the resulting repeated violations of the rights and legal interests of citizens. . . .

6. . . . According to Art. 2 and 45 (part1) of the Constitution of the Russian Federation, the government is required to recognize, respect and protect rights and freedoms by establishing effective legal mechanisms for remedying all violations, among them those of agencies and officials who are involved in the criminal process. This duty falls first on the legislature, which determines the process of review of erroneous decisions with the goal of effective restoration of rights that were violated. These procedures must guarantee that rights and freedoms have the highest priority and prohibit giving preference to even the most important social, departmental or personal interests.

Sharply limiting the understanding of newly discovered evidence as a ground for reopening a criminal case truly permits the government to avoid its responsibility to give priority protection to rights and freedoms in cases where there is judicial error that has not come to light in the usual supervisory procedures, and infringes on the right of every person to protect his or her interests in such cases by any means not prohibited by law (Art. 45, part 2, Constitution of the Russian Federation). . . .

[Point 4 of part 2 of Art. 384 limiting the grounds for reopening] does not comply with Art. 46 of the Constitution of the Russian Federation which guarantees everyone the right to judicial protection of his or her rights and freedoms. Moreover, the right to judicial protection, which is secured by the entire collection of different procedural devices, belongs to that category of rights that may not be limited by the government (Art. 56, part 3, Constitution of the Russian Federation). In addition, justice in its essence may be realized as such only under conditions that comply with the requirements of fairness and assure the effective remedies for violations of rights (Art. 14 of the International Covenant on Civil and Political Rights of 1966; Art. 8 of the General Declaration of Human Rights of 1948). Justice as a fundamental idea finds support also in the introductory provisions of the Constitution of the Russian Federation. An erroneous judicial decision cannot be seen as a just act of justice and must be corrected.

The International Covenant on Civil and Political Rights, as a result of the substantive content of justice and the priority it gives to human rights, emphasizes that the goal of judicial remedies is to serve as a means of reviewing final decisions of courts "if any kind of new or newly discovered circumstances clearly show judicial error" (point 5 of Art. 14). This standard of international law secures broader bases for correcting judicial errors than the existing Criminal Procedure Code of the RSFSR and, by virtue of Art. 15 (part 4) of the Constitution of the Russian Federation, is a constituent part of the legal system of Russia and preempts domestic legislation on issues of human rights and liberties resulting from judicial errors. . . .

[The Court then pointed out that the Russian Constitution secures the right to turn to international human rights organs, such as the European Commission on Human Rights. To do this, however, the person must have exhausted domestic remedies. It observed that it would be illogical to deny the right to correct decisions when that might avoid resort to international tribunals.]

8. . . . Current legislation and application of Art. 384 CrPC RSFSR reveal a tendency toward change in the rule [limiting the bases for reopening cases to circumstances unknown to the court at the time of decision]. Thus, the possible reopening of cases and review of final judgments already confirmed by judicial action because of new legal or factual evaluations flows directly from the law "On the Constitutional Court of the Russian Federation." It provides that any final decisions of courts that are based on statutes held to be unconstitutional must be re-examined (part 3 of Art. 79, part 2 of Art. 100). In reality this reveals another legal situation that is not described in Art. 384 CrPC RSFSR, but which requires re-examination pursuant to its procedures.

The unjustified limited nature of the relevant provisions of Art. 384 . . . that prevent the corrections of errors by the case-reopening procedure is reflected in such laws as the Statute of the RSFSR of October 18, 1991 "On rehabilitation of victims of political repression". . . In connection with these cases, the legislature had to introduce a procedure for re-examination of final judgments that is analogous to the procedure for reopening cases set out in points 1-3 of part 2 of Art. 384 . . .

9. An analysis of the existing legislation shows that in contrast to the strict regulation preventing a higher court from examining a case a second time on supervisory review, the process set out in articles 384-390 CrPC RSFSR could secure to citizens the essential protection of their rights that have been infringed upon by judicial errors. . . .

Alternatively, the legislature could satisfy the need [for a collateral review process] through further legislation by establishing a system of procedural rules currently unknown to the law that would secure the goal of protecting rights of citizens from judicial mistakes. . . . This will not contradict the prohibition on overruling a decision of the Constitutional Court . . . through reenactment of a law declared unconstitutional.

NOTES AND QUESTIONS

1. According to the Court, what grounds for reopening cases were provided for by the applicable articles of the Criminal Procedure Code? Doesn't this pretty much cover the kinds of things that a case should be reopened for? What is not included? According to the Court, what was wrong with limiting collateral review only to those categories of cases?

2. The grounds the petitioners wanted to assert in their collateral attack were "that the courts in trying their cases failed to take into account substantial exculpatory circumstances that bore on the correct decision of their cases, and also committed errors in the application of the criminal law." Since they have already been through various layers of direct review, don't you think that these very issues were reviewed by at least one appellate court? What good does it do them to take yet another trip through the system through the case-reopening procedure? Doesn't a conviction have to become final at some point?

CHAPTER XI

CRIMINAL LAW

A. Introduction

As explained in the last chapter, the Russian Criminal Code and Criminal Procedure Code have been under development for some time and were supposed to be enacted at the same time. While disagreements have held up the Criminal Procedure Code, the Criminal Code was signed into law in July of 1996 and went into effect on January 1, 1997.[1]

The new Criminal Code makes major modifications in Russian criminal law. Compared to the changes to be introduced in the Draft Criminal Procedure Code, the modifications are monumental. In seeking to understand the new Criminal Code, we are fortunate to have both an English-language translation of the new Code and an English-language article outlining it written by its principal drafter, Professor Anatolii V. Naumov.[2]

B. A Glance at Basic Principles and the Structure of the New Code

As is traditional with civil law countries, the Code has a General Part and a Specific Part. The General Part explains provisions that relate to most if not all crimes and to basic concepts and policies. The overall purposes of the Code are stated to be "protection of rights and freedoms of persons and

[1] Ugolovnyi kodeks Rossisskoi Federatsii (Criminal Code of the Russian Federation), Sobranie, No. 25, item 2954 (1996) (effective January 1, 1997), cited as "CrC RF." The old Criminal Code of the RSFSR will be cited as "CrC RSFSR."

[2] See Statutes and Decisions: Laws of the USSR and Its Successor States, vol. 33, nos. 4 and 5 (Sarah Reynolds trans.) (1997); A.V. Naumov, The New Russian Criminal Code as a Reflection of Ongoing Reforms, 8 Criminal Law Forum 191 (1997). See also A.V. Naumov, Kommentarii k Ugolovnomu kodeksu Rossiiskoi Federatsii (Commentary on the Criminal Code of the Russian Federation) (1996). Other commentaries are V.I. Radchenko ed., Novy Kommentarii k Ugolovnomu Kodeksu Rossiiskoi Federatsii (New Commentary on the Criminal Code of the Russian Federation) (1996); V.M. Lebedev, Iu.I. Skuratov eds., Kommentarii k ugolovnomu kodeksu: obshchaia chast' (Commentary on the Criminal Code: The General Part) (1996). A recent textbook is A.I. Rarog ed., Ugolovnoe pravo Rossii: Obshchaia chast' - Uchebnik (Criminal Law of Russia: The General Part - A Textbook) (1997).

citizens, property, and public order and security, of the environment and the constitutional structure of the Russian Federation from criminal attacks, the preservation of peace and security of mankind and the prevention of crime."[3] The Code states five basic principles that underlie the Code: legality, equality before the law, liability solely based on guilt, justice and humanism.[4] These basic principles will not likely decide actual cases under the Code, so it is not necessary to explain them in detail here. But the fact of the statements about protection of the individual discloses immediately some essential differences from the old Soviet Code.

In keeping with the drafters' emphasis on protection of the individual rather than the state, crimes against the person appear in the first section of the Specific Part, rather than crimes against the state, as was the case with the old Code. In keeping with the privatization of society and free enterprise, the section on state offenses is shorter and the section on economic crimes is much longer.

Another interesting change in structure is the order in which the gravity of violations and punishments are listed in the Code. Instead of going from the most serious versions of the offenses and punishments to the least serious, as the old Code did, the 1996 Code does the opposite. This is undoubtedly for the purpose of emphasizing what is a "least restrictive alternative" principle to be applied in sentencing: that in all sentencing, "the more severe form of punishment . . . shall be assigned only if a less severe sanction will not achieve the goals of punishment."[5]

C. The General Part

1. Definition of What Constitutes a Crime

For theoretical reasons, Russian academics have always been critical of Western criminal codes for their "formal definition" of a crime as simply an act made unlawful by the criminal law. This view, they claim, contains "methodological flaws."[6] In contrast to this "formal definition," the concept of a crime under the new Code, contains both "a formal (normative) element, the prohibition of an act by criminal legislation, and a substantive indicium, social dangerousness."[7] Thus, Art. 14(2) provides:

---

[3] Art. 2, CrC RF.
[4] Art. 3-7, CrC RF.
[5] Art. 60(1), CrC RF.
[6] Naumov Article, *supra* note 2, at 205.
[7] *Id.*

> An act or omission to act shall not constitute a crime, although it formally reflects the indicia of an act prohibited by the present Code, if it does not represent a social danger because of its insignificance, i.e., if it has not caused or threatened to cause harm to the individual, to society or to the state.

One can only guess what the practical effect of this provision is. A similar concept was found in the RSFSR Criminal Code and in not one case was the result changed from what it would have been if only the "formal" definition were there. This distinction could be simply another one of those gossamer theoretical distinctions that Russian legal academics love to spin and therefore of no consequence. If it is to be taken seriously, several possible effects come to mind. Among other things, it could form the basis for the complete elimination of "victimless" crimes or for unprecedented broad prosecutorial discretion based on the perceived social dangerousness of each defendant's actions. And one can only imagine to what use the separate requirement of social dangerousness could be put by resourceful defense lawyers in jury trials.[8] More likely, the social dangerousness part of the definition of a crime means nothing at all and will be satisfied in every case automatically based on the social theory that some person—including the defendant — is always harmed by the acts or omissions described by the Code.[9]

The Code does reaffirm the prohibition on using analogies from prohibited conduct to punish conduct not proscribed by the Code. This prohibition was first introduced in the 1958 USSR and 1960 RSFSR Codes. Thus, the elemental notion of *nullum crimen sine lege* (nothing is a crime that is not written in the law) is continued.

2. Categories of Crimes

The categorization of crimes in the Criminal Code is more complex than the felony-misdemeanor division in the U.S. There are four categories of crimes:

Minor Crimes	Up to 2 years deprivation of freedom

---

[8]This is especially so when combined with the open invitation to nullification that the Russian jury trial law provides. *See* Chapter X, pp. ____-____. For example, if taken literally, the absence of social dangerousness of a crime could be argued in the murder of anyone society would be better off without.

[9]However, at least one commentary suggests that a procurator, criminal investigator or court could rely on this article to dismiss charges on the ground that an essential element of the crime is missing. *See* Radchenko Commentary, *supra* note 2, at 20, point 4.

Moderately Serious Crimes	Up to 5 years deprivation of freedom
Serious Crimes	Up to 10 years deprivation of freedom
Very Serious Crimes	Over 10 years, life imprisonment or death

It should be kept in mind, however, that there is a multitude of civil "administrative infractions" many of which correspond to misdemeanors in common law systems.[10] Examples are traffic violations, including drunk driving, littering, jay-walking, creating excessive noise, violating health and work safety standards, defacing monuments and the like. For these, citizens can be fined and in some cases placed in adminis trative detention for up to 15 days.[11] Many of these offenses, especially traffic offenses, are handled by the intervening police officer imposing a fine "on the spot" by writing the person a ticket and collecting the fine. If the person wishes to contest the matter, an administrative or jud icial procedure seeking reversal and return of the fine is provided. Administrative detention can be imposed only on order of a court after a hearing.

3. Level of Culpability for Criminal Responsibility

Regarding general *mens era* requirements, the Code rejects the notion of strict criminal liability and requires that all liability be based on fault. Art. 5 provides that "objective imputation of guilt, i.e. criminal liability for innocent infliction of harm, is not permitted."

Although criminal liability can be based on either intent or negligence, negligence can support liability only if it is specified in the definition of the particular crime.[12] Under the old Code, negligence was sufficient for commission of any crime requiring only general intent.[13]

The "innocent infliction of harm" referred to in Art. 5's prohibition of strict liability is defined in Art. 28 as follows:

> 1. Conduct is totally innocent if the person who engaged in it did not realize and, under the circumstances of the case, could not have realized the social dangerousness of such actions

[10] *Kodeks administrativnykh pravonarushenii* (Code of Administrative Infractions), *Vedomosti Verkhovnogo Sovieta RSFSR*, 1984, N. 27, p. 909 (as amended through July 18, 1997) [hereafter "CAI"].

[11] *See id.*, Art. 27-32.

[12] *See* Art. 24(2), CrC RF.

[13] *See* Art. 24(2), CrC RSFSR.

> (inaction) or did not foresee the possibility of the onset of socially harmful consequences and should not or could not have foreseen them under the circumstances of the case.
>
> 2. Conduct is also considered to be totally innocent if the person engaging in it, although foreseeing the onset of socially harmful consequences as a consequence of such action (inaction), was unable to avert those consequences because the person's psychological or physical attributes were not sufficiently strong to ward off extreme conditions or neuropsychological overload.

The provisions of the second section of Art. 28, in Naumov's view, are aimed primarily at cases of:

> extreme stress on the actor, most often in the operation of sophisticated machinery or equipment. Examples include pilots operating aircraft or drivers operating heavy trucks without adequate rest, and air traffic controllers or railroad engineers working under continual, intense pressure. Although the person who allowed the occurrence of the socially dangerous consequences had foreseen the possibility of their occurrence, he could not have prevented them given the stressful circumstances in which he was working. [It is clear that] this rule is not applicable to situations where socially dangerous consequences resulted from the person's own culpability; for example, in the case of concealing psycho-physiological impairments that would prevent the actor from carrying out a certain type of activity; fraudulently gaining employment requiring special knowledge, skills, or training; or voluntarily becoming intoxicated through the ingestion of alcohol, narcotics, psychotropics, and other controlled substances.[14]

Naumov's comments raise a couple of issues. First, starting with the last observation first, while Naumov interprets Art. 28 as not applying when the "socially dangerous consequences resulted from the person's own culpability," Art. 28 certainly does not say this. Failing to state this in the statute seems to be seriously misleading.

Second, if the infliction of harm is not innocent when the defendant's own culpable conduct caused the "socially dangerous consequences," then there would seem to be no need for Art. 28. This situation is fully addressed by the Code's definition of culpable negligence. Under Art. 26(2) and (3), a crime is committed negligently if harm occurs as a result of the person's conduct and:

> if the person foresaw the possibility of the onset of socially

[14] Naumov Article, *supra* note 2, at 209.

> dangerous consequences as a result of such action (inaction), but unreasonably relied on those consequences not taking place [or] if the person did not foresee the possibility of the onset of socially dangerous consequences as a result of such action (inaction), but should have and would have foreseen such consequences had the person exercised due care and prudence.

Applying this definition of negligence decides the average case of "extreme stress on the actor" with no particular help from Art. 28's "innocent infliction" concept. Assume the case of the truck driver who realizes that he or she should pull over and sleep, but doesn't do so. After driving for over 24 hours straight, the driver dozes off, the truck crosses the center line into oncoming traffic and kills the occupants of a car going in the opposite direction. This would seem to be negligence under Art. 26. And if the truck driver should not have realized that he should have pulled over and slept (say the driver had been driving only an hour), this is apparently not culpable criminal negligence. Art. 28 would not seem to add anything to the analysis.

4. Defenses and Other Means of Avoiding Criminal Responsibility

Under the old Soviet Criminal Code, the only defenses were defense of self and others and extreme necessity. The new code creates several new defenses and other assorted means of avoiding criminal responsibility.

a. Diminished Capacity

Art. 22(1) of the Criminal Code rejects the notion of diminished capacity as a defense to a crime:

> A mentally competent person who, at the time of committing a crime, was unable to comprehend completely the factual circumstances and social dangerousness of his or her actions (omissions) or to be able to control them as a result of a psychological disturbance, is subject to criminal liability.

However, the presence of diminished capacity for understanding due to psychological disturbances does affect punishment. Art. 22 goes on to provide that "psychological disturbance short of insanity shall be considered by the court in determining the punishment and may serve as a basis for compulsory hospitalization." According to Naumov, the legislature had in mind such things as people suffering from chronic alcoholism, organic brain damage and the like.[15]

---

[15] Naumov Article, *supra* note 2, at 207-208.

b. Turning Oneself In and Reconciling With the Victim

In many civil law countries the law flatly states that the prosecutor must prosecute every case in which there is sufficient evidence for a conviction. This may not quite be a description of reality, since there are several ways that such a requirement can be avoided. But it is fair to say that civil law systems tend to closely circumscribe prosecutorial discretion not to prosecute.

In the face of a mandatory prosecution tradition, if the legislature wishes to assure that prosecution of provable cases be declined under certain circumstances, it must set those circumstances out in the criminal law itself. Russian law does this by allowing certain persons to avoid criminal responsibility for otherwise criminal conduct if they voluntarily turn themselves in and confess their guilt, and perform other actions in repentance of their actions.

The Code implements this in two ways. First, "repentance" (*raskaianie)* and "reconciliation" (*primireniie)* are possible for all first-time offenders in cases of minor crimes (punished by up to two years of incarceration). Art. 75 is entitled "Release from Criminal Liability Based on Active Repentance." It provides:

> A first-time offender who has committed a minor crime may be relieved of criminal liability if, after committing the crime, the person turns himself or herself in to the authorities and confesses, assists in investigation of the crime, compensates for the injury caused or in some other way makes amends for the harm that resulted from the crime.

Art. 76 is entitled "Release from Criminal Liability Based on Reconciliation with the Victim." It provides:

> A first-time offender who has committed a minor crime may be relieved of criminal liability if he or she has reconciled with the victim and made amends for the harm caused to the victim.

The second way the concept of "repentance" is implemented is through the provisions of a final section of selected more serious crimes.[16] No less than 14 offenses contain such provisions specifying the conditions under which the offender will be completely relieved of criminal liability. Among them are perjury, bribery, illegal possession of firearms and illegal possession of controlled substances. Also included are some rather serious crimes against

[16] Though these final sections are called "comments" (*primechania*), they are part of the statute.

the state: treason, military desertion, espionage, assassination, terrorism, hostage-taking and forming or participating in an illegal armed group. Each of these crimes has its own requirements for release from liability, some of which require that the person go to the authorities in time to prevent further harm and to turn in co-conspirators. However, only a few require that the person be a first-time offender. Clearly, the "repentance" provisions are there in part to foster defections from criminal groups. And, failing that, they may facilitate negotiations with insurgents by absolving them of criminal responsibility if they give themselves up.

The old RSFSR Criminal Code as amended provided the option of repentance for some crimes, but the number of crimes to which the option applies has been increased.

c. "Necessary Defense" and Detention of an Offender

"Necessary defense" includes self-defense and defense of others, but it is broader than that. Art. 37 provides:

> 1. The infliction of injury on a law-breaker is not a crime if it constitutes a necessary defense, that is, when the actions are for the purpose of protecting the defender's own or another's person or rights, or interests of society or the state that are protected by law from socially dangerous offenses, so long as the actions do not exceed the bounds of a necessary defense.
>
> 2. All persons have an equal right of necessary defense without regard to profession, special training or employment position. A person shall enjoy the right regardless of whether there was a possibility of avoiding the socially dangerous offenses or of turning to other people or to the authorities for assistance.
>
> 3. Actions exceed the bounds of necessary defense if they are intentional actions that obviously are not commensurate with the character and degree of the social dangerousness of the offense.

The old Criminal Code had similar provisions. In 1984, the Court noted the application of "necessary defense" to the activities of the People's Militia Patrol (*druzhina*), groups of citizens who assisted police by patrolling to maintain public order. Often the *druzhinniki* got into scrapes with members of the public—who often resented their high-handed ways—in the process of performing their ill-defined duties. The Court observed:

> The actions of People's Militia and other citizens who are fulfilling their social obligation of supporting the legal order and who inflict injury on a person in connection with suppressing

> that person's socially dangerous actions and seizing and detaining that person immediately after the offense is committed for the appropriate organs of authority must be classified as committed in the process of carrying out a necessary defense.[17]

Art. 37's version of "necessary defense" as it relates to detention of an offender seems to be more open-ended than the old. The old version at least made a distinction between offenders who threaten or employ deadly force and those who do not, permitting "any injury" to be inflicted in "defense" only against deadly force.[18] The new version of "necessary defense" vaguely prohibits injury that is "obviously . . . not commensurate with the character and degree of the social dangerousness of the offense."

The suspicion that the new Code evinces a trend toward greater protection of citizen law enforcement efforts is confirmed in the addition of a new and partially overlapping defense in the very next section of the new Code. Art. 38 is entitled "Infliction of Injury While Detaining an Offender." It provides:

> 1. It is not a crime to inflict injury on a person who has committed a crime while seeking to detain that person to turn him or her over to the authorities or to prevent further crimes from being committed, so long as it was impossible to detain the person in any other way and the measures used to do so did not exceed what was necessary for that purpose.
>
> 2. Exceeding the measures necessary for detention of a person who has committed a crime takes place when those measures clearly do not correspond to the character and social danger presented by the crime committed by the detained person or the detainee is subjected unnecessarily to injury that is clearly not warranted by the situation. Such excesses shall entail criminal liability only when they are intentionally committed.[19]

---

[17] Ruling of the Plenum of the Supreme Court of the RF of August 16, 1984 "*O primenenii sudami zakonodatel'stva, obespechivaiushchego pravo na neobhodimuiu oboronu ot obshchestvenno opasnykh posiagatel'stv*" ("On the Applying the Statutory Provisions Securing the Right of Necessary Defense from Socially Dangerous Violations"), point 3 (on file with the authors). *See also* discussion in Rarog Textbook, *supra* note 2, vol. 1, at 188-189.

[18] *See* Art. 13, CrC RSFSR.

[19] In reading this article, one might envision a police officer who arrests a suspect. However, Art 38 applies to private persons as well. Indeed, one could argue that it was clearly intended to apply *only* to citizen arrests, since it refers to "turn[ing] [the person] over to the authorities." A person arrested by police officers is *already* in the hands of "the authorities."

A textbook on criminal law explains this defense in the following terms:

> The battle against crime as it relates to the arrest of persons committing crimes is the function of the government. However, in a democratic society the government cannot ignore its citizens' efforts in support of law and order, among them efforts to employ coercive measures to detain person who have committed crimes.[20]

There would seem to be several problems with Art. 37 and 38. First, neither article states what grounds the arresting person must have to believe that the prospective detainee "has committed a crime." The Criminal Procedure Code clearly specifies the grounds police officers must have to arrest a suspect.[21] Surely, private citizens should have no greater rights than police officers in apprehending suspects. And private citizens are probably in greater need of guidance than the police as to what grounds they must have. Yet, Art. 38 is silent on the question.

Second, there is no limit to what types of crimes Art. 37 and 38 cover. Apparently, anyone is authorized to attempt physical seizure and detention of persons suspected of *any* crime. The second section of Art. 38 states that the "*measures necessary* for detention" must take into account "the character and degree of social danger" of the crime involved, and Art. 37 provides a similar test. But this simply goes to the question of *how much* "injury" the arresting person can "inflict" in order to effect the detention, not to the issue of whether physical detention is needed *at all.* This means that physical seizure and detention are permitted for the most minor of crimes. One commentary notes this problem with Art. 37 and concludes:

> It is obvious that it would hardly be proper to inflict any form of injury in the process of detaining a person who has committed a crime for which the punishment contemplated

---

[20] *See* Rarog Textbook, *supra* note 2, at 188.

[21] *See* Art. 122, CrPC RSFSR, and Chapter X, p. ____. A police officer can arrest a suspect in only three situations "1) the person is caught in the act of committing the crime or shortly thereafter, 2) eyewitnesses (including victims) immediately point out the person as the one who committed the crime and 3) when contraband or other products of the crime are visible on the person's clothing or in the person's home." Immediate arrest and detention are also possible when "the existence of *other information* provides a basis for suspecting the person of committing a crime," but "only if the person is attempting to flee, has no permanent residence or cannot establish his or her identity." One textbook suggests that Art. 38 applies to "any person, the nature of whose criminal actions are obvious to those nearby." Rarog Textbook, *supra* note 2, at 189, note **. But this is not stated in the Criminal Code.

> would not be imprisonment (for example, insult).[[22]] Even a court (upon conviction of the person for such a crime) would not have the right to limit the freedom of the guilty person. Even more so, infliction of physical injury on a person who has committed such a crime must be "excluded."[23]

Perhaps judicial practice will develop in this direction, but no such exclusion is set out in the statute.

Even when the offense is a more serious one, it apparently does not matter that other methods of dealing with the offender might be more appropriate. Indeed, Art. 37 specifically provides that there is no need to "turn[ ] to . . . the authorities for assistance." Thus, Art. 37 and 38 seem to permit a person to employ the appropriate level of violence to "arrest" his neighbor for failing to pay income taxes—even though the neighbor is unlikely to flee and a quiet report to the tax authorities would do the job.[24]

Similarly, these provisions of the Code do not limit physical seizure and detention to crimes for which detention would be especially justified for additional reasons not related to law enforcement. For example, many states in the U.S. have statutes auth orizing retail store employees to detain suspected shoplifters. One could argue that physical detention of shoplifters is justified to prevent loss of the retailer's property. But neither Art. 37 nor Art. 38 limits its broad sweep to situations where intervention is necessary to prevent loss of property or personal injury.

No comfort can be gained from the fact that the Soviet-era People's Militia Patrol no longer prowls the streets. The virtual army of private security personnel that has grown up in the post-Soviet era will find this provision useful. Thousands of private guards guard entrances and patrol public buildings, businesses and even residences. An unknown number of self-styled bodyguards roam the cities with their charges. Contact by private security personnel with the public is unavoidable. When the result of that contact is that the citizen is injured or killed, these defenses will be useful to private security personnel in escaping criminal liability.[25]

---

[22] *See infra* p. 577, where the crime of insult in discussed.

[23] Radchenko Commentary, *supra* note 2, at 64, point 2.

[24] In this respect, the old Soviet-era encouragement to *inform* on one's neighbors is perhaps to be preferred to the latter-day Russia's encouragement to *arrest* one's neighbors.

[25] The possibility that there will be violence in citizen arrest situations is increased by the fact that private "police" will undoubtedly copy the arrest methods of the real police. It is well known that there is a high level of police brutality in Russia. This was clearly demonstrated in the U.S. television show "Cops," which showed videotapes of several arrests in Russia.

In fact, a number of incidents have arisen in which private security people have come in contact with the public and the member of the public has been killed or seriously injured. In one case, after numerous thefts from a cooperative garden, the cooperative board hired a security guard and even promised him a bonus for each intruder he detained. A drunk citizen on his way back from a party trespassed on the grounds of the garden and began picking gladiolas. The security guard confronted him and the result was that the guard killed the intruder with a knife. Though the guard argued that the intruder attacked him and he was only trying to defend himself, there were indications that the intruder was simply trying to leave and the security guard, seeing his bonus disappear as well, sought to prevent his escape even if it meant stabbing him.[26]

If a state truly wishes to encourage amateur, untrained law enforcers to "inflict injury" on its citizens, it should provide more safeguards than these defenses afford. Safeguards are especially needed given that there are so many "professional" amateurs around acting as private security guards. It is ironic that a Criminal Code so solicitous of *government* violations of the personal rights and liberties of its citizens abandons them to the dangers of *private* oppression. To ascribe the need for such defenses to the demands of a "democratic society" is disingenuous.[27]

d. Duress

Art. 40 of the Criminal Code provides the new defense of duress, which may be physical or mental. This defense is remarkable only for the fact that it was absent from the old Criminal Code, though it blends into the "extreme necessity" defense of the old Code. It is somewhat similar to the Model Penal Code's definition of duress. The most commonly encountered form of duress is psychological duress in the form of threats of violence to the perpetrator of the crime in question or that perpetrator's family. In this situation, duress is a defense only if committing the crime was the perpetrator's only way out and the harm done by the crime was less than the harm that was threatened.

---

[26] *See* W. Burnham, I. V. Reshetnikova, A.D. Proshliakov, *Sudebnaia advokatura* (Trial Advocacy) 101-105 (1996), where this case is used as a criminal trial file for teaching trial advocacy skills.

[27] *See* text *supra* at note 20. In fairness, it should be pointed out that the common law allows for "citizen arrests." However, they can only occur in the case of a felony and must be based on probable cause. Moreover, the common law rule is often superseded and limited by statute.

e. Taking a Justified Risk

A new and unique defense, entitled "justified risk," is provided for in Art. 41 of the Code. It provides:

> 1. It is not a crime to cause harm to interests protected by the criminal law if the conduct entailed a justified risk undertaken to achieve a socially beneficial goal.
>
> 2. A risk is considered to be justified if the above-stated goal could not be achieved without the risky action (inaction) and the person taking the risk took sufficient measures beforehand to prevent harm to legal interests secured by the criminal law.
>
> 3. A risk is unjustified if it clearly entails a threat to the lives of many persons, or a threat of an ecological catastrophe or social disaster.

In socialist societies, it was and is common that managers of government-owned enterprises would be prosecuted criminally for failures that resulted from taking economic risks that Western managers would consider essential for development of the business. Naumov comments that one can apply the concept to "commercial risk (for example, making banking, investment, and other speculative financial decisions)." However, Naumov suggests broader applications to other kinds of risks:

> This innovation reflects the fact that in the modern context of advancing technology, the need to take certain risks of physical harm to life or significant damage to property occurs more often than ever before (for example, during the adoption of new industrial technology or the development of new medical treatment).
>
> Justified risk can arise in any area of professional work. The most common examples are scientific risk (for example, the researchers who invented the polio vaccine tested it on their own children); industrial and economic risk (for instance, making a decision to dismantle a chimney not by ordinary means, which would be very expensive, but by detonation, where the risk lies in deciding on the explosive charge sufficient to do the job but not likely to affect nearby structures) . . . .[28]

As stated in the Code and explained by Naumov, this defense seems rather broad and ill-defined. There is no requirement that the actor be faced with an emergency situation—and the examples Naumov gives belie any such

---

[28] Naumov Article, *supra* note 2, at 212.

requirement. In situations involving "scientific risk," the statute says nothing about getting the *permission* of the potential human subjects of such scientific experiments. The protection of justified risk would seem to provide the basis for at least a modest number of people being exposed to deadly risk (and a larger number being exposed to risk of injury short of death) routinely, unknowingly and involuntarily—so long as the researcher is seeking "to achieve a socially beneficial goal." Mad scientists will certainly welcome this change in the law. Even in the more typical case of non-experimental surgery, surgeons apparently can routinely perform non-emergency, life-endangering operations on patients without warning them of the risks or obtaining their permission to operate even where there is plenty of time to do so.[29]

Taking the two examples Naumov gives, if justified risk excuses these actors, the results seem intuitively wrong. To test the defense's application, we must assume that the actors involved turned out to be wrong in their assessment of the risk. So, the medical researcher, we must assume, has killed his or her children by injecting them (presumably without their knowledge or consent) with a vaccine as yet untested on humans. And, the defense says nothing about the reason *why* the socially beneficial goal "could not be achieved without the risky action," so we can safely assume that the researcher decided to use his or her own children as subjects because the authorities had denied the researcher permission to test the vaccine on adult volunteers because it was deemed as yet too dangerous to test on humans. Unless the researcher has a very large family and thus his or her actions "entail a threat to the lives of *many* people," the researcher is apparently exempt from criminal liability for these killings. Similarly, in the case of the person who dynamited the smokestack instead of dismantling it safely — just to save money—we must assume that he or she has misjudged the size of the charge needed. As a result, several surrounding buildings have been damaged and the lives of less than "many persons" lost. Apparently, justified risk protects this person. Naumov's two examples certainly seem to be cases in which the actors should be subject to *some* form of criminal liability.

It may be that the element of justified risk requiring that the actor "took sufficient measures beforehand to prevent harm" will screen out the most egregious variants of these scenarios.[30] But if this is so, then there does not seem to be any need for a special justified risk defense. Any concerns about

---

[29]The example is suggested in S. Dando, The Criminal Law of Japan: The General Part 113 (1997).

[30]Taken literally, the quoted phrase makes no sense. If the measures taken were *in fact* "sufficient" to prevent the harm, then the need for the defense does not arise. It can be assumed that what was meant was that the actor *reasonably believed* that the measures taken would prevent the injury.

justified or unjustified risk would seem to be adequately covered by the Code's definition of negligence—the usual way to determine what risks are justified. If a risk qualifies as justified under Art. 41, then it would seem to constitute non-negligent conduct, since the person (1) "foresaw the possibility of the onset of socially dangerous consequences" and reasonably "relied on those consequences not taking place," or (2) "did not foresee the possibility of the onset of socially dangerous consequences" and should not have or would not "have foreseen such consequences had the person exercised due care and prudence."[31] If the defendant's actions—whether medical researcher, demolitions expert or other person—do not meet the requirements of culpable criminal negligence, then there in no criminal liability even without Art. 41.[32]

f. Following Orders

Art. 42 of the Criminal Code provides specific direction regarding the defense of "following orders." It provides:

> 1. It is not a crime for a person to inflict injury prohibited by the criminal law when that person is acting pursuant to an obligatory order or directive. A person who issues an illegal order or directive is criminally liable for any resulting injury.
>
> 2. A person who has committed an intentional crime pursuant to a clearly illegal order or directive is criminally liable notwithstanding the order or directive. Failure to carry out a clearly illegal order or directive may not be punished criminally.

The difficulties of such a statute, of course, are in defining what is a "*clearly illegal* order or directive" and imposing the duty of determining that question on the lower-level government functionaries who are most often on the receiving end of orders and directives. But this norm of behavior is consistent with the international standard that has been applied at least since the trial of the Nazi war criminals at Nuremberg.

The only thing remarkable about the duties imposed by Art. 42 is their not-so-curious absence from the Soviet criminal codes for the last 75 years.

---

[31] *See* Art. 26, quoted *supra* at 497.

[32] Similarly, the situation of non-professionals would seem to be covered by the negligence concept as well. Welzel uses the example of "parents who drive their children to school, despite the fact that there is always some element of risk to passengers inherent in driving as an activity." Dando, *supra* note 28, at 113 n. 120, referring to H. Welzel, Das Deutsche Strafrecht (11th ed. 1969).

D. Specific Crimes

It is not possible in the space allotted here to discuss all the types of offenses that are covered in the Criminal Code. And, in any event, the overwhelming number of them have familiar parallels to those in the U.S. and any other developed country. However, four areas should be touched on: provisions of the new Code related to the control of organized crime; changes that reflect the transition from a command economy to private enterprise; some special crimes that do not generally correspond to those in U.S. criminal codes; and decriminalizations reflected in the new Code.

1. Organized Criminal Activities

There are several new crimes that specifically target activities of organized crime and these will be discussed below. However, the general part of the Code also contains some definitional sections that bear on the liability of groups. They were clearly written into the law with organized crime in mind.

Art. 35 provides rules for situations in which a crime is committed by "a group of persons or pursuant to a prior conspiracy of that group or by a criminal organization." Aside from confirming co-conspirator liability, it states in part:

> A person who creates or directs an organized group or a criminal association (organization) is subject to criminal liability for so creating or directing that group as specified in the special part of the present Code, and for all crimes committed by such organized group or association (criminal organization), if such crimes are within the scope of that person's intent.

However, members of an organized group or criminal organization are not liable for "excesses" (*ekstsess*), defined as crimes committed by a member of the group on his or her own initiative and beyond the contemplation of the other members of the group.[33]

Apart from actions taken by organized groups, independent liability is possible for the creation of and participation in a criminal association formed for the purpose of carrying out serious crimes, for directing or supervising such an organization or any of its sub-groups and for the creation of groups of leaders of such organizations for the purpose of planning serious crimes.[34] The last provision mentioned is clearly aimed at coalitions of organized crime

---

[33] Art. 36, CrC RF.
[34] Art. 210, CrC RF.

groups like the "Commission" in New York City which coordinates the activities of the five "families" of the Italian-American Mafia.

In sentencing, one aggravating circumstance the judge must take into account is the fact that the crime was committed by a group.[35] In addition, a number of definitions of particular crimes contain provisions calling for more severe sentences in cases where crimes are committed by organized groups. These include offenses usually associated with organized crime: extortion, drug trafficking, bribery of corporate officers, murder, assault, torture, and forced prostitution. One basis for turning simple murder into aggravated murder, which is punishable by life imprisonment or death, is that the killing was accomplished by an organized group or by prior agreement.[36]

Of particular interest to organized crime groups and well-heeled criminals of all kinds are the provisions on forfeiture of property. Separate articles of the Code provide for different sorts of forfeiture penalties. Unlike the U.S., where defendants convicted of certain offenses forfeit the proceeds or instrumentalities of their crimes, the Code provides that all assets of the defendants beyond a bare minimum necessary to maintain themselves and their dependents are forfeited.[37]

2. Economic Crimes

The Special Part of the new Code introduces a wide array of new economic crimes directed toward control of certain socially harmful business practices and activities. In addition, many of these crimes clearly have in mind business operations controlled by organized crime.

Money laundering, also called "legalization" of money, is prohibited in Art. 174. It makes a crime the use of any unlawfully acquired money or property in a business, commercial enterprise, or financial operation. In addition, a more severe sentence is provided if money laundering is carried out either by a group of persons by prior agreement, by a person in an official position, or by an organized group, or if "a large amount" of money is laundered.

A rather broadly defined crime of "abuse of authority" is punished under Art. 201. Abuse of authority takes place whenever persons "exercising managerial functions in a commercial or other organization" use their position to benefit themselves or others "in disregard of the lawful interests of that organization," if the conduct "caused substantial harm to the rights and legal

[35] Art. 63(1)(c), CrC RF.
[36] Art. 105(2)(g), CrC RF.
[37] Art. 52, CrC RF.

interests of citizens or organizations or the legally protected interests of society and the state." Such actions are punishable by up to 3 years imprisonment, or in the case of certain undefined "serious" consequences, up to 5 years. Art. 201 could be used in any situation in which business managers enrich themselves or others at the expense of the business. In most countries, this sort of action would normally be addressed through civil rather than criminal process. Perhaps in recognition of this, a comment to Art. 201 provides that there is to be no prosecution of officers of purely commercial organizations unless the organization gives its permission.[38]

Other new business crimes include illegal receipt of credit,[39] prohibition of monopolistic and anti-competitive practices,[40] coercion to sign or not sign a contract,[41] infringement of trademarks,[42] false advertising,[43] various offenses related to bankruptcy,[44] consumer fraud,[45] violation of copyright or patent rights,[46] persistent refusal to pay a judgment[47] and commercial bribes, defined as paying money to an officer of a commercial or other enterprise for favors.[48]

3. Assorted Unique Crimes

a. *"Hooliganism" and Its Variants*

Though derived from an English word, "hooliganism" has taken on a special meaning in the lexicon of the Russian criminal law.[49] It has two uses. The first is that "hooliganism" is conduct that is a crime by itself. The other use is that acting "from hooliganistic motives" is an factor that can increase the gravity of some offenses, most notably murder.

[38] Art. 201, Comment 2, CrC RF.
[39] Art. 176, CrC RF.
[40] Art. 178, CrC RF.
[41] Art. 179, CrC RF.
[42] Art. 180, CrC RF.
[43] Art. 182, CrC RF.
[44] Art. 195-197, CrC RF.
[45] Art. 200, CrC RF.
[46] Art. 146-147, CrC RF.
[47] Art. 177, CrC RF.
[48] Art. 204, CrC RF. For a critical analysis of some of the new economic crimes, *see* Sarah Reynolds, The Difficulty of Definition: Precision and Vagueness in the Special Part of the New Russian Criminal Code, 33 Statutes and Decisions 3, 7-9 (1997).

[49] For a book on the subject of hooliganism and its roots in Russian law and culture, *see* Joan Neuberger, Hooliganism: Crime, Culture and Power in St. Petersburg, 1910-1914 (1993).

(1) Hooliganism

Hooliganism as punishable criminal conduct by itself is defined as "a gross disturbance of public order that expresses obvious contempt for society, which is accompanied by violence against citizens or the threat thereof or the destruction or threat of destruction of property of another."[50] "Hooliganism" is punished in three different degrees. Hooliganism in the first degree is the conduct just described. Second degree hooliganism is the same conduct undertaken by a group of persons or by prior agreement, or actions resisting officials who are trying to suppress the hooliganistic activity. Third degree hooliganism is hooliganistic actions committed with weapons. The maximum sentences for the three degrees are respectively 2, 5 and 7 years.

In the following case decided under both the old and the new Criminal Codes, the Russian Supreme Court seeks to draw the distinction between hooliganism and other crimes:

The Supreme Court: *In re Markin*, *BVS*, 1998, No. 1, p. 5

Markin was convicted by the Central District Court of the city of Cheliabinsk under Art. 206(2) CrC RSFSR [hooliganism[51]].

He was found guilty of engaging in aggravated hooliganism. On April 16, 1996, around 8:00 PM outside a house on Kuchatov Street in Cheliabinsk, he intentionally struck the juvenile Shchegolev three times, in the face and chest, starting a fight, and hit the juvenile Romanov in the face, causing minor injuries.

The Judicial Collegium for Criminal Cases of the Cheliabinsk Regional Court affirmed the conviction. . . .

The Deputy Procurator-General of the RF lodged a protest in which he raised the question of reclassifying the actions of the defendant from Art. 206(2) CrC RSFSR to Art. 109(1) CrC RSFSR and Art. 116 CrC RF [inflication of minor bodily injury and assault]. The Judicial Collegium for Criminal Cases of the Supreme Court RF, on April 29, 1997, granted relief on the protest for the following reasons.

According to the law, hooliganism is an intentional crime, one committed with a specific purpose. In effect, the person's actions show that he

---

[50] Art. 213, CrC RF.

[51] This case was prosecuted under the old Criminal Code, but this aspect of the offense has not changed.

is disturbing the public order in a gross way and is demonstrating clear contempt for society.

This fact was not established in the present case.

In classifying the actions of Markin as a violation of Art. 206(2) CrC RSFSR, the court pointed out that they were extraordinarily aggressive, causing bodily injury to Romanov and Shchegolev and entailed what was clear to the defendant to be a gross violation of public order and expressed clear contempt toward society.

However, this view of the court contradicts the record. As Markin explained in the process of the preliminary investigation and at the trial, he hit the juveniles, not from hooliganistic motives, but because of the improper actions of the victims, since he knew that they had broken the glass in the windows of a sports club building.

This explanation is confirmed by the record.

According to the testimony of the victim Shchegolev, on April 16, 1996, the trainer Markin emerged from the sports club, stated "you broke the glass" and hit him three times in the face with his fist. At that point, Romanov came up and Markin hit him, too.

The victim Romanov confirmed Shchegolev's explanation. As witness B. testified, he named the boys who had broken out the window in the club, among them Shchegolev and Romanov. On April 16, 1996, he saw how Shchegolev and Romanov had thrown stones at the club window.

The witness S. reported that Markin told her about some juveniles who had broken the glass in the windows, but that he had not made a written report of it [to the police].

These circumstances give us a basis for believing that Markin caused the bodily injuries to Romanov and assaulted Shchegolev, not from a hooliganistic motivation, but in response to their improper conduct.

In this respect, the actions of the defendant should be reclassified as violations of Art. 109(1) CrC RSFSR (intentional infliction of minor bodily injury) and of Art. 116 CrC RF (assault). . . .

NOTES AND QUESTIONS

1. Now do you understand what hooliganism is? Other hints are provided by the case of Mathias Rust, the young German aviator who in 1987

flew his plane through Soviet air defenses and landed it on Red Square next to the Kremlin (ironically on Border Guard Day). He was prosecuted for "malicious hooliganism." The more normal cases of hooliganism involve rowdy drunkenness. Perhaps 99% of those prosecuted for hooliganism were intoxicated at the time of the offense.

2. Would Markin's situation have qualified for the defense of "detaining a person who has committed a crime" or "necessary defense," discussed *supra* pp. 499-502. Why or why not?

* * * *

(2) Crimes Prompted by "Hooliganistic Motives"

Four specific crimes are more serious if committed "from hooliganistic motives." The most serious of these is murder. Simple intentional murder is punishable by imprisonment of between 6 and 15 years, while murder from hooliganistic motives is aggravated murder, which is punishable by 8 to 20 years or by life imprisonment or death.[52] There are other bases listed in the statute that result in classifying killings as aggravated—killing an obviously pregnant woman, multiple murders, killing with particular cruelty, gang killings or killings that are performed according to a prior agreement among co-conspirators, killings to cover up other crimes, murder in the course of a rape and repeat offenses. But "hooliganistic motives" is by far the most vague basis for increased severity of punishment.

Strangely enough, "hooliganistic motives" are nowhere defined in the Criminal Code and one must extrapolate from the definition of hooliganistic conduct to discover their meaning and then apply that concept to the setting of murder. The Plenum of the Supreme Court provided the following explanation for the lower courts in a general discourse on how to handle murder cases:

> Under point b of Art. 102 CrC RSFSR [murder from hooliganistic motives] it is proper to categorize intentional murder committed on grounds of obvious contempt for society and generally accepted moral norms, when the conduct of the defendant constitutes an open challenge to the public order and resultingly a desire to set oneself apart from those around and to demonstrate scorn toward them. Often this crime is committed without any precipitating factor or with the use of an insignificant event as an excuse for the killing. . . .

---

[52] *See* Art. 105, CrC RF. The other three crimes are assault causing serious injury or disability (Art. 111), assault causing personal injury of a minor nature (Art. 112), and cruelty to animals (Art. 245).

> An intentional murder committed by the accused based on envy, vengeance or other motives arising from personal relations without regard to the place where it is committed should not be categorized [as from hooliganistic motives].
>
> To make clear the proper boundary of murder from hooliganistic motives in the process of an argument or fight, it is appropriate to clarify who the initiator was and whether the conflict was provoked by the defendant as an excuse for the killing. If the instigator of the argument or fight was the victim, and also when the victim's improper conduct was the basis for the conflict, the defendant cannot be held responsible for intentional murder from hooliganistic motives.[53]

On some level one could argue that *any* intentional and unjustified taking of human life automatically expresses "obvious contempt for society and generally accepted moral norms." But "hooliganistic motives" seeks to capture something more specific.

Two cases illustrate the concept in the context of a stabbing murder. One is *In re Barov*, decided by the Supreme Court in 1993.[54] The Court explained the facts and its holding as follows:

> As Barov explained it, [he was drunk] and saw Babina [the female victim] in a state of drunkenness [in a kiosk with a man]. He was upset by her carousing, since she had only recently buried her husband, a friend of the defendant, and he made a comment to her. She responded with an obscenity. Barov then decided to kill her. He went to fetch a knife and then called her out from the kiosk. The argument between them was resumed. He hit her first with his fists and then stabbed her with the knife. . . .
>
> Exactly what Barov did that was a violation of the public order [demonstrating] clear contempt for society is not made clear in the judgment.
>
> At the same time, the facts of the case testify to the fact that the murder was committed during an argument arising from a personal relationship in the nighttime.
>
> Under these circumstances, there is no basis for the conclusion that Barov acted from hooliganistic motives.

---

[53] Ruling of the Plenum of the Supreme Court RF, *"O sudebnoi praktiki po delam ob umyshlennykh ubiistvakh"* (On Judicial Practice in Intentional Murder Cases), *BVS*, 1993, No. 2, item 15, pp. 3-6.

[54] *In re Barov*, *BVS*, 1994, No. 6, p.3.

The second case, decided in 1992 by the Presidium of the Supreme Court, is *In re Sherstnev.*[55]

> On May 27, 1988 at about 7:00 PM, Sherstnev, who was drunk, entered his apartment and hung his bag, which contained his passport and savings account book, on the doorknob of the door of his apartment and immediately went out, as he had just had a fight with his wife. At about 9:00PM, Sherstnev decided to return home, noticed he didn't have his bag and began to look for it in all the places he had stopped. Near the entrance to his apartment building, he approached a group of teenage boys and, suspecting wrongly that one of them had hidden the bag, demanded that he return it.
>
> The teenagers, among them one Serebriakov, told Sherstnev that they had not seen the bag and had not hidden it and offered to look for it in the places he had been drinking. Sherstnev did not believe them. He went home, grabbed a home-made knife, returned to the group of teenagers and, using this insignificant basis for getting even, stabbed the teenager closest to him, Serebriakov, in the heart with the knife. . . .
>
> [It was argued on Sherstnev's behalf] that Sherstnev was honestly mistaken in his suspecting the teenagers about the loss of his bag and their taking it. In stabbing Serebriakov with the knife, he believed that he was doing that as retribution for their taking his bag and laughing at him. . . .
>
> [However,] [t]he trial court correctly pointed out that, in stabbing the teenager on the street in the presence of others, Sherstnev acted from hooliganistic motives, disclosing a clear contempt for society and scorning moral norms.

Based on these cases and the Supreme Court's explanation, it is apparent that hooliganistic motives relate somewhat to evil or unjustified intentions. The Supreme Court Plenum's ruling, for example, states that "it is appropriate to clarify who the initiator was and whether the conflict was provoked by the defendant or an excuse for the killing." In this respect, the general impression one gets from these cases is that hooliganistic motives have some of the characteristics of "malice aforethought" in the common law, perhaps including a lack of definitional clarity.[56]

---

[55] *In re Sherstnev, BVS,* 1993, No. 5, p. 6.

[56] *See People v. Woods,* 331 N.W.2d 707, 728 (Mich. 1982) (in the interest of "avoiding obscure language which has taken on different meanings through the years," henceforth the "elements of murder must be described without use of the terms 'malice' or 'malice aforethought.'")

But murder from hooliganistic motives also concerns the "place where it is committed," the public nature of the act. As the Supreme Court Plenum explained in its ruling, the heart of hooliganistic conduct is its public nature—that it "constitutes an *open challenge* to the public order and [a] resulting[ ] desire to set oneself apart from those around and to demonstrate scorn toward them."[57]

The facts of the murders in both the two cases just discussed are quite grim. But if it is true that the victims were equally innocent (or guilty) in provoking their assailants to kill them, the fact that one defendant stabbed his victim "on the street in the presence of others" while the other did so "in the nighttime" seems to be the only basis for distinguishing them. Certainly, on an intuitive level it is not immediately obvious which murder should result in a maximum of 15 years in prison and which should result in life imprisonment or the death penalty. The Code nonetheless reserves the more severe penalty for those who are indecorous enough to kill in public.[58] One could well make the argument that those who kill by stealth and in secret are the more socially dangerous, even aside from the fact that "secret" murders have no witnesses and are therefore more difficult to solve. Singling out for severe punishment those persons whose acts "constitute[ ] an open challenge to the public order" seems more appropriate to the 1960 Criminal Code's obsession with "security of the public order of the USSR"[59] than the 1996 Criminal Code's focus on "protection of the rights and freedoms of person and citizens."[60]

b. Other Miscellaneous Unique Crimes

Art. 105 of the Criminal Code provides that simple intentional murder is punishable by a sentence of between 6 and 15 years and aggravated murder is punishable by a term of between 8 and 20 or by death or life imprisonment. The next article defines "Murder of a New-Born Baby by Its Mother." It provides:

> Murder of a new-born baby by its mother during or shortly after its birth and murder of a new-born by its mother under circumstances of psychological trauma or while in a state of psychological distress short of insanity—is punishable by imprisonment for up to 5 years.

Two matters normally left to civil litigation in the U.S. are crimes in

---

[57] *See* text *supra* at note 53.

[58] Thus, the thinking murderer should challenge his victim, not to "step outside," but to "step inside."

[59] Art. 1, CrC RSFSR.

[60] Art. 2, CrC RF.

Russia. Art. 129 prohibits slander or libel (*kleveta*) and Art. 130 prohibits insults (*oskorblenie*). One steeped in the common law tradition of prosecutorial discretion might doubt how often such cases would actually be filed in court. However, these crimes are eligible for private prosecution instigated by the victims themselves and are brought quite often.[61] Slander is punishable by up to 3 years in prison, but then only if it falsely accuses someone of a serious or very serious crime. Insult is defined as "impugning the honor and integrity of a person through use of indecent language." It is punishable only by a fine or "corrective labor" of up to 6 months, but by corrective labor of up to one year if the insult is delivered at a public presentation or gathering or through the mass media.[62] The definition of "insult" is rather broad. There is apparently no requirement that the insult be communicated to anyone—including the target of the utterance. And, as to both "insult" and "slander," the U.S. observer familiar with 1st Amendment law will note the absence of any exemption for utterances made regarding public figures or in debates on public issues.

A third matter usually relegated to civil litigation in the U.S. is invasions of privacy. Art. 137 defines invasion of privacy as:

> the illegal gathering or dissemination of information about the personal life of a person which constitutes a personal or family confidence without that person's permission, or the dissemination of such information in public addresses, public presentations or by means of the mass media, if such actions are undertaken for reasons of financial gain or personal benefit and cause harm to the rights and legal interests of citizens.

This is punishable by up to four months in jail or, if the result of use of one's official position, by up to six months in jail and/or a two-to-five year ban on working in a particular position or field of work. Again, as with slander and insult, there is no exemption for situations when such information relates to a public official, even if the information is relevant to that figure's ability to perform his or her duties. In addition, though the invasion of privacy must be "undertaken for reasons of financial gain or personal benefit," this requirement would presumably be automatically satisfied whenever the privacy-invader is a professional journalist or a privately owned television or station, newspaper or magazine.

Art. 136 provides for criminal liability for "Violation of Equality of Citizens." A person steeped in the "state action" requirements of U.S.

---

[61] Private prosecutions were briefly noted in Chapter X, p. ____.

[62] "Corrective labor" is not as bad as it sounds. *See infra* p. 583, text at note 74.

constitutional law might think that this article would apply only to actions by government or its officials, but there is no such requirement for it in the basic article. Moreover, the lack of any need for governmental action is underscored by the second subsection, which provides for enhanced punishment when the violation is committed by an official, raising the maximum punishment from 2 years to 3 years, and adding the possible punishment of banning the offender from working in a particular position or field of work for between two and five years.

Art. 139 prohibits any "Invasion of the Home," defined as the "illegal entry into a home accomplished without the permission of the person living there." There are three levels of the offense. A simple invasion is punishable by up to three months in jail, one undertaken by force or threat of force carries a maximum of up to two years imprisonment, and one accomplished through abuse of official position is punished by up to three years and/or a ban on working in that position or a given field of work for from two to five years.

Art. 144 prohibits "Interference with the Professional Work of Journalists." This crime consists of trying to coerce a journalist to print information or to refrain from printing information. If done in its simple form by an individual, it is punished by correctional labor of up to a year, but if committed through the use of the offender's official position, it is punishable by up to 3 years in prison and up to a 3-year ban on occupying that position or working in a particular field. Presumably refusing to answer a journalist's questions would not violate the statute, although this is not entirely free from doubt. Also, one assumes that attempts to prevent publication of "information about the personal life of a person which constitutes a personal or family confidence"—information protected by the crime of "invasion of privacy" discussed above—would have to be exempt from prosecution under this article, although there is no such exception stated in the statute.

4. Decriminalizations

Crimes of an "anti-Soviet" nature were eliminated from the old Code sometime ago. Principal among them was the infamous crime of "anti-Soviet agitation and propaganda,"[63] which was applied to a wide variety of people who did nothing more than possess "suspect" literature. These prosecutions continued even in the late Soviet period. Another article used against dissidents was Art. 209, which prohibited living a "parasitic way of life." This law was a convenient way to get at dissidents, since the fact they were identified as dissidents usually meant they were fired from their jobs. Because the person was unemployed (and still alive), this could be used as evidence that

[63] Art. 70, CrC RSFSR.

the person was being supported by illicit means or from handouts. More generally, crimes affecting religious freedom[64] and freedom of movement[65] and those prohibiting private entrepreneurial activity[66] were also repealed. There is no resurgence of these crimes in the new Code. And there are some other, perhaps less-expected decriminalizations as well.

The new Code decriminalizes consensual sexual conduct of any kind with anyone over 16 years of age and sexual conduct short of intercourse with anyone over 14. This is quite unlike the old Code, which until 1993 punished all consensual homosexual behavior. However, under Art. 134 of the new Code, "[c]onsensual heterosexual, homosexual or lesbian intercourse committed by someone over 18 years of age with someone known to be under 16 years of age" is punishable by up to 3 years imprisonment. Under Art. 135, sexual activity short of intercourse (*razvratnye deistvie*) with someone under 14, consensual or otherwise, is punished by up to three years. Forcible homosexual rape is punished the same way as heterosexual rape with the same 3-6 year imprisonment range.[67]

The old Soviet Code contained what might be referred to as a "mandatory Good Samaritan" law which required a person who encounters another in danger to render help if the person can do so without serious harm to himself or herself. This does not appear in the new Code. However, the duty to help a sick person whom one is *legally obligated* to help is retained in Art. 124 of the new Code.

Dr. Kevorkian would apparently not run into trouble in Russia. Art. 110 prohibits hounding a person into committing suicide, but there is no prohibition on assisting in a voluntary suicide. However, it would not be surprising if Art. 110 were nonetheless applied to in practice to persons assisting voluntary suicides.

Art. 230 punishes with up to 5 years imprisonment anyone "enticing a person to use narcotic or psychotropic drugs" and punishes the same action

---

[64] Art. 142, CrC RSFSR.

[65] Art. 198, CrC RSFSR.

[66] Art. 153, CrC RSFSR.

[67] Art. 131-132, CrC RF. Male-male homosexual rape may not be classified as rape, however. In defining, the crime of "Rape," Art. 131 uses only the female gender of the term for "victim" (*poterpevshaia*), even though "victim" appears everywhere else in the Code in the male gender (*poterpevshii*). This seems to imply that it would be Art. 132 which defines "Violent Acts of a Sexual Nature" and has the same sentencing range that would be used in the case of male-male homosexual rape. Art. 132 describes the victim in the male gender followed by the female gendered word in parentheses. *See* Reynolds, *supra* note 2, at 76-77, note * and Reynolds, *supra* note 48, at 6.

with up to 12 years if the person dies as a result. It also punishes distribution or possession with or without intent to sell of illegal drugs "in large amounts."[68] However, the Code decriminalizes simple possession of small amounts of illegal drugs. Such possession remains an administrative violation, but even then there is no violation if the person voluntarily turns over the drugs possessed.[69]

In a recent case, some confusion arose over exactly what drug offenses were decriminalized by the new Criminal Code.

The Supreme Court: *In re Okolot, BVS*, 1998, No. 2, p. 7.

The organs of preliminary investigation charged Okolot with a second offense of illegal acquisition, transportation and possession of opium in the amount of 2.6 grams, which he obtained from an unknown person in the middle of September of 1996 in the city of Samara, without intent to sell.

The Krasnoglinski District Court of the city of Samara on January 30, 1997 dismissed the case brought under Art. 224 CrC RSFSR against Okolot because his actions did not satisfy the elements of any crime.

In dismissing the case . . . , the [trial] judge referred to the fact that the current Art. 228(1) CrC RF provides for criminal liability for illegal acquisition and possession of narcotic drugs in large amounts without intent to sell, while Art. 224(4) CrC RSFSR, under which Okolot was charged, does not contain the large amount element. At the time that Okolot acquired and possessed the narcotics, opium in the amount of 2.6 grams was not defined as a large amount. On this basis, in the court's opinion, the case had to be dismissed on the basis of Art. 10 CrC RF.

[Art. 10 provides in relevant part: "A criminal law that eliminates the criminality of conduct, lessens punishment or in some other way improves the position of the person who committed the crime shall have retroactive effect . . ."]

We cannot agree with the trial court's views.

The meaning of Art. 10, CrC RF, is that a law that eliminates the criminality of conduct is a law that decriminalizes that conduct, i.e. that excludes such conduct from the realm of the Criminal Code and, therefore, removes the criminal liability and punishment for engaging in such conduct. Since January 1, 1997, a new Criminal Code has been effective under which

[68] Art. 228, CrC RF.
[69] *See* Art. 44, CAI RSFSR.

the criminal liability for illegal acquisition and possession of narcotics without the intent to sell has not only been preserved, but increased. In fact, Art. 228(1) CrC RF envisions criminal liability for illegal acquisition and possession of narcotics in large amounts. However, this charge was not the one brought against Okolot. He was charged with acquiring and possessing without the intent to sell 2.6 grams of opium, and, according to the record of proceedings No. 54/10-96 of December 17, 1996 of the Committee on Controlled Substances,[70] the above-stated amount of narcotics is a large quantity. Consequently, criminal liability for this conduct has not been eliminated.

The district court and the presidium of the regional court failed to take these circumstances into account, taking the view that the conduct proscribed by Art. 224(4) CrC RSFSR had been decriminalized.

At the new trial, it will be necessary to take into account the requirements of Art. 224(4) CrC RSFSR and Art. 10 CrC RF and, depending on the evidence that is established, decide the question of guilt or innocence of Okolot.

The case is reversed and remanded for a new trial.

NOTES AND QUESTIONS

1. Who has the better of the argument, the trial court or the Supreme Court? Before answering, consider the relevant date the offense was committed and the date the determinations of the Committee on Narcotics Control were issued (see the footnote by the court). When did the elements of the offense finally get determined? When was that in relation to the date the offense was committed? *Cf.* Art. 54(2) of the Constitution: "No one may be held liable for an act which was not recognized as a violation of law at the time of its commission."

2. In the current climate of law and order feeling in Russia, why would the legislature decriminalize simple possession of small amounts of narcotics? Could this be an expression of the notion of the need for "social dangerousness" for there to be a crime (see *supra* pp. 554-555).

3. On the issues of retroactivity of the new Code, the Supreme Court

[70] [footnote by the Court:] The summary table of determinations of the Permanent Committee for Control of Narcotics regarding small, large and very large quantities of narcotics, psychotropic and powerful drugs found in illegal possession or circulation was published in the Bulletin of the Supreme Court of the Russian Federation No. 8 for 1997.

decision in *In re Lukin*[71] is an example of Art. 10 being used to deny retroactive effect. Lukin was convicted of interfering with and assaulting a court officer executing a civil judgment against his son. Lukin was sentenced to one year in prison with the sentence suspended for a probationary period of one year. The prosecutor sought to have the sentence changed to conform to the new Code's provision that the defendant be required to perform certain actions within the probationary period on pain of having the sentence carried out. The Court, citing Art. 10, considered that the new Code's provisions worked a worsening of the defendant's position and therefore could not be applied to his case.

E. Sentences for Crimes

1. Types of Punishment Possible

The new Criminal Code provides an entire menu of 13 different types of sanctions.[72] They range from fines and various forms of corrective labor to life imprisonment and the death penalty. A new category of punishment is something akin to "community service" in the U.S., in which the defendant would be ordered to complete a certain number of hours of work for the local municipality. However, this form of punishment goes into effect only when a new Corrections Code (*Ugolovno-ispolnitel'nyi Kodeks*) goes into effect, but no later than 2001.[73] But even then this form of punishment is dependent on local governments financing it. Given the funding difficulties on every level of government, it may never become a reality in many parts of the country. Another interesting form of punishment we saw when we discussed crimes that were carried out through "abuse" of the offenders "official position," is the possibility of a court-imposed ban on the defendant occupying a particular post or working in a given field for a particular period of time.

The four staples of punishment in the Russian system are now and have always been imprisonment, fines, corrective labor, and conditional convictions or sentences. Imprisonment and fines are self-explanatory. The other two need a brief explanation. "Corrective labor" might conjure up images of back-breaking work on a chain gang, but it is nothing like that.

---

[71] BVS, 1998, No. 1, p. 4.

[72] Art. 44, CrC RF.

[73] Art. 4, *Federal'nyi zakon o vvedenie v deistvie Ugolovnogo kodeksa RF* (Federal Law on the Effective Date of the Criminal Code of the RF), *Sobranie*, 1996, no. 25, item 2955. The same delays are provided for short-term imprisonment (called "*arrest*") and assignment of the first-offenders and those who committed their crimes through negligence to special institutions that would "exercise close supervision" over them, but would not confine them. *See* Art. 53 and 54.

Defendants sentenced to corrective labor are simply required to pay to the state some percentage of their salary from their usual job, usually 25%.[74] Conditional convictions or sentences are somewhat similar to probation or deferred or suspended sentences in the U.S. system. But more than the sentence is held in abeyance. The Code provides that the conviction itself is held in abeyance pending the defendant's staying out of trouble and performing specific tasks, such as undergoing treatment for alcohol or drug addiction, staying away from certain places, supporting his or her family and not changing addresses or work without notification. A defendant who performs all the conditions satisfactorily not only avoids a more serious punishment, but also avoids a record of conviction.[75]

Judges use imprisonment as a sanction in approximately one-third of all cases—a rate that has remained constant from 1990 through the first six months of 1997.[76] Non-custodial punishments were almost identical in the first 6 months of 1996 and 1997, with conditional convictions at 45%, corrective labor at 8% and fines at 9%. From 1990 through 1996, there was a steady decline in the use of corrective labor and an increased use of conditional convictions or sentences. This is apparently because in the years since 1990, those convicted of lesser crimes—the principal objects of corrective labor—have increasingly been people who are unemployed or who have irregular employment. Since ordering a deduction of money from their salary would not constitute any real punishment, judges looking for a meaningful non-custodial sanction have instead resorted to the conditional conviction option.[77]

2. Sentences Under the New Code: Stricter or More Lenient?

The new Code has been declared to be "stricter,"[78] "generally

[74] *See* Art. 50, CrC RF.

[75] *See* Art. 73, 74 CrC RF. Thus, conditional convictions are actually more similar to the "guilty plea held in abeyance," used to assist first-time offenders in parts of the United States in avoiding a criminal record. A difference, of course, is that the conviction that is held in abeyance in the Russian system results from a trial rather than plea of guilty.

[76] All these statistics are based on data supplied by the Ministry of Justice as compiled and reported in T. Foglesong, "The Politics of Fighting Crime in Russia: Out of the Criminal Code and Into the Courts," unpublished paper presented at AAASS Annual Meeting, Seattle, Washington (November 22, 1997), used with permission of the author, whose assistance is gratefully acknowledged.

[77] *See* Foglesong, *supra* note 76, at 7-8. In the overall statistics cited, conditional sentences under the old Code are combined with conditional convictions under the new.

[78] Naumov Commentary, *supra* note 2, at 33.

sterner,"[79] and even "draconian"[80] by people who should know. And there is much in the Code related to sentencing that supports such judgments.

Maximum sentences for the four categories of crimes were described earlier.[81] Those familiar with the old Soviet codes will have noticed that the new Code represents an increase in maximum terms of imprisonment. Under the old Code, the maximum was 15 years and any crime considered worse than 15 years worth of imprisonment was punishable by death, although life imprisonment was possible as a result of commutation of a death sentence. Under the new Code, judges can impose fixed-term imprisonment for a single crime of up to 20 years. Life imprisonment or a 25-year sentence is possible as a result of a death sentence commutation. However, a life sentence may also be imposed in the first instance by the trial court "as an alternative to the death penalty" if the "court considers it appropriate not to apply the death penalty."[82] The minimum sentences for some crimes have also been raised, such as simple intentional homicide for which the minimum was increased from 3 to 6 years. Despite these higher maximum and minimum sentences, an American observer who skims the specific crimes and punishments of the new Code will find that the maximums and minimums for most crimes are in the moderate to low range when compared to most states in the U.S.

Maximum and minimum prison terms do not tell the whole story, however. Longer sentences are also likely to result from a major change in the way sentences are computed. The new Code provides that sentences for multiple offenses will be cumulative or consecutive rather than concurrent. Thus, the court can cumulate the sentences for multiple crimes up to a 25-year maximum and can tack on a new sentence at the end of the unserved portion of an earlier one up to a 30-year maximum.[83] According to Naumov, this change was made so as to eliminate the "absurd" provisions of the old code under which a defendant convicted of multiple offenses simply received the highest punishment possible for the most serious crime committed. In his view, the principle of concurrent sentencing "merely promoted the commission of crimes, especially serious one."[84]

---

[79] Lebedev Commentary, *supra* note 2, at xi. Lebedev is the Chairman of the Supreme Court and Skuratov is the Procurator-General.

[80] V. Radchenko in interview with Todd Foglesong on October 27, 1997, as reported in Foglesong, *supra* note 76. Radchenko is the First Deputy Chairman of the Russian Supreme Court and, according to Foglesong, someone whom "no observer of judicial affairs in Russia would call a 'liberal'."

[81] *See supra* p. 555-556.

[82] Art. 57(1), CrC RF. *See infra* pp. 524-526 for more on the death penalty.

[83] Art. 56(4), CrC RF. *See also* Art. 69 and 70, CrC RF.

[84] Naumov Commentary, *supra* note 2, at 34. *Compare* Art. 17 and 69, CrC RF with Art. 40, CrC RSFSR.

Recidivists are also dealt with more sternly. Among other things, Art. 18 of the new Code omits the option, found in the old Code, of the judge discounting the effect of a prior conviction based on the judge's assessment of "the nature of the first crime."[85] Further, the new Code lowers the age of criminal liability from 16 to 14 for many crimes, thus making many former juvenile defendants subject to adult sentencing ranges and practices.[86]

There are other aspects of the new Code, however, that would seem to be more lenient when it comes to punishment. At both the low and high ends of the punishment spectrum, there is evidence of a reduction in severity. As noted earlier, some offenses have been decriminalized, such as consensual homosexual conduct and simple possession of narcotics. In addition, the number of crimes for which the death penalty is possible has been sharply reduced to only certain forms of aggravated murder.[87] Moreover, the overall penal philosophy represented by the new Code has changed. Under the old Code, "retribution" was unabashedly at the top of the list of the "goals of punishment," though not the only goal.[88] Under the new Code, "punishment is applied with the goal of vindicating social justice, as well as the goals of correction of the offender and deterring new crimes."[89] The general principles of sentencing require that the court take into account, among other things, "the effect of the sentence . . . on the conditions of life of [the defendant's] family."[90] Most importantly, Art. 60, which sets out "General Principles of Sentencing," states a clear preference for the mildest sanction. It states that in all sentencing, "the more severe form of punishment . . . shall be assigned only if a less severe sanction will not achieve the goals of punishment."

The new Code also enumerates more factors in mitigation of punishment than under the old Code. One has been mentioned—the application of a form of "diminished capacity" of the defendant as a factor mitigating punishment.[91] This, when combined with the elimination of alcohol as an aggravating factor, could be important, given the alcohol-besotted nature of

---

[85] *Compare* RSFSR Cr C Art. 39(1), second sentence, *with* Art. 18, CrC RF.

[86] *See* Art. 20(2), CrC RF. Among the crimes for which 14 is the age of criminal responsibility are all forms of homicide, assaults, theft, robbery, rape, kidnaping and aggravated forms of hooliganism. However, neither the death penalty nor life imprisonment may be applied to anyone who committed the offense before reaching 18. Art. 57, 59, CrC RF.

[87] *See* Art. 105, CrC RF. *See also* Art. 59(1), CrC RF.

[88] Art. 20, CrC RSFSR.

[89] Art. 43, CrC RF.

[90] Art. 60(3), Cr C RF.

[91] *See supra* pp. 558-559.

many crimes in Russia.[92] Another is the focus on the conduct of the victim of crime, a relevant factor in many of the 80-plus percent of murder or assault cases where the victim is a family member, friend, acquaintance and/or drinking companion of the defendant. Significantly, Art. 16(2)(h) requires consideration, not just of the "illegality" of the "conduct of the victim that led to the crime," but also the "immorality" of that conduct. This reference is also added to the definition of a lesser form of murder committed in a state of "affect," defined as "strong mental agitation brought on suddenly" by the actions of the victim.[93] Other helpful mitigating factors that are continued are the defendant's minority or pregnancy, the presence of minor children in the defendant's home and the defendant getting medical help for the victim, as well as the defendant's early confession and active assistance in solving the crime, turning in accomplices and recovering any products of the crime. Also, the court may consider whether commission of the crime was the result of "the combination of difficult life circumstances or based on compassion for the victim" or of "physical or psychological compulsion or because of moral, job-related or other conditions of dependence." Also included as factors mitigating punishment are actions of the defendant that come close to qualifying as a complete defense, but exceed the bounds of self-defense, necessity, justified risk, following orders or arresting a criminal.[94]

As in the old Code, the new Code has a provision allowing the sentencing judge to sentence the defendant to a punishment that is below the mandatory minimum sentence in "exceptional circumstances"—what would be in U.S. practice a "departure downward" from the minimum sentence.[95] However, the new Code definition of such circumstances is liberalized in two ways. First, the old provision limited such circumstances to defendants turning themselves in or actively assisting in exposing the crime. The new provision refers to these two grounds, but also broadens such circumstances to include consideration of "the purpose and motives for the crime, the role of the guilty person, [the guilty] person's behavior during and after committing the crime, and other circumstances which substantially reduce the degree of social dangerousness of the crime." Second, the new version allows the "exceptional circumstances" to be based, not only on separate consideration of these mitigating factors, but also on their "totality."[96]

---

[92] *Compare* Art. 39(1), CrC RSFSR *with* Art. 63, CrC RF. It *is* an aggravating circumstance that the defendant sought the participation in the crime of *other* people under the influence of alcohol. Art. 63(d), CrC RF.

[93] Art. 107, CrC RF.

[94] *See* Art. 61, CrC RF.

[95] *See* Art. 43, CrC RSFSR and Art. 64, CrC RF.

[96] Art. 64 CrC RF.

On the other hand, the new basis for departure downward notably fails to include the "personal characteristics of the defendant" (*lichnost'*) and limits the relevant catch-all "other circumstances" to those that "substantially reduce the degree of social dangerousness of the crime." The effect of this is apparently that the "personal characteristics" of the defendant can be relied on to reduce the severity of the sentence *within* the minimum and maximum limits set out in the Code, but not as a basis for a departure downward from the minimum.

3. Judicial Practice in Sentencing

Given that the new Code has both "draconian" and compassionate aspects, judicial practice will play an important role in guiding trial courts in the exercise of their still-considerable discretion in sentencing. It is too soon to tell which aspects of the new Code will be emphasized. However, any future leniency in sentencing that might take place under the new Code would run against the tide, both of recent Russian history in the area of sentencing and of recent pronouncements of the Supreme Court on the subject.

Regarding sentencing history, as of 1992-93, the last years for which comparative statistics are published, Russia had the highest rate of imprisonment of all developed countries in the world, at a rate of 558 incarcerated persons per 100,000 population. The United States ran a close second with 519 per 100,000 population. These rates are quite phenomenal when compared to those of other developed democratic countries: 93 prisoners per 100,000 population in England, 84 in France, 80 in Germany and 49 in the Netherlands. Moreover, for both Russia and the U.S., these figures reflect a considerable increase from just a few years before. In the U.S., these figures represent a 22% increase over 1989. Depending on which estimates one follows for the Soviet Union in 1989, the rate in Russia represents an increase of between 47% and 63%.[97]

Regarding the Supreme Court's position on sentencing in recent years, the Court's Collegium for Criminal Cases has been hard at work dealing with the problem of "excessively mild" sentences. Statistics on cassational review of the judgments of second-level courts (courts in which the most serious cases are tried) indicate that the number of cases in which sentences were reduced fell by 50% between 1994 and 1997, while reversals for leniency on supervisory review increased 200%. The same can be said for the intermediate appellate

[97] M. Mauer, Americans Behind Bars: The International Use of Incarceration, 1992-1993 (The Sentencing Project 1994).

courts, in which reversals for excessive leniency increased almost 100% between 1992 and 1996.[98]

The Supreme Court Plenum also issued a major 1996 supervisory Ruling addressing the use of incarceration in sentencing.[99] The Ruling observed that "some judges have underestimated the increased social danger of crimes against life, health and freedom of citizens." It further noted that "sometimes aggravating circumstances have not been sufficiently taken into account, such as the socially dangerous methods of commission of the crime." This, the Court said, had led to sentences which were "obviously unfair in their leniency." The ruling admonished all courts to take steps to eliminate such "inadequacies." Significantly, the ruling reminds trial courts that they should not depart downward from the minimum punishment except in "exceptional circumstances," which the Court reminds trial courts are only "circumstances that substantially lessen the social dangerousness of the crime."

4. Sentencing Practices in Trial Courts

Despite the Supreme Court's less-than-subtle push for greater use of imprisonment, aggregate statistics disclose little change. As mentioned earlier, judges use imprisonment in approximately one-third of all cases—a rate that has been constant since 1990.[100] The percentage of cases in which imprisonment was used in the first half of 1997 was 36.4%, exactly the same rate as in the first half of 1996. However, there has been a shift toward greater leniency by trial judges within this one-third of cases that would seem to fly in the face of the admonitions from the Supreme Court. There has been a visible *decline*

---

[98] *See* Foglesong, *supra* note 76, at 16-24. Additionally, the Court's work plan for 1995 set for it the task of "securing the participation of judges in work . . . on accelerating the battle against crime" a statement reminiscent of the various Communist Party "campaigns" that enlisted judges in implementing certain party programs in Soviet times.

[99] *See* Ruling of the Plenum of the Supreme Court of October 15, 1996 *'O khode vypolnenia sudami postanovleniq Plenuma Verkhovnogo Suda RF ot 14 Aprelia 1988 g. No. 1 "O praktike naznachenia sudami Rossiiskoi Federatsii nakazania v vide lishenia svobody"* ("On the Progress of Courts Implementing the Ruling of the Supreme Court of the RF of April 14, 1988, No. 1 'On the Practice in the Courts of the Russian Federation of Ordering Sentences of Imprisonment"), BVS, 1997, No. 1, pp. 3-4. *See also Obzor kassatsionnoi praktiki otmeny pregovorov za miagkost'iu naznachenia nakazania* (Study of Appellate Reversals of Sentences for Excessive Leniency), BVS, 1997, No. 7, pp. 20-24.

[100] All these statistics are based on data supplied by the Ministry of Justice as compiled and reported in Foglesong, *supra* note 76, at 7.

in the use of imprisonment for the very serious crimes of homicide, robbery and third degree hooliganism—in some cases up to a 10% decline.[101]

Even more striking is the statistic related to downward departures from mandatory minimum sentences. In comparing the first half of 1996 with the first half of 1997, trial judges increased the number of times that they found downward departures appropriate from 7.2% to 9.6%. Downward departures were even more likely in the cases of crimes for which the new Code increased the minimum punishment for the crime. In cases of second and third degree robbery, downward departures *doubled* from 1996 to 1997, and in cases of third degree hooliganism, they increased by *five times*.[102] Given that the 1997 downward departures were ordered within a few months after the Supreme Court Plenum's October 1996 Ruling — which specifically focussed on unjustified downward departures—the increase is "not just striking, but brazen."[103]

Anecdotal evidence also supports the idea that trial judges view the new Code and the Supreme Court's harsh attitude toward sentencing to be unrealistic. Foglesong relates a conversation with a trial judge from St. Petersburg, who had spent several sleepless nights worrying about a case involving two 14-year-old boys who had stolen two antiques from a local flea market, each worth several hundred dollars U.S. Since the total value of the goods stolen exceeded 500 times the minimum wage and the boys had acted in concert according to a plan, their crime merited a punishment of between 5 and 10 years in prison under the new Code, a sentence he called "idiotic." Yet, there did not appear to be any "exceptional circumstances" in the case that would allow for special leniency. If he nonetheless found such circumstances to exist, he feared reversal and a "tongue-lashing" from the appellate court.[104]

---

[101] The figures for homicide are a decrease in use of imprisonment for aggravated murder of 96.4% to 92.9 and for simple homicide of 95.3% to 88.5%; for first degree robbery, from 79.3 to 69.1 and second and third degree robbery, from 90.1% to 81.7%; and for third degree hooliganism, from 62.9% to 55.4%. These decreases were made up for in other categories of crime, so the aggregate imprisonment rate did not change. *See* Foglesong, *supra* note 76.

[102] It may be that the differences in the wording of the relevant Code provisions discussed earlier account for the difference. *See supra* pp. 585-586. However, one must take into account that grounds for downward departure from the minimum under both versions of the Code are only for "exceptional circumstances" and that a trial judge who takes this step is asking for greater scrutiny on appeal.

[103] Foglesong, *supra* note 76, at 15.

[104] *Id.*, at 15-16. The conversation reported took place at the October 1997 meeting of the Council of Judges of the Russian Federation. Foglesong reports that "several judges complained" about the new Code limiting their discretion in sentencing.

5. The Death Penalty and Russia's Membership in the Council of Europe

Russia has had an off-and-on relationship with the death penalty for some time. As far back as 1753, the Empress Elizabeth abolished the death penalty, but only for a short time. Several other rulers toyed with bans for varying periods of time, without actually changing the law. Then, following the Russian Revolution, the Provisional Government abolished it for several months. It was restored in 1918 by the Bolsheviks. Then in 1920, it was abolished and then reinstated in the same year. In 1947 it was abolished only to be reinstated in 1950. However, the reinstatement applied it only to certain serious state crimes, such as treason and espionage. But in 1954, the death penalty was extended to aggravated murder and the 1960 Criminal Code expanded it to include several other offenses, including economic crimes, such as bribery, counterfeiting, theft of state property and illegal currency transactions in large amounts.[105]

Following the 1991 break-up of the Soviet Union, in keeping with the changes in the nature of government and society, the death penalty was removed for most economic offenses. Since the President of the Russian Federation had the power to pardon, a Clemency Commission was set up in the Administration of the President in 1992 and it included many non-lawyers, such as the poet Bulat Okudzhava (until his recent death), an Orthodox priest, a journalist and a psychologist, as well as several lawyers of different types. The Commission makes recommendations to the President, who has the final say on clemency.

Statistics on the number of executions are available only back to 1985 and even today conflicting numbers are given and the discrepancies are inexplicably large. Nonetheless, by the reckoning of most experts, executions reached a high of 2,000 a year in the 1960s, then dropped to 1,000 per year from the early 1970s to the mid-1980s.[106] In 1985, the number was 770 and this gradually decreased to a low of 4 in 1993, in large part because of the work of the Clemency Commission and, before it, a similar commission attached to the Supreme Soviet.[107]

---

[105] *See* Donald D. Barry and Eric J. Williams, Russia's Death Penalty Dilemma, 8 *Criminal Law Forum* 231, 232-238 (1997), and sources cite therein.

[106] *See* Barry and Williams, *id.* at 240, and sources cited therein.

[107] The figure for 1993 of 4 executions is from the Clemency Commission. For reasons that are not clear, the Clemency Commission and Ministry of Justice figures are substantially different for the two years in which data are available for both. For the years 1991 and 1992, the Commission reported 15 and 1 execution respectively, while the Ministry of Justice reported 59 and 18. There are even discrepancies in Ministry of Justice figures given at different times. For example, one Ministry report places executions in 1989 and 1990 at 93 and 76, while another report states that there were 276 and 195. These are not small discrepancies. Yet they have not been cleared up. *See*

The 1993 Constitution takes a tentative approach to the death penalty. It provides in Art. 20:

> 1. Everyone shall have the right to life.
>
> 2. The death penalty, until its abolition, may be provided for by federal law as an exceptional penalty for particularly grave crimes against life, so long as the accused is given the right to have his or her case tried before a jury.

The primary reason for Russia's backing away from the death penalty has been its wish to become a member of the Council of Europe. Russia was finally admitted as a member in February 1996. In becoming a member, it had to agree to an immediate moratorium on implementation of the death penalty and its elimination within three years. The moratorium was implemented and as of this writing, it is still in place.[108]

From the foregoing, one might suppose that the death penalty is on the verge of extinction in Russia. However, as is clear from discussions elsewhere in this chapter, the 1996 Criminal Code did not abolish the death penalty. The debate over it and the larger debate about the crime problem in Russia are still raging, and both have made themselves felt in the corridors of power. This is represented in a mini-counter-trend of an increase in executions in the years 1993 to 1996. As stated earlier, according to Clemency Commission figures, there was a low of 4 executions in 1993. However, this figure climbed to 19 in 1994, to 86 in 1995 and 56 in 1996 before the moratorium took effect upon Russia's admission to the Council of Europe. And this figure is placed even higher by Amnesty International, which states that there were 140 executions in 1996, 103 of which were carried out after Russian joined the Council of Europe.[109]

Barry and Williamson, *supra* note 105, at 239-241. For this reason, one should rely on published figures with caution.

[108] Art. 59(2) continues the chivalrous approach of the old Code in exempting women from the death penalty and the new Code adds a similar exemption for life imprisonment. The same exemption applies to males who were under 18 when they committed the crime or over 65 at the time of sentencing. The age-based exemptions are required for both sexes by the International Covenant on Civil and Political Rights. *Cf.* 1993 Constitution, Art. 19(1) (insuring equality of men and women).

[109] *Id.*, at 241. It is reported as well that when the Council of Europe bestowed membership on Russia, Council representatives were under the impression that only 16 persons had been executed in 1995, a figure some members of the Council believed was excessive. When the chairman of the Clemency Commission later told Council representatives that the actual number for that year was 86, the Council representatives stated that, had the real figure been known, Russia would never have been admitted to the Council. *Kaznit'? milovat'?, Iuridicheski Vestnik*, 1997, No. 4, at p. 5, as reported in Barry and Williamson, *supra* 105, at 241 n. 32.

These developments and the current climate of public opinion about crime in Russia show how the abolition of the death penalty is not a foregone conclusion. Indeed, the moratorium on executions is only a *de facto* one that has been accomplished through a very low-profile method: the Clemency Commission has simply stopped sending cases to the President for his consideration. With no opportunity for Presidential review, apparently no executions can take place.[110]

Barry and Williamson, in their recent article on the subject, have identified the various positions of the abolitionists, retentionists and "gradualists" involved in the debate.[111] Most of the arguments are familiar to death penalty advocates and opponents in the U.S. — deterrence issues, the danger of errors, the propriety of the state taking retribution and the unfairness of its inconsistent application because of judicial discretion. To the debate have been added additional arguments peculiar to the situation in Russia. The first is the cost of building new prisons to hold all the new inmates serving life sentences who would be produced by abolition and have already been produced by the moratorium. As one Russian commentator bluntly put it, "Bullets are cheaper than bars."[112]

The second argument relates to the nature of the "Russian character." It is used both by those in favor of capital punishment generally and by those who think that the Russian people are "not yet ready" for abolition of the death penalty. The argument is essentially that Russians, being hardened to brutality, are less affected by brutal retribution for their criminal actions. Further, "the succession of wars and cruel repressions [in Russia] has drastically lowered the value of . . . life itself. . . . And this applies all the more to the present situation in Russia."[113] Abolitionists can respond, however, that the brutalizing effects of Russia's history are all the more reason for the state to break with history and refuse to perpetuate that climate of brutality.

F. International Aspects of Russian Criminal Law

1. The Special Problems with Russian Organized Crime

Russian crime has made a name for itself internationally through the

---

[110] *Id.*, at 245.

[111] *Id.*, at 248-256.

[112] Lev Razgon, *Pulia deshevle tiuremnoi reshetki* (Bullets are Cheaper than Bars), *Izvestia*, March 15, 1996, p. 1.

[113] Vladimir Guliev, *Moratorii na smertnuiu kazn' prezhdevremenen* (The Time for a Moratorium on the Death Penalty Has Not Yet Arrived), *Nezavisimaia Gazeta,* December 21, 1996, p. 1.

activities of the "Russian mafia." Use of the term "mafia" implies that it is similar to the better-known Italian-American mafia. However, unlike the Italian-American mafia, family ties are a negligible factor in the Russian mafia if they count at all. Further, the educational level of Russian mafia operatives is much higher and the sophistication of their criminal activities and the types of crimes they commit reflect this. Finally, there is no real hierarchical structure or control, so "free-lance" groups spring up all the time.

A recent law review article describes some of the types of activities in which the Russian mafia excels.[114] One is social security and other entitlement fraud. Another is private insurance fraud. In one case in 1991, Russian emigres in California engaged in "the largest insurance fraud schemes ever perpetrated in the United States." They set up more than "250 bogus medical clinics and mobile laboratories during the middle-to-late 1980s, solicited patients with promises of free physical examinations and tests, and then submitted fraudulent bills to their health insurance providers. The total amount illegally taken by the Smushkevich organization was more than $50 million." In Philadelphia, a group recruited other Russians to stage automobile accidents and then submitted more than $1 million in fraudulent claims to a number of insurance companies. Not only that, after staging their accidents, the "injured" would report for treatment to a medical clinic owned by another co-conspirator which would treat their nonexistent injuries and would then submit claims to their insurance companies.[115]

Perhaps the criminal activity most commonly associated with Russian criminal organizations is fuel tax evasion. Indeed, Russian criminal organizations have almost achieved monopoly status in the field. Fuel tax frauds cost the federal and state governments upwards of $1 billion annually in lost tax revenues and allow lucrative profits to the criminal enterprises engaged in them.[116]

There are also several "spin-off" activities from these primary crimes, most notably money-laundering, which is carried out in the United States, in Western Europe and in various states of the CIS. Counterfeiting is carried out on a massive scale, both as a primary criminal activity and as a means of establishing other criminal operations. Also, criminals from the CIS frequently forge passports, visas, birth certificates, and other forms of identification to

---

[114] Abraham Abramovsky, Prosecuting the "Russian Mafia" Recent Russian Legislation and Increased Bilateral Cooperation May Provide the Means, 37 *Virginia J. of International Law* 191, 195-96, nn. 19 & 20 (1996). Used by permission. Footnotes and other citations to sources have been omitted.

[115] *Id.*

[116] *Id.*

gain entry into the United States and to establish a legitimate American identity.

Both in the United States and Russia, Russian organized crime has been involved in counterfeiting of credit cards on a large scale. The criminal organization takes information obtained by stealing legitimate credit cards or obtaining credit receipts from corrupt retailers and encodes it onto the magnetic strip of a counterfeit credit card. One Russian credit card operation netted its Russian participants more than $500,000 per month in 1994. In another counterfeit credit card operation in 1992, counterfeit credit cards printed in Israel and embossed in the United States were sold to Russian immigrants in Brighton Beach.[117]

2. Dual Prosecution as a Substitute for Extradition

Art. 13 of the new Criminal Code provides that no citizen of the Russian Federation may be extradited to a foreign jurisdiction to answer for crimes committed abroad. Foreign nationals and stateless persons found in Russia may be extradited to a foreign country, but only pursuant to a bilateral extradition treaty, which does not exist between Russia and the United States. However, Art. 12 of the new Code provides:

> Russian citizens and stateless persons permanently residing in the Russian Federation who have committed a crime outside the Russian Federation are subject to the criminal liability provided for in this Code if the activity is [also] considered a crime in the country in which it was undertaken and if such persons have not yet been convicted in the foreign country. Upon conviction of such persons, their sentence may not exceed the upper limit of sanctions provided for in the law of the foreign country on whose territory the activity took place.[118]

Thus, a potential exists for joint cooperative prosecutions of international organized criminals in Russia if their actions violate both U.S. and Russian criminal law. So the new Russian Criminal Code's expansion of economic crimes not only modernizes Russian criminal law to allow Russian authorities to reach the "new generation" of crime in Russia, but also expands the number of crimes for which dual prosecution could be applied.

---

[117] *Id.*

[118] Art. 12(1), CrC RF. Art 12(3) provides that foreign nationals who are not permanent residents of the Russian Federation may be prosecuted in Russia for crimes committed abroad if their crimes were directed against the interests of the Russian Federation or if prosecution is provided for by an international treaty to which the Russian Federation is party.

The kind of relationship between the U.S. and Russia that results from Art. 12 and 13 is similar to the one that exists between the U.S. and Israel. Similar joint prosecutions have taken place in the U.S. and in Israel. U.S. authorities have even shared money obtained in forfeiture actions against organized criminals in the U.S. with the Israeli National Police.[119]

The experience with Israel demonstrates how it is possible to develop joint prosecutions in the absence of an extradition treaty. In order to facilitate joint prosecution, Russian and the U.S. in February 1996 entered into a Mutual Legal Assistance Agreement.[120] That agreement contemplates the parties soon concluding a mutual legal assistance treaty, but as of this writing, the treaty has not yet been concluded.

Joint prosecution is not an ideal solution, however. Unlike cases of extradition, in which U.S. prosecutors and law enforcement officials would handle the prosecutions, joint prosecution for crimes committed in the U.S. would take place in Russia and would be controlled by Russian law enforcement agencies. This poses considerable risks given the potential for corruption in Russian law enforcement and the enhanced power of the Russian mafia on its home turf.

---

[119] *Id.*

[120] St. Dep't No. 96-38 (effective Feb. 5, 1996).

APPENDIX

CONSTITUTION OF THE RUSSIAN FEDERATION

Approved by a popular referendum on December 12, 1993.
Effective date: December 25, 1993

We, the multinational people of the Russian Federation, united by a common destiny in our land, asserting human rights and freedoms, civil peace and accord, preserving the historically established state unity, proceeding from the universally recognized principles of equality and self-determination of peoples, honoring the memory of our ancestors, who have passed on to us their love of and respect for our Fatherland and their faith in goodness and justice, renewing the sovereign statehood of Russia and asserting its immutable democratic foundations, seeking to ensure the well-being and prosperity of Russia, realizing our responsibility for our Fatherland for present and future generations, considering ourselves a part of the world community, hereby approve this CONSTITUTION OF THE RUSSIAN FEDERATION.

PART ONE

Chapter 1. Fundamentals of the Constitutional System

Article 1

1. The Russian Federation - Russia shall be a democratic federal rule-of-law state with a republican form of government.

2. The names "Russian Federation" and "Russia" shall be equivalent.

Article 2

Human beings and their rights and freedoms shall be of supreme value. Recognition of, respect for and protection of the rights and freedoms of the human being and citizen shall be the duty of the state.

Article 3

1. The multinational people of the Russian Federation shall be the bearer of its sovereignty and the sole source of power in the Russian Federation.

2. The people shall exercise their power directly, and also through organs of state power and organs of local self-government.

3. Referenda and free elections shall be the supreme direct manifestation of the power of the people.

4. No one may usurp power in the Russian Federation. Seizure of power or usurpation of state authority shall be prosecuted under federal law.

Article 4

1. The sovereignty of the Russian Federation shall extend to its entire territory.

2. The Constitution of the Russian Federation and federal laws shall have supremacy throughout the entire territory of the Russian Federation.

3. The Russian Federation shall ensure the integrity and inviolability of its territory.

Article 5

1. The Russian Federation shall consist of republics, territories, regions, federal cities, autonomous regions and autonomous areas, which shall be equal subjects of the Russian Federation.

2. The republic (state) shall have its own constitution and legislation. Territories, regions, federal cities, autonomous regions and autonomous areas shall have their own charters and legislation.

3. The federal structure of the Russian Federation shall be based upon its state integrity, the unity of the system of state power, delimitation of jurisdiction and powers between the organs of state power of the Russian Federation and the organs of state power of the subjects of the Russian Federation, and equality and self-determination of the peoples within the Russian Federation.

4. All subjects of the Russian Federation shall be equal in their relationship to the federal organs of state power.

Article 6

1. Citizenship of the Russian Federation shall be acquired and terminated in accordance with federal law and shall be uniform and equal regardless of the grounds on which it has been acquired.

2. Every citizen of the Russian Federation shall have all the rights and

freedoms on its territory and shall have equal duties as provided for in the Constitution of the Russian Federation.

3. No citizen of the Russian Federation shall be deprived of citizenship or of the right to change it.

Article 7

1. The Russian Federation shall be a social state, the policies of which shall aim at creating conditions ensuring dignified life and free development of every individual.

2. The Russian Federation shall protect the work and health of its people, establish a guaranteed minimum wage, provide state support for the family, motherhood, fatherhood and childhood, and disabled and elderly citizens, develop a system of social services and establish government pensions, benefits and other social security guarantees.

Article 8

1. The Russian Federation shall comprise a single economic unit, and free movement of goods, services and financial resources, support for competition and freedom of economic activity shall be guaranteed within the Russian Federation.

2. Private, state, municipal and other forms of property ownership shall be recognized and shall enjoy equal protection in the Russian Federation.

Article 9

1. Land and other natural resources shall be used and protected in the Russian Federation as the foundation of life and activity of the peoples living on the respective territory.

2. Land and other natural resources may be subject to private, state, municipal and other forms of ownership.

Article 10

State power in the Russian Federation shall be exercised on the basis of separation of the legislative, executive and judicial branches. The organs of legislative, executive and judicial power shall be independent.

Article 11

1. State power in the Russian Federation shall be exercised by the President of the Russian Federation, the Federal Assembly (Federation Council and State Duma), the Government of the Russian Federation and the courts of the Russian Federation.

2. State power in the subjects of the Russian Federation shall be exercised by the organs of state power established by them.

3. The jurisdiction and powers of the organs of state power of the Russian Federation and the organs of state power of the subjects of the Russian Federation shall be delineated by this Constitution, the Federal Treaty and other treaties on the delineation of jurisdiction and powers.

Article 12

Local self-government shall be recognized and guaranteed in the Russian Federation. Local self-government shall operate independently within the limits of its authority. Organs of local self-government shall not be part of the system of the organs of state power.

Article 13

1. Ideological pluralism shall be recognized in the Russian Federation.

2. No ideology shall be instituted as the official or mandatory ideology.

3. Political diversity and a multi-party system shall be recognized in the Russian Federation.

4. Public associations shall be equal before the law.

5. The establishment and the activities of public associations, whose aims or actions are directed at forcible alteration of the fundamentals of the constitutional system and disruption of the integrity of the Russian Federation, undermining of the security of the state, the forming of armed units, the incitement of social, racial, national or religious strife shall be prohibited.

Article 14

1. The Russian Federation shall be a secular state. No religion shall be instituted as the official or mandatory religion.

2. Religious associations shall exist separately from the state, and shall be equal before the law.

Article 15

1. The Constitution of the Russian Federation shall have supreme legal force and direct effect, and shall be applicable throughout the entire territory of the Russian Federation. Laws and other legislative acts adopted within the Russian Federation may not contravene the Constitution of the Russian Federation.

2. Organs of state power and organs of local self-government, officials, citizens and their associations shall abide by the Constitution of the Russian Federation and the laws.

3. The laws shall be officially published. Unpublished laws shall not be applicable. No normative legal act affecting the rights, freedoms or duties of the human being and citizen shall be effective if it has not been published officially for general knowledge.

4. The generally recognized principles and norms of international law and the international treaties of the Russian Federation shall constitute an integral part of its legal system. If an international treaty of the Russian Federation establishes rules other than those established by the law, the rules of the international treaty shall apply.

Article 16

1. The provisions of the present Chapter of the Constitution shall constitute the fundamentals of the constitutional system of the Russian Federation and may not be changed except in accordance with the procedure established by this Constitution.

2. No other provisions of this Constitution shall contravene the fundamentals of the constitutional system of the Russian Federation.

Chapter 2. Rights and Freedoms of the Human Being and Citizen

Article 17

1. The rights and freedoms of the human being and citizen shall be recognized and guaranteed in the Russian Federation in conformity with the generally recognized principles and norms of international law and in accordance with this Constitution.

2. Fundamental human rights and freedoms shall be inalienable and shall belong to everyone from birth.

3. The exercise of rights and freedoms of the human being and citizen may not infringe on the rights and freedoms of other persons.

Article 18

The rights and freedoms of the human being and citizen shall have direct effect. They shall determine the meaning, content and application of the laws, the activities of the legislative and executive branches and local self-government and shall be enforced by the judiciary.

Article 19

1. All persons shall be equal before the law and court of law.

2. The state shall guarantee the equality of rights and freedoms of the human being and citizen without regard to sex, race, nationality, language, origin, property or employment status, place of residence, attitude toward religion, beliefs, affiliation with public associations or other circumstances. Any forms of restriction of the rights of citizens on the basis of social, racial, national, linguistic or religious affiliation shall be prohibited.

3. Men and women shall have equal rights and freedoms and equal opportunities to exercise them.

Article 20

1. Everyone shall have the right to life.

2. The death penalty, until its abolition, may be provided for by federal law as an exceptional penalty for particularly grave crimes against life, so long as the accused is given the right to have her or his case tried before a jury.

Article 21

1. The dignity of the individual shall be protected by the state. Nothing may serve as a justification for its diminution.

2. No one shall be subjected to torture, violence or other cruel or degrading treatment or punishment. No one may be subjected to medical, scientific or other experiments without his or her free consent.

Article 22

1. Everyone shall have the right to freedom and personal security.

2. Arrest, detention and custodial confinement shall only be permitted

pursuant to a judicial order. Absent such a judicial order, no person may be detained for more than 48 hours.

Article 23

1. Everyone shall have the right to privacy, to the protection of personal and family confidences, and to the protection of one's honor and reputation.

2. Everyone shall have the right to privacy of correspondence, telephone conversations, postal, telegraph and other messages. Restrictions of this right shall be permitted only pursuant to a judicial order.

Article 24

1. The gathering, storage, use and dissemination of information concerning the private life of an individual without the individual's consent shall not be allowed.

2. The organs of state power and the organs of local self-government and their officials shall be obligated to provide each person with access to documents and materials that directly affect his or her rights and freedoms, unless otherwise specified by the law.

Article 25

The home shall be inviolate. No one shall have the right to enter any home against the will of the occupant, except in cases determined by federal law or pursuant to a judicial order.

Article 26

1. Everyone shall have the right to determine and indicate his or her national identity. No one may be forced to determine or indicate his or her national identity.

2. Everyone shall have the right to use his or her native language, freely choose the language of communication, upbringing of children, education and artistic creation.

Article 27

1. Everyone who is lawfully within the territory of the Russian Federation shall have the right to freedom of movement and the right to freely choose a place of temporary or permanent residence.

2. Everyone shall be free to leave the territory of the Russian Federation. A citizen of the Russian Federation shall have the right to freely return to the Russian Federation.

Article 28

Everyone shall be guaranteed the right to freedom of conscience and freedom of religion, including the right to profess, individually or jointly with others, any religion or to profess none, to freely choose, have and disseminate religious and other beliefs, and to act in conformity with them.

Article 29

1. Everyone shall be guaranteed freedom of thought and speech.

2. Propaganda or agitation inciting social, racial, national or religious hatred or enmity shall not be allowed. The propaganda advocating social, racial, national, religious or language superiority shall be prohibited.

3. No one may be forced either to express his or her opinions and convictions or to renounce them.

4. Everyone shall have the right to freely seek, receive, transmit, produce and disseminate information in any lawful way. The list of information that constitute state secrets shall be established by federal law.

5. Freedom of the mass media shall be guaranteed. Censorship shall be prohibited.

Article 30

1. Everyone shall have the right to association, including the right to establish trade unions in order to protect one's interests. Freedom of activity of public associations shall be guaranteed.

2. No one may be forced to join or maintain membership in any association.

Article 31

Citizens of the Russian Federation shall have the right to assemble peacefully without arms and to hold meetings, rallies, demonstrations, marches and pickets.

Article 32

1. Citizens of the Russian Federation shall have the right to participate in the

administration of the affairs of the state both directly and through their representatives.

2. Citizens of the Russian Federation shall have the right to elect and to be elected to organs of state power and organs of local self-government, and to participate in referenda.

3. Citizens who have been found by a court to be under special disability as well as citizens held in places of detention under a court sentence shall not have the right to vote or to be elected.

4. Citizens of the Russian Federation shall have equal access to public employment.

5. Citizens of the Russian Federation shall have the right to participate in the administration of justice.

Article 33

Citizens of the Russian Federation shall have the right to appeal personally and to send individual and group appeals to state organs and organs of local self-government.

Article 34

1. Everyone shall have the right to freely use his or her abilities and property for entrepreneurial or any other economic activity not prohibited by the law.

2. No economic activity aimed at monopolization or unfair competition shall be allowed.

Article 35

1. The right of private ownership shall be protected by law.

2. Everyone shall have the right to own property and to possess, use and dispose of it both individually and jointly with other persons.

3. No one may be deprived of his or her property except pursuant to a judicial decision. Property may be forcibly taken for state needs only if prior compensation equal to the value of such property is provided.

4. The right of inheritance shall be guaranteed.

Article 36

1. Citizens and their associations shall have the right to hold land in private ownership.

2. Owners may freely possess, use and dispose of land and other natural resources, unless such actions cause damage to the environment or infringe on the rights and legitimate interests of other persons.

3. The conditions of and procedures for land use shall be determined by federal law.

Article 37

1. Labor shall be free. Everyone shall have the right to make free use of his or her abilities to work and to choose his or her occupation or profession.

2. Compulsory labor is prohibited.

3. Everyone shall have the right to work in conditions of safety and hygiene and to receive remuneration for labor without any form of discrimination and in an amount at least equal to the minimum wage established by federal law, and shall also enjoy the right to protection against unemployment.

4. The right to engage in individual and collective labor disputes through the use of means for their resolution specified by federal law for their resolution, including the right to strike, shall be recognized.

5. Everyone shall have the right to rest and leisure. A person working under a labor contract shall be guaranteed the length of working time, days off, holidays, and paid annual vacation time established by federal law.

Article 38

1. Motherhood and childhood, and the family shall be under state protection.

2. The care of children and their upbringing shall be the equal right and duty of parents.

3. Employable children who have reached the age of 18 years shall take care of parents who are unable to work.

Article 39

1. Everyone shall be guaranteed social security in old age, in the event of

sickness, disability or loss of a breadwinner, for the raising of children and in other cases specified by law.

2. State pensions and social benefits shall be established by law.

3. Voluntary social insurance, the development of additional forms of social security and charity shall be encouraged.

Article 40

1. Everyone shall have the right to a home. No one may be arbitrarily deprived of a home.

2. State organs and organs of local self-government shall encourage housing construction and create the conditions essential for the realization of the right to a home.

3. Low-income citizens and other citizens as defined by law, who are in need of housing, shall be housed free or at a reduced rate in state, municipal or other housing in accordance with the law.

Article 41

1. Everyone shall have the right to health care and medical assistance. Medical assistance in state and municipal health care institutions shall be provided to citizens free of charge out of the resources of the appropriate budget, insurance payments and other revenues.

2. The Russian Federation shall finance federal programs for the protection and improvement of the health of the population and take measures to promote state, municipal and private health care systems, and activities contributing to the strengthening of the health of the individual, to the development of physical culture and sports, and to the prevention of environmental, hygienic and epidemiological threats to well-being shall be encouraged.

3. The withholding by officials of facts and circumstances that pose a threat to human life or health shall result in liability in accordance with federal law.

Article 42

Everyone shall have the right to a favorable environment, reliable information on its condition and to compensation for damage caused to his or her health or property by violations of environmental laws.

Article 43

1. Everyone shall have the right to education.

2. Pre-school, elementary, secondary and vocational education in state or municipal educational institutions and at enterprises shall be guaranteed to be accessible to all citizens free of charge.

3. Everyone shall have the right to receive, free of charge and on a competitive basis, higher education in a state or municipal educational institution or at an enterprise.

4. Elementary and secondary education shall be compulsory. Parents or guardians shall ensure that their children obtain a basic general education.

5. The Russian Federation shall establish official federal state educational standards and shall support various forms of education and self-education.

Article 44

1. Everyone shall be guaranteed freedom of literary, artistic, scientific, technical and other types of creative work and teaching. Intellectual property shall be protected by law.

2. Everyone shall have the right to participate in cultural life, to use institutions of culture, and to be exposed to cultural values.

3. Everyone shall be obliged to care for the preservation of historical and cultural heritage and to cherish historical and cultural monuments.

Article 45

1. State protection for the rights and freedoms of the human being and citizen in the Russian Federation shall be guaranteed.

2. Everyone shall have the right to defend his or her rights and freedoms by any means not prohibited by law.

Article 46

1. Everyone shall be guaranteed protection of his or her rights and freedoms in a court of law.

2. Decisions and actions (or inaction) of state organs, organs of local self-government, public associations and officials may be appealed to a court of law.

3. Everyone shall have the right, in accordance with international treaties of the Russian Federation, to apply to international organs concerned with the protection of human rights and freedoms if all available domestic legal remedies have been exhausted.

Article 47

1. No one may be deprived of the right to have his or her case examined by the court and judge under whose jurisdiction the given case falls according to the law.

2. Anyone accused of committing a crime shall have the right to have his or her case tried by a jury in the categories of cases provided for by federal law.

Article 48

1. Everyone shall be guaranteed the right to qualified legal assistance. Legal assistance shall be provided free of charge in cases specified by law.

2. Every arrestee or detainee and the accused in a criminal case shall have the right to utilize the assistance of an advocate (defender) from the moment of arrest, detention or indictment, whichever comes first.

Article 49

1. Everyone accused of committing a crime shall be presumed innocent until his or her guilt has been proved in accordance with the procedure specified by federal law and has been established by final judgment of a court.

2. The defendant shall not be obliged to prove his or her innocence.

3. Remaining doubts about guilt shall be construed in favor of the defendant.

Article 50

1. No one may be convicted twice for the same crime.

2. In the administration of justice, evidence obtained in violation of federal law shall not be admissible.

3. Everyone convicted of a crime shall have the right to have the sentence reviewed by a higher court in accordance with the procedure established by federal law, and shall also have the right to seek pardon or reduction of a sentence.

Article 51

1. No one shall be obliged to testify against himself or herself, or against his or her spouse and close relatives as specified by federal law.

2. Federal law may establish other exemptions from the duty to give testimony.

Article 52

The rights of victims of crimes or abuses of power shall by protected by law. The state shall guarantee victims access to justice and compensation for damage inflicted.

Article 53

Everyone shall have the right to compensation by the state for harm caused by unlawful actions (or inaction) of its organs or its officials.

Article 54

1. Any law that establishes or increases liability shall not have retroactive effect.

2. No one may be held liable for any act which was not recognized as a violation of law at the time of its commission. If liability for a violation of the law was abolished or lessened after that violation was committed, the new law shall apply.

Article 55

1. The enumeration of fundamental rights and freedoms in the Constitution of the Russian Federation shall not be interpreted to deny or diminish other generally recognized rights and freedoms of the human being and citizen.

2. No laws denying or diminishing the rights and freedoms of the human being and citizen may be issued in the Russian Federation.

3. The rights and freedoms of the human being and citizen may be restricted by federal law only to the extent required for the protection of the fundamentals of the constitutional system, morality, health, rights and lawful interests of other persons, or for ensuring the defense of the country and the security of the state.

Article 56

1. Specific restrictions on rights and freedoms, with an indication of the scope

and duration of their operation, may be imposed during a state of emergency to ensure the safety of citizens and protection of the constitutional system in accordance with a federal constitutional law.

2. A state of emergency throughout the territory of the Russian Federation and in its individual areas may be declared under the circumstances and in the manner established by a federal constitutional law.

3. The rights and freedoms specified in Articles 20, 21, 23 (Part 1), 24, 28, 34 (Part 1), 40 (Part 1) and 46-54 of the Constitution of the Russian Federation shall not be subject to any restriction.

Article 57

Everyone shall pay lawfully instituted taxes and levies. Laws that impose new taxes or negatively affect the position of taxpayers shall not have retroactive effect.

Article 58

Everyone shall be obligated to protect nature and the environment and to treat natural resources with care.

Article 59

1. Defense of the Fatherland shall be a duty and responsibility of all citizens of the Russian Federation.

2. All citizens of the Russian Federation shall perform military service in accordance with federal law.

3. In cases where the performance of military service runs counter to a citizen's persuasions or religion, and also in other cases specified by federal law, a citizen of the Russian Federation shall have the right to substitute alternative civilian service for military service.

Article 60

A citizen of the Russian Federation may independently exercise his or her rights and duties in full upon reaching the age of 18.

Article 61

1. A citizen of the Russian Federation may not be deported from the Russian Federation or extradited to another country.

2. The Russian Federation shall guarantee its citizens defense and protection outside its boundaries.

Article 62

1. Citizens of the Russian Federation may have foreign citizenship (dual citizenship) in conformity with federal law or international treaty of the Russian Federation.

2. A citizen of the Russian Federation who has foreign citizenship shall not suffer any diminution of his or her rights or freedoms and shall not be released from duties arising from Russian citizenship, unless otherwise specified by federal law or an international treaty of the Russian Federation.

3. Foreign citizens and stateless persons in the Russian Federation shall enjoy the rights of its citizens and bear responsibilities on an equal basis with the citizens of the Russian Federation, except in cases specified by federal law or an international treaty of the Russian Federation.

Article 63

1. The Russian Federation shall grant political asylum to foreign citizens and stateless persons in conformity with the generally recognized norms of international law.

2. Extradition to other countries of persons persecuted for their political views or for actions (or omissions) which are not recognized as a crime in the Russian Federation shall not be allowed in the Russian Federation. The extradition of persons accused of commiting a crime and the transfer of convicts to other countries to serve their sentences shall be effected on the basis of federal law or international treaty of the Russian Federation.

Article 64

The provisions of this Chapter shall form the basis for the legal status of the individual in the Russian Federation and may not be changed except in conformity with the procedure established by this Constitution.

Chapter 3. Federal Structure

Article 65

1. The Russian Federation shall consist of the subjects of the Russian Federation:

the Republic of Adygeya (Adygeya), the Republic of Altai, the Republic of Bashkortostan, the Republic of Buryatia, the Republic of Daghestan, the Ingush Republic, the Kabardin-Balkar Republic, the Republic of Kalmykia - Khalmg Tangch, the Karachai-Chircassian Republic, the Republic of Karelia, the Republic of Komi, the Republic of Marii El, the Republic of Mordova, the Republic of Sakha (Yakutia), the Republic of North Ossetia, the Republic of Tatarstan (Tatarstan), the Republic of Tuva, the Udmurtian Republic, the Republic of Khakassia, the Chechen Republic, the Chuvash Republic - Chavash Republic;

The Altai Territory, the Krasnodar Territory, the Krasnoyarsk Territory, the Maritime Territory, the Stavropol Territory, the Khabarovsk Territory;

The Amur Region, the Arkhangelsk Region, the Astrakhan Region, the Belgorod Region, the Bryansk Region, the Vladimir Region, the Volgograd Region, the Vologda Region, the Voronezh Region, the Ivanovo Region, the Irkutsk Region, the Kaliningrad Region, the Kaluga Region, the Kamchatka Region, the Kemerovo Region, the Kirov Region, the Kostroma Region, the Kurgan Region, the Kursk Region, the Leningrad Region, the Lipetsk Region, the Magadan Region, the Moscow Region, the Murmansk Region, the Nizhny Novgorod Region, the Novgorod Region, the Novosibirsk Region, the Omsk Region, the Orenburg Region, the Oryol Region, the Penza Region, the Perm Region, the Pskov Region, the Rostov Region, the Ryazan Region, the Samara Region, the Saratov Region, the Sakhalin Region, the Sverdlovsk Region, the Smolensk Region, the Tambov Region, the Tver Region, the Tomsk Region, the Tula Region, the Tyumen Region, the Ulyanovsk Region, the Chelyabinsk Region, the Chita Region, the Yaroslavl Region;

Moscow, St. Petersburg - federal cities;

the Jewish Autonomous Region;

the Aga Buryat Autonomous Area, the Komi-Permyak Autonomous Area, the Koryak Autonomous Area, the Nenets Autonomous Area, the Taimyr (Dolgan-Nenets) Autonomous Area, the Ust-Orda Buryat Autonomous Area, the Khanty-Mansi Autonomous Area, the Chukchi Autonomous Area, the Evenk Autonomous Area, the Yamal-Nenets Autonomous Area.

2. Admission to the Russian Federation and the incorporation within it of a new subject shall be performed in the manner specified by federal constitutional law.

Article 66

1. The status of a republic shall be defined by the Constitution of the Russian Federation and the constitution of the republic.

2. The status of a territory, region, federal city, autonomous region and autonomous area shall be defined by the Constitution of the Russian Federation and the charter of the territory, region, federal city, autonomous region or autonomous area adopted by the legislative (representative) organ of the relevant subject of the Russian Federation.

3. A federal law on the autonomous region or autonomous area may be adopted upon the initiative of the legislative and executive organs of an autonomous region or autonomous area.

4. The relations of autonomous areas that form part of a territory or region may be governed by federal law and a treaty between the organs of state power of the autonomous area and, the organs of state power of the territory or region respectively.

5. The status of a subject of the Russian Federation may be changed by the mutual consent of the Russian Federation and the subject of the Russian Federation in accordance with a federal constitutional law.

Article 67

1. The territory of the Russian Federation shall comprise the territories of its subjects, the internal waters and the territorial sea, and the airspace above them.

2. The Russian Federation shall have sovereign rights and exercise jurisdiction on the continental shelf and in the exclusive economic zone of the Russian Federation in the manner specified by federal law and the rules of international law.

3. The boundaries between the subjects of the Russian Federation may be changed by mutual consent.

Article 68

1. The official language of the Russian Federation throughout its territory shall be the Russian language.

2. The republics shall have the right to establish their own official languages. They shall be used alongside the state language of the Russian Federation in

the organs of state power, organs of local self-government and the state institutions of the republics.

3. The Russian Federation shall guarantee all its peoples the right to preserve their native tongue and to create the conditions for its study and development.

Article 69

The Russian Federation shall guarantee the rights of small indigenous peoples in accordance with the generally recognized principles and rules of international law and international treaties of the Russian Federation.

Article 70

1. The state flag, emblem and national anthem of the Russian Federation, their description and manner of official use shall be established by a federal constitutional law.

2. The capital of the Russian Federation shall be the city of Moscow. The status of the capital shall be established by a federal law.

Article 71

The Russian Federation shall have jurisdiction over:

a) the adoption and amendment of the Constitution of the Russian Federation and federal laws and supervision of their observance;

b) the federal structure and territory of the Russian Federation;

c) the regulation and protection of the rights and freedoms of the human being and the citizen; citizenship of the Russian Federation; the regulation and protection of the rights of national minorities;

d) the establishment of a system of federal organs of legislative, executive and judicial power, the manner of their organization and operation; the formation of federal organs of state power;

e) federal state property and the management thereof;

f) the establishment of the basic principles of federal policy and federal programs in the area of state, economic, ecological, social, cultural and national development of the Russian Federation;

g) the establishment of the basic legal principles of a single market; financial, currency, credit and customs regulation, issuance of money, the basic principles of pricing policy; and federal economic services, including federal banks;

h) the federal budget; federal taxes and levies; federal funds for regional development;

i) federal energy systems, nuclear energy, fissionable materials; federal transport, railways, information and communications; space activities;

j) foreign policy and international relations of the Russian Federation, international treaties of the Russian Federation; questions of war and peace;

k) the external economic relations of the Russian Federation;

l) defense and security; defense industry; determination of the procedures for the sale and purchase of arms, ammunition, military equipment and other military hardware; production of toxic substances, narcotics and procedures for their use;

m) the determination of the status and defense of the state border, the territorial sea, airspace, exclusive economic zone and continental shelf of the Russian Federation;

n) the organization of courts; the Procuracy; criminal, criminal-procedural and criminal-executive legislation; amnesty and pardon; civil, civil-procedural and arbitration-procedural legislation; the legal regulation of intellectual property;

o) federal conflict of laws;

p) the meteorological service, standards, the metric system and time measurement; geodesy and cartography; names of geographic objects; official statistics and bookkeeping systems and procedures;

q) state awards and honorary titles of the Russian Federation;

r) the federal civil service.

Article 72

1. The joint jurisdiction of the Russian Federation and the subjects of the Russian Federation shall comprise:

a) ensuring the conformity of the constitutions and laws of the republics, the charters, laws and other normative legal acts of territories, regions, federal cities, the autonomous region and autonomous areas to the Constitution of the Russian Federation and federal laws;

b) protecting the rights and freedoms of the human being and the citizen; protecting the rights of national minorities; ensuring legality, law and order, and public security; the regime of border zones;

c) issues of the possession, use and disposal of land, subsurface resources, water and other natural resources;

d) the delimitation of state property;

e) the use of natural resources; protection of the environment and ensuring ecological security; specially protected natural reserves; the protection of historic and cultural monuments;

f) general questions of upbringing, education, science, culture, physical education and sports;

g) coordination of health care issues, protection of the family, motherhood, fatherhood and childhood; social protection, including social security;

h) the implementation of measures to cope with catastrophes, natural disasters, epidemics and the elimination of their consequences;

I) the establishment of general principles of taxation and levies in the Russian Federation;

j) administrative, administrative-procedural, labor, family, housing, land, water and forest legislation; legislation on the subsurface resources and on environmental protection;

k) personnel of judiciary and law enforcement agencies; the Advokatura and the Notariat;

l) the protection of the original environment and the traditional way of life of small ethnic communities;

m) the establishment of general principles of the organization of the system of organs of state power and local self-government;

n) the coordination of the international and external economic relations of the subjects of the Russian Federation, the compliance with the international treaties of the Russian Federation.

2. The provisions of this article shall apply equally to republics, territories, regions, federal cities, the autonomous region, and autonomous areas.

Article 73

The subjects of the Russian Federation shall enjoy full state power outside the limits of the jurisdiction of the Russian Federation and the powers of the Russian Federation on issues within the joint jurisdiction of the Russian Federation and the subjects of the Russian Federation.

Article 74

1. The establishment of customs frontiers, duties, levies or any other barriers to the free movement of goods, services and financial resources shall not be allowed within the territory of the Russian Federation.

2. Restrictions on the movement of goods and services may be imposed in accordance with federal law if it is necessary for ensuring the security, protection of life and health of people, the protection of the environment and cultural values.

Article 75

1. The monetary unit of the Russian Federation shall be the rouble. Issuance of money shall be carried out exclusively by the Central Bank of the Russian Federation. The introduction and issue of other money in the Russian Federation shall not be allowed.

2. Protecting and ensuring the stability of the rouble shall be the principal function of the Central Bank of the Russian Federation, which it shall discharge independently from other organs of state power.

3. The system of taxes to be collected for the federal budget and the general principles of taxation and levies in the Russian Federation shall be established by federal law.

4. State loans shall be issued in accordance with the procedure established by federal law and shall be administered on a voluntary basis.

Article 76

1. On issues within the jurisdiction of the Russian Federation, federal constitutional laws and federal laws shall be adopted which shall have direct effect throughout the entire territory of the Russian Federation.

2. On matters within the joint jurisdiction of the Russian Federation and the subjects of the Russian Federation, federal laws shall be adopted and, pursuant to them, laws and other normative legal acts of the subjects of the Russian Federation shall be adopted.

3. Federal laws may not contravene federal constitutional laws.

4. Outside of the jurisdiction of the Russian Federation and the joint jurisdiction of the Russian Federation and the subjects of the Russian Federation, republics, territories, regions, federal cities, the autonomous region and autonomous areas shall effect their own legal regulation, including the adoption of laws and other normative legal acts.

5. Laws and other normative legal acts of the subjects of the Russian Federation may not contravene federal laws adopted in accordance with parts one and two of this Article. In the case of conflict between a federal law and another act adopted in the Russian Federation, the federal law shall apply.

6. In the case of conflict between a federal law and a normative legal act of a subject of the Russian Federation issued in accordance with part four of this Article, the normative legal act of the subject of the Russian Federation shall apply.

Article 77

1. The system of organs of state power of republics, territories, regions, federal cities, the autonomous region, and autonomous areas shall be established by the subjects of the Russian Federation independently in accordance with the fundamentals of the constitutional system of the Russian Federation and the general principles of organization of the representative and executive organs of state power as envisioned by a federal law.

2. Within the jurisdiction of the Russian Federation and the powers of the Russian Federation on issues within the joint jurisdiction of the Russian Federation and the subjects of the Russian Federation, the federal organs of executive power and the organs of executive power of the subjects of the Russian Federation shall form a unified system of executive power in the Russian Federation.

Article 78

1. Federal organs of executive power may, in order to exercise their powers, establish their own territorial organs and appoint appropriate officials.

2. Federal organs of executive power may, by agreement with the organs of

executive power of the subjects of the Russian Federation, delegate to them part of their powers, provided this does not contravene the Constitution of the Russian Federation and federal laws.

3. Organs of executive power of the subjects of the Russian Federation may, by agreement with federal organs of executive power, delegate part of their powers to the latter.

4. The President of the Russian Federation and the Government of the Russian Federation shall ensure, in accordance with the Constitution of the Russian Federation, the exercise of federal state authority throughout the territory of the Russian Federation.

Article 79

The Russian Federation may participate in inter-state associations and delegate some of its powers to them in accordance with international treaties if this does not restrict the rights and freedoms of the human being and citizen and does not contravene the fundamentals of the constitutional system of the Russian Federation.

Chapter 4. The President of the Russian Federation

Article 80

1. The President of the Russian Federation shall be head of state.

2. The President of the Russian Federation shall be the guarantor of the Constitution of the Russian Federation and the rights and freedoms of the human being and citizen. In accordance with the procedure established by the Constitution of the Russian Federation, the President shall take measures to protect the sovereignty, independence and state integrity of the Russian Federation and ensure the coordinated functioning and interaction of the organs of state power.

3. The President of the Russian Federation, in accordance with the Constitution of the Russian Federation and federal laws, shall determine guidelines for the domestic and foreign policy of the state.

4. The President of the Russian Federation, as head of state, shall represent the Russian Federation domestically and in international relations.

Article 81

1. The President of the Russian Federation shall be elected to office for a term

of four years by the citizens of the Russian Federation on the basis of general, equal and direct vote by secret ballot.

2. A citizen of the Russian Federation not younger than 35, who has resided in the Russian Federation for not less than 10 years, shall be eligible for the office of President of the Russian Federation.

3. The same individual shall not be elected to the office of President of the Russian Federation for more than two consecutive terms.

4. The procedure for electing the President of the Russian Federation shall be determined by federal law.

Article 82

1. At his or her inauguration, the President of the Russian Federation shall take the following oath to the people:

> "I solemnly swear that in executing the powers of the President of the Russian Federation I will respect and protect the rights and freedoms of the human being and citizen, observe and protect the Constitution of the Russian Federation, protect the sovereignty, independence, security and integrity of the country and faithfully serve its people."

2. The oath shall be taken in a solemn atmosphere in the presence of the members of the Federation Council, deputies of the State Duma and judges of the Constitutional Court of the Russian Federation.

Article 83

The President of the Russian Federation shall:

a) appoint, with the consent of the State Duma, the Chairman of the Government of the Russian Federation;

b) have the right to preside over meetings of the Government of the Russian Federation;

c) accept the resignation of the Government of the Russian Federation;

d) nominate for approval by the State Duma the Chairman of the Central Bank of the Russian Federation; bring before the State Duma the issue of removing the Chairman of the Central Bank of the Russian Federation from office;

e) appoint, based on proposals by the Chairman of the Government of the Russian Federation, Deputy Chairmen of the Government of the Russian Federation and federal ministers and remove them from office;

f) nominate judges of the Constitutional Court of the Russian Federation, the Supreme Court of the Russian Federation and the Supreme Arbitration Court of the Russian Federation, as well as the Procurator-General of the Russian Federation for appointment by the Federation Council; submit to the Federation Council a proposal for the dismissal of the Procurator-General of the Russian Federation; appoint judges to other federal courts;

g) form and chair the Security Council of the Russian Federation, the status of which shall be defined by federal law;

h) approve the military policy of the Russian Federation;

i) form the Executive Office (Administration) of the President of the Russian Federation;

j) appoint and dismiss the plenipotentiary representatives of the President of the Russian Federation;

k) appoint and dismiss the top commanders of the Armed Forces of the Russian Federation;

l) appoint and recall, after consultations with the respective committees or commissions of the chambers of the Federal Assembly, diplomatic representatives of the Russian Federation in foreign countries and international organizations.

Article 84

The President of the Russian Federation shall:

a) call elections to the State Duma in accordance with the Constitution of the Russian Federation and federal law;

b) dissolve the State Duma in cases and in accordance with procedures stipulated by the Constitution of the Russian Federation;

c) call a referendum in accordance with procedures stipulated by federal constitutional law;

d) submit draft laws to the State Duma;

e) sign and publish federal laws;

f) deliver to the Federal Assembly an annual state of the nation message and a message on guidelines for the domestic and foreign policies of the state.

Article 85

1. The President of the Russian Federation may use mediation procedures to settle differences between organs of state power of the Russian Federation and the organs of state power of the subjects of the Russian Federation, as well as between the organs of state power of the subjects of the Russian Federation. If no agreement is achieved, he or she may submit the dispute for resolution to the appropriate court.

2. The President of the Russian Federation shall have the right to suspend the acts of organs of executive power of the subjects of the Russian Federation if such acts contravene the Constitution of the Russian Federation, federal laws, or the international obligations of the Russian Federation, or if they violate the rights and freedoms of the human being and citizen, pending the resolution of the matter by the appropriate court.

Article 86

The President of the Russian Federation shall:

a) direct the conduct of the foreign policy of the Russian Federation;

b) conduct negotiations and sign international treaties of the Russian Federation;

c) sign instruments of ratification;

d) accept the credentials and instruments of recall of the diplomatic representatives accredited to his or her office.

Article 87

1. The President of the Russian Federation shall be Supreme Commander-in-Chief of the Armed Forces of the Russian Federation.

2. In the event of aggression against the Russian Federation or an imminent threat of aggression, the President of the Russian Federation shall introduce martial law on the territory of the Russian Federation or portions thereof and immediately inform the Federation Council and the State Duma of this action.

3. The regime of martial law shall be determined by federal constitutional law.

Article 88

The President of the Russian Federation shall, under the circumstances and in accordance with the procedure stipulated by federal constitutional law, declare a state of emergency on the territory of the Russian Federation or portions thereof and immediately inform the Federation Council and the State Duma of this action.

Article 89

The President of the Russian Federation shall:

a) decide questions of citizenship of the Russian Federation and of the granting of political asylum;

b) confer state awards of the Russian Federation, honorary titles of the Russian Federation and top military and special titles;

c) grant pardons.

Article 90

1. The President of the Russian Federation shall issue decrees and executive orders.

2. The decrees and orders of the President of the Russian Federation shall be binding throughout the territory of the Russian Federation.

3. The decrees and orders of the President of the Russian Federation may not contravene the Constitution of the Russian Federation and federal laws.

Article 91

The President of the Russian Federation shall have immunity.

Article 92

1. The President of the Russian Federation shall commence executing the powers of the President from the moment of taking the oath of office and shall cease the execution of the powers of the President when his or her term expires and the newly elected President of the Russian Federation takes the oath.

2. The President of the Russian Federation shall cease the execution of the powers of the President before their expiration in cases of resignation, continued inability to discharge the powers of the office for reasons of health or removal from office by impeachment. In such cases, new elections of the

President shall be held no later than three months after the early termination of the execution of the office.

3. In all cases when the President of the Russian Federation shall be unable to execute the powers of the President, they shall be temporarily performed by the Chairman of the Government of the Russian Federation. The acting President of the Russian Federation shall have no right to dissolve the State Duma, call a referendum or submit proposals on amendments to the Constitution of the Russian Federation or revisions of its provisions.

Article 93

1. The President of the Russian Federation may only be removed from office by the Federation Council on the grounds of charges of high treason or other serious crime brought by the State Duma, provided the Supreme Court of the Russian Federation confirms that the President's actions are criminal and the Constitutional Court of the Russian Federation confirms that the established procedure for the bringing of charges has been observed.

2. The decision of the State Duma to bring charges and the decision of the Federation Council to remove the President from office shall be passed by two-thirds of the votes of the total number of deputies in each chamber on the initiative of at least one-third of the deputies of State Duma, provided there is a corresponding conclusion by a special commission formed by the State Duma.

3. The decision of the Federation Council to remove the President of the Russian Federation from office shall be adopted no later than three months after the State Duma brings its charges against the President. If the Federation Council fails to adopt such a decision by this deadline, the charges against the President shall be considered dismissed.

Chapter 5. The Federal Assembly

Article 94

The Federal Assembly - the Parliament of the Russian Federation - shall be the representative and legislative organ of the Russian Federation.

Article 95

1. The Federal Assembly shall consist of two chambers - the Federation Council and the State Duma.

2. The Federation Council shall be composed of two representatives from each

subject of the Russian Federation - one from its representative and one from its executive organ of state power.

3. The State Duma shall be composed of 450 deputies.

Article 96

1. The State Duma shall be elected for a term of four years.

2. The procedure for forming the Federation Council and the procedure for electing the deputies of the State Duma shall be determined by federal law.

Article 97

1. Any citizen of the Russian Federation who has attained the age of 21 and is qualified to vote may be elected deputy to the State Duma.

2. The same individual may not be a member of the Federation Council and a deputy of the State Duma simultaneously. A deputy of the State Duma may not be a deputy of any other representative organs of state power or organs of local self-government.

3. The deputies of the State Duma shall work on a professional permanent basis. The deputies of the State Duma may not hold any government office or engage in any activities for remuneration other than teaching, research or other creative activities.

Article 98

1. The members of the Federation Council and deputies of the State Duma shall have immunity during the entire term of their office. They may not be detained, arrested and searched except when caught in the act of perpetrating a crime, and may not be subject to personal search except when such search is authorized by federal law to ensure the safety of other people.

2. The question of lifting immunity shall be decided by the corresponding chamber of the Federal Assembly on the presentation of the Procurator-General of the Russian Federation.

Article 99

1. The Federal Assembly shall be a permanently working body.

2. The State Duma shall be convened for its first session on the thirtieth day after its election. The President of the Russian Federation may convene a session of the State Duma at an earlier date.

3. The first session of the State Duma shall be opened by the eldest deputy.

4. The powers of the previous State Duma shall end the moment the new State Duma begins its work.

Article 100

1. The Federation Council and the State Duma shall sit separately.

2. The sessions of the Federation Council and the State Duma shall be public. In cases defined by the rules of procedure of a chamber, it may hold closed sessions.

3. The chambers may hold joint sessions to hear the addresses of the President of the Russian Federation, addresses of the Constitutional Court of the Russian Federation and statements by the leaders of foreign states.

Article 101

1. The Federation Council shall elect the Chairman and Deputy Chairmen of the Federation Council from among its members. The State Duma shall elect the Chairman and Deputy Chairmen of the State Duma from among its deputies.

2. The Chairman of the Federation Council and his or her deputies, the Chairman of the State Duma and his or her deputies shall preside over the sessions and supervise the observance of the internal rules governing the activities of the chambers.

3. The Federation Council and the State Duma shall form committees and commissions and hold hearings on the issues within their respective terms of reference.

4. Each chamber shall adopt its own rules of procedure and decide matters pertaining to the regulation of its activities.

5. To supervise the execution of the federal budget, the Federation Council and the State Duma shall form an Accounting Chamber. Its composition and procedure of work shall be determined by federal law.

Article 102

1. The Federation Council shall have power over:

a) approval of changes of borders between the subjects of the Russian Federation;

b) approval of the decree of the President of the Russian Federation on the introduction of martial law;

c) approval of the decree of the President of the Russian Federation on the introduction of the state of emergency;

d) making decisions on the possibility of using the Armed Forces of the Russian Federation beyond its territory;

e) calling the elections of the President of the Russian Federation;

f) the removal of the President of the Russian Federation from office;

g) the appointment of judges of the Constitutional Court of the Russian Federation, the Supreme Court of the Russian Federation and the Supreme Arbitration Court of the Russian Federation;

h) the appointment to office and removal from office of the Procurator-General of the Russian Federation;

i) the appointment to office and removal from office of the Deputy Chairman of the Accounting Chamber and half of its auditors.

2. The Federation Council shall adopt resolutions on the matters within its jurisdiction in accordance with the Constitution of the Russian Federation.

3. The resolutions of the Federation Council shall be adopted by majority vote of the total number of its members, unless a different procedure is provided for by the Constitution of the Russian Federation.

Article 103

1. The State Duma shall have the power over:

a) granting consent to the President of the Russian Federation for the appointment of the Chairman of the Government of the Russian Federation;

b) decision of the question of a vote of confidence with regard to the Government of the Russian Federation;

c) the appointment to office and removal from office of the Chairman of the Central Bank of the Russian Federation;

d) the appointment to office and removal from office of the Chairman of the Accounting Chamber and half of its auditors;

e) the appointment to office and removal from office of the Commissioner for Human Rights, who shall act in accordance with a federal constitutional law;

f) granting amnesty;

g) bringing charges against the President of the Russian Federation for the purpose of removing him or her from office.

2. The State Duma shall adopt resolutions on the matters within its jurisdiction in accordance with the Constitution of the Russian Federation.

3. The resolutions of the State Duma shall be adopted by majority vote of the total number of its deputies, unless a different procedure is provided for by the Constitution of the Russian Federation.

Article 104

1. The President of the Russian Federation, the Federation Council, members of the Federation Council, deputies of the State Duma, the Government of the Russian Federation, and the legislative (representative) organs of the subjects of the Russian Federation shall have the right to initiate legislation. The Constitutional Court of the Russian Federation, the Supreme Court of the Russian Federation and the Supreme Arbitration Court of the Russian Federation shall also have the right to initiate legislation on the matters within their respective terms of reference.

2. Draft laws shall be introduced in the State Duma.

3. The draft laws on the imposition or elimination of taxes, tax exemption, the issue of state loans and changes in the financial obligations of the state and other draft laws providing for expenditures that are covered out of the federal budget may be introduced only if accompanied by a corresponding resolution by the Government of the Russian Federation.

Article 105

1. Federal laws shall be adopted by the State Duma.

2. Federal laws shall be adopted by majority vote of the total number of deputies of the State Duma, unless a different procedure is provided for by the Constitution of the Russian Federation.

3. Federal laws adopted by the State Duma shall be submitted for consideration by the Federation Council within a period of five days of their adoption.

4. A federal law shall be considered adopted by the Federation Council if more than half of the total number of its deputies have voted for it or if it has not been considered by the Federation Council within fourteen days of its submission. If the Federation Council rejects a federal law, the chambers may set up a conciliation commission to settle the differences that have arisen, after which the federal law shall again be considered by the State Duma.

5. If the State Duma disagrees with the decision of the Federation Council, a federal law shall be considered adopted if, in a second voting, at least two-thirds of the total number of deputies of the State Duma have voted for it.

Article 106

The federal laws adopted by the State Duma shall be considered by the Federation Council on a mandatory basis if such laws deal with the issues of:

a) the federal budget;

b) federal taxes and levies;

c) financial, monetary, credit and customs regulations and the issue of money;

d) ratification and denunciation of the international treaties of the Russian Federation;

e) the status and protection of the state border of the Russian Federation;

f) war and peace.

Article 107

1. An adopted federal law shall be sent to the President of the Russian Federation for signing and publication within five days of its adoption.

2. The President of the Russian Federation shall sign the federal law within fourteen days and publish it.

3. If the President of the Russian Federation vetoes a federal law within fourteen days of its submission, the State Duma and Federation Council shall again consider the law in accordance with the procedure stipulated by the Constitution of the Russian Federation. If the federal law is approved during the second hearing in its previous version by majority vote of at least two-thirds of the total number of members of the Federation Council and deputies

of the State Duma, it shall be signed by the President of the Russian Federation within seven days and published.

Article 108

1. Federal constitutional laws shall be adopted on the subject matters provided by the Constitution of the Russian Federation.

2. A federal constitutional law shall be considered adopted if it has been approved by at least three quarters of the total number of members of the Federation Council and by at least two-thirds of the total number of deputies of the State Duma. The adopted federal constitutional law shall be signed by the President of the Russian Federation within fourteen days of adoption and published.

Article 109

1. The State Duma may be dissolved by the President of the Russian Federation in cases stipulated by Articles 111 and 117 of the Constitution of the Russian Federation.

2. In the event of the dissolution of the State Duma, the President of the Russian Federation shall determine the date of elections so that the newly elected State Duma shall convene no later than four months after the dissolution.

3. The State Duma may not be dissolved for the reasons provided for by Article 117 of the Constitution of the Russian Federation within one year of its election.

4. The State Duma may not be dissolved from the moment it brings charges against the President of the Russian Federation and until the adoption of a corresponding decision by the Federation Council.

5. The State Duma may not be dissolved during a time when martial law or the state of emergency is in effect throughout the entire territory of the Russian Federation, as well as during a period of six months before the office of the President of the Russian Federation expires.

Chapter 6. The Government of the Russian Federation

Article 110

1. The executive power in the Russian Federation shall be exercised by the Government of the Russian Federation.

2. The Government of the Russian Federation shall consist of the Chairman of the Government of the Russian Federation, Deputy Chairmen of the Government of the Russian Federation and federal ministers.

Article 111

1. The Chairman of the Government of the Russian Federation shall be appointed by the President of the Russian Federation with the consent of the State Duma.

2. The proposal of a candidate for the office of the Chairman of the Government of the Russian Federation shall be submitted by the newly elected President of the Russian Federation within two weeks of the inauguration or after the resignation of the Government of the Russian Federation, or within one week of the rejection of a candidate by the State Duma.

3. The State Duma shall consider the candidate for the office of the Chairman of the Government of the Russian Federation proposed by the President of the Russian Federation within one week of the submission of the nomination of the candidate.

4. After the State Duma rejects three candidates for the office of the Chairman of the Government of the Russian Federation, the President of the Russian Federation shall appoint a Chairman of the Government of the Russian Federation, dissolve the State Duma and call new elections.

Article 112

1. The Chairman of the Government of the Russian Federation shall submit to the President of the Russian Federation proposals on the structure of the federal organs of the executive power not later than one week after his or her appointment.

2. The Chairman of the Government of the Russian Federation shall propose to the President of the Russian Federation candidates for the offices of Deputy Chairmen of the Government of the Russian Federation and federal ministers.

Article 113

The Chairman of the Government of the Russian Federation, in accordance with the Constitution of the Russian Federation, federal laws and decrees of the President of the Russian Federation, shall determine the guidelines for the activity of the Government of the Russian Federation and organize its work.

Article 114

1. The Government of the Russian Federation shall:

a) prepare and submit to the State Duma the federal budget and ensure its execution; submit to the State Duma a report on the implementation of the federal budget;

b) ensure the implementation in the Russian Federation of a uniform financial, credit and monetary policy;

c) ensure the implementation in the Russian Federation of a uniform state policy in the fields of culture, science, education, health protection, social security and ecology;

d) manage federal property;

e) carry out measures aimed at ensuring the country's defense, state security and the implementation of the foreign policy of the Russian Federation;

f) implement measures to ensure legality, and the rights and freedoms of citizens, and to protect property and public order and combat crime;

g) exercise other powers vested in it by the Constitution of the Russian Federation, federal laws and decrees of the President of the Russian Federation.

2. Procedures for the activity of the Government of the Russian Federation shall be determined by a federal constitutional law.

Article 115

1. On the basis of and pursuant to the Constitution of the Russian Federation, federal laws and normative decrees of the President of the Russian Federation, the Government of the Russian Federation shall issue resolutions and directives and ensure their implementation.

2. The resolutions and directives of the Government of the Russian Federation shall be binding throughout the Russian Federation.

3. The resolutions and directives of the Government of the Russian Federation may be repealed by the President of the Russian Federation if they contravene the Constitution of the Russian Federation, federal laws and decrees of the President of the Russian Federation.

Article 116

The Government of the Russian Federation shall lose its powers upon the election of a new President of the Russian Federation.

Article 117

1. The Government of the Russian Federation may offer its resignation, which may be accepted or rejected by the President of the Russian Federation.

2. The President of the Russian Federation may make a decision on the resignation of the Government of the Russian Federation.

3. The State Duma may adopt a vote of no confidence in the Government of the Russian Federation. The resolution on the vote of no confidence in the Government of the Russian Federation shall be adopted by a simple majority of the total number of deputies of the State Duma. After the State Duma adopts a vote of no confidence in the Government of the Russian Federation, the President of the Russian Federation may announce the resignation of the Government of the Russian Federation or reject the decision of the State Duma. If within the next three months the State Duma again adopts a vote of no confidence in the Government of the Russian Federation, the President of the Russian Federation shall announce the resignation of the Government of the Russian Federation or dissolve the State Duma.

4. The Chairman of the Government of the Russian Federation may put the question of confidence in the Government of the Russian Federation before the State Duma. If the State Duma adopts a vote of no confidence, the President, within seven days, shall make a decision on the resignation of the Government of the Russian Federation or the dissolution of the State Duma and the holding of new election.

5. In the event of the resignation or termination of its office, the Government of the Russian Federation, on instructions from the President of the Russian Federation, shall continue to work until a new Government of the Russian Federation is formed.

Chapter 7. Judicial Power

Article 118

1. Justice in the Russian Federation shall be administered only by courts of law.

2. Judicial power shall be exercised by means of constitutional, civil, administrative and criminal judicial proceedings.

3. The judicial system of the Russian Federation shall be established by the Constitution of the Russian Federation and federal constitutional law. The creation of extraordinary courts shall be prohibited.

Article 119

Citizens of the Russian Federation who have reached the age of 25, have a higher legal education and have a record of work in the legal profession of no less than five years, may become judges. Federal law may set additional requirements for the judges in the courts of the Russian Federation.

Article 120

1. Judges shall be independent and shall obey only the Constitution of the Russian Federation and federal law.

2. A court of law, having established during the consideration of a case that any act of a governmental or other organ does not correspond to the law, shall render a ruling in accordance with the law.

Article 121

1. Judges shall not be removed from office.

2. The powers of a judge may be terminated or suspended only in accordance with the procedure and on the grounds established by federal law.

Article 122

1. Judges shall enjoy immunity.

2. Criminal proceedings may be brought against a judge only in accordance with the procedure established by federal law.

Article 123

1. Proceedings in all courts shall be open to the public. Hearings *in camera* shall only be allowed in cases provided for by federal law.

2. Hearing of criminal cases *in absentia* shall not be allowed except in cases provided for by federal law.

3. Judicial proceedings shall be conducted based on adversarial principles and equality of the parties.

4. In cases stipulated by federal law judicial proceedings shall be conducted with the participation of jurors.

Article 124

Courts shall be financed solely from the federal budget and financing shall ensure full and independent administration of justice in accordance with federal law.

Article 125

1. The Constitutional Court of the Russian Federation shall consist of 19 judges.

2. The Constitutional Court of the Russian Federation, on the request of the President of the Russian Federation, the Federation Council, the State Duma, one-fifth of the members of the Federation Council or deputies of the State Duma, the Government of the Russian Federation, the Supreme Court of the Russian Federation, the Supreme Arbitration Court of the Russian Federation, organs of legislative and executive power of the subjects of the Russian Federation, shall resolve cases concerning the compliance with the Constitution of the Russian Federation of:

(a) federal laws, normative acts of the President of the Russian Federation, the Federation Council, the State Duma and the Government of the Russian Federation;

(b) constitutions of the republics, charters, as well as laws and other normative acts of the subjects of the Russian Federation issued on questions within the jurisdiction of the organs of state power of the Russian Federation and joint jurisdiction of the organs of state power of the Russian Federation and organs of state power of the subjects of the Russian Federation;

(c) agreements between the organs of state power of the Russian Federation and organs of state power of the subjects of the Russian Federation, agreements between the organs of state power of the subjects of the Russian Federation;

(d) international treaties of the Russian Federation that have not entered into force.

3. The Constitutional Court of the Russian Federation shall settle disputes over competence:

(a) between federal organs of state power;

(b) between organs of state power of the Russian Federation and organs of state power of the subjects of the Russian Federation;

(c) between the highest organs of state power of the subjects of the Russian Federation.

4. The Constitutional Court of the Russian Federation, in response to complaints about a violation of the constitutional rights and freedoms of citizens and on the request of the courts, shall verify the constitutionality of a law that has been applied or is due to be applied in a specific case, in accordance with the procedure established by federal law.

5. The Constitutional Court of the Russian Federation, on the request of the President of the Russian Federation, the Federation Council, the State Duma, the Government of the Russian Federation and the organs of legislative power of the subjects of the Russian Federation, shall interpret the Constitution of the Russian Federation.

6. Acts or their individual provisions that have been declared unconstitutional shall be invalid; international treaties of the Russian Federation that contravene the Constitution of the Russian Federation shall not go into effect and shall not be applied.

7. The Constitutional Court of the Russian Federation, on the request of the Federation Council, shall render its opinion concerning the observance of the established procedure for bringing charges against the President of the Russian Federation for high treason or other serious crime.

Article 126

The Supreme Court of the Russian Federation shall be the highest judicial organ for civil, criminal, administrative and other cases falling within the jurisdiction of courts of general jurisdiction, shall exercise judicial supervision of their activities in accordance with the procedure established by federal law, and shall provide explanations on issues pertaining to judicial practice.

Article 127

The Supreme Arbitration Court of the Russian Federation shall be the highest judicial organ resolving economic and other disputes within the jurisdiction of the arbitration courts, shall exercise judicial supervision of their activities in accordance with the procedure established by federal law, and shall provide explanations on issues pertaining to judicial practice.

Article 128

1. Judges of the Constitutional Court of the Russian Federation, the Supreme Court of the Russian Federation, and the Supreme Arbitration Court of the Russian Federation shall be appointed by the Federation Council upon nomination by the President of the Russian Federation.

2. Judges of the other federal courts shall be appointed by the President of the Russian Federation in accordance with the procedure established by federal law.

3. The powers and the procedure for the formation and activity of the Constitutional Court of the Russian Federation, the Supreme Court of the Russian Federation, the Supreme Arbitration Court of the Russian Federation and other federal courts shall be established by federal constitutional law.

Article 129

1. The Procuracy of the Russian Federation shall constitute a single centralized system in which lower-ranking procurators shall be subordinate to higher-ranking procurators and the Procurator-General of the Russian Federation.

2. The Procurator-General of the Russian Federation shall be appointed and dismissed by the Federation Council on the recommendation of the President of the Russian Federation.

3. The procurators of the subjects of the Russian Federation shall be appointed by the Procurator-General of the Russian Federation after consultations with its subjects.

4. Other procurators shall be appointed by the Procurator-General of the Russian Federation.

5. The powers, organization and working procedure for the Procuracy of the Russian Federation shall be established by federal law.

Chapter 8. Local Self-Government

Article 130

1. Local self-government in the Russian Federation shall ensure independent

solution of questions of local importance, possession, use and disposal of municipal property by the population .

2. Local self-government shall be exercised by citizens through referendum, elections and other forms of direct expression of their will, and through elected and other organs of local self-government.

Article 131

1. Local self-government shall be exercised in urban and rural settlements and in other localities taking into account historical and other local traditions. The structure of the organs of local self-government shall be determined by the population independently.

2. The borders of territorial entities under local self-government may be changed after consultations with their population.

Article 132

1. The organs of local self-government shall independently manage municipal property, form, approve and execute the local budget, establish local taxes and levies, maintain public order and decide other questions of local importance.

2. The organs of local self-government may be vested by law with certain state powers and in such cases shall receive the required material and financial means for the implementation of these powers. The state shall oversee the exercise of these powers.

Article 133

Local self-government in the Russian Federation shall be guaranteed by the rights to judicial protection, and to compensation of the additional expenses resulting from the decisions made by the organs of state power, and by the ban on the limitation of the rights of local self-government as established by the Constitution of the Russian Federation and federal laws.

Chapter 9. Constitutional Amendments and Revision of the Constitution

Article 134

Proposals for amending and revising the provisions of the Constitution of the Russian Federation may be submitted by the President of the Russian Federation, the Federation Council, the State Duma, the Government of the Russian Federation, legislative (representative) organs of the subjects of the

Russian Federation, as well as by a group of at least one-fifth of the members of the Federation Council or deputies of the State Duma.

Article 135

1. The provisions of Chapters 1, 2 and 9 of the Constitution of the Russian Federation may not be revised by the Federal Assembly.

2. In the event a proposal to revise the provisions of Chapters 1, 2 and 9 of the Constitution of the Russian Federation is supported by three-fifths of the total number of members of the Federation Council and deputies of the State Duma, a Constitutional Assembly shall be convened in accordance with the federal constitutional law.

3. The Constitutional Assembly shall either confirm the inviolability of the Constitution of the Russian Federation or draft a new Constitution of the Russian Federation, which shall be adopted by two-thirds of the total number of members of the Constitutional Assembly, or shall be put to a nationwide vote. Should the draft of a new Constitution of the Russian Federation be put to a nationwide vote, it shall be considered adopted if more than half of the voters taking part have voted for it, provided that more than half of the eligible voters take part in the vote.

Article 136

Amendments to Chapters 3-8 of the Constitution of the Russian Federation shall be adopted in accordance with the procedure provided for the adoption of a federal constitutional law and shall come into force after their approval by the legislative organs of power of at least two-thirds of the subjects of the Russian Federation.

Article 137

1. Changes in Article 65 of the Constitution of the Russian Federation, which determines the composition of the Russian Federation, shall be made on the basis of the federal constitutional law on admission to the Russian Federation and the formation within it of a new subject of the Russian Federation, and on the change of the constitutional-legal status of a subject of the Russian Federation.

2. In the event of a change in the name of the republic, territory, region, federal city, autonomous region and autonomous area, the new name of the subject of the Russian Federation shall be included in Article 65 of the Constitution of the Russian Federation.

PART TWO

Concluding and Transitional Provisions

1. The Constitution of the Russian Federation shall go into effect on the day of its official publication on the basis of the results of nationwide vote.

The day of the nationwide vote, December 12, 1993, shall be considered the day of the adoption of the Constitution of the Russian Federation.

The Constitution (Fundamental Law) of the Russian Federation - Russia, adopted on April 12, 1978, with subsequent changes and amendments, shall become null and void at the same time.

Should the provisions of the Federal Treaty - Treaty on the Delineation of Jurisdiction and Competency Between the Federal Organs of State Power of the Russian Federation and the Organs of State Powers of the Sovereign Republics Within the Russian Federation, the Treaty on the Delineation of Jurisdiction and Competency Between the Federal Organs of State Power of the Russian Federation and the Organs of State Power of the Territories, Regions and the Cities of Moscow and St. Petersburg, the Treaty on the Delineation of Jurisdiction and Competency Between the Federal Organs of State Power of the Russian Federation and the Organs of State Power of the Autonomous Region and Autonomous Areas within the Russian Federation and other treaties between the federal organs of state power of the Russian Federation and the organs of state power of the subjects of the Russian Federation and treaties between the organs of state power of the subjects of the Russian Federation - contravene the Provisions of the Constitution of the Russian Federation, the provisions of the Constitution of the Russian Federation shall apply.

2. Laws and other legal acts in effect on the territory of the Russian Federation before this Constitution entered into force shall be enforced insofar as they do not contravene the Constitution of the Russian Federation.

3. The President of the Russian Federation, elected in accordance with the Constitution (Fundamental Law) of the Russian Federation - Russia, from the day the present Constitution takes effect, shall exercise the powers established by it until the expiration of the term for which he was elected.

4. The Council of Ministers - Government of the Russian Federation, from the day the present Constitution takes effect, shall assume the rights, duties and responsibility of the Government of the Russian Federation established by the Constitution of the Russian Federation and shall be named henceforth the Government of the Russian Federation.

5. The courts in the Russian Federation shall administer justice in accordance with their powers established by the present Constitution.

After this Constitution becomes effective, the judges of all courts of the Russian Federation shall retain their powers until the expiration of the term for which they were elected. Vacancies shall be filled in accordance with the procedure established by this Constitution.

6. Until the entry into force of a federal law establishing the procedure for trial by jury, the prior procedure for hearing the relevant cases in court shall be preserved.

Until the criminal procedure legislation of the Russian Federation is brought into conformity with the provisions of this Constitution, the former procedure for arrest, custodial confinement and detention of persons suspected of having committed a crime shall be preserved.

7. The Federation Council and the State Duma first convened shall be elected for a term of two years.

8. The Federation Council shall hold its first session on the 30th day after its election. The first session of the Federation Council shall be opened by the President of the Russian Federation.

9. A deputy to the first-convened State Duma may simultaneously be a member of the Government of the Russian Federation. Deputies to the State Duma who are simultaneously members of the Government of the Russian Federation shall not be covered by the provisions of this Constitution concerning the immunity of deputies from responsibility for their actions (or inaction) connected with the performance of their official duties.

Deputies to the first-convened Federation Council shall exercise their powers on a part-time basis.

TABLE OF CASES

[Page references in italic type indicate principal discussion of case.]

A

B

C

[Page references in italic type indicate principal discussion of case.]

[Page references in italic type indicate principal discussion of case.]

[Page references in italic type indicate principal discussion of case.]

[Page references in italic type indicate principal discussion of case.]

L

M

[Page references in italic type indicate principal discussion of case.]

[Page references in italic type indicate principal discussion of case.]

[Page references in italic type indicate principal discussion of case.]

T

U

V

[Page references in italic type indicate principal discussion of case.]

Index

A

B

D

E

F

G

H

I

K

L

M

N

R

S

U

V

W

Z